EXAM KRACKERS

MCAT

101 PASSAGES IN MCAT

VERBAL REASONING

OSOTE
PUBLISHING

2nd Edition

ISBN: 1-893858-55-3
ISBN: 978-1-893858-55-8

To purchase additional copies of this or any other book in the Examkrackers MCAT 5-volume set,
call 1-888-572-2536 or fax orders to 1-859-255-0109.

examkrackers.com
osote.com
audioosmosis.com

OSOTE
PUBLISHING

Printed and bound in the U.S.A.

MCAT is a registered trademark of the Association of American Medical Colleges.

Acknowledgements

This book would not have been possible without Alex Vinnitsky's gathering and editing of the majority of the passages. Thank you, Alex. I also wish to thank Karen Weinshelbaum and Jordan Zaretsky for their comments and help in the proofing and editing of this book. Finally, I would like to thank my wife, Ellis, for her constant loving support and encouragement.

Forward by Jonathan Orsay

Author of Examkrackers *MCAT Verbal Reasoning and Math*

I have long felt that the availability of accurate practice materials for the verbal reasoning section of the MCAT has been limited to the few passages published by the AAMC. It is my opinion that the commercial prep companies have been unable to capture the nuances of this section in their prep materials. Although some gains can be made using less sophisticated MCAT verbal passages, it is mastery of the nuances that allows students to score in the double digits on the real MCAT verbal section. As we all know, 10 is the magic number for the MCAT verbal section, the score that seems to capture the attention of the medical school admissions committees.

Typical inaccuracies found in commercially available verbal materials include too many words per passage, too few words per passage, question stems that are too short, question stems that don't match the language typically found on a real MCAT, and too many correct answers that can be verified directly from the passage by simple logic. It is surprising that such simple aspects of a real MCAT, such as passage and question-stem length, could be overlooked by those writing commercial books, but, unfortunately, this is the case. One explanation might be that companies intentionally lengthen passages in order to make them more difficult. A longer test is a disadvantage for the test taker because it disrupts the sense of timing essential for a double-digit score on the real MCAT.

Matching the language of the MCAT is a more difficult, though no less important, proposition than matching its length. Real MCAT questions are often confounded with peculiar language that makes them difficult to read. Reading question after question written in the MCAT language makes the real MCAT questions easier to understand. In my opinion, before this book was published, prep companies have been unable to duplicate this language.

Perhaps the most disappointing aspect of any commercial practice materials in MCAT verbal reasoning is the way that the answers can be derived through pure logical deduction based upon specific details found in the passages. On a real MCAT, answers to the more difficult questions are often verifiable only through the reader's sense of the feeling, tone, or main idea of the passage. Such questions are difficult to create, and correct answers are difficult to defend satisfactorily, but that is the nature of the MCAT verbal section. Furthermore, those of us with scientific inclination tend to be more comfortable with detailed questions. No matter how difficult a practice exam with only detailed questions may seem, test takers are still in for a shock on the real MCAT.

I asked my brother, David Orsay, to write this book, because I knew his background, personality, and talents were perfect for such a job. David has a mastery of verbal skills possessed by very few, yet he also possesses the trained eye for detail that is required to produce an accurate replication of any exam. He is obsessive in his desire for perfection in every task that he performs. Even as an underachiever in high school, he walked into the SAT with no preparation or even interest and scored in the high 90th percentile on the verbal section. He took the Department of Justice Federal Law Enforcement Exam for U.S. Marshals and achieved what we were told was the only perfect score in the history of that examination. There have been others that have scored 100%, but only because they were given extra points for previous job history. To my knowledge, David was the first and only person to answer every single question on that exam correctly. His military training in not one but two of the most elite special forces units in the U.S. armed services has trained him to be disciplined, precise, and demanding in his tasks beyond what most of us would consider possible. When David accepts a task, it is executed and accomplished with a rare and comforting certainty and effectiveness.

In less than a year working exclusively on MCAT verbal, Dave has become a true expert in how to produce a replica of an MCAT verbal exam. I was anxious to take his first practice exam myself and see if David had succeeded where other prep companies had failed. I was impressed and quite excited by what I found. The mechanics of passage and question length were, of course, accurate. The language was exactly right, but David has done more than just that with this book. I believe that in Examkrackers *101 Passages in MCAT Verbal Reasoning*, David has done what no one else has been able to do. He has captured the essence of the MCAT verbal. These exams aren't just difficult; they are difficult in that peculiar MCAT way. The questions leave you with that uncomfortable feeling in your gut, an uncertainty about your answers.

After taking the first verbal exam in this book, I felt exactly the way I felt after taking the real exam. I wasn't certain I had done well. My score on the real MCAT and my score on the first exam in this book were nearly identical. I scored a perfect score on the real MCAT and missed only two questions on the first test in this book. I find the exams in this book to be an accurate reflection of the exams on a real MCAT. I highly recommend Examkrackers *101 Passages in MCAT Verbal Reasoning* for use as practice for the real MCAT.

Good Luck.
Jonathan Orsay

Table of Contents

Directions

1. Familiarize yourself with the look, feel, and format of the first two Verbal Passages and questions. These appear just prior to Verbal Test 1. You are given 60 minutes for a full-length Verbal Reasoning test. Take the three sample test passages first, allotting yourself about 25 minutes. Grade your test and check the explanations for both correct and incorrect answers at the back of the book.

2. When you are ready to take your first full-length Verbal Test ensure that you will not be bothered for at least an hour. During the test, don't answer the telephone, don't sharpen your pencils, don't sit and stare out the window, and don't get up to go to the bathroom. Treat these practice tests like the real thing.

3. It is not very practical or helpful to write your answers or considerations on a piece of notebook paper. It is always a good idea to mark up the multiple choice questions *on the test itself* as you go through them. If 'A' can't be correct, then mark it off and go to 'B'. If 'B' is *possible*, circle it, and go to 'C', and so on. That way you are at least eliminating and narrowing choices that are *not possible* or are *less likely*. Using the process of elimination is a very helpful technique on the MCAT. The Computer Based Test allows the use of strikethrough and highlight functions right on the screen to help with narrowing down choices.

4. When you are done with your practice test, take a short break. You've earned it.

5. Now grade your test. To find your raw score, count the number of questions that you answered correctly. Use the table at the back of the book to translate your raw score into an MCAT scaled score. How did you do?

6. Turn to the Answers and Explanations section of the book and examine the explanations.

7. Check your schedule for when you will take your next practice test. Between tests you should also concentrate on the MCAT knowledge-based areas of study. Verbal Reasoning is a skills-based area. Practice will improve your scores.

Verbal Reasoning Warm-up
(Three passages only!)
Time: 25 Minutes
Questions 1–17

VERBAL REASONING

DIRECTIONS: There are three passages in this Verbal Reasoning warm-up test. Each passage is followed by several questions. After reading a passage, select the one best answer to each question. If you are not certain of an answer, eliminate the alternatives that you know to be incorrect and then select an answer from the remaining alternatives. Indicate your selection by blackening the corresponding oval on your answer document.

Passage I (Questions 1–6)

There are two basic methods used to teach acting skills: the "external" and "internal" styles. The "external" style, best exemplified by the London-based Royal Academy of Dramatic Art (RADA), emphasizes the technical detail of
5 reproducing voice, facial expression, and body language. Actors trained in this style are taught to mimic the classic external manifestations of emotions, without striving to feel the emotions themselves. To this end, they study what are commonly regarded as obvious physical indicators of the
10 emotional state being portrayed, and incorporate some or all of them into the role. For example, actors, scientists, and most of the public agree that lying is characterized by "shifty eyes," avoidant eye contact, hesitant speech, elevated pitch, sweating, and/or hand wringing. Thus, an "external"
15 actor portraying a liar would consciously perform some or all of these motions while reciting his lines, to suggest to the audience the external traits they are likely to associate with deception.

Therein lies the primary advantage of this classical,
20 "external" style: since it conveys emotions through stylized, visible movements that the public instinctively associates with identifiable feelings, it usually succeeds in letting audiences know which emotion the actor is trying to portray. Audiences are rarely confused, but there is a risk the
25 performance may seem too overt, too melodramatic. This usually happens when an overeager classical actor attempts to work in too many external indicators of the same emotion. The result is a character that obviously feels an identifiable emotion, but seems to either feel it much more strongly than
30 the circumstances warrant or to be exaggerating his feelings to the point of melodrama.

We should note that classical acting evolved on stage and bears the imprint of its origins. Classical actors often practice Shakespearean productions, which affects their
35 style. Since the Elizabethan stage was unamplified and viewed from a distance, classical acting stressed vocal strength, projection, and clear enunciation. It also stressed general posture over small gestures and facial expression, since an Elizabethan audience could see only the former

40 from their seats. But, when this kind of acting is used in film, the actor may appear too rigid and theatrical, conducting a street conversation with a booming, stentorian voice and Oxford-precise enunciation. This is not to say that classically trained actors have not made inroads into American film; consider Patrick Stewart, John Gielgud, and
45 Judy Dench. However, you will notice that such actors are usually typecast as commanding, dignified, well-educated characters, playing basically the same roles in every movie.

The other style of acting is the Stanislavski Method, popularized in America during the 1930s at the prestigious
50 New York–based Actors Studio and exemplified by the young Marlon Brando. "Method" acting is an "internal" discipline that aims to get the actor to actually feel the thoughts, motives, and emotions that the script calls for the character to feel. In Stanislavski's book *An Actor Prepares*,
55 he urges actors to prepare for a role not by mimicking others' mannerisms, but by taking time to contemplate the character's circumstances and motivations, along with his purpose in interacting with the other characters, props, and his environment. Ideally, this preparation lets the actor
60 "get into the mind" of the character and give a "natural," effortless performance by "living the life" of the character on stage/screen. Since Method actors do not focus on mechanical gestures, they give a less mannered, more natural performance when at their best. But Method acting also has
65 its drawbacks. First, it is better suited to the close-up camera than the stage, because Method actors' reliance on facial expression and quieter, natural speaking styles will not project to the stage audience. While Method acting aims for a subtler performance, if the actor does not accompany his
70 understanding of the character with overt actions suggesting his emotions to the audience, his performance may be too subtle for the audience to appreciate.

GO ON TO THE NEXT PAGE.

1. According to the author, Patrick Stewart's success in the role as the commander of the starship *Enterprise* in the series *Star Trek* was in large part the result of his:

   A. previous roles in Shakespearean productions.
   B. ability to make inroads into American film.
   C. previous classical training.
   D. ability to incorporate some of Stanislavski's Method.

2. On the basis of the passage, it is reasonable to conclude that:

   A. Stanislavski probably did not think much of the "external" style.
   B. Marlon Brando would not have done well in an Elizabethan stage production.
   C. an audience might be confused by a Method actor in an Elizabethan stage production.
   D. John Gielgud was probably not capable of acting using the Method.

3. Assume that Judy Dench was interviewed. If Ms. Dench remarked that often, in her film career, she had refused roles after reading scripts and realizing that she could not relate to what her character was feeling, this evidence would *weaken* the passage assertion that:

   A. Ms. Dench was usually typecast, playing the same role in every movie.
   B. the RADA style enabled actors and actresses to mimic emotions.
   C. the Stanislavski Method helps actors to get into the minds of their characters.
   D. Ms. Dench was a classically trained actress.

4. Children may often lie, or say that they will do something while having no intention of actually carrying through with what they are saying. What question might this information reasonably suggest about the author's explanation of acting styles?

   A. Children can be good natural actors.
   B. Isn't the RADA style a more basic or natural style of acting?
   C. Aren't most actors simply 'lying' when they are in a film?
   D. Did Stanislavski analyze children to come up with the basis for his style?

5. According to the passage, the best actress to realistically portray the character of the blind Helen Keller in a television documentary would be one who has been trained primarily in:

   I. the Method.
   II. the RADA style.
   III. the "internal" style.

   A. I only
   B. II only
   C. III only
   D. II and III only

6. According to passage information, when compared to Elizabethan stage characters, characters in films would appear:

   A. more realistic.
   B. larger than life.
   C. as commanding or dignified.
   D. too subtle.

GO ON TO THE NEXT PAGE.

Passage II (Questions 7–12)

It might be argued that the main purpose of modern fashion is to make the wearer appear more attractive. But, at least for men, that is not the main function that clothes fulfill.

5 Fashion-oriented clothing designers have indeed developed diverse methods to create the illusion of more perfect body proportions, and they are remarkably successful in conveying this image. For example, vertical stripes on a garment create an effective optical illusion. They make the 10 wearer himself appear more vertical—taller and thinner— thus improving the physical attractiveness of someone who is shorter and/or heavier than average. On a jacket, padded shoulders convey the appearance of muscular shoulders and arms, while a narrow, tapered waist shows off (or creates 15 the illusion of) trim, athletic abdominals. Similarly, a garment's color, seen juxtaposed against the wearer's skin, affects viewers' perception of skin tone. For example, pale skin seems sallow against a dark, navy blue suit, but tanner with a light shirt and jacket. In high fashion, color aims to 20 mimic the color of the wearer's hair and/or skin undertone, for a more harmonious blend. Again, we should emphasize that these effects are not just overblown claims by clothes peddlers; clothing in the right colors, patterns, and cut will actually make its owner appear more ideally proportioned. 25 Yet the best-designed, most form-flattering clothes are not necessarily the most popular or acceptable.

Tradition played a greater role than any other influence in men's clothing. In the Middle Ages (and probably earlier), clothing was strictly regulated by law; certain colors could 30 be worn only by the upper classes or by certain guilds, on penalty of a fine. Since that time, clothing has become a uniform of class, rank, and calling, which has endured as a "dress code" long after the legal rules were repealed. While the look of "power" clothing has certainly changed, there 35 remains a "power" look, which is expected dress for those in power or aspiring to it.

Currently, the "power" look is the British business suit, with its limited range of dark colors and simple patterns. Simply put, executives are expected to wear a power suit, 40 and the mere wearing of such suits signals subconsciously to viewers that the wearer must be a wealthy and powerful businessman. The power look gravitated toward the British heavy woolen suit because of a historical accident; Englishmen were driven by a combination of jingoism, 45 greed, and gunpowder to become the dominant colonial empire, and thus exported to economically and culturally subjugated nations their dismal fashion sense. Note that English fashion is not badly suited to life in the British Isles. The cold, sodden climate of England and Ireland are well 50 served by heavy woolen suits and hats and heavy brogue shoes. However, these items are not suitable for export to the sweltering dry heat of Africa and the antebellum South,

or humid summers on New York's Wall Street. And yet these ancient uniforms persist throughout all of Britain's former 55 colonies despite their obvious impracticality.

Many items of clothing are worn purely for traditional purposes. For example, the tie has no rational function that anyone can explain, yet most businessmen agree that the tie is a man's most important accessory. The reasons are again 60 historical. The tie evolved from other, more archaic badges of class and rank, whose symbolic implications persist. The traditional, diagonally striped "repp" tie is more properly called the "regimental" pattern, which was once worn by British Army officers to symbolize their high status and 65 access to guns. Similarly, the repeating-patterned "foulard" evolved from ancient heraldic crests, which medieval aristocrats once wore on their shields and pennants to symbolize their connection to wealthy, landowning, arms-bearing clans. Even more recently, the "Ivy League" tie 70 pattern was worn by wealthy East Coast scions to symbolize their elite schooling and connection to the "old boy" power network.

Unfortunately for fashion, these traditions are so deep-seated that they cannot be changed in one lifetime by the 75 average person, or even by vast advertising campaigns by designers. While a businessman would look objectively "better" by eschewing the traditional "red tie, white shirt, blue suit" uniform in favor of a color, cut, and pattern more suited to his individual body, doing so would be unwise. 80 Research shows that a uniform's historical implications trump any aesthetic considerations and have much more of an impact on the viewer. Thus, conformity produces the best results, if not the best fashions.

7. The author most likely believes that one of the main purposes of clothing should be to provide the wearer with:

A. a "power" appearance.
B. a uniform.
C. a more attractive appearance.
D. an appearance appropriate to his employment.

GO ON TO THE NEXT PAGE.

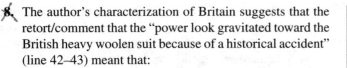

4/6

8. The author's characterization of Britain suggests that the retort/comment that the "power look gravitated toward the British heavy woolen suit because of a historical accident" (line 42–43) meant that:

   A. the author believes the former colonies could have defeated their British subjugators.

   B. the author believes the British business suit is appropriate for the British Isles.

   C. the author does not think much of Britain.

   D. the author does not think much of the British.

9. An appropriate theory based upon the emerging dominance of the British business suit (lines 37–55) is that:

   A. the best designed clothes are not necessarily the most comfortable.

   B. the traditional British 'power' look has even permeated the American business landscape.

   C. people will go to great lengths in their efforts to increase their status.

   D. people usually don't dress appropriately for their prevailing climate.

10. The "expected" business suit jacket invariably has four seemingly useless buttons sewn on the cuff of each sleeve. The information presented on the origins of fashion makes which of the following ideas most plausible?

   A. The extra buttons sewn on the sleeves actually serve to create and enhance the appearance of strength and authority in a man's hands.

   B. The appearance of the "extra" buttons is a relatively new addition to jackets and is believed to somehow render the wearer more attractive.

   C. Traditionally, four buttons have always been sewn on the sleeve of jackets and have never served any useful purpose.

   D. Traditionally, oyster-shell buttons were so susceptible to breaking that "extras" were always sewn on the sleeve.

11. The author implies that the primary purpose of women's fashion is:

   A. to enhance their appearance.

   B. to be more practical.

   C. to promote the "power" look, but in a different manner.

   D. to confront traditional styles.

12. The author probably mentions that "conformity produces the best results, if not the best fashions" (82–83) in order to:

   A. demonstrate the weakness of some fashion designers.

   B. support the claim that there is an expected 'look.'

   C. illustrate the persistence of beliefs that conflict with the demands of the business world.

   D. provide an example of the application of traditional clothing.

_____

GO ON TO THE NEXT PAGE.

Passage III (Questions 13–18)

While Machiavelli's *The Prince* is often hailed as the first breakaway from classical (Greco-Roman) political theory toward the shrewder and more pragmatic modern form, there is clear evidence that his system, "realpolitik"—
5 politics without principles—was practiced extensively long before his day, though it was genteelly omitted from popular political treatises.

One notably evil predecessor to Machiavelli was the early Spanish imperial advisor Ortega Sorolla, a prototypical
10 representative of Spain's early Legalist school. Sorolla openly advocated the perpetuation of the ruling emperor by any means, going so far as to recommend that the state execute men of exceptional talent who might one day aspire to the throne.

15 For Machiavellians, power is tangible and material; the strength of the army that a state can muster is at once the manifestation and measure of its power. Machiavelli considers as strong only those "who can, through abundance of men or money, put together a sufficient army, and hold the
20 field against anyone who assails them." Those who cannot must bargain or assume the defensive, and those that are disarmed become the targets of aggression and contempt. For Machiavelli, the price of ruling is eternal vigilance and constant warfare; he urges aspirants to power to "have no
25 other aim or thought but war … the chief cause of the loss of states, is the contempt of this art."

It is not until Chapter XII that Machiavelli mentions for the first time that a state must also have good laws, but it seems so much like an afterthought that the laws of quality
30 seemingly means little to Machiavelli. For one thing, he never defines what qualities make the laws "good," and his trite statement that "where there are good arms there must be good laws" is unsupportable. Thus, for Machiavelli, the quality of government, and of municipal life under it,
35 appears unimportant.

Machiavelli holds the view that the prince does what he does in order to gain the glory of a good reputation, even if posthumously. He gives an admiring account of Agathocles's rise from poverty to kingship of Syracuse
40 by seizing control of the army and butchering the proper senators and eminent citizens; he gained great power and apparently lived out his natural life. Yet this is still not the Machiavellian ideal; he comments, "… by these methods one may indeed gain power, but not glory … his countless
45 atrocities … do not permit of his being named among the most famous men." Yet if a ruler's self-evaluation in life must include how others will remember him after death, how can any would-be prince rest easy, knowing that if he is defeated, history can be rewritten, and no one will be able to
50 know what his character was truly like?

The ultimate embodiment of realpolitik might well be the totalitarian communist government envisioned in George Orwell's *1984*. In his vision of a future England controlled by communism, he depicts a ruling clique—the Inner
55 Party—which controls the populace through propaganda and "disappearances," by encouraging racial violence and hysteria, and by waging never-ending war with its neighbors simply to destroy surplus wealth, thus keeping the population at subsistence level. Since the propaganda ministries control
60 all information, they control the things posterity will say of them, hence their motto: "Who controls the past controls the future; who controls the present controls the past." At one point, an Inner Party member lays bare the principles of the Party, which illustrates the possible consequences of
65 realpolitik's critical flaw.

"…we are not interested [he says] in the good of others … not wealth or luxury or long life or happiness; only power … the German Nazis and the Russian Communists pretended, that they had
70 seized power unwillingly and for a limited time, and that just around the corner there lay a paradise where human beings would be free and equal. We are not like that. We know no one ever seizes power with the intention of relinquishing it. Power is not a
75 means; it is an end."

13. According to the passage, a ruler's power would be determined by measuring:

A. the qualities of his laws and his renown.
B. his renown and his ability as a strategist.
C. the strength of his army and if he was contemptible.
D. the strength of his army and the qualities of his laws.

GO ON TO THE NEXT PAGE.

3|5

14. Given the fact that George Orwell wrote *1984* after World War II, long after the death of Machiavelli, we may assume, based on passage information, that:

    A.   Orwell admired the Nazis.
    B.   Orwell was satirizing Machiavellian ideas.
    C.   Machiavelli admired the Nazis.
    D.   Orwell admired Machiavelli.

15. According to the passage, Machiavelli believed that the ultimate goal of a ruler is:

    A.   eternal vigilance and constant warfare.
    B.   power.
    C.   the strength of his army.
    D.   his legacy.

16. Elsewhere in *The Prince*, Machiavelli wrote, "States that rise quickly, just as all the other things of nature that are born and grow rapidly, cannot have roots and ramifications; the first bad weather kills them." This most strongly challenges passage descriptions of:

    A.   the Inner Party.
    B.   Agathocles.
    C.   the totalitarian communist government in *1984*.
    D.   Spain's early Legalist school.

17. According to the author, Machiavelli would have considered all of the following to be examples of power EXCEPT:

    A.   extreme loyalty to the ruler.
    B.   a strong army.
    C.   money.
    D.   powerful weapons.

STOP. IF YOU FINISH BEFORE TIME IS CALLED, CHECK YOUR WORK. YOU MAY GO BACK TO ANY QUESTION IN THIS TEST.

STOP.

ANSWERS &
EXPLANATIONS

Verbal Reasoning Warm-up
Answers & Explanations

WARM-UP ANSWER KEY

1.	C	10.	D
2.	C	11.	A
3.	D	12.	B
4.	B	13.	C
5.	B	14.	B
6.	A	15.	D
7.	C	16.	C
8.	D	17.	B
9.	C	18.	A

Passage I (Questions 1–6)

1. According to the author, Patrick Stewart's success in the role as the commander of the starship *Enterprise* in the series *Star Trek* was in large part the result of his:

    A. previous roles in Shakespearean productions.

    WRONG: It is *accurate* that Stewart had "previous classical training." Some "classically trained actors have made inroads into American film; consider Patrick Stewart ..." (lines 45–46). However, it is a major *assumption* that he had *any* previous roles in Shakespearean productions.

    B. ability to make inroads into American film.

    WRONG: This seems merely to be regurgitating passage information. There is no real cause-and-effect relationship between this answer and Stewart's *success* in the role as the commander.

    C. previous classical training.

    CORRECT: It is *accurate* that Stewart had "previous classical training." Some "classically trained actors have made inroads into American film; consider Patrick Stewart" (lines 45–46). Further, Patrick Stewart's role as "commander" (regardless of whether you know anything about *Star Trek* or not) was probably a success because "such actors are usually typecast as *commanding*, dignified, well-educated characters" (lines 47–49).

    D. ability to incorporate some of Stanislavski's Method.

    WRONG: There is no indication that Patrick Stewart used or was even aware of the Stanislavski Method. This is pure conjecture.

2. On the basis of the passage, it is reasonable to conclude that:

    A. Stanislavski probably did not think much of the 'external' style.

    WRONG: This is not a reasonable conclusion. Other than the man's name, there is no specific information on Stanislavski or what he thought.

    B. Marlon Brando would not have done well in an Elizabethan stage production.

    WRONG: This is not a reasonable conclusion. We *can* assume that since "the Elizabethan stage was unamplified and viewed from a distance ... [doing well in an Elizabethan stage production required] vocal strength, projection, and clear enunciation" (lines 36–38). However, it is another assumption altogether that Brando had no training or background in this area and would not have done well.

    C. an audience might be confused by a Method actor in an Elizabethan stage production.

    CORRECT: This is a reasonable conclusion. Notice the word *might*. The inclusion of this 'softener' opens up the possibilities in this answer. Because the "Elizabethan stage was unamplified and viewed from a distance ... [doing well in an Elizabethan stage production required] vocal strength, projection, and clear enunciation" (lines 36–38). And because the "external" style "conveys emotions through stylized, visible movements that the public instinctively associates with identifiable feelings, it usually succeeds in letting audiences know which emotion the actor is trying to portray. *Audiences are rarely confused*" (lines 20–24). In *contrast* to the external style is the Method. "While Method acting aims for a subtler performance, if the actor does not accompany his understanding of the character with overt actions suggesting his emotions to the audience, his performance may be too subtle for the audience to appreciate" (lines 73–75). This *might* confuse an audience.

    D. John Gielgud was probably not capable of acting using the Method.

    WRONG: This is not a reasonable conclusion. There is no way of knowing this. It is pure conjecture.

3. Assume that Judy Dench was interviewed. If Ms. Dench remarked that often, in her film career, she had refused roles after reading scripts and realizing that she could not relate to what her character was feeling, this evidence would *weaken* the passage assertion that:

    The correct answer must satisfy two criteria. The first is that it be an *accurate* passage assertion. In this question, all of the answer choices are accurate passage assertions. Be aware, this is *not* always the case on the MCAT. The question is *not* telling you to assume or trust that all of the following assertions are accurate. You must know! The second criterion is that the assertion be *weakened* by the new information in the assumption.

    A. Ms. Dench was usually typecast, playing the same role in every movie.

    WRONG: This is an accurate passage assertion. However, it is *not* clearly weakened by the passage assumption. For instance, what if the roles she refused were all pretty much *the same*? There is no way of knowing and this is not the best answer.

    B. the RADA style enabled actors and actresses to mimic emotions.

    WRONG: This is an accurate passage assertion. However, it is *not* clearly weakened by the question assumption. Apparently, Ms. Dench did *not* decline the roles because she was unable to "mimic emotions," but because "she could not relate to what her character was [actually] feeling."

C. the Stanislavski Method helps actors to get into the minds of their characters.

WRONG: This is an accurate passage assertion. However, it is *not* weakened by the passage assumption because Ms. Dench was considered a classically trained actress (lines 44–47).

D. Ms. Dench was a classically trained actress.

CORRECT: This *is* an accurate assertion (lines 44–47), which is *weakened* by the assumption in the question. The author used her as one of three examples of a classically trained actor, and therefore one can assume that she was probably *predominantly* an actress in this style. However, refusing roles because "she could not relate to what her character was feeling" is not characteristic of the classical style. This shouldn't have mattered to her. She would only be "mimicking" her characters overt actions. It was Stanislavski's Method actors who would have been concerned with actual feelings (line 56). The assumption would indicate that Ms. Dench was also influenced to a greater or lesser degree by the Method.

4. Children may often lie or say that they will do something while having no intention of actually carrying through with what they are saying. What question might this information reasonably suggest about the author's explanation of acting styles?

A. Children can be good natural actors.

WRONG: The correct answer requires a "question." This answer is *not* a "question."

B. Isn't the RADA style a more basic or natural style of acting?

CORRECT: This answer is reasonably suggested by the information. The London-based Royal Academy of Dramatic Art (RADA) style teaches actors "to mimic the classic external manifestations of emotions, without striving to feel the emotion themselves" (lines 6–8). Contrast this style with the Method style in which actors are taught to "actually feel" the characters emotions, desires, and motivations. The children in the question are clearly exhibiting the RADA style of acting; acting/saying one thing, while thinking/feeling another. They are children-in-general (there is no specificity), and it is logical to assume that most of them have not had any formal acting training, but are doing this 'naturally' as a 'basic' way of behaving.

C. Aren't most actors simply 'lying' when they are in a film?

WRONG: This answer is *not* reasonably suggested by the information. It is possible that if this answer had been more specific in referring to *RADA* actors only, then it would have been reasonable. However, "most" actors is a generalization and severely limits

the 'rightness' of this answer. Notice that this answer even gives you a hint regarding who it is referring to with, "when they are in a *film*." This answer is referring to the Stanislavski-style actors. Thus, there is no comparison or relationship with the "children" in the question.

D. Did Stanislavski analyze children to come up with the basis for his style?

WRONG: This question is *not* reasonably suggested by the information. The "children" in the question are (probably unconsciously) using the *RADA* style "to mimic the classic external manifestations of emotions, without striving to feel the emotions themselves" (lines 6–8). Thus, there is no comparison or relationship with the "children" in the question.

5. According to the passage, the best actress to realistically portray the character of the blind Helen Keller in a television documentary would be one who has been trained primarily in:

I. the Method.

WRONG: This choice is the same as III. An actress *primarily* trained in this style would *not* be the best choice. Stanislavski's Method "urges actors to prepare for a role *not by mimicking others' mannerisms*" (lines 58–59). Yet the question suggests that we *want* someone who can "*mimic*" Helen Keller as closely as possible.

II. the RADA style.

CORRECT: An actress trained *primarily* in this style would be the best choice. The fact that Helen Keller is "blind" is of no consequence to the answer. The fact that she will be portrayed in a "television documentary" is misleading because of the similarity to "film." The key to this question is the *realistic portrayal*. There is no suggestion here of interpreting emotions, motivations, circumstances. Stanislavski's style "urges actors to prepare for a role *not by mimicking others' mannerisms*" (lines 58–59). Yet the question suggests that we *want* someone who can "*mimic*" Helen Keller as closely as possible. The "London-based Royal Academy of Dramatic Art (RADA), emphasizes the technical detail of *reproducing* voice, facial expression, and body language" (lines 3–5).

III. the 'internal' style.

WRONG: This choice is the same as I. An actress *primarily* trained in this style would *not* be the best choice. Stanislavski's internal style "urges actors to prepare for a role *not by mimicking others' mannerisms*" (lines 58–59). Yet the question suggests that we *want* someone who can "*mimic*" Helen Keller as closely as possible.

A. I only

B. II only

CORRECT: See the explanation above.

C. III only

D. II and III only

6. According to passage information, when compared to Elizabethan stage characters, characters in films would appear:

A. more realistic.

CORRECT: The question does not say phrase "would *sometimes* appear" or "*could* appear." The question says, "*would* appear." The reference to "characters in films" clearly refers to actors using the Stanislavski Method. "Since Method actors do not focus on mechanical gestures, they give a less mannered, more natural performance when at their best" (lines 66–68). In contrast, "Since the Elizabethan stage was unamplified and viewed from a distance, classical acting stressed vocal strength, projection, and clear enunciation. … *But, when this kind of acting is used in film*, the actor may appear too rigid and theatrical, conducting a street conversation with a booming, stentorian voice and Oxford-precise enunciation" (lines 36–44).

B. 'larger than life'.

WRONG: It is the Elizabethan characters who would have appeared 'larger than life.' "Since the Elizabethan stage was unamplified and viewed from a distance, classical acting stressed vocal strength, projection, and clear enunciation. … *But, when it is used in film*, the actor may appear too rigid and theatrical, conducting a street conversation with a booming, stentorian voice and Oxford-precise enunciation" (lines 36–44). The phrase "characters in films" clearly refers to actors using the Stanislavski Method.

C. as commanding or dignified.

WRONG: It was the "classically trained actors," whose origins can be traced back to Elizabethan productions, who were "usually typecast as commanding, dignified, well-educated characters" (lines 48–49). The phrase "characters in films" clearly refers to actors using the Stanislavski Method.

D. too subtle.

WRONG: The question does not say "would *sometimes* appear" or "*could* appear." The question says, "*would* appear". *If* a Method actor does not do well, then "his performance *may* be too subtle" (line 76). However, they are not *always* too subtle. This is not the best answer.

Passage II (Questions 7–12)

7. The author most likely believes that one of the main purposes of clothing should be to provide the wearer with:

A. a "power" appearance.

WRONG: The author is not likely to believe this. "*Unfortunately* for fashion, these traditions [i.e. clothing worn for no rational purpose other than to emulate 'power' or 'authority'] are so deep-seated that they cannot be changed in one lifetime by the average person, or even by vast advertising campaigns by designers" (lines 78–81).

B. a uniform.

WRONG: The author is not likely to believe this. "*Unfortunately* for fashion, these traditions are so deep-seated that they cannot be changed in one lifetime by the average person, or even by vast advertising campaigns by designers" (lines 78–81).

C. a more attractive appearance.

CORRECT: Though the author is a 'realist', he is likely to believe this. Consider the disparaging way that he describes the rising dominance of the British business suit (lines 40–59). The author clearly has a preference for "fashion." And, "*Fashion-oriented clothing* designers have indeed developed diverse methods to create the illusion of more perfect body proportions [i.e. a "more attractive appearance"]" (lines 5–7). Consider the author's statement, "*Unfortunately* for fashion, these traditions are so deep-seated that they cannot be changed in one lifetime by the average person, or even by vast advertising campaigns by designers" (lines 78–81).

D. an appearance appropriate to his employment.

WRONG: The author is not likely to believe this. Though the author does apparently believe in comfort over the traditional 'power' look (lines 54–59), there are no other examples regarding other types of employment which would allow us to draw this conclusion. *If* the author had his way, the emphasis would be on making a person appear "more attractive."

8. The author's characterization of Britain suggests that the retort/comment that the "power look gravitated toward the British heavy woolen suit because of a historical accident" (lines 45–47) meant that:

A. the author believes the former colonies could have defeated their British subjugators.

WRONG: This is not the suggested meaning. This answer is obviously on the right track, but too speculative. There is no support for the speculation. We don't specifically know why the author believes that the British becoming "the dominant colonial empire" was an "accident," other than that he *doesn't seem to think much of them* (Answer D).

B. the author believes the British business suit is appropriate for the British Isles.

WRONG: This answer may be attractive because it is an *accurate* statement. However, it is not the suggested meaning of the author's comment. This answer seems to have nothing to do with the comment.

C. the author does not think much of Britain.

WRONG: This answer may be attractive because it is an *accurate* statement. The author's description of the "cold, sodden climate of England and Ireland" (lines 52–53) indicates that this is not his favorite vacation spot. However, this really has nothing to do with the comment.

D. the author does not think much of the British.

CORRECT: This is the suggested meaning. This *encompasses* the possibilities of Answers A and C. We know that the author does not think much of the British from the terms he uses to describe them: "dismal fashion sense," "jingoism, greed." The author would, in a way unrevealed to us in the passage, argue that it was an "accident" that the British were able to "become the dominant colonial empire" and transfer their "dismal fashion sense." This is the best answer choice.

9. An appropriate theory based upon the emerging dominance of the British business suit (lines 40–59) is that:

A. the best-designed clothes are not necessarily the most comfortable.

WRONG: This is not an appropriate theory. The author does *not* imply that the British business suit falls into the category of "the best-designed clothes."

B. the traditional British "power" look has even permeated the American business landscape.

WRONG: This is not an appropriate theory because it is *not accurate*. British business suits "are not suitable for *export* to … the antebellum South, or to the humid summers on New York's Wall Street. And yet these ancient uniforms *persist throughout all of Britain's former colonies* despite their obvious impracticality" (lines 54–59).

C. people will go to great lengths in their efforts to increase their status.

CORRECT: This is an appropriate theory. It is clear that wearing a "power" suit is a *necessity* for increasing one's status. The current "power" look is the British business suit. "And yet these ancient uniforms *persist* throughout all of Britain's former colonies, *despite their obvious impracticality*" (lines 57–59). Further examples of clothing items that

have "no rational function" yet are "important" are replete in the passage (lines 60–77).

D. people usually don't dress appropriately for their prevailing climate.

WRONG: This is not an appropriate theory. If we changed "*usually*" to "*sometimes*" this answer would have a chance. As it stands, it is not accurate. Clearly, "The cold, sodden climate of England and Ireland are *well served* by heavy woolen suits and hats and heavy brogue shoes" (lines 52–54).

10. The "expected" business suit jacket invariably has four seemingly useless buttons sewn on the cuff of each sleeve. The information presented on the origins of fashion makes which of the following ideas most plausible?

This is a common type of supposition question that provides you with information from outside of the passage. You are then expected to extrapolate on the theories or ideas presented by the author. Do *not* get hung up or annoyed if you believe that the extra information or supposition is inaccurate. It obviously does not matter. Choose the best answer.

A. The extra buttons sewn on the sleeves actually serve to create and enhance the appearance of strength and authority in a man's hands.

WRONG: This idea is not the most plausible. The reference to "strength and authority" is an enticing aspect of this answer. However, "enhancing the appearance" is a "fashion-oriented" aspect of clothing, which is *subservient* to "tradition." Particularly when the new information specifies "the expected business suit jacket."

B. The appearance of the extra buttons is a relatively new addition to jackets and is believed to somehow render the wearer more attractive.

WRONG: This idea is not the most plausible. The crux of the passage emphasizes, "tradition played a greater role than any other influence in men's clothing" (lines 29–30). "Relatively new addition" is in conflict with this. Further, "render the wearer more attractive" is a "fashion-oriented" aspect of clothing, which is *subservient* to "tradition." Particularly when the new information specifies "the 'expected' business suit jacket."

C. Traditionally, four buttons have always been sewn on the sleeve of jackets and have never served any useful purpose.

WRONG: This idea is not the most plausible. This answer is attractive because it incorporates "tradition" and alludes to serving "no rational function." However, the author does not say that traditional items of clothing have "*never* served any useful purpose." On the *contrary*, it seems that the purpose of what *now* seems to serve "no rational function" can rather invariably be traced back to its original purpose, such as "guild" designations, warmth, uniforms, and badges (lines 29–39, 52–54, and 60–78).

D. Traditionally, oyster-shell buttons were so susceptible to breaking that extras were always sewn on the sleeve.

CORRECT: This idea is the most plausible. This answer incorporates "tradition," which "played a greater role than any other influence in men's clothing" (lines 29–30). Additionally, in contrast to Answer C, it provides a rational explanation for why there were four buttons. Best of all, the traditional reasoning for having the extra "oyster-shell" buttons serves "no rational function" today.

11. The author implies that the primary purpose of women's fashion is:

A. to enhance their appearance.

CORRECT: This is implied by the author. In other words, the author implies that 'the main purpose of modern fashion is to make women appear more attractive.' The absence of any mention of "women" in the passage is conspicuous. However, the caveat in the second sentence obviously refers to women. "It *might* be argued that the main purpose of modern fashion is to make the wearer appear more attractive. But, *at least for men*, that is not the main function that clothes fulfill" (lines 1–4).

B. to be more practical.

WRONG: This is not implied by the author. See Answer A.

C. to promote the "power" look, but in a different manner.

WRONG: This is not implied by the author. See Answer A.

D. to confront traditional styles.

WRONG: This is not implied by the author. There is no way of knowing what women's "traditional styles" would consist of.

12. The author probably mentions that "conformity produces the best results, if not the best fashions" (lines 87–88) in order to:

A. demonstrate the weakness of some fashion designers.

WRONG: This is not the reason. For one thing, the author apparently thinks that fashion designers are very effective at what they do. "Again, we should emphasize these effects are not just overblown claims by clothes peddlers; clothing in the right colors, patterns, and cut will actually make its owner appear more ideally proportioned" (lines 22–26).

B. support the claim that there is an expected 'look.'

CORRECT: This is the reason. We know that the author believes that there is an "expected look" in the business world. That is the "conformity" he refers to in the question. Further, the quote in the question does support the claim in this answer.

C. illustrate the persistence of beliefs that conflict with the demands of the business world.

WRONG: This is not the reason. This answer is very muddled, and doesn't make much sense. The only *demand* of the business world is to have the "power" look. Who has these persistent beliefs? The author? Certainly not the millions of businessmen who are wearing business suits. It seems that only "designers" and the "average person" have these "persistent beliefs." This is not the best answer.

D. provide an example of the application of traditional clothing.

WRONG: This is not the reason. The quote in the question is *not* an "example." Examples are provided from lines 60–77.

Passage III (Questions 13–18)

13. According to the passage, a ruler's power would be determined by measuring:

A. the qualities of his laws and his renown.

WRONG: The "qualities of his laws" would not be a determiner of a ruler's power; "the law of quality seemingly means little to Machiavelli" (lines 30–31).

B. his renown and his ability as a strategist.

WRONG: These would not be determiners of a ruler's power. Beyond there being no mention of "ability as a strategist," there is no implication of this. An "ability" would not be "tangible and material"; "For Machiavellians, *power is tangible and material*" (line 15), though this is rendered somewhat ambiguous in the passage by references to "contempt."

C. the strength of his army and if he was contemptible.

CORRECT: Both of these qualities are among those that *could* be "measured" to determine power; "the *strength of the army* that a state can muster is at once the manifestation and *measure of its power*" (lines 16–17), and "those that are disarmed become the targets of aggression and *contempt*" (lines 22–23).

D. the strength of his army and the qualities of his laws.

WRONG: The "qualities of his laws" would not be a determiner of a ruler's power; "the laws of quality seemingly means little to Machiavelli" (lines 30–31).

14. Given the fact that George Orwell wrote *1984* after World War II, long after the death of Machiavelli, we may assume, based on passage information, that:

A. Orwell admired the Nazis.

WRONG: This is not a valid assumption. The extensive quote, which is an Inner Party member's soliloquy (lines 69–79) as he "lays bare the principles of the Party" (line 66) revels, according to the author, "realpolitik's critical *flaw*" (line 68). Orwell, who wrote the book and the soliloquy, would have been unlikely to have revealed any flaws in a system which caricatured the Nazis if he so admired them.

B. Orwell was satirizing Machiavellian ideas.

CORRECT: This is the only valid assumption. The extensive quote, which is an Inner Party member's soliloquy (lines 69–79) as he "lays bare the principles of the Party" (line 66) reveals, according to the author, "realpolitik's critical *flaw*" (line 68). Orwell, who wrote the book and the soliloquy, would have been unlikely to reveal *any flaws* in Machiavellian ideas in this fashion if he had been doing anything other than "satirizing" or making fun of them.

C. Machiavelli admired the Nazis.

WRONG: This is not a valid assumption. If, as provided in the question, Machiavelli died long before Orwell and WWII, then the Nazis would not have existed in his lifetime for him to have ever known or admired them.

D. Orwell admired Machiavelli.

WRONG: This is not a valid assumption. The extensive quote, which is an Inner Party member's soliloquy (lines 69–79) as he "lays bare the principles of the Party" (line 66) reveals, according to the author, "realpolitik's critical *flaw*" (line 68). Orwell, who wrote the book and the soliloquy, would have been unlikely to have revealed any flaws in a system which caricatured Machiavelli, among others, if he so admired him.

15. According to the passage, Machiavelli believed that the ultimate goal of a ruler is:

A. eternal vigilance and constant warfare.

WRONG: This was not a *goal* but a "price" to be paid. "For Machiavelli, the price of ruling is eternal vigilance and constant warfare" (lines 23–24).

B. power.

WRONG: This was not Machiavelli's *goal* but the goal of the Inner Party in *1984* (lines 78–79). For Machiavelli, power was not a goal, in and of itself, but a means by which to achieve a goal. "Machiavelli holds the view that the prince does what he does [i.e. establishing and maintaining power] in order to gain the *glory of a good reputation*" (lines 37–38).

C. the strength of his army.

WRONG: This was not Machiavelli's *goal*, but the only way to achieve power. Even power was not Machiavelli's goal, but the goal of the Inner Party in *1984* (lines 78–79). For Machiavelli, power was not a goal, in and of itself, but a means by which to achieve a goal. "Machiavelli holds the view that the prince does what he does [i.e. establishing and maintaining power] in order to gain the glory of a good reputation" (lines 37–38).

D. his legacy.

CORRECT: This was the "ultimate goal of a ruler." For Machiavelli, power was not a goal, in and of itself, but a means by which to achieve a goal (lines 37–52). "Machiavelli holds the view that the prince does what he does [i.e. establishing and maintaining power] in order to gain the *glory of a good reputation*" (lines 37–38).

16. Elsewhere in *The Prince*, Machiavelli wrote, "States that rise quickly, just as all the other things of nature that are born and grow rapidly, cannot have roots and ramifications; the first bad weather kills them." This most strongly challenges passage descriptions of:

A. the Inner Party.

WRONG: The quote in the question does not challenge the description of the Inner Party, the government in Orwell's *1984*. No inference can be made regarding how long this government had been in power.

B. Agathocles.

CORRECT: The quote in the question does challenge the description of Agathocles. Machiavelli "gives an *admiring* account of Agathocles's rise from poverty to kingship of Syracuse" (lines 39–40). "Admiring" seems somewhat strong based upon the quote in this question. For Machiavelli, Agathocles would be doomed because he "rose quickly."

C. the totalitarian communist government in *1984*.

WRONG: For the purposes of this question, you should have recognized the similarity of this answer to Answer A. They are one in the same. The quote in the question does not challenge this description. No inference can be made regarding how long this government had been in power.

D. Spain's early Legalist school.

WRONG: The quote in the question does not challenge this description. No inferences can be made regarding this school, its longevity, or its rise to power.

17. According to the author, Machiavelli would have considered all of the following to be examples of power EXCEPT:

A. extreme loyalty to the ruler.

CORRECT: This *would* be an *exception* to Machiavelli's idea of power. "For Machiavellians, power is tangible and material" (line 15). "Loyalty" is neither tangible nor material.

B. a strong army.

WRONG: This would *not* be an *exception* to Machiavelli's idea of power. "For Machiavellians, power is tangible and material" (line 15). "A strong army" is tangible and material.

C. money.

WRONG: This would *not* be an *exception* to Machiavelli's idea of power. "For Machiavellians, power is tangible and material" (line 15). "Money" is tangible and material and is mentioned in the passage (line 19).

D. powerful weapons.

WRONG: This would *not* be an *exception* to Machiavelli's idea of power. "For Machiavellians, power is tangible and material" (line 15). "Powerful weapons" are tangible and material.

Verbal Reasoning Test 1
Time: 60 Minutes
Questions 1–40

VERBAL REASONING

DIRECTIONS: There are seven passages in this Verbal Reasoning test. Each passage is followed by several questions. After reading a passage, select the one best answer to each question. If you are not certain of an answer, eliminate the alternatives that you know to be incorrect and then select an answer from the remaining alternatives. Indicate your selection by blackening the corresponding oval on your answer document.

Passage I (Questions 1–7)

There are over one hundred small white rabbits here in the laboratory today for the Draize test, immobilized by their positions in their small containers, with only their heads sticking out. An assistant is placing a drop of the newest
5 cologne or perfume directly into each of the animal's eyes. The bucking and kicking of these small subjects seems to indicate that they are experiencing severe pain as a result of this experiment, yet it seems necessary in order to ensure that humans do not experience eye injuries resulting from
10 the use of this product. Later, the animals will be analyzed and destroyed.

Ask the experimenters why they experiment on animals, and the answer is: "Because the animals are like us." Ask the experimenters why it is morally
15 OK to experiment on animals, and the answer is: "Because the animals are not like us." Animal experimentation rests on a logical contradiction.
—Professor Charles R. Magel

Is it right under any circumstances to experiment with
20 animals? Do we have a moral obligation towards animals? What is an animal? Certainly, most humans would think of these small rabbits as animals that deserve our protection. But, do humans generally consider that mosquitoes, spiders, or ticks deserve the same protection? Probably not. They are
25 not "fubsy," the term used to describe the cuddly soft, furry, larger mammals that we generally fawn over and feel the desire to protect. Recognizing this intrinsic tendency and attempting to override it, let us then define animals as any non-human organism. Yet, this is such a wide definition that
30 it could pertain to potential aliens. Will we witness an Alien Rights movement soon? We are then forced to narrow our definition of animals to non-human organisms that remind us of humans and, thus, provoke empathy in us. However, to most advocates this would seem rather unsatisfactory
35 because it is not "fair."

Historically, philosophers like Kant (and Descartes, Malebranche, and even Aquinas) did not favor the idea of animal rights. They said that animals are the organic equivalents of machines, moved by coarse instincts, unable
40 to experience pain (though their behavior sometimes might deceive us into mistakenly believing that they do). Thus, any moral obligation that we have towards animals is a derivative of a primary obligation that we have towards our fellow humans. These are the indirect moral obligations
45 theories. For example, it is wrong to torture animals because it desensitizes us to human suffering and makes us more prone to using violence towards humans.

Empathy as a differentiating principle is of little use because it is primarily structural. If the animal looks like
50 me, resembles me, behaves like me—then it must be like me in other, more profound ways. However, this is a faulty method when used to prove identity; *empathy* is defined in the dictionary as *pathetic fallacy*. This way of thinking is too dependent upon historical, cultural, and personal
55 contexts. That another organism looks like us, behaves like us, and talks like us is no guarantee that it is like us. The creature is not capable of want, and if it were, it would neither necessarily want nor deserve our pity. We cannot determine through empathy whether another creature, like
60 another human, is experiencing pain.

Additionally, pain is a value judgment and the reaction to it is not only relative, but also culturally dependent. In some cases, pain can actually be perceived as positive and be sought after. If we humans cannot agree and separate the
65 objective from the subjective, the rational from the cultural— what gives us the right to decide for other organisms (without getting their approval)? In Aztec culture, being chosen as a sacrifice to the gods was a high honor and a burning desire. We have no way of knowing: perhaps pigs prefer to be
70 slaughtered. We cannot decide right and wrong, good and evil for those with whom communication is barred.

GO ON TO THE NEXT PAGE.

2|7

VERBAL REASONING TEST 1 • 19

TEST 1

1. For which of the following of the author's assertions is NO support provided in the passage?

 A. Empathy is of little use because it is primarily structural.
 B. Pain can, in some cases, actually be perceived positively and sought after.
 C. Human beings have an intrinsic tendency to fawn over and protect "fubsy" animals.
 D. Another creature is not capable of want, and if it were, it would neither necessarily want nor deserve our pity.

2. The author implies that an animal does not:

 A. have enough "fubsy" characteristics to be considered human.
 B. communicate effectively.
 C. benefit from human empathy.
 D. empathize with humans.

3. It has been said that animal experimenters "are using more and more animals whom they consider less 'cute,' because, although they know these animals suffer just as much, they believe people won't object as strenuously to the torture of a pig or a rat as they will to that of a dog or a rabbit." The author would probably disagree by saying that:

 A. Dogs and rabbits are less "cute" than pigs or rats.
 B. People will usually object strenuously to an experiment in which any kind of animal is suffering.
 C. The experimenters cannot know how much the animals suffer.
 D. The experimenters probably realize that non-human organisms cannot suffer as we do.

4. The passage indicates that its author would NOT agree with which of the following statements?

 A. Animals communicate effectively through non-verbal means.
 B. The reaction to pain is culturally dependent and relative.
 C. An organism may look like us, behave like us, and talk like us, yet not be like us at all.
 D. An animal's reaction to a certain stimulus might not lead us to believe that it is experiencing pain.

5. The author's argument that "we cannot decide right and wrong, good and evil for those with whom communication is barred" (lines 70–71) depends on the acceptance of which of the following premises?

 A. The philosophers Kant, Malenbrach, and Aquinas all urged better treatment for animals.
 B. Rabbits undergoing Draize experimentation actually feel little or no pain in the way humans understand it.
 C. Empathy is a false method of communication.
 D. In Aztec culture, being chosen as a sacrifice to the gods was a high honor and a burning desire.

6. The passage suggests that human compassion for other organisms derives from the fact that:

 A. helping other organisms may prevent us from hurting other humans.
 B. the organism looks like us, behaves like us, and talks like us.
 C. other organisms suffer in the same way humans do.
 D. other organisms usually look like us.

7. The author contends that in order to judge whether we have the right to make decisions for other organisms, a researcher would need to determine:

 A. whether or not they are experiencing pain.
 B. if this is a derivative of a primary obligation towards other organisms.
 C. whether or not we have their approval.
 D. if empathy can be used to determine the relative fubsiness of an organism.

Copyright © 2008 Examkrackers, Inc.

GO ON TO THE NEXT PAGE.

TEST 1

Passage II (Questions 8–13)

The preamble to the Declaration of Independence is a masterful work of literary expression. However, beyond the flowery eloquence lies great and significant meaning. No words are wasted here. As it wrote the Declaration with
5 war looming on the horizon, the Continental Congress knew America could not withstand Britain's military might alone. They would require allies and foreign assistance. Nevertheless, they also knew America could not receive assistance as long as the colonies were seen to be fighting
10 a civil war against the ruling British Empire. To help the colonies would constitute interference in Great Britain's internal affairs. As Samuel Adams explained, "No foreign Power can consistently yield Comfort to Rebels, or enter into any kind of Treaty with these Colonies till they declare
15 themselves free and independent." With this in mind, pen was put to paper:

When in the Course of human events, it becomes necessary for one people to dissolve the political bands which have connected them with another, and to assume
20 among the powers of the earth, the separate and equal station to which the Laws of Nature and of Nature's God entitle them, a decent respect to the opinions of mankind requires that they should declare the causes which impel them to the separation.

25 The preamble establishes the document as a "declaration." It is not some attempt to persuade and present the case for independence to a watching world, indeed to "mankind," that the actions of these colonies are righteous and should be supported. It is a bold statement, with the
30 implication that anyone with ears to hear and eyes to see will realize that the words therein merely put to paper the "Laws of Nature and of Nature's God" that "entitle" this declaration. The Declaration goes so far in its assumption that all will see the validity in the revolution that only "a
35 decent respect to the opinions of mankind requires that they should declare the causes which impel them to the separation."

A less bold statement, or an attempt to persuade, on the other hand, would have been a tacit admission that there
40 was another perspective on these unfolding events—that of Britain, which is never mentioned by name. This was a not unimportant factor to an emerging nation well aware that its actions would be challenged and that allies would be critical to success. However, the issue, as the Declaration implies, is
45 not one of interpretation but of observation. The Declaration served to announce and convey only America's side on an issue of international law and sovereignty, and it maintains this perspective throughout.

The first line, "When in the Course of human
50 events," elevates the Declaration to an apogee of historical significance. It is not merely the fledgling utterances of a few colonies attempting to be heard, but the birthing of "one people." This "one people" is America, also never mentioned by name, but bound, nevertheless, by the unification of the
55 phrase. Of no less importance, the phrase "one people" demonstrates the separateness that existed between Britain and the Americas. Already separated geographically, they were now two peoples who could not be made one. This also served to prevent the Declaration from being an act of
60 civil war.

Finally, as Stephen E. Lucas expands upon in his essay "The Stylistic Artistry of the Declaration of Independence," "The most important word in the introduction is 'necessary,' … Revolution was not merely preferable, defensible, or
65 justifiable." According to the international law of nations, "necessity" was a prerequisite for taking up arms against another nation. Again, the Congress recognized that in order for the revolution to succeed it had to be not only allowed by other nations, but aided. The pen—not only mightier than
70 the sword, but also a prerequisite for justifying its use.

8. The central thesis of the passage is that:

   A. the colonies hoped to enlist Britain's help as an ally in the efforts to secede.

   B. the allies, required by the colonies, must perceive the manifest rightness of the independence efforts.

   C. a strong and unequivocal declaration of civil war was a necessity for the colonies.

   D. the preamble to the Declaration of Independence could not have been better written.

9. Implicit in the statement that "a decent respect to the opinions of mankind requires that they should declare the causes which impel them to separation" is the idea that the colonies:

   A. were required by the international laws of that time to declare why they were separating.

   B. were respectful of the opinions of friend and foe alike.

   C. believed their aforementioned "causes" to be self-evident but were sharing them with mankind out of respect.

   D. believed their aforementioned "causes" would impel them to separation.

GO ON TO THE NEXT PAGE.

10. According to the passage, the proper wording of the Declaration was critical to the colonists' independence efforts because they:

    I. would require allies and foreign assistance. ✓

    II. could not afford to have the efforts construed as acts of civil war. ✓

    III. did not want to appear to be attempting to justify and persuade. ✓

A. ~~II only~~

B. ~~I and II only~~

C. I and III only

D. I, II, and III

11. What does Samuel Adams's notion that "no foreign Power can consistently yield Comfort to Rebels, or enter into any kind of Treaty with these Colonies till they declare themselves free and independent" (lines 12–15) imply about foreign interference?

A. That foreign powers would not yield to rebels in their own country.

B. That the colonists considered themselves to be rebels who were not yet worthy of a treaty.

C. Once the colonies had proven that they could win, they could then expect foreign aid.

D. That foreign nations would not help the colonies in a civil uprising.

12. Which of the following statements is NOT presented as evidence for the significance of the phrase "one people"?

A. "One people" served to demonstrate the separateness that existed between America and Britain at that time.

B. The phrase served to prevent the Declaration from being an act of civil war.

C. The phrase emphasized the characteristics of equality, justice, and liberty inherent in the new nation.

D. Though never mentioned by name, America is bound by the unification of the phrase.

13. The passage suggests that the perspective presented throughout the Declaration:

A. eloquently brings forth the stylistic artistry of the men and women who lived during this turbulent period in our nation's history.

B. is balanced.

C. is one-sided.

D. carefully addresses the validity of the arguments of both sides.

GO ON TO THE NEXT PAGE.

Passage III (Questions 14–18)

Arguments abound over whether marijuana should be legalized. Many of these arguments pertain to the federal guidelines for lengthy prison sentences meted out for what is considered a relatively petty crime. Others point out that
5 marijuana is a drug that could, and should, be used for medicinal purposes. But most proponents of legalization ignore the mounting evidence that points to the long-term damage to the user and to society as a whole.

In the Netherlands, marijuana has been legally
10 available since 1976. "Coffee shops" sell cannabis over the counter in many parts of the country. However, more people have tried cannabis since it has been legalized. At the Centre for Drug Research at the University of Amsterdam, Arjan Sas and Peter Cohen divided Amsterdamers surveyed
15 regarding their marijuana use into two groups—those who were born before 1958, in other words who were 18 or older in 1976, and those who were born after 1976, for whom cannabis has always been legal. Only 19 percent of the older people had tried cannabis, compared with 38 percent
20 of the younger group. It would seem then that legalization promotes experimentation with cannabis, if not also even harder drugs.

Medical research has repeatedly provided evidence that marijuana use causes permanent physical, psychological,
25 and thus emotional damage to those who regularly use it. Studies at the University of Maryland and UCLA indicated that the regular smoking of only two marijuana cigarettes a day would tend to promote toe fungus and thrush. But over the years, much stronger claims have surfaced: for example,
30 that heavy marijuana users perform poorly at work or school and are more likely to be delinquent and develop psychiatric problems, or have abnormal brain waves. Repeatedly, however, such studies have encountered the same question: are the problems caused by smoking marijuana, or is it just
35 that people with problems are more likely to end up using marijuana heavily?

Marijuana is addictive. According to Wayne Hall, director of the National Drug and Alcohol Research Centre at the University of New South Wales, Sydney, cannabis is
40 not generally regarded as a drug of dependence because it does not have a clearly defined withdrawal syndrome. But that, he says, is an old-fashioned definition of addiction: "While there may be debate about whether there is a cannabis withdrawal syndrome there is no doubt that some
45 users want to stop or cut down their cannabis use and find it difficult or impossible to do so, and they continue to use cannabis despite the adverse effect it has on their lives."

Research into marijuana's use as a medicine has proven inconclusive or has tended to show that its side
50 effects rendered cannabis unsuitable as a medicinal drug. For instance, one study surveyed the use of cannabinoids to

combat nausea following chemotherapy. While the tablets or injections of cannabinoids were slightly more effective than standard treatments, their side effects, along with the
55 recent development of other, more powerful drugs, makes them a poor choice for nausea relief. "Cannabinoids were no more effective than codeine in controlling acute and chronic pain and they had undesirable effects in depressing the central nervous system," comments Eija Kalso of
60 Helsinki University Hospital in her study. Yet, under mounting pressure, the U.S. Drug Enforcement Agency has reluctantly agreed to provide funds for further testing the efficacy of marijuana as a medicine.

One common finding of the medical research is that
65 the few useful components of marijuana might be extracted and administered in an oral or injectable form. Given the commonly known dangers of cigarette smoking, the smoking of a filterless "joint" of marijuana seems a high-risk exercise. However, it is revealing to interview those
70 who actually want to use marijuana as medicine. With few exceptions, they reject this simple finding and indicate that actually smoking the marijuana is the only acceptable form of medicinal administration. This brings us back full circle to the question, Or is it just that people with problems are
75 more likely to end up using marijuana heavily?

14. The author claims, "Given the commonly known dangers of cigarette smoking, the smoking of a filterless 'joint' of marijuana seems a high-risk exercise" (lines 66–69). The support offered for this conclusion within the passage is:

A. weak; there is no evidence that smoking marijuana cigarettes is dangerous.

B. weak; the dangers of cigarette smoking are not commonly known.

C. strong; the dangers of cigarette smoking are commonly known.

D. strong; the dangers of reefer madness have been well-documented.

15. What is the author implying when referring to information that people who want to use marijuana indicate that "actually smoking the marijuana is the only acceptable form of medicinal administration" (lines 70–73)?

    A. That this is a legitimate alternative point-of-view.
    B. That people who want to use marijuana are stupid.
    C. That these individuals are more interested in recreational use than in the medical benefits of marijuana.
    D. That people with medical problems are more likely to end up using marijuana heavily.

16. Which of the following is offered as support for the statement "marijuana's use as a medicine has proven inconclusive or has tended to show that its side effects rendered cannabis unsuitable as a medicinal drug" (lines 48–50):

    A. Cannabinoids were only slightly more effective than codeine in controlling pain.
    B. The central nervous system was depressed by marijuana.
    C. Marijuana use causes toe fungus and thrush, which in turn cause emotional damage.
    D. The DEA has reluctantly agreed to provide funds for further testing.

17. Assume that the following statements are true. Which one is *inconsistent* with the assertion that "legalization promotes experimentation with cannabis, if not also even harder drugs?"

    A. In the Netherlands today, hard drugs are more difficult to find than in 1976.
    B. In the Netherlands, more people have tried cannabis since it was legalized.
    C. In the Netherlands prior to 1976, drug use in general had diminished.
    D. People who live in Amsterdam come into contact with a wider variety of recreational drugs nowadays.

18. An argument FOR the legalization of marijuana, mentioned in the passage but not expanded upon, is:

    A. the medical uses of marijuana for nausea relief.
    B. the recent support of the DEA.
    C. the benefits of living in Amsterdam.
    D. lengthy prison sentences for drug offenders.

GO ON TO THE NEXT PAGE.

Passage IV (Questions 19–23)

… [In 1996, New York State Governor George] Pataki announced a plan to reduce the cost of care in the state's hospitals. The plan is in response to the state's perceived explosion in health-care spending. The plan's savings
5 come largely in the form of deregulating hospital rates and reducing subsidies for hospital medical training. Under the plan, rate regulation for private insurance will be phased out and will eventually be replaced by competitive bidding. Thus, insurance companies will be able to negotiate bulk-
10 rate discounts with individual hospitals. In addition, Medicaid subsidies for medical training at state hospitals will be reduced.

This plan can be expected to save some money, particularly for New York State itself, through the reduction
15 in Medicaid subsidies. It will probably save more than the current regulatory system, in which total New York State medical spending from 1980 to 1991 outpaced national spending by 22%. Unfortunately, it probably won't achieve a truly dramatic savings (aside from the Medicaid savings from
20 the subsidy cut). From 1980 to 1991, New York's growth in hospital costs only slightly exceeded that of most other states, which operate on a competitive system.

The major concern is that this plan will shift rather than reduce medical costs, thereby creating winners and losers.
25 Among the winners will be, predictably, the state itself, which will reduce the amount it pays for hospital training subsidies through Medicaid (the nationwide program that subsidizes medical care for low-income residents, particularly for emergency hospital care). Insurance carriers
30 are also expected to benefit; by exploiting the state's high concentration of hospitals, insurers will probably be able to negotiate discounts for clients' hospital care, thus cutting costs and increasing their profit margins. Those clients themselves may also share in the savings, depending on
35 what percentage of the discounts will be passed along to consumers. On net, it is anticipated that most will probably enjoy somewhat lower premiums.

Much of the "savings" will fall on the shoulders of New York *City*, which will have to scramble to subsidize
40 costs for the poor and uninsured, who will be turned away from hospitals. Hospitals may opt not to turn away any and, in fact, will be prohibited from turning away certain extremely low income patients, whose right to certain emergency care is protected by the state's Hill-Burton law.
45 Of course, should hospitals continue to offer access to the uninsured, they will effectively be subsidizing the poor and will be rewarded with lower profit margins. Some may be forced to close.

Undoubtedly, the greatest impact will be felt by the
50 uninsured—often the poor and elderly. Since they do not enjoy the negotiated rates set by insurance companies,

costs to the uninsured may rise to cover hospitals' reduced profits on insured patients. Simple economics dictates that uncompensated care will be reduced as a result of lower
55 profit margins.

However, the plan does not take into account the historical fact that, of the increase in the cost of medical care over the past 17 years, the portion attributable to rising salaries among doctors and other hospital staff amounts
60 to only 18.5%, and the portion attributable to insurance costs and insurance abuse only 12.2%. Over 55% of the increase is directly related to the staggering cost of new medical technologies. The unavoidable fact remains that, if Americans insist on receiving state-of-the-art treatments,
65 the money for them will have to come from somewhere.

19. The passage argument suggests that which of the following might benefit from the proposed plan?

    I.   the state of New York
    II.   insurance carriers
    III.   those who have insurance

  A. I only
  B. I and II only
  C. II and III only
  D. I, II, and III

20. According to the author, the governor's plan "probably won't achieve a truly dramatic savings" (lines 18–19). The primary argument given is that:

  A. New York's medical spending from 1980 to 1991 outpaced national spending by 22%.
  B. though state hospital costs compose the bulk of New York's costs, these costs will be relatively unaffected by changing to a competitive system.
  C. state medical costs cannot be changed through deregulating hospital rates.
  D. New York's growth in hospital costs are the result of Medicaid subsidies.

GO ON TO THE NEXT PAGE.

21. According to the passage, the decisive factor in determining whether a patient in New York City will be turned away from the hospital is whether this person requiring care:

A. has insurance or not.
B. is poor or elderly.
C. has an extremely low income.
D. insists on receiving state-of-the-art treatments.

22. Assume that the telephone industry, which had been heavily regulated, was subsequently deregulated and forced to operate on a competitive system. History shows that consumer telephone rates thereafter skyrocketed and efficiency diminished, never again approaching the lower rates or greater efficiency achieved during the period of regulation. This finding:

A. increases the probability that the greatest impact will be felt by the poor and elderly.
B. increases the probability that total New York State medical spending will probably be less than it is under the current regulatory system.
C. decreases the probability of saving through reduction in Medicaid subsidies.
D. reveals nothing about the probability of New York state's hospital costs.

23. Which of the following statements, if true, would most directly *challenge* the assertions of the author?

A. Deregulation and competition in an economic system invariably lead to greater efficiency, productivity, and savings.
B. Most health consumers in New York can be expected to benefit from somewhat lower insurance premiums.
C. It is possible that hospitals in New York City may have to close regardless of how well the plan works.
D. New medical technologies help prevent long-term debilitation and subsequent intensive care of many patients, thereby proportionally reducing medical costs.

Passage V (Questions 24–28)

Among the components of the popular judicial image, which has engendered our enduring cultural respect for judges as lawgivers, is the divided nature of the judicial image. One ancient example is the juxtaposed attributes
5 of the Greek goddess Athena, the ideal "judicial" figure of the Greek world. Some of those attributes, since lost to the common law tradition, may lend new legitimacy to the current legal system if rediscovered.

Athena's essential nature is fundamentally divided; she
10 is at once of the people and impossibly above them. She is undeniably a goddess, who has the ear of the King of Gods and "the sealed chamber's keys where Zeus's thunderbolt/ is stored." As a paragon of both wisdom and of war, she is wiser and more erudite than any mortal. Her identity as
15 a woman is surprising in a role once reserved exclusively for men; it distances her from the commoners and imparts mystique, just as her mythic virginity adds to her aloofness from the people. At the same time, she is more "masculine" than any male; she is a perfect warrior and leader.

20 Yet what is strikingly incongruous with the modern image of a distant apolitical judge is Athena's simultaneous civic involvement in the community as a religious and judicial administrator. The common Anglo-American law judicial tradition has largely abandoned Cicero's early
25 vision of a legal scholar active in the political arena and the community in favor of a bench composed of distant scholars who are physically and intellectually aloof from the litigants before them. While this cultivated persona has increased the mystique and status of the lawyer-judge, it has done so at
30 the expense of trust and popularity.

Furthermore, this choice has largely preempted one possible judicial role, that of the community mediator, which is the judicial tradition Athena represented. With all her superhuman wisdom and power, she is ideally suited to
35 judge by fiat, yet she consciously legislates by consensus; in early Hellenic "courtroom dramas," she is often pictured selecting a jury of citizens to help her in her decision, then persuading the losing side to accept her decision. Such mediation is often useful in modern neighborhood
40 disputes—such as "nuisance" claims and intrafamilial arguments—in which the full force of the law would be too heavy-handed. It offers the advantages of allowing the parties to have their day in "court," but its structure—having the mediator aid the parties in reaching their own agreement
45 rather than hand down a judgment from above—encourages active participation, and likely leaves both parties more satisfied with their outcome than would a judicial decree.

If popular acceptance is the foundation of the law's enduring power, then the image of a justice trained in the
50 academy but dwelling among the people may become the judicial image that endures into the next age of American legal thought.

24. The discussion of Athena and the current legal system includes the assumption that:

   A. most of Athena's admirers were surprised at her gender.
   B. present-day justices are popular and respected.
   C. most litigants consider modern justices to be aloof.
   D. Athena was the ideal "judicial" figure.

25. Which of the following statements, if true, would most WEAKEN the author's contention that "a distant apolitical judge" (line 21) has less legitimacy with the people?

   A. An enemy is anyone who tells the truth about you.
   B. The only normal people are the ones you don't know very well.
   C. To know him is to love him.
   D. Criticism is prejudice made plausible.

GO ON TO THE NEXT PAGE.

TEST 1

26. The author would argue that emulating some of the "juxtaposed attributes" (line 4–5) of Athena is important to the current legal system because it:

   A. explains why the Greeks honored their goddesses.
   B. provides for greater acceptance of judicial decisions.
   C. illustrates Athena's detached judicial renderings.
   D. indicates that current judicial decisions are poorly decided.

27. The main argument of the passage is that:

   A. Athena was a goddess with many admirable human attributes.
   B. the modern judicial system, though much changed, takes its roots from the Greeks.
   C. Greek justices were active in the political arena and the community.
   D. modern judges have become more like gods with godlike attributes.

28. The author most likely believes that one of the main purposes of the judiciary should be to:

   A. render decisions that are fair while remembering that "you can't please them all."
   B. deliver charity to the people and heavy-handed justice to the guilty.
   C. encourage active participation, then rule by fiat.
   D. render fair and equitable decisions that leave the majority satisfied with the outcome.

GO ON TO THE NEXT PAGE.

Passage VI (Questions 29–34)

Immediate postwar planning following World War II has been portrayed by most historians as a confusing time, as conflicting interests within the U.S. military and government tried to exert their influence on future policy.
5 There seem to be a few points of agreement among modern historians to separate the confusion of interests that marked this period. It appears that all the parties involved agreed that the need to severely curtail Japan's military and militarism was the most important priority, and they all had
10 concrete proposals on how to achieve demilitarization; the aims and the means were clear. However, the democratic shape Japanese government and society would be made to take were not as clear in the minds of the planners; they had concrete ideas of what a democratic country should have—
15 civil rights, decentralized government, unions, competitive markets—but there was no single depiction of either the goal or the best method of government for bringing democracy to the Japanese.

Historian Robert E. Ward maintains that even at the
20 pre-surrender stage, there was a consensus that the Japanese emperor would be retained. But Ward is one of only a few historians who claims this as definite; most others saw the fate of the emperor to be very uncertain, at least until a much later date. Even by Ward's own account, Americans at every
25 level, from policymakers to homemakers, saw the emperor as the heart of the Japanese political system, and the reason for all its faults.

This assessment of the emperor as the agent of militarism, nationalism, and the war seems to be a strange
30 one for American political leaders to have made; it does not conform to the views of modern historians about the political role of the emperor. The prevailing opinion now is that Emperor Hirohito was merely a figurehead for the *genro* [capitalist elite], whom he supported, and later became a tool
35 for the military and pro-military bureaucracy, with whom he disagreed but was unwilling to formally oppose. Historian Mikiso Hane says that the emperor was, in fact, so passive that the army actively tried to change his image into that of a war hawk with dramatic photo spreads, but that these
40 attempts were unsuccessful, and the emperor retained the reputation within Japan of being a strictly civilian figure—a dramatic dissimilarity from his image outside of Japan.

How did this flawed perception of the emperor as an aggrandizing military dictator take hold in America? One
45 possible explanation is that, because Japanese soldiers swore allegiance to the emperor and carried on the war effort in his name, Americans believed that he was their actual leader. Whatever the reason, the debate over the emperor's role in the new Japan raged on among the Americans. The question
50 was argued along a concrete line: no one actually liked the institution of the emperor, and everyone blamed him for the war, but he was seen as a crucial tool for the Americans

to promote cooperation and bring about a democracy. If the emperor could be co-opted, he could also be used as
55 a disguised clarion for American mandates to be broadcast to the Japanese, with almost divine authority. If he were deposed or tried as a war criminal, America would incur the undying anger of the Japanese people, and all future reforms would have to be forced on them.

29. Before the onset of World War II, the American public perceived the emperor as a gentle and ineffectual figurehead. The most reasonable explanation on the basis of passage information is that:

   A. the war had not yet begun.
   B. there were no Japanese soldiers killing American soldiers in the name of the emperor.
   C. Americans had always had a flawed perception of the emperor.
   D. this period, as portrayed by most historians, was a "confusing time."

30. The author's apparent point in referring to historian Robert E. Ward's analysis that "there was a consensus that the emperor would be retained" (lines 20–21), is that:

   A. there was a consensus that the emperor would be retained.
   B. this analysis was of critical importance to the passage.
   C. there was actually no clear consensus that the emperor would be retained.
   D. a flawed perception of the emperor by the American people.

GO ON TO THE NEXT PAGE.

31. If the passage information is correct, what inference is justified by the fact that there is still a Japanese emperor, almost sixty years after the period described?

 A. The American debate regarding the role of the emperor had been decided.

 B. The Japanese military had retained much of their political influence.

 C. The Americans had decided that the emperor could be used to their advantage.

 D. The Japanese *genro* had lost much of their power.

32. According to the passage, all American parties agreed that the most important priority was:

 A. reaching a consensus on what should be done about the emperor.

 B. bringing democracy to Japan.

 C. not something that could be determined easily.

 D. restricting Japan's military capabilities.

33. Given the passage implication that the goal of bringing a democracy to Japan was a foregone conclusion (lines 11–18), which of the following passage assertions seems *contrary* to this idea?

 A. Japan would be demilitarized as soon as possible.

 B. The emperor would be retained.

 C. The emperor would be deposed.

 D. The emperor was, in fact, passive.

34. The passage suggests that its author would probably *disagree* with which of the following statements?

 A. The emperor was unwilling to formally oppose the military.

 B. The emperor was actually passive.

 C. The emperor was a member of the *genro*, whom he supported.

 D. The emperor was seen by Americans as a military dictator.

Passage VII (Questions 35–40)

The first psychologist to study memory experimentally in a clinical setting was Dr. Hermann Ebbinghaus. His methodology was to have test subjects memorize word lists of variable length, under varying test conditions. Using this method, Ebbinghaus determined that the average person's memory span is seven units of information. Ebbinghaus also noted that,

"… the memorization of a series of ideas that is to be reproduced is more difficult, the longer the series is. That is, the memorization not only requires more time taken by itself, because each repetition lasts longer, but it also requires more time relatively because an increased number of repetitions becomes necessary. Six verses of a poem require for learning not only three times as much time as two but considerably more."

Initially, this would suggest that word lists are best learned in sub-lists of seven. However, the increase in retention may be less dramatic, in fact. Ebbinghaus goes on to conclude that, if subjects were to memorize a list of words in a certain order and come back to relearn them a day later, but then were given a list of the same words out of sequence, their rate of learning for the new list would be no better for having studied the other sequence before; the savings in time disappears completely. Thus, to memorize single words, it would be more efficient to learn them one at a time, repeating a word, say, 7 times before going on the next, rather than going through the sub-list 7 times before tackling the next sub-list.

Yet it seems that sometimes, the order in which the words are learned can dictate the ease with which they can be recalled, due to the "serial position effect." According to Columbia University's Professor Herbert S. Terrace, when we study a string of words, we tend to remember the words closer to the beginning and end of the list (also known as the "primacy" and "recency" effects), but have a harder time with those in the middle. If this is true, it would make sense to go through a list of words, learning them one at a time, but then rearrange the list so that the elements that were in the center are now near the beginning or end, and then study the list that way the next time. This research may validate the popularity of randomly shuffled flash cards as a study aid.

This serial position theory could also explain why people advise us to spread our studying over a few days, instead of cramming a semester's worth of information into our heads the night before a test. For instance, if we try to read 250 pages of St. Augustine in one sitting, we might remember the first 25 pages and the last 20 fairly well, but that leaves a vast 205 pages that fall into the vaguely remembered middle of the string. If we could read this material over a period of five days, there would be many more beginnings and endings, with fewer pages falling in the middle. Ironically, Dr. Terrace cites a "precipitous decline" in recall in the first hour after learning, so students would be well advised to avoid being tested until at least one hour later.

In his writings on improving memory, Allen Baddeley stresses that monotonous rote learning, without active concentration on the material, makes for very inefficient recall when compared to an interested or critical reading. He gives the example of the mnemonist Shereshevskii, who could seemingly remember any datum for any length of time because of his innate ability to visualize images relating to the subject matter. Baddeley writes,

"In general, this meant that even the driest and most unpromising material created a vivid experience which was represented not only visually but in terms of sound and touch and smell."

Baddeley counsels us to attempt to do the same, to visualize an image or story to go with a word, to stimulate our attention and break the monotony of a long list of data. This is in line with Ebbinghaus, who noted that memorizing a portion of *Don Juan* took 10 times less time than memorizing a series of nonsensical syllables of similar length.

35. According to the passage information, what would most likely happen if a student was tested "in the first hour after learning" (lines 54–55)?

A. Overall, recall would be very poor due to a decline in this first hour.
B. Overall, recall would be strong based on the strengths of short-term memory.
C. The student would be likely to recall only the last part of what he had been studying.
D. The "recency" of the testing would result in better recall than testing done later.

GO ON TO THE NEXT PAGE.

O|6

TEST 1

36. The assertion that Shereshevskii "could seemingly remember any datum for any length of time because of his innate ability to visualize images relating to the subject matter" (lines 63–65) is NOT clearly consistent with the information about:

- A. Terrace's "serial position effect."
- B. memorizing a portion of *Don Juan.*
- C. monotonous rote learning.
- D. Baddeley's quoted description of this ability.

37. According to the information about "serial position effect" (line 32), readers of this passage would find it easiest to recall the information about:

- A. Ebbinghaus's being the first to study memory experimentally and "serial position effect."
- B. "serial position effect" and the memory abilities of Shereshevskii.
- C. the spelling of Shereshevskii's name, and that Ebbinghaus was the first to study memory experimentally.
- D. visualizing an image to go with a word, and that the average person's memory span is seven units of information.

38. According to the passage, prior to the memory studies of Dr. Hermann Ebbinghaus, the study of memory was most probably characterized by which of the following?

- A. Speculation based upon little experimentation within a clinical setting.
- B. Facts observable through experimentation outside of a clinical setting.
- C. Evidence based upon some experimentation within a clinical setting.
- D. Observation without experimentation, outside of a clinical setting.

39. Based upon the Ebbinghaus quotation (lines 8–16), we can conclude that the professor equated:

- A. decreasing difficulty with the increasing speed of recall.
- B. decreasing difficulty with the increasing time it takes to recall.
- C. increasing difficulty with the increasing speed of recall.
- D. increasing difficulty with the decreasing time it takes to recall.

40. Passage information indicates that Ebbinghaus's conclusions regarding memorizing a list of words in a certain order and then changing the sequence of this list (lines 18–29) were most likely based upon:

- I. an experiment conducted in the manner described.
- II. conclusions based upon his other experiments.
- III. speculation with no experimentation.

- A. I only
- B. II only
- C. III only
- D. I and II only

STOP. IF YOU FINISH BEFORE TIME IS CALLED, CHECK YOUR WORK. YOU MAY GO BACK TO ANY QUESTION IN THIS TEST.

STOP.

Verbal Reasoning Test 2
Time: 60 Minutes
Questions 1–40

VERBAL REASONING

DIRECTIONS: There are seven passages in this Verbal Reasoning test. Each passage is followed by several questions. After reading a passage, select the one best answer to each question. If you are not certain of an answer, eliminate the alternatives that you know to be incorrect and then select an answer from the remaining alternatives. Indicate your selection by blackening the corresponding oval on your answer document.

Passage I (Questions 1–5)

The concepts of right and wrong and good and evil, in a universal sense, are irrational, and, as such, are valueless and even damaging to society. Logical concepts are based upon a series of verifiable premises that, when placed side
5 by side, create an argument leading, via the rules of logic, to a conclusion. In order for a concept to have logical clarity, the accuracy of the premises or the validity of the argument may be disputed, but these essentials of logical structure must be present. Traditional moral concepts fail in this
10 regard.

Universal morality is not grounded in verifiable facts, but in faith. Its apologists claim factual basis as evidenced by overwhelming mutual agreement: "We all sense morality, so it must exist." But can mutual sensation evidence fact?
15 Descartes correctly argued, "I think, therefore I am." Though Descartes's example may demonstrate that sensation can evidence fact, it is the certainty founded in self-sensation that compels his argument. This certainty is lost in the mutuality of the group. For instance, "We think, therefore we are,"
20 relies upon faith in the existence of others. How can one be certain that the thought of others is not a self-manufactured illusion? It is this uncertainty of mutuality that undermines any logical validity of a concept of universal morality. Right and wrong in the moral sense rely upon feelings of others
25 that can never be ascertained with confidence.

The damage to a society that blindly accepts such fallacies of reason lies in the fallacy itself; if an action is not truly wrong, it should not be forbidden, punished, or otherwise condemned. Doing so risks condemning right,
30 rewarding wrong, and, thus, perpetuating evil.

Although the concepts of right and wrong cannot stand alone as universal truths, right and wrong can be qualified in a deterministic sense, not only allowing moral judgments but requiring them. If man is a product of his biological
35 makeup as science tells us he is, man must act to reproduce; and not just to reproduce, but also to create an environment that is most conducive to the reproductive efforts of his own offspring. According to the factual findings of science, any

action not conducive to these goals cannot be perpetuated
40 and is, in fact, a waste of energy that would in effect reduce the chance of achievement of these goals. The rules of Darwinism dictate that animals exhibiting such behavior would be less fit. Such animals, their offspring, and their behavior would be doomed to extinction.

45 Actions that are not conducive to the goals of reproduction as prescribed by Darwinism are 'wrong' or 'evil' actions, while those that are conducive are 'right' or 'good' actions.

Upon first reflection, one might conclude that such a
50 philosophy would prescribe a primitive, anarchical society. However, it is the nature of man to be social and to work together. It is often in the best interest of the individual and his own offspring to obey societal rules and regulations even when his fitness may be reduced in the short term. Because
55 offspring are only partially related to their parents, there may be cases where an individual is better served to provide for his brother's offspring or even his neighbor's offspring over one of his own resulting in what outwardly appears as altruistic behavior. The resulting society cannot be anything
60 but what we have today. The very existence of our society is, in itself, the proof.

1. Which of the following assertions in the passage is NOT supported by an example, argument, or by reference to an authority?

   A. The concepts of right and wrong are traditional moral concepts.
   B. Irrational concepts are damaging to society.
   C. Right and wrong in the moral sense rely upon feelings of others that can <u>never</u> be ascertained with confidence.
   D. A Darwinian philosophy would prescribe a primitive, anarchical society.

GO ON TO THE NEXT PAGE.

2. Which of the following would the author believe is the most important factor to consider when making a decision concerning a moral dilemma?

    A. What others in your position would do.
    B. What makes you feel good.
    C. What is best for society. by product of D
    D. What is best for you.

3. A religious man says, "It's *wrong* to have sex before marriage." The author would most likely argue:

    A. Sex before marriage is always right because it results in reproduction.
    B. Sex before marriage may or may not be wrong depending upon the circumstances.
    C. There is no right or wrong concerning sex before marriage.
    D. Sex before marriage is only right if a child is the result.

4. Based on the passage, which statement could most reasonably be attributed to the author?

    A. People who produce offspring are naturally good.
    B. People who produce offspring are naturally bad.
    C. People who produce more offspring are neither bad nor good; they just are.
    D. Modern societies are morally better than ancient ones.

5. Which of the following is the most logical conclusion when applying the author's definition of morality (lines 45–48) to animals?

    A. Only extinct animals were moral.
    B. If animals are proliferating, then they are amoral.
    C. Animals cannot be moral.
    D. If animals are proliferating, then they are moral.

TEST 2

GO ON TO THE NEXT PAGE.

Passage II (Questions 6–12)

Industrial melanism is a phrase used to describe the evolutionary process whereby initially light-colored organisms become dark, as a result of natural selection, in habitats that have been darkened by soot and other forms of
5 industrial pollution. The significance of industrial melanism in the European peppered moth, *Biston betularia*, as one of the first, and still most cited examples of "evolution in action," places importance on the need to be sure that the story is right. In the 50 years since Bernard Kettlewell's
10 pioneering work, many evolutionary biologists, particularly in Britain but also in other parts of Europe, the United States, and Japan, have studied melanism in this species. Their findings show that the precise description of the basic peppered moth story is wrong, inaccurate, or incomplete
15 with respect to most of the original story's component parts.

The story actually began in 1896, when J.W. Tutt noted that the then-typical, light-colored European peppered moths were well camouflaged against the light-colored foliose
20 lichens that grew on tree trunks in unpolluted woodlands. But in woodlands where industrial pollution had killed the lichens, exposing the bark and darkening the tree trunks, the darker-colored melanics were better camouflaged, and, he felt, more prevalent. Since conspicuous moths are
25 more likely to be eaten by predatory birds, Tutt attributed the increase in the proportion of melanic forms to natural selection. In the 1950s, intrigued by his own observations of this phenomenon, Kettlewell tested the idea experimentally by marking several hundred peppered moths (typicals as
30 well as melanics) and releasing them onto tree trunks in a polluted woodland near Birmingham, England. Kettlewell observed through binoculars that melanics seemed less conspicuous than typicals, and that birds took conspicuous moths more readily than inconspicuous ones. That night he
35 recaptured 27.5 percent of the melanics, but only 13.0 percent of the typicals, suggesting that a much higher proportion of melanics had survived predation. Kettlewell later repeated this experiment in unpolluted woodland in Dorset, England, where the recapture percentages were the opposite of those
40 obtained in Birmingham. He concluded that "birds act as selective agents, as postulated by evolutionary theory," and that industrial melanism was "the most striking evolutionary change ever actually witnessed in any organism."

However, when biologists looked beyond Birmingham
45 and Dorset, where Kettlewell had conducted his experiments, they found discrepancies in the expected geographical distribution of melanic moths. In rural East Anglia, where there was little industrial pollution and the light-colored typicals seemed better camouflaged, dark-colored melanics
50 actually reached a frequency of 80 percent. This led D.R. Lees and E.R. Creed to conclude that "either the predation experiments and tests of conspicuousness to humans are misleading, or some factor or factors in addition to selective

predation are responsible for maintaining the high melanic
55 frequencies."

By virtue of the fact that Kettlewell performed his own observations via binoculars using his own natural eyesight, one can surmise that he assumed that a bird's visual perception and abilities were the same as a human's,
60 and further, his own. But, humans and birds see the resting places of moths differently in ultraviolet (UV) light. For birds, black pepper moths are actually camouflaged in unpolluted forests on foliose in pure UV, but the reverse is true in human vision.

65 In his experiments, Kettlewell released moths directly onto tree trunks, and acknowledged that they "were not free to take up their own choice of resting site. I admit that, under their own choice, many would have taken up position higher in the trees." Before the 1980s, many investigators continued
70 to find it convenient to conduct predation experiments using dead specimens glued or pinned to tree trunks. This artificial placement is critically misleading for two reasons. First, as explained previously, an incorrect assumption is immediately made that birds perceive the moths in the
75 same way that humans do. Secondly, one naturally assumes that this is where the moths will actually be found. Yet, in 25 years of fieldwork, one prominent researcher and his colleagues found only one peppered moth on a tree trunk. The moths rarely choose to alight on vertical surfaces, but
80 instead rest high in the understory of trees on the bottoms of the lateral branches. Significantly, the foliose lichens are nonexistent there.

6. According to the passage, which of the following is most likely to be true about the relationship between the foliose lichens and the peppered moths?

   A. Typicals are more difficult for birds to see on unpolluted lichens.
   B. Moths and lichens tend to thrive in the more polluted areas.
   C. Lichens in polluted forests provide concealment for melanics.
   D. Their relationship is based upon Kettlewell's supposition.

GO ON TO THE NEXT PAGE.

TEST 2

7. The author is primarily concerned with demonstrating that:

(A.) Poor experimentation leads to poor findings.
B. Industry has had little effect on populations.
C. Kettlewell knew that his experiment was inaccurate and that his findings were wrong.
D. The scientific community can be fooled.

8. The passage suggests that the discrepancies in the expected geographical distribution of melanic moths can actually be attributed to:

(A.) the relative nonexistence of foliose lichens in the understory.
B. differences between the way humans and birds see, which Kettlewell was not aware of.
C. selective predation.
(D.) This information is not provided.

9. According to the author, melanics and typicals tend to:

A. rest on vertical surfaces.
B. feed on foliose lichens.
(C.) rest where lichens are nonexistent.
D. thrive in industrially polluted areas.

10. The author suggests that Kettlewell:

(A.) knew that certain aspects of his experiment were inaccurate.
(B.) did not know that aspects of his experiment were inaccurate.
C. did not think that his findings were very significant.
D. was devious.

11. According to the author, why is it important to determine if Kettlewell's story is right?

A. If Kettlewell's story is flawed, then we must accept that evolution is flawed.
B. Industrial melanism is significant.
(C.) The European peppered moth story is still one of the most cited examples of "evolution in action."
D. Most biologists sight European peppered moths when they are working on stories about industrial melanism.

12. As it is used in the passage, the phrase *industrial melanism* refers to:

A. the relationship between the foliose and the moths.
B. habitats that have been darkened by soot and other forms of industrial pollution.
C. a process of natural selection, whereby habitats that have been darkened by soot and other forms of industrial pollution attract dark-colored organisms.
(D.) an evolutionary process.

Passage III (Questions 13–18)

Those involved in the production of law and legal texts made it a point to set the language of the law apart from all other types of writing. There has been a continuous philosophical determination, both conscious
5 and subconscious, to present the law as something distinct from "ordinary" language, and thus above the reach of the "laity."

The pronouncement of ancient law was often attributed to a divine lawgiver, or else a messenger with
10 a *visible* connection to the divine or supernatural. Their commandments and prohibitions were transformed into a binding "law" by an external authority, "the lawgiver," or, more precisely, the ancient community's shared belief in the lawgiver's intrinsic power, omniscience, or justice. Examples
15 of the supernatural-authoritative lawgiver abound: the Bible (direct word of God), Moses (messenger of God), Christ (son of God, miracle worker), Athena (goddess, masculine woman, supernatural birth, messenger of Zeus), and the seer Tiresias (venerable, blind, visionary, hermaphrodite) are
20 just a few examples. Sometimes, of course, the lawgivers were undeniably human figures, such as Roman Emperor Justinian, the English kings, or even the town "elders." Yet even then, devices were constructed for them to forge a public link with the divine: Roman emperors typically
25 acted as High Pontiff in taking auguries, while rulers had prophets, priests, and the "divine right of kings," and even old men had "benches of polished stone in the sacred circle" on which to sit in borrowed glory. Thus, ancient law, with its fundamental reliance on *external* authority, had little need
30 to justify its content internally.

Since they drew their legitimacy from fiat—that is, their *lack* of internal reasoning or evidentiary support— ancient laws tended to be simple and absolute. They were also correct, by definition. A quintessential example of
35 ancient law is the single-minded rule of the demonic Furies: "every mortal soul/ whose pride has once transgressed/ the law of reverence due/ to parent, god, or guest,/ shall pay sin's just, inexorable toll." Thus, under ancient law, the innocent are entirely vindicated ("The man whose open
40 hands are pure/ Anger of ours shall not pursue," say the Furies), while the guilty are usually killed outright. Because theirs is a tradition of focusing on absolutes, the Furies are poor at differentiating degrees of guilt and equally poor at articulating the reasoning for their justice.

45 It was the English Judge Thatcher who heralded an important turning point in legal reasoning by identifying himself as an independent legal authority, by virtue of his own self-created legal ability. Yet it was left to the later Judge Edward Coke to define the mode of reasoning that
50 would dominate the common law for more than three centuries. As he prepared to rule on a legal case, King James I was doubtless surprised by Judge Edward Coke's sudden

pronouncement that he could no longer do so, because Coke had perfected a kind of logic, "artificial reason," which
55 was so unique as to make him and his fellow judges the sole proper interpreters of the law. The exact nature of this new method is not immediately ascertainable from Coke's description:

"… reason, which is to be understood as an
60 artificial perfection of reason … gotten by long study, observation, and experience and not every man's natural reason, for [no one is born skillful]. This legal reason [is the highest reason]."

Yet what is discernible is that this method is so
65 esoteric and exclusive that only professional lawyers can comprehend and use it. It was for later legalists to actually invent its processes, but for now, Coke had claimed for the legal profession an exclusive monopoly over it.

13. The central thesis of the passage is that:

A. recently, there has been movement towards rendering legal language more accessible to the "laity."

B. lawgivers and judges have usually considered themselves to have a divine right.

C. since the earliest times, the language of the law has needed to be practical and precise.

D. throughout history, the language of the law has been made purposely beyond the understanding of those lacking a legal background.

14. Which of the following claims is NOT explicitly presented in the passage as an example of an "undeniably" human figure?

      I.   Roman Emperor Justinian ✓
      II. English kings ✓
      III. Moses

  A. I only
  B. II only
  C. III only
  D. I and II only

15. According to the passage, which of the following statements would be the most accurate in describing "the single-minded rule of the demonic Furies" (line 35)?

  A. The accused was either completely guilty or completely innocent.
  B. The guilty stood to benefit because the Furies sought a punishment which fit the crime.
  C. The innocent were often punished because of the Furies disdain for mortals.
  D. The Furies would expound at length upon the reasoning behind their decisions.

16. Which of the following statements is the most reasonable conclusion that can be drawn from the author's description of King James I's surprise at Judge Edward Coke's pronouncement (lines 51–56)?

  A. From that point forward, King James was the sole interpreter of the law.
  B. From this point forward, King James I demanded inclusion in the judges' interpretation of the law.
  C. Prior to this, King James' I judges had not been the only interpreters of the law.
  D. Prior to this, King James I had allowed his judges to be the sole interpreters of the law.

17. Though not mentioned in the passage, the biblical Ten Commandments can best provide an example for which one of the following passage statements?

  A. "Sometimes, of course, the lawgivers were undeniably human figures …"
  B. "The pronouncement of ancient law was often attributed to a divine lawgiver, or else a messenger with a *visible* connection to the divine or supernatural."
  C. "There has been a continuous philosophical determination, both conscious and subconscious, to present the law as something distinct from 'ordinary' language."
  D. "Thus, under ancient law, the innocent are entirely vindicated …"

18. The author's assertion that "even old men had 'benches of polished stone in the sacred circle' on which to sit in borrowed glory" (lines 26–28), supports which of the following conclusions?

  A. These elders required a bench in a sacred place befitting their divine authority.
  B. The benches alone would have imparted a divine connection to these human figures.
  C. The circle 'became' sacred in the presence of these divine elders.
  D. These undeniably human figures gleaned external authority from a divine location.

GO ON TO THE NEXT PAGE.

Passage IV (Questions 19–23)

In society, people tend to base their decisions not on what is true, but rather on what they *perceive* to be true. Sometimes, the two are the same, making the decisions correct. But often they are not. Thus, many decisions are
5 based on first impressions, which are themselves predicated on incomplete information, stereotypes, or even wild guesses extrapolated from a few facts. With this realization, the emerging science of impression management is concerned with teaching people to act in ways that trigger positive
10 responses from others and to avoid common negative stereotypes associated with certain acts or features.

The most important impression is the first one. First impressions tend to be especially lasting, both because people tend to trust their first instincts as correct and
15 because once a person forms a definite positive or negative impression, he subconsciously seeks to validate it by perceiving future actions in a way that is consistent with that impression. For example, once an interviewer decides an applicant is competent, he will view the applicant's
20 later questions as demonstrating valid curiosity; but if the interviewee concluded the interviewer is incompetent, he will perceive the same question as demonstrating ignorance of basic facts.

Impression management is the stock-in-trade of
25 courtroom consultants, since the courtroom is a place where jurors make major decisions about litigants' credibility, demeanor, and worth, often based on nothing more than a few days' rehearsed testimony. One of the pioneering writers on impression management is the jury consultant Jo-Ellen
30 Dimitrius. According to surveys conducted by Dimitrius, the main qualities each person should try to project are, in order of importance, (1) trustworthiness, (2) compassion, and (3) humility and/or competence. Trustworthiness consists of both honesty and reliability (most visibly demonstrated
35 by keeping promises). Compassion is marked by caring, kindness, and graciousness. Competence tends to be inferred from some mix of visible intelligence, confidence, and demonstrations of actual competence at a task. People should at all times strive to project trust and compassion,
40 since the lack of these qualities is always evaluated negatively. However, since visible humility may suggest less competence, people must strike a balance between these two, based on whichever trait is more important to the observer's needs. Generally, in informal social contexts,
45 people should display humility rather than capability, since social acquaintances are relatively unaffected by a stranger's competence but will judge him arrogant for blatant self-promotion. Professionally, people may choose to emphasize either their competence or their caring/humility, depending
50 on which trait people value more in their profession. For example, a personal injury litigator may want to project a tough and competent image to suggest he is a hard bargainer likely to negotiate a large one-time settlement, whereas a

nurse or psychotherapist will want to strive for a "nicer"
55 image, even at the risk of seeming "softer."

There are a few behaviors that seem to *always* improve one's impression, regardless of circumstances. These include direct eye contact (which is invariably perceived as more honest), smiling, good posture, shaking hands, and
60 appropriate enthusiasm. Similarly, there are "toxic traits" that, with the same invariability, detract from one's image. Among these are bad grammar, cursing, sarcasm, obvious aggression, and visible anger. Nonetheless, most traits and behaviors tend to convey some good qualities, but also
65 unavoidably suggest some undesirable connotations. This is due largely to the fact that traits suggesting competence and capability tend to conflict with the aspirational goal of humility. For instance, a man whose image is wealthy, sophisticated, and dominant conveys power, confidence, and
70 leadership, but may seem domineering, arrogant, and aloof, especially to observers that are more low-key. If he changed his image by wearing more casual clothes and adopting a quieter, more subdued approach, he would gain the latter set of desirable associations, but lose the former. The key
75 to effective impression management, therefore, is to find an equilibrium between these traits by assessing which is more likely to be valued by the intended audience under the circumstances, and emphasizing those qualities.

19. The ideas of the author in the passage seem to derive primarily from:

   A. evidence on how people act.
   B. speculation based on observation.
   C. surveys conducted by a researcher.
   D. facts observable in the courtroom.

20. The central thesis of the passage is that:

    I.   a person can learn to 'read' others in order to gain a more accurate impression of them.

    II. a person can learn to convey the appropriate impression to others.

    III. a person can learn to 'read' the impression he is conveying to others.

    A. I only

    B. II only

    C. III only

    D. I and II only

21. The passage discussion most clearly suggests the hypothesis that first impressions are:

    A. trusted by those who make them and usually negative.

    B. long lasting and always harmful.

    C. often wrong, long lasting, and difficult to overcome.

    D. often wrong, trusted by those who make them, and always harmful.

22. What distinction is implied in the passage between professional and informal contexts, respectively?

    A. Either competence or humility and self-promotion

    B. Always competence and humility

    C. Caring/humility and humility

    D. Deciding on which trait is valued more and humility

23. According to the passage descriptions, which of the following "main qualities" (line 31) would be the most difficult to convey in a short first impression?

    A. Trustworthiness

    B. Competence

    C. Compassion

    D. Humility

TEST 2

Passage V (Questions 24–29)

Using extensive survey data, communication specialist Dr. Linda McCallister has identified several distinct "styles" of spoken communications and has studied their interaction. Her book, *Say What You Mean, Get What You Want*, offers
5 a guide to understanding colleagues with different speaking styles and avoiding misunderstandings based on stylistic differences.

She identifies three basic speaking styles. Any person is capable of utilizing all three and may use any one
10 occasionally, but everyone has one preferred, or "dominant," style. The so-called "Noble" style is typically employed by those who believe the main aim of communication is to speak the truth and achieve results quickly. This style is characterized by blunt but honest content, spoken briefly and
15 without great detail. An example of the Noble style is almost any role played by tough cowboy Clint Eastwood, who wastes no time telling people his honest opinion of them. It is generally the style prevalent among males. Another basic style, favored by those who believe the primary aim of
20 talking is to maintain friendly interpersonal relationships, is the so-called "Reflective," identifiable by pleasant, polite, and diplomatic speech, along with a reluctance to tell people anything that might upset them. This style is best illustrated by soft-spoken comedian Woody Allen but is
25 the more dominant style among women. The third basic style is the "Socratic," chosen by those who believe that conversation, debate, and detailed understanding should be the aim of communication. Socratics are much more verbose and rambling and tend to focus on detail and anecdotes, as
30 well as rhetorical questions and linguistically sophisticated arguments. Professors often adopt a Socratic role, encouraging debate to share ideas and sharpen rhetorical skill. In addition to the pure styles, there are two "mixed" or blended styles. The "Magistrate" combines the Noble's
35 candor with the Socratic's verbosity, creating an honest but long and often repetitive speech pattern calculated to "win" conversations by persuading others to adopt the Magistrate's own (honest) opinion. A prime example would be argumentative talk show host Larry King. The other style
40 is the "Candidate," who blends the Reflective's niceness with typically Socratic chattiness, and who tries to persuade others to adopt his positions by first charming them with his politeness and humility.

According to Dr. McCallister, no one style is necessarily
45 "correct" or superior; each one's view of the proper role of communication may be valid, at least under certain circumstances. However, the difficulty of communication is that people of each style tend to prefer speaking in, and listening to, their own style only. Frequently, when
50 confronted with a different style, they react with annoyance and unwarranted assumptions, not realizing the validity and intentions of other styles. For example, the diplomatic and patient Reflective often misperceives the blunt and concise Noble as tactless and abrupt, whereas the Noble
55 may merely be honest and efficient. Similarly, the bottom–line-oriented Noble is frequently annoyed at the Socratic's verbosity and fixation on details, not recognizing it as an attempt at thoroughness. Dr. McCallister's research carries several implications. First, by recognizing each style's
60 inherent strengths and weaknesses, students can tailor their manner of speaking to meet listeners' expectations. For example, if a person works in a field where "toughness" is expected and lauded, he should probably conform to that expectation by favoring the Noble style. The same person
65 might wish to switch to the more pleasant Reflective style socially, or when applying for a position which requires compassion. Moreover, communication is enhanced, and misunderstanding and friction reduced, when speakers meet each other's expectations by mirroring each other's speaking
70 styles. Since a speaker cannot practically expect to change the other person's style in the course of a conversation, he should adapt his own to achieve rapport. Similarly, students exposed to the multiplicity of styles, and taught the valid reasoning behind each, are more likely to develop tolerance
75 for styles other than their own.

24. In the context of the passage, the word *honest* (line 14) means:

   A. not telling lies.
   B. caring enough to say what you mean.
   C. telling the truth.
   D. saying what you mean regardless of the consequences.

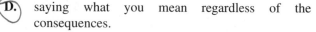

GO ON TO THE NEXT PAGE.

25. Which of the following statements most strongly *challenges* one of the assertions made in the passage?

A. A Socratic will tend to engage in a controlled, concise debate. *Socratic = Verbose*

B. Clint Eastwood's natural style is Socratic.

C. Each of the spoken styles has its place.

D. Reflectives are patient and diplomatic.

26. According to passage descriptions, the title of Dr. McCallister's book *Say What You Mean, Get What You Want* would most characterize which of the following styles?

A. Candidate

B. Reflective

C. Magistrate

D. Noble

27. In order to *Get What You Want*, which of the following styles would probably be the *least* effective?

A. Candidate

B. Magistrate

C. Socratic

D. Reflective *reluctance to upset*

28. According to the passage, "Frequently, when confronted with a different style, [people] react with annoyance and unwarranted assumptions, not realizing the validity and intentions of other styles" (lines 49–52). The 'reaction' of a male Reflective would most likely manifest itself through:

A. keeping an opinion to himself.

B. walking away.

C. not letting it bother him.

D. changing styles in order to respond.

29. According to passage information, a Noble would be most bothered by:

A. thoroughness.

B. verbosity and fixation on details.

C. bluntness.

D. a succinct opposing argument.

GO ON TO THE NEXT PAGE.

Passage VI (Questions 30–34)

Most moviegoers tend to sum up all of a film's features—acting, directing, special effects, and script—into a blanket "I loved it" or "hated it." But movie industry workers, and even film connoisseurs, can attest to the

5 contribution of the movie's "cinematics," or technical features, towards creating any movie's atmosphere.

Artistic movies are composed of a multitude of "shots," or discrete scenes usually lasting only 6 to 20 seconds; together, the hundreds of individual scenes combine to

10 make up the movie. For each shot, the director has many options on how to film the same actors interacting, and his choice has a great influence on how the audience perceives the same action. For example, imagine that the movie's script calls for two actors to speak a fixed dialogue in a

15 specified location. Even while the director stays true to the script, he has considerable leeway in how to film the scene. He may film an "extreme long shot," with the camera far away. This tends to show the setting in panorama, emphasizing the background while underplaying the actors,

20 and is used primarily in outdoor scenes where the backdrop is particularly impressive. Or, he may employ the "long shot," which brings the camera close enough to capture the actors' entire bodies, together with some of the setting. This technique highlights the actors' relation to their setting; it

25 is useful for showing actors interacting with their setting and is a staple of action films. The most common technique, the "medium shot," shows the actors from the waist up, while incorporating a bit of their setting; this shot focuses primarily on the characters rather than their environment and

30 is commonly used to draw attention to important dialogue. At the nearer end of the spectrum is the "close-up," where the camera is brought in close enough to focus on the actors' heads and faces. This has the effect of spotlighting a particular actor, while hiding the setting and other actors.

35 It can emphasize the actor's appearance or gestures and can sometimes suggest the spotlighted character's isolation from his surroundings. There is also the "extreme close-up," where the camera fixates on a single important or dramatic detail, such as the characters' expressive eye gestures or a

40 time bomb ticking towards zero.

Camera "angling" refers to the camera's height from the ground, and thus the vertical angle from which it (and the audience) views the action. The most common angle is filmed at (adult) eye level, though some artistic films for or

45 about children can capture a child's-eye view of the world by filming from a child's eye level, looking up at most things. Similarly, even ordinary films can switch to "low-angle" view by occasionally lowering the camera to look upwards at a character or building. The low-angle format

50 suggests the object or character is somehow larger, grander, dominant, or intimidating. In contrast, the "high-angle" shot positions the camera to "look down on" a character, which often suggests he is inferior, powerless, weak, or in trouble.

A "side-by-side" shot of two characters suggests they are

55 equal in importance, while filming one character as seen over the shoulder of another emphasizes that character, while reminding audiences that he is being observed or heard.

"Optics" refers to the special type of camera lens used to film each scene. Like angling, this is within the director's

60 purview, and directors can switch cameras for each scene. The normal lens attempts to duplicate the human eye's focus and perspective, and thus is used for natural scenes and documentaries. The special wide-angle lens has the artificial ability to take in both the foreground and the background

65 simultaneously, but this exaggerated perspective makes on-screen objects seem farther away. Its opposite, the telephoto lens, can focus on only one plane while blurring others; it makes objects appear closer and is often used in conjunction with the close-up.

70 "Perspective" refers to the camera's ability to make an object seem closer or farther away. The special "soft-focus" mode films foreground objects normally, while blurring the background into a wash of color. This is often used in romantic pictures, to emphasize lovers while evoking a beautiful technicolor environment. The contrasting "deep

75 focus" mode is able to make near and far objects appear equally sharp; it is used to film the foreground while not de-emphasizing the background, and is a staple of "gritty" realistic movies and documentaries.

30. According to the passage, when deciding upon how to film a scene, one must take into account:

- **A.** how the audience is going to perceive the action.
- **B.** the type of camera angles to be used.
- **C.** if the director will approve of the shot.
- **D.** if the audience is going to 'love it,' or 'hate it.'

GO ON TO THE NEXT PAGE.

31. According to the passage, a nature documentary would most likely be filmed using:

    A. a normal lens at 'eye level.'
    B. a wide-angle lens in 'deep focus.'
    C. a 'long shot' in 'deep focus.'
    D. a normal lens in 'deep focus.'

32. The passage discussion most clearly suggests the hypothesis that one of the more important aspects in the making of a film is:

    A. figuring out what 'most moviegoers' are going to love.
    B. deciding how to make a movie 'artistic.'
    C. using a good director.
    D. using a good cameraman.

33. According to the passage, a scene from a horror movie showing two lovers embracing, unaware of the huge monster closing in on them, would be filmed using:

    A. an 'eye level' 'extreme close-up' with a normal lens.
    B. a 'high-angle' 'long shot' with a normal lens.
    C. a 'low-angle' 'long shot' with a normal lens.
    D. a 'child's-eye-level' 'close-up' in deep focus.

34. According to the passage, a child's film with three alternating shots showing a mother scolding her small daughter, the daughter, and the father who is secretly listening would most likely be filmed using which sequence of camera angles, respectively?

    A. 'Low angle,' 'high angle,' and 'over the shoulder.'
    B. 'Low angle,' 'low angle,' and 'high angle.'
    C. 'High angle,' 'high angle,' and 'over the shoulder.'
    D. 'Over the shoulder,' 'high angle,' and 'low angle.'

GO ON TO THE NEXT PAGE.

Passage VII (Questions 35–40)

Under the "axes" theory of music appreciation, music's appeal derives from the impression it leaves on listeners, indexed with their understanding of its technical composition and historical circumstances. It is indeed possible that both
5 factors contribute to one's evaluation, but probable that the emotional impact far outweighs the technical execution in forming our final opinion of it.

Consider the foundations of Western music, its beginnings in the Christian church of the Middle Ages.
10 The scientific rules governing its creation were not yet developed systematically, and there was little knowledge of the mechanisms of sound. Rules of consonance and dissonance were understood only narrowly, and superstition impeded the incorporation of elements such as polyphony
15 and the "devilish" tritone. Notation of music was sparse, with melodies written out without exact instructions on rhythm or pitch. Working with the barest knowledge of acoustics, from laboriously copied texts, and doubtless crude instruments, the early pioneers of church music strove
20 to portray the full glory of nothing less than the divine with the full force of their emotion. The extent to which they succeeded in producing compelling music is amazing; it is a tribute to the sincerity of their emotion, if, even after a millennium, it can still compel admiration and feeling in a
25 less-than-devout society. It is truly timeless music.

To be sure, medieval music was not without its esoteric academic conventions that were doubtless overlooked by most medieval churchgoers. Yet the music cannot be said to have lost its effectiveness, because the composer did
30 not rely on the listener's understanding of the underlying musical theory, but merely transmitted his own reverence into the work.

Since the Middle Ages, … our understanding of sound and composition have increased exponentially to the point
35 where computers can not only synthesize but actually write our music for us. Yet this does not necessarily mean new music has improved. With the scientific study of music theory, psychobiology, and acoustics, revealing whole new worlds of understanding, much of today's music has
40 become obsessed with the minutest esoteric details; and in its drive to become as intellectual and exact as possible, it has lost its appeal to people. Educated listeners who studied principles of twelve-tone composition may just grasp that there is a definite order at work in such pieces. According
45 to the "axes" theory, their intellectual satisfaction at the mathematical correctness of serial music should satisfy them as much as the spirituality of church music, yet the former's unpopularity suggests otherwise.

In fact, some serial music radiates contempt for the
50 listener; it has consciously been made so complex as to be incomprehensible to the listener, who is then made to feel frustrated with his own inability to understand the composer's intention. The medieval-to-Renaissance composer could be accused of dwarfing the listener in his exaltation of God,
55 with the excessive length and complexity of some pieces, but never of composing with the deliberate aim of alienating listeners.

Returning to the "axes" theorem: Of course reason is one appropriate measure, for example, when, having studied
60 the purpose of a piece, one judges whether its emotional tone is appropriate to its stated aim (e.g., requiems should evoke grief, etc.) Yet even in this context, it seems the "axes" model is a poor predictor of music's effect since the emotional impact so outweighs the logical considerations,
65 and music can be judged aesthetically even without knowing the circumstances surrounding it.

35. Which of the following statements provides support for what the author probably means in satating that "even after a millennium, it can still compel admiration and feeling in a less-than-devout society" (lines 23–25)?

A. Millions of people still flock to Egypt each year to admire the ageless wonder of the pyramids.
B. Tourists still stand in awe of the Colosseum of Rome, though it was the site of countless horrible deaths.
C. Though a majority of Americans profess a belief in a supreme being, a minority actually attend any type of religious service.
D. Young and old people alike are increasingly tending to purchase rap music with religious themes.

TEST 2

36. The author of the passage characterizes the "axes" theory of music appreciation as one that:

 A. can help accurately predict why listeners appreciate music or not.
 B. is completely erroneous.
 C. may have been true in the past but is now outdated.
 D. is based upon a false assumption.

37. Suppose it could be established that almost all of the music composed for the Christian church of the Middles Ages could be deconstructed or simplified down to only one or two consistent mathematical themes that seem to hold an almost universal appeal. The author of the passage would be most likely to respond to this development by:

 A. arguing the universal appeal of any musical themes.
 B. pointing out that the composers were unlikely to have been aware of this coincidence.
 C. disputing that the composers would have deliberately set out to alienate their listeners.
 D. agreeing that these early composers were probably aware of universal musical theories.

2 TP, "vaguely aware"

38. If the author of the passage is right that the "axes model" is a poor predictor of music's appeal, then it follows that:

 A. "good" music can usually be created following a set series of guidelines.
 B. music cannot be fully appreciated without some knowledge of its historical circumstances.
 C. the emotional impression that a piece of music leaves on a large group of listeners is unimportant.
 D. the worth of the opinion of a single, highly educated music critic is overrated.

39. Regarding the composing of "serial music," the passage strongly implies that:

 A. alienating listeners was a deliberate goal.
 B. it is comprehensible to the listener.
 C. composers are frustrated by listeners' inability to comprehend.
 D. it is more emotionally appealing to compose this way.

40. If the author's primary criterion for judging the "effectiveness" of music was applied to manmade objects, which of the following creations would be most effective?

 A. an huge underground particle accelerator.
 B. the Alaskan pipeline.
 C. the Vietnam memorial.
 D. the Suez Canal.

STOP. IF YOU FINISH BEFORE TIME IS CALLED, CHECK YOUR WORK. YOU MAY GO BACK TO ANY QUESTION IN THIS TEST.

STOP.

Verbal Reasoning Test 3
Time: 60 Minutes
Questions 1–40

VERBAL REASONING

DIRECTIONS: There are seven passages in this Verbal Reasoning test. Each passage is followed by several questions. After reading a passage, select the one best answer to each question. If you are not certain of an answer, eliminate the alternatives that you know to be incorrect and then select an answer from the remaining alternatives. Indicate your selection by blackening the corresponding oval on your answer document.

Passage I (Questions 1–6)

Imagine a Cartesian coordinate system of three-dimensional space with axes pointing up and down, left and right, and forward and backward. Any point in this space can be described by three terms: the displacement to the left or right (x), the displacement forward and backward (y), and the vertical displacement (z). We can draw a line in this space between any two points, and the distance between the two points is equal to the length of the line. However, life is animated, and just knowing the distance between two points cannot adequately represent animation. In order to describe life, we must have a fourth axis. If a living creature is traveling along our line, we can also ask, "At what time is the creature at a given point?" That point in time must be contiguous with two other points in time: one preceding it and one following it.

Time (t) then is the fourth axis in our space. Like the other axes, the time axis is necessarily perpendicular to all other axes so that that movement parallel to the time axis does not change the value of any coordinate but time. In other words, if our living creature stands perfectly still in our space, his x, y, and z coordinates remain constant, while his t coordinate changes. It is important to note that a point with coordinates x, y, and z at one moment is not the same point in space as a point with the same x, y, and z coordinates a moment later; t has changed. From this point of view, a line parallel to the time axis represents an object that seems to sit perfectly still.

Einstein's theory of relativity tells us that time and space are part of the same entity called the space-time continuum. In such a continuum, time and space are indistinguishable. Our previously described space is a model of this space-time continuum. Einstein also theorized that light moves at a constant speed in a vacuum regardless of the perspective of the observer. In our space-time continuum, a straight line nearly perpendicular to the time axis can represent the path and speed of a photon (a particle of light). The slope with respect to the time axis gives the speed of light. Since this slope must be the same for all observers, observers that move in the x, y, or z direction will experience time more slowly than those that remain still.

Given this information, it is conceivable that time travel in the forward direction is possible. Moving near the speed of light would slow time for the traveler, allowing him to arrive years in the future after what would seem like only moments to his body. But what about going backward in time? If space and time are truly indistinguishable in the space-time continuum, backward time travel might seem as feasible as retracing your own footsteps through the space-time continuum.

The answer may lie not in the characteristics of the space-time continuum, but in the phenomenon of light itself. Time may be an illusion of our perception of the space-time continuum, which seems to be intricately tied to the movement of light. Photons themselves appear to us to have a direction. Light floods a dark room but cannot be absorbed to create darkness.

Or can it? An examination of the human sensory system reveals that we are not equipped to sense light retreating from us. We may routinely move backwards in time without being aware. The space-time continuum may be a four-dimensional stone in which our past, present, and future is etched for us to continually relive each time as if it were the first.

1. Which of the following assertions is most clearly a thesis presented by the author?

   A. Time travel is not possible.
   B. A t axis is necessary to describe life.
   C. A t axis must be parallel to at least one other axis in the model.
   D. Humans are not equipped to sense light.

GO ON TO THE NEXT PAGE.

2. If the hypothesis of the passage is correct, one should find that a change only along the *t* axis:

- A. would indicate photon movement.
- B. would indicate a flaw in the model.
- C. would indicate an object that has traveled backwards in time.
- **D.** would indicate an object that seems to sit perfectly still.

3. Which of the following scientific advances would most seriously *challenge* the hypothesis involving the "space-time continuum" (lines 28–30)?

- A. Association of time and space characteristics
- B. Proof of Einstein's theory of relativity
- C. Further correlation of the consistency of light speed
- **D.** Confirmation of characteristics distinguishing time from space

4. According to the passage information, what would happen if one were to travel near the speed of light?

- A. This person would remain perfectly still.
- B. This person would travel back in time.
- **C.** Time would slow for this person allowing him to travel into the future.
- D. Time would accelerate for this person, allowing him to travel into the future.

5. If the author of the passage is right that the "space-time continuum may be a four-dimensional stone in which our past, present, and future is etched for us to continually relive" (lines 60–63), then it follows that:

- A. the stone must be moving along the *t* axis.
- B. at all times we are on the stone.
- C. we have free will.
- **D.** our lives are predetermined.

6. Which of the following statements is true concerning the four-axes coordinate system described by the author?

- I. Knowing the distance between any two points will adequately represent animation.
- II. All axes are perpendicular to all other axes.
- III. Photons do not appear to us to have direction.

- A. I only
- **B.** II only
- C. I and III only
- D. II and III only

GO ON TO THE NEXT PAGE.

TEST 3

Passage II (Questions 7–13)

The most obvious way for founders of charitable foundations to instruct and control the trustees who administer the foundation's daily activities is for the founder to specify his intended aims for the foundation through its
5 charter documents. These intentions can be enumerated affirmatively (by outlining trustees' explicit duties), or negatively (by listing those acts that the founder prohibits them from doing).

The more explicit the founder's instructions, the
10 less room there is for trustee opportunism. At the same time, explicit aims and prohibitions decrease the trustees' flexibility, and an overly rigid set of instructions may cause the foundation to become obsolete or be dissolved, particularly in light of changing circumstances. For example,
15 if a prosperous buggy-whip manufacturer endowed a foundation that is only empowered to grant scholarships to apprentice buggy-whip makers, the social impact of the foundation will dwindle as the number of apprentices falls. Finally, when there are no more such apprentices,
20 the founder's heirs would be able to petition the courts to dissolve the foundation and assign its assets to them.

Under the legal doctrine of *cy pres* ("close enough"), when changing circumstances render a founder's stated purpose impossible, illegal, or highly impractical, courts
25 may allow trustees to apply the foundation's endowment toward related charitable purposes, so long as they find that the founder's intent was to fund similar charitable projects, rather than the original project exclusively.

Where founders wish to give guidance about their
30 recommended aims without the risks of limiting the foundation's usefulness or causing it to fail, they can attach a "letter of gift." This letter—an expression of the founder's personal preferences—is not legally binding but can be used by trustees and courts to reinterpret the founder's probable
35 intent under changing circumstances.

The foundation documents also include provisions for removing trustees for misbehavior, either by specifying objective infractions (usually absenteeism) that require dismissal, or else by allowing the board of trustees to
40 remove individual members for cause by majority vote. However, oddly enough, the law usually denies the founder any right to sue trustees for failing to enforce the terms of his foundation.

Of course, the founder wields the most power in his
45 initial selection of the original trustees. These original trustees are likely to consist of the founder himself, close friends/family members, business associates, and personal lawyers. Such agents are likely to better understand—and respect—the founder's intent.

50 Once elected, though, most trustee boards are self-perpetuating. Members are routinely re-elected until they die or retire; when they do, the remaining trustees select a replacement. There are methods to prevent trustee entrenchment. Some foundations require term limits for
55 trustees or require retirement at a certain age. This may be effective in preventing entrenchment but is indiscriminate between capable and dishonest trustees. A less mechanical arrangement is to require some "outside" trustees to be selected by independent organizations, corporations,
60 or political divisions. An even more rigorous system of accountability was devised by the Richardson Foundation: it allows donors to elect trustees annually, giving them votes proportional to their dollar contribution to the foundation for that year. This lets those with the most invested in
65 the foundation run it, and probably encourages increased donation by founders seeking to take control of the board.

7. A "letter of gift" (line 32) would most likely be used when:

   A. documentation of a donation was required.
   B. a donor wished to express a personal preference.
   C. the guidance of a trustee was requested.
   D. the founder wished to give some guidance.

GO ON TO THE NEXT PAGE.

8. Suppose a long-dead, affluent lover of birds had expressed his rather vaguely written desire that all of his monies go towards studying and protecting the now-extinct passenger pigeon. Since this activity is no longer possible, the court would most likely:

A. find that another similarly threatened animal species would suffice since the activities are now impossible and the founder was not explicit in his aims.

B. find that another similarly threatened bird species would suffice since the founder loved all birds and was not explicit in his aims.

C. find that the monies should revert to the heirs since there is no other activity that is 'close enough.'

D. find that the monies should revert to the heirs since the founder was explicit in his aims, which are now impossible.

9. According to the passage, "Some foundations require term limits for trustees or require retirement at a certain age" (lines 54–55). However, this might be *disadvantageous* to the founder because:

A. this requirement does not discriminate between capable and dishonest trustees, and the founder wields the most power in his initial selection of the original trustees.

B. this requirement cannot be adequately enforced after the founder is gone, and the founder wields the most power in his initial selection of the original trustees.

C. the original trustees that the founder chose may refuse this short-term occupation, and the requirement to retire cannot be enforced.

D. the law usually denies the founder any right to sue trustees for failing to enforce the terms of his foundation, and the requirement to retire cannot be enforced.

10. Assume that the wealthy buggy-whip manufacturer's heirs would prefer to inherit her wealth rather than see it donated to another 'charitable purpose' where none of them is employed as one of the well-paid trustees. Which of the following hypotheses does this assumption suggest?

A. The trustees would be disappointed by a judge's *cy pres* ruling.

B. The heirs would go to court in an attempt to obtain a *cy pres* ruling.

C. A *cy pres* ruling would satisfy both the trustees and the heirs.

D. The heirs would be dismayed by a judge's *cy pres* ruling.

11. What assumption is implicit in the idea that "an even more rigorous system of accountability … lets those with the most invested in the foundation run it, and probably encourages increased donation by founders seeking to take control of the board" (lines 60–66)?

A. That those donors who have more money to invest will not want to take control of the board.

B. That those donors who seek to take control of the board will be more accountable.

C. That donors are motivated by accountability.

D. That those who have the most invested in the foundation are motivated by founders seeking to take control of the board.

12. According to the passage, the "founder wields the most power in his initial selection of the original trustees" (lines 44–45) for all of the following reasons:

I. All the trustees are probably going to be personally known by the founder. ✓

II. The founder is likely to appoint himself as a trustee.

III. The intent of the founder is most likely to be respected by these trustees. ✓

A. II only

B. I and II only

C. II and III only

D. I, II, and III

13. The passage suggests that its author would probably *disagree* with which of the following statements?

A. There are advantages and disadvantages in very explicit instructions by the founder.

B. Very explicit instructions by the founder are invariably disadvantageous.

C. Very explicit instructions by the founder may cause the foundation to become obsolete.

D. Heirs would have a greater chance of dissolving a foundation based on overly rigid instructions.

GO ON TO THE NEXT PAGE.

Passage III (Questions 14–19)

Sigmund Freud, the "Father of Psychotherapy," is often criticized by modern psychology for the fanciful nature of his theories, which do not seem to have any verifiable basis in either psychological experimentation or normal
5 people's conscious thoughts. For example, the "Oedipal complex" (which supposedly drives all men to desire to kill their father in order to mate with their mother) seems to appear only in a single Greek myth rather than in real life. Correctly, American psychotherapy has largely rejected
10 Freud's theories, but his lively and inventive storytelling ability ensures that his influence lingers on in the popular understanding, with serious implications for women. Freud's famous remark that "anatomy is destiny" means that a woman's anatomical "limitations" (the vagina is seen
15 as a lack of a penis, supposedly a cause of "penal envy") doom her to contribute little towards civilization's material progress.

In *Civilization and its Discontents*, Freud sums up civilization largely in terms of increasing technology,
20 leisure, and protection from nature. Accordingly, he states that the taming of fire was the first step to civilization. But then, Freud invents a bizarre theory of why it had to be a man who first tamed fire: men, he says, view flame as a rival phallus and instinctively desire to extinguish it by urinating
25 on it, which gives them the subconscious impression of winning a quasi homosexual competition. Under Freud's theories, in order for a person to create contributions to civilization, "sublimation" must occur. That is, the instinct toward sexual gratification must be suppressed, so that sexual
30 energy can be channeled into materially productive work. The male alone, because of his penis's long-range urinating capability, had the ability to put out the fire. This ability was unimportant in itself, except that it carried with it the simultaneous possibility of *not* utilizing that ability ("self-
35 suppression"), which would make sublimation possible. Women, because they could not fulfill the instinct, could not suppress or sublimate it either, so they were assigned the role of guardian of a hearth-flame that they were powerless to extinguish. Freud's presentation of his theory deliberately
40 complicates tracing the "role" given to women back to any particular agent, so that their inferior role is meant be seen as natural and immutable.

What implications does this have for women? It seems directly targeted at them, since it presents no
45 limitations for men in creating civilization, but ascribes to women a necessarily lower potential for sublimation-induced achievements, such as art and science. The female's supposed protectiveness towards the fire that the male wants to extinguish, and the resulting competition of the male's
50 ambition against the female's possessiveness predicts a natural antagonism between the sexes. Furthermore, this perpetuates the common ascription of passivity to women and activity to men, a mote that Freud finds unpalatable in

other works but overlooks in his own. The results of women's
55 limits being attributed to a *natural* inequality are that any differences in the social status of women are (a) made to seem beyond correction, (b) made to be beyond grievance, since the agent is nature itself, and (c) permanent. These combine to make Freud's role for women a true "destiny,"
60 in that it is made to seem irrevocable.

Feminist theorists, like Simone de Beauvior, have made some inroads against the influence of Freudians. While de Beauvior concedes that women might be at a slight biological disadvantage by the demands and dangers of pregnancy
65 and menstruation, she argues that this slight difference is insufficient to account for the completely inferior role assigned to women by social constructions. Her *Second Sex* progresses from "biology" to the greater influence of societal constructions. The book rejects biological theories
70 as biased by sexual politics, noting that Freud invented a "sexual" anatomy separate from biological anatomy, and practiced a type of biology that labels female anatomy with a bias toward controlling it by presenting women's bodies as either incomplete, inactive, or weak, and thus in need of
75 men to give meaning to their existence. Faced with a biology that merely reaffirms social prejudices, de Beauvior rejects it as an objective science and explores societal prejudices directly. This is what she means when she says, "One is not born, one becomes, a woman."

14. According to the author, which of the following is most likely to be true about the relationship between the "fire" and "women"?

A. Freud proved that women were protective towards the hearth-fire.

B. There is no relationship between women and the fire.

C. Men will continually put out the fire by urinating on it.

D. Women have been assigned the role of guardian of the hearth-fire.

GO ON TO THE NEXT PAGE.

TEST 3

TEST 3

15. Given the claims made in the passage, the statement "One is not born, one becomes, a woman" (lines 78–79) would suggest that:

   A. unlike Freud, de Beauvior believes that a woman controls her own destiny. ✓
   B. de Beauvior does not believe that a woman can be differentiated biologically at birth from a man.
   C. like Freud, de Beauvior believes that a woman controls her own destiny.
   D. de Beauvior believes that at birth a woman's body is incomplete.

16. Suppose that the majority of Freud's research and theories are based upon dream analysis and a person's unconscious thoughts. This new information would most CHALLENGE the claim that:

   A. Freud was the "Father of Psychotherapy."
   B. Freud's theories do not seem to have any verifiable basis.
   C. "One is not born, one becomes, a woman."
   D. a natural antagonism exists between the sexes.

17. For which of the following conclusions does the passage offer the *least* support?

   A. Freud's theories were fanciful.
   B. Freud believed that men were the first to 'tame' fire.
   C. Freud believed that women were supposed to protect the hearth-fire.
   D. Simone de Beauvior felt women were superior to men. →not a conclusion

18. On the basis of the passage, one can most reasonably infer all of the following EXCEPT:

   A. Freud believed that sex was man's primary motivation.
   B. Freud apparently felt that nature was an antagonist.
   C. Freud viewed a penis-to-penis contest as having homosexual implications.
   D. Freud's ideas were quickly rejected by American psychotherapy.

19. According to one of the positions presented, any differences in the social status of women are (a) made to seem beyond correction and (b) made to be beyond grievance, since the agent is nature itself. If both of these premises are true, what conclusion is most reasonable?

   A. Though women have a right to complain, this will not change their status.
   B. Only through asserting themselves, not by complaining, can women improve their status.
   C. Women cannot change their lot and there is no one to blame.
   D. Women are the only ones who can change their lot, but they must speak with one voice.

GO ON TO THE NEXT PAGE.

Passage IV (Questions 20–24)

Joining two pieces of wood has always presented challenges to wood furniture makers and anyone involved with cabinetry. The organic aspects of this building material, while lending itself to strength, lightness, and beauty, creates
5   its own specific problems for joinery. A poorly planned and constructed piece of wood furniture will literally tear itself to pieces if it does not overcome the method of joinery itself.

During its life as a tree, wood is an ever-changing,
10 living, and breathing piece of material. Simply cutting down a tree and converting it into boards does not turn it into an inert substance. Unlike metal or stone, throughout its existence any object constructed of wood undergoes constant movement in the form of expansion and contraction of
15 every part of its whole. This is due mainly to changes in the humidity of the environment. These changes in turn change the moisture content of the wood. Predictably, an increase in the ambient humidity surrounding the piece of furniture is associated with an increase in the relative humidity of
20 the wood furniture in the area. As the relative moisture of a piece of wood increases so too does its size; the piece expands. In an arid environment, the piece of wood will contract over time. An example of the kind of power that moisture and wood exert can be seen in Italy, where huge
25 blocks of marble are separated by placing wooden wedges in cracks and then pouring water over them, with predictable, irresistible results. Of course, a properly chosen wood finish will affect the degree of change in the piece, to a greater or lesser degree. Interestingly though, it will never completely
30 negate it.

An understanding that wood will continually change size and relative dimension is important. However, more critical is an understanding of exactly how the dimensions of a plank or board will change. The dimensions of any
35 board do change predictably, but do not change uniformly. A plank of black cherry wood, six feet long, eight inches wide, and one inch thick can be used as an example. Generally, the dimensions of this board will change least over time along its six-foot length. The most significant change will
40 be along its eight-inch width, followed by its thickness. The differences are not due to the differences in size but are percentage increases. The caveat "generally" is used here because these changes are based upon the way that the board was cut from the tree.

45 The plank will have been either "plain-sawn" or "quarter-sawn" from the tree. The quarter-sawn method is rather traditional and yields a much more stable piece of wood that is not only less likely to change dimensions, but also less likely to warp or cup. It may also yield particularly
50 beautiful grain patterns, as in the case of the medullary rays in quarter-sawn white oak boards. However, it is also a tremendously wasteful method, and as a result a very

expensive method, of turning a tree trunk into boards and has thus fallen from favor in its use. The now more
55 commonly used method of plain-sawn boards and planks can be distinguished from the quarter-sawn planks by the pattern of grain on the end of each board. The prominent grain or rings on quarter-sawn boards will appear as lines, which are perpendicular to the width of the board and
60 parallel to its thickness. Long grain lines or rings running parallel to the width of the board characterize the grain of the common plain-sawn board. These are most often curved and immediately recognizable as the growth rings of the tree itself.

65 Given two pieces of wood to join, a cabinetmaker should first determine the aforementioned characteristics of the pieces to ascertain how they will change dimension. Only after determining how the pieces will move and change size should the cabinetmaker consider the secondary aspect
70 of the wood's beauty.

20. The author would argue that understanding how the dimensions of a board will change is important to the study of cabinet-making because it:

    A. provides a basis for determining where the wood came from.
    B. explains why previous joints have failed.
    C. indicates how the board can be used.
    D. illustrates the way cabinets are made.

GO ON TO THE NEXT PAGE.

21. The discussion of wood movement includes the assumption that:

  A. the board is plain-sawn.
  B. the board is at least six feet long.
  C. the relative humidity is the same.
  D. the ambient humidity is changing.

22. Which of the following statements is the most reasonable conclusion that can be drawn from the author's description of separating marble blocks in Italy?

  A. The marble contracts upon the wedge and separates.
  B. This is what occurs in a poorly constructed furniture joint.
  C. This is what occurs in a furniture joint in an arid environment.
  D. The wedges are probably from quarter-sawn wood.

23. If one were to examine the construction of an oak rocking chair and find medullary rays throughout the piece, this situation would best support the assertion that:

  A. the rocking chair is made of black cherry.
  B. the rocking chair has probably been made fairly recently.
  C. the rocking chair is expensive.
  D. the rocking chair was made with beauty, rather than longevity, in mind.

24. The claim that cutting up a tree in a quarter-sawn manner is "a tremendously wasteful method, and as a result a very expensive method, of turning a tree trunk into boards and has thus fallen from favor in its use" (lines 51–54), necessitates which of the following conclusions?

  A. Inefficient practices are often used when cutting trees.
  B. Wasteful methods can be efficient and more costly.
  C. Inefficient practices are no longer popular or costly.
  D. Inefficient practices are costly and are no longer popular.

GO ON TO THE NEXT PAGE.

Passage V (Questions 25–29)

On March 14, 1788, Adam Hamilton noted in the Federalist Papers his high regard for the electoral college and its workings. "I venture somewhat further, and hesitate not to affirm, that if the manner of it be not perfect, it is
5 at least excellent. It unites in an eminent degree all the advantages, the union of which was to be wished for." The close and hotly contested race for the presidency for the United States between George W. Bush and Al Gore has once again brought to the forefront of our thinking an aspect
10 of the Constitution that is usually never considered: That is that the citizens of the United States do not directly vote for the president of the United States. The electoral college actually casts the votes deciding who will be the President. Many would argue that the will of the American people
15 needs to be better represented and that the popular vote should be the deciding factor. One might ask, Why not let the popular vote decide our president?

For one thing, the electoral college has a definite tendency to limit third-party candidates. This is a desirable
20 aspect of the college. The apparent greater voter choice among a huge number of candidates is a dangerous illusion. In practice, well-organized minorities have a very good chance to achieve the highest or second-highest share of votes, advancing to a run-off round. Consider the tremendous
25 influence nowadays of political action committees and large corporations. Who do you think would be electing the president of the United States? Do you believe that the majority of Americans, for instance, support homosexual adoptions, the right of every person to own a machine gun,
30 or the legalization of recreational drugs?

The Bush v Gore election demonstrated the futility of attempting to count individual votes beyond a reasonable degree of certainty. Many statisticians found that the commonly reported and scrutinized lead in popular votes
35 in Florida (choose your own candidate for this) was smaller than the reasonable degree of uncertainty associated with any large attempt at counting votes in these elections. Over a year later the election was still being repeatedly debated with various sides claiming that their candidate had actually
40 received a majority of the popular vote. Common sense, stability, and the Constitution of the United States call for the election of a president within a certain time. This could not be met with attempts to precisely count popular votes. The Electoral College vote tends to be less in doubt than
45 the popular vote, for two reasons: 1) only a few states will have close races, even if the national vote is close, and 2) the electoral vote tends to magnify the margin of victory. Under a direct election system, a close race nationwide could realistically depend upon absentee ballots, or upon
50 recounts anywhere. In a direct election, any of the 160,000 polling places in the U.S. could affect the outcome.

Finally, consider where you *live and vote* for the head of the executive branch. If you live in California then you are probably very much in favor of the popular vote. Anywhere
55 else in the country and you may, or should not, be so sure. This is because California, soon stands to become the most populous state in the union. California, by virtue of her climate, topography, and demographic situation has many concerns, needs, and issues, which the rest of the country
60 does not necessarily share. Would you want Californians choosing the next president of the United States while you sit by and watch? Sure, you could cast your vote, but you could rest assured that it would be inconsequential and that your state's desires and viewpoints would be ignored. The
65 electoral college protects the vast union of the states, their varied cultures, desires, and needs, and keeps us from living under the president of California *and* the United States of America.

25. If the hypothesis of the passage is correct, one should find that Presidential elections in the United States:

    A. are usually not indicative of the popular vote.
    B. are not frequently contested.
    C. do not reflect the will of the people.
    D. are almost always contested.

TEST 3

26. According to the passage, any <u>large</u> attempt at precisely counting votes with respect to reasonable degrees of certainty is characteristic of:

     I.   a California election.
    II.   contested leads in popular votes.
   III. the electoral college.

  A. I only
  B. II only
  C. II and III only
  D. I, II, and III

27. The author claims, "In practice, well-organized minorities have a very good chance to achieve the highest or second-highest share [of popular votes], advancing to a run-off round" (lines 22–24). The support offered for this conclusion is:

  A. weak; Bush v. Gore demonstrated the impact of well-organized minorities.
  B. weak; political action committees and large corporations are representative of minorities.
  C. strong; political action committees and large corporations are tremendously influential.
  D. strong; the majority of Americans would support homosexual adoptions.

28. A study of international elections reveals that immediately following an election, governmental instability increases in relation to the amount of time it takes for the results to be announced. This information increases the likelihood of which of the following answers to the author's question about why we should not let the popular vote decide our president?

  A. The electoral college "unites … all the advantages … ."
  B. The electoral college actually casts the votes deciding who will be the president.
  C. The popular vote is a more accurate representation.
  D. The popular vote could depend on vote recounts.

29. The statement is made that "many statisticians found that the commonly reported and scrutinized lead in popular votes in Florida (choose your own candidate for this) was smaller than the reasonable degree of uncertainty associated with any large attempt at counting votes in these elections" (lines 33–37). The excerpted "(choose your own candidate for this)" means that:

  A. the author does not want everyone to be able to choose their own candidate.
  B. the author is aware that opinions on this matter differ.
  C. the author is aware that there are going to be those who are in favor of the popular vote.
  D. the author wants everyone to be happy with the election results.

TEST 3

GO ON TO THE NEXT PAGE.

Passage VI (Questions 30–35)

Book authors' compensation is a tricky and detailed matter, with many countervailing considerations, and authors should not sign a book contract lightly before extensive reflection. Authors are typically paid a small "advance," or
5 cash payment, by the publisher to cover their immediate living expenses and research costs. But the bulk of their compensation comes in the form of "royalty" payments, calculated as a percentage of the publisher's gross receipts from all future sales of the book. Typically, the going rate
10 is 8 to 10% of the first 5,000 copies sold, 12½% of the next 5,000, and 15% of subsequent sales. While the author will want to negotiate the highest possible advance and royalty percentage, there are many other variables that should be considered.

15 First, authors should read their contracts to be sure royalties are calculated based on the "list" (cover) price, not the wholesale price, and not the publisher's net receipts. This is because bookstores buy their stock for resale from the publisher at a 45% discount from the list price. Much
20 of the book receipts are applied by the publisher to cover its costs for editing, manufacturing, advertising, selling, shipping, and warehousing the book, as well as its overhead, including rent, general payroll, and utilities.

The lion's share of an author's compensation depends
25 on strong book sales. But unfortunately, after a book is written and the book contract is signed, there is not much more the author can do to increase sales. The book's success will depend largely on the publisher's efforts at distribution. If the publisher fails to advertise the book widely, or cannot
30 get many bookstores to carry it on their shelves, the book will earn little despite its quality since potential readers are unlikely to even realize that it exists. First-time authors may assume that publishers have every incentive to promote the book effectively since their profits also depend on book
35 sales. But this is not always the case, for several reasons. Some large publishers seek to gain prestige in the industry by publishing a wide assortment of diverse titles, even though they believe many of these will not be profitable. Consequently, they will not promote vigorously those books
40 they assume are loss leaders. Also, some publishers large and small concentrate the bulk of their advertising budget on promoting a few projected bestsellers, while leaving the other titles to split whatever is left. Finally, some smaller publishing houses simply lack the sales force, contacts, and
45 territorial reach to promote a book effectively. If a book fails to sell well for any of these reasons, the result may prove financially disastrous for the author, since bookstores, seeking to carry the newest titles, will often remove from their stocks, and return, any copies unsold after 1–2 months.
50 Thus, writers should investigate the publisher's "backlist" policy for promoting older books and engage in a frank discussion of what kinds of promotion the publisher intends to pursue and what other titles are currently competing for the publisher's budget and attention.

55 To increase sales, authors may want to engage in strategic positioning of their product. After the book is accepted for publication, a wise author will contact the publisher's employees to drum up enthusiasm for the book and to suggest new avenues for promotion. Authors may also
60 engage in self-promotion. For example, if the book relates to current events, the author can obtain free publicity by sending an excerpt to a daily newspaper's Op-Ed or Letters section, with a note that material comes from a book.

In sum, author salary negotiations are not without their
65 perils, and first time authors may want to hire an agent to conduct negotiations. Agents get 10% of the value of any rights that they negotiate away from the publishers, so their incentives tend to be aligned more closely with the writer's.

30. It can most justifiably be said that the main purpose of the passage is:

A. to explain the concepts of book publishing.
B. to examine the authoring of a book.
C. to enlighten publishers regarding common publishing practices.
D. to advise authors about the publishing business.

GO ON TO THE NEXT PAGE.

31. The passage suggests that its author would probably *disagree* with which of the following statements?

 A. The authoring of a book can be very lucrative.
 B. Publisher's profits depend on book sales.
 C. For the most part, royalty payments will determine an author's compensation. *Licn's payment plays*
 D. Most publishers will try to take advantage of a naïve or first-time author. *big role.*

32. The passage offers several examples regarding why publishers might fail "to promote [a] book effectively" (lines 33–34). From the first example to the last, the publishers are designated as:

 A. good promoters to poor.
 B. large to small.
 C. effective to ineffective.
 D. honest to dishonest.

33. According to the passage, from a purely monetary perspective, the worst that could happen to an author would be to:

 A. receive low royalty payments.
 B. accept compensation based upon wholesale prices.
 C. have his book promoted ineffectively by the publisher.
 D. have the public fail to realize that the book exists.

Licn's payment depends on book sales

34. Which of the following would be an example of the "countervailing considerations" (line 2) facing an author?

 A. A publisher who primarily promotes his bestsellers
 B. A publisher who pays an 8% flat rate
 C. A publisher who pays a 15% flat rate
 D. A publisher who lacks a sales force

35. Assume that a book is written and a contract signed with a publisher. Although the book is highly promoted by the author and critically acclaimed, no increase occurs in actual book sales. Which of the following hypotheses about this outcome is the most plausible on the basis of the studies cited?

 A. The author did not negotiate the highest possible royalty percentage.
 B. The book's subject matter was too diverse for wide public acceptance.
 C. The publishing house lacked the necessary contacts.
 D. A first-time author probably wrote the book.

GO ON TO THE NEXT PAGE.

TEST 3

Passage VII (Questions 36–40)

In 1916, on a single battlefield near the small town of Albert, France, more than a half million men were killed or wounded in five months. This battle was to be known as "The Battle of the Somme." Of the initial attacking force, nearly
5 half were killed or wounded in the first day. Laden with heavy gear that severely restricted their speed and mobility, the soldiers advanced across open ground in the light of day into heavy machine-gun fire. Their chances of survival were slim, at best. The deafening roar of battle and seeing their
10 comrades on either side of them being torn to pieces by the hail of flying metal must have been overwhelming. In spite of this, few men disobeyed their orders to advance.

One may wonder why more men did not refuse to go when faced with such a meager chance of surviving.
15 However, the motivating factors to obey were powerful. The first and possibly the strongest motivator was peer pressure, which was especially intense at the Somme, where fighting units were made up of men from the same communities. A man's unwillingness to embarrass himself in the eyes of his
20 lifelong friends may, in itself, have been enough to compel him to go "over the top," out of his trench, and into the hail of enemy fire.

Another strong motivator would have been the so-called herding instinct, where a man finds security in a
25 crowd. Under precise and accurate sniper fire, when a man is part of a group from which individuals are being selected as targets, cohesion breaks down. However, for the soldiers under indiscriminate machine-gun fire at the Somme, a natural reaction would be to try to blend in among the
30 other men, much like the behavior of a herd animal running from a predator. A soldier refusing to advance would be drawing attention to himself and thus acting contrary to this instinct.

There is also the question concerning the moment
35 of decision. At what point does the soldier finally say that he won't go? Refusing an order invites immediate confrontation. As long as he does what he is told, he follows the path of least resistance; he leaves open his option to say "No." In fact, this is itself a security. It is the one thing that
40 the soldier can do that will change his situation. If he refuses to attack, the threat will no longer be the Germans but his own officer; he will no longer be rushing toward the front but sitting in the rear, and his weapon will no longer be his rifle but his powers of persuasion over his officer. His option
45 to say "No" is his only control over an otherwise completely uncontrollable situation. However, once this option is spent, he will have no more alternatives; he will have played all his cards. Here too, it would seem that human nature dictates procrastination; a bad situation is more tolerable when there
50 exists an option.

Finally, there is the obvious to consider. There were serious repercussions for disobedience, including being shot on the spot. In addition, the chances of successfully rebelling against the order to attack were not very good.
55 Thus, when the time came to attack, whether a soldier reasoned to a conscious decision to obey or whether he did what came natural, he was most likely to follow the order—even when those orders sent him charging headlong into blazing machine-gun fire.

36. According to the passage, which of the following is most likely to be true about the relationship between the individual soldier and his comrades at the Battle of the Somme?

A. The individual soldier was motivated to prove his bravery to his lifelong friends. ✓

B. The individual soldier knew that there were repercussions to saying 'No' to an officer. ✓

C. If the individual soldier stayed within a large group of his comrades he was unlikely to be shot.

D. The individual soldier was not willing to be shamed in front of his friends.

37. The author's assertion that soldiers under machine-gun fire trying to "blend in among the other men" is analogous to the "behavior of a herd animal running from a predator" (lines 29–31) suggests that such behavior:

> I.   will ultimately fail.
> II. is instinctual, but not always effective.
> III. stems from not wanting to be singled out. *lines 31-33*

- **A.** I only
- **B.** II only
- **C.** II and III only
- **D.** I and III only

38. The existence of which of the following circumstances would most strongly CHALLENGE the information in the passage?

- **A.** After-action reports indicating that those who had acted autonomously were more likely to have survived the battle
- **B.** Historical research indicating that most of the soldiers had not known one another well prior to their enlistments ✓
- **C.** War diaries indicating that some soldiers had been summarily executed for fleeing the battlefield
- **D.** Historical studies revealing that the majority of soldiers obeyed the orders of their officers

39. The passage suggests that precise shooting that tends to single out individual soldiers would do which of the following to the "herding instinct"?

- **A.** Strengthen it, because there would be even more motivation to "blend in"
- **B.** Weaken it, because the soldiers would want to draw attention to themselves
- **C.** Strengthen it, because the soldiers would be even more motivated to "blend in"
- **D.** Weaken it, because the soldiers realize that there is nowhere to hide

40. Suppose it is found that convicted and sentenced killers on death row experience more serenity and peace when they realize that they have finally run out of appeals and know for certain that they will inevitably be executed within a short time. How would this information affect the author's claims about "procrastination" (lines 48–50)?

- **A.** This information *strengthens* the author's claims because it indicates that 'serenity' was a motivating factor for the soldiers.
- **B.** This information *weakens* the author's claims because it indicates that one can become resigned to anything.
- **C.** This information *weakens* the author's claims because it indicates that a bad situation without options is more tolerable.
- **D.** This information *strengthens* the author's claims because it proves that "human nature dictates procrastination."

STOP. IF YOU FINISH BEFORE TIME IS CALLED, CHECK YOUR WORK. YOU MAY GO BACK TO ANY QUESTION IN THIS TEST.

STOP.

TEST 3

Verbal Reasoning Test 4
Time: 60 Minutes
Questions 1–40

VERBAL REASONING

DIRECTIONS: There are seven passages in this Verbal Reasoning test. Each passage is followed by several questions. After reading a passage, select the one best answer to each question. If you are not certain of an answer, eliminate the alternatives that you know to be incorrect and then select an answer from the remaining alternatives. Indicate your selection by blackening the corresponding oval on your answer document.

Passage I (Questions 1–5)

Too many of our young people are caught up in conflicts every day that they do not know how to manage—teasing, jealousy, and physical aggression. Juvenile delinquency and violence are symptoms of youth's inability to manage
5 conflict in their lives. Teaching youth how to manage conflict in a productive way can help reduce incidents of violent behavior. Conflict-resolution education is a beneficial component of a comprehensive violence prevention and intervention program in schools and communities. It
10 encompasses problem solving in which the parties in dispute express their points of view, voice their interests, and find mutually acceptable solutions. Conflict-resolution education programs help the parties recognize that while conflict happens all the time, people can learn new skills
15 to deal with conflict in nonviolent ways. The programs that appear to be most effective are comprehensive and involve multiple components, such as the problem-solving processes and principles of conflict resolution, the basics of effective communication and listening, critical and creative
20 thinking, and an emphasis on personal responsibility and self-discipline.

Most school violence-prevention programs include conflict-resolution education. According to William DeJong, a lecturer at the Harvard School of Public Health, "the best
25 school-based violence prevention programs seek to do more than reach the individual child. They instead try to change the total school environment, to create a safe community that lives by a credo of non-violence and multicultural appreciation." Effective programs can enable children
30 to respond nonviolently to conflict through processes of negotiation, mediation, and consensus decision-making. They can enable an educator's ability to manage students' behavior without coercion by emphasizing personal responsibility and self-discipline. These programs also
35 mobilize community involvement in violence prevention through education programs and services such as expanding the role of youth as effective citizens beyond the school into the community.

Experts identify four school-based conflict-resolution
40 strategies that can be replicated in other settings. These are commonly referred to as: (1) Peer Mediation, (2) Process Curriculum, (3) Peaceable Classrooms, and (4) Peaceable Schools. The Peaceable Schools model incorporates the elements of the other three approaches. It is up to each local
45 school district to decide how conflict-resolution education will be integrated into its overall educational environment. The expectation is that when youth learn to recognize and constructively address what takes place before conflict or differences lead to violence, the incidence and intensity
50 of these situations will diminish. The program examples empower young people with the processes and skills of conflict resolution. However, youth need to know that conflict resolution does not take precedence over adult responsibility to provide the final word in a variety of
55 circumstances or situations. Conflict resolution can only supplement, not supplant, adult authority.

Recognizing the importance of directly involving youth in conflict resolution, many schools and communities are using the Peer Mediation approach. Under this approach,
60 specially trained student mediators work with their peers to resolve conflicts. Mediation programs reduce the use of traditional disciplinary actions such as suspension, detention, and expulsion; encourage effective problem-solving; decrease the need for teacher involvement in student
65 conflicts; and improve school climate. An example of a Peer Mediation program is We Can Work It Out, developed by the National Institute for Citizenship Education in the Law and the National Crime Prevention Council. The program promotes mediation, negotiation, and other nonlitigating
70 methods as strategies to settle unresolved confrontations and fights.

1. The passage suggests that conflict-resolution education in the schools provides:

 A.   students with the tools to effectively teach these concepts to the community.
 B.   students with the understanding to accept more traditional disciplinary actions.
 C.   changes to the whole school environment.
 D.   teachers with guidelines that emphasize their personal responsibility.

2. According to the passage, to whom might one look to become involved with in order to effectively address the problems of youth violence in schools, rather than using coercion?

 A.   The National Institute for Citizenship Education in the Law
 B.   Parents
 C.   Teachers
 D.   The community

3. Suppose that a study found that in the case of young people, they are incapable of recalling the circumstances that led up to a violent conflict. Which of the following statements is an assumption of the author about conflict resolution strategies that would be called into *question*?

 A.   Effective programs can enable children to respond nonviolently to conflict through processes of negotiation, mediation, and consensus decision-making.
 B.   When youth learn to recognize and constructively address what takes place before conflict, the incidence of these situations will diminish.
 C.   The programs that appear to be most effective are comprehensive and involve multiple components such as the problem-solving processes and principles of conflict resolution.
 D.   Too many of our young people are caught up every day in conflicts every day that they do not know how to manage.

4. According to the passage, reduced incidents of violence with respect to youth quarreling is characteristic of:

 I.   Peer Mediation approaches.
 II. learning to manage conflict in a productive way.
 III. an emphasis on personal responsibility.

 A.   II only
 B.   III only
 C.   II and III only
 D.   I, II, and III

5. Which of the following approaches would most likely be stressed by a school administrator who had an understanding of managing students' behavior without coercion?

 A.   self-discipline
 B.   detention
 C.   litigation
 D.   projection

GO ON TO THE NEXT PAGE.

Passage II (Questions 6–10)

Integrity as we know it today stands for soundness of moral principle and character-uprightness-honesty. Yet there is more. Integrity is also an ideal, a goal to strive for, and for a man or woman to "walk in their integrity"
5 requires constant discipline. The word integrity itself is a martial word that comes to us from an ancient Roman army tradition.

During the time of the twelve Caesars, the Roman army would conduct morning inspections. As the inspecting
10 centurion would come in front of each legionnaire, the soldier would strike with his right fist the armor breastplate that covered his heart. The armor had to be strongest there in order to protect the heart from sword thrusts and arrow strikes. As the soldier struck his armor, he would shout
15 "Integritas!" (in-teg-ri-tas), which in Latin means material wholeness, completeness, and entirety. The inspecting centurion would listen closely for this affirmation and for the ring that well-kept armor would give off. Satisfied that the armor was sound and that the soldier beneath it was
20 protected, he would then move on to the next man.

At about the same time, the Praetorians, or imperial bodyguard, were ascending into power and influence. Drawn from the best "politically correct" soldiers of the legions, they received the finest equipment and armor. They
25 no longer had to shout "Integritas" to signify that their armor was sound. Instead, as they struck their breastplate, they would shout "Hail Caesar!" to signify that their heart belonged to the imperial personage, not to their unit, not to an institution, not to a code of ideals. They had armored
30 themselves to serve the cause of a single man.

A century passed and the rift between the Legion and the imperial bodyguard and its excesses grew larger. To signify the difference between the two organizations, the legionnaire, upon striking his armor, would no longer shout
35 "Integritas!" but would instead shout "Integer!" (In-te-ger). Integer means undiminished, complete, perfect. It not only indicated not only that the armor was sound, but also that the soldier wearing the armor was of sound character. He was complete in his integrity, his heart was in the right place,
40 his standards and morals were high. He was not associated with the immoral conduct that was rapidly becoming the signature of the Praetorian guards.

The armor of integrity continued to serve the Legion well. For over four centuries, they held the line against the
45 marauding Goths and Vandals, but, by 383 A.D., the social decline that infected the Republic and the Praetorian Guard had taken its toll upon the Legion.

As a fourth-century Roman general wrote, "When, because of negligence and laziness, parade ground drills
50 were abandoned, the customary armor began to feel heavy since the soldiers rarely, if ever, wore it. Therefore, they first asked the emperor to set aside the breastplates and mail and then the helmets. So our soldiers fought the Goths without any protection for the heart and head and were often beaten
55 by archers. Although there were many disasters, which led to the loss of great cities, no one tried to restore the armor to the infantry. They took their armor off, and when the armor came off—so, too, came their integrity. It was only a matter of a few years until the Legion rotted from within
60 and was unable to hold the frontiers. The barbarians were at the gates!"

The biblical book of practical ethics—better known as the Book of Proverbs—sums it up very nicely: "The integrity of the upright shall guide them: but the perverseness of
65 transgressors shall destroy them" (Proverbs 11:3).

6. In the context of the passage, the term *politically correct* does NOT refer primarily to:

A. the soldiers who received the finest equipment and armor.

B. the soldiers who were undiminished.

C. differences between the allegiances of the Praetorians and the legionnaires.

D. recognition of Caesar as the imperial personage.

GO ON TO THE NEXT PAGE.

7. According to the author, the reason "integritas" was replaced with "integer" was:

A. that the Praetorians no longer wished to be associated with the legionnaires.

B. that Caesar wanted only the finest equipment for his Guard.

C. to signify the difference between the legionnaires and the Praetorians.

D. that the legionnaires felt somewhat diminished.

8. On the basis of the passage, it is reasonable to conclude that "sword thrusts" and "arrow strikes":

A. could probably penetrate Roman armor.

B. were not something one needed to be concerned about.

C. represented character and integrity.

D. could also symbolize depravity.

9. According to the passage, at some point "customary armor began to feel heavy" (line 50). This was also an indication that:

A. negligence and laziness were easier to bear. ✓

B. negligence and laziness were heavier burdens.

C. the Romans were training harder.

D. Caesar's guards were becoming weaker. ✓

10. Assume that the Roman Empire had not fallen when it did, but continued to reign for another 400 years. What could be the relevance of this continued period of influence to the author's views about the "armor of integrity"?

A. This would demonstrate that integrity is important to an empire's longevity.

B. This would reveal that moral armor was not that important.

C. This would indicate that the Praetorians were better soldiers than described in the passage.

D. This would demonstrate that the Goths were weak enemies.

TEST 4

GO ON TO THE NEXT PAGE.

Passage III (Questions 11–15)

The pioneering clinical research of the Japanese scientist Dr. Yasu Kuno, published in *Ase* [*Perspiration*], reveals several interesting aspects of perspiration. Normal physiological perspiration is an ongoing process that takes

5 place at varying levels, even at room temperature. At low temperatures, perspiration remains undetectable, because the rate of evaporation matches the rate of perspiration. This is the biological mechanism operating at the peak of efficiency. However, at high temperatures, perspiration

10 becomes so copious as to be visible, especially if attended by high humidity, or if evaporation is impaired. In addition to this normal base perspiration, nervousness may produce extra "psychological" perspiration, whose volume often doubles or triples the normal amount of secretions, usually

15 for brief periods.

Normal physiological perspiration, may be reduced by several methods, if need be. One obvious method is the application of cold packs directly to the skin, particularly to areas such as the wrist and carotid artery, where larger blood

20 vessels are closest to the skin's surface, or directly to sweat centers such as the armpit, hand, foot, etc. Interestingly, while the application of cold will prevent sweating for several minutes, perspiration levels have been shown to return to normal quickly despite continued application.

25 However, this effect can be avoided by shifting the location of the cooling pack every five minutes. Kuno speculates that such shifting creates the perception of continuous cold drafts, which signals the body to reduce perspiration levels. One natural method of reducing body temperature without

30 sweating, commonly seen among animals without sweat glands, is panting. A panting animal achieves the same effect—enhanced evaporation of hot fluids from the skin's surface—by exposing its saliva to the open air, whereby the evaporation exerts a cooling influence. While overheated

35 humans can also pant, the gains for them are slighter since their tongues provide (proportionally) less surface area, and the act of panting itself, because it is unnatural, actually faintly increases body temperature with predictable results.

Persons exposed to frequent high heat and/or humidity

40 become acclimatized, developing the habitual tendency to perspire more, regardless of actual ambient heat. While one remains in the environment that one has adapted to, this is a highly efficient and desirable adaptation. However, a situation wherein one adapts to the Sahara desert only

45 to return to humid New Orleans can be imagined, and it is usually not desirable. Presumably, then, progressive reduction in a person's ambient temperature should have the opposite effect.

Dr. Kuno's research also offers promise for those

50 suffering from hyperhidrosis, or excessive sweating. Injections of a 3% hypertonic salt solution have been shown to decrease perspiration by 12–22%. More radical treatments include the application of antiperspirant chloride salts with the aid of a mild electrical current,

55 which increases their absorption into the sweat glands. A solution of 7–10% formaldehyde, when applied to sweat centers, usually "shocks" them into inactivity for several days. Using the same methodology, researchers are now investigating injections of Botox (botulism) directly into

60 the bloodstream. Currently, Botox injections are commonly used as a temporary treatment for facial skin wrinkling. The injection temporarily paralyzes the skin and facial muscles, which relaxes the skin around the wrinkle and also lessens the muscle constrictions that deepen wrinkle lines. Through

65 further research, it is hoped that Botox will have similar dampening effects on overactive sweat glands.

11. Which of the following is *not* a characteristic of perspiration caused by nervousness, as described in the passage?

  I.   It may double or triple the normal amount of secretions.
  II. It may be reduced by several methods.
  III. It may occur in addition to physiological perspiration.

  A. I only
  B. II only
  C. III only
  D. II and III only

GO ON TO THE NEXT PAGE.

12. The term *shocks* (line 57) refers implicitly to formaldehyde's:

   A. paralyzing effect on sweat glands.
   B. application with a mild electrical current.
   C. strong and long-lasting odor.
   D. tendency to irritate the skin.

13. Passage information indicates that which of the following statements must be true?

   A. Panting works as well as Botox injections.
   B. Application of cold packs works because it lowers body temperature.
   C. Nervous perspiration is common to everyone.
   D. A complete failure to perspire indicates that something is wrong.

14. According to the passage, all of the following are *true* about the application of cold packs to reduce perspiration EXCEPT:

   A. The cold packs should be applied directly to sweat centers.
   B. This method works because it reduces body temperature.
   C. The cold packs should be applied directly to areas where large vessels are closest to the skin surface.
   D. After a short time, continued application of the cold packs on the same area ceases to be effective.

15. On the basis of the passage, one may assume that panting is most effective when:

   A. the organism pants naturally and has a proportional tongue.
   B. there is no other way for the organism to cool itself.
   C. cold packs can be applied constantly to the organism's tongue.
   D. the organism's tongue has a proportionally large surface area, and it pants naturally.

TEST 4

GO ON TO THE NEXT PAGE.

Passage IV (Questions 16–20)

What 'Agenda' are you against? If you are pro-life, then you are anti-abortion. How about Big Government? Then you are anti-decentralization. Save the Whales? You are anti-whaling. Dolphin-safe Tuna? Anti–drift nets. But

5 how to get that message across in a not-so-negative manner. We certainly don't want to be labeled as 'antis!' What are the techniques used by the antis in modern democracies? How does the minority put forth their anti-agenda until it is embraced and adopted by the majority? Hitler knew:

10 By means of shrewd lies, unremittingly repeated, it is possible to make people believe that heaven is hell—and hell heaven. The greater the lie, the more readily it will be believed. —Adolf Hitler

15 The first basic technique is the Big Lie. It is simple to use, yet surprisingly effective. It consists of claiming that the Agenda causes harm: cancer, heart disease, poverty, and other serious problems that people fear. The fact that there is no supporting evidence for such claims does not matter. The

20 trick is to keep repeating the lie—because if something is said often enough, people tend to think there must be some truth to it.

A variation of the Big Lie is the Laundry List. List enough "evils" and even if proponents can reply to some

25 of them, they will never be able to cover the entire list. The Laundry List is always impressive since it lends the appearance of tremendous evidence. This technique is most effective in debates, letters to the editor, and television news reports.

30 A key factor in any anti campaign is the use of printed materials and documents. Scientific or academic journals will rarely publish them, but your target audience does not read those anyway, do they? Most local newspapers are more than willing to express minority viewpoints regardless

35 of whether facts support them. A few editors even welcome the controversy the antis generate—expecting that it will increase readership. The aim is to create the illusion of scientific controversy. The documents can quote statements that are out of date or out of context. Quotes from obscure

40 or hard-to-locate journals can often be used. And half-truths always work well. Another favored tactic is to Misquote a pro-Agenda scientist or official, knowing that even if the scientist protests, the reply will not reach all those who read the original misquote.

45 The Conspiracy Gambit is particularly effective when government agencies are providing support for the Agenda. The beauty of the conspiracy charge is that it can be leveled at anyone and there is absolutely no way to disprove it. After all, how does one prove that something is not taking place

50 secretly? Favorite "conspirators" are the U.S. Public Health

Service, the American Medical Association, and almost any government-subsidized industry. It is easy to convince the public that these groups could all be working together to "destroy" and "deceive" the American people! Years ago,

55 conspiracy claims would work primarily with the very paranoid. However, modern-day government scandals may make them seem realistic to a wider audience.

The Slippery Slope claim is a related ploy, and should always be used on the heels of the Conspiracy Gambit. "This

60 is only the beginning!" you should wail. "First they will [Your-Warning-Here], then they will [Oh-My-Goodness], and the next thing you know they will be [Completely-Unacceptable-Goes-Here]!" Who "they" are need not be specified. We know, and so will those you are trying to

65 convince.

Finally, "Let the people decide!" This sounds as if you wish to use the democratic process to make the decision. Nevertheless, experience in many cities has shown otherwise. Curiously, studies have shown that Agendas

70 can fail in referendums even in communities where public opinion favors the Agenda. People will usually go to the polls to vote against what they don't like. Therefore, the crucial factor in many referendums is your ability to mobilize fellow supporters.

16. According to the passage, if you "misquote" (line 41) a pro-Agenda scientist or official, the:

  A. newspapers will be unlikely to run further articles.
  B. editors will likely contact the source and correct the misquote.
  C. scientists and officials will not protest.
  D. protestations by a scientist or official will be to no avail.

GO ON TO THE NEXT PAGE.

17. Given the statements made in the passage, the reference "but your target audience does not read those [scientific journals] anyway, do they?" (lines 32–33) would suggest that:

   A. the author does not think much of scientific journals.
   B. the author does not think that printed materials are useful.
   C. the author is unsure who "your target audience" consists of.
   D. the author does not have high regard for those he must persuade.

18. The concept of the "Slippery Slope" (lines 58–65) would best be compared to the saying:

   A. "give 'em an inch and they'll take a mile."
   B. "a rolling stone gathers no moss."
   C. "the early bird gets the worm."
   D. "the boy who cried wolf."

19. According to the passage, the popularity of your 'anti' claims and position is not important because:

   I.   people will usually go to the polls to vote against what they don't like.
   II. people will usually go to the polls to vote for what they like.
   III. people will usually not go to the polls if your information is not accurate.

   A. I only
   B. II only
   C. I and III only
   D. II and III only

20. According to information in the passage, the best way to convince people to become vegetarians would be to:

   A. convince them that eating vegetables is healthy.
   B. convince them that eating meat is harmful.
   C. persuade them to study scientific journals.
   D. allow them to vote.

GO ON TO THE NEXT PAGE.

Passage V (Questions 25–31)

Cold weather clothing and equipment has evolved radically with the advent of synthetics. Traditional materials such as wools and eider down have given way to polypropylene and a myriad other more plasticlike products.
5 Though the old stand-bys still function as effectively as ever, they are no longer in favor with the more knowledgeable explorers, outdoorsmen, and experienced general consumers. For all but those who are simply traipsing to and fro from the artificial heat of cars and buildings, there are many good
10 reasons for the move to the synthetic materials, particularly when an individual is in a situation wherein he is relying on his own body heat to keep him warm.

Water retention in a material that is being worn or slept in is a critical factor in almost any cold-weather
15 environment. Moisture, either in the form of precipitation, snowmelt, or perspiration, is the bane of the individual who elects to be outdoors. Vapor barrier garments aside, given the choice, one would wear clothing that retained no moisture whatsoever. It is in this area of extremely low water retention
20 that synthetics excel. With synthetics, perspiration working its way to the surface of clothing becomes frost, which can be brushed away.

Surprisingly, the colder the weather, the less important this becomes. The most critical and dangerous temperatures
25 vis-à-vis hypothermia are above thirty degrees and below fifty degrees. This is due to the melt-freeze cycles wherein one is constantly encountering rain, wet snow, and water. In extremely cold weather, it is also very dry. Sleeping bags and the like can actually be thrown out onto the snow in the
30 sunshine to dry.

Wool, the traditional choice of the past, has hollow fibers and retains three percent of its weight in water when completely soaked and then hand-wrung dry. Compared to cottons, this is phenomenal. However,
35 modern polypropylenes, polar fleeces, capilenes, etc., retain only one percent of their weight in water under the same circumstances. This is a remarkable difference. When this synthetic clothing is layered in the correct fashion, the individual's body heat actually causes moisture to move
40 outwards to the surface of the clothing where it evaporates or can be wiped away. Additionally, the synthetics are not scratchy and irritating next to the skin like wool, as can be attested to by anyone who has worn a wool hat for any length of time and then switched to a softer, poly fleece–type hat.

45 Eider down does retain the advantage of being one of the lightest insulating materials and has not been surpassed in situations in which it will maintain its critical loft, even after being tightly compressed over long periods. However, down, the traditional choice for sleeping bags, has several
50 distinct disadvantages for all but the most experienced mountain climber. The most significant disadvantage of

down is the aforementioned tendency to retain water. Down soaks up moisture, in the form of perspiration and ambient humidity, like a sponge. Further, and perhaps most notably,
55 it is very difficult to dry in the outdoors; once wet, it stays wet. With a synthetic sleeping bag on the other hand, it is a common practice to buy the bag large and sleep with wet clothing and boots inside the bag itself. The individual's body heat dries the moisture from the boots and clothing
60 and the synthetic nature of the sleeping bag's filling allows the moisture to pass through to the surface of the bag. Lastly, down is also incredibly expensive, costing more than twice what a comparably temperature-rated bag made of synthetics would cost.

21. The central thesis of the passage is that:

A. synthetic materials are generally more suitable because they retain less moisture.

B. the colder the weather, the more selective one should be regarding one's clothing.

C. synthetic materials are always better than the "old stand-bys."

D. technology has radically changed the way we dress outdoors.

GO ON TO THE NEXT PAGE.

$6/7$

22. According to the passage, an "old stand-by" (line 5) would best be described as an item that:

    A. has outlived its usefulness.
    B. has been improved upon and should not be used.
    C. is still just as effective as what is being used nowadays.
    D. has been improved upon but still functions well.

23. According to the passage, if a person is outdoors in extremely cold weather, then:

    A. the risks of hypothermia significantly increase.
    B. the water-retaining properties of materials are less important.
    C. wool is just as good a choice as synthetics.
    D. one is constantly encountering wet snow and water.

24. An appropriate theory of survival in the outdoors, derived from the information contained in the passage, would state that maintaining body heat involves:

    I.   staying as dry as possible.
    II. using wool instead of cotton.
    III. wearing synthetic clothing.

    A. I only
    B. III only
    C. I and III only
    D. I, II, and III

25. The expression "artificial heat" (line 9) would best support a metaphor that compares computer-generated speech to:

    A. televised talking.
    B. written words.
    C. human vocalizations.
    D. computer-generated writing.

26. According to information in the passage, the best way to dry wet clothing when the temperature is above thirty degrees would be to:

    A. actually thrown them out onto the snow in the sunshine to dry.
    B. allow your body heat to dry them inside a synthetic sleeping bag.
    C. wear the clothing loose and in layers.
    D. wear the "old stand-bys."

27. According to the passage, the descriptive term "melt-freeze cycles" is characterized by all of the following EXCEPT:

    I.   extremely cold weather
    II. the most critical and dangerous temperatures
    III. hypothermia

    A. I only
    B. II only
    C. III only
    D. I and III

TEST 4

GO ON TO THE NEXT PAGE.

Passage VI (Questions 28–33)

"The Polish Rider," ostensibly painted by the legendary Rembrandt van Rijn, was recently deattributed by the Rembrandt Research Project. Its authenticity was previously disputed by critics, but for incorrect reasons.
5 Comparing it to Rembrandt's finest works, critics rejected "Polish Rider" as artistically inferior, saying Rembrandt himself would never have produced a painting of such low quality. Yet such a comparison presupposes that Rembrandt himself never produced anything less than his finest work.
10 By this standard, any one of Rembrandt's earlier, lesser, or more obscure paintings becomes a target for deattribution.

In fact, "Polish Rider" seems a studied attempt to copy Rembrandt's style. If the painting is viewed as a deliberate forgery, features that initially seem like artistic "flaws" will
15 appear to be the result of a calculated but overdone attempt to reproduce Rembrandt's artistic flourishes, with imperfect results. Like all forgeries, it has the telltale signs of trying too hard.

First, there is the apparent similarity of sunlight: a
20 yellow-gold hue colors the land, much like Rembrandt's landscapes circa 1638. The sun is covered in a diffuse golden mist, in Rembrandt's famous style of representing direct sunlight. Yet the light's luminance alone would be too weak and hazy to fully illuminate the contours of the
25 cliffs. We expect a more muted, narrow color band for the background, which would just begin to suggest the details of the cliff face. It seems that this artist lavished great care in rendering the features of the stone, whereas Rembrandt would not have bothered to dwell on such details.

30 Then, there is the horse: its rendering is poor, but flawed in a way that suggests not lack of skill, but overcompensation in copying an unfamiliar style. Art historians note Rembrandt's style grew less precise and more "painterly" with the passage of time. This artist must have
35 known this as well and worked to make his strokes looser and less distinct than was natural for him. An unintended consequence was a noticeable streaking. A wide brush was used to thinly spread a few drops of paint into a broad, loose stroke. Yet it was done to a fault: there was insufficient
40 paint on the brush to cover the canvas from the stroke's start to finish, producing rough, shallow, streaked bands. The strokes became too "painterly"—even looser, rougher, and shallower than Rembrandt's. This exaggerated stroke ended up causing a ghastly illusion of emaciated horse skin over
45 bone.

Finally, there is the rider's pose: attempt to imitate it, and you will discover that it is impossible. The pose is reminiscent of the supinated arm sculpted by Michelangelo; to imitate it, you would need extraordinary flexibility. Even
50 if you could copy the pose, you would find it impossible to clasp your fingers with the strength needed to grip a heavy

wood-and-metal hammer of the type the rider holds; the pressure on your wrist would be too much. Furthermore, the frequent shocks of horseback riding would make this a
55 bizarre contortion for a horseman to maintain.

Such awkward stances are not usually found in Rembrandt's paintings, except in an exceptional pose. Try once again to imitate the same arm position, but, without resting your wrist on your hip, rest your elbow and upper
60 forearm on a supporting surface, such as a table. This requires much less flexibility, and once you manage it, you find yourself in a position Rembrandt used for many self-portraits (such as "Self-portrait with Stone Sill"). Yet in every instance, the arm is supported by a flat surface such
65 as a sill or table. It is my theory that the forger, working without the benefit of a model, copied the pose from a sketch of one of Rembrandt's self-portraits. Not realizing the need for arm support, the forger mistakenly made the wrist into the weight-bearing point. The result is an awkward position
70 that not only defies human anatomy, but also supplies the most telling indication that portions of the painting were an ambitious copy of Rembrandt's own work.

It is fortunate that the "Polish Rider" has been deattributed. Now that it has been removed from the ranks
75 of the master's works, among which it had never found much approval, perhaps it will finally be judged in proper perspective: not as an inferior work of art, but rather as a superior example of forgery that for centuries withstood the test of time.

28. In the context of the passage, the word "painterly" (line 42) may be used to describe:

A. a more experienced style of painting.
B. a style common to forgers.
C. a more distinct style of painting.
D. a more precise style of painting.

GO ON TO THE NEXT PAGE.

29. According to information in the passage, the best way for an art forger to ensure that his forgery is not discovered would be to:

   A.   avoid difficult subject matter.
   B.   ensure that the postures of his subjects are realistic.
   C.   not attempt to imitate too precisely.
   D.   adopt a more 'painterly' style.

30. It is the author's theory that the "impossible" pose of the rider was a result of:

   A.   the forger working from a poor model.
   B.   the forger copying the pose from a subject in one of Rembrandt's other paintings.
   C.   the forger copying the pose from a sketch of a Rembrandt self-portrait.
   D.   the inexperience of the forger.

31. Which of the following examples from the passage would most clearly NOT be an example of a "painterly" (line 34) style?

   A.   The rendering of the "golden mist."
   B.   The rendering of the stone on the cliff face.
   C.   The rendering of the horse.
   D.   The rendering of the rider.

32. The passage suggests that the authenticity of a painting is frequently challenged by critics when the painting is perceived to be of inferior quality. The author argues that this is a poor basis for "deattribution" because:

   A.   not all of an artist's works can actually be attributed to him.
   B.   inferior quality may indicate that the artist was merely growing older.
   C.   basically, beauty is in the eye of the beholder.
   D.   not all of an artist's works are his finest.

33. Passage information indicates that which of the following statements must be true?

   A.   The forger was very familiar with Rembrandt's style.
   B.   The forger could not recreate the colors of Rembrandt's landscapes.
   C.   The low quality of "The Polish Rider" diminished Rembrandt's reputation.
   D.   "The Polish Rider" is actually a painting of Rembrandt himself.

TEST 4

GO ON TO THE NEXT PAGE.

Passage VII (Questions 34–40)

Defining sexual orientation has proven to be a difficult task for researchers. Society's trichotomous labeling of sexuality—as heterosexual, homosexual, or bisexual—leaves little flexibility if one does not "fit the mold" of a
5 particular label. The precise criteria for self-labeling are not specifically defined by society. Therefore, someone who has had a same-sex sexual experience at one time may still label himself heterosexual.

One research pioneer, who recognized that trichotomous
10 labeling produces an inaccurate description of sexuality was Dr. Kinsey, in his 1948 study. Kinsey's measure of sexual behavior consisted of a seven-point continuum, from zero (exclusively heterosexual) to six (exclusively homosexual). A score of three would indicate a person
15 who is equally bisexual in her sexual practices. Kinsey's continuum gave people the freedom to define their sexuality in relative terms, rather than absolutes. Kinsey's method of measuring sexuality challenged conventional labeling, and his research revealed that 37% of men had participated in
20 a post-adolescent same-sex encounter at least once. His continuum was based solely on sexual behavior, although Kinsey admitted that other factors (such as erotic drive and fantasy) play a crucial role in determining individuals' "sexual identity."

25 Another method of assessing sexuality was presented by Drs. Shively and DeCecco (1977), who divided what they termed "sexual identity" into four components. The first aspect was "gender" (male or female). The second was "gender identity," the psychological self-identification of the
30 individual as being male or female. The third was "social sex role," the set of cultural norms propagated by society for each sex. The last aspect Shively and DeCecco cited as composing sexual identity was "sexual orientation," the erotic and/or affectional responses to the same/opposite sex.
35 Under their system, same-sex eroticism did not necessarily detract from heterosexual eroticism. Their framework distinguishes between a person who feels varying amounts of erotic and/or affectional responses. In addition, their definition designated sexual behavior and orientation as two
40 distinct categories.

In the most recent sex survey, conducted by Laumann (1994), sexuality was separated into three components: behavior, desire, and identity (self-labeling). In the general population, 1.4% of women and 2.8% of men labeled
45 themselves homosexual. Of these, 59% of women and 44% of men reported having some same-sex desires, without identifying themselves as gay/lesbian, and without participating in homosexual behavior. Thirteen percent of men and 22% of women who engaged in homosexual
50 behavior neither identified themselves as gay/lesbian, nor reported same-sex desire. Thus, for one to label oneself "gay"/"lesbian," it seems crucial that one have both

homosexual behavior and desire. Self-identification, or "self-labeling," is another important aspect, because, for
55 some, it represents a conscious choice to identify with homosexuals as a group, and thus as part of a larger social identity. For example, some women who have not had sex with another woman nevertheless describe themselves as lesbian, as a feminist statement.

60 The question of fluidity of sexuality orientation complicates the matter further. Models, that acknowledge fluidity of erotic drive to some extent, such as the "development models" espoused by Cass (1987) and others, typically describe the movement of the individual from
65 initial blocking of homosexual desires to a sense of ease regarding homosexual feelings and practices. Thus, even these models view homosexual desire as a progression in which open homosexuality is the final destination. Thus, they typically view bisexuality as an interim "phase," rather than
70 a mature sexual orientation. They assume that, eventually, the individual arrives at a relatively fixed outcome. Among women especially, sexual orientation and self-labeling can change over the course of their lifetime. A woman who at one time was married and considered herself heterosexual
75 may later begin a relationship with another woman and redefine herself as lesbian. Among men, on the other hand, self-labeling tends to be more rigid. It appears that sexual orientation is more fluid for some individuals than for others, suggesting that exogenous forces might be at work, helping
80 some to define and redefine their sexual orientation.

34. The author claims that Doctors Shively and DeCecco's "definition designated sexual behavior and orientation as two distinct categories" (lines 39–40). The support offered for this conclusion is:

A. strong; the doctors' assessment method has a component for each category.

B. strong; the doctors divided "sexual identity" into four components.

C. weak; it is clear from the entire passage that the two are distinct categories.

D. weak; there does not appear to be a distinction in the doctors' assessment method.

GO ON TO THE NEXT PAGE.

35. Using Kinsey's continuum, a person whom Cass (lines 60–80) deemed to be of "mature sexual orientation" would most likely indicate which of the following scores?

   A. Seven
   B. Four
   C. One
   D. Six

36. An important comparison is made in the passage between:

   A. homosexuals and lesbians.
   B. homosexuals and heterosexuals.
   C. society's labeling and self-labeling.
   D. gender identity and gender.

37. Implicit in the author's conclusion that "for one to label oneself gay/lesbian, it seems crucial that they have both homosexual behavior and desire" (lines 51–53), is the assumption that:

   A. both homosexual behavior and desire were expressed by the "1.4% of women and 2.8% of men" in Laumann's survey.
   B. both homosexual behavior and desire were expressed by the "59% of women and 44% of men" in Laumann's survey.
   C. both homosexual behavior and desire were expressed by the "thirteen percent of men and 22% of women" in Laumann's survey.
   D. both homosexual behavior and desire were expressed by the "development models" in Cass's survey.

38. According to passage information, whose method of assessment would best describe a physical male who is attracted to other males but does not self-label as homosexual because he desires to physically become a female?

   A. Laumann
   B. Kinsey
   C. Cass
   D. Drs. Shively and DeCecco

39. Which of the following would Cass regard as in an "interim 'phase' rather than as a mature sexual orientation" (line 69–70)?

   I. Heterosexuals
   II. Homosexuals who had not revealed their sexuality publicly
   III. Bisexuals who were 'open' about their sexuality

   A. I only
   B. III only
   C. II and III only
   D. I, II, and III

40. If the passage information is correct, what inference is justified by the fact that studies conducted after Kinsey's have consistently failed to support his finding that 37% of men have participated in same-sex encounters "at least once," more than fifty years after the period described?

   A. Kinsey's study was not based solely on behavior.
   B. Kinsey's continuum offered more limited choices.
   C. Kinsey admitted that trichotomous labeling produced inaccurate descriptions.
   D. The subsequent studies do not seem to concern themselves with single same-sex encounters.

STOP. IF YOU FINISH BEFORE TIME IS CALLED, CHECK YOUR WORK. YOU MAY GO BACK TO ANY QUESTION IN THIS TEST.

TEST 4

STOP.

Verbal Reasoning Test 5
Time: 60 Minutes
Questions 1–40

VERBAL REASONING

DIRECTIONS: There are seven passages in this Verbal Reasoning test. Each passage is followed by several questions. After reading a passage, select the one best answer to each question. If you are not certain of an answer, eliminate the alternatives that you know to be incorrect and then select an answer from the remaining alternatives. Indicate your selection by blackening the corresponding oval on your answer document.

Passage I (Questions 1–6)

Recently, music historian and professor Mr. Rothstein decried a lack of interest in the new music, attributing it to a century of music appreciation courses. This seemed clearly at odds with everything I saw, which pointed to expanding
5 interest by the public in modern music. Only recently did I realize we were both right.

By "new music," Mr. Rothstein probably meant that of the *avant-garde*, like the music of twelve-tone composers continuing the tradition of theorists Schoenberg and Babbitt.
10 If this is the case, he is partially correct, in that there is no public interest in them, and partially wrong, by attributing this to music appreciation courses. There is no interest in such artists simply because they are uninteresting. Some of them, in their search to challenge the definitions of
15 music, have produced pieces so self-consciously opposed to the current understanding of music that it alienates the majority of the public, and appears to do so deliberately. The problem is accentuated by the fact that some of them do feel contempt for their audience, honestly considering the
20 masses to be asses for not accepting their extreme theories. Those who choose to pursue radically different approaches to composition may achieve personal artistic satisfaction, but they must also be prepared never to gain popular acceptance for their work. Even the most well known of these may
25 achieve little recognition outside academic circles, as was the case with Babbitt himself.

Strictly speaking, works by *avant-garde* artists may be called "new music" due to their recent creation, but the term may be better reserved for referring to those that guide
30 existing trends in new directions and have actual influence on the mainstream. The systematic study of music history must necessarily be the study of popular music. The academically "Certified Masterpieces," it must not be forgotten, are not merely randomly selected pieces, but those that have
35 somehow influenced or represented the mainstream of their time.

Mr. Rothstein will surely recognize that almost all the musicians profiled in the classroom were included not to increase their reputation among future listeners, but because
40 their contemporaries were significantly influenced by them, during or soon after their lifetimes. It would not, therefore, be logical to conclude that the selected musicians only achieved their fame after and because of their inclusion into the curriculum.

45 Mr. Rothstein's criticism, however, becomes valid towards the very end of the modern curriculum, when, probably due to the difficulty of knowing which of several currently active trends will turn out to be the dominant one, teachers turn to studying some of the radical musicians
50 such as those described above, rather than focusing on the more important trends currently exerting an influence on mainstream America.

One way to expand understanding of "new" music would be to include into the curriculum rap music and
55 international music favored by recent immigrants, as representing the product of social forces in the American population and at the same time a force intent on affecting its own social change. By staying alert to current trends, we would keep students equally well educated about their
60 present and their past.

1. The *author* of the passage characterizes the "new music" as:

A. exemplified by rap music and international music.
B. arousing increasing interest by the public.
C. exemplified by that of the twelve-tone composers.
D. exemplified by engendering a lack of interest in the public.

GO ON TO THE NEXT PAGE.

5/6

2. If the public reception of Einstein's theory of relativity repeated the reception that the author claims was given to Schoenberg's and Babbitt's compositions, most people would:

    A. view Schoenberg's and Babbitt's compositions as too radical.

    B. only have heard of Einstein's theory in an appreciation class.

    C. only have heard of Schoenberg's and Babbitt's compositions in an appreciation class.

    D. view Einstein's theory as too radical.

3. The claim that "only recently did I realize we were both right" (lines 5–6), is most in accord with the view that:

    A. the author and Mr. Rothstein are in agreement.

    B. Mr. Rothstein and Babbitt are in agreement.

    C. Mr. Rothstein's statements can be reinterpreted by the author.

    D. Mr. Rothstein presents primarily valid points.

4. The author probably mentions that "some of them do feel contempt for their audience, honestly considering the masses to be asses for not accepting their extreme theories" (lines 18–20) in order:

    A. to show intellectual elitism.

    B. to prove the composers' lack of popularity.

    C. to identify the cause of the problem.

    D. to use alliteration in argumentation.

5. According to the passage, which of the following is most likely to be true about the relationship between music appreciation courses and the music or musicians featured in these courses?

    I. These courses have created a "lack of interest in the new music" (line 2).

    II. The courses present musical works "that have somehow influenced or represented the mainstream of their time" (lines 34–36).

    III. "[S]elected musicians only achieved their fame after and because of their inclusion into the curriculum" (lines 42–44).

    A. I only

    B. II only

    C. I and III only

    D. I, II, and III

6. An appropriate theory of the relationship between artists and their work derived from the information contained in the passage would state that popular acceptance involves:

    I. achieving personal artistic satisfaction.

    II. influencing or representing the mainstream.

    III. creating within the current understanding of the genre.

    A. I

    B. I and II

    C. II and III

    D. I, II, and III

TEST 5

GO ON TO THE NEXT PAGE.

Passage II (Questions 7–11)

One part in particular sticks in my mind from that old animated movie *Donald Duck in MathMagic Land,* and it is a constant irritation to me that my subtle allusions to this movie and the "Golden Proportions" meet with blank stares
5 from my friends and family; subtlety is the basis for humor and I am a subtle and witty guy. Anyway, what amazed me about Donald's discussion with Pythagoras regarding the Golden Proportion is the Proportion's prevalence in the world. Pythagoras danced along violin strings explaining
10 the relationship between the tonal scales and the Proportion. Vivid yellow rectangles were superimposed snugly over the Parthenon and other Greek structures of the day, which then dissolved under the rectangles to be replaced by the paintings of Leonardo da Vinci, Seurat, and Mondrian. I was
15 amazed. With the Golden Rectangle placed directly on top of these architectural icons and well-known paintings, the repetitiveness and prevalence of these proportions was clear. Was this done on purpose? Were the proportions chosen first and then the building built and the paintings painted? Or
20 was this simply an inherent characteristic of "beauty" that artists unknowingly produced again and again?

The Golden Rectangle has been described as one of the most visually satisfying geometric shapes ever discovered. It can be derived repeatedly without mathematics by simply
25 using the relationships of the sides. However, there is a clear mathematical relationship and proportion here that simply explodes in its limitless possibilities as more and more is discovered about it. When the length of the rectangle is divided by the width, the answer is 1.618. If the width is
30 divided by the length, the answer is 0.618. Big deal, huh? Not so, Grasshopper. Solve for x where $1/x = 1 + x. x = 0.618$. The Golden Rectangle can be increasingly enlarged, as Donald seemed to realize, and then superimposed exactly over the logarithmic spirals of a Nautilus or the petals of a
35 flower.

The Golden Rectangle and Proportion are linked inextricably with the Fibonacci Series, which is the complementary view of the Golden Proportion. It is called the Fibonacci Series after Leonardo of Pisa, alias Leonardo
40 Fibonacci, born in 1175, whose great book on arithmetic, *The Liber Abaci* (1202), was a standard work for 200 years and is still considered the best book ever written on arithmetic. Fibonacci discovered the series of numbers beginning: 0, 1, 1, 2, 3, 5, 8, 13, 21, 34, 55, 89, 144, etc.; add
45 the last two numbers to get the next. Notice that the ratios of successive Fibonacci numbers, $F_n/F_n - 1$, approaches the Golden Proportion as n approaches infinity! The Fibonacci numbers form the best whole number approximations to the Golden Number.

50 These numbers are replete throughout nature. Dentists know that as you proceed from the larger teeth at the front of the mouth to the smaller in back, you find in them

the relationships of the Fibonacci numbers—the Gold Proportions. Plastic surgeons use the Golden Proportion
55 when attempting to achieve the ever-so subtle and seemingly indefinable quality of physical beauty in a human being. Golden Proportion calipers, which can be autoclaved for sterility, are available to these surgeons in order to more quickly find this relationship in the operating room. If you
60 count the opposing spirals found on the base of a pinecone, you will always find them to be 5 and 8, or 8 and 13, successive Fibonacci numbers; so too with a pineapple, or a daisy. The technical term for this study of the arrangements of branches, leaves, and seed heads in plants is phyllotaxis.
65 The arrangement of leaves is the same as for seeds and petals. All are placed at 0.618034. leaves, (seeds, petals), per turn. In terms of degrees, this is 0.618034 of 360°.

This is more than just fascinating happenstance. If there are 1.618 leaves per turn (or, equivalently, 0.618 turns
70 per leaf), then we have the best arrangement for each leaf to get the maximum exposure to light, casting the least shadow on the others. This also gives the best possible area exposed to falling rain so that the rain is directed back along the leaf and down the stem to the roots. For flowers or petals,
75 it gives the best possible exposure to insects to attract them for pollination. The whole of the plant seems to produce its branches, leaves, flowerhead, petals, and then seeds based upon the Golden Number. The discoveries of the occurrences of this Proportion and this series continue today. There is a
80 large society devoted to Fibonacci in California. Ha! Who says you can't learn anything watching cartoons.

7. Evidence shows that in Leonardo da Vinci's drawing of an old man, probably a self-portrait, the artist has overlaid the picture with a square subdivided into rectangles, some of which approximate Golden Rectangles. This fact tends to support the hypothesis concerning the "repetitiveness and prevalence of these proportions" (line 17) because:

A. this was "probably a self-portrait."
B. it is likely that da Vinci knew Fibonacci.
C. it is unlikely that this is mere coincidence.
D. it is unlikely that da Vinci knew Fibonacci.

GO ON TO THE NEXT PAGE.

8. Assume that a scroll was unearthed during an archeological dig in Cyprus, and it appeared to instruct architects of the Parthenon to design using Golden Proportions. This information would increase the likelihood of which of the following answers to the author's question, "[W]as this simply an inherent characteristic of 'beauty' that artists unknowingly produced again and again" (lines 20–21)?

A. No, the artists had been specifically instructed to use Golden Proportions.
B. No, the artists were not aware of this characteristic but used it repeatedly.
C. Yes, the artists simply strove for "beauty," and the better ones again and again produced the Golden Rectangles.
D. Yes, the scroll indicates that traditions were important to the Greeks.

9. The author claims that Leonardo of Pisa's "great book on arithmetic *The Liber Abaci* (1202), was a standard work for 200 years and is still considered the best book ever written on arithmetic" (lines 40–43). The support offered for this conclusion is:

A. weak; the author provides only the discovery and prevalence of the Fibonacci series in furtherance of this claim.
B. weak; the passage suggests that Fibonacci stole the concept of the series from the Greeks.
C. strong; the passage repeatedly refers to *The Liber Abaci* in furtherance of this claim.
D. strong; Fibonacci's discovery of leaves, flowerheads, and seeds is provided as support.

10. The passage indicates that the author would NOT agree with which of the following statements?

A. The Golden Proportion is an inherent characteristic of beauty.
B. The discoveries of the occurrences of the Golden Proportion continue today.
C. It is fascinating that the Golden Proportion seems to occur repeatedly throughout nature.
D. It is purely coincidental that the Proportion seems to appear in plants.

11. Suppose the author had inserted the following sentence at line 59: "The Fibonacci series has been used to accurately predict the number of male drones that a given hive will produce." This example would best illuminate the author's discussion of:

A. the relationship between the series and the Proportion.
B. how each succeeding number in the series is derived.
C. the Fibonacci numbers are replete throughout nature.
D. discoveries of the occurrences of this series are continuing, even to this day.

GO ON TO THE NEXT PAGE.

TEST 5

Passage III (Questions 12–17)

> "Spanking is love and scolding is affection."
> —Chinese proverb

Exhaustive research and study on the subject has shown that appropriate corporal punishment, when not
5 used as an impulsive recourse by an out of control parent, does not lead to violent behavior by the child in his or her adult life. Even though research maintained by the U.S. Department of Health and Human Services, National Clearinghouse on Child Abuse and Neglect Information,
10 predominantly indicates that this is true, there has been a growing movement in the past several decades to label any form of corporal punishment "the legitimization of violence," "hitting," and "child abuse." Despite the fact that over the course of 20 years, 27 states have banned school
15 corporal punishment, nearly half of U.S. parents now use physical punishment for disciplining their children. This suggests a trend towards a governmental blanket injunction that contrasts with prevailing parental practices.

The term "spanking" used herein adopts the definition
20 decided upon during an American Academy of Pediatrics conference on the effects of corporal punishment. Conference participants concluded that little evidence could be found for or against the use of spanking, defined as non-injurious physical punishment applied with an open hand
25 to the buttocks or extremities. Recent research has failed to determine whether spanking is an effective form of behavior modification or whether it has long-term negative consequences.

Though some parents may use "discipline" and
30 "spanking" as a prelude and excuse for what is really abuse, it is nevertheless erroneous to extrapolate further to say that all parents who spank are abusive. In a John Hopkins University School of Hygiene and Public Health study titled "Ethnicity, Income, and Parenting Contexts of
35 Physical Punishment in a National Sample of Families With Young Children," by L.S. Wissow, it was discovered that although some studies relate physical punishment and later dysfunction, others suggest that its effects depend on the context in which it is used. The authors analyzed data from
40 the Commonwealth Fund Survey of Parents with Young Children, a national sample of 2,017 parents with children younger than three. Parents reported their use of spanking, five other disciplinary practices, and four nurturing interactions. The authors used cluster analysis to define four
45 groups of parents with distinct patterns of discipline and nurturing. Two groups with above-average use of spanking shared a high prevalence of parent depressive symptoms and a low level of nurturing but had markedly different demographic profiles and use of nonphysical punishment.
50 Interestingly, parents who reported below-average spanking had relatively low levels of both disciplinary and nurturing interactions. Parents who used average levels of spanking made frequent use of nonphysical disciplinary strategies and had high levels of nurturing interactions.

55 In 1996, even the liberal bastion at the U.C. Berkeley Institute of Human Development offered this journal article to the American Academy of Pediatrics: "A Blanket Injunction Against Disciplinary Use of Spanking Is Not Warranted by the Data," which was authored by
60 D. Baumrind. This article explains why current research findings do not provide scientific evidence against spanking by parents. Seven propositions in support of disciplinary spanking are outlined. First, spanking provides adverse consequences for disobedience after reasoning has been
65 used. Second, power-assertive methods such as spanking may enhance the internalization of appropriate behavior that has already been explained through reasoning. Third, spanking has different consequences at each developmental level and is most effective during the child's first six years.
70 Reasoning is most important during adolescence. Fourth, the effectiveness of physical discipline depends on the culture of the family. Working-class and African-American families are more accepting of physical discipline. Fifth, there is no empirical evidence to support the theory that spanking is
75 related to child abuse and aggressive behavior in children. Sixth, research must consider differences between prudent and imprudent application of punishment as well as types of child aggression when examining negative outcomes. Finally, studies that indicate a correlation between physical
80 punishment and negative outcomes do not establish causality.

12. Which of the following research findings would most seriously *challenge* the hypothesis that "spanking may enhance the internalization of appropriate behavior, which has been explained through reasoning" (lines 65–67)?

   A. Evidence that the children were behaving appropriately
   B. Proof of enhanced and appropriate spanking
   C. Further correlation of appropriate behavior by children, in the absence of their parents
   D. Confirmation of inappropriate behavior by the children, in the absence of their parents

GO ON TO THE NEXT PAGE.

13. Which of the following suppositions is most clearly believed by the author?

A. Spanking may not promote discipline, but it is harmful.

B. The trend towards spanking is increasing and should not be studied further.

C. Many parents are spanking their children, and there is nothing wrong with that.

D. It is undisputed that spanking has proven to be an effective means of discipline.

14. In Canada, there are laws against any kind of corporal punishment of children. According to the passage, this trend could lead to:

A. less internalizing of appropriate behavior in the children.

B. more aggressive behavior in children.

C. a lower level of nurturing in children.

D. less child abuse.

15. What is the intended relevance of the quote "Spanking is love and scolding is affection?"

A. To explain the relative futility of nonphysical forms of punishment

B. To express that the more you spank your children, the more you love them

C. To indicate that those who use physical punishment may care for their children more than those who don't

D. To provide a moral justification for requiring obedience in children

16. On the basis of the passage quote, "Despite the fact that over the course of 20 years, 27 states have banned school corporal punishment, nearly half of U.S. parents now use physical punishment for disciplining their children" (lines 13–16), it is reasonable to conclude that the author believes that:

A. spanking is neither good nor bad.

B. teachers should be able to spank students.

C. parental spanking of children will soon be outlawed.

D. pediatricians strongly endorse spanking.

17. The claim that "[p]arents who used average levels of spanking … had high levels of nurturing interactions" (lines 52–54), *and* that nurturing interactions are the equivalent of love, is most in accord with the view that:

A. parents who use average levels of spanking love their children the least.

B. parents who use average levels of spanking love their children the most.

C. parents who use below-average levels of spanking love their children the most.

D. parents who use below-average levels of spanking love their children the least.

TEST 5

GO ON TO THE NEXT PAGE.

Passage IV (Questions 18–24)

From the early English Judge John Hodgekin's pronouncement that legal decisions were properly made only by trained judges by virtue of their superior "artificial reason," modern judicial reasoning continued to evolve to
5 a point where it could become hermetically self-justifying, without needing reference to external authority or divine right. Its novel differentiating concept was the development of a construct called "logic." Such "logic" was presented as the intellectual equivalent of the mechanical scales,
10 the universal symbol of justice, which, according to historians Curtis and Resnick, "suggest that an objective standard, independent of the whim of any ruler (as well as of the judge), governs the outcome." Like the scales, judicial reasoning (i.e. logic) promised both procedural and
15 substantive fairness; it operated by neutral and predictable principles, just as a scale operates by the constant law of gravity, and its outcome was always certain, predictable, and objectively (and visibly) "correct." The perceived neutrality of the law made it seem applicable to resolving any dispute
20 between any parties; simply "weigh" the logic of their arguments, and the weightier reasoning inevitably triumphs. This purported inclusiveness of legal reasoning and, by extension, of the law itself emboldened justice-minded statesmen to try structuring entire national legal regimes
25 founded upon an objective and impartial common[-to-all] law, since the law was seen as able to regulate all things. Recent academic discussions have largely undermined the image of an impartial legal process based on logic.

The legal realists rejected the notion of all-pervasive
30 legal reasoning, and instead made each lawsuit the analytic unit for examining judicial reasoning. Supreme Court Justice Oliver Wendell Holmes first rejected the fallacy that "the only force at work in the development of the law is logic"; instead, he said, the true basis for judicial decisions was
35 usually the underlying (and sometimes subconscious) *social* policy judges wished to promote. Yet Holmes had little to say about what social theories judges *should* promote; he suggested only that judges explain their reasoning and policy choices more honestly. Similarly, theorist-judge Richard
40 Posner exposed many of the classical methods of legal reasoning as subjective, fact-selective, or unsupported by reliable data. Yet after advocating "reasoning skepticism"— the belief that there is no single correct analytical method— Posner merely calls for greater judicial candor in explaining
45 the true reasoning behind judicial decisions, rather than greater coherence in reaching them.

Where legal realism dropped the ball, feminist legal theory picked it up, making a profound philosophical change in our understanding of legal reasoning. The legal
50 realists had noted that the neutral, mechanical language of judicial reasoning often obscured the vast discretion judges possessed in deciding outcomes. Feminist legal theory goes further, noting that, because the process and language of

legal "reasoning" was developed by men, it systematically
55 disadvantages certain groups, namely women and some racial minorities. Historian [Ms.] West, for example, argues that the very image of judicial scales and the balancing of competing interests is the product of an exclusively male outlook. This outlook views all others as rivals and
60 effectively creates a contest where none might have existed naturally, thus making even intrinsic rights subject to counterclaims. In any such legally created conflict, the male interest is typically privileged over the female; traditionally male work, for instance, is assigned a monetary value that
65 is recoverable in contract disputes, while traditionally female "house work" is not. Unlike the realists, however, this movement offers two distinct options for change. The first is to remain within the current legal framework but to correct the gender biases of the language of legal reasoning.
70 The more radical option is for women to invent their own language and methodology of legal reasoning.

Of all modern philosophic schools, critical legal studies offers the most revolutionary prospect for changing the inadequacies of the current methodology of legal reasoning.
75 It holds that "law provides only a conflicting variety of stylized rationalizations from which courts pick and choose," thus providing "a falsely legitimizing justification for a decision that is ultimately social and political." Critical legal studies offers the liberating possibility of abandoning
80 the very notion of salvaging a neutral, mechanical method for determining the objectively "correct" allocation of rights to each in favor of a more honest political discourse about group needs and desires, and a more democratic political process that would allow everyone to participate in making
85 an informed vote towards his or her political preferences.

18. One of the references used in the passage is to "Historian [Ms.] West" (line 56). What is the most likely reason for the choice of these words?

   A. Ms. West probably has a first name that would not clearly indicate her gender.
   B. The author felt it important to indicate that she is a historian.
   C. It was deemed important to indicate that historian West is a woman.
   D. It is surprising that a female historian would disagree with feminist legal theory.

GO ON TO THE NEXT PAGE.

19. The statue of Justice is a blindfolded woman holding scales, indicating that Justice is eminently fair and unrelated to anything other than reason. The author of the passage would be most likely to respond to this information by:

    A. suggesting this entire concept of justice has been largely undermined and superseded.
    B. proposing that the statue of the woman not be blindfolded but gagged.
    C. asserting that justice is not fair to women and that only the scales are representative.
    D. explaining that the idea of the scales has been refuted.

20. Which of the following conclusions about the author's beliefs can be inferred from the passage?

    A. The more radical option of feminist legal theory is the more appropriate.
    B. Critical legal studies offers the best ideas for changing the methodology of legal reasoning.
    C. Traditional legal reasoning was the most satisfactory.
    D. The current methodology of legal reasoning is inadequate.

21. What is the relation of other passage information to the assertion that "an objective standard, independent of the whim of any ruler (as well as of the judge), governs the outcome" (lines 11–13)?

    A. The implication that Judge Hodgekin disagreed undermines it.
    B. The difference between Judges Holmes and Posner weakens it.
    C. The information concerning Oliver Wendell Holmes weakens it.
    D. The contrast between Judges Holmes and Posner clarifies it.

22. What assumption is implicit in the phrase "hermetically self-justifying" (line 5)?

    A. A judge's legal decisions are not subject to the ravages of time in the way that 'oxidation' or rust can affect metals.
    B. A judge's legal decision stands alone and is unrelated to peripheral influences.
    C. If there are no external authorities to challenge a decision, it is self-justifying.
    D. When the legal language is genderless, there will be less conflict.

23. The passage argument suggests that judicial methodology might benefit from:

    I. clearer explanations of the true reasons for a decision.
    II. less bias in a judge's decision making.
    III. more women in judicial positions.

    A. I only
    B. II only
    C. I and II only
    D. I, II, and III

24. Elsewhere, the author of the passage states that people are the sum of their experiences, and thus, true objectivity is not possible. This statement most directly supports the passage assertion that:

    A. those in positions of authority try to hide the fact that they have tremendous discretion in the decisions that they make.
    B. the male interest is typically privileged over the female.
    C. Holmes suggested only that judges explain their reasoning and policy choices more honestly.
    D. logic was presented as the intellectual equivalent of mechanical scales.

TEST 5

GO ON TO THE NEXT PAGE.

Passage V (Questions 25–29)

Since its foundation, America has been a land of opportunity and freedom, promoting a tradition of self-reliance and independence. Our country has flourished because it has embodied a commitment to human freedom,
5 human rights, and human dignity. However, since the Roe vs. Wade decision of 1973, which legalized the abortion of unborn babies, our country has undergone a radical moral decline. As the "right to life" is snatched away at the moment of birth, and even before, the fundamental rights,
10 on which America was established, are being denied and trampled upon. This poses a serious threat to our nation, for "the future of democracy … depends on a culture capable of forming men and women who are prepared to defend certain truths and values" (pg. 439).

15 On December 3, 1998, the National Conference of Catholic Bishops, addressing this very issue, put out a document titled "Living the Gospel of Life: A Challenge to American Catholics." The document holds that the ideals and beliefs of the country will continue to be diminished,
20 and further rights will be forfeited, until all citizens recognize the dignity of human life and strive to support and defend its sanctity. Since the bishops believe that the universal understandings of freedom and truth are written on every human heart, they profess that everyone is called
25 to acknowledge and defend the right to life. However, it is specifically intended for American Catholics, and even more particularly for Catholic politicians. "In a special way, we call on U.S. Catholics, especially those in positions of leadership—whether cultural, economic or political—to
30 recover their identity as followers of Jesus Christ and to be leaders in the renewal of American respect for the sanctity of life."

A political community is supposed to exist for the common good. "This is its full justification and meaning,
35 and the source of its specific and basic right to exist" (pg. 433). Yet, the common good cannot be obtained without recognizing and standing up for the right to life because all other inalienable rights of humanity are founded upon and derived from it. Therefore, "Catholic public officials are
40 obliged to address each of these issues as they seek to build consistent policies which promote respect for the human person at all stages of life" (pg. 434). Moreover, "Catholics who are privileged to serve in public leadership positions have an obligation to place their faith at the heart of their
45 public service, particularly on issues regarding the sanctity and dignity of human life" (pg. 435).

Since the entry of Catholics into the realm of politics, believers have struggled to balance their faith with the perceived demands of democratic pluralism. However, the
50 issue of abortion is not religious but scientific. Furthermore, the sanctity of human life is not simply a Catholic doctrine, but a law inscribed on the heart of every human

being. Therefore, Catholic politicians should defend these principles, not solely because they are the teachings of the
55 Church, but because they represent the fundamental rights of humanity.

Failure to bring about change, through the renewal of a national respect for the rights of the unborn and a return to the founding principles of America, could be devastating
60 for this country. "The future of a nation is decided by every new generation" (pg. 436). If this generation desires that America continue to flourish and to be a land of opportunity, then it needs to maintain and embrace freedom. However, "Freedom always implies the ability to choose between two
65 roads: one which leads to life: the other, death" (pg. 436).

25. In the context of the passage, the term *sanctity* refers primarily to:

A. the fundamental rights on which America was established.
B. certain truths and values.
C. the human life.
D. the Catholic Church.

26. The author's argument is based upon the idea that:

    A. everyone is called to recognize the Catholic Church.
    B. freedom can be lost.
    C. politicians have undergone a radical moral decline.
    D. our country has flourished because of a good political system.

27. Which of the following assertions in the passage is NOT supported by an example, argument, or reference to an authority?

    A. A political community is supposed to exist for the common good.
    B. Catholic politicians should defend the principle of sanctity.
    C. Freedom implies the ability to choose.
    D. The issue of abortion is not religious but scientific.

28. Which of the following would the author probably consider the best evidence of the moral regeneration of the country?

    A. Catholic churches have been reporting that ever-increasing numbers of parishioners are donating money to the Church.
    B. Findings that young people are more supportive than ever of an unborn child's right to life.
    C. Catholic politicians, when asked, admitted that they always tended to vote in a manner that was very representative of their constituency.
    D. Voters are voting increasingly for Catholic politicians.

29. The author's reasoning that "the common good cannot be obtained without recognizing and standing up for the right to life because all other inalienable rights of humanity are founded upon and derived from it" (lines 36–39) could most reasonably be extended to questions about:

    A. communism.
    B. animal rights.
    C. capital punishment.
    D. the elderly.

TEST 5

GO ON TO THE NEXT PAGE.

Passage VI (Questions 30–34)

In 1978, Argentinean President Spinoza announced economic reforms to open the Argentinean economy to the world market. Among the propositions was the encouragement of joint ventures (JVs) between Argentinean
5 state-owned enterprises (SOEs) and foreign partners. This JV policy, as iterated by national-level leaders, was vague. Its exact meaning evolved through daily negotiations shaped not only by the national Communist Party itself, but also by regional officials and even by the managers of the SOEs
10 themselves.

The central government's decision to move away from a planned economy was pragmatic, considering the unsuccessful record of economic planning in Argentina. Prior planning had favored heavy industry over consumer
15 manufacturing; in order to raise the stagnant standard of living of Argentinean consumers, future production would have to focus on everyday items.

The national government had strong interests in encouraging cooperation between domestic firms and
20 foreign investors; in the short run, it was hoped the union would remove the drain of unprofitable SOEs on the national budget. Tax revenues from JVs would be paid partially in hard currency, which the national government needed to import goods from abroad, especially those of strategic,
25 military, or economic importance.

More fundamentally, the joint ventures themselves were a gateway for the immediate acquisition of advanced foreign technology, as part of the capital, training, and expertise foreign partners would invest into the mergers. Since
30 Argentina did not (then) recognize patent rights, its leaders no doubt realized that foreign blueprints and proprietary technology could be duplicated and disseminated throughout the nation, at no cost. Finally, as part of the desire for greater enterprise efficiency, it was intended that working alongside
35 foreign managers would allow the Argentinean workers to learn foreign management and accounting methods.

At the same time, enterprise-level SOE managers— those who saw their SOEs converted to JVs—exerted their own influence, because they were responsible for actually
40 negotiating the terms of the JV contracts with foreign partners. As a group, they hindered the implementation of the JV policies favored by the central and local authorities. Unlike those authorities, they stood to gain little from the success of the JVs. Some theorists attribute these delays to
45 Argentina's different method of capital budgeting, which, because there was no regular inflation of administrative prices, did not include the concept of the time value of money. Yet this argument overlooks the basic incentive structure facing the Argentinean managers. While managers
50 gained relatively little, in either money or prestige, from organizing a profitable JV, they stood to damage their political

careers in the Party hierarchy if their hastily contracted JV encountered visible problems. Thus, Argentinean managers acted rationally in delaying JV implementation to gain a
55 fuller knowledge of the partner's motives and capabilities.

Faced with scant monetary incentives, managers maximized the nonpecuniary benefits of their positions— the opportunity to further their Party careers—through their JVs. Thus, the decisions they made were often ones that
60 maximized not the long-term profitability of the venture, but rather its short-term political appeal. Political careers would be hurt if leaders were seen by the Party as "giving away the shop" to foreigners by offering too many concessions. They would not be affected if JV implementation was delayed.
65 Thus, leaders could hold out indefinitely in the hope of receiving a bargain from the foreign delegation, which *was* anxious to return home with a signed contract.

30. According to the passage, which of the following is most likely true about the JV policy?

A. The policy was also fashioned by managers of the SOEs.

B. The policy heavily favored foreign investors.

C. The policy heavily favored the SOEs.

D. The sole architect of the policy was the Communist Party.

GO ON TO THE NEXT PAGE.

31. Which of the following assertions most clearly exemplifies the motivations of the central government?

   A. The central government delayed JV implementation in order to assess the foreigners' motivations.

   B. The central government hoped that transition to joint ventures would render the SOEs more efficient.

   C. The central government presumed that the profitable SOEs could be maintained.

   D. The central government intended to convert all of the manufacturing into SOEs.

32. On the basis of the passage, it is reasonable to conclude that:

   A. The SOE managers did their utmost to comply with the reforms, though the reforms were not a good idea.

   B. The JV managers attempted to hinder the transition to becoming SOEs.

   C. Foreign investors were not highly motivated to help with the reforms.

   D. Though the reforms were a good idea, giving the SOE managers so much responsibility for the reforms was not.

33. On the basis of the passage, one may assume that central and local authorities might benefit by:

   A. advancing heavy industry over consumer manufacturing.

   B. indefinitely delaying the signing of a contract.

   C. hindering the joint venture policies.

   D. promoting the joint venture policies.

34. Which of the following conclusions about the pre-1978 Argentinean economy can be inferred from the passage?

   A. Its emphasis on heavy industry was closed to the world market, relying primarily on JVs.

   B. It was a planned economy that focused on heavy industry and state-owned enterprises.

   C. It was a planned economy that had a fairly successful record.

   D. It was closed to the world market but open to some foreign investors.

TEST 5

GO ON TO THE NEXT PAGE.

Passage VII (Questions 35–40)

Towards the end of their first year of life, most babies have learned to sit up by themselves. Many have become regular in their patterns, too. This often applies to regular bowel movements. A mistake often made by young parents
5 who are misled into believing that their life will somehow be easier when their child is toilet trained is to begin placing the child on the toilet or a child's toilet seat around the time of the child's regular bowel movements. Of course, if the child is left in this position long enough a bowel movement in the
10 toilet will result. However, this should not be construed as toilet training and actually achieves a rather poor result, both in expectations and time. The child is not truly in control of his bowels, nor is she necessarily aware of the fact that she is eliminating at all.

15 Take it from a parent of four that once a child is potty trained, life does not get any easier. Sure, the expense of either disposable diapers or cleaning cloth ones is forgotten, but you pay for it with your time. Consider first that though you do not want to wait all day, when your child is wearing
20 diapers and has a bowel movement, if there is something pressing such as a telephone call, lunch that needs to be made, or another sibling requiring immediate attention, these more pressing needs can be met, and the soiled diaper can wait. You can even try to trick your spouse into
25 changing the dirty diaper if you're sly about it. You can put off, for a short time, the diaper change. Secondly, think for a moment how long it actually takes you to change a diaper. If you have even one child and are not new to it, you should be pretty fast. However, when your child is finally toilet
30 trained and comes running to you telling you that she must use the toilet, she means now! You had better drop what you are doing, whatever it is, and immediately get the process moving along. She has prioritized this task for you with your help. Next, you must undress your child; depending on
35 the day or time of the year, this may be relatively easy or a chore. Now you place her on the toilet. Oh, is the child's seat already on the toilet or do you have to do that also? You say your child doesn't want you to stay with her while she goes? Nonetheless, you must now situate yourself where you can
40 at least hear her when she tells you that she is done. When she is done you end up in the same situation you were in when you were simply changing a diaper in the first place. That is, you are wiping little bottoms and cleaning them up; albeit with toilet paper and in a rather awkward position as
45 opposed to the handy 'on-the-back-with-the-feet-in-the-air' using moist and convenient baby wipes. Beginning to get the picture?

Remember that we haven't even approached, nor will we, any of those sacred-cow psychological implications
50 of toilet training 'too early.' If you are starting your child early enough with this silliness (remember that we are still discussing your attempts prior to her expressing the desire to go in the toilet or even being aware that she can control

this function), then she is probably not protesting too much
55 as you strap her on the toilet for however long it takes to get her to go. However, in a few months, when she can walk and begin to move around more, she is going to complain bitterly about this process that so resembles the beloved disciplinary "time-out" punishments. You have actually made your
60 eventual task of having this child come voluntarily to you to help her go to the toilet much more difficult, because it requires her happy cooperation.

Don't rush to toilet train your child. Research has shown that no matter when you begin toilet training your
65 child, she will, on average, be able to keep herself reliably clean and dry by her third year. Enjoy your child as she is, while she is. It doesn't last long.

35. Which of the following statements is an example of what the author probably means in implying that it may be more difficult to undress your child depending on the day or time of year (lines 34–36)?

   A. In the summer, the child would not want to be undressed.

   B. People usually wear more clothes while they sleep.

   C. Undressing the child in the dead of winter would take more time.

   D. For instance, Christmas day would be easier than Easter.

GO ON TO THE NEXT PAGE.

36. Which of the following assertions is most clearly a thesis presented by the author?

    A. Toilet training a child early will only save you time.
    B. Most parents assume that life gets easier after their children are toilet trained. ✓
    C. You don't save any money through early toilet training.
    D. There are many false assumptions regarding toilet training. ✓

37. According to the passage, what is the period of time between when a child may first become "regular" and the "average" age at which the child becomes reliably trained?

    A. "forever"
    B. 1 year
    C. Two years
    D. Three years

38. Which of the following suppositions is most clearly believed by the author?

    A. The psychological implications of early toilet training are exaggerated.
    B. A child with a soiled diaper does not have to be changed immediately.
    C. You can't really toilet train a child until three years of age.
    D. It seems as if you'll be changing diapers 'a long time.'

39. What is the author's response to the standard story about the one- or two-year-old child who is already toilet trained?

    A. The parents are wasting their money.
    B. This is actually not that hard to teach a child.
    C. The parents are probably just leaving the child on the toilet until she poops.
    D. At any rate, the parents now have more time on their hands.

40. The statement that towards the end of their first year of life many babies may have "regular bowel movements" (lines 3–4) probably means that:

    A. these babies have movements in their bowels.
    B. the baby's defecations are a regular size.
    C. these babies defecate at least once a day.
    D. these babies defecate at regular times each day.

STOP. IF YOU FINISH BEFORE TIME IS CALLED, CHECK YOUR WORK. YOU MAY GO BACK TO ANY QUESTION IN THIS TEST.

TEST 5

STOP.

Verbal Reasoning Test 6
Time: 60 Minutes
Questions 1–40

VERBAL REASONING

DIRECTIONS: There are seven passages in this Verbal Reasoning test. Each passage is followed by several questions. After reading a passage, select the one best answer to each question. If you are not certain of an answer, eliminate the alternatives that you know to be incorrect and then select an answer from the remaining alternatives. Indicate your selection by blackening the corresponding oval on your answer document.

Passage I (Questions 1–7)

Video games have become an almost integral part of the popular culture of America's youth in the past several years. The craze has spread with increasing speed since the 1980s. As video game graphics have become more precise
5 and realistic, the violence in them has also become more graphic. With some notable exceptions, typically, the image of the aggressive male hero and the submissive, curvaceous female persists.

In the early 1980s, during the initial video game
10 craze, psychologists and educational professionals began to notice the tremendous impact the video game medium had on learning and the development of motor skills. Dr. Greenfield writes that video games, as opposed to other forms of media, encourage the active development of visual
15 skills, spatial ability, hand-eye coordination, and creativity: "The interactive quality of both video games and computers forces children actively to create stimuli and information, not merely consume them." However, concern was already beginning to develop regarding the violent content of these
20 games. A 1992 Gallup poll revealed that the most popular games among America's youth were violent in nature.

The medium was receiving considerable attention in the world of research even when the home video game market took a turn for the worse. Judging from a number of
25 studies that drew upon papers presented at the 1983 Harvard symposium "Video Games and Human Development: A Research Agenda for the 80s," researchers aptly figured that this form of entertainment would grow to play a tremendous role in education; the dynamic imagery in the medium
30 and its ability to help children with difficulties in abstract thinking was often noted.

However, violence and aggression in video games is still a new topic of research. Conflicting evidence has been found regarding how violent video games influence
35 children's behavior. The research uses children of different ages, different games, and different definitions of violence, so that one cannot make any comparisons among the different studies. It is important to note that video game

violence has evolved with violence in other media (i.e.,
40 television, movies). The fact that these media have become closely intertwined cannot be overlooked.

In 1984, Dr. Dominick concluded that "playing video games is evidently one part of a cluster of activities that center around television." He found that children who played
45 more video games tended to watch more television. The link is strong in part because they are both primarily visual media that involve many of the same cognitive and spatial skills. In recent years, video games, television, and film have been used together to create an all-encompassing popular culture
50 for children. The three share common subject matter and are used to market a specific set of characters.

In the early 1980s, investigators set out to discover exactly what was fun about video games. Thomas Malone found the presence of a goal to be the most important
55 determinant of a game's popularity. He concluded that a fantasy-inducing environment that evoked mental images and social situations assigning a definite role to the player were among the aspects that determined the amount of pleasure derived from the game. While Malone does not
60 expressly mention violence as an enjoyable aspect of video games, other investigators discuss the attraction to danger and alternate worlds—for example, that one has another chance if one gets "hurt" or "dies" in video games. One can learn from experience and eliminate regret by acting
65 aggressively and defeating danger. At present, less abstract, more realistic violent themes dominate the most popular games for the target group, boys age 8–18.

GO ON TO THE NEXT PAGE.

1. The passage implies that video games may help children with difficulties in:

    I.   visual skills.
    II. spatial ability.
    III. abstract thinking.

  A. I only
  B. I and II only
  C. II and III only
  D. I, II, and III

2. According to the passage, a child who plays more video games will also be likely to:

  A. have better spatial ability and watch less television.
  B. display more creativity and watch less television.
  C. watch more television and display more creativity.
  D. watch more television and display diminished hand-eye coordination.

3. Dr. Greenfield writes, "The interactive quality of both video games and computers forces children actively to create stimuli and information, not merely consume them." (lines 16–18). What question might this information reasonably suggest about the author's comment that "video game violence has evolved with violence in other media" (lines 38–40)?

  A. Aren't video games and television equally responsible for violence in children?
  B. Won't children learn violence from video games rather than just consume it on television?
  C. Is television as stimulating as video games?
  D. Didn't video game violence evolve after the violence we see on television?

4. The author of the passage would be most likely to agree with which of the following ideas expressed by other researchers?

  A. Since it is still a new topic, very little research has been done into how violent video games influence children's behavior.
  B. Children's behavior is tremendously influenced by the increasing violence of video games.
  C. Violence in video games has little, if any, influence on children's behavior.
  D. No real inferences can be drawn from research into how violent video games influence children's behavior.

5. The passage argument suggests that children might benefit from:

    I.   certain types of video games.
    II. certain types of television programming.
    III. violent video games.

  A. I only
  B. II only
  C. III only
  D. I and II only

6. One can infer from the passage that the underlying goal of creating "an all-encompassing popular culture for children" (lines 48–49) was:

  A. to aid the active development of visual skills, among others.
  B. to sell more video games.
  C. to offer an alternative to violent programming and games.
  D. to get children to play more video games and watch more television.

7. The author's argument that video games are becoming increasingly realistic is most *weakened* by which idea implicit in the passage?

  A. Video game violence is still not very realistic because it has evolved with television violence.
  B. Video games, television, and film are creating a culture for children.
  C. The main characters in the games are not very realistic.
  D. If you are killed in a video game you get another chance.

TEST 6

GO ON TO THE NEXT PAGE.

Passage II (Questions 8–13)

The Whistleblower's Protection Act of 1989 was instituted to protect those who came forward, or "blew the whistle," regarding instances of fraud, waste, and abuse in the federal government. However, for various reasons, 5 it is an abysmal failure. There really is no protection for the whistleblower. A quick perusal of the stories behind those who have broken ranks to expose gross instances of what can roughly be characterized as "cheating" shows that whistleblowers are invariably castigated by their employers 10 and then punished. What then would motivate someone to come forward in this fashion, knowing that their selfless decrying of wrongs would come to nothing, or worse?

It may often seem to an introspective society that corrective or punitive acts are lowly and beneath us. These 15 acts or the urge to commit them seem unforgiving or selfish. We prefer to reflect, for instance, on prisons providing rehabilitation, not discipline. However, recent experiments and studies by various researchers point to a less intuitive basis for these urges, which we all share. Only lately have 20 researchers realized that a willingness, even eagerness, to punish transgressors of societal trust is at least as important to the maintenance of social harmony as are regular displays of common human decency. And while the punitive urge may seem like a lowly and unsavory impulse, scientists 25 point out that the effort to penalize cheaters is very often a selfless act.

The societal acts of trusting, sharing, giving, and working for the common good can be easily undermined by cheaters. Such a readiness to trust others, to behave civilly 30 in a crowd, to share and empathize, to play the occasional good Samaritan—all the behaviors that we laud and endorse and vow to cultivate more fully in ourselves—could not have evolved without a corresponding readiness to catch, and to punish, the Cheat. Nevertheless, we generally tend 35 to work and move towards the common good, content in the knowledge that the majority of others are doing the same. Predictably, this characteristic description begins to break down when individuals either realize or believe that someone else within the group is cheating. If the selfish cheater 40 can continue to cheat without rebuke or consequence, the functioning of the group (society) begins to decline.

At first glance, it may seem selfish that if so-and-so has something that I don't have, I won't cooperate, perform, or help until I get it also. However, Dr. David Sloan Wilson, an 45 evolutionary biologist at the State University of New York at Binghamton, said, "People are used to thinking of social control and moralistic aggression as forms of selfishness, and that you must be punishing someone for your own benefit. But if you look at the sort of punishment that 50 promotes altruistic behavior, you see that it is itself a form of altruism." In "Altruistic Punishment in Humans," which appears in the January 10, 2002 issue of the journal *Nature*,

Dr. Ernst Fehr, of the University of Zurich and Dr. Simon Gachter, of the University of St. Gallen in Switzerland, offer 55 evidence that people will seek to punish a cheat even when the punishment is costly to them and offers no material benefit—the very definition of altruism. The researchers propose that the threat of such punishment may have been crucial to the evolution of human civilization and all its 60 parallel achievements.

Perhaps part of the reason it feels good to rail against the cheater is that not to do so seems irresponsible, if not cowardly. "Once you think of punishment as a form of altruism, then the kind of person who doesn't punish 65 emerges as a kind of freeloader too," said Dr. David Wilson, author of *Unto Others: The Evolution and Psychology of Unselfish Behavior.*

But always remember, "No good deed goes unpunished."—Clare Booth Luce

8. The author would look upon "whistleblowers" with:

A. suspicion.
B. envy.
C. admiration.
D. altruism.

GO ON TO THE NEXT PAGE.

9. The author's reasoning about "societal acts" could most reasonably be extended to questions about:

    A. "Eat Meat," and vegetarianism.
    B. "Give a hoot, don't pollute" and littering.
    C. "Don't do the crime if you can't do the time" and prison sentences.
    D. "Just say 'No'" and drugs.

10. Suppose researchers discover that only in nondemocratic forms of government are high-ranking transgressors punished, whereas in the United States those found cheating at the highest levels of government are almost never punished. Which of the following hypotheses is most compatible with passage information?

    A. Nondemocratic forms of government will decline.
    B. Democratic forms of government will decline.
    C. The United States is exceptionally corrupt.
    D. Democratic forms of government prefer rehabilitation not discipline.

11. The people who cheat are described as "transgressors." What is the most likely reason for the choice of this word?

    A. The word contrasts with the author's use of "moralistic" aggressors.
    B. This is a commonly known biblical term, that evokes shame in all of us.
    C. The word is widely encompassing and applies to breaking civil or moral rules, whether expressed or implied.
    D. It can be used to describe anyone who follows the rules.

12. The aphorism "No good deed goes unpunished" (lines 68–69), means that whistleblowers should:

    A. not go unpunished.
    B. expect their transgressors to be punished.
    C. be better protected for whistleblowing.
    D. expect retaliation for whistleblowing.

13. The ideas discussed in this passage would likely be of most use to:

    A. a general preparing for battle.
    B. a senator engaged in a serious debate.
    C. a casino manager promoting ethics.
    D. a zookeeper training animal behaviorists.

TEST 6

GO ON TO THE NEXT PAGE.

Passage III (Questions 14–18)

A defining feature of life in America's schools today is the increasing incidence of violence. Nearly three million crimes take place in or near schools annually—one every six seconds of the school day. These increases are occurring
5 nationwide. Eighty-two percent of school districts surveyed by the National School Boards Association (NSBA) reported increasing violence within their schools during the past five years. Incidents of violence involving deadly weapons reported in schools are on the upswing. More than sixty
10 percent of school districts have reported weapons violations among their students.

One prominent legislative and policy measure to ensure a safe school environment has been to require removal of disruptive and dangerous students. Typically,
15 this is accomplished through expulsions and long-term suspensions. For example, the Federal Gun-Free Schools Act of 1994 requires a minimum 1-year expulsion for any student found to have carried a firearm on school grounds.

However, school districts across the country report
20 experiencing significant increases in both the number of students expelled and the length of time they are excluded from their schools. The consensus among educators and others concerned with at-risk youth is that it is vital for expelled students to receive educational counseling to help
25 modify their behavior and possibly other support services while they are away from their regular schools. Without such services, students generally return to school no better disciplined and no better able to manage their anger or peacefully resolve disputes. They will also have fallen
30 behind in their education, and any underlying causes of their violent behavior may be unresolved. Research has shown a link between suspension/expulsion and later dropping out of school, with resulting personal and social costs.

One reservation about providing services to expelled
35 students has been the cost. However, data show it is less costly to address the problem behavior and its underlying causes as quickly as possible than to wait until the student becomes involved with the criminal justice or welfare system later in life. The American Federation of Teachers
40 has estimated that "for the [$1,750] additional dollars spent on each [disruptive] student attending an alternative school, the public annually gains $14,000 in student learning time that would have been lost, $2,800 in reduced grade repetition costs, $1,750 in reduced welfare costs, and $1,500
45 in reduced prison costs." This is a total savings of $18,300 per student.

School systems across the country are turning to alternative education programs to deliver educational and other services to expelled students. Some school systems
50 are modifying existing programs to accommodate the larger numbers of students expelled for disruptive behaviors, while others are creating new programs, often in collaboration with social agencies or nonprofit service organizations.

The programs typically differ from the expelled
55 students' regular schools in these dimensions: the ratio of students to teachers; the way academic subject matter is presented; the setting of the program; the linkage of the school to the community or workplaces; the emphasis on behavior modification; the emphasis on counseling
60 for conflict resolution and anger management; and the availability of comprehensive support services. Programs have been created for students as young as elementary age. Some seek to prepare students to return to their regular schools, and others prepare students to graduate from high
65 school and enter the workforce or postsecondary education directly from the alternative program.

Once again, there is the problem of limited resources. The argument has been made that any number of other students might benefit as well from these "dimensions" that
70 are actually improvements to the existing school system— improvements such as a low student-to-teacher ratio for instance. Further, there is little stomach for the perceived "coddling" of troublemakers. Nevertheless, it seems that if the violence of youth in the school setting is not to bloom
75 and bear the fruit of criminal adulthood, then emphasis must be placed on behavior modification early on in life.

14. The passage states that "school districts across the country report experiencing significant increases in both the number of students expelled and the length of time they are excluded from their schools" (lines 19–22). According to the author, this increase would probably have resulted from:

I. the passage of the Federal Gun-Free Schools Act of 1994.
II. National School Boards Association (NSBA) reporting of the increasing violence within their schools during the past five years.
III. the lack of alternative schools and other support services while students are away from their regular schools.

A. I only
B. II only
C. III only
D. I, II, and III

GO ON TO THE NEXT PAGE.

15. The contention that "research has shown a link between suspension/expulsion and later dropping out of school, with resulting personal and social costs" (lines 31–33), can most justifiably be interpreted as support for the idea that:

   A. reduced prison costs may be achieved through providing educational services that will keep students in school.

   B. in cases of suspension/expulsion and later dropping out of school, alternative education may cost a great deal of money.

   C. students who are expelled and return to school are able to modify their behavior and peacefully resolve disputes.

   D. personal and social costs should prompt us to link suspension/expulsion and later dropping out of school.

16. Evidence shows that violent youth have a greater tendency to end up in prison as adults. This fact tends to support the hypothesis concerning "the violence of youth in the school setting [may] bear the fruit of criminal adulthood" because:

   A. most people in prison are violent criminals.

   B. adult criminals are usually violent.

   C. criminal adulthood can lead to incarceration.

   D. adults in prison who were violent as youths probably were expelled or suspended from school.

17. Which of the following conclusions can justifiably be drawn from the required removal of disruptive and dangerous students as mentioned in the passage?

   A. Society has tired of "coddling" troublemakers.

   B. It has been decided that this is one method that can be used to ensure a safe school environment.

   C. Violent students should be placed directly into alternative schools.

   D. Youth violence has increased dramatically.

18. The passage suggests that alternative education should be:

   A. provided not just to expelled students, but to all other students who might benefit as well.

   B. provided primarily to students who were expelled because of violence at school.

   C. provided to all expelled students despite the problem of limited resources.

   D. carefully managed by the National School Boards Association (NSBA) in order to husband scarce resources.

GO ON TO THE NEXT PAGE.

TEST 6

Passage IV (Questions 19–23)

Beyond the question of his guilt or innocence, the "American Taliban," John Walker Lindh, provides a classic example of why one should never talk to or provide information to a law enforcement officer when
5 being questioned by them. In a press release, Attorney General Ashcroft announced that Walker will be facing serious criminal charges that may result in a life sentence. Significantly, as pointed out by Ashcroft, these charges are based almost exclusively on information that Walker
10 provided voluntarily to law enforcement officers during his detention, after waiving his right to an attorney. If John Walker is found guilty and does serve the rest of his life in prison, he will have put himself in this position—not only by virtue of the acts that he allegedly committed and the law
15 that he allegedly violated, but also because he then provided law enforcement, prosecuting attorneys, and the United States government, with the information and evidence that they required to prove these violations.

If you are "read your rights" by a police officer, you
20 know that you are in trouble. However, it is important to understand that simply because you are *not* "read your rights," not to mention handcuffed or detained, does not mean that you are not under suspicion. Any information you provide when being questioned still "can and will
25 be used against you in a court of law"; this occurs under circumstances that the police are aware of and you are not. The police have a right to attempt to question you and do not have to read you your rights if they are not detaining you and you are free to go at any time. This should be your first
30 litmus test. When the police officer starts questioning you, before answering any questions, ask, "Am I free to go?" If the answer is 'yes,' then tell the officer that you would prefer to leave and not to answer any questions. At that point, you may be detained or arrested by them, but not because you
35 refused to answer their questions. They were going to arrest you anyway and were attempting to lull you into a false sense of security. They were playing upon the fact that deep down we all want to cooperate and want others to like and respect us. If you are ever read your rights, or "Mirandized,"
40 you should never agree to waive any of your rights. Why would you? You are simply providing information to people and a system that will use it against you regardless of your guilt or innocence.

No attorney who had been assigned to provide
45 representation to John Walker would ever have allowed him to speak with law enforcement officers or other agents of the United States. However, Walker waived his rights to an attorney both verbally and in writing during interrogation sessions. This may have been for selfless reasons, because
50 Walker realized that what he had gotten himself involved with was wrong and he wished to help right these wrongs. However, Walker undoubtedly hoped that his cooperation would help his situation. It was even widely reported in

the press that the government was considering how this
55 cooperation would help his case. Maybe it did help. Maybe he would have been facing the death penalty instead of life in prison, but this is not likely. What is likely is that if Walker had stated, even once, that he did not want to speak with anyone before he spoke with an attorney, he would, very
60 possibly, today be free.

19. Which of the following statements best summarizes the main idea of the passage?

A. When being questioned by police, any information you provide can and will be used against you.
B. The police, and law enforcement in general, are dishonest and unscrupulous.
C. John Walker is most probably innocent.
D. Always have an attorney present when you answer questions from police.

GO ON TO THE NEXT PAGE.

20. The "'American Taliban,' John Walker Lindh" (lines 1–18) best illustrates the author's point that:

   A. if you are not being detained by police, they do not have to read you your rights.
   B. cooperating with the police when you are under suspicion will not benefit you.
   C. cooperating with the police may help to allay their suspicion of you.
   D. you may wish to help the police for the benefit of everyone else.

21. Which of the following statements, if true, would most WEAKEN the author's contention that Walker, if found guilty, will have "put himself in this position" (line 13)?

   A. The incriminating information provided by Walker to law enforcement was, in fact, not true.
   B. The information provided by Walker is the sole evidence used to place him in prison for life.
   C. The defense counsel files a legal brief outlining its evidence for an insanity plea.
   D. The prosecution announces that it has several witnesses to its allegations and will not be using Walker's statement.

22. In advising a group of foreign exchange students who are preparing to go out 'partying' in New York, the author would most likely tell them to:

   A. ensure that they have an attorney before they get into any trouble.
   B. call an attorney and refuse to answer any questions from police if they get in trouble.
   C. not get into any trouble while they are in the city.
   D. ask the police officer if they are being detained.

23. The California Highway Patrol has found that when their troopers simply asked for permission to search vehicles that they had pulled over, drivers invariably consented, even when the drivers knew that the vehicle was filled with illegal drugs. If the author were to include this description in the passage, it would probably be used to:

   A. illustrate the point that if you are under suspicion, you will probably be arrested.
   B. emphasize that you should cooperate if you want leniency.
   C. support the point that we all want to cooperate.
   D. explain the author's own experiences with being pulled over.

GO ON TO THE NEXT PAGE.

Passage V (Questions 24–29)

The Cambrian period lasted approximately forty million years. According to the fossil record, animals showed dramatic diversification during this episode of Earth's history. With this diversification occurring over a time period that was short enough to call our previous theories of evolution into question, it has rightly been called an explosion—the "Cambrian Explosion." More startling still, when the fossil record is scrutinized closely, it turns out that the fastest growth in the number of major new animal groups took place during the Tommotian and Atdabanian stages of the early Cambrian, a period of time that may have been as short as five million years! In that time, the first undoubted fossil annelids, arthropods, brachiopods, echinoderms, mollusks, onychophorans, poriferans, and priapulids began to show up in rocks all over the world.

The largest landmass during this time was Gondwana, which was then a collection of today's southern continents. The Cambrian world was concentrated in the southern hemisphere and flourished between two ice ages—one ice age during the late Proterozoic and the other during the Ordovician. During these ice ages, the decrease in global temperature led to mass extinctions. Cooler conditions eliminated many warm-water species, and glaciations lowered global sea level. However, during the Cambrian there was no significant ice formation. None of the continents was located at the poles, and so land temperatures remained mild. In fact, the global climate was probably warmer and more uniform than it is today. With the beginning of the Cambrian, at the retreat of Proterozoic ice, the sea level rose significantly. Lowland areas such as Baltica were flooded, and much of the world was covered by epeiric seas. These rising sea levels opened up new habitats where marine invertebrates, such as the trilobites, radiated and flourished. Plants had not yet evolved, and the terrestrial world was therefore devoid of vegetation and generally inhospitable to life as we know it. Photosynthesis and primary production were the monopoly of bacteria and algal protists that populated the world's shallow seas.

Also during the Cambrian, oxygen first mixed into the world's oceans in significant quantity. Although there was plentiful atmospheric oxygen by the opening of the Cambrian, only during the Cambrian period did the numbers of oxygen-depleting bacteria become sufficiently reduced in numbers to permit the high levels of oxygen we know of today. This made dissolved oxygen available to the emerging diversity of animals and may have helped trigger the "Cambrian Explosion."

Almost every metazoan phylum with hard parts, along with many that lack hard parts, made its first appearance in the Cambrian. The only modern phylum with an adequate fossil record to appear after the Cambrian was the phylum Bryozoa, which is not known before the early Ordovician.

A few mineralized animal fossils, including sponge spicules and probable worm tubes, are known from the Vendian period immediately preceding the Cambrian. Some of the odd fossils of the *Ediacara biota* from the Vendian may also have been animals in or near living phyla, although this remains a somewhat controversial topic.

Nonetheless, the Cambrian was a time of great evolutionary innovation, with many major groups of organisms appearing within a span of only forty million years and perhaps as few as five million. Trace fossils made by animals also show increased diversity in Cambrian rocks, indicating that the animals of the Cambrian were developing new ecological niches and strategies such as active hunting, burrowing deeply into sediment, and making complex branching burrows. Finally, the Cambrian saw the appearance and/or diversification of mineralized algae of various types, such as the coralline red algae and the dasyclad green algae.

24. According to the passage, Gondwana was:

A. a collection of present-day southern continents.
B. concentrated in the southern hemisphere.
C. the second largest landmass.
D. predominantly an ice age phenomenon.

GO ON TO THE NEXT PAGE.

25. According to the passage, the growth in the number of major new animal groups during the Cambrian period is best shown by analysis of the:

   A. shifting southern continents.
   B. mass extinctions during the ice ages.
   C. metazoan phylum.
   D. fossil record.

26. According to the passage, the Cambrian Explosion is considered a result of all of the following factors EXCEPT:

   A. rising sea levels opening up new habitats.
   B. high levels of dissolved oxygen.
   C. high numbers of oxygen-producing bacteria.
   D. warmer climates.

27. The author implies that "previous theories of evolution" (lines 5–6) included the idea that:

   A. diversification is always a dramatic process.
   B. diversification can occur within relatively short "explosions" of time.
   C. diversification usually occurs over many millions of years.
   D. the continents did not develop from a single large landmass.

28. According to the passage, which of the following is most likely to be true about the relationship between oxygen and the emerging diversity of animals?

   A. Oxygen diffused from the oceans into the atmosphere and may have helped trigger the Cambrian Explosion.
   B. Bacteria helped to produced the high levels of oxygen necessary to the Cambrian Explosion.
   C. Atmospheric oxygen may have helped trigger the Cambrian Explosion.
   D. Oxygen in the oceans may have helped trigger the Cambrian Explosion.

29. According to the passage, if we were to compare the global climate of the Cambrian world with today's climate, we would find that:

   A. the climate of today is more uniform than the climate of the Cambrian.
   B. the climate of today is warmer than the climate of the Cambrian.
   C. the climate of the Cambrian was more uniform than the climate of today.
   D. the climate of the Cambrian is colder than the climate of today.

TEST 6

GO ON TO THE NEXT PAGE.

Passage VI (Questions 30–35)

[Economists] Cooter and Ulen have hypothesized that, "[e]conomic theory of property suggests that ownership claims should be granted to any resource if the bundle of rights called property will lead to a more efficient use of
5　that resource and thus an increase in social wealth, and if the costs of establishing and enforcing those ownership claims is less than the benefits."

Under this theory, if the costs of "production" to natural parents are lower than the "value" that many childless people
10　attach to children, then there should be a legal market for selling babies because the social benefits would outweigh the social costs.

In fact, such legislation, if enacted, might, through economic incentives, be more effective in reducing the
15　number of abortions than moral persuasion has been. If parents could sell unwanted, "surplus" children, they would come to see their children as valuable liquid assets rather than just another mouth to feed, and even the most heartless, profit-maximizing mothers would be reluctant to
20　destroy such a precious asset. Similarly, legalizing child-selling should reduce instances of child abuse, as parents who despise their children would probably choose to sell rather than keep them and would be given an incentive to keep their "product" in good condition, if only to recoup a
25　higher price.

One theoretical economic objection to legalizing the sale of children is that the costs of establishing and enforcing "ownership" claims may outweigh the social benefits. Not only would it be somewhat costlier to verify ownership
30　and birth records of available babies on a larger scale than already exists on the adoption market, but the wholesale exchange of babies for money also creates incentives for wholesale kidnapping. If this became rampant, the costs of proving identity, arresting kidnappers, and recovering
35　pilfered infants might well outweigh the social benefit to childless couples. In this case, the system would become economically untenable.

Of course, the main objection to a system for selling babies is not theoretical, but moral. In our society, it is
40　simply seen as "immoral" to sell a person, especially one's own child. Most lawmakers will reject such proposals reflexively, without entertaining the thought or evaluating the economic incentives, simply because our society has conditioned us that it is "wrong" to sell people, regardless
45　of circumstances. Thus, most people would rather doom unwanted children to abortion, abuse, and neglect, rather than consider new approaches that are economically feasible and may be more moral than the status quo.

However, it is gratifying to know that, even under the
50　current system, there is limited system in place to allow the transfer of unwanted children to desirous parents. That system is surrogacy, which is perfectly legal. Surrogacy does offer several advantages over the free-market sale of infants. In the case of surrogacy, the identity of a baby is more easily
55　verifiable, and there is no chance that the baby is being stolen from the surrogate against her will because there is a contract between her and the buyer prior to birth. The costs of establishing ownership are, therefore, presumably lower than the social benefit to the adoptive parents, so this system
60　has positive social benefit.

30. In discussing the theory of property the author argues that there should be a legal market for selling babies "because the social benefits would outweigh the social costs" (lines 11–12). According to the passage, all of the following would fall under the category of "social costs" EXCEPT:

   I.　abortions of babies.
   II.　establishing ownership claims of babies.
   III.　proving identity of babies.

   A. I only
   B. II only
   C. III only
   D. II and III only

GO ON TO THE NEXT PAGE.

31. According to the passage, "ownership claims should be granted" (lines 2–3) for all of the following EXCEPT:

A. a toxic waste site bought in order to be restored and made into a park.

B. a precious gold mine purchased for the purpose of shutting it down.

C. a baby purchased by a family who intends to raise him as their own.

D. an airline acquired for expansion.

32. In order to evaluate if the author's idea of 'selling babies' is viable under the economic theory of property, one would first have to determine:

A. if the selling of babies is a moral or a theoretical issue.

B. whether "surrogacy" actually has "positive social benefit."

C. whether "surrogacy" is more advantageous.

D. if the costs of production are lower than the value placed upon the child by childless parents.

33. The author's discussion of 'selling babies' includes the assumption that:

A. surrogacy allows the transfer of children to parents.

B. legalizing "child-selling" has not been tried yet.

C. parents who are abusive despise their children.

D. parents usually want the best for their children.

34. According to the passage, a central problem to be solved in an emerging lucrative "free-market" is:

A. the cost of "production."

B. hoarding of available resources.

C. a proportional increase in crime.

D. the success of the program itself.

35. The author argues that "our society has conditioned us that it is 'wrong' to sell people, regardless of circumstances" (lines 43–45). According to the passage, these beliefs imply that:

A. society is not as moral as it could be.

B. society is more moral than it should be.

C. the status quo is more concerned with theory than morality.

D. the legacy of slavery has left its impact on society.

GO ON TO THE NEXT PAGE.

Passage VII (Questions 36–40)

In American perception, the judge (and especially the chief justice of the Supreme Court) is a quintessentially divided figure. As a political appointee, he is expected to rise above politics. As an unelected official, he must check a
5 popularly elected president and Congress when they violate a Constitution whose interpretation is unclear and fluid. He must privately decide controversies before him, then publicly present, justify, and defend his decisions—to litigants, the electorate, the president, Congress, legal scholars, and
10 even dissenting justices—in a public document, the judicial opinion. As Justice Brennan noted, a justice's "personal reading inevitably occurs in a public context and is open to critical scrutiny from all quarters."

Under the American common-law philosophic legacy,
15 the Supreme Court is simultaneously urged to view both judicial activism and restraint as coexisting virtues.

The justifications given for restraint are surprisingly divergent. [Early English Judge] Bracton, while acknowledging the need for "rule of law" and an independent
20 judiciary, nevertheless felt it was not his proper role to judge the king's actions. Bracton left that responsibility to the "Divine Law," and to the King's own conscience in adhering to it. Similar reasoning is visible in formative American cases. However, this principle is premised on a number
25 of problematic assumptions; namely, that the executive is persuadable and can be punished by some extralegal mechanism such as election, impeachment, or perdition. It also undermines a cornerstone of the perceived legitimacy of the American charter—the rule of law—because it denies
30 a legal remedy for wrongs committed by political officials.

A more convincing reason for restraint is a lack of expertise on the part of the Supreme Court in some areas: for example, those requiring extensive evidentiary hearings on a scale which only Congress or an executive agency
35 can conduct. This reason becomes especially compelling if one is convinced that all judicial decisions are, by their very nature, inescapably political. This leads straight into the "countermajoritarian difficulty," which posits that the Supreme Court's perceived legitimacy among the
40 government and electorate will drop if it arrogates to itself the right to make purely political decisions on behalf of the electorate. This loss of legitimacy would present a very real practical problem for a Court that relies on the executive branch for its enforcing "sword" and on the legislature for
45 its jurisdiction. There is no simple answer to this critique. Yet in America, as commentator Alexis de Tocqueville noted, "[T]he most fundamental issues confronting our democracy finally arrive in the Supreme Court for judicial determination. Not infrequently, these are the issues upon
50 which contemporary society is most deeply divided. [and] judges must resolve them." Since it is impossible for the Supreme Court to constantly sidestep judicial resolution

while still preserving its popular support, the best advice for a chief justice may be simply, "tread cautiously … ."

55 At the same time, our common law tradition elevated the activist judge to the status of hero. Inherent in the image of the activist judge is the idea of a great man single-handedly dispensing corrective justice. The simultaneous lionization of judicial activism also has its roots, ironically enough, in Bracton. He popularized the enduring common law image of
60 an all-powerful judge possessing an authority independent of his appointer's and, like a king, held to account under divine law alone, by God himself. Bracton added to the judicial image a myth of the judge's amazing individual ability to sort out conflicting precedents and accounts and to
65 discover something called the truth. Tellingly, this ability is not granted by God, but self-acquired through the study of law and "not without working long into the night watches." These two myths—the common law judge's divine mandate and unique truth-finding ability—have not only survived, but
70 embedded themselves so strongly in American legal culture that even in 1789 Justice Chase claimed the right to overrule legislative acts because of his own superior understanding of "natural law." Furthermore, it seems that this admiration of the activist judicial figure, as popularized by the "great
75 judge" view of legal history, is currently strong among the electorate, if not academics.

36. Which of the following statements is the most reasonable conclusion that can be drawn from the author's description of the "countermajoritarian difficulty" (line 37)?

A. The Court will lose perceived legitimacy if it votes for a particular branch of government.

B. The Court will lose faith in the government if it makes findings based solely on the popular vote.

C. The government and the voting public will lose faith in the Court if the Court goes completely against the majority vote.

D. The voting public will lose faith in the Court if the Court makes findings based solely on their majority vote.

GO ON TO THE NEXT PAGE.

37. If the averred "number of problematic assumptions" *are* true, that "the executive is persuadable, and can be punished by some extralegal mechanism, such as election, impeachment, or perdition" (lines 25–27), then which of the following must also be true?

A. The members of the executive are going to hell.
B. The members of the executive care enough about something to modify their behavior.
C. The executive does not care about impeachment, among other things.
D. The executive is not going to be re-elected because they are persuadable.

38. According to the passage, Judge Bracton felt that "it was not his proper role to judge the king's actions" (lines 21–22). Bracton's reasoning behind this idea paralleled his other belief that:

A. a judge was accountable only to those he represented.
B. a judge was accountable only to his appointer.
C. a judge was accountable only to God.
D. a judge was accountable only to the king.

lines 60–63

39. According to the passage, a practical problem for the Court is that the executive branch of government provides:

A. for the actual enforcement of the Court's decisions.
B. the actual monies from which the Court operates.
C. some of the most difficult issues with which the Court struggles.
D. little, if any, popular support for the Court.

40. The contention that, "it seems that this admiration of the activist judicial figure, as popularized by the 'great judge' view of legal history is currently strong among the electorate, if not academics." (lines 73–76), can most justifiably be interpreted as support for the idea that:

A. those who study and teach law for a living do not think so highly of the electorate.
B. the academicians generally admire an activist judge, while the public prefers a more populist one.
C. the electorate strongly supports the idea of a "great judge" who can discern the truth, as do the academicians.
D. the public loves the idea of a judge who will "stand up" to Big Government.

STOP. IF YOU FINISH BEFORE TIME IS CALLED, CHECK YOUR WORK. YOU MAY GO BACK TO ANY QUESTION IN THIS TEST.

TEST 6

STOP.

Verbal Reasoning Test 7
Time: 60 Minutes
Questions 1–40

VERBAL REASONING

DIRECTIONS: There are seven passages in this Verbal Reasoning test. Each passage is followed by several questions. After reading a passage, select the one best answer to each question. If you are not certain of an answer, eliminate the alternatives that you know to be incorrect and then select an answer from the remaining alternatives. Indicate your selection by blackening the corresponding oval on your answer document.

Passage I (Questions 1–6)

In a popular 1962 textbook, referring to Charles Darwin's works *On the Origin of Species* and *The Descent of Man,* science editors confidently asserted, "When [Darwin] finished, the fact of evolution could be denied only by an
5 abandonment of reason." And, "[Darwin's] books did not so much undermine the old, comfortable order of things as simply overwhelm it." However, in the ensuing half a century, this rather haughty point of view has *evolved.* New scientific discoveries have not provided the expected
10 irrefutable evidence for evolution that had been hoped for. Though the same individuals who wrote and believed the above statements would be unlikely to embrace scientific creation, evidence for evolution has not advanced as they would have hoped. The universe and our formation within it
15 appear to be increasingly too complex to be answered by the theories of Charles Darwin. However, perhaps the greatest failing of early evolution proponents was in wholeheartedly and blindly embracing a theory in the same fashion that they would have attributed to believers in scientific creation
20 theory.

Humans are large animals that fall under the categorization of K-strategists, unlike many species of annual plants, bacteria, insects, and small animals (r-strategists) that have very fast rates of population growth,
25 among other strategies. Many factors work to limit large animals' capacity for natural-process change, or evolution. These same factors make large animals especially vulnerable to rapid extinction; the increasing tendency towards rapid extinction bodes ill for the opportunities to evolve.

30 The seven most significant factors are: their relatively small population levels their long generation spans (the time between birth and the ability to give birth) their low numbers of progeny produced per adult their high complexity of morphology and biochemistry their enormous body sizes;
35 their specialized food supplies and their relatively advanced cultural and social structures. These all apply to *Homo sapiens* and back down the long list of large mammals from which *H. sapiens* allegedly evolved.

These factors limit the capacity of animals not only
40 to change through natural selection and mutations, but also to adapt to environmental changes. A fundamental problem biologists observe is that deleterious mutations vastly outnumber beneficial mutations (by anywhere from 10,000 to 1 up to 10,000,000 to 1). Thus, a species needs
45 an enormous population, a very short generation time, and a small body size if it is going to survive long enough to benefit from mutations. Deleterious mutations and environmental stresses drive most animal species to extinction. New species of K-strategists actually arising (evolving) Phoenix-like
50 from these ashes has never been proven to have occurred.

Crude mathematical models indicate that a species capable of significant evolutionary advance rather than doomed to eventual extinction must have a population of one quadrillion individuals, a generation time of three months,
55 and a body size of one centimeter. These conclusions are confirmed by field observations.

It is true that human beings have come to use their culture to avoid or postpone the effects of most limitations on their population size. However, this was not an advantage
60 of nomadic hunter-gatherer societies of early man. Even the relatively recently existing cultures of the American Indian were severely restricted by their environment. Their populations would fluctuate accordingly. Human culture, which would satisfy the definition of reducing limitations
65 on population size, has only come about recently with technological, pastoral, and industrial advances.

GO ON TO THE NEXT PAGE.

1. According to information in the passage, evolution would be most likely to occur when an animal exhibits:

   A. long generation spans.
   B. simple social structures.
   C. high complexity of morphology.
   D. small population levels.

2. According to information in the passage, "r-strategists" (line 24) would be characterized by:

   I. low numbers of progeny produced per adult.
   II. generalized food supplies.
   III. advanced cultural and social structures.

   A. I only
   B. II only
   C. I and III only
   D. I, II, and III

3. If the public reception of scientific creation repeated the reception that the author claims was given to Darwin's ideas, most people would:

   A. resist the theory initially but gradually modify their view of natural selection.
   B. claim to believe the theory but ignore its profound implications.
   C. reject its version of reality as contrary to common sense.
   D. accept the theory readily and quickly revise their theories about natural selection.

4. Which of the following statements is most clearly NOT supported by the author?

   A. Evolution is possible.
   B. An occurrence of a new species has never been proven.
   C. A K-strategist's capacity for change is limited.
   D. *H. sapiens* did not evolve.

5. The author's characterization of the science editors who reviewed Darwin's works suggests that the retort/comment "in the ensuing half a century, this rather haughty point of view has *evolved*" (lines 7–8), meant that:

   A. the editors have abandoned Darwin's ideas.
   B. the editors probably embrace the concept of scientific creation.
   C. the editors' arrogant perspective has changed.
   D. the editors had been wrong.

6. The claim that "a species capable of significant evolutionary advance rather than doomed to eventual extinction must have a population of one quadrillion individuals, a generation time of three months, and a body size of one centimeter" (lines 51–55) necessitates which of the following conclusions?

   A. *H. sapiens* will become extinct.
   B. There is no species capable of "significant evolutionary advance."
   C. All species are doomed to eventual extinction.
   D. *H. sapiens* must increase their generation time to three months, or else they will become extinct.

GO ON TO THE NEXT PAGE.

Passage II (Questions 7–11)

The United States overseas presence, which has provided the essential underpinnings of U.S. foreign policy for many decades, is near a state of crisis. Insecure and often decrepit facilities, obsolete information technology,
5 outmoded administrative and human resources practices, poor allocation of resources, and competition from the private sector for talented staff threaten to cripple our nation's overseas capability, with far-reaching consequences for national security and prosperity.

10 In its relations with the world, America has always stood for freedom, democracy, and the principled pursuit of global commerce. Our foreign policy has sought to tear down barriers and to form ever wider links among the world's people based on the rule of law and the
15 advancement of human rights. While these overriding goals are a constant, specific objectives and strategies change with the geopolitical realities of an era.

The structure of America's overseas presence today is an outgrowth of World War II and the demands of the
20 Cold War. America's foreign policy then focused largely on maintaining military preparedness and on influencing the alignment of nations. Geopolitical and security considerations took priority over economic interests and other foreign policy concerns. Information gathering and
25 reporting were necessarily among the central activities at our embassies.

A vital concern of this period was denying adversaries access to military technology and sensitive information and countering political movements hostile to American
30 interests. The need for secrecy and tight control led to a highly centralized and hierarchical approach to managing both people and information. Inevitably, these activities shaped the U.S. overseas presence in almost every way. In retrospect, we can see a consistent logic, shape, and style
35 to the organization and functions of American foreign operations, which could be called the Cold War design. This design evolved to advance our primary strategy: containment. For our overseas presence during the Cold War period, this was enormously successful. However, what
40 was suited to our strategy then is not necessarily well suited to our strategies today and in the future.

The condition of U.S. posts and missions abroad is unacceptable. Since the end of the Cold War, the world's political, economic, and technological landscape has
45 changed dramatically, but our country's overseas presence has not adequately adjusted to this new reality. Thirty federal agencies now operate internationally, yet they lack a common Internet/e-mail-based communications network through which to communicate with one another. There is no
50 interagency process to "right-size" posts as missions change, nor are agencies required, with a few exceptions, to pay their share of the cost of maintaining and renovating facilities. It is ironic that, at the moment when our nation's message resonates through history, its voice has been rendered nearly
55 mute by antiquated technologies. Our overseas presence is perilously close to the point of system failure.

Such failure would have serious consequences: less effective representation and advocacy of U.S. interests abroad; a loss of U.S. exports, investment, and jobs;
60 inadequate political and economic information leading to unexpected crises; less effectiveness in promoting democracy and the rule of law; and a weakening of the fight against international terrorism and drug trafficking. U.S. citizens traveling abroad would not get the assistance that
65 they need and deserve. Our nation would be less able to forge global alliances to respond to regional conflicts or to solve global environmental and social problems. Only by maintaining a robust global presence can our government protect U.S. interests and promote its values throughout the
70 world.

7. In the context of the passage, the word *containment* (line 38) means:

A. poor allocation of resources and competition from the private sector for talented staff.

B. an interagency process for each agency to pay its share of the cost of maintaining and renovating facilities.

C. outmoded administrative and human resources practices.

D. countering political movements hostile to American interests.

GO ON TO THE NEXT PAGE.

8. The author's reference to the relationship of "our nation's message" and "antiquated technologies" (lines 53–55) implies that:

   A. as a result of older technologies, it is more difficult to communicate throughout the world.

   B. the people of the world would have no recourse but to use old radios to get their information.

   C. America's values of freedom and the principled pursuit of global commerce are antiquated.

   D. as a result of archaic technology, our nation's message cannot be adequately expressed throughout the world.

9. According to the passage, "system failure" of United States overseas presence would result in all the following EXCEPT:

   A. U.S. citizens traveling abroad would not get the assistance that they need and deserve.

   B. Our nation would be less able to solve global environmental problems.

   C. a loss of U.S. imports.

   D. a loss of U.S. jobs.

10. According to the passage, the Cold War design (line 36) is considered a result of all of the following factors EXCEPT:

    A. denying adversaries access to military technology and sensitive information.

    B. circumventing international terrorism.

    C. countering political movements hostile to American interests.

    D. the need for secrecy and tight control.

11. According to the passage, why is "[o]ur overseas presence … perilously close to the point of system failure" (lines 55–56)?

    A. Our country's overseas presence has not adequately adjusted to the end of the Cold War.

    B. We are no longer maintaining a robust global presence.

    C. Our Cold War strategy was enormously successful.

    D. We are less effective in promoting democracy and the rule of law.

TEST 7

GO ON TO THE NEXT PAGE.

Passage III (Questions 12–17)

If public schools experience high levels of violence and drug use, school officials may wish to consider adopting search policies that permit them under certain circumstances to screen students and search school property for weapons
5 and drugs.

Public school officials, like law enforcement officers, are State officers bound by the Fourth Amendment. Thus, school officials must understand the basic dictates of the Fourth Amendment—both to comport themselves within
10 the bounds of the law and to implement an effective drug and weapons search policy. The information contained in this section is meant to give school officials some basis for considering whether to pursue a search policy in their schools or school districts. Before implementing a search
15 policy, schools should be sure to contact the school attorney, the local district attorney, or the state attorney general.

The Fourth Amendment prohibits all unreasonable searches and seizures by state officers. Reasonableness is determined by balancing the government's interest behind
20 the search against the privacy intrusion of the search. The Supreme Court has held that students have a legitimate expectation of privacy for their persons and accompanying possessions. However, the Court also has held that schools have a substantial interest in maintaining security and order
25 in the classroom and on school grounds. The Court has determined that this interest justifies a more flexible standard of reasonableness for searches of students that are conducted by school officials as opposed to law enforcement officers. Thus, the Court has held that school officials, unlike the
30 police, do not need to obtain a warrant prior to conducting a search. Nor do they need probable cause to believe that a violation of the law has occurred.

School officials need only have "reasonable suspicion" that a particular search will reveal evidence that the student
35 has violated or is violating either the law or the rules of the school. Even if reasonable suspicion exists, to be permissible the scope of the search must be such that the measures used are reasonably related to the purpose of the search and not excessively intrusive in light of the age and gender
40 of the student and the nature of the suspected infraction. The Supreme Court has upheld searches that comply with this standard only insofar as such searches are initiated and conducted by school officials. A more stringent legal standard likely applies to searches conducted in conjunction
45 with or at the behest of law enforcement officers.

In interpreting and applying the "reasonable suspicion" standard set forth by the Supreme Court, lower courts generally have required more than general suspicion, curiosity, rumor, or a hunch to justify searches of students
50 and their possessions. Factors identified by courts in sustaining a search of a student include the observation of specific and describable behavior leading one reasonably to believe that a particular student is engaging in or has engaged in prohibited conduct. The more specific the evidence in
55 support of searching an individual student, the more likely that the search will be upheld.

When reasonable suspicion exists, school officials may search students, but only within reasonable limits. Such limits require school officials to adopt measures that
60 are reasonably related to the purpose behind the search. In addition, the search may not be excessively intrusive in light of the age and gender of the particular student and the nature of the infraction.

Generally, the more intrusive the search, the greater
65 the justification the courts will require. Thus, a search of a student's jacket or book bag requires less suspicion than a physical "pat down" or, at the extreme, a strip search. Courts consider strip searches highly intrusive of an individual student's privacy; thus, they should be premised only on
70 probable cause.

12. An important comparison is made in the passage between:

A. weapons and drugs.
B.) school officials and law enforcement officers.
C. a student's jacket and book bag.
D. searches and seizures.

GO ON TO THE NEXT PAGE.

13. If a local police officer, assigned to provide security at a public school, heard of an infraction that would require the search of a student, the author's ideas suggest that the police officer should:

    A. be careful in how he conducts the search.
    B. first place the student under arrest.
    C. handcuff the student for his safety.
    D. obtain a warrant prior to conducting the search.

14. The phrases "*more stringent legal standard*" and "*school officials*" can be connected, respectively, to:

    A. "law enforcement officers" and "more flexible standard of reasonableness."
    B. "law enforcement officers" and "nature of the infraction."
    C. "school officials" and "more flexible standard of reasonableness."
    D. "school officials" and "premised only on probable cause."

15. If the information that "students have a legitimate expectation of privacy for their persons and accompanying possessions" (lines 21–23) is accurate, then:

    A. students have an expectation of privacy with respect to their wall lockers.
    B. students have no expectation of privacy with respect to their wall lockers.
    C. students have no expectation of privacy with respect to their clothing.
    D. students should never be strip searched.

16. Which of the following more likely *violates* the basic dictates of the Fourth Amendment, as described in the passage?

    A. A female school official opens and searches the wall locker of a male student.
    B. A female school official asks for a male student's book bag, which she then searches.
    C. A male school official physically pats down a male student.
    D. A male school official physically pats down a male student at the behest of a male police officer.

17. According to the passage, "reasonable suspicion" (lines 46–47) would best be described as:

    A. balancing school officials' and police interests.
    B. more than general suspicion or a hunch.
    C. specific curiosity or rumor.
    D. the Court's reaction to a strip search.

TEST 7

GO ON TO THE NEXT PAGE.

Passage IV (Questions 18–23)

When I hear that someone has published a successful novel, bought an awesome stock, or filled the racks of a pottery story with her wares, my heart constricts with jealousy. Damn! How come they can do that and I can't?
5 Another opportunity gone. Now I'll never be able to get my foot in the door. This jealousy also manifests itself through demeaning introspection and self-evaluation: I'm such a loser. Actually, it's worse. I read just the other day that there is no such thing as a "lost opportunity"; somebody else
10 always takes advantage of it.

What I usually have to remind myself of is, in the first place, that I've never actually written a novel, bought any stock, or gone out and tried to sell any of my ceramics pieces. But, writing a novel or a book is something that I've
15 always dreamed of doing. My image of myself as a rich author includes my rather simple and unpretentious (given the large amounts of money that I will be making, and that everybody knows that I make) white clapboard house in Cornwall, Connecticut, next to the covered bridge, where
20 I hobnob in the afternoons with the other Pulitzer Prize-winners about cerebral topics and issues, which only we really understand. I've considered buying stock before. It seems like everybody does it. And makes good money at it, too. How about that Microsoft? All it takes is a little analysis
25 of the stock pages in the newspapers each day. Boring! And people are always telling me that I should sell my pottery and sculptures. "You could be an artist!" Thanks a lot. What, because I don't sell the stuff I'm *not* an artist?

When I think that it's too late, that I'll never be able
30 to get my foot in the door, it does sink me into the abyss and tends to breed apathy. Why bother writing my novel or analyzing the stock. All the good books have already been written. All the really good stock (like Microsoft) has been bought up. There aren't anymore good deals left in the
35 world. The pie is shrinking and I haven't even gotten my piece yet! Well, there's nothing to be done about it now. Too late. Too late. And if I had only done what they have done when they did it, I'd be where they are now. Look at them! I am a loser by virtue of where I am.

40 Upon reflection, I realize that the big difference between them and me is that they took action. They tried and, I'm sure at times failed. What's that quote by Theodore Roosevelt about the only real losers being those who do not have the courage to try, perhaps fail, and then try again?
45 I do hope for their sakes that those whose successes I so admire and covet are more satisfied with what they have at the moment than I seem to be. Perhaps, though, it is an inability to be satisfied that drives them. But if I want more, I have to at least try to go out and get it.

50 Hey, the pie gets bigger all the time. I have to realize that someone else's good fortune is certainly not my personal misfortune. Someone else's good fortune actually increases the opportunities for all of us. I mustn't measure my life or career by the successes of another. The only yardstick to
55 measure success with is the satisfaction and contentment we find within ourselves.

18. According to the author, his perceptions of his shortcomings were in large part the result of his:

   A. apathy.
   B. unrealistic expectations.
   C. being too late to do anything about them.
   D. inability to write, choose stocks, or create ceramic art.

GO ON TO THE NEXT PAGE.

19. What is the author's initial response to the standard story about the successes of others?

   A. "That guy is such a loser."
   B. "I could do that."
   C. "They got the last piece of pie."
   D. "I've got to sell one of my books."

20. The assertion that "[p]erhaps though, it is an inability to be satisfied that drives them" (lines 47–48) is NOT clearly consistent with the information about:

   A. Theodore Roosevelt.
   B. those who are successful.
   C. the author's background and interests.
   D. the author's own situation.

21. Which of the following descriptions most clearly exemplifies the skills of the author?

   A. professional artist
   B. ceramic hobbyist
   C. stock analyst
   D. novelist

22. The author's characterization of himself suggests that the comment "My image of myself as a rich author includes my rather simple and unpretentious (given the large amounts of money that I will be making, and that everybody knows that I make) house in Cornwall" (line 15–19) meant that:

   A. he plans on making large amounts of money.
   B. he is very serious.
   C. he is a humble person.
   D. he was being sarcastic.

23. Which of the following assertions is the most effective argument *against* the author's suggestion that "[s]omeone else's good fortune actually increases the opportunities for all of us" (line 52–53)?

   A. The early bird gets the worm.
   B. Slow and steady wins the race.
   C. A stitch in time saves nine.
   D. All's well that ends well.

GO ON TO THE NEXT PAGE.

Passage V (Questions 24–29)

In their wisdom, America's Founding Fathers instituted the rule of law to do away with arbitrary justice and absolute power; to this end, they issued their famous Constitutional prohibition against "cruel and unusual punishments." In
5 this, they must be praised for not only protecting the rights of the innocent, but also for extending their protection to those already convicted of crimes. Though it was vital for them that convicts, though a hated minority, should not be abused by the majority, it appears that the Founding Fathers
10 themselves didn't object to capital punishment for grave crimes, as we can deduce from the persistence of executions, especially hangings, in the post-revolutionary period.

Thus, the Eighth Amendment should not be taken to mean that the Constitution's framers objected to any sort
15 of punishment that might be considered "cruel"—what punishment, after all, could be considered kind?—but that they forbade penalties that were *unusually* cruel, meaning those that singled out certain people for "special" retribution. A study of the practices of that period suggests
20 that, by including this provision, they sought to save the American people from practices like the *amende honorable*, which was still practiced in France and elsewhere at the time. The *amende honorable* was both cruel and unusual; it was imposed not on all murderers, but only on those
25 who killed the privileged aristocrats or kings, and the penalty was arbitrarily set *ex post facto*. On one occasion, it included tearing away chunks of the regicide's flesh, filling his wounds with molten lead and burning oil, melting away his hand with sulfur, followed by drawing and quartering,
30 and ending with his trunk being burned to ash and scattered. There has been nothing in the American legal system that has subjected anyone to any such tortures; on the contrary, in our efforts to reduce the cruelty inherent in punishment, we have striven to develop increasingly painless methods
35 of execution, culminating in the gas chamber. At the same time, America's history has shown increasing equality for all people before the law, thereby moving us further from both cruelty and irregularity in our punishments.

But does the state have the moral right to kill a person
40 for the crime of murder when it would seem that the act of killing is equally harmful for the individual as for the state? To understand this seeming contradiction, we must look at what it is that we seek to punish. There are some cases where murder is allowed—in self-defense, for example—
45 and in other cases we make a distinction between accidental, negligent, and premeditated murder. I would posit from this that we are punishing not the action itself, but the *intent* behind the murder. ... Most people would agree that the police need to be armed to keep order, and sometimes they
50 must shoot in the line of duty, yet no one would say they should be tried as murderers. The state should be accorded the same leeway, because its intent is not to harm, not to kill for cruelty, revenge, or selfish gain, but to protect us from

those who do. Besides, are critics of the state's right to kill
55 really willing to argue for a total equivalence of the state and the individual? Remember that, though few oppose the state's right to imprison, an imprisonment by an individual is kidnapping; similarly, we agree the state has the right to impose fines as punishment, but which individual can
60 impose fines on another without becoming an extortionist? By limiting the right of the state to punish by obvious and direct channels, we leave the justice system little choice but to invent truly cruel and unusual punishments.

24. It is clear from the passage that the author believes that the state should administer sentences to criminals in order to:

    I.   abuse the criminal.
    II. protect society.
    III. punish the criminal.

A. II only
B. III only
C. II and III only
D. I, II, and III

GO ON TO THE NEXT PAGE.

25. Which of the following opinions would the author be most likely to endorse?

    A. The Founding Fathers were against punishment that might be considered "cruel."
    B. Capital punishment is cruel, but not unusually so.
    C. Capital punishment is cruel.
    D. The Founding Fathers meant to single out only certain people for capital punishment.

26. Assume that recently obtained medical studies of capital executions over the last twenty years show conclusive evidence that lethal injection is by far the most painless method of execution. This finding:

    A. increases the probability that the author's argument is valid.
    B. increases the probability that the use of capital punishment will become greater.
    C. decreases the probability that the author's argument is valid.
    D. reveals nothing about the validity of the author's arguments.

27. If the author were a warden in a prison, he would most probably tend to place the *least* emphasis on:

    A. ensuring that the prisoners did not escape.
    B. ensuring that the prisoners had adequate nutrition.
    C. ensuring that adequate rehabilitative programs were available.
    D. ensuring that the prisoners were not beaten.

28. According to the passage, one drawback to eliminating capital punishment is that it can lead to:

    A. cruel and unusual punishments.
    B. excessive fines on the citizenry.
    C. an equivalence of state and citizens' rights.
    D. prison overcrowding.

29. According to the passage, the Founding Fathers would consider the *amende honorable* (line 21) to be:

    A. unusual and unjust.
    B. arbitrary justice.
    C. appropriate, given the circumstances of the crime.
    D. cruel and unjust.

GO ON TO THE NEXT PAGE.

TEST 7

Passage VI (Questions 30–35)

The Russian morality play "Case of the Dead Infant" makes excellent use of early Russian readers' expectations, giving seemingly good and proper actions unforeseen consequences. What begins as a lightly introduced piece,
5 billing itself as "a story about enticing a widow to lose her chastity," quickly plunges into an explicit tale of murder and sexual blackmail. Yet as in most Russian short stories of the period, harsh retribution falls surely on the offenders in the end, as the earthly authorities, working with Heaven's help,
10 bring him to justice and restore order to the world.

Like an experienced judge, the story's (anonymous) author makes clear from the first that the case we are about to hear is no new pattern, but rather falls in line with an established literary precedent. In all such familiar stories
15 an unloving person is tricked into abandoning her chastity by the plotting of another. Knowing such "historical" precedents allows readers to make definite inferences about the characters in this tale. For example, we can infer of the widow Svetlana Dunyevskaya that her fall was merely "due
20 to the victim's momentary failure to withstand temptation" rather than chronic amoral laxity. Svetlana is indeed represented not so much as a sexual transgressor, but as the victim of a far more malevolent transgressor, one who will, "without cause, set a snare to humiliate" her.

25 Yet whereas traditional Russian short stories often pay homage (or at least lip service) to conventional morality, harshly censuring the infidelity of faithless wives, this storyteller unexpectedly softens his rebuke of Svetlana to the point of almost a backhanded compliment. [When] her
30 husband dies suddenly, young Svetlana resolutely rejects her parents' proffered suitor and vows never to remarry, in order to honor her husband's memory. Here, instead of praising her determination and morals, the narrator takes a different view (for that society), saying "… if you can
35 swallow three gallons of vinegar at one sitting, you can live on as a lone widow. Widowhood is not easily maintained. The best long-term course for Svetlana would have been to take another husband openly. Although then she would not have rated in the top category of women, still she would
40 not have missed being counted in the middle group, and would not have come to disgrace in the end." Another couplet dismisses "hollow reputation" in favor of worldly security. By recognizing the difficulty for a young widow to lead her life in accordance with moral dictates, and pointing
45 out that it is sometimes necessary, and even praiseworthy, to compromise morality, he is definitely leading readers to question the value of tradition. In White Russian literature, which elevates acts of maniacal loyalty, his compromising moral attitude is puzzling, perhaps even risqué. There is the
50 strong implication that it was not neglect of, but excessive preoccupation with, propriety that led Svetlana to ruin.

In fact, the villainous seducer Sergei Yanin only manages to catch a glimpse of her when she dutifully performs her ritual obligations at a Russian Orthodox
55 ceremony in honor of her husband, which is the only time in ten years that she had ever ventured past the middle door of her house. As Sergei lies in wait for her to light candles and come out, he waits to draw her out of safety using the lure of propriety. Even as Sergei sees her and resolves to seduce her,
60 it is her very purity of motive that makes her a target. What draws him to her is her reputation as a beautiful yet chaste widow; when he sees her, she appears doubly desirable, just because she is forbidden and unattainable. He laments, "A widow in white/Ravishes one's sight."

65 As the story unfolds, we see that it is Svetlana's innocence that indirectly provides the means for her own seduction.

For a story with such an unconventional moral attitude, the resolution of the affair may be unsatisfying—it is exactly
70 the same as a traditional ending, which runs something like this: the lover dies (suddenly), the (guilty?) adulteress kills herself, and various other people are executed by the law as punishment for their greed.

30. The word *chastity* (line 6) is most likely being used to describe:

A. a woman who is religious.
B. a woman who is pure.
C. a woman who has never had sexual intercourse.
D. a woman who is currently celibate.

GO ON TO THE NEXT PAGE.

31. According the passage description, Sergei Yanin waits outside of the church in order to draw Svetlana "out of safety using the lure of propriety" (lines 58–59). What was this "lure of propriety"?

   A. He offered her a position within the top category of women.
   B. The passage does not specify.
   C. He was wealthy and, thus, she would have owned property as well.
   D. He offered to have sex with her.

32. According to the passage, "Knowing such 'historical' precedents allows readers to make definite inferences about the characters in this tale" (lines 16–18). The author most likely meant that:

   A. historical precedents were not often included in plays such as this one.
   B. the readers were bound to be surprised by the characters when they read a play.
   C. the readers were expected to add their own details to the story based upon previous dramas.
   D. without such precedents it would not be possible to understand the play.

33. Based upon the numerous quotations in the passage from the play, we can discern that the play was most likely:

   A. written from Sergei's perspective.
   B. written from a second-person perspective.
   C. written in the third person as a narrative.
   D. written without the character of a narrator.

34. On the basis of the passage, it is reasonable to conclude that:

   A. the author who wrote this play would have been considered somewhat radical by his peers.
   B. the author who wrote this play would have been widely accepted.
   C. this play is indicative of White Russian literature.
   D. White Russian literature questioned the value of tradition.

35. Assume that the following statements are true. Which one is *consistent* with the assertion that "[t]here is the strong implication that it was not neglect of, but excessive preoccupation with, propriety that led Svetlana to ruin" (lines 49–51)?

   A. Sergei specifically chose to victimize Svetlana because it was well known that she was chaste and had not left her home in over ten years. ✓
   B. Ten years of almost total isolation had left Svetlana with an unquenchable sexual desire, which Sergei was able to take advantage of.
   C. It was well known that Svetlana's chastity was a front, and that her "No," really meant "Yes."
   D. Svetlana had led a very poor life and would do almost anything for money and property.

TEST 7

GO ON TO THE NEXT PAGE.

Passage VII (Questions 36–40)

People are living longer today than at any other time in human history. The graying of America is a phenomenon and issue that generates a plethora of discussion because of its present and continued effects on the economic, health,
5 social, and legislative landscape of this country. By means of surveys, statistics, and other data sources, we can measure and attempt to foresee the impact this will have in the future. However, we may feel uncomfortable with our ability to understand *why* America is getting older. Fortunately, with
10 the scientific work being conducted by a group of researchers in a new field known as biogerontology, we are beginning to understand how and why we age.

If aging is a function of time, then there must be a clock. Dr. Leonard Hayflick, a professor of anatomy at
15 the University of California, does not address a clock in a molecular way at the cellular level, but rather as normal rhythms associated with biological functions and circadian rhythms. The master clock for these rhythms has been located in an area of the brain in the anterior portion of the
20 hypothalamus. It is known as the suprachiasmatic nuclei or SCN.

Yet this cannot be the only clock or even a clock at all in the traditional sense. There are only three groups of cells in the body that continue to endlessly divide. They
25 are skin cells, cells of the digestive tract, and cells in the bone that produce red and white blood cells. Why these particular cells do so may be explained by their function and evolution. However, all other cells in the body have a finite number of divisions. Something allows some cells to divide
30 indefinitely and others only a finite number of times.

For years, it was thought that if a cell were removed from tissue, it would continue to divide endlessly, in an essentially immortal fashion. However, closer scrutiny of the experiment that originally promoted this fallacy indicated
35 that it was a preparation technique that perpetuated the cell's life. It was a pair of inquisitive graduate students (Dr. Hayflick being one of them) who discovered that their own cells actually had a limited number of divisions, around fifty.

40 At the time of the students' experiment that led to this discovery, there was a technique used in the cattle industry to preserve bull semen. This technique prevented ice crystals from forming inside of the cell where they could permanently damage the cell by rupturing the wall. The students used
45 this technique to freeze cells to see if they would remember the point at which they had stopped dividing. Every cell that they defrosted completed its fifty divisions from the point of freezing. The cells somehow remembered where they had left off. Also, it was noticed that throughout cellular division
50 the cells exhibited an "aging effect" similar to the decreasing level of functionality noticed in elderly adults.

Nevertheless, Dr. Hayflick does not believe that death occurs because cells cease to divide. He believes that other factors and changes in the body bring this about. Despite
55 this, it is interesting to note that the longevity of a species is proportional to the number of the species' cellular divisions. A species with a short life span has fewer divisions than a species with a long one. Evidently, there is "something" governing the number of cellular divisions, possibly located
60 on the DNA. Speculation would lead us to believe that if this "clock" governing the number of divisions is located, it may be possible to manipulate the number of divisions. However, would this merely extend our longevity or have a direct bearing on aging? The burgeoning field of biogerontology
65 is in its infancy and only time will tell; pun intended.

36. Which of the following conclusions can justifiably be drawn from the experience of the pair of inquisitive graduate students mentioned in the passage?

   A. Don't assume that someone has done something incorrectly.

   B. Don't assume that an experiment has been performed inaccurately.

   C. It is sometimes helpful to question that which has been accepted.

   D. Grad students are more careful than professors.

GO ON TO THE NEXT PAGE.

37. The author asks, "However, would this merely extend our longevity or have a direct bearing on aging?" (lines 62–64). By "longevity" he most probably means:

   A. living longer with a decreasing level of functionality.
   B. maintaining our functionality into old age.
   C. staying young but not living any longer.
   D. living longer without aging.

38. The author contrasts our inability to understand why we are getting older with:

   A. people living longer today than at any other time.
   B. the field of biogerontology.
   C. a pun.
   D. what the impact will be on this country.

39. According to the passage, in the graduate students' experiment, cells that had already divided twenty times prior to freezing, when thawed would:

   A. divide a finite number of times while exhibiting almost no aging.
   B. continue to divide endlessly.
   C. divide around thirty more times.
   D. divide around fifty more times.

40. Based on passage information, if bulls have shorter lifespans than humans, their semen after freezing, would probably divide:

   A. endlessly.
   B. less than fifty times.
   C. around fifty times.
   D. more than fifty times.

STOP. IF YOU FINISH BEFORE TIME IS CALLED, CHECK YOUR WORK. YOU MAY GO BACK TO ANY QUESTION IN THIS TEST.

TEST 7

STOP.

Verbal Reasoning Test 8
Time: 60 Minutes
Questions 1–40

VERBAL REASONING

DIRECTIONS: There are seven passages in this Verbal Reasoning test. Each passage is followed by several questions. After reading a passage, select the one best answer to each question. If you are not certain of an answer, eliminate the alternatives that you know to be incorrect and then select an answer from the remaining alternatives. Indicate your selection by blackening the corresponding oval on your answer document.

Passage I (Questions 1–6)

Imagine that 95% of the world shared a language, called "Esperanto," so versatile and all-pervasive that people could not help but communicate in it, even when they refused to say a word. Further, imagine this "Esperanto" being
5 spoken by even the deaf, dumb, blind, insane, and children. Now imagine that you had already learned "Esperanto" in passing but were no longer proficient because of disuse. Wouldn't you, as a professional negotiator, invest a few hours in brushing up on it so you could speak fluently the
10 language that everyone else speaks? Body language, also called Proxemics, is the closest method of communication that we have to Esperanto, the "universal language," and should be a part of every negotiator's tool kit.

It is said that actions speak louder than words. Yet the
15 world is apparently full of foolish negotiators who routinely disregard nonverbal cues and are regularly taken in by verbal lies.

True, learning to perceive body language accurately is added work, requiring some additional training prior
20 to the negotiation in order to recognize it, and greater concentration during negotiation in order to notice it. So why should negotiators bother undergoing such training?

For one thing, learning to 'read' non verbal cues makes you more alert to lying. Lying is a constant problem (or
25 tool) and will remain a fixture in the arena of the negotiator. Therefore, sorting lies from truths is a critical skill. Body language is always more truthful than the spoken word because people are rarely as adept at pantomiming lies as they are at speaking them. This is true even for people who
30 lie (verbally) for a living.

Unfortunately, studies show untrained people are, on average, poor at nonverbal lie detection; they swallow 75% of lies without realizing it. Ironically, research studies show that professional negotiators who have not been trained in
35 the vagaries of Proxemics are actually no more accurate at discerning falsehoods. However, with training, people can learn to detect lies correctly 75% of the time. Incidentally, a 75% "hit" rate is every bit as accurate as a polygraph, which is legally prohibited in some circumstances, inappropriate
40 in others, and generally not very convenient.

The ability to read body language is also important because it is easier to convey emotion physically rather than verbally. Words are often clumsy tools for describing feelings. Many negotiators aim to hide or deny their
45 emotions during negotiations, perhaps feeling negotiations should be about "issues" and "positions" rather than feelings. However, any poker player will tell you that veiled negative emotions will still be apparent and may remain an obstacle to resolution. This requires skilled negotiators to
50 make a tactical choice: either confront the problem directly, or just keep its existence in the back of their mind.

There are some statements that cannot be voiced credibly, but that can be communicated believably through gesture. In negotiation, it is common but pointless to say,
55 "I'm being honest," or "I can't pay more than that," since no strategist will ever admit his dishonesty or reservation price. Yet these messages can be conveyed by gestures, and it is these nonverbal messages that tend to be believed over the words, whether they are true or just cleverly faked.
60 Thus, learning to use body language can make all your statements—true or not—seem more truthful.

GO ON TO THE NEXT PAGE.

1. Suppose an armed bank robber has failed in his robbery attempt and has taken several hostages within a nearby building. The robber knows nothing about Proxemics but that the concept exists and that the negotiator has been trained in its use. Which of the following negotiating scenarios would be most advantageous to the bank robber, based solely upon passage information about Proxemics?

   A. The robber would meet the negotiator within a dimly lit room inside of the building.
   B. The robber would insist on negotiating over the telephone from the building.
   C. The robber would wait until after darkness and meet the negotiator from a short distance away.
   D. The robber would seek a face-to-face meeting with the negotiator on the roof of the building.

2. Which of the following statements most strongly *challenges* one of the assertions made in the passage?

   A. The biggest obstacle to Proxemics is that it is only as accurate as a polygraph.
   B. An understanding of body language can make all of your statements seem more truthful.
   C. The main stumbling block to the passage's "universal language" is the need for everyone to learn it and stay proficient in its use.
   D. Apparently, everyone speaks this language but few are actually fluent in it.

3. Which of the following suppositions is most clearly believed by the author?

   A. The untrained negotiator must rely more heavily on the polygraph, which is often not convenient.
   B. The ability of the negotiator to convey his messages depends very much on the training of the recipient.
   C. Proper training in nonverbal communication will allow you to read and convey messages more clearly.
   D. Esperanto will someday be the primary form of nonverbal communication.

4. The passage implies that, without formal training in the area, who among the following may already be proficient in 'reading' nonverbal cues?

   A. 95% of the world
   B. polygraphers
   C. professional negotiators
   D. poker players

5. The ideas discussed in this passage would likely be of most use to:

   A. detectives.
   B. lovers.
   C. radio disc jockeys.
   D. police dispatchers.

6. The passage asks that the reader, "[i]magine that 95% of the world shared a language, called 'Esperanto'" (lines 1–2), and then uses Esperanto as an anology for Proxemics. However, the passage *weakens* this analogy through which of the following quotations?

   I. "[P]eople could not help but communicate in it."
   II. "Esperanto [is] spoken by even the deaf, ... blind, insane ..."
   III. "Esperanto [is] spoken by even the ... dumb, blind, ... and children."

   A. II only
   B. III only
   C. II and III only
   D. I, II, and III

TEST 8

GO ON TO THE NEXT PAGE.

Passage II (Questions 7–11)

Societal stigmatization of homosexuals declined throughout the 1970s to such a degree that homosexual groups were able to forge a group identity and began to foster pride in the fact that they identified as homosexual.
5 The rise of consolidated groups of gays, lesbians, and bisexuals has helped to change the feelings of those who discover themselves as such from shame to pride. Recently, there has been a move toward recognizing homosexual and bisexual persons as members of a minority group, rather
10 than as psychologically disordered individuals.

This is not a unique phenomenon in cultures or in history. Almost all minority groups go through this transition. Homosexuals are simply a group that is perceived as a minority by virtue of their behavior. In fact, those who
15 are categorized as "social deviants" often take pride in their stigmatized attribute and have frequently banded together to protect themselves. When one member of a group is attacked, the rest of the group rallies in support to protect him. In this way, the homosexuals who have forged a minority status
20 can be seen as a group that takes pride in its difference from "normal" society.

Researchers have studied the self-esteem of minority group members, who are almost always confronted with societal prejudices. It was expected that this prejudice would
25 be found to have lowered the self-image of these members. A study by Crocker and Major (1989) addresses the issue of stigma and its effects on minority group members' self-concept. They were particularly interested in "global" self-esteem—feelings about one's own self-worth—as opposed
30 to feelings about the minority group. In their hypotheses, they cite the "reflected appraisals theory," which suggests that members of stigmatized groups may develop negative self-concepts, either because specific persons with whom they interact view them negatively, or because society as a whole
35 devalues their group. Another theoretical perspective, "self-fulfilling prophecies," suggests that they may internalize the negative stereotypes held by society, so that they come to fulfill the stereotype.

However, the empirical evidence on stigma and self-
40 esteem reveals that these theoretical perspectives are not confirmed. Self-identified homosexuals' self-esteem has not been found to be consistently lowered. In fact, most research has found that homosexuals are as diverse with regard to their self-esteem as any other population. To explain this
45 result, Crocker and Major concluded that membership in a stigmatized group enables the individual to protect himself from lowered self-esteem by attributing any negative events or attitudes as being directed at the group and due to societal prejudices, rather than toward himself. In other words, the
50 individual attributes these prejudices, which often result in personal setbacks and obstacles, to negative feelings toward the group, not himself. Thus, belonging to a hated or socially

ostracized group appears to be a buffer against lowering the individual's self-esteem.

55 However, we should not forget that homosexuals' minority status is different from that of other minorities,' in that it may be relatively private. That is, a homosexual may, if he chooses, be able to hide his sexuality and "pass" for a heterosexual, which may allow him to escape direct social
60 prejudice. Yet he, at least, would still know that he was a homosexual. Furthermore, such a masquerade would also deprive him of the ability to attribute others' reactions to society's stance towards homosexuals as a whole, and not to him personally.

65 There have recently been further studies that document the positive association between "coming out" (revealing one's homosexuality) and self-esteem, giving support to Crocker and Major's theory. Prior to openly accepting and unabashedly revealing to his family and colleagues that he
70 is a homosexual, this individual is actually participating in a farce, perpetuating his own stigmatization and denigration (and those of other homosexuals), to the detriment of his own self-worth. The seemingly simple act of "coming out" seems to free the individual from the confines of his having
75 adopted societal restrictions and prejudices and enables him to identify openly with members of his own group, leading to a healthier lifestyle.

7. The passage suggests that the self-esteem of individual homosexuals:

A. is somewhat higher than the self-esteem found in individuals of other populations.
B. is somewhat lower than the self-esteem found in individuals of other populations.
C. varies widely depending upon social stigmatization.
D. is similar to the self-esteem found in the individuals of any other population.

GO ON TO THE NEXT PAGE.

8. Which of the following best characterizes the study by Crocker and Major (1989)?

   A. They hypothesized that homosexuals were experiencing prejudice.
   B. Their hypotheses and assumptions prior to the study were disproved.
   C. Their hypotheses and assumptions prior to the study were proved.
   D. They hypothesized that being part of a group would insulate individuals from diminished self-esteem.

9. The author of the passage would be most likely to agree with which of the following ideas expressed by other researchers of societal prejudice?

   A. Members of stigmatized groups may develop negative self-concepts because society as a whole devalues their group.
   B. The individual will often come to accept and believe societal perspectives about his group.
   C. Being part of a group seems to buffer the individual from the prejudice and stigmatization of society.
   D. Societal prejudice falls more heavily upon those whose 'unacceptable' proclivities may be hidden.

10. In the context of the passage, the term 'global' self-esteem refers primarily to the:

    A. sense of worth that the world provides you.
    B. way in which the individual believes the world values him or her.
    C. sense of worth the individual has about himself.
    D. feelings about society's perspective.

11. Regarding the ability of homosexuals to forge a group identity, the passage strongly implies that:

    A. this was only possible because of diminished societal stigmatization.
    B. this was a unique phenomenon in a global sense.
    C. prior to this, it was rare for a homosexual to "come out."
    D. the self-esteem of individual homosexuals might have been stronger.

TEST 8

GO ON TO THE NEXT PAGE.

Passage III (Questions 12–17)

In their recruiting, cults use surprisingly scientific principles of manipulation (also known, more euphemistically, as "persuasion"). These techniques are amusingly similar to those employed by Madison Avenue, only adapted to less acceptable purposes. First, cultists will canvass their existing membership to obtain a "prospects list" of members' friends and acquaintances, since people are always more receptive to requests from "friends and family." Still, cults face the challenge of transforming a socially derided institution into something that the target can rationalize as legitimate.

Psychological studies show that the best way to encourage a person to do the socially unacceptable (or to conquer an abnormal phobia) is to show many others doing the same. This works especially well if those others are either like them or like what the target believes himself to be. For this reason, having a celebrity member is priceless, since most people have no trouble picturing themselves as rich, famous, attractive, and adulated. Failing that, the cult can attempt the classic "man-on-the-street" testimonial, recruiting the target via an ordinary person who appears so similar to the target that he can picture himself in the same position. Additionally, cults may portray themselves as a spin-off of a more legitimate religion, since joining a cult is considered ridiculous, while joining a "religion" is seen as acceptable, even laudable.

The cult recruiter will often do the target a small favor, like giving his target a free copy of the *Bhagavad Gita* or a flower. The Hare Krishna cult is known for this seemingly innocent gesture, but it is not mere generosity. The psychological phenomenon of "reciprocity" encourages people to return favors reflexively, even if they do not like the person who originally did them the favor. The recruiter's strategy, of course, is to do a small favor, but ask a much larger one in return. Usually, the favor involves coming to view the cult's headquarters, for further indoctrination.

At the headquarters, control over the visitor is intensified. Cult compounds are invariably located in isolated people-free areas, where only the faithful are admitted. Thus, inside the headquarters, the cultists become the only role models to follow; within that context, their behavior becomes the "norm," lending it an air of legitimacy. The headquarters itself has an extremely pleasant facade, conditioning the target to associate the cult with pleasant things. Everyone in view is blissfully happy and will tell the visitor how the cult leader changed their lives. Seeing so many people obeying the cult leader, the target is acclimatized to view life in the compound as the norm, especially if the cultists are similar to the target in age and background.

Later, after being "primed" with members' positive descriptions and testimonials, the target will get to meet the cult's leader. The leader will assume a grand title of authority, usually as a prophet purporting to speak with the voice of God. Great effort will be made to display how the cultists obey the leader absolutely, in the same manner that televangelists "salt" their audience with paid applauders, vocal supporters, faked testimonials, and actors casting off their crutches.

Finally, after one or several visits, the target is ready for the "pitch." He is asked to join the cult. Often, he must make a massive sacrifice to do so, burning all his bridges to the outside world, renouncing his job and family, donating all his possessions, etc. This not only removes him from the steadying influence of outsiders, but ensures his commitment. If the recruit has to suffer, sacrifice all, and burn his bridges to join, he will be more loyal. After all, how could he admit afterwards, to himself or to others, that he did it all for nothing? It is this realization that explains why cultists remain with apocalyptic cults even after their "doomsday" has come and gone without incident.

12. Which of the following statements is the most reasonable conclusion that can be drawn from the author's description of why cults might value celebrity members?

A. Most people have an unrealistic image of themselves.

B. Celebrities would be difficult to recruit into a cult.

C. Celebrities are no more difficult than anyone else to recruit into a cult.

D. An ordinary person would be the best 'bait' for a celebrity.

GO ON TO THE NEXT PAGE.

4|6

13. Evidence shows that in the heat of battle, a soldier is much less hesitant to kill in order to defend himself than a civilian alone in an urban environment. This fact tends to support the hypothesis concerning "socially unacceptable" behavior (lines 12–26) because:

A. the civilian, in this instance, is not affected by 'reciprocity.'
B. the civilian does not have the soldier's background and training.
C. the soldier is surrounded by killing and is seeing many others doing the same as he is.
D. the soldier has been trained to consider this behavior acceptable.

14. According to the author, what motivates a member of a cult to remain loyal even "after their 'doomsday' has come and gone without incident" (lines 69–70)?

A. strong beliefs
B. shame
C. generosity
D. stubbornness

15. Implicit in the passage is the assumption that:

A. the cult cannot survive without the outside world.
B. cults should be made illegal.
C. peer groups are tremendously influential.
D. after her first visit to the cult compound, the target is inevitably going to become a member.

16. According to information in the passage, the best way to overcome a fear of heights would be to:

A. take a friend and stand on the edge of a tall cliff.
B. gradually stand on higher and higher platforms or places.
C. parachute out of a plane with a friend.
D. go to a drop zone and watch as many people as possible skydiving.

17. In describing the first meeting with the cult leader, the author writes, "Great effort will be made to display how the cultists obey the leader absolutely, in the same manner that televangelists 'salt' their audience with paid applauders, vocal supporters, faked testimonials, and actors casting off their crutches" (lines 54–58). In the context of the passage, this most reasonably implies that:

A. some of the cultists are not genuine in their support for their leader.
B. televangelists are just like cult leaders.
C. belief is critical to the success of the cult.
D. the "pepper" is composed of all new recruits.

TEST 8

GO ON TO THE NEXT PAGE.

Passage IV (Questions 18–23)

Many barbers and hairstylists consider their profession an art form. They are wrong. Styling is in fact a science, which can achieve its consistent results only by applying certain fixed principles. The function of styling is to create
5 an optical illusion that makes the client's features appear to conform to current standards of beauty, or to certain positively perceived images. Hairstyles that follow these scientific principles will be successful; that is, they will improve the client's appearance. Those that go against these
10 principles, or are executed without regard for them, can never do so.

The most important function of hairstyling is to make the facial proportions appear to conform to classical standards of beauty. While the issue of what constitutes facial beauty
15 is much debated and still unresolved, most psychometric research suggests it depends largely on the proportions of the facial features in relation to each other, rather than the exceptional beauty of each individual feature. Ideally, the "perfect" face should be roughly oval shaped (though, for
20 men, it may be somewhat squarer-jawed). Within the face itself, each of the three vertical thirds, hairline-to-eyebrow, eyebrow-to-nasal tip, and nose-to-chin, should ideally be of equal length. Optimally, the two sides of the face should also be reasonably symmetrical.

25 Hair, by virtue of "framing" the face, has the ability to create an optical illusion; when the hairstyle assumes a certain shape, the face itself is seen as having a shape more nearly similar to the hairstyle's. Thus, for example, a square, flat-topped haircut makes the entire face appear squarer,
30 including both the forehead and the jaw line. If we take as the ideal the oval shape, most hairstyles should make the face seem nearer to ovoid. Thus, round faces are enhanced by the flat top style. Oblong faces, those that are longer and thinner, can be "widened" by leaving the hair longer on
35 the sides and by leaving some hair visible behind the ears. Overly square faces can be "rounded" by round-topped cuts. As for the vertical proportion, the most easily altered proportion is the top third of the face. It may be reduced by wearing the hair hanging down over the face, or lengthened
40 by combing it straight back, creating the appearance of a more continuous surface, and thus a longer one.

Aside from the basic shape, the hair's length adds another dimension. Short hair, whose length is two inches or less, tends to emphasize the facial bone structure by reducing
45 the "frame" visible around it. Purely aesthetic considerations aside, fairly short hair is the socially accepted norm for men and is associated with masculinity and athleticism. Longer hair, measuring four inches or longer, deemphasizes the face. While it is often the better choice for those with
50 unattractive facial features, stylists should be aware that it is often considered foppish or self-indulgent when worn by men and is not judged acceptable in some occupations.

Of course, the possibilities of a hairstyle are limited by the client's hair thickness, texture, and waviness. Still,
55 there are advanced techniques that can appear to alter these aspects. For example, "diffusing" hair, cutting the ends at an angle so that each hair stands up and supports the surrounding hairs, can add volume to flat, limp hair. Volume can be decreased by "thinning," or removing every other
60 hair, to remove bulk without changing the hairstyle's basic shape.

The fact that hairstyling is governed by such scientific principles does not detract from the importance of stylists' skill at haircutting; a well-conceived style can still be ruined
65 by clumsy execution. But knowing such principles gives every stylist the potential to recognize the best possible haircut, and produce a finished product equal to that of overpriced "top" designers who claim to possess a sort of gift or unique talent, when in fact it is a science that can be
70 learned by all.

18. Which of the following opinions would the author be most likely to endorse?

A. A person without hair could never achieve the facial beauty of one with hair.

B. A person without hair might be more facially beautiful than a person with hair who had a 'perfect' haircut.

C. A 'perfect' haircut can render anyone facially 'beautiful.'

D. All hairstylists use scientific principles, whether they realize it or not.

TEST 8

19. With which of the following opinions would the author be most likely to *disagree*?

   A. A hairstyle rendered without regard for the scientific principles, can never improve the client's appearance.
   B. Without applying certain fixed principles, consistent results in hair styling cannot be achieved.
   C. Scientific styling principles are more important than execution by the stylist.
   D. Classical standards of beauty vary over time and from place to place.

20. Assume that recently obtained lesson plans from an ancient art school in Venice indicate that students were taught classical facial proportions in order to more beautifully recreate the subjects of their portraiture. This finding:

   A. increases the probability that artists do not require scientific principles.
   B. increases the probability that beauty depends on the proportionality of the features.
   C. decreases the probability that hairstyles can alter our perceptions of beauty.
   D. reveals nothing about beauty and proportionality.

21. An unstated assumption in the author's discussion of hairstyling is that:

   A. people generally get their hair styled in order to become more attractive.
   B. a person without hair could enhance his appearance with this information also.
   C. overpriced designers need to learn scientific principles.
   D. anyone who learns hairstyling's scientific principles can give a good haircut.

22. In the passage, when the hairstyle assumes a "certain shape," it is described as creating an "optical illusion" (lines 26–27). What is the most likely reason for the choice of this phrase?

   A. A false impression can be created that the actual hairstyle has changed.
   B. The face can be changed to a shape more nearly similar to the hairstyle's.
   C. The eye cannot quickly grasp the true nature of the changes.
   D. The hairstyle can create the impression that the actual shape of the face has changed.

23. According to the passage, if a client has a roughly ovoid face with generally unattractive facial features, the hair stylist should:

   A. leave the client's hair longer.
   B. provide a flat-top style.
   C. advise the client to let the hair hang down over the face.
   D. frame the face by leaving the hair longer on the sides.

TEST 8

GO ON TO THE NEXT PAGE.

Passage V (Questions 24–28)

Under the Clinton administration in 1994, the "Risk Rule," designed to exempt women from especially dangerous missions within the United States military, was retracted. "Direct ground combat," from which women remained
5 excluded, was restricted to mean, "being exposed to hostile fire and to a high probability of direct physical contact" with hostile forces and to being situated "well forward on the battlefield." As a direct result of this, over 90 percent of military occupational career fields became open to women.
10 Nevertheless, for good reason, women are still excluded from several tier-one career fields within each branch of the United States military.

Currently, there are no women in the Rangers, Special Forces, or Delta Force, or any flying Army Special Operations
15 helicopters. According to one Army source, though women are allowed to fly and have flown in combat as helicopter pilots, they are nonetheless excluded in the aforementioned instance because the Special Operations helicopter pilot jobs necessitate close coordination with ground troops and
20 have a high risk of the possibility of hand-to-hand combat.

Regardless of whether or not women can handle the mental stresses of combat, many studies have shown that, physically, women are unable to stand shoulder to shoulder with men. A British army study's findings concluded that
25 women should continue to be prevented from occupying front-line combat positions. Among the findings was that women were not as strong as men in combat-related tasks. For instance, 70% of women were not able to carry 90 pounds of artillery shells over a fixed distance as compared with
30 20% of men. And 48% of women failed a 12-mile rucksack march carrying 60 pounds of equipment as compared to only 17% of the men. Finally, a later study found that under combat conditions, while under fire, women were unable to "dig in" to hard ground. The U.S. Army also
35 performed strength-test studies on women and found that, not surprisingly, women were simply not as strong as men. These lesser physical abilities argue strongly that women, in general, would not be able to adequately support their male comrades in combat, or perhaps, even adequately support
40 themselves.

To say that these physical differences could be ignored or that they would not affect a unit's training and fighting regimen and capabilities is to ignore example after example to the contrary. The *Washington Times* reported in August
45 of 2001 that the U.S. Southern Command had canceled a mandatory weekly training run after a female officer complained that the run was "demeaning" because slower runners like her were being ridiculed. Several months later, the runs had not been reinstated, with the Southern Command
50 responding to inquiries by saying that the "matter was still under investigation." These types of stories and reports are not 'politically correct.' This means that the seriousness and

frequency of these problems are being underreported, not the opposite.

55 Beyond the ramifications of a lesser physical ability, studies of mixed-gender armed forces units have shown that training and performance are diminished. There are lower physical standards for everyone throughout the selection and training of these units based upon the fact that women
60 are members of the unit. However, there are the additional negative repercussions of decreased discipline, cohesion, and morale within these mixed-gender units. The reasons for this are not completely understood but may have to do with the manner in which men and women relate to one another
65 when faced with sharing hard physical tasks. Finally, the example during Desert Storm of the USS Acadia may be a forewarning. The Acadia was widely dubbed "The Love Boat" because over 36% of the women on board became pregnant and were thus nondeployable.

70 In combat, there is no equal opportunity. Women will not be given due consideration and equal opportunity to survive or to help their fellow soldiers to survive.

24. Which of the following assertions is the most effective argument *against* the author's supposition that "In combat, there is no equal opportunity" (line 70):

A. Men who were less physically fit were more likely to be killed during sustained ground combat.
B. Female soldiers are not as strong as male soldiers are.
C. Women fighting in the Battle of Stalingrad were frequently better able to survive and help their comrades survive than their male counterparts.
D. Men are smarter than women are.

GO ON TO THE NEXT PAGE.

5/5

25. Suppose it could be established that Civil War diaries and memoirs indicated that women disguised as men and fighting alongside them were rarely discovered to be females. Which of the following hypotheses is most compatible with passage information?

A. In combat, strong men tend to help their weaker comrades without question.

B. The Civil War offered more "equal opportunity".

C. Women in the Civil War were weaker than women today.

D. It is the women's perceptions of men in combat that leads to problems.

26. If the author of the passage admired the exploits and life-saving actions of the Revolutionary War battlefield nurse, Betsy Ross, this admiration would be most *discrepant* with the passage assertion that:

A. while under fire, women were unable to "dig in" to hard ground.

B. these types of stories are not politically correct.

C. physical differences can be ignored.

D. in combat, there is no equal opportunity.

27. What is the intended relevance of the comment, "These types of stories and reports are not 'politically correct'" (lines 51–52), to the rest of the passage?

A. To explain that the stories and reports are not accurate

B. To indicate that the occurrences are more prevalent than they appear

C. To show that women are as strong as men

D. To provide a feminist viewpoint

28. Because of a shortage of people, the Israeli Defense Force (IDF) has traditionally relied upon women to fill the ranks of its armed forces. The argument presented on the cost of placing women with previously all-male units suggests that this policy most probably:

A. increased physical standards.

B. decreased morale throughout the IDF.

C. decreased morale in IDF mixed-gender units.

D. increased combat effectiveness.

TEST 8

GO ON TO THE NEXT PAGE.

Passage VI (Questions 29–33)

While Western readers are used to reading Homer's *Odyssey* as an epic tale of the Trojan War hero Odysseus's homecoming, it also provides a survey of the hospitality accorded to strangers by different peoples of the Hellenic
5 world, as the oft-detoured Odysseus seeks shelter at various points on his voyage home. It is clear that the ancient Greeks took the ceremony of hospitality very seriously. In Greek mythology/religion, to harm a guest after offering him hospitality under your roof was considered a mortal sin
10 punishable by Zeus, the ruler of the gods.

Social and religious customs often have their basis in worldly necessity. For example, incest likely became taboo because inbreeding was known to result in birth defects. Similarly, Hebrews and Muslims may have
15 been instructed by their clerics to avoid pork because the cooking methods used in the Middle East were inadequate to prevent trichinosis from undercooked meat. The Greeks' strong emphasis on hospitality may have had its basis in geography; the Hellenes and their neighbors were seafarers,
20 but with their small-capacity longships and primitive food-preservation techniques, they were dependent on frequent stops in various city-states to rest and replenish supplies.

As the *Odyssey* reveals, the Greeks of Homer's time considered the treatment a host accorded his visitors to
25 be a crucial indication of his character. The perversion of hospitality, or the welcome feast, is a recurring theme in Greek myth, and those who violate their guests at the dinner table earn the hatred of men and the damnation of the gods. For example, King Tantalus was damned for serving
30 the gods a dish of food made from his own son, and King Aigisthos was reviled in the *Iliad* for murdering the hero Agamemnon over dinner.

In the Hellenic legendary world, a sea-roving traveler could expect to encounter a wide range of "hospitality,"
35 ranging from the embarrassingly generous to the horrific. As a rule, the respect accorded to a stranger is based on his fame. If he himself is an unknown, then his welcome depends on his father's renown. Thus, the renowned Odysseus's young son Telemachus finds his first visit to the courts of foreign
40 kings very warm, owing to his father's fame.

While the Achaean veterans of the Trojan War show all due courtesy to a hero's son, it is the Phaiakians who humble all others in hospitality, promising Odysseus safe passage, sacrifices, and a princess bride, before learning that
45 he is the enemy of their patron god, Poseidon. If anything, the Phaiakians are seen as *too* hospitable, for in appeasing Zeus (patron of suppliants) they incur the wrath of their own patron god.

But the Greeks had no requirement that hosts entertain
50 an uninvited guest. Consider the hospitality of the Cyclops, Polyphemos. Fearing the justice of neither man nor god, he laughs outright at Odysseus's very expectation of hospitality upon entering his cave and devours his "guests" rather than feed them. Similarly, it seems the gods of Greece had no
55 quarrel with the irate host who resorted to any means to rid himself of unwelcome guests, as shown by the lack of divine retribution for Odysseus's wholesale slaughter of the suitors who had encamped at his wife's household in his absence and helped themselves to his hospitality.

29. According to the passage, which of the following is most likely to be true about the relationship between the person providing the hospitality and the person enjoying the hospitality?

A. Though uninvited, the child of a famous person would be generously welcomed by a good host.
B. If respectful, a host of good character could count on many visits by people of fame.
C. A host of good character would generously welcome the child of a famous person.
D. Less respect would be accorded a famous person who was invited by a host.

GO ON TO THE NEXT PAGE.

30. Some of the first outsiders to make contact with scattered tribes of Arctic Eskimos brought home stories of frequent instances in which they were encouraged to have sexual intercourse with the women in the tribe. Given the information in the passage, this 'hospitality' was probably due to:

A. a strong sense of welcome and nothing more.

B. the Eskimos requiring compensation for the services of their women.

C. Eskimo religious customs, which prohibited being inhospitable.

D. a perceived necessity by the Eskimos, perhaps to enlarge their genetic pool, that had become a social custom.

31. The contention that "[s]ocial and religious customs often have their basis in worldly necessity" (lines 11–12), can most justifiably be interpreted as support for which of the following ideas?

A. Certain religious customs and restrictions, such as not eating meat on Fridays, were handed down through apostolic tradition.

B. Out of the need to determine that another person was not armed arose the custom of shaking hands upon first meeting.

C. Customary observances, such as stores being closed on Sundays, can be traced back to historical religious requirements.

D. Carrying a young bride 'over the threshold' had its basis in the belief that this would ensure a long and happy marriage.

32. Evidence shows that during the early days of expansion westward from the Mississippi River, the small isolated groups of settlers tended to be initially cautious of strangers but were extremely welcoming and generous to the travelers arriving by stagecoach. This fact tends to support the hypothesis concerning the wide range of Greek 'hospitality' because:

A. the settlers had often learned that uninvited strangers meant trouble, and this attitude carried over to the stage travelers who were actually like the Greeks' 'uninvited' guests.

B. the stage travelers had learned that, though uninvited, they could rest and replenish their supplies, since they and the settlers needed one another.

C. the settlers were not obligated to trust and welcome the stage travelers since they were uninvited guests.

D. though the stage travelers were not invited guests, they, like the Hellenic travelers, were frequent and regular visitors upon whom the settlers were dependent for news, if nothing else.

33. On the basis of the passage, it is reasonable to conclude that:

A. Zeus was the patron of supplicants, and his patron god was Poseidon.

B. Poseidon was the patron god of supplicants and the ruler of the gods.

C. Poseidon was the ruler of the gods, and Zeus was the patron of supplicants.

D. Zeus was the patron of supplicants and the ruler of the gods.

TEST 8

Passage VII (Questions 34–40)

"an average man of middle class origins and normal middle class upbringing, a man without identifiable criminal tendencies."
—Von Lang & Sibyll, *Eichmann Interrogated*

5   Dr. Stanley Milgram's classic experiment on obedience began with a seemingly innocent ad in a local paper soliciting volunteers to participate in a psychology experiment at Yale University in exchange for a small payment. There in the psychology department's waiting room they met their co-
10 participant, who was sercretly, in fact, Milgram's confederate. The impostor "volunteer" struck up a conversation with the other participants, portraying himself as a likeable and mild-mannered man, and casually let them know he had a weak heart. Soon after, Dr. Milgram entered, introducing himself
15 as the experimenter and describing the experiment. As the doctor explained, the project was meant to measure people's tolerance for electrical shock. In an adjoining one subject would be strapped to a machine room that could deliver jolts of electricity of increasing voltage. Once the subject was
20 strapped in, he could not free himself without help. The other volunteer would remain in the control room with Milgram to operate the control panel under Milgram's direction. Thus, volunteers could not see the subject in the next room but could still hear him through the closed door. Using a
25 prearranged method, the confederate was "randomly" selected as the subject to receive the shock, administered by the volunteer. Then, Milgram led the confederate next door and pretended to strap him into the apparatus. Milgram returned to the control room, and instructed the volunteer
30 to begin delivering shocks, at small but increasing doses. As the "shocks" got stronger, the actor would make noises from the next room, showing increasing pain. Periodically, Milgram called out to him, asking if he was all right and could continue. At first, he agreed, but grew increasingly
35 reluctant. Later, when he complained of increasing pain and heart trouble and asked to stop, Milgram instructed the volunteer to continue increasing the voltage.

      Contrary to all predictions, an amazing 63% of volunteers were willing to administer a shock of 450 volts
40 to a person who had stopped responding to questions and was likely unconscious. Most volunteers showed signs of extreme tension—sweating, trembling, stuttering, and hysterical laughing that were occasionally so strong that Milgram had to stop the scenario—yet 26 of the 40 subjects
45 nevertheless completed the experiment.

      If asked beforehand, those 26 would doubtless have asserted that neither they nor most anyone else would submit to an immoral authority, yet the fact remains that they did. When interviewed after the experiment, none could
50 articulate a logical reason for why they obeyed. There just seemed to be reason to obey the experimenter; there was no chance of punishment for refusing, no chance of demotion,

as Eichmann faced. The experimenter, who posed as a Yale professor, may have had some authority by virtue of
55 his position, but it did not extend over people unaffiliated with Yale. The most he could have done was to deny the subjects their small, promised travel stipend, though he had assured them that they would receive it whether or not they completed the experiment. At no time did the experimenter
60 make specific threats; he only said, "You have no choice. You must continue."

      Why do we obey? Milgram theorizes that a hierarchy of obedience became necessary for human survival, so it became socially conditioned. As people obeyed their
65 superiors, they were often rewarded by a promotion to a higher stage, thus reinforcing the hierarchy for themselves and those who witnessed their rise. There is the implication that we tend to generalize the obedience we must give to the powers that be, either by seeing someone with no real
70 authority as having connections with something higher that we are bound to respect, or by allowing someone in a position of authority to exceed his jurisdiction.

34. Evidence shows that juries tend to assume that a clergyman who is giving testimony in a court of law is telling the truth, unless proven otherwise. This fact tends to support the hypothesis concerning authority because:

A. the clergy are perceived as having connections with a higher authority.

B. the clergy can generally authorize people to do certain things.

C. a clergyman would not have sanctioned Milgram's experiments.

D. a clergyman would not make specific threats but only say, "You have no choice. You must continue."

GO ON TO THE NEXT PAGE.

35. It is currently possible to more accurately evaluate a person's perceptions of who is in authority by standardized psychological testing. Such information would be relevant to Milgram's theory presented in the passage because it would:

   A. show that the results of Milgram's experiment were accurate.
   B. indicate whether the participants might have merely enjoyed inflicting pain.
   C. prove that the participants truly believed that Milgram was in charge.
   D. prove that Milgram's experiment was flawed.

36. According to the passage information, what would have happened if the participant administering the shocks had refused to continue the experiment?

   A. Nothing. However, he or she would have been denied the travel stipend.
   B. He would have been unstrapped from the apparatus.
   C. He would certainly have lost his Yale affiliation.
   D. There were no specific threats made.

37. Which of the following scientific advances would most seriously *challenge* the hypothesis involving Milgram's experiments and authority?

   A. Association of obedience with perceived authority
   B. Proof of the predictions made prior to the experiment taking place
   C. Further correlation of the necessity of obedience for human survival
   D. Confirmation of the extreme tension shown by the participants

38. If the hypothesis of the passage is correct, one should find that if a policeman ordered several bystanders to restrain someone while the policeman "beat information out of him," that:

   A. it is unlikely that the bystanders could be enlisted to help the policeman.
   B. it is likely that the bystanders might cooperate by doing so.
   C. a small majority of the bystanders might come to the aid of the person being restrained.
   D. a majority of the bystanders might not stand by and do nothing.

39. Which of the following suppositions is most clearly believed by the author?

   A. The experiment was meant to measure people's tolerance for electric shock.
   B. Identifiable criminal tendencies are not an indication of future problems.
   C. To follow instructions that will result in hurting another is immoral.
   D. Most people will obediently submit to rightful authority.

40. The quotation by Von Lang & Sibyll refers to the notorious Nazi Adolf Eichmann, who was responsible for ordering the deaths of millions of Jews. According to the passage, the behavior of the soldiers who followed Eichmann's orders could be described as:

   A. quite normal.
   B. criminal.
   C. aberrant.
   D. socially conditioned.

STOP. IF YOU FINISH BEFORE TIME IS CALLED, CHECK YOUR WORK. YOU MAY GO BACK TO ANY QUESTION IN THIS TEST.

TEST 8

STOP.

TEST 8

Verbal Reasoning Test 9
Time: 60 Minutes
Questions 1–40

VERBAL REASONING

DIRECTIONS: There are seven passages in this Verbal Reasoning test. Each passage is followed by several questions. After reading a passage, select the one best answer to each question. If you are not certain of an answer, eliminate the alternatives that you know to be incorrect and then select an answer from the remaining alternatives. Indicate your selection by blackening the corresponding oval on your answer document.

Passage I (Questions 1–6)

Effective speed-readers must do two things. First, before reading, they must plan which sections to focus on and which to skim. Then, they should practice learning efficient eye movements.

5   Before reading, readers should ask themselves *why* they are reading—i.e., what information they need to extract. If they need information from only one section of a text, they should focus on that section only and ignore irrelevant parts. Before reading, they should consider their
10 existing knowledge of the topic, to ascertain what gaps exist. If they are entirely unfamiliar with the topic, they may wish to get an encyclopedic overview to determine how the current reading's topic fits into the overall subject.

To maximize recall, readers should structure their
15 reading time into sessions of roughly 30 minutes. This avoids the boredom and distraction of exceeding the normal attention span, which averages only 20–30 minutes. Further, since the psychological phenomenon of the "primacy" and "recency" effects dictate that students tend to remember
20 the beginnings and endings of passages much better than the material in between, breaking reading into many small blocks ensures more of the memorable beginnings and endings.

While reading, readers should concentrate the bulk
25 of their time on those sections most likely to contain valuable information. Usually, this means concentrating on understanding the main point/plot while skimming over details. Sometimes, it may require picking out a certain useful detail and ignoring the others. To that end, readers
30 should focus on any summaries within the text or conclusory paragraphs, which usually restate the main points in the fewest words. Failing that, readers should focus on each chapter's introduction and each paragraph's opening and concluding sentences, since these often summarize what will
35 be stated, or has been stated, in the rest of the paragraph.

The more commonly known aspect of speed-reading is eye control. The main impediments to efficient reading are fixating on one word at a time and momentarily 'back-skipping' to previously read sections before returning
40 to the current position. The eye is designed to focus only when fixated, and so cannot read while moving. Thus, too-swift scanning will prevent readers from seeing the words, much less understanding them. Yet making each fixation takes time, so that fixations that occur too frequently are
45 counterproductive. This dilemma can be overcome by making fewer fixations, but also by expanding the peripheral vision to take in larger blocks of text during each fixation. Experienced speed-readers will "sweep" half the page's horizontal length, and several lines, at any time. This is
50 best done by reading down the line's center and scanning each line in a z-shaped pattern, fixating on only two points per line. The larger problem is back-skipping to already-read sections, which is an obvious distraction and waste of time but is very common. Practice, possibly with a pointer,
55 should overcome this counterproductive habit. Another common habit is reading aloud, or subvocalizing. While this carryover from elementary school reading practice had its place in teaching pronunciation, continuing this habit slows reading, since an adult should be able to read faster than he
60 can speak.

After reading, readers should test the effectiveness of their efforts by attempting to recall the major points, or plot, of the passage that they have read. This serves a dual purpose, telling readers whether their reading was too fast to
65 understand and letting them consider whether their original purposes or questions have been satisfied.

GO ON TO THE NEXT PAGE.

1. Which of the following sections of a text would be the most effective areas upon which to focus in order to glean the most useful details, according to passage indications?

   A. conclusory paragraphs or within the text summaries
   B. a chapter's introduction or conclusory paragraphs
   C. a paragraph's opening or concluding sentences
   D. in-text summaries or a paragraph's opening

2. Some timed verbal reasoning tests, such as the MCAT, require the test-taker to be prepared to answer questions that may be drawn from any area of the text or passage. An appropriate clarification of the passage would be the stipulation that the author's argument applies only to:

   A. tests other than the verbal section of the MCAT.
   B. back-skipping when not taking a timed verbal test.
   C. skimming when the reader already knows what information he requires from the text.
   D. concentrating on those sections most likely to contain valuable information.

3. For which of the following conclusions does the passage offer the most support?

   A. Subvocalization is an important skill for reading comprehension.
   B. Readers must skim over details that are not important.
   C. Readers should practice learning efficient eye movements.
   D. Readers should test the effectiveness of their efforts.

4. According to the passage, the effectiveness of a course in speed reading could be determined by first having the reader speed-read a passage and then measuring:

   A. the reader's attention span.
   B. the ability to recall the plot.
   C. the ability to recall each paragraph's opening and concluding sentences.
   D. the reader's ability to concentrate.

5. In the context of the passage, the word *primacy* (line 19) means:

   A. the first or start.
   B. the most important.
   C. apelike.
   D. the main.

6. According to the passage, a very common problem is:

   A. eye control.
   B. structuring time poorly.
   C. inability to recall major points.
   D. back-skipping.

GO ON TO THE NEXT PAGE.

Passage II (Questions 7–12)

Efforts to legalize physician-assisted suicide and euthanasia, wherein the physician actively involves himself in the death of the patient, are laden with misconceptions and poorly understood. Misleading images of those who
5 might wish for assisted euthanasia abound among those who can scarcely relate or understand.

These efforts at legalization are not a recent phenomenon born of medical advances that keep us alive longer than we wish, as one would be led to believe.
10 Society has grappled with these issues since rudimentary medicine first began. Proponents of assisted suicide argue that continuing medical advances now allow people to live far beyond the point at which they would have naturally passed away. Consequently, the medical community should
15 be involved with when they should be allowed to die, when they should be helped to die. However, this ignores efforts going back to the ancient Hippocratic oath, which enjoins physicians to "neither give a deadly drug to anybody if asked for it, nor make a suggestion to this effect." This oath
20 was a direct response to physicians of the day purposely giving mortal doses of medicines for what they knew to be rather minor ailments.

People who are healthy have a strong tendency to extrapolate understanding from the suffering of others
25 in ways that those who are in fact suffering would not allow. For instance, many of us look at a crippled, blind, or otherwise handicapped person and say that we would rather be dead than in that position; would they? One of the most misleading images is that of the lucid, communicative
30 patient lying in intensive care, wracked with pain, being kept alive against his will by the use of respirators, dialysis machines, artificial nutrition, or other medical means. The patient who is being kept alive artificially has always had the legal option of refusing life-support technology. They do
35 not need physician-assisted suicide or euthanasia. Moreover, the image is also inaccurate because of the perceived association between pain and the wish to die. Empirical studies of physician-assisted suicide and euthanasia in the Netherlands (where the practices have long been accepted),
40 the United States, and elsewhere indicate that pain plays a minor role in motivating requests for the procedures. No study has ever shown that pain plays a major role in motivating patient requests for physician-assisted suicide or euthanasia.

45 It is, in fact, not physical pain, but depression and emotional pain that lead patients to consider suicide. A study of Washington State physicians found that the leading factors driving requests for assisted suicide were fear of a loss of control or of dignity, of being a burden, and of being
50 dependent. Among New York HIV-infected patients, the leading factors were depression, hopelessness, and having few—and poor-quality—social supports. This seems then to

be a societal problem requiring more supportive institutions and mental health care. But this is, of course, a labor- and
55 money-intensive proposition.

Finally, could we one day find ourselves in a situation in which euthanasia is no longer voluntary but the rule? Would you be required to die though you cried out to live? We are already struggling with national health care issues
60 revolving around how much can be spent, and on whom, to keep them alive. Given these pressures, it is not unreasonable to assume that at some point you would have no choice but to die and have your organs harvested for the good of all. You would first see this applied to those who were least able to
65 provide consent or express their opinions and those without advocacy: the unconscious, the demented, the mentally ill, the homeless, and children. They already have little voice in this world and rely upon a healthy society to care for them, whether they ask for it or not.

TEST 9

7. The passage states that the Hippocratic oath "was a direct response to physicians of the day purposely giving mortal doses of medicines for rather minor ailments" (lines 20–22). According to the author, this ancient form of euthanizing would probably have resulted from:

A. ever increasing health care costs.
B. empathy for the person suffering.
C. poor understanding of the ailment.
D. a desire to rid society of the aged.

GO ON TO THE NEXT PAGE.

8. Based upon information in the passage, which of the following statements would NOT be an argument given by *proponents* of assisted suicide?

    A. Those fearing a lack of social supports and suffering extreme emotional pain should be allowed to die if they wish.
    B. Medical advances now allow people to live far beyond the point at which they would have naturally passed away.
    C. Often, people are kept alive artificially against their will.
    D. Extreme physical pain can commonly lead someone to consider suicide.

9. According to the author, a healthy person's perceptions regarding what the suffering are feeling is:

    A. based upon a variety of factors.
    B. a valid component of the assisted-suicide debate.
    C. what may determine our fate.
    D. how children and the elderly really feel.

10. Which of the following is most clearly believed by the author?

    A. A human can never live too long.
    B. Suicide is wrong.
    C. Those who wish to die can be helped through means other than assisted suicide.
    D. Healthy adults are sound advocates for all of society.

11. The passage provides that the wish to die is "a societal problem requiring more supportive institutions and mental health care" (lines 55–57). The reason given is that:

    A. there are poor quality "social supports" for depressed HIV-infected patients in New York.
    B. the requests for assisted suicide were driven by a fear of a loss of control or of dignity.
    C. at some point you would have no choice but to die and have your organs harvested for the good of all.
    D. in the long run this would cost society less money.

12. The author probably mentions having "your organs harvested for the good of all" (lines 66–67) in order:

    A. to illustrate that society could make good use of your body after you have died.
    B. to support his argument that the debate surrounding assisted suicide is an old one.
    C. to offer an alternative to an otherwise bleak prediction.
    D. to provide an example of mandatory euthanasia.

GO ON TO THE NEXT PAGE.

Passage III (Questions 13–18)

"Copywriting" is the art of writing advertisement text, also known as "ad copy." Its aim, like rhetoric, is not just to inform, but to persuade consumers to buy. Unlike most other writing, its effectiveness is immediately apparent, as
5 evidenced by the sales generated when a new advertisement is run. Thus, copywriters use a markedly different writing style than that used by academics; it is a style that subordinates technical perfection to psychological impact.

The copywriter's first task is to get the readers'
10 attention. This must usually be done immediately in the advertisement's headline or caption, since research shows that fully 80% of magazine readers scan only an advertisement's headline, in decideing whether to continue reading, or to skip it. A common, if crude, technique is to get readers'
15 attention immediately through provocative visuals. Often, the images that generate initial attention do so because they exploit instincts, such as sex appeal (e.g., attractive women used to sell cars or beer); maternal instinct (e.g., pictures of babies' faces); or the attraction to "cuteness" (e.g., images
20 of puppies and kittens). However, the problem with such images is that they are unrelated to the product, so while the reader notices them, and may take great interest in them, this interest does not translate into reading the ad, or into sales. The more effective approach is to offer the promise
25 of free and useful information if the reader reads the rest of the advertisement.

The copy's body text must keep the reader's interest. Thus, it must constantly focus on the customer's needs, rather than the copywriter's or that of his client company.
30 All too often, ineffective ads describe the company's history or its current events. However, this is, strictly speaking, of no interest to a reader. What is consistently compelling to the reader is how the company's product can meet his needs and/or wants. One way to relate this is to translate
35 the product's features into tangible benefits. This has two advantages. First, recounting purely technical features will tend to alienate nonspecialists. Second, and more importantly, benefits let the reader understand exactly what the product will do for him, and also let him picture himself
40 enjoying the product. It is perfectly acceptable to note the product's technical features, especially when selling to specialists; however, features are always more effective in generating demand when linked to specific benefits. Thus, for example, an advertisement for a computer may mention
45 that its system speed is 433 megahertz, but it should also explain that this allows it to run certain programs faster than competitors.

If the product is readily available from many sources, the ad should differentiate the client's product from that
50 of competitors. It would be ironic for the ad to succeed in stimulating demand, only to encourage the reader to buy from a competitor. Most products can be differentiated on the basis of features, such as price. However, if the product is a generic commodity, such that the item itself is fairly
55 similar across all sellers, the copywriter must stress another "feature," such as the manufacturer's service, expertise, or warranty.

Next, the ad must establish credibility and prove its case. Naturally, neither the manufacturer nor its copywriter
60 is necessarily objective, so people tend to distrust claims originating from these sources. Much more effective are testimonials from third parties, such as customer testimonials, reviews, and industry awards.

Most books on advertising advise copywriters to end
65 with a "call to action," telling readers what they should do next. Obviously, the ad should tell the reader to buy. But an often overlooked point is that it should also tell the reader to buy *now*. This is critical, because if the customer does not perceive the need as pressing, he is likely not to
70 get around to ordering. Psychological research shows the most effective call to action is the threat of loss—that is, that a desirable product will no longer be available if the customer delays. Thus, wise copywriters usually give some sort of deadline, real or artificial, after which the product
75 will become unavailable, more expensive, or otherwise less desirable.

13. The passage provides examples for the assertion that copywriters often use "provocative visuals" (line 17). Which of the following examples would be commonly considered "provocative?"

 I. images of puppies and kittens
 II. pictures of babies' faces
 III. attractive women used to sell cars or beer

 A. I only
 B. II only
 C. III only
 D. I and II only

TEST 9

14. Which of the following approaches to selling horses would be most likely to be stressed by an advertiser who had an understanding of how best to translate a product's features?

   A. Describe the height of the horse.
   B. Explain the different types of horses that are available.
   C. Emphasize that the reader shoulder 'buy now' or the horse will be sold.
   D. Depict how the entire family will enjoy riding the horse.

15. Which of the following products most clearly exemplifies a "generic commodity" (line 57)?

   A. Dishwashers
   B. Computers
   C. Contact lenses
   D. Running shoes

16. According to the passage, all of the following may be considered product "features" EXCEPT:

   A. free and useful information.
   B. service.
   C. manufacturer's expertise.
   D. warranties.

17. According to the passage, which of the following would be the most effective "call to action" (line 68)?

   A. "Let's leave now."
   B. "If we don't leave now, then I'm not going."
   C. "I want you to leave now."
   D. "If you leave now, then I'll go with you."

18. According to the passage, which of the following would be the most effective in credibly promoting a movie?

   I. Publicized positive audience responses
   II. An Academy Award
   III. Positive interviews with the more famous actors who starred in the movie

   A. I only
   B. II only
   C. I and II only
   D. II and III only

TEST 9

GO ON TO THE NEXT PAGE.

Passage IV (Questions 19–24)

Gays, lesbians, and bisexuals have traditionally been the victims of shame and persecution in our society. Studies report that as many as 66% of Americans have expressed feelings that homosexuality is wrong or sinful. Historians
5 examining the increasing trend of homosexuals as a persecuted and ostracized American minority cite the 1870's to 1930's as the period in American history when there first emerged an actual 'community' of people whom openly recognized erotic interest in members of their own sex.
10 Until that time, although people did engage in homoerotic activity, homosexuality was not considered a sexuality but a deviant and disgusting (sinful or immoral) activity. Society's attitudes towards homosexual practices are evident in the laws condemning these practices, laws which have existed
15 in every American state at one time or another.

In addition to the moral condemnation imposed by religious institutions and punishments imposed by law, homosexuals were also harmed by the fact that the medical profession regarded homosexuality as a disease.
20 Throughout the 1880's and 1890's, doctors engaged in heated debates regarding the "cause" of this "disease." While some argued that homosexuality was an acquired form of insanity that surfaced in weak-willed individuals, others claimed it was a congenital defect that indicated
25 evolutionary degeneracy. Among those who advanced a medical model for the "cause" of homosexuality, most agreed, by the early twentieth century, that it was hereditary in its origin. The "disease" model removed some prejudices attendant to homosexuality, as those who believed in this
30 model concluded that homosexuals should not be punished for their sexual orientation. Still, those who engaged in homosexual practices were viewed as disordered individuals in need of curing.

Sigmund Freud's theory of psychosexual development,
35 promulgated in 1905 as part of Freud's famous essays on sexuality, played a large role in influencing the "disease" model. Freud felt that human beings were born bisexual, with the infant having an inclination toward either sex as a possible love object. Over the course of psychosexual
40 development, the child learns to identify with the same-sex parent. While the precise workings of development are different for boys and girls, heterosexuality was the expected result. That is, attraction only to the opposite sex was what Freud considered a successful resolution to the
45 problems encountered during the course of psychosexuality, problems that he saw as an indication of inhibited psychosexual development. Therefore, while Freud viewed homosexuality as an abnormal outcome, he recognized the capacity of all individuals to wish to partake in homosexual
50 activities at some level or point in their lives. Freud referred to homosexuals as "inverts" who needed further help to resolve their emotional conflicts. Despite Freud's equation of homosexuality with pathological psychosexual

development, his assumption that bisexuality was innate,
55 and his recognition that heterosexuality was "created" during development and could be influenced by external factors, changed the medical view of homosexuality. If the maintenance of a heterosexual identity could be due, in part, to external influences (e.g., familial or societal expectations),
60 then homosexuality or bisexuality could not be viewed as inherently pathological.

Today, a fair number of psychologists maintain that a theory assuming bisexual tendencies is necessary to explain psychosexual development in "normal" individuals.
65 Yet the search for a biological abnormality as the cause of homosexuality, along with the idea that homosexuality should be "cured," persists. In fact, homosexuality was recognized as a disorder by the American Psychological Association as late as 1973.

19. Regarding the increasing persecution of homosexuals (lines 1–15), the passage strongly implies that:

A. persecution increased as society felt that this 'disease' could be passed on to others.
B. homosexuals were increasingly perceived by society as immoral.
C. this might not have occurred without the increasing openness of homosexuals themselves.
D. the sexuality aspect has always been recognized.

GO ON TO THE NEXT PAGE.

20. According to the passage, Freud's theory of psychosexual development most clearly resulted in:

- **A.** only increased persecution of homosexuals.
- **B.** increasing homosexual openness.
- **C.** an impact only on the perceptions of the medical community.
- **D.** diminishing punishment for homosexual behavior.

21. In order to distinguish the nature of who was being persecuted and punished, the author of the passage implies a distinction between:

  I. orientation and activity.
  II. homosexuals and bisexuals.
  III. religious institutions and the law.

- **A.** I only
- **B.** II only
- **C.** III only
- **D.** I and II only

22. The contention that "a fair number of psychologists maintain that a theory assuming bisexual tendencies is necessary to explain psychosexual development in 'normal' individuals" (lines 62–64), can most justifiably be interpreted as support for the idea that:

- **A.** homosexuals are normal individuals.
- **B.** homosexuals are "normal" individuals.
- **C.** homosexuals are abnormal.
- **D.** homosexuality is a disease.

23. Which of the following statements, if true, would most directly *challenge* the principles of Freud?

- **A.** A child is not sexually attracted to the same-sex parent.
- **B.** Homosexuality is not a disease.
- **C.** Bisexuality is a 'normal' phase in development.
- **D.** Homosexuality is probably genetic.

24. Which of the following opinions would the author be most likely to endorse?

- **A.** The medical community has finally accepted homosexuality as normal.
- **B.** The idea that homosexuality is abnormal and can be treated still endures.
- **C.** The American Psychological Association still believes that homosexuality is a disorder.
- **D.** Nowadays, most Americans accept homosexuality.

GO ON TO THE NEXT PAGE.

Passage V (Questions 25–30)

An estimated 22 million Americans are projected to be afflicted with Irritable Bowel Syndrome (IBS), a digestive disorder usually characterized by chronic, alternating bouts of diarrhea and constipation. As the term "syndrome"
5 implies, the condition is diagnosed on the basis of its symptoms, though the exact origin is unclear. Currently, researchers are divided as to possible causes; approximately half believe the condition is caused primarily by stress or a similar psychosomatic factor, while others attribute the
10 ailment to one or more food allergies and/or intolerances. The fact that the condition seems to be, at least to some degree, hereditary vitiates against the theory that it is psychological.

As previously mentioned, the exact cause of IBS is
15 not understood. The difficulty of diagnosing this condition is that the primary symptom—diarrhea—is simultaneously a symptom of a wide variety of digestive disorders, from temporary food poisoning to simple but constant food intolerances, to diverticulosis or blockages in the stomach
20 and intestines. For example, if a congenital defect left the patient's large intestine "smooth"—devoid of the cilia that normally aid nutrient absorption—the symptoms would include chronic to constant diarrhea, though likely not frequent constipation. There is concern that, without a better
25 differentiation of its causes, the diagnosis of IBS may be a convenient catch-all for any unidentified digestive disorder. Some methods have been developed for differentiating possible causes. For example, an elimination diet—in which the patient shifts to eating commonly tolerated foods, then
30 gradually adds new foods to see if any of these additions causes digestive disruptions—is useful to isolate food allergies and intolerances. Similarly, a gradual introduction of lactobacillus acidophilus bacteria into the lower intestine, if effective, will show the cause to have been lactose
35 intolerance. However, the temptation to conveniently label an unknown case as IBS often prevents further investigation, which may reveal a far more serious condition.

Since medical science has not found a single underlying cause, treatment of IBS focuses on treating
40 the individual symptoms separately, through conventional methods. In a 'take two aspirin and call me in the morning' approach, patients are most commonly advised to avoid foods that generally cause intolerance, especially milk and dairy products, fruit sugars, alcohol, caffeine, fat, and
45 gluten. They are urged to drink more water and to gradually increase their intake of dietary fiber. In addition to many other known benefits, interestingly, fiber is known to prevent both diarrhea and constipation. This is because the source of fiber—plant products, with their attendant cellulose—
50 usually contains fiber of both the soluble and insoluble varieties. The former tends to slow movements, while the latter bulks stools, making elimination easier. Constipation may be treated by various stimulant laxatives, such as malt or magnesium citrate. Similarly, simple diarrhea is easily
55 treated by commonly available antispasmodics, such as loperamide and attapuglite. While these over-the-counter laxatives and antispasmodics will effectively cure or prevent the symptoms of IBS temporarily, their addictiveness and increasing side effects do not permit their continuous use.

25. What is the author's response to the passage statement that "approximately half [of the researchers] believe the condition [IBS] is caused primarily by stress or a similar psychosomatic factor" (lines 7–9)?

A. Further research has indicated that this theory is probably correct.

B. The likelihood that this is true renders finding a cure more problematic.

C. The likelihood that this is true renders finding a cure much easier.

D. The likelihood that the condition is inherited shows that this is probably not correct.

GO ON TO THE NEXT PAGE.

26. According to passage information, a person whose large intestine is devoid of cilia would most likely be exhibiting which of the following symptoms?

    I.   probably not constipation, but constant diarrhea
    II. alternating attacks of diarrhea and constipation
    III. primarily constipation with some diarrhea

  A. I only
  B. II only
  C. III only
  D. II and III only

27. If certain patients were to eat large amounts of primarily soluble fiber instead of insoluble varieties of fiber, how would their elimination be affected?

  A. This would prevent both diarrhea and constipation.
  B. They would tend towards being constipated.
  C. They would tend towards having diarrhea.
  D. They would experience alternating bouts of diarrhea and constipation.

28. An unstated implication of diarrhea in the author's discussion of treatments is that:

  A. laxatives may actually be helpful.
  B. it is not easily treated by available medicines.
  C. those who are afflicted may experience spasms.
  D. the medicine is not available over-the-counter.

29. What is the intended relevance of the comment, "In a 'take two aspirin and call me in the morning' approach ..." (lines 41–42), to the rest of the passage?

  A. To explain the prevailing belief that IBS is caused primarily by stress or a similar psychosomatic factor.
  B. To show that to conveniently label an unknown case as IBS often prevents further investigation.
  C. To express the general inadequacy of any treatments of IBS.
  D. To indicate that physicians do not understand the underlying causes of IBS and treat it like a syndrome.

30. The author suggests that the difficulty of using medicines to treat constipation and diarrhea results from the fact that those afflicted:

  A. must get a prescription because the medicines are addictive.
  B. can become addicted to the medicine, though it can be purchased without a prescription.
  C. must get a prescription for the medicine, though there is no danger of addiction.
  D. must decide if the increasing side effects of the medicine are worth the trouble.

TEST 9

GO ON TO THE NEXT PAGE.

Passage VI (Questions 31–35)

Cryptography is the science of encoding communications so that they are understandable only to the intended recipients. Its counterpart is crypto analysis, which involves deciphering another's cryptogram through various
5 analytical means. Cryptography's applications are primarily military; indeed, it was originally developed to transmit tactical instructions to friendly units, without the risk of the message being intercepted and used by the enemy. However, civilians who wish to transmit confidential information—
10 for example, diplomats and businesspersons—also use it. Occasionally, cryptography was even used without any intention of hiding messages; in the days of telegraphs (whose cost was dictated by a message's length), businesspersons routinely transmitted messages through a public system of
15 4-letter codes that represented common words or sentences, purely to save money on transmission.

There are two primary types of cryptograms, or encoded messages. One system for encoding messages is the "code," in which a set of 5,000 to 20,000 preset words,
20 numbers, and/or symbols are assigned a meaning unrelated to their ordinary meaning. For example, the word "glass" or the number "13072" might be preset to refer to "Israel." Codes work only if both the transmitter and receiver know each coded word and its real meaning (the "clear"). For this
25 purpose, both parties must be issued a special "dictionary" that lists all the possible code words and the meaning of each. The code system's advantage over other encryption systems is that it is virtually undecipherable without the dictionary (or a turncoat or prisoner familiar with it). In our example,
30 there is nothing in "glass" or "13072" that would suggest to an interceptor that it refers to "Israel." However, the security of codes comes at a price. A code is inflexible; once the code words are determined and the "dictionary" is written, new words cannot be coded without sending an update to both
35 the sender and receiver. More importantly, every intended user of the code must be given a copy of the dictionary, in either printed or electronic form. The practical difficulty of using codes today is the ease with which a dictionary can be copied, stolen, or bought from an inside source. Still, codes
40 continued to be a popular form of cryptography as late as the 1940s.

The other, better-known type of encoding is the "cipher." In this method, what is transmitted is the message itself, rather than a series of unrelated code words that
45 represent the message. But the message is "scrambled" according to some regular pattern ("key"), which is known to the receiver. The receiver then deciphers (unscrambles) it. There are many patterns of enciphering. One of the simplest, the substitution cipher, has each letter of the alphabet stand
50 for another letter, according to a pattern. For example, the "Caesar cipher," supposedly used by Julius Caesar, was to have each letter in the enciphered text refer to the letter two spaces forward in the alphabet. Thus, in the English version,

"CAESAR" would be encrypted as "AXBPXO." An alternate
55 type of enciphering methodology is the transposition system, whereby the letters are simply rearranged according to a predictable pattern. Ancient Spartans, who invented a primitive enciphering machine, used this type. When a Spartan commander wished to encipher a message, he would
60 wrap a strip of paper, 'candy-cane style,' down the length of a wooden pole called a "scytale." Then, he would write his message down the paper wrapped across the rod. When the paper was unwound, the letters would become disconnected. To decipher the message, a recipient would have to wrap the
65 ribbon around a scytale of similar thickness (and know to do so). The cipher offers the advantage of flexibility; any word can be enciphered, so messages are not limited to preset signals. But, since enciphering must follow some regular, predictable pattern, it can be deciphered by an interceptor
70 who finds the pattern. Before the 1940s, 'cracking' ciphers was achieved by analyzing normal letter frequencies and noting probable letter combinations, often manually. Today, both encryption and decryption are computerized, allowing for stunningly complex keys, but also superhumanly fast
75 analysis.

31. According to one authority on illiteracy and public safety, efforts to render all public transportation signs and directions into more easily understood 'symbols,' rather than written directions and words, must continue. This authority would probably:

   A. agree with the passage suggestion that written communication is sometimes unclear.
   B. agree with the passage suggestion that what is communication for one group is a code to another.
   C. disagree with the passage suggestion that encryption promotes simpler communication.
   D. disagree with the passage suggestion that codes are most often used by the military.

GO ON TO THE NEXT PAGE.

32. According to the passage, the Spartan's "scytale" (lines 58–70) was characteristic of:

   A. the substitution code.
   B. the substitution cipher.
   C. the 'alternate' type of cipher.
   D. the 'alternate' type of the "code".

33. According to the passage, which of the following was a *drawback* to the "code" (line 19)?

   A. Every intended user required a copy of the dictionary.
   B. Without the dictionary, it was virtually indecipherable.
   C. An interceptor who had found the pattern could decipher it.
   D. It was a flexible system.

34. An important comparison is made in the passage between:

   A. computers and "scytales."
   B. cryptograms and substitution ciphers.
   C. businesspersons and the military.
   D. scrambling and encoding.

35. According to the passage, all of the following are true of the cipher EXCEPT:

   A. the scrambled message itself is transmitted instead of code words.
   B. the cipher must follow some regular, predictable pattern.
   C. the system was relatively inflexible.
   D. the "scytale" is an example.

GO ON TO THE NEXT PAGE.

Passage VII (Questions 36–40)

In response to growing levels of violence in the nation's schools, many parents, teachers, and school officials have come to see school uniforms as one positive and creative way to reduce discipline problems and increase school

5 safety. They observed that the adoption of school-uniform policies could promote school safety, improve discipline, and enhance the learning environment. The potential benefits of school uniforms include decreasing violence and theft— even life-threatening situations—among students over

10 designer clothing or expensive sneakers; helping prevent gang members from wearing gang colors and insignia at school; instilling discipline in students; helping parents and students resist peer pressure; helping students concentrate on their school work; and helping school officials recognize

15 intruders who come to the school.

As a result, many local communities are deciding to adopt school-uniform policies as part of an overall program to improve school safety and discipline. California, Florida, Georgia, Indiana, Louisiana, Maryland, New York,

20 Tennessee, Utah, and Virginia have enacted school-uniform regulations. Many large public school systems have schools with either voluntary or mandatory uniform policies, mostly in elementary and middle schools. In addition, many private and parochial schools have required uniforms for a number

25 of years. Still other schools have implemented dress codes to encourage a safe environment by, for example, prohibiting clothes with certain language or gang colors.

The decision to adopt a uniform policy is made by states, local school districts, and schools. However, for uniforms to

30 be a success, as with all other school initiatives, parents must be involved. Parental support of a uniform policy is critical for success. Indeed, the strongest push for school uniforms in recent years has come from parent groups that want better discipline in their children's schools. Parent groups have

35 actively lobbied schools to create uniform policies and have often led school task forces that have drawn up uniform guidelines. Many schools that have successfully created a uniform policy first survey parents to gauge support for school-uniform requirements and then seek parental input

40 in designing the uniform. Parent support is also essential for encouraging students to wear the uniform.

A school-uniform policy must accommodate students whose religious beliefs are substantially burdened by a uniform requirement. As U.S. Secretary of Education

45 Richard W. Riley stated in *Religious Expression in Public Schools*, a guide he sent to superintendents throughout the nation on August 10, 1995, students may display religious messages on items of clothing to the same extent that they are permitted to display other comparable messages.

50 Religious messages may not be singled out for suppression, but rather are subject to the same rules as generally applied to comparable messages. When wearing particular attire,

such as yarmulkes and headscarves, during the school day is part of students' religious practice, under the Religious

55 Freedom Restoration Act schools generally may not prohibit the wearing of such items.

Some schools have adopted wholly voluntary school-uniform policies that permit students to freely choose whether and under what circumstances they will wear the school

60 uniform. Alternatively, some schools have determined that it is both warranted and more effective to adopt a mandatory uniform policy. When a mandatory school-uniform policy is adopted, the school must still determine whether to have an "opt-out" provision. In most cases, school districts with

65 mandatory policies allow students, normally with parental consent, to "opt out" of the school-uniform requirements. Some schools have determined, however, that a mandatory policy with no "opt-out" provision is necessary to address a disruptive atmosphere. However, in the absence of a finding

70 that disruption of the learning environment has reached a point at which other, lesser measures have been or would be ineffective, a mandatory school-uniform policy without an "opt-out" provision could be vulnerable to legal challenge.

36. The author suggests that a school-uniform policy is likely to be much more effective when it:

A. includes an "opt-out" provision.
B. enlists parental involvement.
C. responds to growing levels of violence.
D. is voluntary.

GO ON TO THE NEXT PAGE.

37. Given the information in the passage, Los Angeles inner-city schools that are experiencing increasingly violent levels of gang activity most likely are undergoing this tribulation because:

   A. the school has allowed an "opt-out" provision.
   B. the school is accommodating of the parents' wishes.
   C. the school has not enlisted parental involvement.
   D. the school is permissive with its dress policy.

38. The commonly recognized meaning of the word "uniform" is most DISCREPANT with which of the following ideas from the passage?

   A. Many schools that have successfully created a uniform policy first survey parents to gauge support for school-uniform requirements and then seek parental input in designing the uniform.
   B. Religious messages may not be singled out for suppression, but rather are subject to the same rules as generally applied to comparable messages.
   C. Some schools have adopted wholly voluntary school uniform policies that permit students to freely choose whether and under what circumstances they will wear the school uniform.
   D. Some schools have determined that it is both warranted and more effective to adopt a mandatory uniform policy.

39. The passage indicates that its author would agree with all of the following statements regarding the potential benefits of school uniforms EXCEPT:

   A. help school officials to recognize intruders who come to the school
   B. help parents to resist peer pressure
   C. help students to concentrate on their school work
   D. help to overcome religious persecution

40. What distinction is implied in the passage between dress codes and uniform policies, respectively?

   A. uniform requirement versus a certain style of dressing
   B. mandatory style of dressing versus voluntary policy
   C. prohibiting certain clothing versus adopting a type of clothing
   D. adopting guideline codes versus adopting restrictions

STOP. IF YOU FINISH BEFORE TIME IS CALLED, CHECK YOUR WORK. YOU MAY GO BACK TO ANY QUESTION IN THIS TEST.

TEST 9

STOP.

TEST 9

Verbal Reasoning Test 10
Time: 60 Minutes
Questions 1–40

VERBAL REASONING

DIRECTIONS: There are seven passages in this Verbal Reasoning test. Each passage is followed by several questions. After reading a passage, select the one best answer to each question. If you are not certain of an answer, eliminate the alternatives that you know to be incorrect and then select an answer from the remaining alternatives. Indicate your selection by blackening the corresponding oval on your answer document.

Passage I (Questions 1–5)

The current stock exchange system often gives institutional investors poor execution prices when they attempt to buy large numbers of shares of stock on the open market over short periods, for example, when buying the
5　shares necessary to acquire voting control of a corporation. Since they are unlikely to find a single source that owns all the shares they need (and is willing to sell them all), they must instead advertise their willingness to buy on the open market, a few shares at a time. Consequently, sellers who see
10　the institution buying up shares piecemeal will realize that it is intent on amassing an unusually large position and will raise their selling price, knowing the institution is willing to pay a premium over the "fair" market value to achieve its objectives. Thus, as soon as the institution advertises its
15　desire and makes its first few purchases on the open market, it cannot help "tipping its hand" to all other sellers.

The exchanges have developed some solutions to the problem. Instead of buying on the open market, the institutional buyer may use the "order-matching" system,
20　whereby it advertises its offer price to large institutional sellers only. However, this does not resolve the problem entirely, since posting the "buy" order still tips their hand, albeit to a smaller group of players. Another currently available tactic is "crossing sessions," in which a
25　computerized system attempts to match a large buy order with an equally large block seller. If successful, this would of course solve the price-creeping problem, but the problem is that such large sellers usually don't exist.

A newly developed solution to this problem is
30　OptiMark, a computerized block-trading service. It allows two unique results. First, when a seller enters a "sell" order into OptiMark, it commits to selling the entire block at the same price per share. This guarantees a block buyer that the seller will not raise prices for later sales of stock.
35　Second, OptiMark allows the buyer to make a "contingent" purchase—that is, contingent on receiving a minimum number of shares. If supply is insufficient, the trade is automatically reversed, with no seller learning about the

buyer's intentions. OptiMark's aggregation capability may
40　also be better at matching fragmented buy and sell orders.

Can OptiMark be profitable? Possibly. OptiMark earns profit on commission; therefore, it earns more if more shares are traded using it. If broker-dealers (who currently make stock trades on the exchanges) decide against using
45　OptiMark, it will earn little. Of course, it could still earn commissions even if it were used only by institutions trading outside the traditional markets, though apparently there is not enough volume in those markets to make OptiMark worthwhile. Alternately, if OptiMark could convince the
50　exchanges to *require* its use (over broker-dealers' protests), it could earn commissions from exchange trading.

If adopted, OptiMark would (hopefully) undermine the entire trading system of the New York Stock Exchange (NYSE). NYSE is composed of member brokerages that, in
55　exchange for a large fee, are allowed to trade in listed stocks on behalf of customers. These brokerages then charge monopolistic "rents" in the form of commissions, since they are the only ones allowed to take orders on the NYSE, which offers access to a large variety of popular stocks. If
60　ordinary traders could place trades through OptiMark for a smaller commission, they would not need to place them with NYSE brokers.

1.　According to the passage, an existing solution that closely resembles some aspects of OptiMark is:

A.　the system of "order matching."
B.　the tactic of "crossing sections."
C.　the NYSE's "rents."
D.　a "contingent" purchase.

GO ON TO THE NEXT PAGE.

2. On the basis of information in the passage, one would generally expect the required use of OptiMark to be received most favorably by:

   A.   institutional investors and NYSE member traders.
   B.   ordinary traders and institutional buyers.
   C.   NYSE member brokerages.
   D.   broker-dealers and institutional buyers.

3. Which of the following statements is the most reasonable conclusion that can be drawn from the author's description of OptiMark?

   A.   If OptiMark could develop a computerized block-trading service, they could become profitable.
   B.   It is likely that OptiMark would be charging monopolistic "rents" if it became widely accepted.
   C.   The larger the number of shares an institution is willing to buy, the better the price that institution may obtain for those shares.
   D.   Institutional investors attempting to acquire voting control of a corporation is an infrequent occurrence.

4. If the description of OptiMark in lines 29–40 is correct, one could most reasonably conclude that:

   A.   using OptiMark, a "match" of the seller's offer must be made with the buyer's offer before any intent is revealed.
   B.   using OptiMark, the buyer would know the seller's intentions, but not vice versa.
   C.   using OptiMark, the seller would know the buyer's intentions, but not vice versa.
   D.   using OptiMark, a seller's offer must match the buyer's offer before the buyer's intent is revealed.

5. According to the passage, in the existing system, institutional investors looking to buy large numbers of shares cannot avoid:

   A.   the price-creeping problem.
   B.   paying large commissions to NYSE brokerages.
   C.   revealing their intentions to other sellers.
   D.   buying their shares in a piecemeal fashion.

TEST 10

GO ON TO THE NEXT PAGE.

Passage II (Questions 6–11)

The full-time prostitute is the most highly paid professional woman in America. An average streetwalker can expect to earn from five hundred up to one thousand dollars per day, a salary that translates easily into an annual income of several hundred thousand dollars, all tax-free. However, the primary beneficiary of these earnings is often not the prostitute herself, but her pimp, who, for "managing" a prostitute, usually keeps for himself an amazing 85% of her earnings. Since a successful pimp has a "stable" of two to twelve women, his earning power is enormous.

It is commonly believed that a pimp provides for his women a variety of services amusingly akin to those offered by mainstream talent agents—publicity, networking, costumes, money management, legal expenses, etc. Sometimes, he fills even more basic needs. Many prostitutes begin their professional careers after having an illegitimate child at an early age, forcing them to leave home and fend for themselves and their child. Often, they leave the child behind in the care of a relative. Such single mother prostitutes' first goal is often to earn enough quickly to bring their child to live with them. Ironic as it sounds, the pimp often doubles as day care for the prostitute's children. For such women, having a pimp with his own house/apartment enables them to work long days, while knowing their children are (relatively) safe. Further, the pimp acts as a banker to his stable. For obvious reasons, a prostitute cannot deposit a thousand dollars a day in a bank without declaring taxable income.

Prostitution penalties are notoriously low, often amounting to no more than a night in jail and a miniscule fine. But streetwalkers are arrested frequently, and a long record of prostitution arrests makes it impossible to legitimately obtain credit, credit without which they cannot put a down payment on a home or business. As the majority of prostitutes begin desperately poor, the pimp's immediate "loan" of food, clothing, housing, a lawyer, and bail money may seem to be worth the exorbitant "interest."

And for a novice prostitute, a pimp's advice—on the most profitable and least competitive streets, on avoiding police patrols and arrests, and on ways of extracting the most money from clients—may indeed be valuable. But with even minimal experience, a rational prostitute would find that her pimp provides precious little to justify his exorbitant fee. This cannot be otherwise, since most pimps admittedly do nothing but recruit new girls, or else lounge while waiting for their stable to bring home their night's earnings. However, even mature prostitutes often remain with a pimp (perhaps replacing their current pimp with another, similar one), even though they themselves realize he takes their hard-earned money in exchange for nothing tangible. As one prostitute says, "My man doesn't do anything. But he does it beautifully." Why, then, do they continue to turn over the bulk of their earnings to a pimp who, even they realize, provides almost nothing in return?

The reasons appear to be delusional rather than rational. Pimps often promise their women that, at the end of their careers, after they have accumulated enough money for them, the pimp will marry them, buy a house and business, invest their earnings, and bring them into the respectable middle class. Needless to say, this promise is rarely fulfilled. But while a young and naïve prostitute may be excused for believing it, more experienced streetwalkers, who have been abandoned by a succession of pimps, cannot still harbor the hope of it happening. Their continued reliance on the pimp is likely a manifestation of their underlying psychological needs. Most of the women who turn to street prostitution share a remarkably similar upbringing: a lack of a strong father figure early in childhood (e.g., raised by a single mother or an abusive father/stepfather), and an early and traumatic experience with sex (e.g., a teen pregnancy, rape, or often incest). Psychologists posit that such experiences early in life effectively teach these women that men are unreliable as providers, that marital relationships are unstable, and that sex is a commodity to be exploited. Also, it leaves them with the craving for a powerful male figure to substitute for the absent father/husband figure. The pimp appears to fill this need, as an exploitative and abusive but powerfully macho and male figure who promises to provide them with financial and emotional fulfillment, the absence of which most likely drove them to embrace prostitution.

6. It can most justifiably be said that the main purpose of the passage is:

A. to describe the life and difficulties of a prostitute.
B. to explain the relationship between a prostitute and her pimp.
C. to illustrate the reasons why a woman would become a prostitute.
D. to deemphasize the role of prostitutes as bad mothers.

7. What is the most serious apparent *weakness* of the research described?

   A. The penalties for prostitution are notoriously low.
   B. The mature prostitutes are described as both delusional and realistic.
   C. A long record of arrests makes obtaining credit impossible.
   D. A prostitute's wages are tax-free.

8. Which of the following opinions would the author be most likely to endorse?

   A. In the case of more mature prostitutes, their pimps are often their lovers and boyfriends.
   B. In the case of more mature prostitutes, they realize the importance of what they pay their pimp.
   C. In the case of a novice prostitute, the pimp provides them valuable information on safety.
   D. In the case of the novice prostitute, they recognize the pimp provides them with little.

9. The author of the passage would be most likely to agree with which of the following ideas expressed by other researchers?

   A. Pimps usually remain with the prostitute for her entire working career.
   B. Prostitutes enjoy their work.
   C. Prostitutes often drift away from stable upbringings.
   D. The pimp acts as a father figure for the prostitute.

10. The author claims that "the pimp acts as a banker to his stable" (lines 27–28). The support offered for this conclusion is:

    A. strong; the author argues that, for obvious reasons, a prostitute cannot deposit a thousand dollars a day in a bank without declaring taxable income.
    B. strong; the author argues that prostitution penalties are notoriously low.
    C. weak; the author argues that, for obvious reasons, a prostitute cannot deposit a thousand dollars a day in a bank without declaring taxable income.
    D. weak; the author argues that prostitution penalties are notoriously low.

11. The passage states that prostitutes are:

    A. likely to have an illegitimate child before beginning prostitution.
    B. not likely to care for their illegitimate children.
    C. likely to have an illegitimate child early on in their career.
    D. likely to keep their children with them while they work.

GO ON TO THE NEXT PAGE.

TEST 10

Passage III (Questions 12–17)

The art of "people-reading," assessing people's character and actions from visible characteristics and appearance, can, of course, be a very powerful predictive tool. Most of the time, people are, in fact, what they appear
5 to be; even if they attempt to disguise their character, their disguise will have imperfections visible to a trained and conscientious observer. Indeed, there are many books available on decoding body language, and their assessment of what psychological traits each gesture suggests is largely
10 accurate.

However, to avoid mistaken snap judgments based on a single trait or action, people-reading must be done systematically. Of course, "readers" should remain observant and attempt to take in all available information
15 before making their decision. But a person's presentation contains too many attributes for any reader to observe them all fully in any single encounter. That is why expert people-readers focus on observing only those traits that are relevant to the purposes for which they are evaluating their target.

20 The experienced observer will seek to locate patterns of behavior rather than isolated traits or gestures since patterns are more predictive of general behavior over time and less likely to be caused by situational factors. For example, poor posture is generally a sign of poor self-confidence. Other
25 signs of low self-esteem include soft or mumbled speech, downcast eyes, anxiety, etc. Thus, if the reader sees an elderly person with poor posture, he should look for the presence of these other indicators before deciding the person is unassertive, rather than a confident individual suffering
30 from spinal curvature.

Watchers will sometimes want to focus both on traits "relevant" to the situation, and on those traits that tend to be the most revealing of a person's general character. Research shows the most predictive traits tend to be the person's levels
35 of compassion, satisfaction, and socioeconomic fulfillment. The level of each of these traits tends to influence the person's broader outlook on a wide range of issues. Generally, compassionate people tend to be generous, fair, sincere, affectionate, family-oriented, and both understanding and
40 forgiving of mistakes or misdeeds. In contrast, uncaring people tend to be critical, intolerant, harsh and punitive, and prone to impetuous snap judgments. People who are socioeconomically fulfilled, as measured by a combination of wealth and/or familial support, tend to be more confident,
45 kind, tolerant, and forgiving, though they also have greater than average chances of being lazy, vain, and materialistic. The unfulfilled tend to be more callous, intolerant, and defensive, though they also are often more focused and hardworking. Finally, those who are subjectively satisfied
50 with their status in life—often through having achieved their career aspirations—tend towards compassion, optimism, and industriousness. Those disappointed with life tend to

see themselves as victims, becoming bitter, pessimistic, vengeful, and less driven.

55 Other predictive traits tend to be those that deviate from the norm, either the cultural norm or the person's other normal attributes. For example, if a banker wears a suit at work, this has no predictive value because it is the cultural norm, and most bankers do so by rote. However, if
60 he dresses casually in an atmosphere in which formal dress is accepted, this indicates a strong personal preference. A person's "rogue" traits are those inconsistent with his other apparent attributes and are almost always predictive of his true nature. For example, a man who is unusually on his best
65 behavior, but is prone to rare fits of anger or cursing, is likely possessed of this tendency but trying to hide or control it.

Finally, watchers should consider any trait in the context of the person's own culture. If a seemingly nonconformist trait has its basis in the person's foreign ancestry, it may
70 actually signal a desire for conformity, rather than a rebellion against society.

12. The central thesis of the passage is that:

I. a person can learn to 'read' others in order to gain a more accurate impression of them.

II. a person can learn to convey the appropriate impression to others.

III. a person can learn to 'read' the impression he is conveying to others.

A. I only
B. II only
C. III only
D. I and II only

GO ON TO THE NEXT PAGE.

13. According to the passage, the only real limitations to "people-reading" would be the evaluator's:

   I.   inability to hear.
   II. lack of background information on the 'target.'
   III. inability to see.

   A. I only
   B. II only
   C. III only
   D. II and III only

14. The author's example of the significance of "a man who is usually on his best behavior, but is prone to rare fits of anger or cursing" (lines 64–65) is most weakened by which idea that is implicit in the passage?

   A. Traits that deviate from the norm are also good predictive traits.
   B. To determine general behavior over time, patterns should be used.
   C. Almost everyone has gotten very angry at one time or another in their lives.
   D. Anger and cursing are usually caused by situational factors that can be ignored.

15. According to the ideas presented, people-reading must be done systematically to avoid snap judgments, and "uncaring people tend to be critical, intolerant, harsh and punitive, and prone to impetuous snap judgments" (lines 40–42). If both of these premises are true, what conclusion is most reasonable?

   A. A good people-reader should be somewhat critical.
   B. A critical person would make a poor people-reader.
   C. Uncaring people would make poor people-readers.
   D. The best people-readers are usually uncaring people.

16. In the last paragraph, the author writes, "If a seemingly nonconformist trait has its basis in the person's foreign ancestry, it may actually signal a desire for conformity, rather than a rebellion against society" (lines 68–71). By this, the author most likely means that:

   A. this person is attempting to conform to his/her own culture.
   B. the person is wrongly perceived as rebelling against his/her ancestry.
   C. the person is attempting to conform to his/her new culture.
   D. the person's ancestry is nonconformist.

17. According to the passage, an inexperienced people-reader might most easily make the mistake of:

   A. making a snap judgment about a "rogue" trait.
   B. trying to observe only traits that he/she felt were relevant to their purposes.
   C. making broad generalizations regarding compassion or socioeconomic fulfillment.
   D. dismissing a "rogue trait."

Passage IV (Questions 18–22)

For Muslims the Koran is the very word of God, who spoke through the Angel Gabriel to Muhammad: "This book is not to be doubted," the Koran declares unequivocally at its beginning. Scholars and writers in and outside of Islamic
5 countries who have ignored that warning have sometimes found themselves the target of death threats and violence, sending a chill through universities around the world. Extrareligious examination and interpretation of this Islamic holy book is regarded as profane and sacrilegious
10 by most of the followers of Islam. Interestingly, unfettered secular thought in Europe could only have been achieved after centuries of close textual study of Jewish and Christian Scripture. This study gradually evolved into questioning of the Scriptures and, eventually, the Church's role and
15 domination of thought. Perhaps familiarity does breed contempt. "The Muslims have the benefit of hindsight of the European experience, and they know very well that once you start questioning the holy scriptures, you don't know where it will stop," a scholar, who wishes only to be
20 identified by a pseudonym, Mr. Luxembourg, explained. Yet despite the dangers, a small group of scholars continues to closely examine, study, and question the Koran, its origins, and its meaning.

As long ago as 1977, John Wansbrough of the School of
25 Oriental and African Studies in London wrote that subjecting the Koran to "analysis by the instruments and techniques of biblical criticism is virtually unknown." Mr. Berlin, a scholar of ancient Semitic languages in Germany, believes that the Koran has been misread and mistranslated for centuries. His
30 work, based on the earliest copies of the Koran, maintains that parts of Islam's holy book are derived from pre-existing Christian Aramaic texts that were misinterpreted by later Islamic scholars who prepared the editions of the Koran commonly read today. Modern researchers are increasingly
35 returning to the earliest known copies of the Koran in order to grasp what it says about the document's origins and composition. Mr. Luxembourg explains that these copies are written without vowels and diacritical dots that modern Arabic uses to make it clear what letter is intended. In
40 the eighth and ninth centuries, more than a century after the death of Muhammad, Islamic commentators added diacritical marks to clear up the ambiguities of the text, giving precise meanings to passages based on what they considered their proper context. Mr. Luxembourg's radical
45 theory is that many of the text's difficulties can be clarified when the text is seen as closely related to Aramaic, the language of most Middle Eastern Jews and Christians at the time. In many cases, after taking into account the revision and interpretation of the ancient Islamic commentators, the
50 differences can be quite significant. For instance, Mr. Berlin points out that in the early archaic copies of the Koran, it is impossible to distinguish between the words "to fight" and "to kill." In many cases, he said, Islamic exegetes added diacritical marks that yielded the harsher meaning, perhaps

55 reflecting a period in which the Islamic Empire was often at war.

However, the prevailing attitude is strongly, and dangerously, against any but traditional interpretations or methods of study of the Koran. Mr. Berlin would love to
60 see a "critical edition" of the Koran produced, one based on recent philological work, but, he says, "the word critical is misunderstood in the Islamic world—it is seen as criticizing or attacking the text." Yet, "between fear and political correctness, it's not possible to say anything other
65 than sugary nonsense about Islam," said one scholar at an American university who asked not to be named, referring to the threatened violence as well as the widespread reluctance on United States college campuses to criticize other cultures.

18. According to one authority on the Bible, "centuries of faithless secular analysis of the Bible was one of the primary reasons for the Protestant exodus from the Catholic Church." This authority would probably:

   A. consider the fears of extrareligious examination of the Koran by followers of Islam as valid.
   B. support further analysis of the Koran within the context of diacritical marks.
   C. not consider either the Koran or the followers of Islam to have any valid concerns.
   D. approve of analysis by Middle Eastern Jews and Christians only.

TEST 10

19. The author suggests that the difficulty of performing a critical analysis of the Koran and then publishing the findings results from:

   A. the Judeo-Christian experiences of studying the holy Psalms.

   B. reluctance to criticize other cultures.

   C. instructions within the Koran "to kill" those who would perform such an act.

   D. an inability to understand the ancient Aramaic scripts.

20. What is the intended relevance of the comment that "between fear and political correctness, it's not possible to say anything other than sugary nonsense about Islam" (lines 63–65) to the rest of the passage?

   A. Islamic people are difficult to understand.

   B. Religious books such as the Koran and the Bible cannot be critically analyzed without danger.

   C. The Koran is probably not "the very word of God."

   D. A critical analysis of the Koran has not been accomplished.

21. Assume that scientists and physicists studying Genesis, the first book of the Bible, discover that it actually gives an accurate explanation of the beginnings of the universe. Which of the following hypotheses does this assumption suggest?

   A. Scientists and physicists have a great deal to learn about the Koran.

   B. Extrareligious examination and interpretation of sacred texts continues to undermine their credibility.

   C. Extrareligious examination and interpretation of sacred texts does not necessarily undermine their credibility.

   D. Extrareligious examination and interpretation of the Koran will help to prove its accuracy.

22. According to the passage, which of the following is most likely to be true about the relationship between Muslims and Jews?

   A. They are both people of great religious fervor.

   B. Centuries of hatred have brought them to the brink of war.

   C. The language of the Muslim's Koran is closely related to Jewish Aramaic.

   D. They have learned not to allow their Koran to be criticized.

TEST 10

GO ON TO THE NEXT PAGE.

Passage V (Questions 23–28)

Research on African-American Vernacular English (AAVE) conducted during the 1960's was primarily concerned with developing improved methods of teaching reading and language arts to African-American children

5 in the inner cities. The seminal work on dialect readers was summarized in a collection, *Teaching Black Children to Read* (1969), which set the stage for producing reading materials in the AAVE dialect. There seemed to be good and positive evidence to bolster the tenet that these readers were

10 effective in helping students bridge the gap from dialect to Standard English use. None of the efforts lasted long, mainly because there was a negative reaction to using the readers. This issue and the use of this dialect were to resurface, and they were characterized as Ebonics.

15 In the Oakland school districts, what seemed to be occurring was that some African-American children were unable to understand or to be understood by their teachers in school. They were unable to effectively communicate. Unable to communicate, they did poorly in school and thus

20 were failing to learn the skills and *ways of speaking* that were required in order to be successful in the world outside of their local neighborhoods. In instances in which children are unable to communicate effectively, they have often been ignored and allowed to languish. Without ridiculing or

25 demeaning the children's way of speaking, it was hoped that AAVE would serve as a "bridge" to help the children learn to speak a more commonly used dialect: Standard English.

As Charles Fillmore points out in his essay "A Linguist Looks at the Ebonics Debate," "One uncontroversial

30 principle underlying 'Ebonics' is the truism that people can't learn from each other if they don't speak the same language." One of the first jobs of missionaries traveling to other countries is to learn the local language and to help the natives to learn to speak English, in order for them to be

35 able to understand one another. Moreover, the missionaries are less effective if they simply ignore the native tongue or demean it as inferior to English. What is ironic is that, in a larger sense, communication relates not only to the issue of Ebonics, but also to the debate *about* Ebonics. There was

40 an absolute failure of communication between the Oakland School District and the world at large.

The school district's resolution asked that the schools acknowledge that AAVE is the "primary language" of many of the children who enter Oakland schools. What this meant

45 was that it was the children's primary *home* language: the language they spoke with their families and friends. In fact, all over the world children show up in school speaking a variety of dialects that differ in some great or small way from the standard language they're about to start learning.

50 Where the discrepancy is slight, the difference can be easily bridged. This phrase "*primary language*," but not necessarily its meaning, was seized upon by the outside world.

The *Chronicle* (12/20) asked readers to send in their opinions "on the Oakland school board's decision to

55 recognize Ebonics, or Black English, as a *primary language*." An *Examiner* writer editorialized (12/20) that "[i]n the real world of colleges and commerce and communication, it's not OK to speak Ebonics as a *primary language*. Job recruiters don't bring along a translator." The *Chronicle*

60 (12/24) accounted for the Oakland School District's sudden notoriety as happening "all because the school board voted to treat Black English like any other *primary language* spoken by students."

The misunderstandings revolving around this phrase

65 were only the tip of the iceberg in this ironic debate about communication in which no communication took place. Nevertheless, it was enough to sink the AAVE ship '*Titanic*.' She was filled with young African-American children this time out as she moved deeper into the waters of the world.

70 and they were unable to communicate with others about the rough seas ahead.

23. The main argument of the passage is that:

A. Oakland wished to teach Ebonics to African-American children.

B. it is incontrovertible that Ebonics is a proven method of teaching Standard English.

C. we cannot learn from one another if we cannot communicate.

D. the label Ebonics was being used in a pejorative way.

GO ON TO THE NEXT PAGE.

24. In the context of the passage, the phrase *"rough seas"* refers primarily to the:

    A.   cultural attacks on the children's primary language.
    B.   opportunity offered to teach AAVE in Oakland.
    C.   children's chances for success in the outside world.
    D.   death of the original *Titanic* passengers.

25. The passage implies that teaching is less effective when it:

    A.   is attempted in the native tongue.
    B.   is performed in a demeaning fashion.
    C.   is scrutinized by the media.
    D.   involves missionaries.

26. The passage suggests that objection to the phrase "primary language" derives from the fact that:

    A.   most people did not want their children to be taught to speak AAVE.
    B.   most people did not want their children to be taught to speak Ebonics.
    C.   Standard English is the only acceptable primary language.
    D.   the true meaning of this phrase was not communicated.

27. According to the passage, why did the school district refer to AAVE as the "primary language"?

    A.   This was the language spoken at the children's home with their friends and families.
    B.   This was to be the language that all African-American children learned to speak in school.
    C.   This name was more acceptable than 'Ebonics.'
    D.   This language was considered the equivalent of Standard English.

28. The discussion of missionaries and their efforts to teach English in other countries (lines 35–41) shows primarily that:

    A.   teachers must speak only English when trying to teach English.
    B.   teachers can teach more effectively if they learn to speak and understand the native language.
    C.   missionaries never demeaned their pupils.
    D.   students are more willing to learn if their teacher is a missionary.

TEST 10

GO ON TO THE NEXT PAGE.

Passage VI (Questions 29–34)

During World War II, the Germans herded innocent men, women, and children into shower rooms and gassed them to death; the Allies bombed German cities relentlessly also killing innocent men, women, and children. With both
5 actions having the same result, how can we consider the former a crime and not the latter? When killing is the norm as it is during a war, what is the moral standard by which we judge a war crime? I would propose that the standard by which we distinguish between morally acceptable and
10 unacceptable behavior should not change whether in times of peace or times of war. Under either circumstance, our moral judgment of a specific action is intrinsic to the control held by an actor over his situation. This control provides him with the opportunity to show compassion.

15 Criminal laws reflect this concept accurately. For instance, an insane man has no control over his own actions and cannot be held responsible; he can commit no crime. Along the same lines, one man who is assaulted by another may use reasonable force to defend himself, yet he must
20 resist his attacker no more than is necessary to regain control of the situation. Our criminal penalties also reflect this ethical standard. Premeditated murder, for example, in which the offender plans and then commits his crime under circumstances of his choosing, receives a harsher penalty
25 than a murder of sudden passion. In each case, the offender's ability to control his situation is the pivotal factor on which our moral judgment of his actions is based.

Likewise, in war we use the same standards. The most notorious war crimes were unarguably committed
30 in the concentration camps of the Holocaust under the most controlled circumstances imaginable. It is precisely that control that makes them intolerable. We shudder at the callousness required to perform such calculated and deliberate acts of cruelty. In comparison, other war crimes,
35 such as the shooting of momentarily unarmed combatants during a battle, do not conjure up the same intensity of outrage. The unpredictable circumstances, which we know exist in battle, induce our empathy. When allied planes bombed German cities killing noncombatants, no one
40 was directly deciding who lived and who died. In fact, bombing is generally a very inefficient method for killing. It lacks precision, virtually removing the offender from the selection process. Such uncertainty absolves him of direct responsibility for any single individual's death. Thus,
45 bombing is not a war crime.

However, if calculated and premeditated control is introduced to the bombing, as in the case of the neutron bomb, which neatly kills its victims without disturbing inanimate objects, the act is judged immoral and unacceptable.
50 Moreover, in the intricate control of which pinpoint bombing is capable, as was done in Baghdad, we require detailed explanations for any loss of noncombatant life.

In the final analysis, our standards of justice do not really change when we go to war. We continue to demand
55 compassion whenever possible and judge the morality of individual actions in direct proportion to the amount of control possessed by the actor. Thus, we are left with the paradox in which two morally different actions can have the same results; one is judged to be a war crime, while the
60 other is just one of the many ineluctable horrors of war.

29. The author's central thesis is that:

A. there should be two sets of standards for judging morality.
B. violence is inevitable.
C. "control" determines culpability.
D. the Germans were amoral.

GO ON TO THE NEXT PAGE.

30. The passage suggests that if a perfectly functioning precision "smart bomb" hits a hospital, producing many civilian casualties, it may be reasonable to assume that:

    A. the pilot who caused the bomb to hit the hospital should not be held responsible.

    B. 'smart bombs' are not as useful as one might think.

    C. the pilot who caused the bomb to hit the hospital should be charged with murder.

    D. the officer back at the base, who initially ordered the bombing of the area but not the hospital, is at fault.

31. Which of the following assertions does the author support with an example?

    I. Criminal laws accurately reflect the concept of "control."

    II. Unpredictable circumstances in battle induce our empathy.

    III. In wartime, where intricate control is possible, we require detailed explanations for any loss of noncombatant life.

    A. I only

    B. I and II only

    C. I and III only

    D. I, II, and III

32. The men, women, and children whom the Germans herded into the gas chambers are described as "innocent." What is the most likely reason for the choice of this word?

    A. They all were actually innocent of any crimes.

    B. To more intensely convey the horror of this fate.

    C. They were sentenced to death even though a jury had found them innocent.

    D. This is only the author's opinion.

33. According to the passage, which of the following actions is/are unacceptable?

    I. A soldier killing an armed enemy soldier

    II. A soldier killing an armed child who is trying to kill him

    III. A soldier killing a restrained enemy soldier who has surrendered within the last two days

    A. II only

    B. III only

    C. II and III only

    D. I, II, and III

34. The author suggests that high-ranking German generals were considered "criminals" because they:

    A. had the ability to prevent civilian deaths.

    B. were on the losing side of the conflict.

    C. did not have precision-bombing capabilities.

    D. actually put to death innocent men, women, and children.

TEST 10

GO ON TO THE NEXT PAGE.

Passage VII (Questions 35–40)

In the early 1900's, Dr. Frederick S. McKay began an almost 30-year search for the cause of the staining of teeth that was then prevalent in Colorado, where he practiced dentistry. In his investigation, McKay found a condition
5 common in other states, including Texas, where it was known as "Texas teeth." In 1928, he concluded that such teeth, although stained, showed "a singular absence of decay," and that both the staining and the decay resistance were caused by something in the water. In 1931, the "something" was
10 identified as fluoride.

By the 1950's, the cities of Newburgh and Kingston, New York, underwent the first studies to determine whether fluoride should be introduced into the nation's water. First, children in both cities were examined by dentists and
15 physicians; then fluoride was added to Newburgh's water supply. After ten years, the children of Newburgh had 58% fewer decayed teeth than those of nonfluoridated Kingston. Children who had drunk the fluoridated water since birth obtained the greatest benefits. Other studies showed that
20 teeth made stronger by fluoride during childhood would remain permanently resistant to decay. As the evidence supporting fluoridation accrued, thousands of communities acted to obtain its benefits.

In those early days, drinking water was one of the
25 few avenues through which children might obtain fluoride. Today, all that has changed: it is difficult to find toothpaste that does not contain fluoride. Fluoride may also be found in canned drinks, fruit juices, tea, meat, vegetables—in fact, in all foods that have been grown or manufactured using
30 fluoridated water. So is it really necessary to add more to tap water? The evidence suggests strongly that it is not. Fluoridation of tap water forces us all to take the risk of this dubious and, for most, unnecessary medication, whether we want to or not, as domestic water filters do not filter fluoride
35 out and bottled water is both suspect and expensive. Further, fluoride can be dangerous. Since 1997, all toothpaste tubes have carried a warning label that cautions, "If you swallow more than used for brushing, contact a poison control center immediately."

40 In their article entitled "Fluoridation: Don't Let the Poisonmongers Scare You!," Bob Sprague, Mary Bernhardt, and Stephen Barrett, react, saying, "Although fluoridation is safe and effective in preventing tooth decay, the scare tactics of misguided poisonmongers have deprived many
45 communities of its benefits." These dentists and doctors argue that the scientific community is so solidly in favor of fluoridation that the "poisonmongers" must resort to conspiracy theories and worse to advance their cause. And it is easy to find antifluoride websites with such slogans as
50 "It is not the business of government to use the water supply to medicate the population without their consent."

Yet, despite the protestations of some dentists and doctors, no one has ever been shown to suffer from a 'deficiency' of fluoride. There is also recent evidence
55 suggesting that fluoride in milligram-per-day doses may have zero health value. Moreover, who regulates the amount of fluoride our children take in? Consider that the amount of fluoride we get depends on how much water we drink, which is strongly influenced by the climate in which we
60 live. In warmer climates people usually drink more water, and in cooler climates they drink less. So, it seems that the only justification for putting fluoride in drinking water is that the small fraction of children who do not brush their teeth with fluoride toothpaste or who do not use fluoride
65 mouthrinses might miss out on a possibly small topical benefit from this nonessential substance. However, they may also miss out on the chronic toxic effects of swallowing fluoride: dental fluorosis, skeletal fluorosis, bone fractures, and hypersensitivity reactions.

35. The passage suggests that fluoride provides:

   A. an excuse to medicate tap water.
   B. an alternative to tap water.
   C. no benefits whatsoever.
   D. prevention from tooth decay.

GO ON TO THE NEXT PAGE.

36. According to the passage, outside of fluoridated tap water, where might one look to obtain fluoride?

    A. Foods that have been grown using fluoridated water
    B. Nonfluoridated mouthrinses
    C. Coffee or tea
    D. Fluoride tablets

37. Suppose that researchers discovered that the human body safely regulated the amount of fluoride that it absorbed even when increasingly large amounts of fluoridated water are drunk. The lesson of this experience for local water districts, in general, would be:

    A. to attempt to medicate the population more regularly during winter months.
    B. to compete more intensely for fluoride contracts during the winter months.
    C. to focus less attention on monitoring levels of fluoride in relation to the weather.
    D. to cooperate more fully with the government on fluoride research.

38. According to the passage, unlimited intake with respect to fluoride is characteristic of:

    I. "Texas teeth."
    II. staining.
    III. decay resistance.

    A. II only
    B. III only
    C. II and III only
    D. I, II, and III

39. Which of the following conclusions can justifiably be drawn from the experience of the authors who wrote the article entitled "Fluoridation: Don't Let the Poisonmongers Scare You!" (lines 40–42) mentioned in the passage?

    A. The "Poisonmongers" have some solid scientific bases for their warnings.
    B. Many communities that may need fluoridated water have been deprived of it.
    C. Many communities are fortunate enough to have been able to choose.
    D. The government may try to medicate the population for its own good.

40. Assume that the FDA official who was instrumental in pushing legislation requiring "warning labels" was interviewed. If this official remarked that he had done this only to avoid class-action litigation against the government, this remark would *weaken* the passage assertion that:

    A. fluoride can cause "Texas teeth."
    B. fluoride can cause staining.
    C. fluoride can be dangerous.
    D. fluoride can prevent tooth decay.

_____

STOP. IF YOU FINISH BEFORE TIME IS CALLED, CHECK YOUR WORK. YOU MAY GO BACK TO ANY QUESTION IN THIS TEST.

_____

TEST 10

STOP.

Verbal Reasoning Test 11
Time: 60 Minutes
Questions 1–40

VERBAL REASONING

DIRECTIONS: There are seven passages in this Verbal Reasoning test. Each passage is followed by several questions. After reading a passage, select the one best answer to each question. If you are not certain of an answer, eliminate the alternatives that you know to be incorrect and then select an answer from the remaining alternatives. Indicate your selection by blackening the corresponding oval on your answer document.

Passage I (Questions 1–7)

Video games introduced children in the United States to the world of microcomputers at a time when computers were becoming increasingly important in many jobs and in daily life. The first successful electronic video game was
5 Pong, an electronic version of ping-pong, which appeared on the scene in 1971. Pong was a nonviolent video game that gained wide acceptance in a relatively short amount of time. It was eased into polite society by appearing in airports, train stations, and other establishments that were
10 not of the typical seedy quality that one associates with game arcades and smoke-filled pool halls. The founders of Pong eventually created the company Atari, and by 1976 Atari Video Computer Systems became available for the home. Shortly thereafter, a variety of other video games
15 could be played in front of the television while sitting on the couch.

By 1979, Atari's home video game system was so popular that other companies developed their own video game systems in order to enter the market, but none rivaled
20 Atari's success. Games like "Break Out" (a game in which the player attempts to break through a three-colored wall) brought Atari more wealth and fame. However, between 1983 and 1985, home video games experienced an immense downward plunge in the market, which was partially due to
25 some unsuccessful game programs and partly due to poor marketing strategies. Critics are not specific about what was bad about Atari's marketing strategies. Perhaps Atari's technology was not advancing fast enough, and new games were not differing enough from those that had preceded them
30 (an apparent reason for Nintendo's and Genesis's modern game consoles recent successes). The company lost over $600 million, and the home video game market appeared to be completely dead. Meanwhile, video arcade games, which had been thriving since the introduction of the first games,
35 continued to provide a social gathering place for children.

In 1985, Nintendo, a Japanese company that had previously made toys, card games, and video arcade games like Donkey Kong, revived the home video game craze in America. In 1989, the introduction of Nintendo's handheld
40 "Game Boy" game machine meant that video games could provide a means of entertainment almost anywhere. By 1990, more American homes had a Nintendo than a personal computer. A combination of ingenious marketing strategies and excellent software gave Nintendo a lock on the market
45 for quite some time.

However, it is virtually impossible to pinpoint exactly what it was about Nintendo's approach that allowed the company to experience such success. A few conversations with experts and enthusiasts revealed that the graphics were
50 much better than those of the Atari video game system. Also, Nintendo marketed a magazine offering tips on how to play the games and held conventions on Nintendo game-playing strategies, which helped to hype up its products. In addition, Nintendo was never behind in developing new
55 games. Nintendo even developed a "Game Genie," which enabled players to alter the games' parameters (e.g., making their characters invincible so they could get to the next "level" of the game). But recently, rival companies such as Sega have been successfully competing with Nintendo, and
60 Atari is now attempting to reenter the market.

The interactive element of video games has become more and more pronounced. Today, there is a move to put the player "inside the action" through the development of virtual reality. Indeed, the high resolution of today's video
65 games has allowed programmers to display violence in a more realistic manner. Nintendo's advertising slogan "Now You're Playing with Power!" gives some insight into the connection that these games have with a feeling of self-efficacy that is partially dependent on a player's
70 identification with the protagonist.

GO ON TO THE NEXT PAGE.

1. The contention that "[b]y 1990, more American homes had a Nintendo than a personal computer" (lines 41–43) can most justifiably be interpreted as support for the idea that:

   A. there were not many personal computers in American homes by 1990.
   B. there were many Nintendos in American homes by 1990.
   C. there were not many Nintendos in American homes by 1990.
   D. there were many personal computers in American homes by 1990.

2. According to the passage, which of the following is most likely to be true about the relationship between the video games and the home computer?

   A. The advent of the personal computer enabled children to play the video games at home.
   B. Prior to the advent of video games, children had little contact with computers.
   C. Video games became increasingly realistic because of home computers.
   D. Initially, video games were played in front of the television.

3. According to the passage, which of the following is most likely true about "game arcades" (line 11)?

   A. Video games thrived in arcades without decline.
   B. Video games experienced an immense downward plunge in arcades between 1983 and 1985.
   C. Pong never gained wide acceptance in the arcades.
   D. Early on, children were not allowed in the arcades.

4. The ideas in the passage seem to derive primarily from:

   A. facts observable to the author.
   B. speculation based upon written accounts.
   C. evidence from studies and research.
   D. conversations with others knowledgeable in these areas.

5. It has been said that in violent video games, children usually identify with the villains because they have superhuman strengths. The author would probably:

   A. agree, pointing out how realistic today's games have become.
   B. agree, pointing to the companies as the main culprits.
   C. disagree, arguing that most players identify with the hero.
   D. disagree, citing Pong and Donkey Kong as nonviolent examples.

6. Based upon the passage, if the society of the 1970's were a person, this person would most likely be:

   A. a well-educated soldier.
   B. a well-mannered gentleman.
   C. a rude businessman.
   D. a violent young person.

7. According to the passage, which of the following descriptions was/were common to Atari *and* Nintendo?

   I. Japanese company
   II. Video arcade games
   III. Home video games

   A. I only
   B. III only
   C. II and III only
   D. I, II, and III

GO ON TO THE NEXT PAGE.

Passage II (Questions 8–13)

In our earliest historical references to stuttering, the Book of Exodus finds Moses replying to God's request that he go before Pharaoh to deliver the Hebrews by saying, "They will not believe me, nor hearken unto my voice …
5 I am not eloquent, neither heretofore, nor since thou hast spoken unto thy servant, but I am slow of speech and of a slow tongue." Even today, the symptoms of stuttering may be described, yet definitions of the condition are more difficult to come by.

10 The American Psychiatric Association's Diagnostic and Statistical Manual of Mental Disorders (DSM-IV), identifies stuttering as a communicative disorder. Stuttering has received the dubious honor of being listed in the DSM-IV because it meets three of the four criteria for abnormal
15 patterns of behavior, despite the fact that speech is not a behavior. The three said criteria are Deviant, Distressful, and Dysfunctional (the only omission being Dangerous). This classification as a communicative disorder is only partly correct. It is doubtful that stuttering's genesis is of a
20 psychological nature; it is most likely organic. Unfortunately, because the psychological profession has deemed stuttering abnormal, numerous theories as to its etiology have been purported, with an excess spewing from the Freudian's and Neo-Freudian's.

25 Dr. Otto Fenichel (Freudian) described stuttering as an anal fixation. "Children who have difficulty being toilet trained may displace their anxiety about moving their bowels, to their mouth. Stuttering is thus a kind of verbal constipation." Dominick A. Barbara, director of speech in
30 the clinic established by the noted psychoanalyst Karen Horeny, states that a stutterer "stutters not with his mouth alone but with his whole body. Its cause is primarily due to the anxiety of the stutterer in coping with the world he lives in and his chaotic attempt to adjust to other people.
35 The confirmed stutterer presents a picture of an insecure, chronically anxious, highly excitable, emotionally immature person and a morbidly fearful person in speech situations."

Historically there have been two opposing views about the origins of stuttering and the relationship of physiological
40 and psychological aspects of the phenomenon. At one extreme is the position that stuttering reflects a psychological or emotional disturbance. At the other extreme is the position that stuttering reflects a physiological or neurological anomaly, and that whatever emotional or psychological
45 concomitants there may be are consequences and not the cause of stuttering.

It is hypothesized that compromised functioning of the right hemisphere of the brain may place stutterers at higher risk for stuttering because of the disruptive effect of
50 emotional functions, purportedly subserved by the right side of the brain. That is, compromised functioning of the right

hemisphere would reduce an individual's ability to effectively modulate emotion (either positive or negative) and place him or her at greater risk of consequent disruption of fluent
55 speech. This disruption of speech is further hypothesized to be the result of interference effects of the right hemisphere on the left hemisphere's functional executive control of the motor systems, both at cortical and subcortical levels of the brain, during speech production. This was confirmed
60 to some degree by Dr. William Webster in 1993 when he undertook to compare repetitive finger tapping and then demonstrated the existence of an inefficiency in the correct sequencing of this tapping. The errors were not corrected when the rapidity of the motion was decreased. These errors
65 in proper sequencing pointed to an inherent inefficiency in motor coordination, which is also involved in the generation of speech. Positron Emission Tomography (PET) scans have further supported these findings.

Despite differing opinions, two irrefutable truths
70 emerge from the jungle of information available on stuttering. There is no single, accepted, and provable explanation for stuttering, and, there is no cure.

8. If the author of the passage is right about stuttering, then it follows that:

   A. stuttering begins with psychological manifestations.
   B. the PET scans were wrong or misinterpreted.
   C. stuttering is not a communicative disorder.
   D. he holds a rather extreme point of view.

TEST 11

9. Regarding the research of Dr. William Webster (lines 60-69), the passage strongly implies that:

   A. finger tapping is the same as stuttering.
   B. stutterers had more difficulty with the sequencing of tapping.
   C. PET scans were conducted subsequent to the tapping.
   D. these experiments were conclusive.

10. Suppose it could be established that the majority of those who stutter are, in fact, morbidly fearful in speech situations. The author of the passage would be most likely to respond to this information by:

   A. suggesting that this indicates it is even more necessary to find a cure.
   B. proposing that this still does not prove that stuttering's primary cause is anxiety.
   C. asserting that 'left hemisphere explanations' account for this.
   D. explaining the psychological genesis of stuttering.

11. For which of the following of the author's assertions is NO support provided in the passage?

   A. There is no single, accepted, and provable explanation for stuttering.
   B. Speech is not a communicative disorder.
   C. Abnormal speech is not dangerous.
   D. Speech is not a behavior.

12. The author implies that a person who stutters is not:

   A. stuttering because of a psychological problem.
   B. suffering from any psychological problems.
   C. suffering from any physiological problems.
   D. constipated.

13. Which of the following suppositions is most clearly believed by the author?

   A. There is relatively little information available on stuttering.
   B. Stuttering reflects a physiological or neurological anomaly.
   C. The basis for stuttering is the left hemisphere of the brain.
   D. There are only two irrefutable facts with regard to stuttering.

TEST 11

GO ON TO THE NEXT PAGE.

Passage III (Questions 14–19)

Particularly in public schools today, there is an emphasis on mediocrity. The children who have difficulty academically struggle, while the brighter ones languish as the teachers attempt to present a curriculum that the
5 majority can understand and learn. In this instance, the teachers may have no choice, but in many other situations there is a conscious effort to praise and lift the self-esteem of malingerers. It is politically correct to ensure that everyone feel good about themselves, regardless of what they are not
10 doing or have not accomplished. Remember Ebonics? If students are failing to learn and have adopted some strange form of illiteracy, then let's not fight the trend, but adopt it as a curriculum. Let's promote the accomplishments of one and all, even if there are actually no accomplishments to
15 speak of.

In examining this strange perspective, it might do us well to listen to those who, by the old standards, are actually successful. I choose Bill Gates for this, not because he has the most money in the world, but because he gives away the
20 most money in the world. His money is a byproduct of his success.

Recently, Bill Gates gave a speech at a high school, in which he came pretty close to the truth. It was about 11 rules the graduating students had not been taught in school.
25 He talked about how feel-good politically correct teachings have created a generation of kids who have no concept of reality and how this lack of a concept sets them up for failure in the real world. Here is what he said:

Rule 1: Life is not fair—get used to it.

30 Rule 2: The world won't care about your self-esteem. The world will expect you to accomplish something BEFORE you feel good about yourself.

Rule 3: You will NOT make 40 thousand dollars a year right out of high school. You won't be a vice-president with
35 a car phone, until you earn both.

Rule 4: If you think your teacher is tough, wait till you get a boss. He doesn't have tenure.

Rule 5: Flipping burgers is not beneath your dignity. Your grandparents had a different word for burger flipping;
40 they called it opportunity.

Rule 6: If you mess up, it's not your parents' fault, so don't whine about your mistakes, learn from them.

Rule 7: Before you were born, your parents weren't as boring as they are now. They got that way from paying your
45 bills, cleaning your clothes, and listening to you talk about how cool you are. So before you save the rain forest from

the parasites of your parents' generation, try delousing the closet in your own room.

Rule 8: Your school may have done away with winners
50 and losers, but life has not. In some schools they have abolished failing grades, and they'll give you as many times as you want to get the right answer. This doesn't bear the slightest resemblance to ANYTHING in real life.

Rule 9: Life is not divided into semesters. You don't
55 get summers off, and very few employers are interested in helping you find yourself. You have to do that on your own time.

Rule 10: Television is NOT real life. In real life, people actually have to leave the coffee shop and go to jobs.

60 Rule 11: Be nice to nerds. Chances are you'll end up working for one.

If this seems harsh as you read it, you have been betrayed by your school system. These rules provide a framework of self-discipline within which to succeed, and a
65 healthy dose of reality.

14. The author's claim that "in public schools today, there is an emphasis on mediocrity" (lines 1-2) is supported by:
A. testimony adopted by the author.
B. examples of specific public schools.
C. comparison with private instruction.
D. an analysis of job performance.

GO ON TO THE NEXT PAGE.

15. The author most likely believes that one of the main purposes of pre-college education should be to provide students with:

    A. an awareness of their own importance.
    B. a sense of self-discipline.
    C. a sense of self-esteem.
    D. engaging experiences.

16. Given the information in the passage, if a "concept of reality" (lines 26–27) were taught to students in public schools, which of the following outcomes would most likely occur?

    A. There would be fewer students who would have to be "flipping burgers."
    B. Politically correct concepts could be utilized more effectively.
    C. Teachers would be more accountable for what they are teaching.
    D. Students would be much more successful in the real world.

17. The author suggests that praise and rewards are much less effective when they:

    A. are only given to actually promote accomplishments.
    B. are doled out indiscriminately.
    C. enhance the performance of all the students.
    D. are only given to those who make a lot of money.

18. Suppose that the majority of high-school students have, at one time or another, held a rather low-paying job, such as working in a MacDonald's restaurant. This new information would most CHALLENGE the claim that:

    A. students believe that this type of work is beneath their dignity.
    B. your school may have done away with winners and losers, but life has not.
    C. employers are not interested in helping you find yourself.
    D. you won't be a vice-president with a car phone, until you earn both.

19. According to the passage, the author feels that Bill Gates is successful because:

    A. he has the most money.
    B. he gives away the most money.
    C. his money is what made him successful.
    D. he seems to understand the problems with the school system.

GO ON TO THE NEXT PAGE.

Passage IV (Questions 20–24)

My students often ask me what I consider to be the most practical style of martial art for real fighting and self-defense. In reality, the effectiveness of any fighter depends not on the fighting style he uses, but (of course) on how long he has trained in it, and, more importantly, how practical his training has been.

When my preferred style, karate, developed on the Japanese island of Okinawa during the Shogunate, it was intended as a practical response to a concrete problem. The Shogun [of that era], having just subdued the island and fearful of armed rebellion, forbade the Okinawans from carrying swords or other weapons. Suddenly, the Okinawans could no longer rely on sword skills to defend themselves from marauding troops or native bandits, and were forced to use their bare hands. Thus, they developed a system of blocking, punching, and kicking that has survived to this day. While the system was certainly innovative, students must remember that it was a product of its times, which have long passed. For example, ancient practitioners learned blocks effective against the various swords, clubs, and polearms wielded by Shogunate-era soldiers. Many of these sword-blocks are still taught today. Because the soldiers wore lacquered-wood armor, dissident karatekas learned bare-hand armor-breaking techniques, which survive today in the form of board-breaking exercises that often accompany a student's promotion to a higher-ranking belt. At the time, unarmed attacks and blocks were taught in the form of *kata*, which were a complex series of combination moves. These combinations of up to 34 movements were taught as a series, by rote, simply because rote learning was the norm in feudal Japan and throughout most of Asia.

Today, the requirements of fighting arts have changed. Hand weapons are no longer carried; if they are, they are guns rather than swords. Armor is no longer worn. People cannot kill their attackers with impunity, without facing serious legal repercussions.

Similarly, the martial arts should stay true to their origins by adapting to meet the defensive needs of modern times. They should begin by teaching students how to make themselves less of a target for street crimes, and how to defuse arguments through words before resorting to fists, because any fight puts the fighter at risk of serious injury and criminal charges. For the same reasons, they should eliminate training in the use of ancient Asian weapons (as remains the tradition in Chinese *gunfu*), both because modern criminals no longer carry such weapons, and because carrying them is now criminal. …

Most of all, martial arts *dojos* that advertise themselves as schools of serious self-defense, rather than simply schools of Asian history and tradition, should adapt their martial arts for the demands of modern self-defense. Each style boasts hundreds of advanced, flashy, and complex attacks and defenses, but schools should consider restricting their repertoires to only those techniques that are safe and effective. For example, karate includes several spinning punches and kicks, jump kicks, and even somersaulting attacks and evasions. These certainly demand impressive athleticism to execute and often draw crowds at demonstrations. However, it is unclear whether they deliver a blow that is more forceful than a simple but well-executed punch or low kick. What is clear is that they are strenuous and difficult to remember, leaving the person open to injury from faster and simpler counterattacks, and dangerous to the person who executes them incorrectly.

Furthermore, the method of teaching should itself be altered. Returning to the *kata*—it is true that they do develop in students the ability to use combinations of several strikes, or a block followed by a counterstrike. Properly used, these combinations would be useful in actual fighting, since a single blow may not incapacitate an attacker each time, and because a combination may help throw a well-guarded attacker off balance, allowing a more effective counterstrike against him. But it is unrealistic to continue teaching traditional kata of two dozen strikes and blocks, especially when they include simulations of blocks against numerous attackers on all sides and simulated blocks against traditional weapons. If kata are to be retained, they must be shortened to the number of strikes that will foreseeably be needed to immobilize an attacker, and redesigned to reflect the types of attacks the modern martial artist is more likely to encounter.

20. The passage suggests that the author is most likely:

A. a martial arts instructor.
B. a martial arts student.
C. the developer of his own martial arts style.
D. a historian.

GO ON TO THE NEXT PAGE.

21. The author of the passage characterizes modern martial arts *dojos* as:

    A. schools of serious self-defense.
    B. intentionally deceptive.
    C. schools that should adapt to the times.
    D. practitioners of Asian history and tradition.

22. Regarding the concept of modern martial arts instruction, the author asserts that the teaching should concentrate first on:

    A. being safe and effective.
    B. eliminating training in the use of ancient weapons.
    C. making students less of a target for street crimes.
    D. hand weapons.

23. According to the author, the real effectiveness of a martial artist depends upon:

    I.   his athleticism.
    II. how long the artist has trained.
    III. the type of attacks he is more likely to encounter.

    A. I only
    B. II only
    C. III only
    D. II and III only

24. Assume that many forms of martial arts arose first as spiritual mind-body exercises and only secondarily as forms of self-defense. The author of the passage would be most likely to respond to this information by:

    A. suggesting that this is not contrary to modernizing the combat aspects of the art.
    B. proposing that the primary emphasis should always have been placed on the martial aspects of the art.
    C. asserting that the spiritual aspect of martial arts is indeed very important.
    D. explaining that if spirituality is the primary focus, then the discipline should not be called a 'martial' art.

TEST 11

GO ON TO THE NEXT PAGE.

Passage V (Questions 25–29)

Some recent developments in the study of the psychology of emotion offer new avenues for better emotional control. Unfortunately, prior research has demonstrated conclusively that some sudden emotions, most notably anger,
5 are often accompanied by the release of various hormones and chemicals, that contribute to sustaining the emotional reaction. For instance, psychologically caused anger triggers the release of adrenaline, which itself heightens and sustains the aroused state of anger. The adrenaline, once released,
10 will continue to be effective until it dissipates, and its rate of dissipation cannot be controlled consciously. Thus, emotions, *once triggered*, tend to bypass the conscious mind and are temporarily beyond its effective control. This has several important implications for emotional-impulse
15 control.

One of the best ways to avoid triggering improper impulses is to cultivate an awareness of one's personal "construals," or the ways in which one perceives an event. This is popularly known as "not jumping to conclusions,"
20 the oppostie of which is frequently the cause of sudden emotional responses. Two people may observe the same event but reach different conclusions about its significance; one will accept it rationally, while another will misconstrue it and be overcome with emotion. For example, upon
25 seeing two people pointing in their direction and laughing, many people will assume that the two are laughing at *them* personally, become angry, and challenge the two while "under the influence" of adrenaline and rage. A less impulsive person will similarly perceive that the two are
30 laughing and pointing, but will not necessarily assume the two are pointing or laughing *at* them; this less impulsive person may respond by waiting for the two to reveal more, by addressing them calmly or by ignoring them.

What sets the "impulsive" person apart from the
35 "level-headed" one is often the act of realizing that he *may* be misconstruing a given event and should investigate further before acting on his construal. Thus, it is possible to avoid misconstruals by using rational thought to counter irrational impulses, preventing these impulses from building
40 to uncontrollable levels.

The first step towards cultivating emotional control is for each person to become aware of his personal sensitivities or the types of misconstruals he is prone to making. This will depend largely on the person's own experiences and
45 persepective; for example, a person who has often been victimized by racism (or who *believes* he has) is more likely to assume that injurious acts are motivated by racism. There are many common irrational thought patterns, but each can be countered by a corresponding rational pattern.
50 Gradually, with practice, this rational self-correction becomes habitual. Generally, before acting on emotions, everyone should take at least a few seconds to pause and

think. This is effective against any rash construal. Other thought patterns require more individualized solutions.
55 For example, before interpreting an apparent slight as a personal insult, or assuming it is intentional, one should consider other possible causes. Before "catastrophizing," or overestimating each setback's importance, one should attempt to put it into perspective by considering the
60 setback's *worst possible* consequence, which often reveals it is really quite acceptable. This strategy is effective against 'categorical thinking' (viewing events as total successes or absolute failures, preventing one from recognizing partial successes), prejudices/labeling, and feeling threatened by
65 change or challenge.

Even if awareness proves unsuccessful at preventing the occurrence or intensification of an irrational response, it can also be used after the fact, to shorten the *duration* of the response. With practice, one can learn to recognize sudden
70 or prolonged surges of emotion. Instead of resigning oneself to the idea that emotional fugues are "natural," one should try to identify a physical source or reason for the emotion. Tracing the emotional response back to its source often shows it to be grounded in a misconstrual, which prevents
75 further rumination and re-irritation, and helps the response subside more quickly.

25. An unstated assumption in the author's example of "a person who has often been victimized by racism (or who *believes* he has)" (lines 45–46) is that:

   A. beliefs are not as important as actual events.
   B. memories can be misleading.
   C. repeated injury can increase sensitivity.
   D. most people probably weren't actually victims.

GO ON TO THE NEXT PAGE.

26. In another essay, the author is quoted as saying, "Instead of seeing it as an unqualified disappointment, I prefer to look at a setback as an 'alternative'." This quotation could best be used in the passage to illustrate the concept of:

A. categorical thinking.
B. catastrophizing.
C. misconstrual.
D. positive thinking.

27. The passage discussion most clearly suggests the hypothesis that we must learn:

A. to live with and accept our emotions for what they are.
B. to avoid acting on our impulses through re-channeling our emotions during events.
C. to control our sudden emotions and sustained emotional reactions.
D. to understand the ways in which we perceive in order to avoid inappropriate emotions and actions.

28. The author suggests that the difficulty of controlling some sudden emotional reactions results from:

A. our giving in to them.
B. uncontrollable physiological responses.
C. our not being 'level-headed.'
D. recent experiences.

29. According to information in the passage, the best way to avoid 'misconstruals' and develop emotional control would be to:

A. use self-correction.
B. become aware of your irrational thought patterns.
C. use 'categorical thinking.'
D. not overestimate a failure.

GO ON TO THE NEXT PAGE.

TEST 11

Passage VI (Questions 30–35)

When it comes to the quest for beauty in physics, even Einstein was a piker compared with the British theorist Paul Dirac, who once said that "it is more important to have beauty in one's equations than to have them fit [the] experiment."

An essay by Dr. Frank Wilczek, a physics professor at the Massachusetts Institute of Technology, recounts how the 25-year-old Dirac published an equation in 1928 purporting to describe the behavior of the electron, what was then known as the most basic and lightest elementary particle at the time. Dirac had arrived at his formula by "playing around" in search of "pretty mathematics," as he once put it. Dirac's equation successfully combined the precepts of Einstein's relativity with those of quantum mechanics, the radical rules that prevail on very small scales. But there was a problem. The equation had two solutions, one representing the electron, another representing its opposite, a particle with negative energy and positive charge, which had never been seen or considered before.

Dirac eventually concluded that the electron (and, it would turn out, every other elementary particle) had a twin, an antiparticle. In Dirac's original interpretation, if the electron was a hill, a blob, in space, its antiparticle, the positron, was a hole—together they equalled zero, and they could be created or destroyed in matching pairs. His equation had given the world its first glimpse of antimatter, which makes up, at least in principle, half the universe.

The first antimatter particle to be observed, the antiproton, was found in 1932, and Dirac won the Nobel Prize the next year. His feat is always dragged forth as Exhibit A in the argument to show that mathematics really does seem to have something to do with reality. "In modern physics, and perhaps in the whole of intellectual history, no episode better illustrates the profoundly creative nature of mathematical reasoning than the history of the Dirac equation," Dr. Wilczek wrote. In hindsight, what Dirac was trying to do was mathematically impossible. But, like the bumblebee who doesn't know it can't fly, through a series of inconsistent assumptions, Dirac tapped into a secret of the universe.

Dirac had started out thinking of electrons and their opposites, the "holes," as fundamental entities to be explained, but the fact that they could be created and destroyed meant that they were really evanescent particles that could be switched on and off like a flashlight. What remains as the true subject of Dirac's equation, and as the main reality of particle physics, are fields, in this case the electron field, which permeate space. Electrons and their opposites are only fleeting manifestations of this field, like snowflakes in a storm.

Analyzing this lapse, Dr. Steven Weinberg, a 1979 Nobel laureate in physics from the University of Texas, wrote, "This is often the way it is in physics. Our mistake is not that we take our theories too seriously, but that we do not take them seriously enough. It is always hard to realize that these numbers and equations we play with at our desks have something to do with the real world."

As it happens, however, Dirac's 'quantum field theory,' as it is known, must jump through the same mathematical hoops as Dirac's electron, and so his equation survives as one of the cathedrals of science. "When an equation is as successful as Dirac's, it is never simply a mistake," wrote Dr. Weinberg. Indeed, as Dr. Weinberg has pointed out in an earlier book, the mistake is often in not placing enough faith in our equations. In the late 1940's, a group of theorists at George Washington University led by Dr. George Gamow calculated that the birth of the universe in a big bang would have left space full of fiery radiation, but they failed to take the result seriously enough to mount a search for the radiation. Another group later discovered it accidentally in 1965 and won a Nobel Prize.

30. Based upon its metaphorical usage in the passage, one can make the following assumption about the bumblebee:

A. A bumblebee knows that it cannot fly, but flies nonetheless.
B. Inconsistent assumptions would add up to show that a bumblebee can fly.
C. Common assumptions about flight would tend to show that a bumblebee cannot fly.
D. A bumblebee doesn't know that it can't fly, which allows him to do so.

GO ON TO THE NEXT PAGE.

31. According to the passage, Dirac's "feat is always dragged forth as Exhibit A" (lines 31–32). The defensive context of this statement would lead one to the conclusion that:

    A. mathematics is usually considered to be reality-based.
    B. mathematicians require examples of successes to reassure themselves.
    C. Dirac was unwilling to have the 'exhibit' brought forth.
    D. mathematics often seems to have nothing to do with reality.

32. The statement that "even Einstein was a piker compared with the British theorist Paul Dirac" (lines 1-3) could lead one to the following conclusion:

    A. Einstein sought beauty in his equations.
    B. Dirac did not care for Einstein.
    C. Einstein did not care if his equations fit the experiment.
    D. Dirac felt it important to have his equations fit the experiment.

33. One source provides that, unlike applied mathematicians, pure mathematicians "see their work as an art and judge its value by the brilliance and beauty of its logic. They pay no attention to the practical application of their research." Dr. Steven Weinberg (line 52) is most likely:

    A. a pure mathematician.
    B. a physicist who loves applied mathematics.
    C. a physicist who enjoys pure mathematics.
    D. an applied mathematician.

34. The passage describes Dirac's antiparticles variously as all of the following EXCEPT:

    A. a positron
    B. a hole
    C. evanescent
    D. fields

35. The word *cathedral* (line 62) is used in the sense of:

    A. a place of worship.
    B. an enduring symbol of truth.
    C. a perpetual icon of veneration.
    D. a vessel of adoration.

GO ON TO THE NEXT PAGE.

Passage VII (Questions 36–40)

Once a charitable foundation bestows a grant of money on a chosen recipient, or "beneficiary," the foundation's main defense against misuse/waste of its grant is the individual contractual agreement between foundation and beneficiary.
5 These contracts tend to be idiosyncratic, varying with the specific purposes of the foundation and the grant; thus, they have not been the focus of much academic study.

However, scholars have identified informal non-contractual control mechanisms by which foundations
10 guard against misuse of their investments. Such mechanisms arise at three points: in the initial screening of projects, in the decision of how much funding to allocate, and in the contract between foundation and beneficiary.

Needless to say, a foundation's power over beneficiaries'
15 activities is greatest before it has committed money to them. Foundations can best protect against unsatisfactory use of their grants by awarding grants only to beneficiaries that intend to use the money for projects that the foundation encourages. Screening may be done in two ways. First,
20 foundations can issue public statements on types of programs they will, or will not, fund. This will prevent mistaken misuse by recipients, though not fraudulent abuse. Foundations may issue absolute (negative) prohibitions: for example, a clause that no money will be given for personal charity
25 or religious education. Conversely, they may affirmatively announce types of projects that they *will* fund. This latter method has obvious advantages; not only is it more helpful to applicants, it may also encourage beneficiaries who are *capable* of undertaking desired projects, but have not yet
30 done so for lack of funds, to apply.

Second, foundations can take a proactive role by working with promising applicants to propose new projects or define the goals/parameters of existing ones. A foundation exercises considerable power through its grasp of the purse
35 strings, and the manner in which it doles out its grants. This is done at the budgeting stage. Most fundamentally, a foundation can specify what types of expenses it will, or will not, reimburse. Furthermore, foundations can grant themselves more discretion, and retain more of their
40 bargaining power with beneficiaries, by disbursing only part of the total projected cost at regular intervals. This allows them to monitor a project to ensure that it has not strayed from the desired parameters, to demand correction of wayward projects through threats of withdrawal, and
45 to withhold funding from uncorrected projects. Also, this partial disbursement encourages beneficiaries to meet deadlines and disclose results.

Once the foundation has disbursed some/all of its funding and the beneficiary's project is underway, the
50 foundation may want to continue monitoring progress to prevent misuse of funds or unwanted deviations from the originally planned project. This supervision can be accomplished through several methods. First, the foundation can specify in its agreement with the beneficiary that its
55 grant is a *conditional grant* contingent on specified uses. Presumably, if the beneficiary diverts the money for other purposes, the foundation can recover the money through a lawsuit for breach of contract. An alternate approach is for the foundation to appoint monitors to work with
60 the beneficiary throughout the project. This is a common practice for venture capital "foundations" in monitoring the start-up companies that are the beneficiaries of their seed capital. There is even some evidence that this approach is sometimes used by foundations in dealing with mutual
65 funds with which they invest their endowment; their directors sometimes try to steer fund managers' investment choices toward socially oriented public corporations (for instance, ones that practice reforestation, equal opportunity employment, corporate philanthropy, etc.). However, in
70 cases in which the foundation is commissioning an impartial research report from the beneficiary, such close supervision may be seen as tainting the objectivity of the results.

There are several clever funding strategies available to incentivize recipients. *Declining grants*—in which award
75 amounts decrease annually until they are phased out—can be given to recipients who pledge to start a self-sustaining program. *Matching grants*—in which the foundation matches contributions made by the beneficiary or third parties—encourage recipients to apply for grants from other
80 philanthropic sources as well and encourage third-party contributions.

36. In the context of the passage, the word *incentivize* (line 74) means:

A. to induce recipients to distribute their funds in a nonfraudulent manner.
B. to stimulate the foundation to give more to the beneficiaries.
C. to motivate recipients to use funds as the foundation had intended.
D. to encourage beneficiaries not to mislead the foundations.

GO ON TO THE NEXT PAGE.

37. The passage suggests that public statements by foundations on what types of programs they will or will not fund are effective because:

   A. funds that are misused can be recovered through a lawsuit for breach of contract.
   B. they will prevent fraudulent abuse by recipients.
   C. they may persuade beneficiaries with less money to apply.
   D. a foundation can specify what type of funds it will, or will not, reimburse.

38. According to passage information, at what point is the foundation's control over a beneficiary's activities the greatest?

   A. When the monies can be distributed in partial disbursements
   B. Prior to the foundation committing money to the beneficiary
   C. Upon the signing of a conditional grant
   D. When a foundation can appoint a monitor to work with the beneficiary throughout the project

39. According to the passage, all of the following are *true* regarding the advantages of "partial disbursement" (line 46) of funds by the foundation EXCEPT:

   I.   allows the foundation to monitor a project to ensure that it has not strayed from the desired parameters
   II. encourages recipients to apply for grants from other philanthropic sources as well
   III. encourages beneficiaries to meet deadlines and disclose results

   A. I only
   B. II only
   C. III only
   D. I and III only

40. According to the passage, informal control mechanisms that are not contractual arise at all of the following periods EXCEPT:

   A. during the initial screening of projects.
   B. when making the decision regarding how much funding to allocate.
   C. as the foundation decides which projects to support.
   D. upon conferring a conditional grant.

STOP. IF YOU FINISH BEFORE TIME IS CALLED, CHECK YOUR WORK. YOU MAY GO BACK TO ANY QUESTION IN THIS TEST.

TEST 11

STOP.

Verbal Reasoning Test 12

Time: 60 Minutes

Questions 1–40

VERBAL REASONING

DIRECTIONS: There are seven passages in this Verbal Reasoning test. Each passage is followed by several questions. After reading a passage, select the one best answer to each question. If you are not certain of an answer, eliminate the alternatives that you know to be incorrect and then select an answer from the remaining alternatives. Indicate your selection by blackening the corresponding oval on your answer document.

Passage I (Questions 1–5)

Major record labels and some music artists complain that online web sites such as Napster, which allow music fans to download popular songs for free, take away their profitsby reducing CD sales. The record executives and band
5 members claim they deserve every cent of the value that is being siphoned off by downloaders. Meanwhile, music fans can read in the trade papers that Danny Goldberg, who parlayed a career as a hanger-on to the popular band The Doors into a record industry executive position, will not be
10 getting his five-million-dollar bonus this year; or, that rock group Metallica's drummer, Lars Ulrich, is selling off part of his collection of Old Masters paintings, from which he is supposed to reap in excess of fifteen million dollars. Fans' hearts should not be bleeding.

15 Some 10 years ago, I took a friend to see a live performance of [the heavy-metal rock band] Metallica. Even then, tickets cost $45 each, which is expensive for the ordinary working people who comprise most of their audience. Back then, Metallica's CDs cost some $15 each.
20 True fans were likely to have bought all of them. If we analyze the industry's cost structure, we find that it costs about twelve cents to produce a CD, and perhaps another five cents to re-draw the CD's covers. That's about 17 cents, total. The distributor pays about $2 to buy the CD, then
25 resells it. Once it hits the stores, it is marked up to $10–18. What happens to the money?

The recording industry universally decries CD piracy. Technically, a "pirated" CD is an unauthorized duplication of an officially released song or entire CD's song collection. The
30 pirated CD is sold illegally, usually through street vendors connected with the pirate copying operation, at much lower cost than the prices at legitimate music stores. Needless to say, no one connected with the band or its promoters sees any profit from sales of pirated CDs. Furthermore, the
35 pirates pay no taxes on their profits because their business is illegal and thus undeclared. Therefore, I cannot condone actual music piracy, which benefits no one but the pirates themselves.

A grayer area is the "boot" CD. A "boot," short for
40 "bootleg," is a recording of previously unreleased material, often from a band's earlier live performances made while on tour. It is usually created after material is lifted from the band's recording studio archives by someone connected with the band. A recent bootleg of 60's legend Bob Dylan's
45 1962 European tour (which, incidentally, features the most-professional packaging I've ever seen in a CD) shows signs of having been made by someone intimately connected with the tour; after all, who else would have had access to *every* night's board tapes? Sometimes, the bootleg is supplied by
50 a former band member who has been summarily dismissed from the group after an altercation with the other band members, or after trying to renegotiate a fairer contract with the band's record label. Typically, under the record company's standard contract, dismissed band members give
55 up their right to most of the band's profits, even if they were fired without good cause. In the case of boot CDs, it cannot be said that former band members should have *no* right to release and profit from music that they themselves created.

Also, the music industry's antipiracy crusade can
60 expect little support from fans because the industry has done little to give value to customers. CD rereleases have become record a company's license to steal. Typically, the record label reissues a band's CDs in a multi-CD boxed set, of which three-quarters of the songs are previously unreleased.
65 This is still good value for the money. But then, they release a "Best of" set for $15, with most of the same songs, plus *one* new song. So, die-hard fans basically must pay $15 to get a single new song. Popular performers like Britney Spears typically put one or two good songs on each CD and
70 surround it with filler. Not surprisingly, more and more fans are either copying their friends' CDs, or else purchasing superior-quality boots of several good songs for $5.

GO ON TO THE NEXT PAGE.

1. Which of the following suppositions is most clearly believed by the author?

   A. The recording industry's complaints about CD piracy are legitimate.
   B. Most band members make plenty of money.
   C. The recording industry's complaints about 'boot' CDs are legitimate.
   D. All reissued CDs are a poor value.

2. According to the passage, the author's primary reason for justifying individuals' copying CDs off of a website seems to be that:

   A. there is no specific law against doing this.
   B. record labels and band members make plenty of money.
   C. record label re-releases invariably contain mostly re-issued music.
   D. everybody else does it.

3. For which of the following of the author's assertions is NO support provided in the passage?

   A. CD markups are exorbitant.
   B. Fans shouldn't feel sorry for record industry executives, because they make plenty of money from the industry.
   C. Fans shouldn't feel sorry for band members, because they make plenty of money in the band.
   D. 'Boots' usually come from someone connected with the band.

4. Which of the following conclusions about the author's beliefs can be inferred from the passage?

   A. There is no real value in record company re-releases anymore.
   B. Music piracy and downloading songs for free using Napster are basically the same thing.
   C. The only difference between actual music pirates and downloading off Napster is in the selling of the CDs.
   D. Band members who sign record-company contracts should be bound by them.

5. What distinction is implied in the passage between a "pirated" CD and "bootleg" CD, respectively?

   A. no one connected with the making of the CD makes a profit, and unreleased material
   B. illegal, and illegal
   C. cannot be condoned, and should not be condoned
   D. someone connected with the band, and an officially released song

GO ON TO THE NEXT PAGE.

Passage II (Questions 6–10)

The ancient Greek historian Thucydides, a participant in, and chronicler of the *History of the Peloponnesian War*, provides valuable insight into the actual resolution of political questions in the Hellenic world, which is far
5 removed from the intellectual abstractions characteristic of Greek political philosophy.

Modern students of political thought should focus on the speeches and debates recorded by Thucydides. To say he "recorded" them is misleading. His introduction contains the
10 bizarre admission: " ... my method has been, while keeping as closely as possible to the general sense of the words that were actually used, to make the speakers say what, in my opinion, was called for by each situation." While this may disappoint modern historians, it means the contents express
15 Thucydides's own views, and as such they are valuable glimpses of ancient military/political theory.

Thucydides suggests wealth is the key to power, as when he says of the Hellenic navies, "They brought in revenue and they were the foundation of empire." We might
20 expect he is referring to mercantile trade; in fact, they were warships whose "revenues" were probably paid in plunder and tribute. Thucydides does not consider a state's wealth useful other than to expand its army, which for him is the yardstick of political power. In Thucydides's account of
25 "cyclical" empire-building, a stronger nation conquers a people and exacts tribute, then uses these spoils to expand its military, and finally finds that added soldiers must be stationed in the conquered province to suppress revolts. Thus, ancient military theory considered a strong army to
30 be an end in itself.

The purest instance of political realism in *Peloponnesian War* is the frank discussion between the Melians and invading Athenians, which is remarkable for its bluntness. In this "Melian Dialogue," the mighty Athenians
35 demand the surrender of a small and unoffending city, proclaiming: "you should try to get what it is possible for you to get, taking into consideration what we both really do think, since ... the standard of justice depends on the equality of power to compel, and, in the fact, the strong do
40 what they have the power to do and the weak accept what they have to accept."

In the ensuing debate, it becomes apparent that the two sides are really speaking of different things; the Melians maintain that, because theirs is the just cause, they
45 are destined to prevail. For example, they venture, "[W]e trust that the gods will give us fortune as good as yours, because we are standing for what is right ..." The Athenians scornfully dismiss the Melians' claim as wishful thinking, saying, "[Only] if one already has solid advantages to fall
50 back on, one can indulge in hope ... ." As for the other foundation of the Melians' hope, it is a military intervention

by the Spartans, "who are bound, if for no other reason, than for honor's sake, and because we are their kinsmen, to come to our help."

55 The outcome of the ensuing battle was exactly as predicted: the Spartans, who were distant and unresolved, offered the Melians no aid, and the small Melian army was predictably destroyed, after which the greater part of the city's population was either destroyed or enslaved by
60 Athens.

The type of warfare described by Thucydides was characterized by a successful state surrounded by subjugated enemies rather than willing allies, a circumstance that required an ever-larger army if it was to be maintained.
65 Thucydides notes that a powerful state will never be loved, as shown when he says to the Athenians, "[Because Athens is a democracy,] fear and conspiracy play no part in your daily relations ..., [so] you imagine ... the same ... is true of your allies .... [W]hat you do not realize is that your empire
70 is a tyranny exercised over subjects who do not like it and are always plotting against you ... your leadership depends on superior strength and not on any goodwill of theirs."

This system seems unconcerned with the condition of people living under it. It is never mentioned that they should
75 be content or prosperous, only obedient, nor does it seem especially important whether they are given good laws or secure lasting peace and freedom from fear; if military might is the only virtue, then a state's entire budget might well be used to expand the army and to pursue endless conquest.

6. According to the passage, when studying the works of Thucydides, one must take into account:

   A. the abstract characteristics of Greek political philosophy.
   B. Thucydides's own views.
   C. that he fabricated the statements of historical figures.
   D. the *History of the Peloponnesian War*.

GO ON TO THE NEXT PAGE.

7. Regarding the concept of Athenian democracy, Thucydides asserts that:

   A. a powerful state will never be esteemed.
   B. the Athenians were the most powerful of the nation states.
   C. the Athenians were actually living under tyranny.
   D. their existence depended upon the goodwill of their subjects.

8. Passage information indicates that if a strong nation were to begin empire-building, it would probably most benefit from:

   A. using most of its resources to expand its military.
   B. offering full citizenship to those it has conquered.
   C. destroying or enslaving those it has conquered.
   D. requiring only obedience.

9. An important relationship is suggested in the passage between:

   A. political philosophy and the Athenians.
   B. mercantile trade and power.
   C. strong armies and suppressing revolts.
   D. wealth and armies.

10. The opinion that, "[t]he purest instance of political realism in *Peloponnesian War* is the frank discussion between the Melians and invading Athenians" (lines 31–33) is *challenged* in the passage by the argument that:

    A. Thucydides did not focus on political thought.
    B. this discussion was not really "frank."
    C. the Athenians were not invading at that point.
    D. Thucydides fabricated what people said.

GO ON TO THE NEXT PAGE.

Passage III (Questions 11–16)

In examining the causes of the Chinese Ch'ing dynasty's collapse, it is crucial for historiography to avoid the generalization that the blame rests solely with the West's activities in China. It is a tempting line for Chinese and
5 Western historians alike to take, which allows Euro centrists to fuel the flames of self-importance by asserting that Western influence alone successfully changed the course of an ancient civilization. Simultaneously, Chinese nationalists can use Western imperialism as the all-explanatory factor,
10 conveniently sidestepping the embarrassing examination of how China as a polity interacted with the West. A better-balanced analysis should begin by looking at the Ch'ing-era Chinese as a national polity—a group with some unity of purpose, and a system of shared culture that held them
15 together on a national level.

Historian Jacques Gernet characterizes the dynastic China of the 1820's onward as being in "social deterioration" due to problems it inherited from the prior Ch'ien-lung emperor's lavish spending and widespread corruption. A
20 list of China's problems should also enumerate the K'ang-hsi emperor's benevolent but ill-advised decision to freeze official taxes at the 1712 level, which, when combined with the overspending of later emperors, caused the shortage of national tax revenue that held back industrialization and
25 forced dependence on foreign capital in order to build the armies necessary to repel foreign military influence. This policy, which provided fewer tax incentives to keep families small, may have contributed to the population explosion of the 18th century. Fundamentally, the Ch'ing could be said
30 to have inherited the continuation of the general problems inherited by all dynasties since the Han; in addition, there was ever-present tension between landlords and tenant farmers, which was worsened by overcrowding and exacerbated by later taxes instituted to bolster stagnant revenue.

35 Traditional historiography makes the First Opium War (1839–42) the watermark for imperialist intervention and unequal trade agreements. But the war began as an economic reaction by Great Britain against its trade deficit with the Chinese. The decision was made by
40 the British East India Company to send Indian opium, then still legal, to China. The first shipments of opium were only 28,000 pounds annually before the 1729 ban, though its effects were concentrated in Canton. This quantity of opium had minimal effect on the trade
45 deficit and could have been crushed by the authorities soon after 1729 had it not been for the collaborators within China who abetted British smugglers. The first collaborators were on the demand side—the recreational users of opium, a surprisingly large number of whom were low-
50 level government officials. Simultaneously there arose a network of Chinese pirates, smugglers, and corrupt customs inspectors who distributed the drug. The prohibition that could have wiped out the fledgling opium trade in China had

a national consensus existed, became a telling revelation of
55 the disunity and profiteering in Chinese society, both inside and outside the government.

The transition from economic imperialism to armed intervention dated from 1839, when the British sent an armed force to Canton to legalize opium. The British
60 attackers numbered only 2,400, in ships of not much more sophisticated capabilities than those that the Chinese navy had at its disposal. Exactly why the Chinese defenders were defeated is unclear. It would have been a relatively easy matter for the Ch'ing military, at full strength, to destroy the
65 British expedition. However, in later encounters, widespread theft and embezzlement among the Chinese military leaders reduced their impressive army to complete ineffectiveness. Also, vital militia units that could have reinforced the Canton defenders were withheld because government
70 ministers were more wary of the threat from arming their own people than the threat from outside attack. Few realized the snowball effect the halfhearted defeat at Canton would set in motion.

Now legalized in Canton, the trade in British opium
75 swelled until it completely reversed the trade deficit in Britain's favor. The British took much of their share of the profits back home, causing a drain of silver currency away from China [which, in turn] caused hyperinflation in the copper currency held mostly by peasants and poor urban
80 laborers. To make up for lost revenue, the Ch'ing government raised taxes, aggravating the burden on the poor.

11. The passage indicates that its author would NOT agree with which of the following statements?

A. The West actually had little to do with the Ch'ing dynasty's collapse.

B. The activities of the West were not the sole reason for the Ch'ing dynasty's collapse.

C. Many Western historians place too great an emphasis on European activities.

D. Many Chinese historians place too great an emphasis on European activities.

GO ON TO THE NEXT PAGE.

12. The author is primarily concerned with demonstrating that the causes of the Ch'ing dynasty's collapse:

    A.   began with the First Opium War (1839–42) and British armed intervention.

    B.   have been accurately described by both Western and Chinese historians.

    C.   were much more the fault of China than of any Western activities or influences.

    D.   stemmed from longstanding problems within China that were aggravated by Western activities.

13. Which of the following discoveries, if genuine, would most *weaken* the author's arguments?

    A.   The Chinese army at Canton in 1839, for various reasons, had been rendered almost completely ineffective.

    B.   The British had badly miscalculated the strength of their armed forces necessary to a successful engagement at Canton in 1839.

    C.   The Chinese naval commanders considered the number of British ships at Canton in 1839 to be inconsequential.

    D.   Many modern Chinese historians are at a loss to explain why the British were not simply destroyed at Canton in 1839.

14. Passage information indicates that which of the following statements must be true?

    A.   In 1839, the Chinese were defeated in Canton because of widespread theft and embezzlement.

    B.   Opium was legal in China in 1839.

    C.   Silver was more popular with the British because it was actually worth more than copper.

    D.   Those Chinese who were not peasants, or poor urban laborers, dealt predominantly in silver.

15. According to one historical authority on the 1729 ban of opium in China, "because no national [Chinese] consensus existed [on the ban], even a concerted effort by customs inspectors and the government was unable to stem the tide of opium into Canton." This authority would probably:

    A.   support the author's assertions fully.

    B.   approve of the author's description of the government's efforts, but disagree with the idea of a 'consensus.'

    C.   not consider the author's portrayal of customs inspectors and government officials to be accurate.

    D.   consider the author's narrative regarding this ban to be completely incorrect.

16. According to the passage, which of the following is most likely to be true about the relationship between the government and the Chinese people during the period of the First Opium War?

    A.   After the 1839 initial British invasion at Canton, the government ministers armed the Chinese people to repel the invaders.

    B.   Both the government ministers and the Chinese people dealt primarily in copper currency.

    C.   Government ministers were less worried about the British than they were about an internal revolt.

    D.   The Chinese people unsuccessfully revolted against higher government taxes.

GO ON TO THE NEXT PAGE.

Passage IV (Questions 17–22)

In the Metropolitan Museum's nineteenth-century room stands an extravagant oak armoire decorated with silver sculpture, whose central plaque shows a chariot bearing King Merovich of Gaul flanked by a group of festive
5 soldiers and musicians. His chariot is drawn by oxen, guided by an irate oxherd over the prone corpses of armored men. Unexpectedly, the Gallic king is being celebrated by Gauls and Romans alike. Ostensibly, this artwork commemorates the brilliant victory of King Merovich over Attilla the Hun
10 in 451 A.D. on the plains of Catalaunum.

History paints King Merovich's battle with Attilla in grayer strokes. The battle at Catalaunum culminated Attilla's aborted foray into Gaul in his failed bid to conquer the remnants of the Western Roman Empire The Roman army
15 he faced a there was a pale shadow of its former glory, bled by embezzlement, neglect, and years of paying tribute. It was forced into an unlikely alliance with its bitter enemies, the Visigoth tribesmen of Gaul, for mutual defense. On the Catalaunian Plains, Attilla's force of a quarter million
20 faced battle with a roughly equal army. In the fray, strategy disintegrated into confused and desperate infighting that ended only when both sides were forced to separate by exhaustion and impending nightfall. They camped within easy attack range of each other, but neither army had strength
25 enough to resume the attack. With sunrise came the daunting realization of the full extent of casualties; as accounts came in, they showed fully 100,000 dead, with roughly equal losses on each side. Among them was the Visigoth king, pulled dead from the wreckage. Fearing desertion by their
30 allies, the Roman armies retreated. Attilla, dismayed by his losses, waited long enough to watch the Romans leave, then himself called a retreat. He returned home, where he died planning his next invasion.

History rarely remembers King Merovich, who was
35 no more than a minor commander in the battle. It is Attilla who is renowned, though historiography is divided. Some portray him as a brutal fighter incapable of administering the territories he had seized, or controlling his hordes. Others view him as an ambitious underdog, an orphan prince who,
40 while a hostage in Rome, wisely used his time to study the weaknesses of the Romans, a leader who maintained and encouraged a Spartan lifestyle in the hope that his people would never experience the decadence of the late Romans, but would be free to enjoy greater social mobility, religious
45 tolerance, and gender equality than was possible in Rome.

The historical King Merovich was one of many leaders among the Gallic Visigoth tribesmen who collectively ruled an area that would later encompass France.

Not coincidentally, the armoire's sponsor, Charles-
50 Guillaume Diehl, was a Frenchman. Neither is it coincidental that the work was commissioned during the 19th century, which for France was a time of rebuilding and reassessment. Just as their capital, Paris, was redesigned to more modern specifications, the French reworked their conception of
55 national identity in a period of renewed French nationalism. Diehl chose the Huns, whose brutality was mostly proverbial, to represent the forces of barbarism over which French civilization triumphed. The vision of France as the center of "civilized" civilization, is a long-standing national myth
60 among the French. The artwork produced in that period shows how history can be as much a blank canvas for the historian as wood and metal can be for the artist.

17. According to the passage, "With sunrise, came the daunting realization of the full extent of casualties; as accounts came in, they showed fully 100,000 dead" (lines 25–27). Roughly how many men did Attilla have left in his army?

   A. 250,000
   B. 200,000
   C. 150,000
   D. 50,000

GO ON TO THE NEXT PAGE.

18. Which of the following statements is the most reasonable conclusion that can be drawn from the author's description of the battle at Catalaunum?

    A. The Huns were stalemated.
    B. King Merovich was the victor.
    C. Attilla was the victor.
    D. The Gauls stalemated the Romans.

19. The passage states, "Ostensibly, this artwork commemorates the brilliant victory of King Merovich over Attilla the Hun in 451 A.D., on the plains of Catalaunum" (lines 8–10). According to the author, this rendition of the battle would probably have resulted from:

    A. the fact that Merovich was the only surviving Visigoth king.
    B. a renewed interest in this time period and that battle.
    C. Roman attempts to rewrite the battle.
    D. French efforts to rewrite history.

20. The contention that "[t]he artwork produced in that period shows how history can be as much a blank canvas for the historian as wood and metal can be for the artist" (lines 60–62) can most justifiably be interpreted as support for the idea that:

    A. artists often more accurately illustrate on blank canvas than with wood and metal.
    B. historians should restrict their portrayals to books.
    C. historians must be free to recreate history as they see it.
    D. artists are not restricted to realistic portrayals of their subjects.

21. On the basis of the passage, one may assume that from the perspective of Attilla, Roman society was characterized by:

    A. equality between men and women.
    B. social stratification.
    C. great wealth.
    D. vast empires.

22. According to the passage, which of the following statements is true about the alliances in 451 A.D. on the plains of Catalaunum?

    A. The Spartans and the Romans were led by King Merovich against the Huns.
    B. In an unusual arrangement, the Romans had allied themselves with their former enemies, the Gauls.
    C. The Visigoth tribesman had allied themselves with the Romans in order to attack the Huns.
    D. The Gauls and the Visigoth tribesman had allied themselves for mutual defense against the Huns.

GO ON TO THE NEXT PAGE.

Passage V (Questions 23–28)

In this country, without regard to sentencing, the actual administration of the death penalty has experienced a tremendous resurgence. There are now more people, not only on death row, but actually being put to death, than at
5 any other time in the past forty years. Perhaps this is due to the seemingly more humane method of lethal injection as opposed to Old Sparky, which gained some further, recent notoriety from the movie *The Green Mile*. However, advances in DNA technology and its use in forensics as an
10 investigate tool have cast a spotlight on the inevitability of the death penalty as an irrevocable act from which there is no appeal.

From a purely economic standpoint, the costs of the death penalty are not intuitive. It would seem that the person
15 has been executed and that is the end of it. However, that less-than-inevitable outcome takes years to achieve. Prior to the execution, the appeals processes, which the accused are entitled to and which include legal representation, prisoner housing, and court costs, among other things, are
20 horrendous. Is the answer then to limit these processes?

It is argued by many that the death penalty is discriminatory and is often used disproportionately against the poor, minorities, and members of particular racial, ethnic, and religious communities. It is further argued that it is
25 imposed and carried out arbitrarily. From a purely statistical standpoint, it is difficult to ascertain if these arguments are relevant. Yet it is irrefutable that for a disenfranchised individual who cannot afford his own attorney, the likelihood that he will obtain good representation and counsel at this
30 critical first trial is slim. Many of the appeals now pending in death penalty cases revolve around the inadequacy of defendants' public-appointed attorneys who had not bothered to attempt to obtain further exculpatory evidence, were inexperienced in the law at hand, or were simply semi-
35 conscious throughout the proceedings. Moreover, it is this first court proceeding and trial upon which all subsequent appeals will be based. The death penalty entails the risk of judicial errors, which, unlike imprisonment, can never be corrected.

40 It is difficult to know if the innocent have been put to death by the state for crimes that they did not commit. It is easy to deny that innocent men are charged with crimes and then forced to serve their sentences. Yet this perspective is becoming increasingly naïve in the face of the fact that
45 several individuals who were awaiting executions on death row have been freed recently—not simply removed from death row to serve out less punitive sentences, but actually freed; a tacit acknowledgement that they had not actually committed the heinous crimes of which they had been
50 accused. Of course, protestations of O.J. Simpson and the mob bosses aside, a finding of "not guilty" or the inability of the state to pursue a prosecution does not mean that the accused has been "proven innocent." Nevertheless, in many of the instances in which the condemned have walked free,
55 the reason is not simply because their guilt could not be proven beyond a reasonable doubt, but that someone else had been determined to have commited the crime; these people who had been condemned to death had been found not to have committed the crime at all.

60 Our system of justice was not designed so that we let no guilty man go free. We are innocent until proven guilty precisely to ensure that no innocent man is punished for a crime that he did not commit. The death penalty legitimizes an irreversible act of violence by the state, and it will
65 inevitably claim innocent victims. As long as human justice remains fallible, the risk of executing the innocent can never be eliminated.

23. According to the passage, when a person is found "not guilty," one must take into account:

    A. that he was accused in the first place.
    B. that he has not been "proven innocent."
    C. that he may still have committed the crime.
    D. that he has been "proven innocent."

GO ON TO THE NEXT PAGE.

24. The passage implies that "our system of justice" should:

   A. ensure that no guilty man go free.
   B. eliminate costly appeals for those facing death.
   C. ensure that all death sentences are carried out swiftly.
   D. ensure that mistakes are not made that cannot be rectified.

25. On the sole basis of the passage, determine which of the following acts the author would most want to see forbidden by international law, regardless of the heinousness of the offense.

   A. Using private property for state purposes
   B. Placing certain restrictions on prosecution investigators in death penalty cases
   C. Suspending appeals in death penalty cases
   D. Torturing prisoners facing the death penalty

26. Which of the following statements most strongly *challenges* one of the assertions made in the passage?

   A. One only has to watch an execution to see that lethal injection is more humane than Old Sparky.
   B. Death row is actually very different from how it is depicted in the movie *The Green Mile*.
   C. Our system of justice ensures that society is protected from those who commit violent crimes.
   D. The death penalty saves money in the long run.

27. Which of the following conclusions about the death penalty can be inferred from the passage?

   A. It is possible that people have been put to death for crimes they did not commit.
   B. It is unlikely that people have been put to death for crimes they did not commit.
   C. Our system of justice ensures that no innocent people are convicted.
   D. Our system of justice ensures that no guilty people go free.

28. With regard to our present system of justice, the author most clearly believes that:

   A. justice is blind.
   B. a minority person is at a disadvantage.
   C. a poor person is at a disadvantage.
   D. DNA testing will always determine innocence.

GO ON TO THE NEXT PAGE.

Passage VI (Questions 29–34)

Yamamoto, the admiral of the Japanese Pacific fleet, spoke prophetically when, after the Japanese attack on Pearl Harbor, he said Japan had "awakened a sleeping giant." At the same time, Iwakuro Hideo, a Japanese colonel,
5 calculated the advantage in wartime production to be ten-to-one in favor of the United States. However, Pearl Harbor was such a decisive victory that the Japanese held a significant material advantage until June of 1942 at the Battle of Midway. Carriers being the new dominant weapon in open-
10 sea warfare, Japan had five in the central Pacific while the United States had only three, one of which had been hastily repaired after Pearl Harbor. Yamamoto understood that if Japan were to have any chance of defeating the United States, she needed to exploit this edge in carriers early on. Thus,
15 although Japan's tactical objective was to capture the island of Midway, this was simply a ploy to bring the remaining enemy carriers to battle at a numerical disadvantage. Japan's strategic, and more important, objective was to put these carriers out of action, leaving her in undisputed control of
20 the entire Pacific. Unfortunately, the Japanese lost sight of this goal and, as a result, lost their advantage in the Pacific permanently.

The first sign of ambiguity in Japanese strategy appeared in their plan of attack against Midway. At Pearl
25 Harbor, they had converged their total available forces onto a single point and achieved a decisive victory; at Midway, instead of using the same tactics, they divided their force, holding a large group in reserve too far from the battle to be of any use. Although this reserve force did have tactical
30 value (it served to protect Japanese invasion forces in the Aleutians from Allied reinforcements), its remote position eliminated its threat to the American carriers. In their tactical positioning of the reserves, the Japanese overlooked the strategic implications.

35 In fact, given the goal of destroying the carriers, the invasion of the Aleutians was a waste of resources. The islands were of little strategic value, and both the invading force and the previously mentioned reserve force could have been concentrated against the U.S. carriers. The Midway
40 attack was meant to bring the carriers to battle; a feint at the Aleutians could only have caused the carriers to go north, taking them away from the Japanese main strength. The Aleutian attack was inspired by the tactical objective of taking Midway, but it actually worked against the strategic
45 objective of sinking the carriers.

The last indication that the Japanese had lost their focus was Nagumo's decision to rearm his planes with bombs to attack Midway. Bombs were less effective against the carriers than the torpedoes with which the planes had
50 been previously armed. Clearly, if the main objective was to sink the carriers, the act of rearming the planes with bombs diminished the Japanese ability to do so. However, Nagumo chose to soften Midway for the invasion force and felt that this called for the rearming of the planes. This decision
55 alone may have saved the carriers. Once again, the strategic objective was sacrificed for the less important tactical objective.

The battle at Midway was more closely contested than the results indicate. In *The Price of Admiralty* John Keagan
60 talks about a crucial five minutes in which the battle was lost. In such a closely fought battle, any small difference in command decisions might have drastically changed the outcome. Clearly, if the Japanese had maintained their focus on the sinking of the carriers, they could not have lost.

29. In order to distinguish the nature of the Japanese loss at Midway, the author of the passage draws a distinction between:

    I.   the Aleutian Islands and Pearl Harbor.
    II. planes and aircraft carriers.
    III. strategic and tactical objectives.

    A. I only
    B. II only
    C. III only
    D. I, II, and III

TEST 12

GO ON TO THE NEXT PAGE.

30. From the Japanese perspective, an important lesson of war implied in the passage is:

    A.   never split available forces.
    B.   a reserve force has little tactical value.
    C.   position reserve forces to protect against reinforcements.
    D.   position reserve forces closer to the battle.

31. What distinction is implied in the passage between tactical and strategic, respectively?

    A.   long term, short term
    B.   more important, less important
    C.   small scale, large scale
    D.   Pearl Harbor, Midway

32. Suppose it is discovered that Yamamoto wanted the American carrier forces split at Midway in order to ensure that Nagumo's advantage in carrier strength was overwhelming. Does this discovery support the author's argument?

    A.   Yes. The Aleutian invasion would have accomplished this.
    B.   Yes. This would have enhanced chances of Nagumo's victory.
    C.   No. The author asserts that a feint at the Aleutians was a poor decision.
    D.   No. Nagumo still should not have been using bombs.

33. Passage information indicates that which of the following statements must be true?

    A.   Strategic objectives should remain within the confines of the overall tactical plan.
    B.   Tactical objectives must remain subordinate to the strategic plan.
    C.   The Japanese strategic plan was flawed.
    D.   If the Japanese had destroyed the American carriers at Midway, they might well have won the war.

34. According to the passage, all of the following are true about Nagumo's decision to rearm his airplanes with bombs (lines 46-57) EXCEPT:

    A.   This decision may have saved the American aircraft carriers from destruction.
    B.   This was an example of a tactical decision taking precedence over the strategic plan.
    C.   Nagumo seemed to be more concerned about the welfare of his Midway invasion forces.
    D.   This tactic had been used successfully at Pearl Harbor.

TEST 12

GO ON TO THE NEXT PAGE.

Passage VII (Questions 35–40)

The many and oft-noted psychological differences between men and women may have their source in evolved divisions of labor. We must remember that humankind had existed in its primitive, prehistoric state for millions of years
5 before the period of recorded civilization, which has lasted a mere 3,000 years. Thus, most of human evolution occurred during the prehistoric period, in response to the prevailing conditions of that time. While the responses that evolved during this vast but influential period are often startlingly
10 inapplicable to the recently modernized world—a world of birth control, automation, and more equal earning capacity—they persist, a testament to the durability of evolutionary influences.

For most of (pre-agricultural) prehistory, men assumed
15 the role of "hunter." This role was largely predetermined due to their greater height, reach, lung capacity, muscle mass, and strength. Their culture evolved to revolve around the hunt—physical accomplishment, strength, visible achievement (capturing the animal), and violence.
20 Women, with their lesser physical strength and childbearing responsibilities, evolved as caretakers of the young, and later, with postsexual pair bonding, as "wives" or domestic partners.

This "role" is today visible in each sex's social aims.
25 Men's conversations tend to focus on concrete goals, their status within the "tribal" hierarchy, "winning" at various tasks, and competitive sports. Linguistic studies show men aspire to qualities like "bold," "capable," "dominant," and "admired." Women's conversations tend to revolve
30 much more around their romantic relationships, children, promoting communication, and ensuring harmony in and outside the family. Their desired qualities tend to be described as "generous," "attractive," "friendly," and "giving." Both sexes' divergent sexual preferences can also
35 be understood as a function of their evolution. The biological basis of the sex drive is to propagate the individual's genes to maximize the number, quality, and/or survival probability of their offspring. To that end, men evolved as opportunistic, fast, and polygamous, with a high sex drive and a desire
40 for intercourse with numerous different women. For the male, whose reproductive "aim" was largely accomplished after several sessions of sex (at least, in the millennia before effective birth control), opportunistic sex with many women was the most efficient method of spreading his genetic
45 material, maximizing the chance that at least some of those matings would yield children who would similarly survive long enough to reproduce. In order to achieve this, the main quality sought by men in women was youth, beauty, and easy availability; youth, in fact, was the main predictor that
50 the woman would be able to give birth to a healthy baby.

Needless to say, women evolved a different set of desires. For the woman, sex was likely to become a
long-term investment, which would render her unable to provide for herself for some portion of nine months, and
55 then require many additional resources to ensure that the child would have the food and shelter needed to survive infancy. Thus, women tended to analyze potential sex partners as potential newborns' caretakers, and thus valued commitment, emotional connection, status, and material
60 resources in a mate, much more than transient good looks and easy availability. Similarly, women desired pair bonding (later institutionalized as marriage) and were conditioned to seek a long-term sexual bond with one male, because such a bonding would increase the chances that the male would
65 continue to provide resources for the woman and child over the long term.

35. The claim that "[w]e must remember that humankind had existed in its primitive, prehistoric state for millions of years before the period of recorded civilization, which has lasted a mere 3,000 years" (lines 3–6) necessitates which of the following conclusions?

A. Most of humankind's responses evolved during prehistory.
B. Most of humankind's responses evolved during the last 3,000 years.
C. Before humans developed the ability to record, there was no civilization.
D. Writing heralded the end of prehistory.

36. The author claims that in order to maximize the chances that his children would survive and then reproduce themselves, "the main quality sought by men in women was youth, beauty, and easy availability" (lines 47–49). The support offered for this conclusion is:

   A. strong; the passage indicates that beauty would not help his female children reproduce.
   B. strong; the passage indicates that beauty would help his male children reproduce.
   C. weak; there is no indication that beauty would help his male children reproduce.
   D. weak; there is no indication that beauty would help his female children reproduce.

37. The author's argument that men's culture evolved to focus around the hunt is most *weakened* by which idea that is implicit in the passage?

   A. This had to have occurred within a relatively short time.
   B. Women's culture also included hunters.
   C. Women were not as physically capable of hunting as men.
   D. This had to have occurred prior to agriculture.

38. Taking into consideration passage information on male desires, the claim that "women desired pair bonding (later institutionalized as marriage), and were conditioned to seek a long-term sexual bond with one male" (lines 60–62) necessitates which of the following conclusions?

   A. Men probably ensured that divorce was an option.
   B. Men would stay married just long enough to inseminate the women.
   C. Marriage was developed and promoted by women.
   D. Women and men evolved in their desires for marriage.

39. An unstated assumption in the author's discussion of humankind's evolution is that:

   A. it was predominantly determined by women.
   B. it has been outstripped by civilization.
   C. the majority of this evolution took place over a period of 3,000 years.
   D. it was predominantly determined by men.

40. Suppose it could be established that many, many women and men do *not* exhibit the tendencies described in the passage. The author of the passage would be most likely to respond to this information by:

   A. claiming that they had "adapted" to their more modern surroundings.
   B. arguing that, likely, this supposition was flawed.
   C. explaining that his arguments were obviously generalizations.
   D. describing evidentiary research that backs his claim.

STOP. IF YOU FINISH BEFORE TIME IS CALLED, CHECK YOUR WORK. YOU MAY GO BACK TO ANY QUESTION IN THIS TEST.

STOP.

Verbal Reasoning Test 13
Time: 60 Minutes
Questions 1–40

VERBAL REASONING

DIRECTIONS: There are seven passages in this Verbal Reasoning test. Each passage is followed by several questions. After reading a passage, select the one best answer to each question. If you are not certain of an answer, eliminate the alternatives that you know to be incorrect and then select an answer from the remaining alternatives. Indicate your selection by blackening the corresponding oval on your answer document.

Passage I (Questions 1–5)

Philosophers Francis Bacon and René Descartes both proposed new philosophical systems for acquiring scientific knowledge, as they were impelled by the belief that existing methods were not systematic enough in
5 filtering out falsehoods, which contaminated the body of commonly accepted knowledge with many misconceptions and misapplied half-truths.

Bacon introduces his "New Organon" by saying the "entire work of understanding [must] be commenced
10 afresh" by setting out a more rigid system of gradual degrees of understanding, with sense perception, aided by observational equipment, as the only feasible means of acquiring information. To reduce subjective-reasoning error, he rejects all conclusions based on pure logic. Thus,
15 he denies the importance of intellect, allowing anyone with senses to enter the search for truth on a level field. He notes that errors are frequently propagated through imprecise language and seems to call for a standard technical vocabulary. The aim of science, he says, should be practical
20 application of discoveries so "that human life be endowed with new … powers," and having opened up science for the masses, he entreats them to unite with him in a search for a better life for mankind through science.

Descartes is even more ambitious; he expounds
25 a system that generates pure, incontrovertible truth by rejecting anything that is in doubt. His necessary first principle is that, in order to doubt, there must be a doubter, so that each person may be assured of the definite existence of that part of him that thinks, which is his essence or "soul."
30 Since the senses can deceive, their evidence is rejected, and reason (including abstract mathematical truths) becomes the sole tool for generating information. Descartes then uses his method to prove that God must exist, to impart true thoughts to the thinker where none had previously existed.

35 While both authors' theories suggest nihilism, neither is willing to call for the rejection of *all* previous knowledge. Bacon blasts ancient philosophers as superstitious "spiders" who spun tangled fantasies, and frequently attacks theologians for perverting and hindering science, yet he
40 does not call for the abolition of philosophy or religion, but only for their respectful separation from natural science. To avoid alienating influential academics and clerics, he reluctantly says that classical philosophers were intelligent though misguided men, and through their philosophy may
45 be useful for "winning assent" (i.e., persuasion), he calls it a lesser science, with the strong implication that it wins assent through falsehood and obfuscation.

Likewise, Descartes, aware of the example of Galileo and eager to prevent Rome from sinning twice against
50 science, goes out of his way to appease churchgoers. In "Discourse," he cautions against discarding all knowledge through the metaphor of demolishing a home to rebuild a better one, yet in the interim being left without any place to live. He gives four trite maxims, one of them being to follow
55 the laws of God—and the Church—before proving that God exists. Once he presents his proof, it is obvious that it rests on faith, and should have been rejected on these grounds. The role he assigns to God—the giver of knowledge, to the exclusion of all else—fails to establish God's omnipotence
60 (since God has no power over the existence of the thinker), and it would seem that God could not even choose to impart false knowledge, since that would compromise God's goodness, in addition to his power.

Descartes again violates his strict system by allowing
65 for the existence of the physical body merely because it *seems* more real to his senses than other bodies do; he is unable to prove, by reason, that it necessarily must exist.

GO ON TO THE NEXT PAGE.

TEST 13

1. According to the passage, Francis Bacon believed in "setting out a more rigid system of gradual degrees of understanding, with sense perception, aided by observational equipment, as the only feasible means of acquiring information" (lines 10–13). This technique could most reasonably be *contrasted* with:

   A. pure discernment.
   B. practical testing.
   C. experimentation.
   D. subjective reasoning.

2. Which one of the following most closely describes the author's characterization of Bacon's and Descartes's attitude toward the Church, respectively?

   A. Criticism while avoiding alienation, avoidance of conflict
   B. Criticism, careful criticism while avoiding alienation
   C. Avoidance of conflict, avoidance of conflict
   D. Blunt criticism and rejection, avoidance of conflict

3. According to the passage, which of the following could be an example of Bacon disagreeing with Descartes?

   A. The evidence of the senses must be rejected unless aided by observational equipment.
   B. Information cannot be generated by reason.
   C. God does not exist.
   D. There is no way of knowing if our physical bodies actually exist.

4. According to the passage, Francis Bacon "rejected pure logic" and believed that it was possible for "anyone with senses to enter the search for truth on a level field" (lines 14–16). This concept is most *discrepant* with Bacon's specific statement regarding which of the following?

   A. the Church
   B. God
   C. classical philosophers
   D. ancient philosophers

5. According to the passage, Descartes's "proof" of the existence of God "rests on faith, and should have been rejected on these grounds" (lines 56–57). This conclusion of the author's can best be supported from the passage information that:

   A. Descartes fails to establish God's omnipotence.
   B. the senses can deceive.
   C. shows that Descartes goes out of his way to appease churchgoers.
   D. indicates that Descartes did not believe faith could generate information.

GO ON TO THE NEXT PAGE.

TEST 13

Passage II (Questions 6–11)

Tanning is a simple but necessary process for prolonging the usefulness of an animal's skin by turning it into leather. Prior to the advent of weaving and creating cloth, tanning was critical to the production of clothing,
5 housing, tools, and other necessities for the survival of hunter-gatherer societies.

Hides and skins may be tanned with the hair on or off depending on what their eventual use will be. The essential step common to all tanned hides is that, after
10 being removed from the animal and having undergone some cleaning and fleshing, they then undergo a process that removes the proteins from the hide. This is accomplished by the application of an acid. Upon completion of the tanning process, the acid is neutralized and washed from the
15 skin, which is now considered leather. The leather is then "broken," or softened, and ready to be manufactured into its final form.

Tanning itself may be subcategorized into two methods. chemical or vegetable tanning. The resultant
20 characteristics of the leather obtained will differ depending upon the method used. Chemical tanning, also known as "chrome tanning," which has become the modern industry standard, is very quick and produces a consistently high quality leather. Because this method is relatively swift, there
25 is little chance that the hair on a skin will "slip," or come off, and it is used for all furs. It is also used for hides that are destined to become furniture coverings, and other leathers that will not be exposed to water. The resultant hides, furs, and skins are white and must be dyed if another color or a
30 more natural color is desired. The American Indian method of brain tanning is actually a chemical tanning process in which the qualities of water-resistance and color are added later through slow smoking over a low-burning fire.

Vegetable tanning is a much slower process suitable
35 only for skins and hides that will eventually be hairless. Usually, the hair is removed from the skins prior to the vegetable tanning process. A strong base, such as lye, wood ashes, or lime is applied to the skin until the hair comes away easily. Vegetable tanning, using tannic acid, or gallotannic
40 acid from oak, walnut, or sumac leaves and husks, is actually where the term "tanning" derived from. However, any plant or vegetable that is high in acid can be used. Legumes such as alfalfa are particularly suitable for this sort of tanning. Unlike chemically tanned skins, vegetable-tanned skins
45 assume the soft natural color of the plant used for the tanning. Skins tanned using this method can be "tooled" and decorated with impressions, and indentations can be made in the leather itself. Vegetable-tanned leather is used in saddles and bridles because of its natural abilities to remain flexible
50 and malleable after repeated contact with water.

Freshly tanned leather must go through many additional steps in order to be useful. Even the thickness of the leather may have to be reduced depending on what it will be used for. First, though, the leather must be "broken." This involves
55 physically stretching, oiling, and slowly drying the freshly tanned wet leather. As the water leaves the skin, warmed neatsfoot oil, made from the boiled hooves of cattle, is generously applied to the leather and rubbed in. When the leather is but damp, it is then drawn repeatedly in a vigorous
60 fashion over a dull edge of some sort. This action is similar to that of buffing a shoe and is physically quite rigorous and taxing. It is at this point that the home tanner begins to appreciate the price that he pays for fine leather. Care must be taken that only the "bottom grain" of the leather,
65 and not the fine outer surface is drawn against the edge, or deep scratching may result. The piece is constantly rotated in order for the stretching to take place over the entire skin from all directions. This breaking will, over time, soften the leather and break down its fibers.

6. According to the passage, water-resistance with respect to skins that have been tanned in some fashion is characteristic of:

    I.   chrome tanning.
    II. vegetable tanning.
    III. smoking.

A. I only
B. II only
C. II and III only
D. I, II, and III

GO ON TO THE NEXT PAGE.

7. On the basis of the passage, it is reasonable to conclude that the term *top grain*, when used to describe leather, refers to:

   A. the outer surface of the animal's skin.
   B. the finest leather.
   C. the inner surface of the animal's skin.
   D. the least desirable leather.

8. An important comparison is made in the passage between:

   A. tooling and dyeing.
   B. dyeing and coloration achieved through tanning.
   C. clothing and tools.
   D. lye and wood ashes.

9. The author suggests that the difficulty of tanning leather at home results from:

   A. the necessity of reducing the leather's thickness.
   B. the tendency of the hair to "slip."
   C. obtaining the necessary materials.
   D. softening the leather.

10. According to information in the passage, the fastest way to "remove the proteins from the hide" (line 12) would be to:

    A. apply a very strong base.
    B. first remove the hair.
    C. chrome tan the skin.
    D. apply very concentrated legumes.

11. Suppose that "prior to the advent of weaving and creating cloth," the hunter-gatherers were to find themselves in a lush prairie environment, but one that was devoid of trees. In order to make leather, the author's ideas suggest that they should:

    A. tan using oak, walnut, or sumac leaves.
    B. gather alfalfa or other legumes.
    C. use wood ashes or lime.
    D. first de-hair the skins with the animal's brains.

GO ON TO THE NEXT PAGE.

TEST 13

Passage III (Questions 12–16)

Throughout history, various types of finishes have been used for preserving and protecting wood furniture while maintaining or enhancing the beauty of the wood itself. This has met with varying degrees of success and
5 has evolved to a large degree based upon the availability of the finishing materials themselves, not only geographically, but also through time as new discoveries have occurred. That fine bare wood is subject to moisture absorption and staining and, therefore, should be protected, there is no
10 doubt. However, the myth that the older furniture makers knew best has been perpetuated by ignorance regarding the materials used in these finishes and what wood finishes actually do, in and on the wood itself.

Wood finishes are in fact wood "coverings." What they
15 do not do, despite the promotions of manufacturers and the yearnings of consumers, is "penetrate" the wood. Only in the softest of woods, such as pine, and the oiliest nondrying finishes is there any discernible penetration of the wood itself. Even in this instance, penetration of the wood is negligible
20 and neither pine nor nondrying oil finishes are suitable for fine furniture. By contrast, commonly and traditionally used hardwoods, such as black cherry, mahogany, and oak, are very dense. Cross-sectional analysis of any commonly used finish such as a "penetrating" Danish oil will reveal
25 the finish to be only molecules thick. Moreover, unless this "oil" is allowed to generously soak into the 'end-grain' of the board, resulting in predictable darkening in this area, there is no discernible penetration of the wood itself.

One of the most common wood finishes is simply paint.
30 Paint is immediately recognizable as a wood "covering" and commonly referred to as a "coat" of paint. It is actually one of the most effective at the extreme end of the spectrum of finishes that protect wood. The layer of paint upon and adhering to the wood may be made as thick as required.
35 This coating then absorbs glancing blows, inhibits moisture, and protects the underlying wood from heat and sunlight. What it does not do is allow the natural beauty of the wood itself to be seen and felt. This can be either a boon or a bane depending on the desires of the manufacturer. A beautiful
40 cabinet may be built of wood that is ugly and filled with knots. The coating of paint itself provides the aesthetic appeal based upon its hue. However, any antique collector can regale the listener with stories of beautiful oak, cherry, or mahogany pieces hidden for years under coatings of
45 paint. In this instance, the choice of paint as a covering or finish is clearly inappropriate.

One of the older traditional coatings is shellac. Shellac is composed of the residue or resin left by the tiny lac insect. In a fashion similar to paint, shellac forms a protective
50 coating over wood. Unlike paint, shellac is transparent, allowing one to admire the characteristic swirls and patterns of the wood grain. In a more modern era, when polyurethane

coatings and finishes are available, shellac has received a reputation for fragility. Though it is true that alcohol will
55 penetrate and degrade this finish, and that water left on its surface may form white rings, shellac is rather easy to apply and actually does provide good protection, taking into account what it can and cannot do. Additionally, those same characteristics of solvency that have led to a common
60 consideration that shellac is too fragile, lend themselves to relatively easy repairs of a marred surface. A scratched or cracked polyurethane surface, which is impervious to solvents, must be physically reduced and then rebuilt, while the same situation in a shellac finish may be fixed rather
65 quickly through an alcohol solvent or the addition of more shellac.

12. The passage implies that wood finishes are MORE effective when they:

    A. protect from moisture and beautify that which is covered.
    B. inhibit moisture, protect that which is covered, and remain impervious to solvents.
    C. beautify the underlying wood, protect from moisture, and penetrate to some degree.
    D. inhibit moisture, allow for easy repairs to that which is covered, and remain transparent.

GO ON TO THE NEXT PAGE.

TEST 13

13. The passage suggests that people generally believe that a wood finish will actually penetrate the wood, and that this belief derives from the fact that:

    A.   the finish appears to penetrate.
    B.   consumers promote this idea.
    C.   this idea is actually advertised.
    D.   there exists a "myth that the older furniture makers knew best."

14. According to the passage, any actual penetration that is going to occur is predominantly:

    A.   going to be only one molecule thick.
    B.   from an oily nondrying finish left to soak too long on oak or cherry.
    C.   at the 'end-grain' of the piece.
    D.   the promotions of the manufacturer.

15. The central thesis of the passage is that:

    A.   wood finishes actually coat and protect the wood.
    B.   it is a myth that the older furniture makers knew best.
    C.   wood finishes penetrate very little.
    D.   paint is still the best.

16. According to the passage, which of the following wood finishes is/are a good choice for a wood surface that will be exposed to an outdoor environment?

    I.   shellac
    II.   polyurethane
    III.   paint

    A.   II only
    B.   III only
    C.   I and III only
    D.   II and III only

GO ON TO THE NEXT PAGE.

Passage IV (Questions 17–21)

An examination of the causes and aftermath of China's T'ai-P'ing Rebellion might lead historians to appreciate the cyclical nature of history; this type of revolt has clearly happened before in China. What is apparent is its continuity
5 with previous religious uprisings. The messiah this time, Hung Hsiu-ch'uan, recruited his followers from the traditional malcontents of Chinese society: the overtaxed peasantry, resentful of the growing gap between landlords and tenant farmers; the newly unemployed urban shippers
10 and other laborers; and ethnic minorities like the Hakka and the aborigines, who resented encroachment on their land and culture. These groups, understandably enough, were the likely suspects to be behind a revolt, such as the previous Yellow Turban uprising. The form of the revolt—a
15 utopian-minded peasant insurrection led by a secret society incorporating Buddhist and Taoist views and headed by a leader who ruled as an incarnation of a god—has been seen in China before. It is true that there was a Western influence on the ideology, which was obviously quasiChristian, but
20 there are few indications to suggest that the uprising was in any way planned or even desired by foreign powers. Hung Hsiu-ch'uan's religious advisor, the American priest Roberts, does not seem to have been anything of a provocateur for foreign nations, especially since these same powers rejected
25 the T'ai-P'ing regime's diplomatic overtures and even sent a token military force to aid China's Ch'ing government in putting down the revolt, at great cost to the near-bankrupt dynasty.

Thus, the forces that reduced the last Chinese dynasty to
30 virtual ineffectiveness were internal forces of dissatisfaction with Chinese society. This most painful shock came not from abroad, but from within.

Of course, the economic imperialism of the West, often in the form of oppressive indemnities and forced
35 trade concessions backed by military threats, was an ever increasing drain on the Ch'ing government's revenues, one which held back its best efforts at regaining control of the finances and politics of China.

Yet despite the seriousness of foreign encroachments
40 (especially after imperialist nations began seizing portions of China's land in the 1860's), it should be remembered that such usurpations were only possible because central authority in China had been rendered so weak by internal dissention. The deep-rooted nature of that dissent was
45 visible later, when neither the fall of the Ch'ing nor the cutbacks of Western encroachment did anything to stop civil strife in China; in fact, factional hostility continued through the 1910's among the warlords, and then intensified in the struggle between the nationalist Kuomintang regime
50 and the Communist rebels at a time when a socially united China might have realized great achievements in peacefully rebuilding the damage done to its nation.

The opportunity costs of China's social disunity on the eve of dynastic collapse did not escape the leading
55 intellectuals, many of whom, in fact, saw introspection and internal reform as the necessary first step for China in battling foreign imperialism. Wei Yuan angrily proclaimed, "Away with the nurturing of private evils and the tolerating of private gain at the expense of the public interest! Then the
60 minds of men will be aroused from their ignorant lethargy," and men like Ch'u Ch'eng-po wrote of the uselessness of technological advancement without an effort to eliminate the corruption that in fact rendered these attempts ineffective, saying, "If the proposals had been carried out gradually and
65 persistently, China would have long ago become invincible. But these far-reaching plans failed because we only put up an ostentatious facade behind which were concealed the avarice and selfishness [of the officials]."

Unfortunately for China, the traditionally aloof
70 intellectuals' calls for unity and morality went unheard among the people, paving the way for further humiliation of China by the foreign powers.

17. According to the passage, which of the following is most likely to be true about the relationship between Wei Yuan and the followers of Hung Hsiu-ch'uan?

A. They would have agreed with him.
B. He felt that public interest was sacrificed for technological advancement.
C. He felt that they were being selfish.
D. They believed he was a god.

GO ON TO THE NEXT PAGE.

18. According to the passage, the question of whether or not the rebellion was purposefully aided by the West is best shown by analysis of the:

   A. nationalist Kuomintang regime.
   B. West's trade concessions.
   C. Western nations' seizures in the 1860's.
   D. subsequent Western military actions.

19. The author is primarily concerned with demonstrating that:

   A. the internal dissent in China is deep and longstanding.
   B. the Ch'ing dynasty was the root of the strife.
   C. Western encroachment was the root cause of the strife.
   D. the rebellion was supported by the intellectuals.

20. The author argues that the uprising was more internal than it was influenced from outside the country. Which of the following claims, if true, would most WEAKEN the argument?

   A. Hung Hsiu-ch'uan was not really considered a "messiah."
   B. The author was wrong about the economic imperialism of the West.
   C. The author was wrong about Roberts.
   D. The intellectuals were correct.

21. According to the passage, prior to the rebellion, which of the following is most likely to be true about the relationship between the intellectuals and the people?

   A. The intellectuals had not been involved with the people.
   B. The intellectuals had a strong base within the communities.
   C. The intellectuals had urged the people to try to act in the public interest.
   D. The people had looked to the intellectuals for guidance.

Passage V (Questions 22–28)

A fine finish on a piece of handmade wood furniture immediately reveals whether the piece was made by an experienced craftsman or a novice. The characteristics of this finish may be beyond visual cues such as depth, clarity,
5 and reflection. They additionally include the sense of touch. Closing one's eyes and lightly caressing the piece will reveal much with regard to the care taken in the production and crafting of the piece.

Most people, with only a passing understanding of
10 woodworking and furniture craftsmanship, would choose sandpaper for smoothing and finishing a wood surface. Depending on the level of smoothness sought and the type of wood to be smoothed, there are varying "grits" and types of sandpaper. However, there are inherent problems with
15 attempting to achieve a fine finish with sandpaper.

Sandpaper, by its nature, scratches and wears down the high spots on a wood surface until the surface is finally uniform. One uses successively finer and finer grits of sandpaper. Each higher number is a finer grit and scratches
20 out the scratches made by the previously used grit. This is one reason why it is important not to skip grits of sandpaper when attempting to achieve a highly reflective surface. At some point, the scratches may no longer be visible to the naked eye. At some further point, the scratches may no
25 longer be felt by a light caress of the wood surface. However, it can be envisioned that a scratch or rough spot is relative to the examiner. Sandpaper, by its nature, will always leave scratches in the wood surface, no matter how minute. It will always tear and never cut.

30 Sandpaper is not, and was not, always a fine craftsman's first choice. Harkening back first to its lack of availability, when sharkskin was actually used as one of the first sandpapers, other methods were used quite successfully. Most of these methods involved a very sharp cutting tool,
35 which would actually sever the tight wood fibers and scrape down the high spots on a wood surface.

One of the lesser-known tools most frequently used in the past was the scraper. As the name suggests, this tool scrapes off the high surfaces of the wood to create an
40 increasingly level surface that can be recognized by its highly reflective nature. However, 'scraping' mischaracterizes what this simple tool actually does. Like the plane, the scraper actually cuts the high spots and wood fibers to a uniform level. The advantages of the scraper go beyond efficiency
45 and the beauty imparted to the surface of the wood. There are no dust particles to be inhaled or cleaned up when using a scraper. The cost of a set of scrapers is less than a sleeve of sandpaper, which must be constantly replenished. And finally, considering that almost no one hand-sands, the
50 noise of an electric sander, and the lack thereof when using scrapers, should be considered.

The scraper itself is a very thin flat piece of steel varying in size but generally around three by five inches. Before it can be used, its long edge must be sharpened
55 perpendicular to its plane. Then a 'burr' must be produced along the sharpened edge. The skills necessary to accomplish this task are not complex; however, in an age when tools and materials are "disposable," it is rare to find a craftsman who is adept in its preparation. It is this rather laborious
60 preparation of the scraper that allows it to do its work, and is probably the chief reason why it is no longer widely used.

22. Suppose you are in the process of finishing a fine wooden rocking chair and given the availability of 200, 400, 80, and 120 sandpaper, but no scrapers. From the grit used first to the grit used last, which of the following choices of sandpaper "grits" (line 13) would be best when finishing this rocker?

   A.   120, 200, then 400
   B.   80, 120, 200, then 400
   C.   400, 200, 120, then 80
   D.   80, 200, 120, then 400

23. According to the passage, the biggest drawback to sandpaper is that:

   A.   it will never allow one to achieve a 'reflective surface.'
   B.   it always leave scratches.
   C.   it is rather labor intensive.
   D.   almost no one hand-sands.

GO ON TO THE NEXT PAGE.

24. The passage suggests that determining the very finest finish may be best accomplished by:

    A. looking closely at the surface to determine that no scratches are visible.
    B. looking for a highly reflective surface.
    C. the sense of touch.
    D. ensuring that the maker used the correct sandpaper grits in the right order.

25. Which of the following quotations of passage information provides the LEAST support for the author's thesis?

    A. "There are no dust particles to be inhaled or cleaned up when using a scraper."
    B. "Sandpaper, by its nature, will always leave scratches in the wood surface, no matter how minute."
    C. "The cost of a set of scrapers is less than a sleeve of sandpaper, which must be constantly replenished."
    D. "[C]onsidering that almost no one hand-sands, the noise of the electric sander, and the lack thereof when using scrapers, should be considered."

26. What does the author's concept of "an age when tools and materials are 'disposable'" (lines 57–58) imply about the author's values?

    A. The author would tend to value more traditional tools and materials that could be reused, even if they were not quite as efficient.
    B. The author would value efficiency and the ability to reuse a material or tool above all else.
    C. The author is a proponent of this age and its advances.
    D. The author would probably be considered lazy by today's standards.

27. The author mentions the use of "sharkskin" (line 32) to indicate a general time period to the reader. According to the passage, the aforementioned period was characterized by all of the following EXCEPT:

    A. sharkskin being used as sandpaper.
    B. the use of scrapers.
    C. the use of sharp cutting tools.
    D. the availability of sandpaper.

28. According to the passage, "One of the lesser-known tools most frequently used in the past was the scraper" (lines 37–38), and "Harkening back first to its lack of availability, when sharkskin was actually used as one of the first sandpapers, other methods were used quite successfully" (lines 31–33). If both of these premises are true, what conclusion is most reasonable?

    A. Sharkskin was known as a tool to a greater extent than the scraper.
    B. Though the scraper was successfully used in the past, it is less well known today.
    C. The scraper was used quite successfully, if infrequently, in the past.
    D. Sharkskin was used quite successfully, although less frequently than the scraper.

GO ON TO THE NEXT PAGE.

Passage VI (Questions 29–34)

In a curious paradox, as civilization advances, warfare becomes less civilized. Progressive technology makes killing psychologically easier and physically more efficient. With each passing century, we are able to make war at a
5 greater distance, until we no longer need to see our enemies in order to kill them. Since we do not see our foe, he is dehumanized, easing our guilty conscience. Advances in weapons technology also enable us to kill more people with less effort. With each improvement in weaponry, we are
10 compelled to change the rules of war in order to encompass these new methods. Far from being more restrictive than preceding rules, these new rules do nothing to limit the old way of violence. Instead, they merely specify under what circumstances the new methods will be acceptable and add
15 those to an ever increasing list.

In the Middle Ages, knights in heavy armor dominated the battlefield and dictated a certain style of fighting. The rules of chivalry formed in response. Without these rules, battle in full armor would have quickly become unthinkable.
20 The heavy armor made retreat slow, difficult, and dangerous. Unlimited warfare would have resulted in huge casualties to the retreating army. Chivalry adjusted for this by requiring capture for ransom whenever possible rather than killing. This meant the knights could approach close enough for
25 hand-to-hand combat and, win or lose, have a reasonable expectation to live to fight again. Also, their armor often protected them from severe wounds. This allowed combat to continue until fatigue overcame one of the combatants at which point he surrendered and paid a ransom for his
30 freedom. Since only a minority could afford armor, the class of knights could not tolerate high casualties in their warfare. Thus, chivalry allowed knights to use the superior technology of armor to control the battlefield but prevented them from destroying themselves in the process.

35 Eventually, the advent of an effective missile weapon, the long bow, forced a change in the code of chivalry and ended the reign of the armored knight. Chivalry was adapted. Due to the long range and potent nature of missile weapons, surrender was not easily recognized and capturing an
40 opponent was a far more dangerous enterprise. In addition, bowmen were not wealthy and could not pay a ransom for their release. On the other hand, due to more affordable weapons, the armies were larger and more prisoners were actually taken. With more prisoners taken, but no ransoms
45 being paid for their release, the rules regarding treatment of prisoners changed. Killing a captured prisoner was still illegal; however, in contrast with the luxury enjoyed by the captured knight, the new captive was provided with only the minimum for his survival. This change allowed a greater
50 number of prisoners to be accommodated, even if only meagerly so. Thus, the new rules of missile warfare were strictly a response to a new technology, allowing its use, yet preventing it from becoming so deadly as to exterminate its combatants.

55 The rifle, machinegun, airplane, gas, atom bomb, and nuclear missiles: each weapon is more destructive than the previous one, from mass annihilation until finally we reach weapons of extinction. Still, rules do not abolish these weapons; they only limit their usage. Rules of war allow
60 new technology to be used to the point at which war is as lethal as possible and yet still perpetuates itself. The rules of chivalry allowed war to be fought in armor. Missile warfare was too deadly to fight under the same rules, so the were rules adapted.

65 Through rules, war works on mankind like a parasite, taking as much as possible from the host without killing him. If it killed the host, the parasite would die as well, so it insidiously sucks the life from its host, taking care to hold him above the threshold of death. In the same way, through
70 rules, war acquires the most lethal technology but in such a fashion as to prevent our extinction.

29. Some scientists believe that the author's "weapons of extinction," such as modern thermonuclear devices, actually do have the capability of exterminating the human race. The author would argue that:

A. these weapons exist only to scare nations and would be used only as a last resort.
B. the "rules of war" dictate that these types of weapons would actually cause the extinction of the human race.
C. these weapons will, in fact, one day lead to the extinction of the human race.
D. though these weapons exist, the "rules of war" would preclude their ever actually being used.

GO ON TO THE NEXT PAGE.

30. Implicit in the passage is the assumption that:

    A.   weapons will one day cause our extinction.

    B.   economics is also a critical factor in determining the "rules of war."

    C.   war is an inanimate entity.

    D.   a limited war will never be fought again.

31. The author provides that the "parasite" (line 65) takes care to hold man "above the threshold of death" (line 69). An appropriate clarification of the passage would be the stipulation that the author's argument applies only to:

    A.   certain kinds of parasites.

    B.   the period of time preceding the invention of "weapons of extinction."

    C.   extermination of the enemy forces.

    D.   the most lethal technology.

32. The author's major thesis is that:

    A.   if we do not change course, our extermination is inevitable.

    B.   missile warfare has had a dramatic impact.

    C.   the "rules of war" change with increasingly deadly technology to avert our extinction.

    D.   the "rules of war" will not prevent our extinction.

33. What is the most serious apparent *weakness* of the theory described?

    A.   Why couldn't the knights in heavy armor tolerate high casualties?

    B.   How does warfare become less civilized?

    C.   Why would the parasite want lethal technology?

    D.   What is the difference between mass annihilation and extinction?

34. According to the passage, "Chivalry adjusted for [the problems of fighting in heavy armor] by requiring capture for ransom whenever possible rather than killing" (lines 22–23). This 'requirement' is later explained to have meant that:

    A.   otherwise, huge casualties would have been incurred.

    B.   killing a captured prisoner was actually illegal.

    C.   it was more lucrative to capture than to kill.

    D.   the new captive was provided with only meager subsistence

GO ON TO THE NEXT PAGE.

Passage VII (Questions 35–40)

The Chinese Communist Party governs China through parallel rule, which closely resembles the Soviet system. The so-called 'parallelism' arises because the national Communist Party is structured to duplicate the structure of the official government itself, with virtually all government officials simultaneously enrolled in the Party. Thus, whatever their official capacity, all government officials are ultimately responsible to their Party superiors, who can promote, demote, or purge them based on "loyalty." This makes it unlikely that openly radical officials will be promoted within the Party.

In theory, China's legal system grants regional governments broad legal discretion. But practically, intra-Party accountability leaves regional authorities with little formal power to alter national laws. China operates under a system of common law, which lacks a rigid legal hierarchy. This means that, technically, regional institutions are not bound to obey national precedents to guide their individual policies. In practice, however, the legal flexibility of the regional governments under common law is undermined by their ultimate political accountability to the Party. However broad the scope of regional leaders' legal authority, it rests on their maintaining their favor in the parallel level of the government.

An interesting and unique feature of the regional legal system is the existence of "internal laws" at the regional level. It is difficult to call them "laws" in the Western sense, since they are often unpublished, obscure, and very vague even when known. The majority seem to have originated as semi-legal directives from the national authorities to the local ones. The reason for disseminating them clandestinely was to hide national priorities from foreign negotiators, who, knowing what concessions the regional governments were empowered to grant, would naturally strike a hard bargain.

In terms of their institutional powers, regional authorities have the means to delay, but not to stop, certain policies ordered by the national government. In 1979, regional authorities had no say in policies at the top; namely, they had no seats on the State Council, and through the late 1980's they managed to acquire only a deliberative, not an executive, role. Their institutional role came in the form of their local bureaucratic control. Most powerful, in its potential at least, was the regional bureau that was authorized to give preliminary approval to national projects; it could delay or reject feasible projects. Equally importantly, once a venture had been approved, this regional "supervisor" had to integrate its raw materials purchases from, and product resales to, the region's other (state-owned) enterprises. Specifically, the supervisor authorized requisitions of raw materials, recruited workers and managers, and sometimes requisitioned hard currency disbursements directly from the Bank of China.

Also, regional governments are able to influence national policies, predominately through their informal relationship with the national government. This is due largely to the tradition of "reciprocal accountability" between the national and regional Party organizations. The entire Party jointly elects the Central Committee, a group of 200, from the national and local governments. This Central Committee then elects the top Party leadership. The regional government Party members are compelled to follow the policies of their elected leaders, but at the same time, the Party leadership relies on the national officials' support to retain their posts. Therefore, much like the relationship between a democratically elected official and his/her constituency, accountability runs both ways.

In daily operations, China's entire government structure functions on the principle of "delegation by consensus." Decisions are given for ratification to the subordinate bodies most affected by them. For example, if the State Council wishes to adopt a proposal that primarily affects the provincial governments, it delegates the decision to the Central Committee, which, in turn, delegates it to the provincial authorities themselves. This enables subordinates with greater proximity to and knowledge of the issue to be involved in the chain of decision. If there is unanimous agreement at the lowest level of delegation, the decision is automatically ratified by all higher-level bodies. If, however, subordinates cannot agree unanimously, then the higher-level authority may either approve the decision over the objection of the subordinates, or reject it. (Both are embarrassing options; the former is an obvious method of strong-arming opposition, while the second is an admission of an unpopular decision.)

35. The passage implies that laws in the "Western sense" (line 27) are:

A. ambiguous, though clearly written and published.
B. often unpublished, obscure, and very vague.
C. clear, though often unpublished and vague.
D. unambiguous, and published.

TEST 13

36. In another publication, the author claims that the Chinese government's "delegation by consensus" is very efficient. The support offered for this conclusion in *this* passage is:

    A. weak; those making the final decisions are invariably the State Council members.
    B. weak; those who are involved often use strong-arm tactics.
    C. strong; those most affected by, and with the most knowledge of the issue are involved in the decisions.
    D. strong; the decisions are made only after it has been determined that raw materials and recruits are available.

37. According to the passage, after the late 1980's, the regional authorities were able to exert an influence on the national policies by:

    A. electing the members of the Central Committee, who in turn elect the Party leadership.
    B. electing their local Party representatives, who in turn elect the Central Committee.
    C. failing to follow the policies of their elected leaders.
    D. electing a group of 200, who then elect the Central Committee.

38. The claim that the "Chinese Communist Party governs China through parallel rule, which closely resembles the Soviet system" (lines 1–2) necessitates which of the following conclusions?

    A. The Soviet legal system grants little legal discretion to regional governments.
    B. The Soviet Central Committee elects the top Party leadership.
    C. It is likely that openly radical officials will be promoted within the Soviet Communist Party.
    D. The Chinese system is based upon the Soviet system.

39. The term *radical* (line 10) refers implicitly to Chinese officials who:

    A. hold Party positions, but have opinions that differ from the Party.
    B. hold Party positions, but have opinions that differ from the official government.
    C. hold government positions, but have opinions that differ from the Party.
    D. hold government positions and Party positions, but have opinions that differ from the Party.

40. What assumption is implicit in the sentence, "Both are embarrassing options; the former is an obvious method of strong-arming opposition, while the second is an admission of an unpopular decision" (line 81–84)?

    A. The Party does not like to be embarrassed.
    B. The higher-level governing bodies prefer unanimous decisions by their subordinates.
    C. The provincial authorities will usually make unanimous decisions.
    D. The higher-level governing bodies prefer making the decisions themselves.

STOP. IF YOU FINISH BEFORE TIME IS CALLED, CHECK YOUR WORK. YOU MAY GO BACK TO ANY QUESTION IN THIS TEST.

TEST 13

STOP.

Verbal Reasoning Test 14
Time: 60 Minutes
Questions 1–40

VERBAL REASONING

DIRECTIONS: There are seven passages in this Verbal Reasoning test. Each passage is followed by several questions. After reading a passage, select the one best answer to each question. If you are not certain of an answer, eliminate the alternatives that you know to be incorrect and then select an answer from the remaining alternatives. Indicate your selection by blackening the corresponding oval on your answer document.

Passage I (Questions 1–5)

While courts generally require strict compliance with legal contracts' explicit terms, they have also learned that defining successful "performance" (completion) of the contract too strictly can give opportunistic parties ample
5 occasion to declare their counterparts to be in breach of the literal terms. The quintessential example of such opportunism is the famous case of *Jacob & Youngs*, in which the owner of a newly built mansion, dissatisfied with the results or simply hoping to extort an *ex post* discount, pored over the
10 blueprints, finally finding the builder to have breached the contract by using a different brand of sewer pipes.

Fortunately, courts have a small arsenal of methods by which they can stretch the terms of a contract to accommodate the minor imperfections and dissatisfactions
15 incident to most business contracts, thus avoiding complete "forfeiture" of the entire contract and the need for extensive reparations.

The first is "substantial performance," the doctrine that an error must be "substantial" to require forfeiture of the
20 entire contract. An error that is found to be "insubstantial" may oblige the responsible party to reduce its price or correct the problem, but it will not void the entire contract. A number of factors go into deciding whether or not a breach is material, but most of them allow some room for judicial
25 interpretation. The court has leeway in deciding whether the error deprives the work of its utility, and whether it is possible to "cure" the defect.

In addition, courts can limit the amount of "damages" (monetary compensation) sought when errors do occur,
30 which limits incentives for the opportunism seen in *Jacob & Youngs* above. When the measure of damages is the "cost of replacement," there is the temptation to wait until the other party's obligation is almost completed, then find some minor detail that is, nevertheless, not replaceable except at
35 prohibitive cost. Often, in these situations, the plaintiff does not actually want the "error" corrected, but simply wants money. Instead, courts have the option of awarding merely

the resulting reduction in market price, which tends to be much smaller.

40 In addition, courts can discourage opportunism by putting a greater burden on prospective plaintiffs to show good cause for their grievance.

Even if the error in fulfilling the contract is substantial, courts are not without their options. If the contract is
45 only partially completed, the court may find the contract 'divisible,' which means that the breaching party must refund only a prorated portion of the contract price for the work that remains undone. This is only possible, though, when the contract is amenable; it must have distinct parts,
50 each of which confers some benefit and has a quantifiable value. Thus, if, for example, a seller delivers only half the logs promised, the court will likely require half payment. On the other hand, if a company contracts to research and then produce a product, and its research proves that production
55 is not feasible, the court may decide that the research is worthless without actual production.

1. Which of the following statements is the most reasonable conclusion that can be drawn from the author's description of "the minor imperfections and dissatisfactions incident to most business contracts" (lines 14–15)?

    A. If the literal terms of the contract were followed as precisely as possible, then both parties to the contract would be always be satisfied.

    B. If the parties to a contract were required to abide precisely by the exact terms of the contract, someone could always be declared in breach of contract.

    C. In general, parties should be more careful than they are now when they are writing their contracts.

    D. Usually, both parties to a contract are satisfied with the work that has been accomplished.

GO ON TO THE NEXT PAGE.

2. The word *opportunistic* (line 4) is used in the sense of:

  A. a party that is ruthless in its business dealings.
  B. a party that would attempt to fairly make the most of a business relationship.
  C. a party that would take advantage of another, given the chance.
  D. a party that will use illegal means to achieve its goals.

3. According to the passage, which of the following is true regarding the "owner" in the "the famous case of *Jacob & Youngs*" (lines 7–11) and (28–31)?

   I. The owner had used a different brand of sewer pipes than the one specified in the blueprints.
  II. The owner might have been hoping to extort a discount from the builders.
  III. The owner might have been dissatisfied with his newly built mansion.

  A. I only
  B. II only
  C. II and III only
  D. I, II, and III

4. Suppose that the court finds that the contractor hired to build a barn had placed the wall studs on 24" centers rather than the specified 18" centers, but that this error was *not* substantial and does not deprive the work of its utility. According to the passage, the court would most likely:

  A. declare the contractor in forfeiture of the contract.
  B. direct the contractor to tear down the barn and rebuild it according to contract.
  C. oblige the contractor to reduce his price.
  D. decide it was not possible nor necessary to 'cure' this defect.

5. An important comparison is made in the passage between:

  A. opportunistic parties and the leeway of the court.
  B. substantial performance and correcting the problem.
  C. a substantial forfeiture and an entire contract.
  D. a substantial error and a material breach.

GO ON TO THE NEXT PAGE.

TEST 14

Passage II (Questions 6–10)

Joining two pieces of rope is generally something that we do almost every day, at least once, often without conscious thought, as in the instance of tying our shoes. At other times considerable conscious thought is given, again
5 to a seemingly noncritical task such as wrapping the ribbon on a gift or securing luggage on the top of the car. The act of joining may assume more critical importance, such as when one attaches a child's tree swing or rigs his own system to help tow someone's car. Concern should be given to the
10 knot selected, the rope material, and the degree to which the rope and knot or splice will be relied upon. For, indeed, the user will rely upon the method of joining that has been selected, whether used to tie his shoes or to "rope up" prior to his climb, and this point of joining will almost invariably
15 be the weakest part of his rope system.

The ubiquitous Granny is the knot most commonly used by the unschooled when he or she is asked to join two pieces of string or rope. This knot should actually not be considered a knot at all and should never be used in any
20 situation. It deserves no mention at all except for the fact that the common inherent tendency to tie this Granny knot over all others requires one to be able to immediately recognize this silly and often dangerous knot in order for it to be retied in an appropriate manner. To see what a Granny knot looks
25 like you should consciously tie one and then examine it. Take an end of the rope in each hand. Pass your left hand over your right and then pass the rope under. Now drop the rope ends and regrasp the ends nearest where your hands were originally. Again pass your left hand over your right
30 and then pass the rope under. (Those who have learned to tie a square knot will immediately recognize the similarity of these instructions, while at the same time seeing the error in the methodology.) Now gently "dress" or tighten the knot. What you should see is the two ends sticking out
35 at right angles to the attached ropes themselves. This is as opposed to the appearance of the aforementioned, very useful square knot, whose ends lie back along the attached ropes. Recognize this Granny knot; don't ever use it.

For the most part, recreational users will be concerned
40 with ropes other than wire rope. Wire rope, more commonly referred to as cable, consists of woven and braided strands of varying gauges. It is never appropriate to knot wire rope; splicing, or crimping, is the method of joining. Splicing, unlike knotting, rarely weakens that section of any type
45 of joined rope. However, it requires some specialized knowledge in all cases, and, in the case of wire rope, requires a considerable degree of physical effort. Rope made of other substances, whether manmade or natural, however, is readily amenable to splicing or knotting, depending on the
50 intended use of it.

One should bear in mind that synthetics such as polyurethane and nylon ropes are 'self-lubricating' and will
have a marked tendency to slip when placed under tension. Anyone who has ever water-skied may have experienced
55 this phenomenon and the potentially catastrophic results of improperly chosen or applied rope joinery. Water-skiing ropes are placed under tremendous strain and are very elastic. The manufacturer usually splices these ropes, obviating the need for the end-user to knot them in any way.
60 When a knot is improperly tied in a broken ski rope and it pulls through under pressure, the resulting reaction of the rope whipping back into the boat is a scary event to behold. Ropes made of natural materials are not only less elastic, but they also have the tendency to grip themselves, which
65 lends to knotting. Here the knot selected must usually have the additional quality of being easy to remove.

6. Evidence shows that, under a variety of situations, when left to tie their own knots, people tie knots that are inappropriate for that situation. This fact tends to support the hypothesis concerning Granny knots because:

   A. Granny knots should never be used in any situation.
   B. a Granny knot is easy to recognize.
   C. these people are probably tying Granny knots.
   D. people usually don't know which knot is appropriate in a given situation.

GO ON TO THE NEXT PAGE.

7. If the hypothesis of the passage is correct, one should find that manufacturers of water-skiing ropes:

A. use ropes made of natural materials as much as possible.
B. use special knots on their ropes to keep them from pulling through under pressure.
C. probably don't recommend that the consumer repair a broken tow rope themselves.
D. know a lot about knots.

8. Assume that most children's tree swing ropes are made from thick natural materials. The passage information presented on ropes and knots makes which of the following suggestions the most plausible?

A. The swing should be checked frequently to make sure the knot hasn't pulled through itself.
B. When the family decides to relocate and take the swing, the knot will be difficult to untie.
C. Whoever put up the swing probably didn't use a Granny knot to attach it to the tree.
D. The swing would have to be retied frequently because of the elasticity of the rope.

9. The author claims that the Granny knot is an "often dangerous knot" (line 23). The support offered for this conclusion is:

A. weak; there are no examples or evidence of this.
B. weak; the author provides only one example in which this is the case.
C. strong; there are no examples or evidence of this.
D. strong; the author provides an example in which this is the case.

10. Which of the following *violates* the guidelines and suggestions for wire rope or cable (lines 39–50) described in the passage?

I. Splicing rarely weakens a cable.
II. Cable should be knotted if possible.
III. Crimping of cables should be avoided.

A. I only
B. II only
C. I and II only
D. II and III only

Passage III (Questions 11–17)

Reacting to the changes the end of World War II brought to Japanese society, Japanese novelist Mishima turned to the samurai-era feudal manual *Hagakure*, reissuing it with his commentary (as *Way of the Samurai*) to lament
5 the degeneracy of his times and to propose a solution. It mattered little that *Hagakure* had been written in an era over two centuries before Mishima's own; the complaints Mishima leveled against postwar youth's "effeminacy, profiteering, and shallowness" seem to transcend the times.

10 Yet while the original *Hagakure* certainly glorified death in the service of a lord, Mishima's reading, colored by his personal obsession with beauty and death, makes the way of the modern samurai lead invariably to suicide as the ultimate expression of freedom and purpose.

15 For Mishima, being a "modern samurai" embodies a contradiction. He recognizes that the samurai is a relic of the feudal past, with no place in the postwar world. Yet Mishima sees in this "conscious anachronism," with his inevitable extinction, something transcendentally noble and
20 pure, which makes such doomed lives worth living.

Despite critiques that label Mishima basically asocial, he is aware that the samurai needs a social context to be meaningful. Simply put, the samurai must perceive his era as decadent, and in order to cultivate eccentricity, he must
25 go head-on against social norms. But, Mishima argued that, "the premise of the democratic age is that it is best to live as long as possible." So the samurai must choose the unpopular course, the pursuit of hardship and early death, to create their artistic statement. In scanning *Way of the Samurai*, we
30 see an amazing lack of purpose to the samurai's life outside of his duty to himself. In *Hagakure*'s time, samurai still had a social position as retainers; postwar samurai had no such position.

Instead, Mishima instructs young men to live their
35 lives with intense dignity, always projecting a strong and active image. In order to be thought strong and heroic, it is necessary to look the part. Thus, Mishima transfers his obsession with personal beauty into the only instruction for living.

40 An interesting corollary to this, not found in *Hagakure*, is the need for an audience to observe the demeanor of the samurai. This must be an audience totally unlike the samurai, one of weak and effeminate men, to whom a samurai will be seen as rash and ferocious. The beauty that Mishima sees in
45 the samurai is for the sake of being feared.

For the living, then, Mishima's philosophy offers no radical new target towards which to direct one's energies, only a grimmer, more hopeless perspective. Here is the major departure from the original *Hagakure*, which recognized

50 death as an occupational hazard and admonished samurai to overcome their fear of it. In Mishima's era, when there are neither lords nor battles, where can that death come from, unless it is self-inflicted?

It becomes apparent that Mishima views "heroic"
55 death—i.e., suicide—as the necessary conclusion of the heroic life. At what point should one choose suicide? The ideal death should come immediately after a notable moment—either a crisis or a notable success. This is why he says that "the greatest calamity for the man of action is
60 that he fail to die even after that last unmistakable point has been added."

Yet once the moment of suicide is reached, Mishima describes it in such a transcendental way that it has the power to redeem almost anyone. The meaning of life is
65 accomplished in a moment. It is an act that is meant to make a statement to the world, yet is above the morality and judgment of others. Though later historians may second-guess the motivations, it is for the individual, in the last tragic moment of his life, to come to terms with the
70 purity and voluntarism of his own action. It "can only be made in the cool, grim reality of an individual facing death; it is a question of the human spirit in the ultimate state of tension."

11. Which of the following statements most clearly exemplifies Mishima's concept of a modern samurai's primary obligation?

A. The samurai's foremost duty is to himself.
B. The samurai's main duty is to his lord.
C. The primary obligation of the samurai is to society.
D. The most important obligation of the samurai is to commit suicide.

GO ON TO THE NEXT PAGE.

12. In the passage, the author contrasts *Hagakure* with *Way of the Samurai* by pointing out that:

A. the modern samurai does not need society.

B. for the ancient samurai, self-inflicted death brought honor.

C. for Mishima's samurai, death always comes by suicide.

D. for the ancient samurai, death should come immediately after a notable success.

13. Which of the following statements is the most reasonable conclusion regarding Mishima that can be drawn from the passage?

A. His philosophy required selflessness and strength.

B. His goal was to promote the construction of a new society of samurai warriors.

C. He was a man whose philosophy required the society he reviled.

D. He hated society, but felt that it could be redeemed.

14. Given an understanding of *Way of the Samurai*, which of the following would be most *discrepant* with this philosophy?

A. To be strong and heroic and to look the part

B. To become primarily devoted to oneself

C. To dedicate oneself to being feared by all

D. To seclude oneself in total devotion to the pursuit of strength and heroism

15. During the feudal samurai-era of ancient Japan, committing suicide was considered a final honorable act, which was required as a result of dishonor. This information would be most *discrepant* with which of Mishima's views?

A. The ideal death should come immediately after a notable success.

B. The most honorable death is one in the service of a lord.

C. Mishima describes death in such a way that it has the power to redeem almost anyone.

D. As an act, suicide is above the morality and judgment of others.

16. According to the author, Mishima's sole teaching for living was:

A. to imagine oneself as strong and heroic.

B. to serve your lord.

C. to look the part of a samurai.

D. to serve society.

17. What assumption is implicit in the phrase "conscious anachronism" (line 18)?

A. Mishima is aware that his ideas belong to another time.

B. The behavior is no longer relevant and Mishima knows it.

C. Mishima believes that society is out of date.

D. Everyone knows that Mishima's ideas are relics, except him.

TEST 14

GO ON TO THE NEXT PAGE.

Passage IV (Questions 18–22)

The current proliferation of women's self-defense courses throughout the United States is a disturbing trend. These courses vary in the technique they teach, along with the credentials of those teaching them. Some promote

5 initial passivity to lull the attacker into a sense of security or even to discourage him, assuming that the attacker will only enjoy the encounter if the woman is struggling. Others teach "self-soiling" to dissuade the attacker. Still others seek to "empower" women with a sense of self-confidence by

10 teaching them a few seemingly simple but "foolproof" self-defense techniques. The graduation consists of a pretend "attacker," heavily padded, screaming obscenities, whom the graduate inevitably drives off, to the tearful cheers of her classmates. All uphold the supposition that any woman,

15 given the proper training, is capable of beating off her attacker. It is this theory that not only lacks any merit, but is incredibly dangerous to teach and rely upon.

Martial artists and those who box train for years in their craft. Actually, to mention most martial arts in the same

20 sentence with pugilists is an incredible insult to the boxer. Boxers spar and fight for real, requiring heavy sixteen-ounce gloves and full headgear when training so that they do not permanently damage one another. Even sparring for training is done only a few times a week because of the

25 resultant trauma. If two boxers were to get together in a ring wearing no head protection and the same soft hand guards that martial artists wear, they would kill each other. The stylized dance of martial arts bears little resemblance to the quick and brutal violence of actual combat. It is the average

30 martial artist's mentality toward his craft that promotes the unrealistic expectations being perpetuated in women's self-defense courses. Bearing this in mind, let us consider what boxers do and do not do in their craft.

Boxers fight in weight classes. You will not see a 200

35 pounder fighting a 140 pounder. The weight difference is too significant. The 140 pounder may be a Golden Gloves boxer, but the impact of that additional sixty pounds landing on him from the blows landed by his sparring partner would quickly take their toll. How often will a male boxer fight a

40 female boxer? Never. He would kill her. This is due in part to the aforementioned differences in weight between the male and the female. It is due moreover to the fact that females are built differently than males. Pound for pound, they are not as strong as a male of the same size. It is also rare to find

45 a male and a female of the same size and muscular stature. Women naturally have a higher percentage of fat in their bodies than men. When they weigh as much as men they are generally quite overweight.

An instructor has an obligation to teach the truth to his

50 students. This is particularly important in the area of self-defense, as a student may some day be called to act upon the beliefs and skills instilled by her instructor. The belief

that a woman can physical overpower a man is ridiculous. It matters not that the woman has paid good money for her

55 two-day seminar and successfully "fought off" the carefully choreographed attack of her ineffectual assailant.

What needs to be taught are preventive measures and tactics—prevention of the circumstances that could lead to the meeting of this woman and her assailant in the first

60 place. These measures and tactics involve common sense habits and approaches, such as traveling with a companion, not walking down dark alleys, and being aware of your surroundings and those around you, to name a few. For the woman who is aware and careful, it is her job to make herself

65 a "harder" target for the assailant. In the end, he should realize that there are other, easier targets of opportunity out there and hopefully he will move on.

18. An important comparison is made in the passage between:

A. the boxer mentality and the martial artist's abilities, or lack thereof.
B. the expectations in women's self-defense courses and the martial artist's mentality.
C. women's self-defense courses and the way in which boxers train.
D. the women taking the self-defense courses and their assailants.

GO ON TO THE NEXT PAGE.

19. The word *tearful* (line 14) is used in the sense of:

   A.   outraged.
   B.   exultant.
   C.   tragic.
   D.   happy.

20. What would be the author's response to the standard story about the smaller, mild-mannered child who finally turns on and defeats the schoolyard bully?

   A.   The author would first ask about the gender of the child and the bully.
   B.   The author would respond that this is wishful thinking and unlikely to happen.
   C.   The author would want to know if the child had any martial-arts training.
   D.   The author would think that this is very possible if both the child and the bully are the same gender.

21. A women's self-defense course that would best represent the author's concept of *realistic* as opposed to "unrealistic expectations" (line 31) would probably have:

   A.   a female assailant attacking females, and vice versa.
   B.   a two-hour block of boxing training.
   C.   more martial arts-type sparring.
   D.   an assailant attacking to the utmost of his abilities.

22. Which of the following assertions is the most effective argument *against* the author's conclusion that "[i]n the end, he should realize that there are other, easier targets of opportunity out there and hopefully he will move on." (lines 65–67)?

   A.   If a 'stalker' realizes that his victim is wary, he will be dissuaded from further activities.
   B.   Victims are frequently chosen at random based upon their perceived vulnerability at that moment.
   C.   Feelings of vulnerability, denial, and loss of love infrequently motivate the assailant who is looking for targets of opportunity.
   D.   A stalker's choice of victim is predicated primarily upon his perceptions of such factors as celebrity status and/or affection.

GO ON TO THE NEXT PAGE.

Passage V (Questions 23–28)

Psychologist Sigmund Freud and social philosopher Friedrich Nietzsche were both aware of society's seeming inability to provide lasting happiness for its people, and so they undertook a study of conflict as inherent in
5 civilization.

Freud's clinical work taught him that, when people developed neuroses, the cure was not achieved by relieving the outward symptoms, but by finding the origin of the problem, usually in the patient's early childhood. Freud saw
10 conflicts within the individual that were similar to those that, he felt, existed within society. This led him to psychoanalyze society, looking back to events that might have occurred in civilization's prehistory, events that might explain the pattern of current developments as he saw them.

15 Freud's human is basically animated by hedonism, or the pleasure principle, an unrestrained pursuit of pleasure. Yet to enjoy more than momentary pleasure, he needs the security and leisure provided by society. However, paradoxically, in order for civilization to develop, the instinct
20 for pleasure must be suppressed and the energy "sublimed" (transformed) into something productive. Additionally, to keep a society together, man's natural aggressive instinct must be repressed. Each of these repressions reduces man's enjoyment of life, and may even drive some individuals to
25 neurosis, but they are the price man must pay to achieve and enjoy the protection and material conveniences of civilization.

Nietzsche, who denies that morality has any intrinsic worth, is more interested in a historical study of it, from its
30 origins to the present, as a reflection of the dominance of certain groups who were able to produce "knowledge" (i.e., make their texts the socially accepted ones). For Nietzsche, the conflict that has historically accompanied civilization produced neither universal repression nor progress. The
35 conflict was a power struggle between the nobles and the slaves, in which the nobles adopted a hedonistic and materialistic morality, and the lower classes countered it with a passive Judeo-Christianity. When either side comes to power, it institutes its morality on the other, so that,
40 instead of all individuals being repressed in order for the society to achieve a common goal, repression is used by one faction to repress another. For the present, Nietzsche says, the Christians (slaves) have won in caging the amoral nobles through a religious society. This was in order to
45 save themselves and their society from the nobles' natural aggressive instincts. Nietzsche, who clearly identifies himself with the repressed nobility, or as a "noble beast," says that such a repression causes society to stagnate, since the lower classes are incapable of anything but mediocrity.
50 It may be supposed that when the nobles were dominant, they similarly repressed the slaves' desires, but Nietzsche would not claim any disservice to civilization from this. For

progress, Nietzsche would say, some repression is always necessary, but it must consist of keeping useless people
55 powerless, rather than hampering both the ambitious and the apathetic alike.

23. According to the author, which of the following best describes an aspect of Freud's theories?

A. In society, without hedonism man can only realize momentary pleasure.

B. Hedonism is provided by society.

C. The nobles' natural aggressive instincts are repressed by society.

D. Man's aggressive instinct is natural and pleasurable to him.

24. Which of the following statements is the most reasonable conclusion that can be drawn from the author's description of Friedrich Nietzsche?

A. Nietzsche felt that the individual needs the security and leisure provided by society.

B. Nietzsche was more interested in civilization as it reflected dominance.

C. Nietzsche felt that societal conflict produced progress, but not necessarily universal repression.

D. Nietzsche felt that societal conflict produced universal repression, but not necessarily progress.

GO ON TO THE NEXT PAGE.

25. Which of the following approaches to relieving a patient's neurosis would be most likely to be stressed by a clinician who had an understanding of and belief in the work and theories of Sigmund Freud?

A. The clinician would carefully prescribe the appropriate drug that would alleviate all of the symptoms of his patient.

B. The clinician would compare his patient's neurosis with the societal problems during that time.

C. The clinician would spend however long was required attempting to determine the origin of the neurosis.

D. After extensive psychoanalysis, the clinician would be able to trace the neurotic manifestations back to their sexual roots.

26. The assertion that civilization is "a reflection of the dominance of certain groups who were able to produce 'knowledge' (i.e., make their texts the socially accepted ones)" (lines 31-33) is NOT clearly consistent with the information about:

A. lower classes countering with a passive Judeo-Christianity.

B. society providing security and leisure.

C. repression being used by one faction to stifle another.

D. man needing to repress his natural aggressive instinct.

27. Which of the following statements is the most reasonable conclusion that can be drawn from the author's description of Sigmund Freud's theories?

A. Society can be 'cured' if one can only determine the origin of its problems.

B. The individual would be happiest if allowed to do exactly as he pleased.

C. Until society is fully developed, the individual will not be able to fully enjoy life.

D. The individual will never be able to fully enjoy life without periodic repressions of this enjoyment.

28. On the basis of the passage, it is reasonable to conclude all of the following EXCEPT that:

A. Nietzsche felt that he had natural aggressive instincts.

B. Freud felt that he had natural aggressive instincts.

C. Nietzsche fancied himself a hedonist.

D. Nietzsche was religious.

Passage VI (Questions 29–35)

In 1998, American investment banking giant Morgan Stanley will begin the second stage of its long-touted expansion into the Chinese financial markets.

5 The most immediate draw is, of course, the lucrative infrastructure-project finance work, which is expected to proceed on a massive scale now that China's Communist Party has openly embraced the prospect of capitalism, in practice if not in name. This reorganization is also likely to be followed by privatization and restructuring of many large-10 scale Chinese state-owned enterprises, again promising large consulting and capital-raising fees. Morgan Stanley's managers' analysts have predicted increased international investment in Chinese companies once investment barriers are lowered, two draws being their high growth rates and 15 return on investment from 1992 to 1997. Further, Morgan Stanley's Private Client Group foresees a brisk trade in marketing asset-management services and American global financial products to Asia's financial elite. However, analysts should note that the Chinese market is not necessarily 20 limited to the upper echelon; the high (forced) savings rate among Chinese consumers could well be channeled into investment, as could the high cash reserves held by Chinese banks.

Morgan Stanley expects that helping Asian companies 25 to raise funds would simultaneously allow it to perform due diligence on these companies, allowing Morgan Stanley to recommend increased investment in the more promising companies to their existing clients. It would also create contacts in government, which might perhaps 30 give it influence over legislation on privatization, securities markets, and foreign investment.

For this reason, Morgan Stanley has chosen to establish its China operation in partnership with the Chinese government, though of course it would have been perfectly 35 legal to simply go in alone and set up a branch office in China. This structure will create instant government contacts and state-sponsored projects through Morgan Stanley's cooperation with the Chinese Commercial Bank and others, along with access to vast amounts of capital. 40 Needless to say, Morgan Stanley's minority ownership stake in the venture will yield inevitable challenges. It will have to govern through compromise and negotiation, which is not a role it is accustomed to assuming in its American operations. There is also the possibility of incongruent 45 and conflicting interests between Morgan Stanley and the Chinese government; for instance, the Chinese may want to transfer as much technology and expertise as possible to Chinese state-owned firms.

For the venture to succeed, necessary ingredients 50 include brand recognition. The Chinese central government, anxious to make its first attempts at capitalism a public

success, may refuse to deal with unknowns, or, if it does, may use its vast bargaining power to dictate very unattractive terms. Further, Morgan Stanley will need to develop a strong 55 sales-distribution network, a factor sorely neglected under the centrally planned Chinese regime. In addition, Morgan Stanley will be responsible for importing its own information gathering and transfer technology, to compensate for the often underdeveloped foreign communications systems.

60 Morgan Stanley's challenges will include staffing its office with a workable mix of expatriates or nationals (who know the language, business etiquette, and political climate) and foreigners (who are experienced in the more sophisticated techniques of Western financing). This 65 involves obtaining work visas, setting compensation rates, retraining Chinese workers in American standards of ethics and finance, etc. Also important is bringing quick decision-making to a culture used to consensus management and centralized planning, continuous education of Chinese 70 (and American) staff on changing legal issues, reconciling partners' conflicting interests, and correcting linguistic miscommunications.

29. The author of the passage states that, "though of course it would have been perfectly legal to simply go in alone and set up a branch office in China" (lines 34–36), Morgan Stanley expects to enjoy which of the following advantages through cooperating with and helping the existing state-owned companies?

    A. Morgan Stanley expects challenges in the staffing of its Chinese offices.
    B. Morgan Stanley foresees great autonomy in the terms it will dictate, based primarily upon its close relationship with these companies.
    C. Morgan Stanley anticipates creating contacts within the Chinese government, which may give them some influence in certain areas.
    D. Morgan Stanley looks forward to raising funds from these state-owned companies.

GO ON TO THE NEXT PAGE.

TEST 14

30. Based upon passage information, one can assume the following regarding the operations of Morgan Stanley in America:

   A. Morgan Stanley governs through compromise and negotiation.

   B. Staffing of its offices is not a challenge for Morgan Stanley in America.

   C. From 1992 to 1997, Morgan Stanley enjoyed unusually high growth rates.

   D. Morgan Stanley does not usually govern through compromise and negotiation.

31. Based upon passage information, one can assume the following regarding the Chinese business culture EXCEPT:

   A. It is characterized by centralized planning.

   B. It is characterized by rapid decision-making and centralization.

   C. The culture is accustomed to consensus management.

   D. Business is conducted in a different fashion than it is in America.

32. Based upon passage information, why does Morgan Stanley predict that there may be increased international investment in Chinese companies?

   A. These companies are embracing the prospect of capitalism.

   B. These companies have been dramatically overhauled in the last several years by the state.

   C. These companies are expected to experience tremendous growth once investment barriers are lowered.

   D. These companies have experienced high growth rates.

33. Which of the following has been ignored under the Chinese government?

   A. A strong sales-distribution network

   B. Brand recognition

   C. Privatization and restructuring

   D. Raising funds

34. According to the passage, which of the following is INACCURATE regarding China?

   A. The Chinese market is not limited to the upper ranks.

   B. Chinese banks hold high cash reserves.

   C. Chinese consumers choose to save a large portion of their money.

   D. The Chinese government may refuse to deal with unknown brands.

35. The passage indicates that its author would NOT agree with which of the following statements?

   A. Helping Asian companies to raise funds is one of the necessary inconveniences of the Morgan Stanley expansion.

   B. Western financing is more sophisticated than Chinese financing.

   C. The communications system of the Chinese is often underdeveloped.

   D. Determining compensation rates for workers will be one of Morgan Stanley's challenges.

GO ON TO THE NEXT PAGE.

Passage VII (Questions 36–40)

Is human evolution finally over? That is the stark, controversial view of a group of biologists who believe a Western lifestyle now protects humanity from the forces that used to shape *Homo sapiens*. "If you want to know what
5 Utopia is like, just look around—this is it," said Professor Steve Jones, of University College London. "Things have simply stopped getting better, or worse, for our species."

In support of this, biologists compare modern man with his early counterparts. "If you had looked at Stone Age
10 people in Europe a mere 50,000 years ago, you would assume the trend was for people to get bigger and stronger all the time," said Professor Chris Stringer of the Natural History Museum, London. Yet, after immediate environmental stimulations like increased access to milk and beef are taken
15 into account, our physiques are actually becoming less robust. Are we instead growing in intelligence or intellectual capability? Not if you depend upon the size of the brain as an indicator. Brain size has, in fact, decreased over the past 10,000 years. Some scientists believe humans are becoming
20 less brainy and more neurotic. Though whether neurosis has anything to do with evolution is not clear.

The Western lifestyle, which has been postulated to have halted or impeded natural selection, is characterized by better nutrition, health care, and medicine. "Until recently,
25 there were massive differences between individuals' life spans and fecundity," said Jones. "In London, the death rate outstripped the birth rate for most of the city's history. If you look at graveyards from ancient to Victorian times, you can see that a half of all children died before adolescence,
30 probably because they lacked genetic protection against disease. Now, children's chances of reaching the age of 25 have reached 98 percent. Nothing is changing. We have reached stagnation."

One of the problems with this perspective is that it is a
35 purely Western-based one. It is not likely that children from Afghanistan and India would recognize and be receiving the aforementioned benefits of this lifestyle. It is only in the West that these advances are keeping virtually every member of society alive and able to pass on his or her genes.
40 In the developing world, no such protection exists.

Though it is difficult to say which direction evolution would continue to take, it is certainly based upon the ability of humans to pass on their genetic code, to have children. The more children, the more genetic material. Thus, it is
45 fascinating to observe that most of the biologists studying and arguing naturally assume that people who are more intelligent, have more money, and live longer will have more children. For example, the biologist Christopher Wills of the University of California, San Diego, who argues that ideas
50 are now driving our evolution, says, "There is a premium on sharpness of mind and the ability to accumulate money.

Such people tend to have more children and have a better chance of survival." In other words, intellect—the defining characteristic of our species—is still driving our evolution. If people start to live to 150 through genetic engineering,
55 and are capable of producing children for more than 100 of those years, the effects could be dramatic, he says. "People will start to produce dozens of children in their lifetimes, and that will certainly start to skew our evolution. These people will also have more chance to accumulate wealth as well.
60 So we will have created a new race of fecund, productive individuals and that could have dramatic consequences."

These arguments would seem to fly in the face of the remarkably declining populations and birth rates of the Western world. Why would these people of greater intellect,
65 who were living longer and had more money, suddenly decide to start having all of these children?

36. In the context of the passage, the term *utopia* refers primarily to:

  A. the apogee of *Homo sapiens*' evolution.
  B. Afghani lifestyle and society.
  C. a perfect futuristic society.
  D. the ability to have more children.

37. According to two of the positions presented, evolution as it is occurring nowadays places a premium on sharpness of mind and the ability to accumulate money, *and* Western lifestyle has been postulated to have halted or impeded natural selection. If both of these premises are true, what conclusion is most reasonable?

A. Increasingly, Western societies will be more intelligent and more able to accumulate money.

B. Increasingly, Western societies will be less intelligent and less able to accumulate money.

C. Members of Western society will become increasingly able to accumulate money.

D. No reasonable conclusion can be drawn.

38. According to the passage, "Until recently there were massive differences between individuals' life spans and fecundity" (lines 24–26). This meant that:

A. people would live long lives and have few children.

B. people would live long lives and have many children.

C. people would live short lives and have few children.

D. people would live short lives and have many children.

39. Assume that in the West, less-educated, poverty-stricken women have three times as many children as their better-educated, wealthier, counterparts. If, in the West, "virtually every member of society" is being kept alive and able to pass on his or her genes, this evidence would *weaken* the passage assertion that:

A. we will have created a new race of fecund individuals.

B. evolution is certainly based upon the ability of humans to pass on their genetic code.

C. our physiques are actually becoming less robust.

D. there is a premium on sharpness of mind and the ability to accumulate money.

40. The opinion that "[p]eople will start to produce dozens of children in their lifetimes, and that will certainly start to skew our evolution" (lines 56–58) is challenged in the passage by the argument that:

A. wealthy people generally have many children.

B. populations and birth rates are declining.

C. studies indicate that wealthy people generally do not have many children.

D. most of these new members of society will be able to pass on their genes.

STOP. IF YOU FINISH BEFORE TIME IS CALLED, CHECK YOUR WORK. YOU MAY GO BACK TO ANY QUESTION IN THIS TEST.

STOP.

Verbal Reasoning Test 1
Answers & Explanations

TEST 1 ANSWER KEY

1.	D	11.	D	21.	C	31.	C
2.	B	12.	C	22.	D	32.	D
3.	C	13.	C	23.	D	33.	B
4.	A	14.	A	24.	C	34.	C
5.	C	15.	C	25.	B	35.	A
6.	B	16.	B	26.	B	36.	D
7.	C	17.	A	27.	D	37.	D
8.	B	18.	D	28.	D	38.	D
9.	C	19.	D	29.	B	39.	A
10.	D	20.	B	30.	C	40.	B

Passage I (Questions 1–7)

1. For which of the following of the author's assertions is NO support provided in the passage?

    The key words are "author's assertion," and "NO support" or argument provided by the author. The correct answer must satisfy both of these requirements.

    A. Empathy is of little use because it is *primarily* structural.

    WRONG: Though this IS an assertion by the author, support for it is prevalent; see "fubsy."

    B. Pain can, in some cases, actually be perceived positively and sought after.

    WRONG: This, too, IS an assertion made by the author, but he *supports* it with the example of the Aztecs.

    C. Human beings have an intrinsic tendency to fawn over and protect "fubsy" animals.

    WRONG: This IS an assertion made by the author, and he supports it with an explanation.

    D. Another creature is not capable of want, and if it were, it would neither necessarily want nor deserve our pity.

    CORRECT: This is an almost verbatim quote from lines 56–58 though there the author refers specifically to "The creature." However, these lines indicate clearly that he is speaking generally, which makes this answer one of the "author's assertions." There is *no* support for this assertion. The author does not say definitely that animals are not capable of want, only that it would be false thinking to *empathize* with them—projecting want, needs, feelings, etc. Previous references to animals "deserving" anything refer to protection.

2. The author implies that an animal does not:

    This is a difficult question because we are asking for the author's *implications*. You cannot simply go back to line such and such and pick this out. Additionally, this is the type of answer wherein you must follow the original MCAT instructions and pick the *one best* answer, as unsatisfactory as that may feel.

    A. have enough "fubsy" characteristics to be considered human.

    WRONG: The author never implies that "that an animal does not have enough 'fubsy' characteristics to be considered human." This is much too vague a statement. The author recognizes an "intrinsic tendency towards "cuddly soft, furry, larger mammals that we generally fawn over and feel the desire to protect" (lines 25–27).

    B. communicate effectively.

    CORRECT: The author does imply this. "We cannot decide right and wrong, good and evil for those with whom communication is barred" (lines 70–71). Communication between animals and humans is mentioned with finality in this last sentence. The implication of a large portion of the passage is that direct or effective communication with animals is impossible and without direct communication, we are unable to "determine whether another creature … is experiencing pain … " The author implies that empathy and all other forms of communication are misleading.

    C. benefit from human empathy.

    WRONG: The author never implies "that an animal does not benefit from human empathy." In contrast, his references to "fubsy" animals show that some are at least considered for protection. There are animals that we "generally fawn over and feel the desire to protect" (lines 26–27). With regard to empathy, the author merely considers it a pathetic fallacy, but would probably admit that some animals do benefit from it.

    D. empathize with humans.

    WRONG: The author never implies that "that an animal does not empathize with humans." This is a silly answer; animals empathize with humans? About what? Though empathy is defined in derogatory terms as a pathetic fallacy, it would still require that animals have intellect, which the author would clearly argue against.

3. It has been said that animal experimenters "are using more and more animals whom they consider less 'cute,' because, although they know these animals suffer just as much, they believe people won't object as strenuously to the torture of a pig or a rat as they will to that of a dog or a rabbit." The author would probably disagree by saying that:

    You should immediately grasp the flavor of the quote because of the word "torture." We are looking for an answer in which the author would *disagree*. What would the author's response be?

    A. dogs and rabbits are less "cute" than pigs or rats.

    WRONG: The author would clearly discount any efforts to quantify the unquantifiable; i.e., "cuteness." Therefore, he would never respond with "less cute." Additionally, he discounts structural differentiation and fubsiness throughout the passage.

    B. people will usually object strenuously to an experiment in which any kind of animal is suffering.

    WRONG: In the passage the author makes very few sweeping statements about animals. This answer is an all-inclusive type of statement, which you should be wary of. You might imagine that this answer is so, imagining yourself in the lab with the rabbits. The author does imply that we would *not* care if "mosquitoes, spiders, or ticks" were suffering (lines 23–24).

C. the experimenters cannot know how much the animals suffer.

CORRECT: This is the recurrent theme throughout the passage, that animals cannot tell us if they are suffering, how much they are suffering, or whether or not they want to suffer. "We have no way of knowing: perhaps pigs prefer to be slaughtered" (lines 69–70).

D. the experimenters probably realize that non-human organisms cannot suffer as we do.

WRONG: This is not the *one best* answer. Again (see explanation of the CORRECT answer), the author argues that animals cannot tell us if they are suffering, how much they are suffering, or whether they want to suffer or not. According to the author, we actually cannot know and do not know.

4. The passage indicates that its author would NOT agree with which of the following statements?

Note that if the author would NOT agree with one of the following statements it is *probably not* going to be a statement that you remember having read in the passage! The exception would be if the author had offered counterpoint in the passage.

A. Animals communicate effectively through non-verbal means.

CORRECT: The author would *not* agree with this statement. This is the best possible answer. The author clearly feels that non-verbal means are a poor method of communication, and what meaning there might be could be misconstrued; remember, empathy is a *pathetic fallacy*.

B. The reaction to pain is culturally dependent and relative.

WRONG: The author would agree. This statement is essentially one of the author's own but rewritten (lines 60–62). It advances the author's thesis.

C. An organism may look like us, behave like us, and talk like us, yet not be like us at all.

WRONG: The author would agree. This statement is also rewritten from a passage sentence (lines 55–56). It, too, advances the author's thesis.

D. An animal's reaction to a certain stimulus might not lead us to believe that it is experiencing pain.

WRONG: The author would agree. This can be a true statement by anyone's reckoning. The "certain stimulus" could be *petting* the animal; it is not specified. If you chose this answer, you *assumed*

that the "certain stimulus" was one that might evoke pain. You probably recalled that the author mentions the philosophers and there is the implication that he agrees with their positions. In lines 40–41 he paraphrases them admitting that an animal's behavior, presumably in response to a stimulus of some kind, "might deceive us into mistakenly believing that they do" experience pain. Note, however, that Answer D adds the word *not*, negating the philosopher's idea, and most importantly does not define the "certain stimulus."

5. The author's argument that "[w]e cannot decide right and wrong, good and evil for those with whom communication is barred" (lines 70–71) depends on the acceptance of which of the following premises?

The "whom" of the argument are the animals. The answer must have to do with them. The correct answer will probably be a restated premise or argument from the passage. However, it must still be the best possible answer and refer to the argument which is presented in the question, not an unrelated quotation.

A. Philosophers Kant, Malenbrach, and Aquinas all urged better treatment for animals.

WRONG: The "whom" is correct, but the "philosophers … did not favor the idea of animals rights" (lines 36–38).

B. Rabbits undergoing Draize experimentation actually feel little or no pain in the way humans understand it.

WRONG: The rabbits would fall into the "whom" category of the question. However, it is not necessary to accept that rabbits "actually feel little or no pain" in order to accept the premise of the question. This is not the best answer.

C. Empathy is a false method of communication.

CORRECT: First, this answer does not *contradict* the argument, so it *is* a *possible* answer. Second, according to the author, empathy is a false method of communication and the *only* method of communication we have with animals. Conversely, if empathy *were* a *valid* method of communication the author's argument would not be acceptable. This is the best possible answer.

D. In Aztec culture, being chosen as a sacrifice to the gods was a high honor and a burning desire.

WRONG: The "whom" of the argument stated in this question refers to animals, not humans. We can throw this information out and it will not render the author's argument unacceptable, as the question calls for.

6. The passage suggests that human compassion for other organisms derives from the fact that:

Remember, "suggests" means that the answer *may* not be exact, but only the best possible answer. If you were not able to eliminate the alternatives and determine that three of the four answers were *definitely wrong*, then this could have been a difficult question.

A. helping other organisms may prevent us from hurting other humans.

WRONG: This seemingly familiar piece of information stems from the "indirect moral obligation theories" of the philosophers: "[I]t is wrong to torture animals because it desensitizes us to human suffering and makes us more prone to using violence towards humans" (lines 45–47). Further, opining that it is wrong to "torture animals" is not the same as saying "helping other organisms." You have extrapolated from the information.

B. the organism looks like us, behaves like us, and talks like us.

CORRECT: This answer provides a good example of why going back to the passage is not a good strategy. If you had the time to go back to the passage" to lines 49–50—"the animal looks like me, resembles me, behaves like me"—you would not see anything about "talks like us." This might lead you to believe that this is *not* the correct answer. However, shortly thereafter, at lines 55–56—"That another organism looks like us, behaves like us and talks like us is no guarantee that it is like us"—this answer occurs verbatim. Further, you may see that regarding being "fubsy" there is no mention made of 'talking.' However, the above references are taken from the paragraph on empathy and the author does *suggest* that human compassion is empathic. This is the best possible answer.

C. other organisms suffer in the same way humans do.

WRONG: The author probably does not believe this and certainly would make no arguments regarding the level of suffering for any organisms "with whom communication is barred."

D. other organisms usually look like us.

WRONG: They do not, and the passage does not say that they do.

7. The author contends that in order to judge whether we have the right to make decisions for other organisms, a researcher would need to determine:

Lines 65–67, "what gives us the right to decide for other organisms (without getting their approval)?" The question does not *specify* whether these decisions regard pain, suffering, or being chosen as a sacrifice to the gods.

A. whether or not they are experiencing pain.

WRONG: The author does not argue that we need to determine whether or not animals are experiencing pain. However, he goes on to argue that even if the organisms *are* experiencing pain, pain "can actually be perceived as positive and be sought after" (lines 63–64).Thus rendering this answer moot.

B. if this is a derivative of a primary obligation towards other organisms.

WRONG: There is no mention of an obligation towards other organisms. The "primary obligation" mentioned by the philosophers is towards "our fellow humans."

C. whether or not we have their approval.

CORRECT: The question clearly refers to lines 66–67. In parentheses is the single caveat to the extensive line of reasoning by the author that we do not have the right to make decisions for other organisms.

D. if empathy can be used to determine the relative fubsiness of an organism.

WRONG: This answer merely uses terms that you have become familiar with from reading the passage, making them seem more attractive to you.

Passage II (Questions 8–13)

8. The central thesis of the passage is that:

You may feel that you could have better stated the thesis of the passage than the choices here do. However, you must pick the best possible answer from the choices given.

A. the colonies hoped to enlist Britain's help as an ally in the efforts to secede.

WRONG: Britain was the nemesis of the colonies.

B. the allies, required by the colonies, must perceive the manifest rightness of the independence efforts.

CORRECT: The author emphasizes several times that the colonists "would require allies" (lines 7, 43–44). The "rightness" refers to efforts to ensure that the revolution was not perceived as a "civil war," which would have precluded help from other nations (lines 8–10, 12–15, and 59–60). "Manifest" refers to efforts to make this perception self-evident, for which examples are replete throughout the passage.

C. a strong and unequivocal declaration of civil war was a necessity for the colonies.

WRONG: There is no evidence for this statement. The Declaration was clearly not a declaration of civil war "To help the colonies [in a civil war] would constitute interference in Great Britain's internal affairs" (lines 10–12).

D. the preamble to the Declaration of Independence could not have been better written.

WRONG: The author makes no secret of his admiration for the way the Declaration was written. However, this is not the main theme, nor is it the best answer available among the choices. The passage is about the remarkable conveyance of so many levels of depth and meaning in the effort to gain independence and prepare for the onslaught of Britain.

9. Implicit in the statement that "a decent respect to the opinions of mankind requires that they should declare the causes which impel them to the separation," is the idea that the colonies:

This quote appears twice in the passage. Once in the blocked quotation (lines 22–24), and for answer purposes, again in lines 34–37.

A. were required by the international laws of that time to declare why they were separating.
WRONG: "According to the international law of nations, necessity was a prerequisite for taking up arms against another nation." This is not the same as declaring causes. This is not the best answer.

B. were respectful of the opinions of friend and foe alike.
WRONG: There is no evidence for this idea in the passage. The colonists would not even dignify Britain by mentioning the country by name in the Declaration.

C. believed their aforementioned "causes" to be self-evident but were sharing them with mankind out of respect.
CORRECT: The passage emphasizes that this was a 'declaration' and not meant to persuade; what was written was already known.

D. believed their aforementioned "causes" would impel them to separation.
WRONG: This sentence does not make sense. If you do not understand the sentence or it does not make sense, do not fall into the trap of choosing it just because it sounds intellectual.

10. According to the passage, the proper wording of the Declaration was critical to the colonists' independence efforts because they:

Notice that these types of questions on the MCAT *always* ask for decisions based upon the information in Roman numerals. Therefore, do *not* go to Answer A, then back up to the numerated information, but *begin* with the information in Roman numerals. After quickly determining what is true and what is not true, go down and find the correct answer among A, B, C, or D.

I. would require allies and foreign assistance.
CORRECT: Lines 7, 41–44.

II. could not afford to have the efforts construed as acts of civil war.
CORRECT: Lines 8–10, 12–15, 59–60.

III. did not want to appear to be attempting to justify and persuade.
CORRECT: Lines 26–29, 38–40.

A. II only
B. I and II only
C. I and III only
D. I, II, and III
CORRECT: The passage emphasizes all three of the given choices.

11. What does Samuel Adams's notion that "No foreign Power can consistently yield Comfort to Rebels, or enter into any kind of Treaty with these Colonies till they declare themselves free and independent" (lines 12–15) imply about foreign interference?

A. That foreign powers would not yield to rebels in their own country.
WRONG: This is not a reference to the foreign powers' "own country." It is the rebels' "own country."

B. That the colonists considered themselves to be rebels who were not yet worthy of a treaty
WRONG: We do not know and it is not important whether the colonists considered themselves to be rebels. We do know the context of the question and quotation (See Answer D.). Further, there is no mention of "worthiness" in the passage.

C. Once the colonies had proven that they could win, they could then expect foreign aid.
WRONG: This idea seems to make sense but is not provided or suggested in the information in the passage.

D. That foreign nations would not help the colonies in a civil uprising.
CORRECT: Throughout, the passage stresses the importance of this answer (lines 8–10, 59–60). The introduction of the Samuel Adams quote is "As Samuel Adams explained … ." This refers specifically to the information regarding "civil war" (line 10) and help from other nations (lines 10–12). The context of the quotation from the passage clearly refers to answer D.

12. Which of the following statements is NOT presented as evidence for the significance of the phrase "one people"?

Be wary of these types of questions that ask for negative conclusions. It is very easy to get mixed up.

A. "One people" served to demonstrate the separateness that existed between America and Britain at that time.

WRONG: This is presented as evidence (lines 55–57).

B. The phrase served to prevent the Declaration from being an act of civil war.

WRONG: This is presented as evidence (lines 59–60).

C. The phrase emphasized the characteristics of equality, justice, and liberty inherent in the new nation.

CORRECT: This answer is not presented as evidence for the phrase. This is the best answer.

D. Though never mentioned by name, America is bound by the unification of the phrase.

WRONG: This is presented as evidence (lines 53–55).

13. The passage suggests that the perspective presented throughout the Declaration:

Lines 45–48: "The Declaration served to announce and convey *only America's side* on an issue of international law and sovereignty, and it maintains this *perspective throughout*." In the way they wrote the Declaration, the colonists *avoided* "a tacit admission that there was another perspective" (lines 39–40).

A. eloquently brings forth the stylistic artistry of the men and women who lived during this turbulent period in our nation's history.

WRONG: Though this might be inferred, it is never stressed. With regard to 'eloquence,' the point of the passage is that "*beyond* the flowery eloquence lies great and significant meaning" (lines 2–3). There is no mention of "women." This answer itself is "flowery" but certainly not the *best* answer.

B. is balanced.

WRONG: Notice the similarity between this wrong answer and Answer D. The passage takes pains to point out that the Declaration is *not* balanced. It never even mentions Britain, whose 'perspective' would have been that the colonies were declaring civil war. "The Declaration served to announce and convey only America's side on an issue of international law and sovereignty, and it maintains this perspective throughout" (lines 45–48).

C. is one-sided.

CORRECT: This is the *best* answer. "The Declaration served to announce and convey only America's side on an issue of international law and sovereignty, and it maintains this perspective throughout" (lines 45–48).

D. carefully addresses the validity of the arguments of both sides.

WRONG: Notice the similarity between this wrong answer and Answer B. The passage points out that the Declaration *purposely avoids* any mention of perspectives other than the colony's own. "The Declaration served to announce and convey only America's side on an issue of international law and sovereignty, and it maintains this perspective throughout" (lines 45–48).

Passage III (Questions 14-18)

14. The author claims "Given the commonly known dangers of cigarette smoking, the smoking of a filterless 'joint' of marijuana seems a high-risk exercise" (lines 66–69). The support offered for this conclusion within the passage is:

This is a typical MCAT question. Remember to *first* ascertain if the *second* clause of the answer is accurate and true, thereby eliminating some choices. Then decide if the second clause strengthens (strong), or weakens (weak) the author's claim.

A. weak; there is no evidence that smoking marijuana cigarettes is dangerous.

CORRECT: It is true that we have no "evidence" from within the passage that smoking marijuana cigarettes is dangerous. And, though the dangers of cigarette smoking *are* commonly known and the author refers to marijuana "joints" being smoked in a filterless fashion, the author still wishes for the reader to draw conclusions for which there is only a *weak* basis—not non-existent but weak. This is the best answer.

B. weak; the dangers of cigarette smoking are not commonly known.

WRONG: The second part of this answer is clearly *not* correct. Whether you believe in the dangers or not, the dangers of cigarette smoking are commonly known. The surgeon general's mandatory warning on the package is evidence of this.

C. strong; the dangers of cigarette smoking are commonly known.

WRONG: The second part of this answer is correct. Whether you believe in the dangers or not, the dangers of cigarette smoking are commonly known. The surgeon general's mandatory warning on the package is evidence of this. However, the relationship between marijuana "joints" and cigarettes is not provided *within the passage*. There would need to be more linkage or argument within the passage for the answer to be "strong."

D. strong; the dangers of reefer madness have been well-documented.

WRONG: This is a silly answer, and the "dangers" are *not* well-documented *within the passage*.

15. What is the author implying when referring to information that people who want to use marijuana indicate that "actually smoking the marijuana is the only acceptable form of medicinal administration" (lines 72–73)?

The author is obviously implying *something*, because he refers to this as "revealing." Overall, the tone of the passage towards marijuana smokers is disparaging. The author obviously feels that smoking marijuana is "a high-risk exercise" (lines 68–69). He also provides that there is an alternative in oral and injectable form (lines 65–66).

A. That this is a legitimate alternative point-of-view

WRONG: 'Alternative-ness' does not necessarily go hand-in-hand with 'legitimacy'. The author obviously feels that smoking marijuana is "a high risk exercise" (lines 68–69). He provides that there is an alternative in oral and injectable form (lines 65–66).

B. That people who want to use marijuana are stupid.

WRONG: Though the author is disparaging, he does not provide information or argument for you to assume that people who want to use marijuana are stupid or unintelligent. Besides lacking support, the use of the word "stupid" is vague. This is not the best answer.

C. That these individuals are more interested in recreational use than in the medical benefits of marijuana.

CORRECT: "This brings us back full circle to the question, Or is it just that people with problems are more likely to end up using marijuana heavily?" (lines 73–75). This "full circle" is a reference to the paragraph wherein the physical and emotional dangers for regular users is elaborated upon. The implication in that paragraph and in the final paragraph, from which the quote comes, is that those who ignore the documented dangers of marijuana use simply want to smoke marijuana, to use it recreationally. Just as these individuals were not interested in the dangers and damage outlined in lines 23–36, they are not really interested in the medicinal benefits, which the author feels are almost non-existent.

D. That people with medical problems are more likely to end up using marijuana heavily.

WRONG: There is no evidence for this in the passage, nor is this an implication of the author.

You would have to assume that the "problems" are medical problems.

16. Which of the following is offered as support for the statement "marijuana's use as a medicine has proven inconclusive or has tended to show that its side effects rendered cannabis unsuitable as a medicinal drug" (lines 48–50):

Notice that you cannot answer this question by simply pulling out information from the passage. The question is asking, 'What does the passage *offer as support* for the statement?' not 'What can you find in the passage that would support this statement?'

A. Cannabinoids were only slightly more effective than codeine in controlling pain.

WRONG: This answer offers *no* support for the quote in the question. This is an appealing answer because it is offered in *what appears to be* (but is not) the same sentence (lines 56–59) as the quote from the question. Nevertheless, this is neither "inconclusive" nor does it mention any "side effects."

B. The central nervous system was depressed by marijuana.

CORRECT: This answer offers support for the quote in the question. In response to the question, marijuana "had undesirable effects in depressing the central nervous system," comments Eija Kalso of Helsinki University Hospital" (lines 58–59). Note that the paragraph in which this information appears specifically discusses why "cannabis is unsuitable as a drug."

C. Marijuana use causes toe fungus and thrush, which in turn cause emotional damage.

WRONG: This answer offers *no* support for the quote in the question. Look at the format of this answer; *"which in turn cause ...."* It is never stated that 'toe fungus and thrush cause emotional damage!' References to this answer are at lines 27–28. If this answer stated that "use causes toe fungus and thrush, *and* can cause emotional damage," then this could also arguably support the statement in the question; these are "side effects." *However*, there is no evidence that the research was being conducted in order to evaluate "marijuana's use as a medicine."

D. The DEA has reluctantly agreed to provide funds for further testing.

WRONG: This answer offers *no* support for the quote in the question. And, this is not responsive to the question. The reference reads, "Yet, under *mounting pressure*, the U.S. Drug Enforcement Agency has *reluctantly* agreed to provide funds for further testing of the efficacy of marijuana as a medicine" (lines 60–63). Though this is not a ringing endorsement for medical use, neither does it provide *support* for "inconclusiveness" as a medicine or "side effects."

17. Assume that the following statements are true. Which one is *inconsistent* with the assertion that "legalization promotes experimentation with cannabis, if not also even harder drugs"?

This is a common type of MCAT verbal question. Notice that you could throw out the first part of the question and still answer correctly. It is really *not* necessary to "assume that the following statements are true." The point is to cause you to juggle unnecessary aspects of the question as you attempt to answer.

A. In the Netherlands today, hard drugs are more difficult to find than in 1976.

CORRECT: The passage states, "In the Netherlands, marijuana has been legally available since 1976" (lines 9–10). If legalization promoted experimentation with harder drugs you would expect it to be *easier* to find them. This answer is correct because *it is inconsistent* with the assertion.

B. In the Netherlands, more people have tried cannabis since it was legalized.

WRONG: This answer is *consistent* with the assertion.

C. In the Netherlands prior to 1976, drug use in general had diminished.

WRONG: The passage states, "In the Netherlands, marijuana has been legally available since 1976" (lines 9–10). Thus, the information which is limited to "prior to 1976" in this answer is irrelevant and non-responsive to the question.

D. People who live in Amsterdam come into contact with a wider variety of recreational drugs nowadays.

WRONG: This answer implies increased drug visibility and is therefore *consistent* with the assertion and therefore a wrong answer. In the most favorable light, this answer is certainly *not inconsistent* with the assertion or the best answer.

18. An argument FOR the legalization of marijuana, mentioned in the passage but not expanded upon, is:

A. the medical uses of marijuana for nausea relief.

WRONG: This information *is* mentioned in the passage but is *not* an argument FOR. In context, the information is that "recent development of other, more powerful drugs, makes them a *poor choice* for nausea relief" (lines 55–56).

B. the recent support of the DEA.

WRONG: The passage does not mention any recent support of the DEA. This misstates information from the passage. In context, the information is that

under mounting pressure, i.e., *reluctantly*, the U.S. Drug Enforcement Agency has agreed to provide funds for further testing of the efficacy of marijuana as a medicine" (lines 60–63).

C. the benefits of living in Amsterdam.

WRONG: The passage does not mention that living in Amsterdam is of any benefit. A drug-user might conclude that there is a benefit, but even this is not mentioned or implied in the passage.

D. lengthy prison sentences for drug offenders.

CORRECT: This is an argument "FOR the legalization of marijuana." Additionally, it is not further expanded upon. "Many of these arguments [over whether marijuana should be legalized] pertain to the federal guidelines for lengthy prison sentences meted out for what is considered a relatively petty crime" (lines 2–4).

Passage IV (Questions 19-23)

19. The passage argument suggests that which of the following might benefit from the proposed plan?

  I. the state of New York
  CORRECT: "Among the winners will be, predictably, the state itself … " (lines 25–26).

  II. insurance carriers
  CORRECT: "Insurance carriers are also expected to benefit …" (lines 29–30).

  III. those who have insurance
  CORRECT: "Those clients themselves may also share in the savings … On net, it is anticipated that most will probably enjoy somewhat lower premiums" (lines 33–37).

A. I only
B. I and II only
C. II and III only
D. I, II, and III
  CORRECT: See above explanations.

20. According to the author, the governor's plan "probably won't achieve a truly dramatic savings" (lines 18–19). The primary argument given is that:

A. New York's medical spending from 1980 to 1991 has outpaced national spending by 22%.

WRONG: This is not the primary argument given. This *is information* provided by the author but is *not* an *argument* given in support of the quotation. It is an attractive answer because it is regurgitating passage information in an answer, albeit unresponsively.

B. though state hospital costs compose the bulk of New York's costs, these costs will be relatively unaffected by changing to a competitive system.

CORRECT: This is the primary argument given. "The plan's savings come largely in the form of deregulating hospital's rates and reducing [Medicaid] subsidies for hospitals' medical training" (lines 4–6). "… From 1980 to 1991, New York's growth in hospital costs only slightly exceeded that of most other states, which [already] operate on a competitive system" (lines 20–22).

C. state medical costs cannot be changed through deregulating hospital rates.

    WRONG: It is not asserted by the author that the "state medical costs cannot be changed."

D. New York's growth in hospital costs are the result of Medicaid subsidies.

    WRONG: This is not the primary argument given and is apparently only a small component of the costs.

21. According to the passage, the decisive factor in determining whether a patient in New York City will be turned away from the hospital is whether this person requiring care:

A. has insurance or not.

    WRONG: First, this is *not* specific to New York *City* (line 39). Secondly, "Hospitals [in New York *City*] … will be prohibited from turning away certain extremely low income patients [whether they have insurance or not], whose right to certain emergency care is protected by the state's Hill-Burton law" (lines 41–44).

B. is poor or elderly.

    WRONG: "Undoubtedly, the greatest impact will be felt by the uninsured—often the poor and elderly" (lines 49–50). This is not specific to New York City (line 39).

C. has an extremely low income.

    CORRECT: Giving the italicized reference to New York City (line 39), this same paragraph asserts that "Hospitals … will be prohibited from turning away certain extremely low income patients, whose right to certain emergency care is protected by the state's Hill-Burton law" (lines 41–44).

D. insists on receiving state-of-the-art treatments.

    WRONG: This is not yet the decisive factor, particularly when given the helpful clue, "New York City."

22. Assume that the telephone industry, which had been heavily regulated, was subsequently deregulated and forced to operate on a competitive system. History shows that consumer telephone rates thereafter skyrocketed and efficiency diminished, never again approaching the lower rates or greater efficiency achieved during the period of regulation. This finding:

The assumption you are asked to make is that deregulation is not only not helpful, but is also deleterious in the long term. The best answer choice must be based upon this assumption.

A. increases the probability that the greatest impact will be felt by the poor and elderly.

    WRONG: It might, *or* it might *not*. This is not the best answer.

B. increases the probability that total New York State medical spending will probably be less than it is under the current regulatory system.

    WRONG: This is probably not true. Further, since this savings is projected, not as a free-market result but as a result of a reduction in Medicaid subsidies, this is unrelated to deregulation.

C. decreases the probability of saving through reduction in Medicaid subsidies.

    WRONG: The Medicaid subsidies are unrelated to the deregulation.

D. reveals nothing about the probability of New York state's hospital costs.

    CORRECT: This is the best answer. The author clearly believes that New York's hospital costs are not tremendous or out of proportion when compared to those of other states. "From 1980 to 1991, New York's growth in hospital costs has only slightly exceeded that of most other states, which operate on a competitive system" (lines 20–22). Therefore, they will not be significantly impacted whether deregulation is successful or not.

23. Which of the following statements, if true, would most directly *challenge* the assertions of the author?

A. Deregulation and competition in an economic system invariably lead to greater efficiency, productivity, and savings.

    WRONG: This does not challenge the author. Though the author is not so clearly strident, he nevertheless does not give the impression that he is against or does not believe in deregulation or competition. He simply believes that there may be aspects of medical costs that have been overlooked.

B. Most health consumers in New York can be expected to benefit from somewhat lower insurance premiums.

    WRONG: This is an assertion of the author and does not challenge him. "[I]t is anticipated that most will probably enjoy somewhat lower premiums" (lines 36–39).

C. It is possible that hospitals in New York City may have to close regardless of how well the plan works.

WRONG: This does not challenge the author. "Of course, should hospitals continue to offer access to the uninsured, they will effectively be subsidizing the poor and will be rewarded with lower profit margins. Some may be forced to close" (lines 45–48).

D. New medical technologies help prevent long-term debilitation and subsequent intensive care of many patients, thereby proportionally reducing medical costs.

CORRECT: This answer most directly challenges the assertions of the author. The author asserts, "Over 55% of the increase [in medical care costs] is directly related to the staggering cost of new medical technologies" (lines 61–63). If this were true, but the technologies reduced medical costs through some other means, this "staggering cost" and the author's final point would be greatly diminished.

Passage V (Questions 24–28)

24. The discussion of Athena and the current legal system includes the assumption that:

A. most of Athena's admirers were surprised at her gender.

WRONG: There is no indication that anyone was surprised at her gender, much less that "most" were surprised. Though "she is more 'masculine' than any male" (lines 18–19), she is the mate of a male god, Zeus, and she does not try to hide her gender.

B. present-day justices are popular and respected.

WRONG: This idea is certainly not implied or assumed by the passage. Quite the opposite. Modern justices have sought "mystique and status" "at the expense of trust and popularity" (lines 29–30).

C. most litigants consider modern justices to be aloof.

CORRECT: The author's discussion includes this assumption. It is an assumption because there really is no direct evidence supporting this idea. Modern justices are "intellectually aloof from the litigants before them" (lines 27–28). This assumption is further promoted as it contrasts with Athena the popular mediatrix.

D. Athena was the ideal "judicial" figure.

WRONG: "Athena, the ideal 'judicial' figure of the Greek world" (lines 5–6). This is not an "assumption" of the passage; it is an explicit/verbatim quote from the passage! Further, it has no relation to the "current legal system."

25. Which of the following statements, if true, would most WEAKEN the author's contention that "a distant apolitical judge" (line 21) has less legitimacy with the people?

A. An enemy is anyone who tells the truth about you.

WRONG: This statement does not weaken the contention because it is completely unrelated to the contention.

B. The only normal people are the ones you don't know very well.

CORRECT: This statement weakens the author's contention. The inverse of this is that "if you know someone well, then they don't seem normal," or "if the judges were not distant, then they wouldn't seem normal." The judges made a conscious decision to become "distant" and "apolitical" apparently because this "cultivated persona has consciously increased the mystique and status of the lawyer-judge" (lines 28–29).

C. To know him is to love him.

WRONG: This statement does not weaken the contention. If this were true, then it would support the author's contention that "love" equals increased "legitimacy." If you did not assume or agree with the aforementioned, then this statement would still not weaken the contention.

D. Criticism is prejudice made plausible.

WRONG: This statement does not weaken the contention because it is completely unrelated to the contention.

26. The author would argue that emulating some of the "juxtaposed attributes" (line 4) of Athena is important to the current legal system because it:

A. explains why the Greeks honored their goddesses.

WRONG: The author would not argue this because it is inaccurate. There is no discussion of why "the Greeks honored their goddesses" in the passage, therefore it would be inaccurate to assume that the author would "argue" it.

B. provides for greater acceptance of judicial decisions.

CORRECT: The author would, and does "argue" this. "One ancient example is the juxtaposed attributes of the Greek goddess Athena, the ideal 'judicial' figure of the Greek world. Some of those attributes, since lost to the common law tradition, may lend new legitimacy to the current legal system if rediscovered" (lines 4–8).

C. illustrates Athena's detached judicial renderings.

WRONG: The author would not argue this because it is inaccurate. Athena's judicial renderings were certainly not "detached."

D. indicates that current judicial decisions are poorly decided.

WRONG: The author does not imply this in his passage, therefore it would be inaccurate to assume that he would "argue" it.

27. The main argument of the passage is that:

A. Athena was a goddess with many admirable human attributes.

WRONG: This is accurate. However, it is not the main argument of the passage. This is a mechanism through which the author contrasts the humanlike goddess to the judges-now-like-gods.

B. the modern judicial system, though much changed, takes its roots from the Greeks.

WRONG: This is not implied in the passage. It is definitely not a "main argument" of the passage.

C. Greek justices were active in the political arena and the community.

WRONG: Though this answer, like Answer D, is strongly implied, it is definitely not a "main argument" of the passage. It is merely implied for the purposes of showing Athena's desirable earthly attributes.

D. modern judges have become more like gods with godlike attributes.

CORRECT: This is one of the "main arguments" of the passage. This is not explicitly presented but is strongly implied as the author contrasts Athena, the goddess with earthly attributes, with "modern judges [who] have become more like gods with godlike attributes." There is the goddess Athena whose earthly attributes include being "of the people," her "civic involvement," her "legislation by consensus," her "encouragement of active participation by mortals," etc. Modern judges, on the other hand, more and more exhibit "godlike attributes" and are "physically distant," "aloof," have a "mystique." The passage urges that modern justices and the "current legal system" regain new legitimacy.

28. The author most likely believes that one of the main purposes of the judiciary should be to:

A. render decisions that are fair, while remembering "you can't please them all."

WRONG: The author does not clearly believe this. The "remember that you can't please them all" remark in this answer is not supported within the passage. Thus, it would be pure conjecture to say that the "author most likely believes" this answer.

B. deliver charity to the people and heavy-handed justice to the guilty.

WRONG: The author does not believe this. The "heavy-handed justice to the guilty" aspect in this answer is not supported within the passage. Thus, it would be pure conjecture to say that the "author most likely believes" this answer.

C. encourage active participation, then rule by fiat.

WRONG: The author does not believe this. Ruling by fiat (a summary ruling without consensus) does not lend itself to a popular or satisfying decision with the litigants according to lines 31–47. If you did not know what "fiat" meant, you could discern the meaning in the context of the sentence from the passage. "With all her superhuman wisdom and power, she is ideally suited to judge by fiat, yet she consciously legislates by consensus" (lines 33–35).

D. render fair and equitable decisions that leave the majority satisfied with the outcome.

CORRECT: The author points with obvious favor to Athena's "fair" and "equitable" decisions which "leaves both parties more satisfied with their outcome than would a judicial decree."

Passage VI (Questions 29–34)

29. Before the onset of World War II, the American public perceived the emperor as a gentle and ineffectual figurehead. The most reasonable explanation on the basis of passage information is that:

A. the war had not yet begun.

WRONG: This is not the most reasonable explanation. This answer is vague and not as explanatory as Answer B.

B. there were no Japanese soldiers killing American soldiers in the name of the emperor.

CORRECT: This is the only answer given which is based on passage information. "How did this flawed perception of the emperor as an aggrandizing military dictator take hold in America? One possible explanation is that, because Japanese soldiers swore allegiance to the emperor and carried on the war effort in his name, Americans believed that he was their actual leader" (lines 43–47).

C. Americans had always had a flawed perception of the emperor.

WRONG: This is not a reasonable explanation. There is no basis for it in the passage. The explanatory quotation from Answer B actually offers a different explanation and suggests that the perception had not always been flawed.

D. this period, as portrayed by most historians, was a "confusing time."

WRONG: This is not the most reasonable explanation. The "confusing time" is an allusion to the "postwar," not "before the onset" of the war.

30. The author's apparent point in referring to historian Robert E. Ward's analysis that "there was a consensus that the emperor would be retained" (lines 20–21), is that:

A. there *was* a consensus that the emperor would be retained.

WRONG: This is not the author's point. "Ward is one of only a few historians who claims this as definite; most others saw the fate of the emperor to be very uncertain" (lines 21–23).

B. this analysis was of critical importance to the passage.

WRONG: This is not the author's point. The passage could have survived just as well without this quotation and Ward's analysis, which was shared by almost no one else. The quotation bolstered the author's argument that there was actually no clear consensus that the emperor would be retained. However, Ward's was a lonely voice. "Ward is one of only a few historians who claims this as definite; most others saw the fate of the emperor to be very uncertain" (lines 21–23).

C. there was actually *no* clear consensus that the emperor would be retained.

CORRECT: This is the author's point. Ward's definitive assertion "makes him one of only a few historians" (lines 21–22) who felt this way. Two of the main themes of the passage are the "confusing time", and "lack of consensus." This quotation, when taken in the context of the passage, clearly supports this assertion as simply another historian/person/American in disagreement over the emperor. "Ward is one of only a few historians who claims this as definite; most others saw the fate of the emperor to be very uncertain" (lines 21–23).

D. a flawed perception of the emperor by the American people.

WRONG: This is not the author's point. This quote has nothing to do with the American's people's "perception" of the emperor.

31. If the passage information is correct, what inference is justified by the fact that there is still a Japanese emperor, almost sixty years after the period described?

A. The American debate regarding the role of the emperor had been decided.

WRONG: This inference is vague when compared with Answer C, which states everything this answer states and is more definitive.

B. The Japanese military had retained much of their political influence.

WRONG: This inference is not justified. The army's "political influence" is dubious based on passage information, though there was a "pro-

military bureaucracy, with whom [the emperor] disagreed but was unwilling to formally oppose" (lines 35–36). However, lines 36–42 explain that the army's efforts to use the unwilling emperor were largely ineffective. Would the army have used their "retained political influence" to keep the emperor? This answer does not approach Answer C.

C. The Americans had decided that the emperor could be used to their advantage.

CORRECT: This is the only inference that can be justified. The passage provides only one response to why the emperor would be kept on, because "no one actually liked the institution of the emperor, and everyone blamed him for the war, but he was seen as a crucial tool for the Americans to promote cooperation and bring about a democracy. If the emperor could be co-opted, he could also be used as a disguised clarion for American mandates to be broadcast to the Japanese, with almost divine authority" (lines 50–56).

D. The Japanese *genro* had lost much of their power.

WRONG: This inference is not justified as "Emperor Hirohito was merely a figurehead for the *genro* [capitalist elite]" (lines 33–34). If the genro had gained or increased much of their power then this could have been a possible answer.

32. According to the passage, all American parties agreed that the most important priority was:

A. reaching a consensus on what should be done about the Emperor.

WRONG: This might have been a high priority, but it is never mentioned explicitly as "the most important priority" in the passage. Demilitarization is explicitly referred to as the "most important priority." Therefore, this is not the best answer.

B. bringing democracy to Japan.

WRONG: This might have been a high priority, but it is never mentioned explicitly as "the most important priority" in the passage. Demilitarization is explicitly referred to as the "most important priority." Therefore, this is not the best answer.

C. not something that could be determined easily.

WRONG: "It appears that all the parties involved agreed that the need to severely curtail Japan's military and militarism was the most important priority" (lines 7–9).

D. restricting Japan's military capabilities.

CORRECT: This answer is explicitly mentioned in the passage: "It appears that all the parties involved agreed that the need to severely curtail Japan's military and militarism was the most important priority" (lines 7–9).

33. Given the passage implication that the goal of bringing a democracy to Japan was a foregone conclusion (lines 11–18), which of the following passage assertions seems *contrary* to this idea?

 A. Japan would be demilitarized as soon as possible.
 WRONG: This is not contrary to the idea of democratization.

 B. The emperor would be retained.
 CORRECT: This answer is contrary to the idea of democratization. Most democracies do not have a king or an emperor. This seems contrary to the idea of bringing a democracy.

 C. The emperor would be deposed.
 WRONG: This is not contrary to the idea of democratization. Most democracies do not have a king or an emperor.

 D. The emperor was, in fact, passive.
 WRONG: This is not contrary to the idea of democratization. Most democracies do not have a king or an emperor. It would be better to have a "passive" one than a despot. This answer is less contrary to the idea of democratization than Answer B and is, therefore, not as good an answer.

34. The passage suggests that its author would probably *disagree* with which of the following statements?

 A. The emperor was unwilling to formally oppose the military.
 WRONG: The author would not disagree with this statement. "Emperor Hirohito ... later became a tool for the military ... with whom he disagreed but was unwilling to formally oppose" (lines 33–36).

 B. The emperor was actually passive.
 WRONG: The author would not disagree with this statement. "Historian Mikiso Hane says that the emperor was, in fact, so passive ..." (lines 37–38).

 C. The emperor was a member of the *genro* whom he supported.
 CORRECT: The author would probably disagree with this statement. There is no basis for this in the passage. Thus, we can assume that the author would probably disagree. "Emperor Hirohito was merely a figurehead for the *genro* [capitalist elite], whom he supported" (lines 33–34). "Merely" means that is all that he was.

 D. The emperor was seen by Americans as a military dictator.
 WRONG: The author would not disagree with this statement. "How did this flawed perception of the emperor as an aggrandizing military dictator take hold in America?" (lines 43–44).

Passage VII (Questions 35–40)

35. According to the passage information, what would most likely happen if a student was tested "in the first hour after learning" (lines 55)?

 A. Overall, recall would be very poor due to a decline in this first hour.
 CORRECT: This would be most likely to happen. "Dr. Terrace cites a 'precipitous decline' in recall in the first hour after learning, so students would be well advised to avoid being tested until at least one hour later" (lines 54–57).

 B. Overall, recall would be strong based on the strengths of short-term memory.
 WRONG: This would not be most likely to happen. There is no mention of "short-term memory" in the passage. You are bringing outside information into the question. "Dr. Terrace cites a 'precipitous decline' in recall in the first hour after learning, so students would be well advised to avoid being tested until at least one hour later" (lines 54–57).

 C. The student would be likely to recall only the last part of what he had been studying.
 WRONG: This would not be most likely to happen. The "only" aspect of this answer negates its accuracy. Based upon the "serial position effect," the student would be able to recall the first part of what he had been studying equally well. See the explanation for Answer A.

 D. The "recency" of the testing would result in better recall than testing done later.
 WRONG: This would not be most likely to happen. This is not an accurate characterization of the concept of "recency." Further, "Dr. Terrace cites a 'precipitous decline' in recall in the first hour after learning, so students would be well advised to avoid being tested until at least one hour later" (lines 54–57).

36. The assertion that Shereshevskii "could seemingly remember any datum for any length of time because of his innate ability to visualize images relating to the subject matter" (lines 63–65) is NOT clearly consistent with the information about:

 A. Terrace's "serial position effect."
 WRONG: The two ideas are not clearly related in any way. Consistency is not expected, nor required here, because the two ideas are mutually exclusive. It is clear that Shereshevskii's abilities were beyond the norm, and thus might be expected to fall outside what was expected from the results of regular clinical experimentation and theories.

B. memorizing a portion of *Don Juan*.

WRONG: The two ideas are not clearly related in any way. Consistency is not expected, nor required here, because the two ideas are mutually exclusive. It is clear that Shereshevskii's abilities were beyond the norm, and thus might be expected to fall outside what was expected from the results of regular clinical experimentation and theories.

C. monotonous rote learning.

WRONG: This answer is consistent with the assertion.

D. Baddeley's quoted description of this ability.

CORRECT: This answer and the quote it refers to are NOT clearly consistent with the assertion in the question. The assertion in the question from the passage emphasizes Shereshevskii's ability to "visualize images," without reference to any other senses being involved. Apparently continuing to refer to Shereshevskii, Baddeley's quote stated, "In general, this meant that even the driest and most unpromising material created a vivid experience which was represented not only visually but in terms of sound and touch and smell" (lines 66–69). All of a sudden, Shereshevskii is using not only "visual" senses, but also "sound and touch and smell" to aid him in memorization.

37. According to the information about "serial position effect" (line 34), readers of this passage would find it easiest to recall the information about:

Based upon the "serial position effect" and the increased ability to recall "primacy" and "recency" information better than information in the middle (which is even exemplified in the passage with the St. Augustine reading) the answer must contain passage information from the *beginning*/primacy and the *end*/recency of the passage.

A. Ebbinghaus's being the first to study memory experimentally and "serial position effect."

WRONG: This answer does not contain passage information from the beginning/primacy and the end/recency of the passage. Information about the "serial position effect" is from the approximate middle of the passage.

B. "serial position effect" and the memory abilities of Shereshevskii.

WRONG: This answer does not contain passage information from the beginning/primacy and the end/recency of the passage. Information about the "serial position effect" is from the approximate middle of the passage.

C. the spelling of Shereshevskii's name, and that Ebbinghaus was the first to study memory experimentally.

WRONG: This answer does not contain passage information from the beginning/primacy and the end/recency of the passage. Shereshevskii's name first appears on line 62, which is not close enough to the end of the passage for this to be the best answer.

D. visualizing an image to go with a word, and that the average person's memory span is seven units of information.

CORRECT: This answer does contain passage information from the beginning/primacy and the end/recency of the passage. The information in the answer is from the first paragraph and the last paragraph of the passage.

38. According to the passage, prior to the memory studies of Dr. Hermann Ebbinghaus, the study of memory was most probably characterized by which of the following?

Note that it is necessary to remember what was novel about the studies of Ebbinghaus in order to characterize prior studies. We know that "[t]he first psychologist to study memory *experimentally in a clinical setting* was Dr. Hermann Ebbinghaus" (lines 1–2). Therefore, look for an answer which is the opposite of this, i.e. non-experimental and outside of a clinical setting.

A. Speculation based upon little experimentation, within a clinical setting.

WRONG: This is not a probable characterization of the studies prior to Ebbinghaus. "The first psychologist to study memory experimentally in a clinical setting was Dr. Hermann Ebbinghaus" (lines 1–2). Therefore, those who had studied "prior" to Ebbinghaus would not have done so "within a clinical setting."

B. Facts observable through experimentation outside of a clinical setting.

WRONG: This is not a probable characterization of the studies prior to Ebbinghaus. We are looking for studies without experimentation.

C. Evidence based upon some experimentation within a clinical setting.

WRONG: This is not a probable characterization of the studies prior to Ebbinghaus. We are looking for studies outside of a clinical setting.

D. Observation without experimentation, outside of a clinical setting.

CORRECT: This is a probable characterization of the studies prior to Ebbinghaus. "The first psychologist to study memory experimentally in a clinical setting was Dr. Hermann Ebbinghaus" (lines 1–2).

39. Based upon the Ebbinghaus quotation (lines 8–16), we can conclude that the professor equated:

A. decreasing difficulty with the increasing speed of recall.

CORRECT: This is the only valid conclusion. "… the memorization of a series of ideas that is to be reproduced is more difficult, the longer the series is. That is, the memorization not only requires more time taken by itself, because each repetition lasts longer, but it also requires more time relatively because an increased number of repetitions becomes necessary" (lines 8–14).

B. decreasing difficulty with the increasing time it takes to recall.

WRONG: This is not a valid conclusion. Why would it take more time to recall easier problems?

C. increasing difficulty with the increasing speed of recall.

WRONG: This is not a valid conclusion. Why would it take less time to recall more difficult problems?

D. increasing difficulty with the decreasing time it takes to recall.

WRONG: This is not a valid conclusion. Why would it take less time to recall more difficult problems?

40. Passage information indicates that Ebbinghaus's conclusions regarding memorizing a list of words in a certain order and then changing the sequence of this list (lines 17–29) were most likely based upon:

I. an experiment conducted in the manner described.

WRONG: This is *not* likely. There had been no actual experiment. Read the explanation for Answer Choice II carefully.

II. conclusions based upon his other experiments.

CORRECT: This is most likely. If you look carefully at the use of the verbs in the quotation, it becomes clear that an experiment of this sort had *not* actually been conducted. "Ebbinghaus goes on to conclude that, if subjects *were to* memorize a list of words in a certain order and came back to relearn them a day later, but then *were given* a list of the same words out of sequence, their rate of learning for the new list *would be* no better for having studied the other sequence before" (lines 19–24).

III. speculation with no experimentation.

WRONG: This is *not* likely. Though not based on an actual experiment, it is *speculation* to base Ebbinghaus's conclusions on "speculation." We do know that Ebbinghaus

had conducted experiments on memory and recall in a clinical setting (lines 1–2).

A. I only

B. II only

CORRECT: See above answer explanations.

C. III only

D. I and II only

Verbal Reasoning Test 2
Answers & Explanations

TEST 2 ANSWER KEY

1.	A	11.	C	21.	C	31.	D
2.	D	12.	D	22.	D	32.	C
3.	B	13.	D	23.	A	33.	B
4.	A	14.	C	24.	D	34.	A
5.	D	15.	A	25.	A	35.	C
6.	D	16.	C	26.	D	36.	D
7.	A	17.	B	27.	D	37.	B
8.	D	18.	D	28.	A	38.	D
9.	C	19.	C	29.	B	39.	A
10.	A	20.	B	30.	A	40.	C

Passage I (Questions 1–5)

1. Which of the following assertions in the passage is NOT supported by an example, argument, or reference to an authority?

  A. The concepts of right and wrong are traditional moral concepts.

  CORRECT: This assertion comes from the first paragraph. "*Traditional moral concepts* fail in this regard" (lines 9–10). The concepts the author has been denigrating are those from line 1, "The concepts of right and wrong." Notice that the author labels the concepts of right and wrong "traditional moral concepts" without providing any evidence for this.

  B. Irrational concepts are damaging to society.

  WRONG: Support *is* provided for this: "The damage to a society that blindly accepts such fallacies of reason lies in the fallacy itself; *if an action is not truly wrong, it should not be forbidden, punished, or otherwise condemned*" (lines 26–29).

  C. Right and wrong in the moral sense rely upon feelings of others that can never be ascertained with confidence.

  WRONG: This answer is verbatim from lines 23–25. It *is* supported through building upon the reference to Descartes. For instance, the "certainty [of self-sensation] is lost in the mutuality of the group" (lines 18–19).

  D. A Darwinian philosophy would prescribe a primitive, anarchical society.

  WRONG: It is true that this is *not* supported. However, this is not actually an "assertion" by the author and thus, would not be responsive to the question. The beginning of this line reads, "Upon first reflection ..." (lines 49–50). The author uses this as a foil to prove his point and in no way supports the idea.

2. Which of the following would the author believe is the most important factor to consider when making a decision concerning a moral dilemma?

  Think in terms of the *author's* definition of the Darwinian philosophy. The author's morals rely on Darwin and the *ability* and *intention* to reproduce. "Actions that are not conducive to the goals of reproduction ... are 'WRONG' or 'evil' actions" (lines 45–47).

  A. What others in your position would do.

  WRONG: If you did this, you would be promoting other's "reproductive efforts" and would be "doomed to extinction."

  B. What makes you feel good.

  WRONG: This is not the best answer. "What makes you feel good" is not always "what is best for you." If you do something that is not the best for you, then you are diminishing your capacity to reproduce. Masturbation may "feel good," but it diminishes your capacity to reproduce by using reproductive energy.

  C. What is best for society.

  WRONG: According to the author, society is the *result* of his philosophy and its proof (lines 59–61). Society is a by-product of doing what is best for you; that which furthers your reproductive efforts.

  D. What is best for you.

  CORRECT: The Darwinian philosophy is the primary espousal in the passage, and thus, the touchstone to be used when confronting a moral dilemma. "[M]an must act to reproduce; and not just to reproduce, but also to create an environment that is most conducive to the reproductive efforts of his own offspring" (lines 35–38). This is an environment, that (in the first person) "is best for you." This is further supported by referring to possible instances of deviation from these factors, such as, "It is *often in the best interest of the individual* and his own offspring to obey societal rules and regulations even when his fitness may be reduced in the short term" (lines 52–54). Here the "individual," though appearing to help society, is actually primarily helping himself.

3. A religious man says, "It's *wrong* to have sex before marriage." The author would most likely argue:

  We must equate "sex" with the reference to information regarding "reproduction." This is implied by the passage. However, "reproduction" is more constraining than "sex," which, in another context, might mean "homosexual sex" or "masturbation." Masturbation, or homosexual sex, may "feel good," but it diminishes your capacity to reproduce by using reproductive energy.

  A. Sex before marriage is always right because it results in reproduction.

  WRONG: This is not the best answer. It is simplistic. Sex before marriage does not *always* result in reproduction so it cannot *always* be right. According to information in the passage, there are "often" situations where an individual might do something "even when his fitness [i.e., personal reproductive efforts] may be reduced in the short term" (lines 53–54). Therefore, personal "reproduction" is not "right" in all situations and not necessarily "right" outside of the context of marriage.

  B. Sex before marriage may or may not be wrong depending upon the circumstances.

CORRECT: Referencing the explanation given to Answer A. According to information in the passage, there are "often" situations in which an individual might do something "even when his fitness [i.e., personal reproductive efforts] may be reduced in the short term" (lines 53–54). Therefore, personal "reproduction" is not "right" in all situations.

C. There is no right or wrong concerning sex before marriage.

WRONG: The author *never* argues that there is "no right or wrong." On the contrary, he refers to the concepts of right and wrong as being *required* (lines 31–34). The author restates these concepts in a nontraditional fashion. Thus, any answer, which includes the assertion that "there is no right and wrong", is incorrect.

D. Sex before marriage is only right if a child is the result.

WRONG: The author asserts that "man must *act* to reproduce" (line 35). No mention is made of the commonly known fact that reproductive efforts/acts do not always produce a child. It is the *intention* and the *act* that are important to the author. The consequences of these acts, *perceived as a whole* [society], are evidenced by the existence of society (lines 59–61).

4. Based on the passage, which statement could most reasonably be attributed to the author?

Remember that the author *does* believe in a right v. wrong and a good v. evil (lines 45–48).

A. People who produce offspring are naturally good.

CORRECT: The author argues that 'goodness' is based upon actions that are "conducive to the goals of reproduction" (lines 45–46). He also argues that anything other than this "behavior" of 'goodness' and we would be "doomed to extinction" (lines 41–44). To the author, "the very *existence* of our society [our *being*] is, in itself, the proof" (lines 60–61). Our *being* validates our goodness—our willingness to conduct, and be conducive to, reproduction.

B. People who produce offspring are naturally bad.

WRONG: This is diametrically opposed to the author's main point.

C. People who produce more offspring are neither bad nor good; they just are.

WRONG: The author is not ambivalent regarding his beliefs on good and evil. They are linked to reproduction.

D. Modern societies are morally better than ancient ones.

WRONG: If we had information from the passage that modern societies are based upon reproduction (which is morally better) and ancient ones were based upon traditional moralities (which are damaging to society), then this might be the best answer. This information is not in the passage.

5. Which of the following is the most logical conclusion when applying the author's definition of morality (lines 45–48) to animals?

"*Actions* that are *not conducive* to the goals of *reproduction* as prescribed by Darwinism are 'WRONG' or 'evil' actions, while those that are conducive are 'right' or 'good' actions" (lines 45–48). Notice that the author describes "*actions*" as good and evil and does not label animate objects as such. He may even believe in the "traditional" perspective of "love the sinner, hate the sin."

A. Only extinct animals were moral.

WRONG: This diametrically opposes what the author would say. The whole point to morality, according to the author, is reproduction leading to proliferation and the opportunity to evolve. If the animals became extinct, it is reasonable to assume that they were not reproducing enough to confront whatever threatened them.

B. If animals are proliferating, then they are amoral.

WRONG: The whole point to morality, according to the author, is reproduction leading to proliferation and the opportunity to evolve.

C. Animals cannot be moral.

WRONG: There is no evidence for this in the passage. Man is the only animal who would prioritize a desire or drive over reproduction, rendering him the only animal that cannot be moral, that can be completely *amoral*. There is not enough information in the passage to choose this answer.

D. If animals are proliferating, then they are moral.

CORRECT: The author would agree. If it could be determined that some animals had a *more effective reproductive strategy* (i.e. were proliferating more) than others did, that animal might be considered moral in the author's eyes. Man is the only animal who would prioritize a desire or drive over reproduction, rendering him the *only* animal that can be amoral (without a morality). Given that there are animals that have become extinct, we know that these animals were probably less fit, that their "actions" might have been less good.

Passage II (Questions 6–12)

6. According to the passage, which of the following is most likely to be true about the relationship between the foliose lichens and the peppered moths?

The question asks which of the following is most likely "to be true" about the relationship. Remember that the main point of the passage is to *refute* the findings, suppositions, and observations of Kettlewell and Tutt. The answer would *not* consider a Kettlewell observation as "most likely to be true!"

A. Typicals are more difficult for birds to see on lichens.

WRONG: This is a *false* assumption of Kettlewell and Tutt. "For birds, *black* [*melanic*] pepper moths are *actually camouflaged* in unpolluted forests on foliose in pure UV" (lines 61–63).

B. Moths and lichens tend to thrive in the more polluted areas.

WRONG: This is patently false. Lines 21–22 indicate the reason for the darker trunks required for the story, "in woodlands where industrial *pollution had killed the lichens*, exposing the bark and darkening the tree trunks."

C. Lichens in polluted forests provide concealment for melanics.

WRONG: This is false. In the polluted forests, the trunks were darker because the *pollution had killed the lichens*; there were no lichens in the polluted forests.

D. Their relationship is based upon Kettlewell's supposition.

CORRECT: This answer correctly implies that there is no relationship between the moths and the lichens. "[I]n 25 years of fieldwork, one prominent researcher and his colleagues found only one peppered moth on a tree trunk" (lines 76–78). Foliose lichens *grow on tree trunks* and are almost nonexistent in the understory where moths alight (lines 19–20, 80–82). Even Kettlewell admitted this. Besides Kettlewell's and Tutt's own observations and suppositions, which are the passage's main targets, there is no evidence that there even *is* a relationship between the moths and the lichens.

7. The author is primarily concerned with demonstrating that:

Do not frustrate yourself if your conclusion regarding what the author was concerned with demonstrating differs from the available choices. Look for the best answer.

A. Poor experimentation leads to poor findings.

CORRECT: This is demonstrated throughout the passage. The author takes pains to explain Kettlewell and Tutt's methods of experimentation, then refutes their findings as sloppy and poorly accomplished.

B. Industry has had little effect on populations.

WRONG: This *may* be true based upon the figures and findings of later researchers cited by the author. However, there is not enough information to determine if this is so. Moreover, this idea is not of primary concern to the author, particularly when compared with Answer A.

C. Kettlewell knew that his experiment was inaccurate and that his findings were wrong.

WRONG: This answer implies that Kettlewell was dishonest or intent on purposely misleading. We have very little evidence or indication from the author that this was so. There is one quote from Kettlewell admitting that his placement of moths was not completely representative. However, any further evidence regarding the motives and awareness of Kettlewell is lacking. This is not a primary concern if a concern at all.

D. The scientific community can be fooled.

WRONG: This is certainly a true statement but not of *primary* concern to the author, particularly when *compared* with Answer A. The author's reference to "the European peppered moth, *Biston betularia*, as one of the first, and still most cited examples of 'evolution in action'" (lines 6–8) does not say that the scientific community is making the citations. Further, the purpose of these lines is not to denigrate the scientific community. Later on in the passage, it is the scientific community that the author relies upon to prove Kettlewell wrong. The author would be unlikely to hold up Kettlewell as an example of the "scientific community."

8. The passage suggests that the discrepancies in the expected geographical distribution of melanic moths can actually be attributed to:

Note that "discrepancies" and "expected" are terms that relate to the geographical distribution data of Kettlewell. Thus, any possible correct answer would have to suggest an *attribute for the later findings* of biologists who established that Kettlewell's data was not correct. Referencing this question, the *only* suggestion regarding the discrepancies provided by the passage is at lines 50–55.

A. the relative nonexistence of foliose lichens in the understory.

WRONG: Though the foliose are relatively nonexistent in the understory, this is not offered as a response to the question.

B. differences between the way humans and birds see, which Kettlewell was not aware of.

WRONG: This is a correct answer to a question *other* than the one being asked. This answer responds to 'what led Kettlewell to reach conclusions that were later found to be incorrect.'

C. selective predation.

WRONG: This is not offered as a response to the question. See D.

D. This information is not provided.

CORRECT: A verbatim quote of the question can be found at lines 46–47. Referencing this question, the *only* suggestion regarding the discrepancies provided by the passage is that "[t]his led D.R. Lees and E.R. Creed to conclude that 'either the predation experiments and tests of conspicuousness to humans are misleading, or some factor or factors in addition to selective predation are responsible for maintaining the high melanic frequencies'" (lines 50–55).

9. According to the author, melanics and typicals tend to:

Notice the "and" in the question. Thus, the question is, "Moths tend to *what*?"

A. rest on vertical surfaces.

WRONG: "[I]n 25 years of fieldwork, one prominent researcher and his colleagues found only one peppered moth on a tree trunk [vertical surface]. The moths rarely choose to alight on vertical surfaces," (lines 76–79).

B. feed on foliose lichens.

WRONG: There is no information regarding the moths eating anything.

C. rest where lichens are nonexistent.

CORRECT: This is a tendency of the moths. The passage takes pains to *refute* Tutt and Kettlewell; theirs is the only information that asserts that moths rest on lichens; or describeswhere lichens exist. We know that: A) Moths *do not* rest on vertical surfaces but in the understory of trees (lines 79–81), and B) Lichens *do not* grow in the understory of trees but do grow on tree trunks/vertical surfaces (lines 20, 79–82). Thus, moths tend to rest where lichens are nonexistent.

D. thrive in industrially polluted areas.

WRONG: There is no suggestion of this in the passage. If Kettlewell is incorrect, we might be forced to conclude that we do not know what impact industrial pollution has had on the moths, but further than this we cannot say at this point.

10. The author suggests that Kettlewell:

A. knew that certain aspects of his experiment were inaccurate.

CORRECT: This is a suggestion of the author. "In his experiments, Kettlewell released moths directly onto tree trunks, and acknowledged that they were not free to take up their own choice of resting site. I admit that, under their own choice, many would have taken up position higher in the trees" (lines 65–69).

B. did not know that aspects of his experiment were inaccurate.

WRONG: This is *not* a suggestion of the author. See lines 65–69 and the explanation for A.

C. did not think that his findings were very significant.

WRONG: This is *not* a suggestion of the author. Given that Kettlewell felt he had proven industrial melanism, and then said that "industrial melanism was 'the *most striking evolutionary change ever actually witnessed in any organism*'" (lines 42–43), one can not choose this answer.

D. was devious.

WRONG: This not suggested. Simply because Kettle "knew that certain aspects of his experiment were inaccurate" (i.e., A., the correct answer), does not mean that he was devious. Apparently, Kettlewell freely admitted this inaccuracy, possibly feeling it was unimportant.

11. According to the author, why is it important to determine if Kettlewell's story is right?

Ensure that the answer is responsive to the question and not just a correct piece of information.

A. If Kettlewell's story is flawed, then we must accept that evolution is flawed.

WRONG: This is not asserted in the passage and is not the best answer when compared with C.

B. Industrial melanism is significant.

WRONG: This is not asserted by the author.

C. The European peppered moth story is still one of the most cited examples of "evolution in action."

CORRECT: This answer is almost verbatim from lines 5–8.

D. Most biologists sight European peppered moths when they are working on stories about industrial melanism.

WRONG: Sight or *cite*, this answer is silly; do most biologists actually *see* European peppered moths when …? This answer does *not* say that "most biologists *cite* European peppered moths …."

12. As it is used in the passage, the phrase *industrial melanism* refers to:

Ensure that the answer is responsive to the question and not just a correct piece of information.

A. the relationship between the foliose and the moths.

WRONG: "Industrial melanism" is not a "relationship." "Industrial melanism is a phrase used to describe the evolutionary *process*, whereby …" (lines 1–2).

B. habitats that have been darkened by soot and other forms of industrial pollution.

WRONG: This answer is not responsive to the question. This type of habitat is *a part* of the requirement for the theory of industrial melanism. However, where is the melanism aspect? This requires an organism of some sort.

C. a process of natural selection, whereby habitats that have been darkened by soot and other forms of industrial pollution attract dark-colored organisms.

WRONG: This answer is attractive because it begins well with "a process of natural selection." If you did not read the *entire* answer carefully, you might have chosen this one. However, according to the passage, industrial melanism refers in part to "initially light-colored organisms becom[ing] dark, as a result of natural selection" (lines 2–3) *not* the *migration* suggested by this answer.

D. an evolutionary process.

CORRECT: "Industrial melanism is a phrase used to describe the evolutionary *process* whereby …" (lines 1–2).

Passage III (Questions 13–18)

13. The central thesis of the passage is that:

A. recently, there has been movement towards rendering legal language more accessible to the "laity."

WRONG: This is not accurate. The passage conclusion is that legal language "is so esoteric and exclusive that only professional lawyers can comprehend and use it" (lines 64–66).

B. lawgivers and judges have usually considered themselves to have a divine right.

WRONG: This is not accurate, according to the passage. "Sometimes, of course, the lawgivers were *undeniably* human figures …" (lines 20–21).

C. since the earliest times, the language of the law has needed to be practical and precise.

WRONG: This is not accurate. There is no "need" stated, particularly in light of the fact that "[s]ince they drew their legitimacy from fiat—that is, their *lack* of internal reasoning or evidentiary support—

ancient laws tended to be simple and absolute" (lines 31–33).

D. throughout history, the language of the law has been made purposely beyond the understanding of those lacking a legal background.

CORRECT: From the first paragraph to the final paragraph, from the Furies to King James I, the author expounds on this theme. "There has been a continuous philosophical determination, both conscious and subconscious, to present the law as something distinct from 'ordinary' language, and thus above the reach of the 'laity.'" (lines 3–7).

14. Which of the following claims is NOT explicitly presented in the passage as an example of an "undeniably" human figure?

I. Roman Emperor Justinian

WRONG: This answer *is* explicitly presented in the passage as an example. "Sometimes, of course, the lawgivers *were* undeniably human figures, such as Roman Emperor Justinian, the English kings" (lines 20–22).

II. English kings

WRONG: This answer *is* explicitly presented in the passage as an example. "Sometimes, of course, the lawgivers *were* undeniably human figures, such as … the English kings …." (lines 20–22).

III. Moses

CORRECT: This answer is *not* explicitly presented in the passage as an example. The author makes no effort to claim that Moses is "undeniably" human or even human at all. "Examples of the *supernatural-authoritative lawgiver* abound: [such as] … Moses (messenger of God)" (lines 14–16).

A. I only
B. II only
C. III only

CORRECT: See above explanation.

D. I and II only

15. According to the passage, which of the following statements would be the most accurate in describing "the single-minded rule of the demonic Furies" (line 35)?

A. The accused was either completely guilty or completely innocent.

CORRECT: This is the most accurate statement. "Because theirs is a tradition of focusing on *absolutes*, the Furies are *poor at differentiating degrees of guilt* …" (lines 41–43).

B. The guilty stood to benefit because the Furies sought a punishment which fit the crime.

WRONG: There is no mention of the guilty benefiting, nor is this conceivable based upon passage information. Furthermore, "the Furies are *poor* at differentiating degrees of guilt" and, thus, would hardly have "sought a punishment which fit the crime."

C. The innocent were often punished because of the Furies disdain for mortals.

WRONG: There is no mention of "disdain for mortals" in the passage.

D. The Furies would expound at length upon the reasoning behind their decisions.

WRONG: "Because theirs is a tradition of focusing on *absolutes*, the Furies are *poor* ... at articulating the reasoning for their justice" (lines 41–44).

16. Which of the following statements is the most reasonable conclusion that can be drawn from the author's description of King James I's surprise at Judge Edward Coke's pronouncement (lines 53-58)?

A. From that point forward, King James was the sole interpreter of the law.

WRONG: This is clearly not the case. "*As he prepared to rule on a legal case*, King James I was doubtless surprised by Judge Edward Coke's sudden pronouncement *that he could no longer do so ...*" (lines 51–53).

B. From that point forward, King James I demanded inclusion in the judges' interpretation of the law.

WRONG: This is not the case. "*As he prepared to rule on a legal case*, King James I was doubtless surprised by his Judge Edward Coke's sudden pronouncement *that he could no longer do so ...*" (lines 51–53).

C. Prior to this, King James I's judges had not been the only interpreters of the law.

CORRECT: "*As he prepared to rule on a legal case*, King James I was doubtless surprised by his Judge Edward Coke's sudden pronouncement *that he could no longer do so ...*" (lines 53-58). From this we can discern that "prior to this," King James had *also* been an interpreter of the law.

D. Prior to this, King James I had allowed his judges to be the sole interpreters of the law.

WRONG: This is clearly not the case. "*As he prepared to rule on a legal case*, King James I was doubtless surprised by Judge Edward Coke's sudden pronouncement *that he could no longer do so ...*" (lines 51–53).

17. Though not mentioned in the passage, the biblical Ten Commandments can best provide an example for which one of the following passage statements?

It is common knowledge that the biblical Ten Commandments were supposedly given by God. Furthermore, this divinity can be *inferred* by the adjective "biblical." It is also professed, though not necessarily common knowledge (*nor necessary to answer this question*), that the Commandments were given to Moses on a mountaintop, to be delivered to the people by him. However, neither knowledge of Moses nor knowledge of the specific Commandments themselves is necessary to answer this question.

A. "Sometimes, of course, the lawgivers were undeniably human figures ...."

WRONG: Though you may know that Moses delivered the Ten Commandments, he is noted in the passage as an example of a "supernatural-authoritative lawgiver" (line 15), not as an undeniably human figure.

B. "The pronouncement of ancient law was often attributed to a divine lawgiver, or else a messenger with a *visible* connection to the divine or supernatural."

CORRECT: Here, the question provides a good example for this statement/answer. If you knew that Moses had received these Commandments from God and delivered them, you would have noted that the passage provides Moses as an example of a "supernatural-authoritative lawgiver" (line 15). A basic knowledge of the biblical Ten Commandments would have indicated that they were delivered by "a messenger" (regardless of his identity) with "a *visible* connection to the divine or supernatural." If all else failed, it is common knowledge that in the Judeo-Christian tradition, the Ten Commandments were believed to have come from God (capital 'G') who is certainly considered a "divine lawgiver."

C. "There has been a continuous philosophical determination, both conscious and subconscious, to present the law as something distinct from 'ordinary' language."

WRONG: The question really does not provide an example for this statement. Although a tenuous connection could be made between this statement and the Ten Commandments, it would be a stretch and not the best answer. This statement/answer has to do with language, while the question does not. But for the "thou," the Ten Commandments are not written as "something distinct from 'ordinary' language."

D. "Thus, under ancient law, the innocent are entirely vindicated ..."

WRONG: The question really does not provide an example for this statement. The Ten Commandments do not 'entirely vindicate' the innocent.

18. The author's assertion that "even old men had 'benches of polished stone in the sacred circle' on which to sit in borrowed glory" (lines 26–28), supports which of the following conclusions?

A. These elders required a bench in a sacred place befitting their divine authority.

WRONG: This conclusion is not supported by the assertion in the question. The example of the "old men" is provided to show "ancient law, with its fundamental reliance on *external* authority, had little need to justify its content internally" (line 28–30). The "elders" had no divine authority.

B. The benches alone would have imparted a divine connection to these human figures.

WRONG: This conclusion is not supported by the assertion in the question. The benches of polished stone existed inside of the "sacred circle." It was apparently the "circle" that was sacred.

C. The circle 'became' sacred in the presence of these divine elders.

WRONG: This conclusion is not supported by the assertion in the question. The example of the "old men" is provided to show "ancient law, with its fundamental reliance on *external* authority, had little need to justify its content internally" (line 28–30). The "elders" had no divine authority.

D. These undeniably human figures gleaned external authority from a divine location.

CORRECT: This conclusion is supported by the assertion in the question. The example of the "old men" is provided to show "ancient law, with its fundamental reliance on *external* authority, had little need to justify its content internally" (line 28–30). The "elders" had no divine authority. However, the "circle" itself, a location, is described as "sacred" and is the "external authority."

Passage IV (Questions 19–23)

19. The ideas of the author in the passage seem to derive primarily from:

A. evidence on how people act.

WRONG: There is no strong basis for this answer. Further, the correct answer is taken verbatim from the passage.

B. speculation based on observation.

WRONG: There is no strong basis for this answer. Further, the correct answer is taken verbatim from the passage.

C. surveys conducted by a researcher.

CORRECT: This answer is almost verbatim from the passage. Dimitrius provides the basis for almost the entire passage. "One of the pioneering writers on impression management is the jury consultant Jo-Ellen Dimitrius. ... *According to surveys* conducted by Dimitrius" (lines 28–30).

D. facts observable in the courtroom.

WRONG: There is no strong basis for this answer. Further, the correct answer is taken verbatim from the passage.

20. The central thesis of the passage is that:

On a question of this type, *don't* pause to think about what might be the "central thesis" or the "main point" of the passage before reading the answer choices. You may be wasting your time. Regardless of your opinion, you must choose the *best* "central thesis" from among the choices offered!

I. a person can learn to 'read' others in order to gain a more accurate impression of them.

WRONG: This is *not* the central thesis. The passage information pertains only in the most incidental way to 'observing' or 'reading' others. The passage is about '*conveying* impressions' and "impression management" (line 75).

II. a person can learn to convey the appropriate impression to others.

CORRECT: This is the central thesis of the passage. This entire passage is about '*conveying* impressions' and "impression management" (line 75).

III. a person can learn to 'read' the impression he is conveying to others.

WRONG: This is *not* the central thesis. The passage is about '*conveying* impressions' and "impression management" (line 75). This answer is a very poor way of explaining "impression management." One would not generally speak of reading an impression that one is giving. This passage is more about how one might "craft" or "be aware of" it. The passage offers generalities, which are appropriate to almost all situations, such as the three "main qualities" a person should try to project. The *only* very indirect inference to 'reading' others is in determining "which trait people value more in their profession" (line 50).

A. I only
B. II only

CORRECT: See above answer explanations.

C. III only
D. I and II only

21. The passage discussion most clearly suggests the hypothesis that first impressions are:

A. trusted by those who make them and usually negative.

WRONG: The second aspect of the answer, "and usually negative", is *not* clearly suggested. "First impressions tend to be especially lasting, ... because once a person forms a definite *positive or negative* impression ..." (lines 13–16).

B. long lasting and always harmful.

WRONG: The second aspect of the answer, "and always harmful", is *not* clearly suggested. "First impressions tend to be especially lasting, ... because once a person forms a definite *positive or negative* impression ..." (lines 13–16). If a first impression is "positive", then it is certainly not harmful to the one who has conveyed this impression.

C. often wrong, long lasting, and difficult to overcome.

CORRECT: This hypothesis is clearly suggested. The first aspect, "often wrong," can be gleaned from the beginning of the passage: "In society, people tend to base their decisions not on what is true, but rather on what they *perceive* to be true. Sometimes, the two are the same, making the decisions correct. *But often they are not. Thus, many decisions are based on first impressions* [which are not correct],which are, themselves predicated on incomplete information, stereotypes, or even wild guesses extrapolated from a few facts" (lines 1–7). Lines 12–23 provide evidence for the subsequent ideas. First impressions are "difficult to overcome" because the person who makes them attempts to "validate [the first impression] by perceiving future actions in a way that is consistent with that impression" (lines 16–18).

D. often wrong, trusted by those who make them, and always harmful.

WRONG: This is *not* clearly suggested. The last aspect of this answer, "always harmful," is *not* clearly suggested. "First impressions tend to be especially lasting, ... because once a person forms a definite *positive or negative* impression ..." (lines 13–16). If a first impression is "positive," then it is certainly not harmful to the one who has conveyed this impression.

22. What distinction is implied in the passage between professional and informal contexts, respectively?

A. Either competence or humility and self-promotion

WRONG: This is inaccurate with respect to an 'information context' and "self-promotion." "Generally, in informal social contexts, people ...

will judge him arrogant for blatant self-promotion" (lines 44–48).

B. Always competence and humility

WRONG: This is inaccurate with respect to a 'professional context' and "always competence." "Professionally, people may choose to emphasize *either* their competence *or* their caring/humility" (lines 48–49).

C. Caring/humility and humility

WRONG: Though the information in the answer is technically fairly accurate, since these two aspects are so similar, this is not a *distinction* but a *similarity* or comparison. "Professionally, people may choose to emphasize *either* their competence *or* their caring/humility" (lines 48–49). This is not the best answer.

D. Deciding on which trait is valued more and humility

CORRECT: This distinction is implied (and even explicit). "Professionally, people may choose to emphasize either their competence or their caring/humility, *depending on which trait people value more* in their profession" (lines 48–50). "Generally, in informal social contexts, people should display *humility ...*" (lines 44–45).

23. According to the passage descriptions, which of the following "main qualities" (line 31) would be the most difficult to convey in a short first impression?

Notice that the correct answer choice must first be one of the "main qualities" offered in the passage. All of the below listed happen to be so, but this is not always the case with these types of questions.

A. Trustworthiness

CORRECT: This would be the most difficult to convey in a *short* first impression. "Trustworthiness consists of both honesty and reliability (most visibly demonstrated by keeping promises)" (lines 33–35). But it would be very difficult to keep a promise, or demonstrate reliability, in a "short first impression." Granted, one could use "direct eye contact (which is invariably perceived as more honest)" (lines 58–59), but honesty is only one small aspect of trustworthiness.

B. Competence

WRONG: This would *not* be the most difficult to convey in a *short* first impression. "Competence tends to be inferred from some mix of *visible* intelligence, confidence, and demonstrations of actual competence at a task" (lines 36–38). Simple conversation can serve to project intelligence and confidence (if any actually exists).

C. Compassion

   WRONG: This would *not* be the most difficult to convey in a *short* first impression. "Compassion is marked by caring, kindness, and graciousness" (lines 35–36). These characteristics can be easily conveyed through courtesy, asking gentle questions about health and family, etc.

D. Humility

   WRONG: This would *not* be the most difficult to convey in a *short* first impression. We can discern that this is the opposite of "blatant self-promotion" (lines 47–48) and deduce that to remain respectfully attentive, quieter, and interested in others might serve to convey our humility.

Passage V (Questions 24–29)

24. In the context of the passage, the word *honest* (line 14) means:

A. not telling lies.

   WRONG: This is *not* the most likely meaning. This answer is the same as Answer C, and too literal and simplistic. The meaning of *honest* "in the context of the passage" has little to do with "not telling lies" or "telling the truth." The word is describing the Noble, and has everything to do with bluntly telling people what you perceive to be the truth, regardless of the consequences. This is the proverbial "bull in the China shop," "get to the point," or "don't beat around the bush" mentality.

B. caring enough to say what you mean.

   WRONG: This is *not* the most likely meaning. The word is describing the Noble style. Is the Noble characterized as "caring?" He *could* be, but he is more likely to be perceived as "tactless and abrupt" (line 54). Think of Clint Eastwood's characters. This is not the best answer "in the context of the passage."

C. telling the truth.

   WRONG: This is *not* the most likely meaning. This answer is the same as Answer A, and too literal and simplistic. The meaning of *honest* "in the context of the passage" has little to do with "not telling lies" or "telling the truth." The word is describing the Noble, and has everything to do with bluntly telling people what you perceive to be the truth, regardless of the consequences. This is the proverbial "bull in the China shop" or "don't beat around the bush" mentality.

D. saying what you mean regardless of the consequences.

   CORRECT: This is the most likely meaning. The words "honest" (lines 14 and 55), "speak the truth"

(line 13), and "candor" (line 35) are used to repeatedly characterize the Noble style of speaking. "This style is characterized by *blunt but honest* content" (lines 13–14), for example, Eastwood's character "telling people his honest opinion of them" (line 17). This is the proverbial "bull in the China shop," "dispense with the niceties and get to the point," or "don't beat around the bush" mentality.

25. Which of the following statements most strongly *challenges* one of the assertions made in the passage?

A. A Socratic will tend to engage in a controlled, concise debate.

   CORRECT: This statement most strongly *challenges* a passage assertion. Socratics are *not* "concise," but are "verbose and rambling" (lines 28–29).

B. Clint Eastwood's natural style is Socratic.

   WRONG: This statement is inaccurate and does not *challenge* a passage assertion. You didn't read this answer carefully. The passage does *not* provide any information regarding what Clint Eastwood's "*natural* style" is. Eastwood is an actor by trade. The passage does tell us what types of *characters* Eastwood *portrays*. "An example of the Noble style is almost any *role* played by tough cowboy Clint Eastwood …" (lines 15–16).

C. Each of the spoken styles has its place.

   WRONG: This statement does not *challenge* a passage assertion. "According to Dr. McCallister, no one style is necessarily 'correct' or superior; each one's view of the proper role of communication may be valid, at least under certain circumstances" (lines 44–47).

D. Reflectives are patient and diplomatic.

   WRONG: This statement does not *challenge* a passage assertion. For instance, "the diplomatic and patient Reflective …" (line 52–53).

26. According to passage descriptions, the title of Dr. McCallister's book *Say What You Mean, Get What You Want* would most characterize which of the following styles?

A. Candidate

   WRONG: This style is *not* characterized by the book's title. The Candidate is one who "blends the Reflective's niceness with typically Socratic chattiness, and who tries to persuade others to adopt his positions by *first* charming them with his politeness and humility" (lines 40–43). If you are "first charming," then you are not "saying what you mean."

B. Reflective

WRONG: This style is *not* at all characterized by the book's title. The title *least* characterizes the "Reflective, identifiable by pleasant, polite, and diplomatic speech, along with a reluctance to tell people anything which might upset them" (lines 21–23). The Reflective would certainly not abruptly and bluntly "say what she means." Notice, too, that the Reflective is the only style which does not *persuade*.

C. Magistrate

WRONG: This style is *not most* characterized by the book's title. The Magistrate is too verbose to be the best answer. The Magistrate engages in a "long and often repetitive speech pattern" (line 36). This is not the best answer.

D. Noble

CORRECT: This style is most characterized by the book's title. The title is blunt, honest, abrupt, and to the point—all characteristics of the Noble. If the Noble were to write a title, this would be it.

27. In order to *Get What You Want*, which of the following styles would probably be the *least* effective?

A. Candidate

WRONG: This would *not* be the *least* effective style. Unlike the Reflective, the Candidate is able "to *persuade* others to adopt his positions" (lines 41–42).

B. Magistrate

WRONG: This would *not* be the *least* effective style. Unlike the Reflective, the Magistrate is capable of "*persuading* others to adopt the Magistrate's own (honest) opinion" (lines 38–39).

C. Socratic

WRONG: This would *not* be the *least* effective style. Unlike the Reflective, the Socratic (here in comparison with the Candidate) is able "to *persuade* others to adopt his positions" (lines 41–42).

D. Reflective

CORRECT: This would be the *least* effective style. The Reflective has "a reluctance to tell people anything that might upset them" (lines 22–23). Thus, if the Reflective wanted something from someone that might upset him or her, the Reflective would be reluctant to do anything about it. Most importantly, the Reflective is the only style which is not described as being '*persuasive*' or even attempting to '*persuade.*' In order to *Get What You Want*, it is probably necessary to persuade somebody. All the other styles are better at persuading. Thus, this answer can also be determined through process of elimination.

28. According to the passage, "Frequently, when confronted with a different style, [people] react with annoyance and unwarranted assumptions, not realizing the validity and intentions of other styles" (lines 49–52). The 'reaction' of a male Reflective would most likely manifest itself through:

A. keeping an opinion to himself.

CORRECT: This is the most likely manifestation. Notice that the adjective "male" is irrelevant to the question. Though the passage provides that the Reflective "is the more dominant style among women" (line 25), the author offers an example of a male, Woody Allen, with this style. Remember that the Reflective manifests "a reluctance to tell people anything which might upset them" (lines 22–23). It is reasonable to assume then that the Reflective would say and do nothing.

B. walking away.

WRONG: This is *not* the most likely manifestation. See the explanation for Answer A. This might upset the other person. And, though the Reflective manifests "a reluctance to *tell* people anything which might upset them" (lines 22–23), one can assume that *actions* would also be included in this reluctance. This is not the best answer.

C. not letting it bother him.

WRONG: This is *not* the most likely manifestation. See the explanation for Answer A. As a matter of fact, the "Reflective often misperceives the blunt and concise Noble as tactless and abrupt" (lines 53–54). Since there is no real passage information on how a person with a given style 'feels,' this answer is highly speculative.

D. changing styles in order to respond.

WRONG: This is *not* the most likely manifestation. See the explanation for Answer A. Though we all use these styles to express ourselves, we might do it knowingly or unknowingly. Further, it is the people who have been 'trained' in these styles in order to further facilitate communication who will end up "mirroring each other's speaking styles" (lines 69–70). Besides the question of whether or not "changing styles" would aid the situation, this is also a speculative answer requiring that we assume that the "male Reflective" *knows* to change styles.

29. According to passage information, a Noble would be most bothered by:

A. thoroughness.

WRONG: This would *not* most bother the Noble. In the passage, "the bottom line–oriented Noble is frequently annoyed at the Socratic's verbosity and fixation on details, *not recognizing it as an attempt at thoroughness*" (lines 55–58). Presumably then, if the Noble *had* recognized it as an attempt at "thoroughness," he would not have been annoyed as long as the explanation was concise.

B. verbosity and fixation on details.

CORRECT: This would *most* bother the Noble. In the passage, "the bottom line–oriented Noble is frequently *annoyed* at the Socratic's *verbosity* and *fixation on details*" (lines 55–58). This *verbatim* answer effectively precludes the argument that the other answers are just as acceptable.

C. bluntness.

WRONG: This would *not* most bother the Noble. The Noble *is* "blunt" (line 14). The passage suggests that if we "mirror" each other, or speak in the same style, then communication is facilitated.

D. a succinct opposing argument.

WRONG: This would *not* most bother the Noble. Unless we are assuming that the "opposing argument" would bother the Noble (and there is no passage information to substantiate this), this is not the best answer. The "succinct" aspect is part of the Noble's makeup.

Passage VI (Questions 30–34)

30. According to the passage, when deciding upon how to film a scene, one must take into account:

A. how the audience is going to perceive the action.

CORRECT: This must be taken into account by the director. The movie is ultimately made for an *audience* to watch and enjoy! "For each shot, the director has many options on how to film the same actors interacting, and his choice has a great influence on how the audience perceives the same action" (lines 10–13).

B. the type of camera angles to be used.

WRONG: It is true that this must be taken into account, but this answer is too specific when compared to Answer A. Thus, this answer would be correct were it standing alone. However, in this instance, it is not the best answer.

C. if the director will approve of the shot.

WRONG: It is *not* clear at all that this must be taken into account. The passage tells us that it *is* the director who is making the decision regarding the shot (and everything else in the passage)! This answer *assumes* that someone else is making the decision regarding the shot, requiring the director's approval.

D. if the audience is going to 'love it' or 'hate it.'

WRONG: Though this is an alluring answer, it is *not* at all clear from the passage that this must be taken into account. The passage makes clear only that one

must take into account the audience's perception of the action. This is not the same as taking into account whether an audience will 'love it' or 'hate it.'

31. According to the passage, a nature documentary would most likely be filmed using:

Note that when you come upon a passage that is primarily informative, or explaining how you do something, you may expect several questions asking you to *use* the information that you have been provided based upon suppositions. The testers expect that you have learned what information is in the passage and can extrapolate and make decisions based upon that information.

A. a normal lens at 'eye level.'

WRONG: This is not likely. "The normal lens … is used for *natural scenes and documentaries*" (lines 61–63). However, the use of 'eye level' is "the most common angle," but it is still speculative with regards to documentaries. Thus, this answer is not as good an answer as the inclusion of 'deep focus' in Answer D. Read Answer D.

B. a wide-angle lens in 'deep focus.'

WRONG: This is not likely. "The contrasting 'deep focus' mode is … a staple of 'gritty' realistic movies and *documentaries*" (lines 75–79). However, the use of a wide-angle lens is not nearly as appropriate as the normal lens. See Answer D.

C. a 'long shot' in 'deep focus.'

WRONG: This is not likely. "The contrasting 'deep focus' mode is … a staple of 'gritty' realistic movies and *documentaries*" (lines 75–79). However, the 'long shot' is speculative and not a clear choice for "nature documentaries." 'Long shot' is not even close to the choice of a normal lens. See Answer D.

D. a normal lens in 'deep focus.'

CORRECT: Based upon the passage, this answer is the most likely. "The normal lens … is used for *natural scenes and documentaries*" (lines 61–63). "The contrasting 'deep focus' mode is … a staple of 'gritty' realistic movies and *documentaries*" (lines 75–79).

32. The passage discussion most clearly suggests the hypothesis that one of the more important aspects in the making of a film is:

A. figuring out what 'most moviegoers' are going to love.

WRONG: This is *not* provided as one of the more important aspects in the making of a film.

B. deciding how to make a movie 'artistic.'

WRONG: If Answer C were not available, then this might be a good choice, since we know that 'artistic movies' are composed of 'shots' to which the rest of the important information in the passage is relevant. *However*, this answer is very vague when compared with Answer C, since it is the *director* who does the "deciding [on] how to make a movie 'artistic.'"

C. using a good director.

CORRECT: This is the most important aspect provided in the answer choices. The distance of the shot, the angle of the shot, the optics, and the perspective are *all* decided by the *director*. If you don't have and use a good director, the passage provides no other way to make a quality film.

D. using a good cameraman.

WRONG: This is not provided as one of the more important aspects in the making of a film. Though there is *probably* a cameraman involved, and he *probably* is important, no mention is made of him in the passage. From what little we know based upon passage discussion, it could be a computer doing the filming—but only *after* the *director* decides upon the angle of the shot, the optics, the perspective, and the distance of the shot!

33. According to the passage, a scene from a horror movie showing two lovers embracing, unaware of the huge monster closing in on them, would be filmed using:

Notice that the question *never* says that the monster is *shown*, only that the two lovers are shown. Thus, the presence of the monster *may* be unseen but is apparently meant to be felt or perceived in the film.

A. an 'eye level' 'extreme close-up' with a normal lens.

WRONG: This is not likely. Though the 'eye level' is the most common shot, it adds nothing to the scene. The 'extreme close-up' *detracts* from the 'horror movie' quality of the scene and the impending doom by focusing on some small detail of the lovers embracing. The 'long shot' is more appropriate.

B. a 'high-angle' 'long shot' with a normal lens.

CORRECT: This is the most likely answer. "[t] he 'high-angle' shot positions the camera to 'look down on' a character, which often suggests he is inferior, powerless, weak, *or in trouble*" (lines 51–53). Further, the addition of the normal lens does not detract from this answer since it "attempts to duplicate the human eye's focus."

C. a 'low-angle' 'long shot' with a normal lens.

WRONG: This is not likely. The 'long shot' is a staple of action films, fine. And, the "low-angle format suggests the object or character is somehow larger, grander, dominant, or intimidating" (lines 49–51). That would be fine for filming the monster. *However*, notice that the question *never* says that

the monster is *shown, only that the two lovers are shown*. It would *not* be appropriate to film the two lovers in a 'low angle' shot.

D. a 'child's-eye-level' 'close-up' in deep focus.

WRONG: This is not likely. The passage tells us that a 'child's eye level' is similar to the 'low angle' shot. And, the "low-angle format suggests the object or character is somehow larger, grander, dominant, or intimidating" (lines 49–51). That would be fine for filming the monster. *However*, notice that the question *never* says that the monster is *shown, only that the two lovers are shown*. It would *not* be appropriate to film the two lovers in a 'low angle' shot. Further, it is very questionable whether 'deep focus' would be appropriate if the audience knows that a monster is "closing in on them."

34. According to the passage, a child's film with three alternating shots showing a mother scolding her small daughter, the daughter, and the father who is secretly listening would most likely be filmed using which sequence of camera angles, respectively?

A. 'Low angle,' 'high angle,' and 'over the shoulder,'

CORRECT: This is the most likely combination. First, mother: 'low angle,' or "child's-eye-level, looking up at most things, … suggests the object or character is somehow larger, grander, dominant, or intimidating" (lines 46–51). Second, "small" daughter: 'high angle' "look down on' a character, which often suggests he is inferior, powerless, weak, or in trouble" (lines 51–53). Third, "father who is secretly listening," though this is somewhat more ambiguous because the answer suggests that the mother may be included in the shot also: 'over the shoulder' "filming one character as seen over the shoulder of another emphasizes that character, while reminding audiences that he is being observed or heard" (lines 55–58).

B. 'Low angle,' 'low angle,' and 'high angle.'

WRONG: This is not likely. The second aspect, 'low angle' would *not* be an appropriate way to *show* the daughter: 'low angle', or "child's eye level, looking up at most things", "suggests the object or character is somehow larger, grander, dominant, or intimidating" (lines 46–51). The daughter being scolded should clearly be filmed from a 'high angle'.

C. 'High angle,' 'high angle,' and 'over the shoulder.'

WRONG: This is not likely. The first aspect, 'high angle,' would not be an appropriate way to film the "scolding," dominating, intimidating mother. 'High angle' is used in order "to 'look down on' a character, which often suggests he is inferior, powerless, weak, or in trouble" (lines 51–53). The mother should be filmed as if being looked up at, from a 'low angle.'

D. 'Over the shoulder,' 'high angle,' and 'low angle.'

WRONG: This is not likely. The question calls for a "respective" answer. This answer is out of sequence.

Passage VII (Questions 35–40)

35. Which of the following statements provides support for what the author probably means in stating that "even after a millennium, it can still compel admiration and feeling in a less-than-devout society" (lines 23–25)?

The two key aspects of the quotation are 1) older music still compelling admiration, and 2) "a less-than-devout society." One of the answer choices will support *either* one or both aspects, but *at least one* aspect.

A. Millions of people still flock to Egypt each year to admire the ageless wonder of the pyramids.

WRONG: This statement does not provide support for the quotation. There is no parallelism in this statement to 'devotion' or lack thereof.

B. Tourists still stand in awe of the Colosseum of Rome, though it was the site of countless horrible deaths.

WRONG: This statement does not provide support for the quotation. There is no parallelism in this statement to 'devotion' or lack thereof.

C. Though a majority of Americans profess a belief in a supreme being, a minority actually attend any type of religious service.

CORRECT: This answer supports the author's implication of "a less-than-devout society."

D. Young and old people alike are increasingly tending to purchase rap music with religious themes.

WRONG: This statement does not provide support for the quotation. Here we have *newer* music, which contrasts with "even after a millennium." Further, an increasing tendency to purchase religious music does *not* support the idea of "a less-than-devout society."

36. The author of the passage characterizes the "axes" theory of music appreciation as one that:

"Under the 'axes' theory of music appreciation, music's appeal derives from the impression it leaves on listeners, indexed with their understanding of its technical composition and historical circumstances" (lines 1–4).

A. can help accurately predict why listeners appreciate music or not.

WRONG: This is not an accurate description of the author's characterization. We know from the passage that the author is not a big supporter of the "axes" theory. The author asserts that "music can be judged aesthetically *even without knowing* the circumstances surrounding it" (lines 65–66).

B. is completely erroneous.

WRONG: This is not an accurate desciption of the author's characterization. He does *not* believe that the theory is "completely" erroneous.

C. may have been true in the past but is now outdated.

WRONG: This is not an accurate description of the author's characterization. The author would assert that it was probably never completely accurate and is certainly not accurate now.

D. is based upon a false assumption.

CORRECT: There are two assumptions upon which axes theory is based: appreciation and technical understanding. "It is indeed possible that *both* factors contribute to one's evaluation, but probable that the emotional impact far outweighs the technical execution in forming our final opinion of it" (lines 4–7). However, the author finally dismisses completely the second assumption: "music can be judged aesthetically *even without knowing* the circumstances surrounding it" (lines 65–66).

37. Suppose it could be established that almost all of the music composed for the Christian church of the Middles Ages could be deconstructed or simplified down to only one or two consistent mathematical themes that seem to hold an almost universal appeal. The author of the passage would be most likely to respond to this development by:

On these types of questions one must attempt to use the author's ideas, motivations, and arguments. In an instance such as this one, where the supposition seems to refute the author's arguments, look for the answer that would best 'rehabilitate' or 'salvage' the author's line of reasoning.

A. arguing the universal appeal of any musical themes.

WRONG: This is not the most likely response. For instance, lines 49–50 give an example of recent 'serial' music that is not popular.

B. pointing out that the composers were unlikely to have been aware of this coincidence.

CORRECT: This is the most likely response. In the second paragraph, the author argues that early composers were only vaguely aware of any type of music theory and, in fact, were dissuaded from any attempt at establishing rules in this area by the church. Finally, the other possible answers are clearly *not* points that the author would argue and are not correct.

C. disputing that the composers would have deliberately set out to alienate their listeners.

WRONG: This is not the most likely response. This answer makes little sense.

A & E 2

D. agreeing that these early composers probably were aware of universal musical theories.

WRONG: This is not the most likely response. In the second paragraph, the author argues that early composers were only vaguely aware of any type of music theory and, in fact, were dissuaded from any attempt at establishing rules in this area by the church.

38. If the author of the passage is right that the "axes model" is a poor predictor of music's appeal, then it follows that:

A. "good" music can usually be created following a set series of guidelines.

WRONG: This does not follow. It is this aspect of the "axes model" that the author disagrees with.

B. music cannot be fully appreciated without some knowledge of its historical circumstances.

WRONG: This does not follow. It is this aspect of the "axes model" that the author disagrees with.

C. the emotional impression that a piece of music leaves on a large group of listeners is unimportant.

WRONG: This does not follow. The author believes that the emotional impression of music is important.

D. the worth of the opinion of a single highly-educated music critic is overrated.

CORRECT: Axes theory postulates that music is appreciated 1) because of the impression it leaves, and 2) "with their understanding of its technical composition and historical circumstances" (lines 3–4). This latter aspect (which the author disagrees with) is not something one is born with, and thus can only be acquired through education. Further, the author clearly feels that music should appeal to the masses and not just to a single individual.

39. Regarding the composing of "serial music," the passage strongly implies that:

A. alienating listeners was a deliberate goal.

CORRECT: This is strongly implied. The author *contrasts* the composers of serial music with earlier composers: "The medieval-to-Renaissance composer could [never] be accused … of composing with the *deliberate aim of alienating listeners*" (lines 53–57). "In fact, some serial music radiates contempt for the listener; it has *consciously* been made so complex as to be incomprehensible to the listener …" (lines 49–51).

B. it is comprehensible to the listener.

WRONG: This is the opposite of what the passage states. "In fact, some serial music radiates contempt for the listener; it has consciously been made so

complex as to be *incomprehensible* to the listener …" (lines 49–51).

C. composers are frustrated by listeners' inability to comprehend.

WRONG: This is not a passage implication. There is no information regarding the feelings of "composers." Further, only the 'serial' composers would be frustrated by a lack of comprehension due to the deliberate complexity of their music.

D. it is more emotionally appealing to compose this way.

WRONG: The author *contrasts* the composers of serial music with earlier composers: "The medieval-to-Renaissance composer could [never] be accused … of composing with the *deliberate aim of alienating listeners*" (lines 53–57). "In fact, some serial music radiates contempt for the listener; it has *consciously* been made so complex as to be incomprehensible to the listener …" (lines 49–51). It is unlikely that such music would be emotionally appealing to the listener. This is not the best answer.

40. If the author's primary criterion for judging the "effectiveness" of music are applied to manmade objects, which of the following creations would be most effective?

A. an huge underground particle accelerator.

WRONG: This would not be the most "effective." The crux of this question is that the author *refutes* "axes" theory by saying that "*emotional* impact far outweighs the *technical* execution" (line 6). This is a technological marvel eliciting little or no emotion.

B. the Alaskan pipeline.

WRONG: This would not be the most "effective." The crux of this question is that the author *refutes* "axes" theory by saying that "*emotional* impact far outweighs the *technical* execution" (line 6). This is a technological marvel eliciting little or no emotion.

C. the Vietnam memorial.

CORRECT: This would be the most "effective." The Vietnam memorial is very simple yet inspires tremendous emotion. Even if you are unfamiliar with the specifics of the 'Vietnam' memorial, this is the *only* memorial choice. The crux of this question is that the author *refutes* "axes" theory by saying that "*emotional* impact far outweighs the *technical* execution" (line 6). All the other answers are technical 'wonders,' but they certainly do not inspire any emotion beyond perhaps, awe at the human endeavor required to create them.

D. the Suez Canal.

WRONG: This would not be the most "effective." The crux of this question is that the author *refutes* "axes" theory by saying that "*emotional* impact far outweighs the *technical* execution" (line 6). This is a technological marvel eliciting little or no emotion.

_____

Verbal Reasoning Test 3
Answers & Explanations

TEST 3 ANSWER KEY

1.	B	11.	B	21.	D	31.	C
2.	D	12.	D	22.	B	32.	B
3.	D	13.	B	23.	C	33.	D
4.	C	14.	B	24.	D	34.	A
5.	D	15.	A	25.	B	35.	C
6.	B	16.	B	26.	B	36.	D
7.	D	17.	C	27.	C	37.	C
8.	B	18.	D	28.	D	38.	B
9.	A	19.	C	29.	B	39.	D
10.	D	20.	C	30.	D	40.	C

Passage I (Questions 1–6)

1. Which of the following assertions is most clearly a thesis presented by the author?

Remember that the correct answer choice must satisfy the necessity of being one of the author's "assertions."

A. Time travel is not possible.

WRONG: This assertion is not clearly a thesis presented by the author. Though the author does not *unequivocally* state that time travel *is* possible, only "conceivable" or seemingly "feasible," it is incorrect to assume that he thinks that time travel is *not* possible.

B. A *t* axis is necessary to describe life.

CORRECT: This assertion is most clearly a thesis presented by the author. "In order to describe life, we must have a fourth axis" (lines 10–11). The author goes on to describe this fourth axis as the *t* axis. Therefore, a *t* axis, as described by the author, is necessary to describe life.

C. A *t* axis must be parallel to at least one other axis in the model.

WRONG: This assertion is not clearly a thesis presented by the author. In describing the *t* or time axis, the author suggests that "the time axis is necessarily *perpendicular* to all other axes" (lines 17–18).

D. Humans are not equipped to sense light.

WRONG: This assertion is not clearly a thesis presented by the author. "An examination of the human sensory system reveals that we are not equipped to sense light *retreating from us*" (lines 57–59). Humans are not equipped to sense that light is *doing* or *exhibiting* certain characteristics.

2. If the hypothesis of the passage is correct, one should find that a change only along the *t* axis:

A. would indicate photon movement.

WRONG: There is no suggestion that this is the case; in fact, "a straight line nearly *perpendicular* to the time axis can represent the path and speed of a photon (a particle of light)" (lines 34–36). A change perpendicular to the *t* axis would not change the *t* axis at all.

B. would indicate a flaw in the model.

WRONG: The author offers no instances that there are flaws in the model, yet he does mention what it means to have a change only along the t axis.

C. would indicate an object that has traveled backwards in time.

WRONG: It might "indicate an object that has traveled backwards in time"; however, it could

also indicate an object that has traveled forwards in time. For the most part, a change along the t axis merely indicates that time has moved forwards or backwards. This is not the best answer.

D. would indicate an object that seems to sit perfectly still.

CORRECT: If no other axis indicates change then the object is clearly not moving: "a line parallel to the time axis [which by definition must be perpendicular to all other axes] represents an object that seems to sit perfectly still" (lines 25–27).

3. Which of the following scientific advances would most seriously *challenge* the hypothesis involving the "space-time continuum" (line 29)?

"Einstein's theory of relativity tells us that time and space are part of the same entity called the space-time continuum. In such a continuum, time and space are indistinguishable." (lines 28–30).

A. Association of time and space characteristics

WRONG: This would further the hypothesis, not challenge it. "Einstein's theory of relativity tells us that time and space are part of the same entity called the space-time continuum. In such a continuum, time and space are indistinguishable." (lines 28–30).

B. Proof of Einstein's theory of relativity

WRONG: This would further the hypothesis, not challenge it, since the hypothesis is Einstein's theory of relativity.

C. Further correlation of the consistency of light speed

WRONG: This does not challenge the hypothesis since "Einstein also theorized that light moves at a constant speed in a vacuum regardless of the perspective of the observer" (lines 32–34).

D. Confirmation of characteristics distinguishing time from space

CORRECT: This advance would most seriously challenge the hypothesis. "Einstein's theory of relativity tells us that time and space are part of the same entity called the space-time continuum. In such a continuum, time and space are *indistinguishable*." (lines 28–30).

4. According to the passage information, what would happen if one were to travel near the speed of light?

"Moving near the speed of light would slow time for the traveler, allowing him to arrive years in the future after what would seem like only moments to his body" (lines 42–45).

A. This person would remain perfectly still.

WRONG: Though it is a matter of the viewer's perspective, if you are "traveling" or moving near the speed of light you are not remaining perfectly still. This is not the best answer.

B. This person would travel back in time.
WRONG: This is the antithesis of passage information. See Answer C.

C. Time would slow for this person allowing him to travel into the future.
CORRECT: "Moving near the speed of light would *slow time for the traveler*, allowing him to arrive years in the future after what would seem like only moments to his body" (lines 42–45).

D. Time would accelerate for this person, allowing him to travel into the future.
WRONG: This is the antithesis of passage information. See Answer C.

5. If the author of the passage is right that the "space-time continuum may be a four-dimensional stone in which our past, present, and future is etched for us to continually relive" (lines 60–62), then it follows that:

The author is using a metaphor, suggesting that our lives are "written in stone."

A. the stone must be moving along the *t* axis.
WRONG: There is no basis for this answer.

B. at all times we are on the stone.
WRONG: The author is suggesting that our lives are "written in stone." The "stone" is a *metaphor*. The author would not actually say "at all times we are on the stone." Additionally, the quote and passage information might just as well lead us to the assumption that we are "*in*" the stone. This is not the best answer.

C. we have free will.
WRONG: If we have free will, we can change our future by the decisions we make, rendering an 'etching' of our future impossible.

D. our lives are predetermined.
CORRECT: If the "future is *etched* for us to continually relive" then it is predetermined. The author is suggesting that our lives are "written in stone".

6. Which of the following statements is true concerning the four-axes coordinate system described by the author?

I. Knowing the distance between any two points will adequately represent animation.
WRONG: "However, life is animated, and just knowing the distance between two points cannot adequately represent animation" (lines 8–10).

II. All axes are perpendicular to all other axes.
CORRECT: "Like the other axes, the time axis is necessarily perpendicular to all other axes …" (lines 16–18).

III. Photons do not appear to us to have direction.
WRONG: "Photons themselves appear to us to have a direction" (lines 54–55).

A. I only
B. II only
CORRECT: See the above answer explanations.
C. I and III only
D. II and III only

Passage II (Questions 7–13)

7. A "letter of gift" (line 32) would most likely be used when:

A. documentation of a donation was required.
WRONG: There is no such passage information.

B. a donor wished to express a personal preference.
WRONG: There is no such passage information.

C. the guidance of a trustee was requested.
WRONG: There is no such passage information.

D. the founder wished to give some guidance.
CORRECT: "Where founders wish to give guidance … they can attach a 'letter of gift.'" (lines 29–32).

8. Suppose a long-dead, affluent lover of birds had expressed his rather vaguely written desire that all of his monies go towards studying and protecting the now-extinct passenger pigeon. Since this activity is no longer possible, the court would most likely:

A. find that another similarly threatened animal species would suffice since the activities are now impossible, and the founder was not explicit in his aims.
WRONG: This is only remotely possible and not nearly as specific as Answer B. "Another similarly threatened *animal* species" is *not* necessarily a "bird" species. The founder was a "lover of birds." This answer is not "close enough" and violates the concept of "*cy pres.*"

B. find that another similarly threatened bird species would suffice since the founder loved all birds and was not explicit in his aims.
CORRECT: This is most likely. This answer requires an understanding of "the legal doctrine of *cy pres* ('close enough'), when changing circumstances render a founder's stated purpose impossible" (lines 22–24). Since the founder was a "lover of [all or many; plural]birds" and his desire

was "rather vaguely written" the court may find that "the founder's intent was to fund similar charitable projects, rather than the original project exclusively" (lines 27–28).

C.   find that the monies should revert to the heirs since there is no other activity that is 'close enough.'

WRONG: This is not likely and is wrong in the same way that Answer D is wrong. Since the founder was a "lover of [all or many; plural]birds" and his desire was "rather vaguely written," the court may find that "the founder's intent was to fund similar charitable projects, rather than the original project exclusively" (lines 27–28).

D.   find that the monies should revert to the heirs since the founder was explicit in his aims, which are now impossible.

WRONG: This is not likely and is wrong in the same way that Answer C is wrong. Since the founder was a "lover-of-[all or many; plural]birds" and his desire was "rather vaguely written" the court may find that "the founder's intent was to fund similar charitable projects, rather than the original project exclusively" (lines 27–28).

9.   According to the passage, "[s]ome foundations require term limits for trustees or require retirement at a certain age" (lines 54–55). However, this might be *disadvantageous* to the founder because:

A.   this requirement does not discriminate between capable and dishonest trustees, and the founder wields the most power in his initial selection of the original trustees.

CORRECT: This answer provides two *disadvantages*. This answer is almost verbatim from the passage: "… term limits for trustees or require retirement at a certain age. This may be effective in preventing entrenchment but is indiscriminate between capable and dishonest trustees" (lines 55–57) and "the founder wields the most power in his initial selection of the original trustees" (lines 44–45).

B.   this requirement cannot be adequately enforced after the founder is gone, and the founder wields the most power in his initial selection of the original trustees.

WRONG: This answer is inaccurate. There is no indication from the passage that "this requirement cannot be adequately enforced after the founder is gone".

C.   the original trustees that the founder chose may refuse this short-term occupation, and the requirement to retire cannot be enforced.

WRONG: This answer is inaccurate. There is no indication from the passage that either assertion in this answer is true.

D.   the law usually denies the founder any right to sue trustees for failing to enforce the terms of his foundation, and the requirement to retire cannot be enforced.

WRONG: This answer is inaccurate. There is no indication from the passage that "the requirement to retire cannot be enforced."

10. Assume that the wealthy buggy whip manufacturer's heirs would prefer to inherit her wealth rather than see it donated to another 'charitable purpose' where none of them is employed as one of the well-paid trustees. Which of the following hypotheses does this assumption suggest?

A.   The trustees would be disappointed at a judge's *cy pres* ruling.

WRONG: This is not suggested by the assumption in the question. Presumably, the "well-paid trustees" are happy with their jobs, which they would lose if the foundation were dissolved. A *cy pres* ("close enough") ruling would keep them employed since the foundation would be able to continue operating and "to fund similar charitable projects" (lines 22–28).

B.   The heirs would go to court in an attempt to obtain a *cy pres* ruling.

WRONG: This is not suggested by the assumption in the question. Presumably, the heirs want the foundation dissolved so that they get the monies. A *cy pres* ("close enough") ruling would prevent the heirs from dissolving the foundation or receiving the monies since the foundation would be able to continue operating and "to fund similar charitable projects" (lines 22–28).

C.   A *cy pres* ruling would satisfy both the trustees and the heirs.

WRONG: This is not suggested by the assumption in the question. Presumably, the *heirs* want the foundation dissolved in order that they get the monies. A *cy pres* ("close enough") ruling would prevent the heirs from dissolving the foundation or receiving the monies since the foundation would be able to continue operating and "to fund similar charitable projects" (lines 22–28).

D.   The heirs would be dismayed by a judge's *cy pres* ruling.

CORRECT: This is suggested by the assumption in the question. Presumably, the *heirs* want the foundation dissolved so that they get the monies. A *cy pres* ("close enough") ruling would prevent the heirs from dissolving the foundation or receiving the monies since the foundation would be able to continue operating and "to fund similar charitable projects" (lines 22–28).

11. What assumption is implicit in the idea that "[a]n even more rigorous system of accountability … lets those with the most invested in the foundation run it, and probably encourages increased donation by founders seeking to take control of the board" (lines 60–66)?

Notice that the question is based solely upon the quote from the passage that appears in this question and so can be answered even if one has not read the passage.

A. That those donors who have more money to invest will not want to take control of the board.

WRONG: This contravenes the idea in the question. The idea implies that donors are motivated by "seeking to take control of the board," and that those who have more money and the desire will succeed at it.

B. That those donors who seek to take control of the board will be more accountable.

CORRECT: It is clear that the idea implies that those making the donations and seeking to take control of the board will be increasingly "even more rigorous" regarding accountability.

C. That donors are motivated by accountability.

WRONG: No. The motivation in the idea seems to be "seeking to take control of the board." The accountability is, apparently, somehow a byproduct of the donors taking care of their "increased donation."

D. That those who have the most invested in the foundation are motivated by founders seeking to take control of the board.

WRONG: This answer does not make sense and is not implied by the idea in the question.

12. According to the passage, the "founder wields the most power in his initial selection of the original trustees" (lines 44–45) for all of he following reasons:

  I. All the trustees are probably going to be personally known by the founder.

CORRECT: "These original trustees are likely to consist of the founder himself, close friends/family members, business associates, and personal lawyers" (lines 45–48).

  II. The founder is likely to appoint himself as a trustee.

CORRECT: "These original trustees are likely to consist of the founder himself …" (lines 45–48).

  III. The intent of the founder is most likely to be respected by these trustees.

CORRECT: "These original trustees … are likely to better understand—and respect—the founder's intent." (lines 45–49).

A. II only
B. I and II only
C. II and III only
D. I, II, and III

CORRECT: See above answer explanations.

13. The passage suggests that its author would probably *disagree* with which of the following statements?

A. There are advantages and disadvantages in very explicit instructions by the founder.

WRONG: The author would *agree* with this statement. Answer C provides a disadvantage, and Answer B provides an advantage to very explicit instructions.

B. Very explicit instructions by the founder are invariably disadvantageous.

CORRECT: The author would *disagree* with this statement. For instance: "The more explicit the founder's instructions, the less room there is for trustee *opportunism*" (lines 9–10), and, "These intentions [of the founder] can be enumerated affirmatively (by outlining trustees' explicit duties), or negatively (by listing those acts that the founder prohibits them from doing)" (lines 5–8). According to the passage, there is somewhat of a 'balancing act' whereby the founder has intentions for his money and wants to maintain some control but must realize that "changing circumstances" might render his wishes "impossible," causing his foundation to be dissolved.

C. Very explicit instructions by the founder may cause the foundation to become obsolete.

WRONG: The author would *agree* with this statement. If "changing circumstances render a founder's stated purpose impossible" and his instructions were too explicit, the foundation may be dissolved (lines 22–28).

D. Heirs would have a greater chance of dissolving a foundation based on overly rigid instructions.

WRONG: The author would *agree* with this statement. If "changing circumstances render a founder's stated purpose impossible" and his instructions were too explicit, the foundation may be dissolved (lines 22–28).

Passage III (Questions 14–19)

14. According to the author, which of the following is most likely to be true about the relationship between the "fire" and "women"?

    A. Freud proved that women were protective towards the hearth-fire.

    WRONG: Not according to the author. Freud didn't "prove" anything. Most importantly, it is clear from the passage that the author does not agree with Freud. He thinks that Freud's ideas are "fanciful." The author provides that "American psychotherapy has largely rejected Freud's theories" (lines 9–10).

    B. There is no relationship between women and the fire.

    CORRECT: This is most likely to be true according to what the author says and how he says it. The author does not believe Freud and thinks that his ideas are "fanciful." The author provides that "American psychotherapy has largely rejected Freud's theories" (lines 9–10).

    C. Men will continually put out the fire by urinating on it.

    WRONG: This is not likely to be true according to the author. The author does not believe Freud and thinks that his ideas are "fanciful." The author provides that "American psychotherapy has largely rejected Freud's theories" (lines 9–10).

    D. Women have been assigned the role of guardian of the hearth-fire.

    WRONG: This is not likely to be true according to the author. The author does not believe Freud and thinks that his ideas are "fanciful." The author provides that "American psychotherapy has largely rejected Freud's theories" (lines 9–10).

15. Given the claims made in the passage, the statement "One is not born, one becomes, a woman" (lines 78–79) would suggest that:

    A. unlike Freud, de Beauvior believes that a woman controls her own destiny.

    CORRECT: The expression suggests this answer. "These combine to make Freud's role for women a true 'destiny,' in that it is made to seem irrevocable" (lines 58–60); however, de Beauvior refutes this idea (lines 61–79).

    B. de Beauvior does not believe that a woman can be differentiated biologically at birth from a man.

    WRONG: The statement does not suggest this answer. The statement in the question addresses a woman's destiny, not anything physical.

    C. like Freud, de Beauvior believes that a woman controls her own destiny.

    WRONG: The statement does not suggest this answer. According to the passage, Freud did not believe this. "These combine to make Freud's role for women a true 'destiny,' in that it is made to seem irrevocable" (lines 58–60).

    D. de Beauvior believes that at birth a woman's body is incomplete.

    WRONG: The statement does not suggest this answer. The statement in the question regards a woman's destiny, not anything physical.

16. Suppose that the majority of Freud's research and theories are based upon dream analysis and a person's unconscious thoughts. This new information would most CHALLENGE the claim that:

    Notice that the "claim" has to be one made in the passage. If it isn't, then it is not correct.

    A. Freud was the "Father of Psychotherapy."

    WRONG: This claim is made in the passage; however, the supposition really has nothing to do with it and does not challenge it.

    B. Freud's theories do not seem to have any verifiable basis.

    CORRECT: This claim is made in the passage, and the supposition in the question would *challenge* it. The author argues that Freud's theories "do not seem to have any verifiable basis in either psychological experimentation or normal people's *conscious* thoughts" (lines 3–5). Given the supposition in the question, the author was either misquoted or incorrect.

    C. "One is not born, one becomes, a woman."

    WRONG: This claim is made in the passage. However, it is de Beauvior who makes the claim and it really has nothing to do with the supposition.

    D. a natural antagonism exists between the sexes.

    WRONG: This claim is made in the passage; however, the supposition really has nothing to do with it and does not challenge it.

17. For which of the following conclusions does the passage offer the *least* support?

    Notice that there may be no support for an answer. However, you must ensure that the answer choice falls into the category of being a "conclusion!"

    A. Freud's theories were fanciful.

    WRONG: There is a great deal of support for this conclusion. "Sigmund Freud, the 'Father of Psychotherapy,' is often criticized by modern psychology for the *fanciful* nature of his theories" (lines 1–3). The author then mentions a basis on "a single Greek myth" and the entertaining story of the fire-fighting penis.

B. Freud believed that men were the first to 'tame' fire.

WRONG: There is a great deal of support for this conclusion. The entire story of the fire-fighting penis is provided as support, allegedly from Freud's book.

C. Freud believed that women were supposed to protect the hearth-fire.

CORRECT: This is a passage conclusion, according to the author; there is a reference to the "female's supposed protectiveness towards the fire" (lines 47–48). However, other than that Freud believed women could not effectively extinguish the fire, there is no reason given for their wanting to protect it.

D. Simone de Beauvior felt women were superior to men.

WRONG: There is no support for this; however, *this is not a passage conclusion*. It would take some real extrapolation on passage information to come up with this idea as a conclusion. De Beauvior is simply trying to overcome what she feels is "the completely inferior role assigned to women by social constructions" (lines 66–67).

18. On the basis of the passage, one can most reasonably infer all of the following EXCEPT:

A. Freud believed that sex was man's primary motivation.

WRONG: We can infer this from the passage. "That is, the instinct toward sexual gratification must be suppressed, so that sexual energy can be channeled into materially productive work" (lines 28–30). In other words, sexual energy is the only energy lying around with which to do work. Man will either have sex, or suppress this desire (but not eliminate it) and work.

B. Freud apparently felt that nature was an antagonist.

WRONG: We can infer this from the passage. Excuse the personification, but "Freud sums up civilization largely in terms of increasing technology, leisure, and *protection from nature*" (lines 18–20). If man has to be protected or protect himself from nature, one can assume that nature is dangerous in some way.

C. Freud viewed a penis-to-penis contest as having homosexual implications.

WRONG: We could infer this from the passage. "[M]en, he says, view flame as a rival phallus and instinctively desire to extinguish it by urinating on it, which gives them the subconscious impression of winning a *quasi homosexual competition*" (lines 23–26).

D. Freud's ideas were quickly rejected by American psychotherapy.

CORRECT: This *cannot* be inferred from the passage. "Correctly, American psychotherapy has largely rejected Freud's theories" (lines 9–10). However, there is absolutely *no* implication that they were "*quickly* rejected"!

19. According to one of the positions presented, any differences in the social status of women are (a) made to seem beyond correction and, (b) made to be beyond grievance, since the agent is nature itself. If both of these premises are true, what conclusion is most reasonable?

A. Though women have a right to complain, this will not change their status.

WRONG: This is not a reasonable conclusion. Though the position does not specifically preclude having a "right" to complain, any differences "are beyond grievance," therefore 'complaining' is a waste of time. This is not the best answer.

B. Only through asserting themselves, not by complaining, can women improve their status.

WRONG: This is not a reasonable conclusion. If the differences are "beyond correction," then 'asserting themselves' will be to no avail.

C. Women cannot change their lot and there is no one to blame.

CORRECT: This conclusion is most reasonable because it essentially restates the position presented in the question.

D. Women are the only ones who can change their lot, but they must speak with one voice.

WRONG: This is not a reasonable conclusion. Any differences "are beyond grievance," therefore 'speaking' is of no use.

Passage IV (Questions 20–24)

20. The author would argue that understanding how the dimensions of a board will change is important to the study of cabinet-making because it:

The author provides practical reasons for understanding these changes.

A. provides a basis for determining where the wood came from.

WRONG: This is not accurate.

B. explains why previous joints have failed.

WRONG: This is not the best answer. The problem with this answer is the relative timing involved. The cabinetmaker does not so much repair furniture [there is no evidence that he does so at all in the passage] as build furniture. The cabinetmaker is not so concerned with "why previous joints have failed" as he is with ensuring that joints he is making will not fail after he makes the piece of furniture.

C. indicates how the board can be used.

CORRECT: Someone who studies cabinetmaking is going to make furniture. "A poorly planned and constructed piece of wood furniture will literally tear itself to pieces if it does not overcome the method of joinery itself" (lines 5–8). "[The] cabinetmaker should first determine the aforementioned characteristics of the pieces to ascertain how they will change dimension" (lines 65–67). The cabinetmaker cannot "determine" this unless he "understands" it.

D. illustrates the way cabinets are made.

WRONG: The cabinetmaker is not an "illustrator", or someone primarily interested in 'showing' the way cabinets are made. He actually builds the cabinets. Moreover, this answer is not as responsive to the question of cabinetmakers because it assumes that the cabinetmaker is only interested in "cabinets"; it is too specific. This would be an assumption based upon the name of the craft, but it is not information from the passage. Cabinetmakers build furniture of many types.

21. The discussion of wood movement includes the assumption that:

"This [movement of wood] is due mainly to *changes* in the *humidity* of the environment" (lines 15–16). The answer must provide an "assumption" that is true in *all* instances of wood movement. It does not say "most of the time" or "sometimes."

A. the board is plain-sawn.

WRONG: This is a false assumption. This answer is too specific. It *could* include a discussion of whether the board was plain-sawn to determine how much and in what manner the wood might move; *but it might not*. Whether the board is plain-sawn or not is *not necessary* to *all* discussions of wood movement.

B. the board is at least six feet long.

WRONG: This is a false assumption. The passage describes a board six feet long, along with some other measurements, but this is for the purpose of visualizing the board as movement is described. The "six foot" measurement is not provided for the purposes of specifying at what length in a board movement occurs.

C. the relative humidity is the same.

WRONG: There must be a change in humidity for wood to change dimension. "This [movement of wood] is due mainly to changes in the humidity of

the environment" (lines 15–16). If there was a great deal of humidity, but it had always been extant, this would not cause wood movement because the wood would [How much wood can a woodchuck ... never mind.] have already stabilized relative to the ambient humidity level. See the explanation for Answer D.

D. the ambient humidity is changing.

CORRECT: The passage makes a clear correlation between changes in humidity and wood movement. "This [movement of wood] is due mainly to changes in the humidity of the environment" (lines 15–16). We must assume, based on information from the passage, that a change in humidity is necessary for this to occur. If there was a great deal of humidity, but it had always been extant, this would not cause wood movement because the wood would have already stabilized relative to the ambient humidity level.

22. Which of the following statements is the most reasonable conclusion that can be drawn from the author's description of separating marble blocks in Italy?

"An example of the kind of power that moisture and wood exert can be seen in Italy, where huge blocks of marble are separated by placing wooden wedges in cracks and then pouring water over them, with predictable, irresistible results" (lines 23–27).

A. The marble contracts upon the wedge and separates.

WRONG: This is not a reasonable conclusion. Based upon information provided prior to the Italian example, we can deduce that the wooden wedges expand because of water being poured over them, while we have been told that the marble ["stone" (lines 12–14)] is inert.

B. This is what occurs in a poorly constructed furniture joint.

CORRECT: This is the most reasonable conclusion. The passage is primarily about wood movement, joinery, and furniture. The entire second paragraph (lines 9–30) is devoted to explaining the effects of humidity on wood. A "reasonable conclusion" is that the author is providing an example of "what occurs in a poorly constructed furniture joint"; Answer B.

C. This is what occurs in a furniture joint in an arid environment.

WRONG: This is not a reasonable conclusion. Based upon information provided prior to the Italian example, we can deduce that the wooden wedges expand because of water being poured over them, while we have been told that the marble ["stone" (lines 12–14)] is inert. The answer would be more acceptable if it read, "This is what occurs in a furniture joint in a humid environment." However, it would then be too specific and still not the best answer.

D. The wedges are probably from quarter-sawn wood.

WRONG: This is not a reasonable conclusion. It would matter only a little whether the wedges were of quarter-sawn wood. In fact, quarter-sawn wood is relatively "stable," and we know that plain-sawn wood expands more dramatically and would therefore make a better wedge for the purpose of splitting the marble.

23. If one were to examine the construction of an oak rocking chair and find medullary rays throughout the piece, this situation would best support the assertion that:

The quarter-sawn method "may also yield particularly beautiful grain patterns as in the case of the medullary rays in quarter-sawn white oak boards" (lines 49–51).

A. the rocking chair is made of black cherry.

WRONG: This assertion is not supported by the question's "situation." The passage speaks of "medullary rays in quarter-sawn white *oak* boards" (lines 50–512).

B. the rocking chair has probably been made fairly recently.

WRONG: This assertion is not supported by the question's "situation." First, medullary rays are characteristic of quarter-sawn wood. Second, "The quarter-sawn method is rather traditional [denoting *older, more aged*]" (lines 46–47). Finally, quarter-sawing "has … fallen from favor in its use" (lines 53–54). It is most likely that the rocker is *older*, or even an antique.

C. the rocking chair is expensive.

CORRECT: This assertion *is* supported by the question's "situation." We know that the rocker was made of quarter-sawn wood because of the medullary rays. Second, quarter-sawing is a "very expensive method" (lines 52–53), meaning that the materials used to construct the chair were very expensive. Finally, the quarter-sawn method is rather traditional [denoting *older, more aged*]" (lines 46–47). It is most likely that the rocker is *older*, or even an antique.

D. the rocking chair was made with beauty, rather than longevity, in mind.

WRONG: This assertion is not supported by the question's "situation." There is no certain way to know if this is true; therefore, this is *not* the *best* answer. Further, this answer is probably *not* true. Quarter-sawn wood, by virtue of its inherent stability (lines 46–49) enhances the characteristics associated with longevity in furniture.

24. The claim that cutting up a tree in a quarter-sawn manner is "a tremendously wasteful method, and as a result a very expensive method, of turning a tree trunk into boards and has thus fallen from favor in its use" (lines 52–54), necessitates which of the following conclusions?

The answer must be a conclusion, arrived at by deductive or inductive reasoning. Thus, it cannot simply restate what is already explicitly stated. The best answer should be a conclusion drawn from the most elements of the quote.

A. Inefficient practices are often used when cutting trees.

WRONG: This conclusion is *not* necessitated by the claim. First, they methods "have fallen from favor" therefore, these are *not* "often used." Further, we know that quarter-sawing is only one method used to cut up trees. This is a poor answer.

B. Wasteful methods can be efficient and more costly.

WRONG: This conclusion is *not* necessitated by the claim. "Wasteful" methods *are not usually* "efficient." These wasteful methods are certainly not averred to be more efficient in this passage.

C. Inefficient practices are no longer popular or costly.

WRONG: This conclusion is *not* necessitated by the claim. This answer can accurately be restated as "Inefficient practices are no longer *costly* or popular," clearly not a conclusion necessitated by the quote in the question.

D. Inefficient practices are costly and are no longer popular.

CORRECT: This conclusion is necessitated by the claim. This answer embodies *all* the elements in the statement, "waste" to "expensive" to "out of favor." It not only restates the essential elements of the quote, it is a "conclusion" because it goes from the specifics in the quote to a generality. It concludes that because the 'sawing practice' is "wasteful" (i.e., inefficient), leading to such-and-such, it follows that all inefficient practices will lead to the same thing.

Passage V (Questions 25–29)

25. If the hypothesis of the passage is correct, one should find that presidential elections in the United States:

There is no specification of the *main* hypothesis in the question. Further, you must choose from the answers provided whether you believe there is a better answer or not. On the MCAT, you may frequently find the answer choices unsatisfying.

A. are usually not indicative of the popular vote.

WRONG: This is not a valid conclusion, particularly with the inclusion of the word "*usually*" in the answer. The electoral college *is* "considered" when the question arises whether the popular vote has been circumvented. This happens very infrequently, according to the passage. Usually the electoral college is "never considered".

B. are not frequently contested.

CORRECT: This is a valid conclusion. The passage tells us that it is the "*contested* race" of Bush v. Gore that has reminded us of the electoral college, which is usually "*never considered*" (i.e., it is taken for granted). The passage reminds us that "to count individual votes beyond a reasonable degree of certainty" (lines 32–33), "third-party candidates" (line 19), and "close races" (lines 45–50) all serve to render a presidential election in doubt. The electoral college "tends to magnify the margin of victory" (line 47).

C. do not reflect the will of the people.

WRONG: This is not a valid conclusion. The entire purpose of the elections is to reflect the will of the people. The author and Hamilton feel that this is accomplished.

D. are almost always contested.

WRONG: This is not a valid conclusion. This would be the antithesis of the passage. Bush v. Gore reminds us of the electoral college because it was a "contested" race, which is rare.

---

26. According to the passage, any large attempt at precisely counting votes with respect to reasonable degrees of certainty is characteristic of:

I.   a California election.

WRONG: This answer does not make sense. There is not enough specificity.

II. contested leads in popular votes.

CORRECT: The "scrutinized lead in popular votes … was [and will be in the future] smaller than the reasonable degree of uncertainty associated with any large attempt at counting votes in these elections" (lines 34–37). The Bush v. Gore race was "scrutinized" because it was "contested"; but the author alleges that this would not be an infrequent occurrence, by contrasting this with electoral college votes which "tend to magnify the margin of victory" (line 47). Of course, not *all* leads in popular votes would be scrutinized or contested because the lead would be so vast that there would be no need to "precisely" count votes "to reasonable degrees of certainty."

III. the electoral college.

WRONG: "[L]arge vote counts" are certainly not characteristic of the electoral college.

A. I only

B. II only

CORRECT: See above explanations.

C. II and III only

D. I, II, and III

---

27. The author claims "In practice, well-organized minorities have a very good chance to achieve the highest or second-highest share [of popular votes], advancing to a run-off round" (lines 22–24). The support offered for this conclusion is:

In order to answer this question correctly you would have to remember that political action committees are synonymous with "organized minorities" for the author. Then, notice that the question *seems* to be asking you for an *opinion*; did you *think* the "support offered was *weak*?" Like all of the other questions in this book, this is an actual style of MCAT test question. It may be answered by *initially* ignoring the references to "weak" and "strong." These are value judgments. Ask instead, "What support was offered by the author?" You will find that the aspect of the answer following the "weak" or "strong" is either accurate or inaccurate; it *is* either the support offered or it is not. However, if the answer is premised with "weak," it may accurately repeat passage assertions, but *negate* them, if it is the correct answer. See Answer B's explanation.

A. weak; Bush v. Gore demonstrated the impact of well-organized minorities.

WRONG: First, this is *not* offered as support for the conclusion. The Bush v. Gore contest had no relation [according to the passage] to the question of "well-organized minorities" and thus did not demonstrate the futility of it. Second, if the assertion were true, then it would have to be prefaced with "strong; Bush v. Gore demonstrated …"

B. weak; political action committees and large corporations are representative of minorities.

WRONG: The second aspect of this answer is accurate. The passage does support the quoted conclusion with this implication. However, it does not make sense to say that "the support offered for this conclusion is weak" and then simply reiterate a passage assertion.

C. strong; political action committees and large corporations are tremendously influential.

CORRECT: In order to answer this question correctly you would have to remember that political action committees are synonymous with "organized minorities" for the author. This sentence, coming on the heels of the quoted "conclusion" from the question, responds directly to, and is in support of, that "conclusion." "Consider the tremendous influence nowadays of political action committees and large corporations" (lines 24–26).

D. strong; the majority of Americans would support homosexual adoptions.

WRONG: This is not offered as support for the quoted conclusion. Further, it is not an accurate representation of information in the passage.

28. A study of international elections reveals that immediately following an election, governmental instability increases in relation to the amount of time it takes for the results to be announced. This information increases the likelihood of which of the following answers to the author's question about why not let the popular vote decide our president?

The "study" reveals that it is important to quickly announce election results. In order to do this, you must *first know who the winner is*. The answer must be responsive to the question of "time" and, because the question is about why we should *not* let the popular vote decide, it must either promote the *faster results* with the electoral college or display the *slower results* of the popular vote.

A. The electoral college "unites ... all the advantages ...."

WRONG: This is not responsive to the question. It is attractive because it is a quote from lines 5–6.

B. The electoral college actually casts the votes deciding who will be the president.

WRONG: This is true but vague. It is not responsive to the question.

C. The popular vote is a more accurate representation.

WRONG: This is not responsive to the question and it is a vague answer. Further, the author would not assert that this is true.

D. The popular vote could depend on vote recounts.

CORRECT: The passage implicitly and explicitly refers to "vote recounts," which occur only with a popular vote, requiring a great deal of time. Implicitly—"Over a year later the election was still being repeatedly debated with various sides claiming that their candidate had actually received a majority of the popular vote" (lines 37–40). Explicitly—"Common sense, stability, and the Constitution of the United States call for the election of a president within a certain time. This could not be met with attempts to precisely count popular votes" (lines 40–43).

29. The statement is made that, "[m]any statisticians reported that the commonly reported and scrutinized lead in popular votes in Florida (choose your own candidate for this) was smaller than the reasonable degree of uncertainty associated with any large attempt at counting votes in these elections" (lines 33–37). The excerpted "(choose your own candidate for this)" means that:

A. the author does not want everyone to be able to choose their own candidate.

WRONG: This is meaningless and not supported within the passage.

B. the author is aware that opinions on this matter differ.

CORRECT: The purpose of the quote in the question and reference is not to debate who *really* won Bush v. Gore. It is offered to show the problem with vote recounts, which are a hallmark of the popular vote. "*Over a year later* the [Bush v. Gore] election was *still* being repeatedly debated with various sides claiming that their candidate had actually received a majority of the popular vote" (lines 37–40). It still *is* being debated. It actually strengthens the author's position to show that he is aware and to remind the reader that *there still exist differences of opinion on this election*!

C. the author is aware that there are going to be those who are in favor of the popular vote.

WRONG: Yes, he is aware of this or he would not be writing a persuasive passage. However, the excerpt is not written for this purpose.

D. the author wants everyone to be happy with the election results.

WRONG: This is naïve and rather silly.

Passage VI (Questions 30–35)

30. It can most justifiably be said that the main purpose of the passage is:

A. to explain the concepts of book publishing.

WRONG: This is not justifiably the main purpose of the passage. Whom is the passage specifically addressed to? Anyone? Compare this answer with Answer D. Answer D encompasses all of the aspects of this answer and includes the target, i.e. authors, to whom these concepts were explained. This is not the most complete answer, and therefore, not the best answer.

B. to examine the authoring of a book.

WRONG: This is not justifiably the main purpose of the passage. There is really no explanation about "authoring a book." This passage concerns advice to authors who have already written a book, or are going to write a book. This answer is well outside of the scope of the passage.

C. to enlighten publishers regarding common publishing practices.

WRONG: This is not justifiably the main purpose of the passage. This passage cannot justifiably be said to be directed at publishers. By virtue of the fact that it is not directed at just 'anyone,' but is specifically directed at "authors," the purpose can actually be said to exclude enlightening publishers, or anyone besides authors.

D. to advise authors about the publishing business.

CORRECT: This is the main purpose of the passage. From beginning to end, this passage is directed towards authors with advice for authors, carefully explaining the "tricky and detailed matter" of a book contract with a publisher.

31. The passage suggests that its author would probably *disagree* with which of the following statements?

The correct answer choice must *first* satisfy the condition of being responsive to *some* aspect or issue in the passage. Otherwise, there is no basis for a conclusion regarding whether the author would agree or disagree.

A. The authoring of a book can be very lucrative.

WRONG: The passage does not suggest this statement. Therefore, we cannot argue that the author would agree or disagree based upon passage information.

B. Publisher's profits depend on book sales.

WRONG: The passage does not suggest this statement. Therefore, we cannot argue that the author would agree or disagree based upon passage information.

C. For the most part, royalty payments will determine an author's compensation.

CORRECT: The author would clearly disagree. Though "the bulk of [the author's] compensation comes in the form of 'royalty' payments" (lines 6–7), "The lion's share of an author's compensation depends on strong book sales" (lines 24–25). In an extreme example, one can surmise that even 50% royalty payments mean nothing without at least some book sales, while tremendous book sales coupled with a relatively low royalty payment could still be quite lucrative.

D. Most publishers will try to take advantage of a naïve or first-time author.

WRONG: The passage does not suggest this statement. Therefore, we cannot argue that the author would agree or disagree based upon passage information. Though "[f]irst-time authors may assume that publishers have every incentive to promote the book effectively, since their profits also depend on book sales" (lines 32–35), this is not the fault of the publishers, but the fault of the unseasoned or 'naïve' author. There is no suggestion or implication that a publisher would seek to take advantage of this naïveté.

32. The passage offers several examples regarding why publishers might fail "to promote [a] book effectively" (lines 33–34). From the first example to the last, the publishers are designated as:

A. good promoters to poor.

WRONG: The publishers are not described this way.

B. large to small.

CORRECT: The progression is from "large publishers" (line 36) to "publishers large and small" (lines 40–41), and finally, "some smaller publishing houses" (lines 43–44).

C. effective to ineffective.

WRONG: The passage does not use this method of designation, neither is there any progression or continuity in it.

A. honest to dishonest.

WRONG: The publishers are not described this way.

33. According to the passage, from a purely monetary perspective, the worst that could happen to an author would be to:

A. receive low royalty payments.

WRONG: From a monetary standpoint, this is not the worst that could happen. Remember that the "lion's share of the author's compensation depends on strong book sales" (lines 24–25). In an extreme example, one can surmise that even 50% royalty payments mean nothing without at least some book sales, while tremendous book sales coupled with a relatively low royalty payment could still be quite lucrative.

B. accept compensation based upon wholesale prices.

WRONG: From a monetary standpoint, this is not the worst that could happen. Remember that the "lion's share of the author's compensation depends on strong book sales" (lines 24–25). In an extreme example, one can surmise that even compensation based upon retail prices means nothing without at least some book sales, while tremendous book sales couple with compensation based upon wholesale prices could still be quite lucrative.

C. have his book promoted ineffectively by the publisher.

WRONG: From a monetary standpoint, this is not the worst that could happen. This might result in poor book sales, but it might not. This answer is encompassed and included in Answer D. In other words, if Answer C occurs, then it is possible (but not inevitable) that Answer D occurs. Therefore, this is not the best answer.

D. have the public fail to realize that the book exists.

A & E 3

CORRECT: From a "purely monetary standpoint," this is the worst that could happen to the author. Remember that the "lion's share of the author's compensation depends on strong book sales" (lines 24–25). Therefore, "If the publisher fails to advertise the book widely, or cannot get many bookstores to carry it on their shelves, the book will earn little despite its quality since potential readers are unlikely to even realize that it exists" (lines 29–32).

34. Which of the following would be an example of the "countervailing considerations" (line 2) facing an author?

A "countervailing consideration" is similar to a "double-edged sword" that 'cuts both ways.' There are advantages and disadvantages to these types of considerations.

A. A publisher who primarily promotes his bestsellers
CORRECT: This is a countervailing consideration. If the author has a mediocre book, the publisher will not promote it as heavily as the bestsellers. On the other hand, if the author is sure that he has a bestseller, this publisher will put an inordinate amount of resources behind the book in order to promote it. See the question explanation.

B. A publisher who pays an 8% flat rate
WRONG: This is not a countervailing consideration. On the one hand, this publisher is paying the lowest rate there is (lines 9–11), and it is a "flat rate" so it is not going to go up. On the other hand … there is no other hand; this deal stinks. See the question explanation.

C. A publisher who pays a 15% flat rate
WRONG: This is not a countervailing consideration. On the one hand, this publisher is paying the highest rate there is (lines 9–11), and it is a "flat rate" so the author will get it immediately no matter how good the book is. On the other hand … there is no other hand; this is a good deal! See the question explanation.

D. A publisher who lacks a sales force
WRONG: This is not a countervailing consideration. On the one hand, the disadvantage to this publisher is that he has no sales force, on the other hand … there is no other hand; this deal stinks! The only consideration is a negative one. See the question explanation.

35. Assume that a book is written and a contract signed with a publisher. Although the book is highly promoted by the author and critically acclaimed, no increase occurs in actual book sales. Which of the following hypotheses about this outcome is the most plausible on the basis of the studies cited?

A. The author did not negotiate the highest possible royalty percentage.
WRONG: This is not the most plausible hypothesis. The royalty percentages have no clear connection to the "actual book sales."

B. The book's subject matter was too diverse for wide public acceptance.
WRONG: This is not the most plausible hypothesis. This answer may seem plausible, but there is no basis for this hypothesis in the passage. The reference to "diversity" has to do with a publisher's preferences.

C. The publishing house lacked the necessary contacts.
CORRECT: This is the most plausible hypothesis. Note in the question that it is only the "author" who has "highly promoted" this book so far. From the passage, which provides our basis, we know that "some smaller publishing houses simply lack the sales force, contacts, and territorial reach to promote a book effectively" (lines 43–45).

D. A first-time author probably wrote the book.
WRONG: This is not the most plausible hypothesis. This answer *seems* plausible. However, there is *no* basis for this hypothesis in the passage. The reference to "first-time authors" has to do with misunderstanding a publisher's incentives (lines 32–35).

Passage VII (Questions 36–40)

36. According to the passage, which of the following is most likely to be true about the relationship between the individual soldier and his comrades at the Battle of the Somme?

A. The individual soldier was motivated to prove his bravery to his lifelong friends.
WRONG: This is not implied. The motivator was not to prove bravery, but to prove that one was not a coward: "A man's unwillingness to embarrass himself in the eyes of his lifelong friends" (lines 18–20). Further, to prove bravery would have removed him from the "herd" and his ability to "blend in."

B. The individual soldier knew that there were repercussions to saying 'No' to an officer.
WRONG: This is attractive because it is an accurate statement based upon the passage. However, it is not responsive to the question, which is asking about the relationship between the "individual and his comrades." The "officers" are distinct in the passage from the individual soldier's "comrades."

C. If the individual soldier stayed within a large group of his comrades he was unlikely to be shot.

WRONG: This is not an accurate paraphrasing of the "herding" concept. It does not say anywhere in the passage that the individual soldier would "actually" be any safer within a large group. Read the third paragraph carefully. It implies that he would feel safer. "Another strong motivator would have been the so-called herding instinct, where a man finds security in a crowd" (lines 23–25).

D. The individual soldier was not willing to be shamed in front of his friends.

CORRECT: This is most likely true. "A man's unwillingness to embarrass himself in the eyes of his lifelong friends" (lines 18–20).

37. The author's assertion that soldiers under machinegun fire trying to "blend in among the other men" is analogous to the "behavior of a herd animal running from a predator" (lines 30–31) suggests that such behavior:

I.   will ultimately fail.

WRONG: Common sense and experience tell us that not only is the predator not always successful, but also that he cannot bring down all of the animals in the herd. Thus, the "behavior" will not "ultimately fail."

II. is instinctual, but not always effective.

CORRECT: The behavior of animals other than humans is, by definition, instinctual. Additionally, the author refers to "this instinct" (lines 32–33). However, it is commonly understood that predators are occasionally successful, or else there would be no more predators! Further, though the author asserts that the soldiers were 'herding,' he also submits that a huge number of them were killed.

III. stems from not wanting to be singled out.

CORRECT: "A soldier refusing to advance would be *drawing attention to himself* and thus acting contrary to this instinct" (lines 31–33).

A. I only
B. II only
C. II and III only
    CORRECT: See above explanations.
D. I and III only

38. The existence of which of the following circumstances would most strongly CHALLENGE the information in the passage?

A. After-action reports indicating that those who had acted autonomously were more likely to have survived the battle

WRONG: This answer would not challenge the information in the passage. This answer appeals to you if you assumed that the "herding instinct" strategy was usually successful. Acting "autonomously," in this answer, suggests that the soldier did not "herd," and thus better survived the battle. However, it does not say anywhere in the passage that the individual soldier would "actually" be any safer within a large group. Read the third paragraph carefully. It implies that he would feel safer. "Another strong motivator would have been the so-called herding instinct, where a man finds security in a crowd" (lines 23–25).

B. Historical research indicating that most of the soldiers had not known one another well prior to their enlistments

CORRECT: This answer would challenge the information in the passage. The author bases many of his assertions on the information that "fighting units were made up of men from the same communities … [and] … his lifelong friends" (lines 17–20).

C. War diaries indicating that some soldiers had been summarily executed for fleeing the battlefield

WRONG: This answer would not challenge the information in the passage. This could either be true or untrue, and it would still have very little bearing on passage information. It does not even challenge the passage assertion that "few men disobeyed their orders to advance" (line 12).

D. Historical studies revealing that the majority of soldiers obeyed the orders of their officers

WRONG: This answer would *not* challenge the information in the passage. The author asserts that "*few* men disobeyed their orders to advance" (line 12).

39. The passage suggests that precise shooting that tends to single out individual soldiers would do which of the following to the "herding instinct"?

Notice that there are two aspects to each answer. Don't even consider the first initially. Determine if the second aspect of the answer is accurate according to the passage. This immediately narrows your answer choices. Now determine if the accurate suggestion 'strengthens' or 'weakens' the "herding instinct."

A. Strengthen it, because there would be even more motivation to "blend in"

WRONG: There is no basis for the second aspect of this answer. "Under precise and accurate sniper fire, when a man is part of a group from which individuals are being selected as targets, cohesion breaks down" (lines 25–27). The first aspect is therefore, irrelevant.

B. Weaken it, because the soldiers would want to draw attention to themselves

WRONG: There is no basis for the second aspect of this answer. One cannot imagine why soliders would want to draw attention to themselves while being shot at. The first aspect is, therefore, irrelevant.

C. Strengthen it, because the soldiers would be even more motivated to "blend in"

WRONG: The second aspect of this answer is incorrect. The first aspect is, therefore, irrelevant.

D. Weaken it, because the soldiers realize that there is nowhere to hide

CORRECT: The second aspect of this answer is accurate, and it does weaken the "herding instinct." Precision shooting would tend to do this, because "a man finds security in a crowd. [However, u]nder precise and accurate sniper fire, when a man is part of a group from which individuals are being selected as targets, cohesion breaks down" (lines 24–27).

40. Suppose it is found that convicted and sentenced killers on death row experience more serenity and peace when they realize that they have finally run out of appeals and know for certain that they will inevitably be executed within a short time. How would this information affect the author's claims about "procrastination" (lins 48–50)?

In this type of question where a 'supposition' or new information is provided your strategy is somewhat different. Quickly understand the supposition and its relation to the passage and determine if it weakens or strengthens the passage. In this specific instance, we know from the supposition in the question that the information *weakens* the author's claims. This immediately narrows the answer choices down to two. Alternatively, you could examine the second aspect of the question for accuracy. Both methods will give you Answer C.

A. This information *strengthens* the author's claims because it indicates that 'serenity' was a motivating factor for the soldiers.

WRONG: The information in the supposition definitely weakens the author's claims about procrastination.

B. This information *weakens* the author's claims because it indicates that one can become resigned to anything.

WRONG: The information in the supposition definitely weakens the author's claims about procrastination. But this is not why. The second aspect of this answer is inaccurate. The author does not mention or imply anything about becoming "resigned."

C. This information *weakens* the author's claims because it indicates that a bad situation without options is more tolerable.

CORRECT: The information in the supposition definitely weakens the author's claims about procrastination. And this answer explains why. The author claims that "… human nature dictates procrastination; a bad situation is more tolerable when there exists an option" (lines 48–50). However, this is not true according to the supposition.

D. This information *strengthens* the author's claims because it proves that "human nature dictates procrastination."

WRONG: The information in the supposition definitely *weakens* the author's claims about procrastination.

A & E 3

Verbal Reasoning Test 4
Answers & Explanations

TEST 4 ANSWER KEY

1.	C	11.	B	21.	A	31.	B
2.	D	12.	A	22.	D	32.	D
3.	B	13.	D	23.	B	33.	C
4.	D	14.	B	24.	D	34.	D
5.	A	15.	D	25.	C	35.	D
6.	B	16.	D	26.	B	36.	C
7.	C	17.	D	27.	A	37.	A
8.	D	18.	A	28.	A	38.	D
9.	A	19.	A	29.	C	39.	C
10.	B	20.	B	30.	C	40.	D

Passage I (Questions 1–5)

1. The passage suggests that conflict-resolution education in the schools provides:

    A. students with the tools to effectively teach these concepts to the community.

    WRONG: This is not provided by conflict resolution. "*Teaching*" concepts to the community is not the same as "expanding the role of youth as effective citizens beyond the school into the community" (lines 36–38).

    B. students with the understanding to accept more traditional disciplinary actions.

    WRONG: This is not provided by conflict resolution. According to the passage, there is an effort to "*reduce* the use of traditional disciplinary actions" (lines 61–62).

    C. changes to the whole school environment.

    CORRECT: This is provided by conflict resolution. "They instead try to change the *total school environment* ..." (lines 26–27).

    D. teachers with guidelines that emphasize their personal responsibility.

    WRONG: This is not provided by conflict resolution. The programs "can enable an educator's ability to manage students' behavior without coercion by emphasizing [the *students'*] personal responsibility and self-discipline" (lines 32–34).

2. According to the passage, to whom might one look to become involved with in order to effectively address the problems of youth violence in schools, rather than using coercion?

    A. The National Institute for Citizenship Education in the Law

    WRONG: This is not where one might look to become involved in addressing youth violence in schools. There is no implication that it is even possible to become involved with the Institute.

    B. Parents

    WRONG: This is not where one might look to become involved in addressing youth violence in schools. Parents are not even mentioned in the passage.

    C. Teachers

    WRONG: This is not where one might look to become involved in addressing youth violence in schools. There is no implication that it is even possible to become involved with the teachers.

    D. The community

    CORRECT: This is an almost verbatim response to the question of where one might look to become involved. "These programs also mobilize *community*

involvement in violence prevention ..." (lines 34–35).

3. Suppose that a study found that in the case of young people, they are incapable of recalling the circumstances that led up to a violent conflict. Which of the following statements is an assumption of the author about conflict resolution strategies that would be called into *question*?

    A. Effective programs can enable children to respond nonviolently to conflict through processes of negotiation, mediation, and consensus decision-making.

    WRONG: This is an assumption of the author. However, it has nothing to do with the supposition and is not *questioned* by it.

    B. When youth learn to recognize and constructively address what takes place before conflict, the incidence of these situations will diminish.

    CORRECT: This is an assumption of the author and the supposition plainly calls it into question. This is the only answer in which there is a 'time' aspect that matches the supposition. "Circumstances *which led up to*" and, in the answer, "what takes place *before*."

    C. The programs that appear to be most effective are comprehensive and involve multiple components such as the problem-solving processes and principles of conflict resolution.

    WRONG: This is an assumption of the author. However, it has nothing to do with the supposition and is not *questioned* by it.

    D. Too many of our young people are caught up every day in conflicts that they do not know how to manage.

    WRONG: This is an assumption of the author. However, it has nothing to do with the supposition and is not *questioned* by it.

4. According to the passage, reduced incidents of violence with respect to youth quarreling is characteristic of:

    I. Peer Mediation approaches.

    CORRECT: Lines 57–71 provide a plethora of supporting examples for this answer.

    II. learning to manage conflict in a productive way.

    CORRECT: "Teaching youth how to manage conflict in a productive way can help reduce incidents of violent behavior" (lines 5–7).

    III. an emphasis on personal responsibility.

    CORRECT: "The programs that appear to be most effective [in reducing violence] ... involve ... an emphasis on personal responsibility" (lines 15–20).

A & E 4

A. II only

B. III only

C. II and III only

D. I, II, and III

   CORRECT: See above answer explanations.

5. Which of the following approaches would most likely be stressed by a school administrator who had an understanding of managing students' behavior without coercion?

   A. self-discipline

   CORRECT: This approach is most likely to be stressed. "[The approaches] can enable an educator's ability to manage students' behavior without coercion by emphasizing personal responsibility and *self-discipline*" (lines 32–34).

   B. detention

   WRONG: This approach is not likely to be stressed by an administrator who had an understanding of managing without coercion. Detention would be considered "coercion."

   C. litigation

   WRONG: Litigation could broadly be considered a form of "coercion." Further, this is not an "approach" at all, but a final legal activity in response to an incident of some type.

   D. projection

   WRONG: This is not mentioned in the passage.

Passage II (Questions 6–10)

6. In the context of the passage, the term *politically correct* does NOT refer primarily to:

   The wrong answers should be answers that this term DOES "refer primarily to." The term *politically correct* is an adjective referring to the Praetorians of Caesar.

   A. the soldiers who received the finest equipment and armor.

   WRONG: The term *does* refer to this answer. These soldiers were the Praetorians who the term describes.

   B. the soldiers who were undiminished.

   CORRECT: The term does *not* refer primarily to this answer. These soldiers were the legionnaires who would shout "Integer!" (lines 32–36). They were the antithesis of the politically correct Praetorians.

   C. differences between the allegiances of the Praetorians and the legionnaires.

   WRONG: "Politically correct" does refer to differences such as what the soldiers would shout, what they professed, and where their "heart" or allegiance belonged.

   D. recognition of Caesar as the imperial personage.

   WRONG: The term *does* refer to this answer. This was the essence of the Praetorians political correctness.

7. According to the author, the reason "integritas" was replaced with "integer" was:

   "To signify the difference between the two organizations [Praetorians and legionnaires], the legionnaire, upon striking his armor, would no longer shout 'Integritas!,' but instead would shout 'Integer!'" (lines 32–35).

   A. that the Praetorians no longer wished to be associated with the legionnaires.

   WRONG: This is not the reason. It was not the Praetorians but the legionnaire who wished to "signify the difference between the two organizations" (lines 32–33).

   B. that Caesar wanted only the finest equipment for his Guard.

   WRONG: This answer is accurate, but it predates and precedes the question and is not responsive to it.

   C. to signify the difference between the legionnaires and the Praetorians.

   CORRECT: This is the reason. "To signify the difference between the two organizations, the legionnaire, upon striking his armor, would no longer shout 'Integritas!,' but instead would shout 'Integer!'" (lines 32–35).

   D. that the legionnaires felt somewhat diminished.

   WRONG: This is not the reason. There is no evidence for this answer.

8. On the basis of the passage, it is reasonable to conclude that "sword thrusts" and "arrow strikes":

   A. could probably penetrate Roman armor.

   WRONG: Actually, though this might *seem* like a reasonable conclusion, and might be true, this is not a reasonable conclusion you could reach from any information in the passage. You could just as reasonably conclude from the passage that the thrusts and strikes could NOT penetrate Roman armor.

   B. were not something one needed to be concerned about.

   WRONG: Besides being very vague, by virtue of the fact that the centurion was inspecting his men in the mornings to ensure that the armor had integrity, this answer would not be a valid conclusion.

   C. represented character and integrity.

   WRONG: This is not a reasonable conclusion. This answer is not supported by the passage. The rather obvious metaphor throughout the passage is that the soundness of the armor represented soundness of character.

D. could also symbolize depravity.

CORRECT: This is the most reasonable conclusion. The armor is a metaphor for integrity. Both clearly provide protection. The physical armor provided protection from sword thrusts and arrow strikes in the same way that the armor-of-integrity provided protection from immoral conduct (i.e., depravity).

9. According to the passage, at some point "customary armor began to feel heavy" (line 50). This was also an indication that:

Notice that the proper answer can also be found through elimination of weaker choices.

A. negligence and laziness were easier to bear.

CORRECT: Lines 48–51 indicate that negligence and laziness were chosen in the 4th century. Continuing the metaphor of bearing the armor of integrity, one can expand this to include "bearing" negligence and laziness because they were easier. Additionally, the passage makes clear that the metaphorical armor of integrity was difficult to bear and required "discipline" and inspections.

B. negligence and laziness were heavier burdens.

WRONG: The "customary armor" was a metaphor, but not for negligence and laziness.

C. the Romans were training harder.

WRONG: Not only is this not supported in the passage, it is not even a logical conclusion. If they were training harder, the armor would feel lighter.

D. Caesar's guards were becoming weaker.

WRONG: We do not know if Caesar's guards, the Praetorians, were becoming weaker. Additionally, and more importantly, the quote refers to the legionnaires, not the Praetorians.

10. Assume that the Roman Empire had not fallen when it did, but continued to reign for another 400 years. What could be the relevance of this continued period of influence to the author's views about the "armor of integrity"?

A. This would demonstrate that integrity is important to an empire's longevity.

WRONG: This answer does *not* indicate the relevance of the assumption in the question. It is clear from the passage that integrity had been lost, "so too came their integrity" (lines 57–58), by the end of the period of time mentioned in the passage.

B. This would reveal that moral armor was not that important.

CORRECT: This answer does indicates the relevance of the assumption in the question. The armor is a metaphor for integrity. Again, it is clear from the passage that integrity had been lost, "so too

came their integrity" (lines 57–58), by the end of the period of time mentioned in the passage. Therefore, it would be difficult to argue that this moral armor/integrity was important.

C. This would indicate that the Praetorians were better soldiers than described in the passage.

WRONG: This answer does *not* indicate the relevance of the assumption in the question. The Praetorians are described in disparaging terms. It is not indicated that the Praetorians did any fighting. It is the fighting, and ultimately the lost battles (and lost integrity), that the author would assert contributed to the fall of the Roman Empire.

D. This would demonstrate that the Goths were weak enemies.

WRONG: This answer does *not* indicate the relevance of the assumption in the question. The Goths (line 53) are the enemy mentioned in the passage. However, there is not enough information about them to come to the conclusion offered by this answer. This is clearly not the best answer.

Passage III (Questions 11–15)

11. Which of the following is *not* a characteristic of perspiration caused by nervousness, as described in the passage?

I. It may double or triple the normal amount of secretions.

WRONG: This is a characteristic described in the passage: "nervousness may produce extra 'psychological' perspiration, *whose volume often doubles or triples the normal amount of secretions*, usually for brief periods" (lines 12–15).

II. It may be reduced by several methods.

CORRECT: This is inaccurate. There is no description of, or reference to, any methods that would reduce amounts of nervous or "psychological" perspiration.

III. It may occur in addition to physiological perspiration.

WRONG: This is a characteristic described in the passage: "nervousness may produce *extra* 'psychological' perspiration, whose volume often doubles or triples the normal amount of secretions, usually for brief periods" (lines 12–15).

A. I only
B. II only

CORRECT: See above answer explanations.

C. III only
D. II and III only

12. The term *shocks* (line 57) refers implicitly to formaldehyde's:

A. paralyzing effect on sweat glands.

CORRECT: "[F]ormaldehyde, when applied to sweat centers, usually 'shocks' them into inactivity for several days. *Using the same methodology*, researchers are now investigating injections of Botox [which] … temporarily *paralyzes* the skin and facial muscles …" (lines 56–62).

B. application with a mild electrical current.

WRONG: This is *not* referred to regarding either formaldehyde or shock. "More radical treatments include the application of *antiperspirant chloride salts* with the aid of a mild electrical current, which increases their absorption into the sweat glands" (lines 52–55).

C. strong and long-lasting odor.

WRONG: This is *not* referred to regarding either formaldehyde or shock. There is actually no implication of or reference in the passage to odors.

D. tendencies to irritate the skin.

WRONG: This is *not* referred to regarding either formaldehyde or shock. There is actually no implication of or reference in the passage to skin irritation.

13. Passage information indicates that which of the following statements must be true?

A. Panting works as well as Botox injections.

WRONG: It is *not* indicated that this statement *must* be true. There is no way to correlate the two methods.

B. Application of cold packs works because it lowers body temperature.

WRONG: It is *not* indicated that this statement *must* be true. The cold packs cease to be effective after a short time unless they are rotated. Even then there is no indication that the body is cooled, but "Kuno speculates that such shifting *creates the perception of continuous cold drafts, which signals the body to reduce perspiration levels*" (lines 26–28).

C. Nervous perspiration is common to everyone.

WRONG: It is *not* indicated that this statement *must* be true. First, "nervousness *may* produce extra 'psychological' perspiration" (lines 12–13). You would also have to assume that "everyone" gets nervous.

D. A complete failure to perspire indicates that something is wrong:

CORRECT: This must be true based on the descriptions of perspiration in the passage. "*Normal, physiological perspiration is an ongoing process,*

that takes place at varying levels, even at room temperature … This is the biological mechanism operating at the peak of efficiency" (lines 3–9).

14. According to the passage, all of the following are *true* about the application of cold packs to reduce perspiration EXCEPT:

A. The cold packs should be applied directly to sweat centers.

WRONG: This is not an exception but is true according to the passage: "the application of cold packs directly to … sweat centers" (lines 17–21).

B. This method works because it reduces body temperature.

CORRECT: This is an exception. There is no information or indication from the passage that this is true. The cold packs cease to be effective after a short time unless they are rotated. Even then there is no indication that the body is cooled, but "Kuno speculates that such shifting *creates the perception of continuous cold drafts, which signals the body to reduce perspiration levels*" (lines 26–28).

C. The cold packs should be applied directly to areas where large vessels are closest to the skin surface.

WRONG: This is not an exception but is true according to the passage: "the application of cold packs directly to the skin, particularly to areas … where larger blood vessels are closest to the skin's surface…" (lines 17–20).

D. After a short time, continued application of the cold packs on the same area ceases to be effective.

WRONG: This is not an exception but is true according to the passage. "Interestingly, while the application of cold will prevent sweating for several minutes, perspiration levels have been shown to return to normal quickly despite continued application. However, this effect can be avoided by shifting the location of the cooling pack every five minutes" (lines 21–26).

15. On the basis of the passage, one may assume that panting is most effective when:

A. the organism pants naturally and has a proportional tongue.

WRONG: This may *not* be assumed to be most effective. A "proportional tongue" is too vague. Proportional to what? Proportional in what way?

B. there is no other way for the organism to cool itself.

WRONG: This may *not* be assumed to be most effective. Conceivably, an animal that perspired through its skin *and* panted naturally might cool itself even more effectively.

C. cold packs can be applied constantly to the organism's tongue.

WRONG: This may *not* be assumed to be most effective. Remember that the cold packs must be *rotated*, not applied "constantly" to one perspiration area. "Interestingly, while the application of cold will prevent sweating for several minutes, perspiration levels have been shown to return to normal quickly despite continued application. However, this effect can be avoided by shifting the location of the cooling pack every five minutes" (lines 21–26).

D. the organism's tongue has a proportionally large surface area, and it pants naturally.

CORRECT: This may be assumed based upon the following passage information: "While overheated humans can also pant, the gains for them are slighter, since their tongues provide (proportionally) less surface area, and the act of panting itself, since it is unnatural, actually faintly increases body temperature with predictable results" (lines 34–38).

Passage IV (Questions 16–20)

16. According to the passage, if you "misquote" (line 41) a pro-Agenda scientist or official, the:

"Another favored tactic is to Misquote a pro-Agenda scientist or official, knowing that even if the scientist protests, the reply will not reach all those who read the original misquote" (lines 41–44).

A. newspapers will be unlikely to run further articles.

WRONG: This is a possible answer, but is not as inclusive as Answer D. In other words, there are other reasons that the misquote is effective. The reason the misquote is effective is Answer D.

B. editors will likely contact the source and correct the misquote.

WRONG: This is not supported in the passage.

C. scientists and officials will not protest.

WRONG: This is not supported in the passage.

D. protestations by a scientist or official will be to no avail.

CORRECT: The Misquote is effective because "even if the scientist protests, the reply will not reach all those who read the original misquote" (lines 42–44) (i.e. the "protestations by the scientist or official will be to no avail").

17. Given the statements made in the passage, the reference "but your target audience does not read those [scientific journals] anyway, do they?" (lines 32–33) would suggest that:

The complete sentence is, "Scientific or academic journals will rarely publish them, but your target audience does not read those anyway, do they" (lines 31–33).

A. the author does not think much of scientific journals.

WRONG: The reference does *not* suggest this answer. The author "thinks enough of science" to see the value of misquoting scientists and misusing scientific documents and materials. If he could get materials published in the scientific journals, he probably would.

B. the author does not think that printed materials are useful.

WRONG: The reference does *not* suggest this answer. This is clearly inaccurate. "A *key factor* in any anti campaign is the use of printed materials and documents" (lines 30–31).

C. the author is unsure who "your target audience" consists of.

WRONG: The reference does *not* suggest this answer. This is not true. The author's target audience is anyone and everyone who will pay attention to him.

D. the author does not have high regard for those he must persuade.

CORRECT: The reference does suggest this answer. The author is implying that the "target audience" does not consist of the "sharpest pencils in the box." He would probably characterize them as *National Enquirer* readers rather than readers of *The Economist*. The author offers his anti-Agenda persuasion with a tongue-in-cheek attitude. He is clearly at least somewhat *derisive* of a "majority" who, for instance, would "go to the polls to vote against what they don't like" (lines 71–72), but would *not* go to the polls to vote for something they *do* like.

18. The concept of the "Slippery Slope" (lines 58–65) would best support a metaphor that compares to:

The "Slippery Slope" is only cryptically explained, but relates to "incrementalism"; convince people that if you compromise on the smaller things that you will incrementally be forced to compromise on more and more. Your opponents or rivals can never be satiated.

A. "give 'em an inch and they'll take a mile."

CORRECT: The "Slippery Slope" is only cryptically explained but relates to "incrementalism"; convince people that if you compromise on smaller things, you will incrementally be forced to compromise on more and more. Your opponents or rivals can never be satiated.

B. "a rolling stone gathers no moss."

WRONG: This answer has to do with ideas such as continually making life changes and 'moving on' in order not to stagnate, "gather dust," "moss," or cobwebs and the like. It does not have anything to do with "incrementalism as explained in Answer A.

C. "the early bird gets the worm."

WRONG: This answer has to do with getting there *early* to get the best or the most. It does not have anything to do with "incrementalism" as explained in Answer A.

D. "the boy who cried wolf."

WRONG: This answer has to do with telling the truth so that you will be believed in the future.

19. According to the passage, the popularity of your 'anti' claims and position is not important because:

"People will usually go to the polls to vote against what they don't like" (lines 71–72).

I. people will usually go to the polls to vote against what they don't like.

CORRECT: This responds to why the "popularity" of your 'anti' claims and position is not important. "People will usually go to the polls to vote against what they don't like. Therefore, the *crucial factor* in many referendums is your ability to mobilize fellow supporters" (lines 71–74).

II. people will usually go to the polls to vote for what they like.

WRONG: This is not accurate passage information.

III. people will usually not go to the polls if your information is not accurate.

WRONG: This is not accurate passage information.

A. I only

CORRECT: See above answer explanations.

B. II only
C. I and III only
D. II and III only

20. According to information in the passage, the best way to convince people to become vegetarians would be to:

Remember that this passage is about "anti" persuasion.

A. convince them that eating vegetables is healthy.

WRONG: The passage says nothing about convincing people in any *positive* way through endorsement of your own product.

B. convince them that eating meat is harmful.

CORRECT: If you are pro-vegetarianism, then you are *anti*-meat. Through the methods described in the

passage, you could go to great lengths to convince people not to eat meat.

C. persuade them to study scientific journals.

WRONG: But "your target audience does not read those anyway, do they."

D. allow them to vote.

WRONG: Not unless the vote was *against* meat, you were sure that your constituency was *against* meat, *and* you could mobilize your constituency. "People will usually go to the polls to vote against what they don't like" (lines 71–72).

Passage V (Questions 21–27)

21. The central thesis of the passage is that:

A. synthetic materials are generally more suitable because they retain less moisture.

CORRECT: This is the central thesis of the passage. Notice the difference between the "generally" in this answer and the "always" in Answer C.

B. the colder the weather, the more selective one should be regarding one's clothing.

WRONG: This is not the central thesis of the passage. In fact, "[s]urprisingly, the colder the weather, the less important [proper clothing selection] becomes" (lines 23–24).

C. synthetic materials are always better than the "old stand-bys."

WRONG: This is not accurate. The "always" is an extreme suggestion that should alert you immediately in an answer unless it is provided by the author. "Though the old stand-bys still function as effectively as ever … " (line 5). Further, "eider down" is an "old stand-by," and it is still *more* appropriate in some situations.

D. technology has radically changed the way we dress outdoors.

WRONG: This is *accurate* and may, therefore, be an *attractive* answer. However, this is not the central thesis of the passage.

22. According to the passage, an "old stand-by" (line 5) would best be described as an item that:

"Though the old stand-bys still function as effectively as ever … " (line 5).

A. has outlived its usefulness.

WRONG: This is not accurate. "Though the old stand-bys still function as effectively as ever … " (line 5). Further, "eider down" is an "old stand-by," and it is still *more* appropriate in some situations.

B. has been improved upon and should not be used.

WRONG: This is not accurate. In most situations they may have been improved upon. However, "eider down" is an "old stand-by" and it is still *more* appropriate in some situations. Finally, the "should not be used" is too strong. The "old stand-bys *still* function as effectively as ever ... " (line 5).

C. is still just as effective as what is being used nowadays.

WRONG: This is not accurate. "What is being used nowadays" is a reference to synthetics. In most situations the author clearly argues for the newer synthetics as being *more* effective than the old "stand-bys."

D. has been improved upon but still functions well.

CORRECT: This answer accurately represents the authors arguments from the passage. In most situations the author clearly argues for the newer synthetics as being *more* effective than the old "stand-bys." However, "... the old stand-bys still function as effectively as ever ... " (line 5).

23. According to the passage, if a person is outdoors in extremely cold weather, then:

A. the risks of hypothermia significantly increase.

WRONG: In "extremely cold weather," what you wear becomes *less* important. "The most critical and dangerous temperatures vis-à-vis are above thirty degrees and below fifty degrees for hypothermia" (lines 24–26).

B. the water-retaining properties of materials are less important.

CORRECT: "Surprisingly, the colder the weather, the less important this [water retention] becomes" (lines 23–24).

C. wool is just as good a choice as synthetics.

WRONG: The author clearly does not believe that "wool is just as good a choice as synthetics." The old stand-bys still work just as well as they used to, but not nearly as well as the newer synthetics.

D. one is constantly encountering wet snow and water.

WRONG: Not in "extremely cold weather" as characterized by the author. It is common knowledge that a melt-freeze cycle would be occurring around 32 degrees Fahrenheit.

24. An appropriate theory of survival in the outdoors, derived from the information contained in the passage, would state that maintaining body heat involves:

I. staying as dry as possible.

CORRECT: "Moisture ... is the bane of the individual who elects to be outdoors. " (Lines 15–17).

II. using wool instead of cotton.

CORRECT: "Wool ... retains three percent of its weight in water when completely soaked and then hand-wrung dry. Compared to cottons, this is phenomenal" (lines 31–34).

III. wearing synthetic clothing.

CORRECT: The entire passage is evidence for this choice. For instance, "... there are many good reasons for the move to the synthetic materials, particularly when an individual is in a situation wherein he is relying on his own body heat to keep him warm" (lines 9–12).

A. I only
B. III only
C. I and III only
D. I, II, and III

CORRECT: See reasons above for each.

25. The expression "artificial heat" (line 9) would best support a metaphor that compares computer-generated speech to:

"... the artificial heat of cars and buildings, ... [versus] body heat to keep him warm" (lines 9–12).

A. televised talking.

WRONG: The comparison is not heat-to-heat, nor is it speech-to-talking. This answer omits the 'natural' or 'human' aspect of the comparison.

B. written words.

WRONG: This answer omits the 'natural' or 'human' aspect of the comparison. There is no specificity as to who is doing the writing; is it a computer? The comparison is not heat-to-heat, nor is it speech-to-written-words.

C. human vocalizations.

CORRECT: The "computer-generated speech" is the "artificial" aspect. From "artificial heat" to human "body heat," we compare "computer-generated speech" to "human vocalizations."

D. computer-generated writing.

WRONG: The comparison is not heat-to-heat, nor is it speech-to-writing. This answer omits the 'natural' or 'human' aspect of the comparison.

26. According to information in the passage, the best way to dry wet clothing when the temperature is above thirty degrees would be to:

A. actually thrown them out onto the snow in the sunshine to dry.

WRONG: Above thirty degrees there is no indication from the article that anything would dry on the snow. One could reasonably expect that the snow might be beginning to melt! "In *extremely cold weather*, it is also very dry. Sleeping bags and the like can actually be thrown out onto the snow in the sunshine to dry" (lines 27–30).

B. allow your bodyheat to dry them inside a synthetic sleeping bag.

CORRECT: This answer can be decided upon via process of elimination if nothing else. "With a synthetic sleeping bag on the other hand, it is a common practice to buy the bag large and sleep with wet clothing and boots inside the bag itself" (lines 56–58).

C. wear the clothing loose and in layers.

WRONG: This is not offered in the passage as a method to dry wet clothing.

D. wear the "old stand-bys."

WRONG: This is not responsive to the question.

27. According to the passage, the descriptive term "melt-freeze cycles" is characterized by all of the following EXCEPT:

    I. extremely cold weather

CORRECT: This is an *exception* to the characterization of "melt-freeze cycles." We know from common experience that a melt-free cycle might be expected around 32 degree Fahrenheit. The author's characterization of "extremely cold weather" falls well below this range.

    II. the most critical and dangerous temperatures

WRONG: This is *not* an exception to the characterization of "melt-freeze cycles." "The most critical and dangerous temperatures vis-à-vis hypothermia are above thirty degrees and below fifty degrees. This is due to the melt-freeze cycles …" (lines 24–26).

    III. hypothermia

WRONG: This is *not* an exception to the characterization of "melt-freeze cycles." "The most critical and dangerous temperatures vis-à-vis hypothermia are above thirty degrees and below fifty degrees" (lines 24–26).

A. I only

CORRECT: See above answer explanations.

B. II only
C. III only
D. I and III

Passage VI (Questions 28–33)

28. In the context of the passage, the word *painterly* (line 42) may be used to describe:

A. a more experienced style of painting.

CORRECT: "Art historians note Rembrandt's style grew less precise and more 'painterly' with *the passage of time*" (lines 32–34). "[T]he passage of time" denotes increased experience, which occurs over time.

B. a style common to forgers.

WRONG: This is not the intended use of the word. A "style" common to forgers would be the style that they are attempting to forge!

C. a more distinct style of painting.

WRONG: Not necessarily. An illustrator such as Norman Rockwell has a "distinct" style of painting. This is not the best answer.

D. a more precise style of painting.

WRONG: This is the antithesis of "painterly." "Painterly" can mean "even looser, rougher, and shallower than Rembrandt's" (lines 42–43).

29. According to information in the passage, the best way for an art forger to ensure that his forgery is not discovered would be to:

A. avoid difficult subject matter.

WRONG: This is not mentioned in the passage and is pure conjecture.

B. ensure that the postures of his subjects are realistic.

WRONG: Not necessarily. Picasso's subjects, for instance, are hardly even recognizable as human.

C. not attempt to imitate too precisely.

CORRECT: This answer relates directly to forgery. "'[F]laws' will appear as the results of a calculated but overdone attempt to reproduce Rembrandt's artistic flourishes, with imperfect results. Like *all* forgeries, it has the telltale signs of trying too hard" (lines 14–18).

D. adopt a more 'painterly' style.

WRONG: *Only* if the style of the artist he is trying to imitate is 'painterly' and the forger doesn't try "too hard."

30. It is the author's theory that the "impossible" pose of the rider was a result of:

A. the forger working from a poor model.

WRONG: This is not the author's theory nor is it mentioned in the passage.

B. the forger copying the pose from a subject in one of Rembrandt's other paintings.

WRONG: This is not the author's theory. NOT one of "Rembrandt's *other* paintings." The author is very specific: "It is my theory that the forger, working without the benefit of a model, copied the pose from a *sketch* of one of Rembrandt's *self-portraits*" (lines 65–67).

C. the forger copying the pose from a sketch of a Rembrandt self-portrait.

CORRECT: "It is my theory that the forger, working without the benefit of a model, copied the pose from a *sketch* of one of *Rembrandt's self-portraits*" (lines 65–67).

D. the inexperience of the forger.

WRONG: This is not the author's theory. The author is actually somewhat impressed with the forgery and refers to it as "a superior example of forgery that for centuries withstood the test of time" (lines 78–79).

31. Which of the following examples from the passage would most clearly NOT be an example of a "painterly" (line 36) style?

"Painterly" is characterized as being "less precise" and "even looser, rougher, and shallower" (lines 42–43).

A. The rendering of the "golden mist."

WRONG: From the passage we know that the forger does a good job rendering the "golden mist, in Rembrandt's famous style of representing direct sunlight" (lines 22–23). However, there is nothing to lead us to believe that the style was either more or less "painterly." This is not the best answer.

B. The rendering of the stone on the cliff face.

CORRECT: This would most clearly *not* be an example of "painterly," which is characterized as being "less precise" and "even looser, rougher, and shallower" (lines 42–43). Thus we can assume that there are fewer details present. "We expect [to] … just begin to suggest the *details of the cliff face*. It seems that this artist lavished great care in *rendering the features of the stone*, whereas Rembrandt [who had grown more 'painterly'] would not have bothered to dwell on such details" (lines 25–29).

C. The rendering of the horse.

WRONG: The horse *IS* an example of a "painterly" style. "The strokes became … too 'painterly,'—even looser, rougher, and shallower than Rembrandt's. This exaggerated stroke ended up causing a ghastly illusion of emaciated horse skin over bone" (lines 41–45).

D. The rendering of the rider.

WRONG: The rider is mentioned for the purposes of criticizing his posture. There is no way of judging the 'painterly-ness' of the style in which he is rendered.

32. The passage suggests that the authenticity of a painting is frequently challenged by critics when the painting is perceived to be of inferior quality. The author argues that this is a poor basis for "deattribution" because:

A. not all of an artist's works can actually be attributed to him.

WRONG: This does not make any sense in the context of the question.

B. inferior quality may indicate that the artist was merely growing older.

WRONG: Not unless you assume that "painterly" means growing inferior. Or, if you *suppose* that as an artist ages his work becomes increasingly inferior. There is no basis for this answer in the passage.

C. basically, beauty is in the eye of the beholder.

WRONG: This is not a passage argument.

D. not all of an artist's works are his finest.

CORRECT: This is the basis of the author's argument. Critics argue that "Rembrandt himself would never have produced a painting of such low quality. Yet such a comparison presupposes that Rembrandt himself never produced anything less than his finest work. By this standard, any one of Rembrandt's earlier, lesser, or more obscure paintings becomes a target for deattribution" (lines 6–11).

33. Passage information indicates that which of the following statements must be true?

A. The forger was very familiar with Rembrandt's style.

WRONG: This is not true. "Then, there is the horse: its rendering is … overcompensation in *copying an unfamiliar* style" (lines 30–33).

B. The forger could not recreate the colors of Rembrandt's landscapes.

WRONG: This is not true. Actually, the passage suggests that the forger did rather well with the color. "First, there is the apparent similarity of sunlight: a yellow-gold hue colors the land, *much like Rembrandt's landscapes* circa 1638. The sun … is covered in a diffuse golden mist, *in Rembrandt's famous style* …" (lines 19–22).

C. The low quality of "The Polish Rider" diminished Rembrandt's reputation.

CORRECT: This must be true. "Now that it has been removed from the ranks of the master's works, *among which it had never found much approval*. perhaps *it will finally be judged in proper perspective: not as an inferior work of art* …" (lines 74–77).

D. "The Polish Rider" is actually a painting of Rembrandt himself.

WRONG: It is *possible* that it is Rembrandt himself, according to the author. "It is my theory that the forger, working without the benefit of a model, copied the pose from a sketch of *one of Rembrandt's self-portraits*" (lines 65–67). But even the author admits that this is his "theory," and suggests that the forger was copying the "pose." He does not suggest that the forger copied the likeness. The question asks for an answer which "*must* be true"; this is not the best answer.

Passage VII (Questions 34–40)

34. The author claims that Doctors Shively and DeCecco's "definition designated sexual behavior and orientation as two distinct categories" (lines 39–40). The support offered for this conclusion is:

Note that there could actually be quite a bit of support offered within the passage for the "author's claims." However, that may not matter! You can't simply decide that the passage "strongly" supported the author's claim, then run down the list of choices and find "strong" based on the aforementioned. That support still needs to be *restated* somewhere in these answer choices! Remember that a correct answer requires that the answer meet *two* criteria. First, the second aspect of the answer (after the "strong" or "weak") must be *accurate* based upon passage information. Second, *if* this second aspect is accurate and *supportive* then it must be prefaced with "strong" to be a correct choice. *If* this second aspect is accurate and *challenges* the author's claims, then it must be prefaced with "weak" to be a correct answer choice.

A. strong; the doctors' assessment method has a component for each category.

WRONG: The second aspect (after "strong") is *inaccurate*. The component for "sexual *behavior*" does *not* appear and does not clearly fall under any of the other three components. They offer "gender," "gender identity," "social sex role," and "sexual orientation" (lines 27–33). Thus the "strong" aspect of this answer is moot.

B. strong; the doctors divided "sexual identity" into four components.

WRONG: The second aspect of this answer only *seems* accurate, because the doctors do in fact offer four components. However, it is *not* accurate. The component for "sexual *behavior*" does *not* appear, and does not clearly fall under any of the other three components. They offer "gender," "gender identity," "social sex role," and "sexual orientation" (lines 27–33). Thus the "strong" aspect of this answer is moot.

C. weak; it is clear from the entire passage that the two are distinct categories.

WRONG: The second aspect of this answer is not accurate. This is not at all clear "from the passage." Most importantly, the question does not refer you to "the entire passage!" Your answer must support the author's claim regarding the doctors, a dramatically narrowed range within which to find an answer.

D. weak; there does not appear to be a distinction in the doctors' assessment method.

CORRECT: This second aspect is accurate. The component for "sexual *behavior*" does *not* appear and does not clearly fall under any of the other three components. They offer "gender," "gender identity," "social sex role," and "sexual orientation" (lines 27–33). Thus, the second aspect does *not* support the author's claim and is, in fact, "weak."

35. Using Kinsey's continuum, a person whom Cass (lines 61-83) deemed to be of "mature sexual orientation" would most likely indicate which of the following scores?

First, you must know whom Cass would define as being of "mature sexual orientation." These would be openly homosexual or heterosexual persons (though openness is not a factor in Kinsey's continuum). Bisexuals were of an "interim phase." Then, "Kinsey's measure of sexual behavior consisted of a seven-point continuum, from zero (exclusively heterosexual) to six (exclusively homosexual). A score of three would indicate a person who is equally bisexual in her sexual practices" (lines 11–15).

A. Seven

WRONG: Kinsey's continuum was a seven-point one. But it began with zero and ran through six. Seven was not on the scale.

B. Four

WRONG: Cass felt that a person of "mature sexual orientation" was openly either homosexual or heterosexual. In-between would have been a less mature "interim phase." To Kinsey, this 'four' would have been very close to a three, a bisexual (line 15).

C. One

WRONG: Cass felt that a person of "mature sexual orientation" was openly either homosexual or heterosexual. In-between would have been a less mature "interim phase." To Kinsey, this 'one' would have been a person who tended more toward bisexuality than a zero. This is not as correct an answer as Answer D, and thus not the *best* answer.

D. Six

CORRECT: Based on Kinsey's continuum, Cass's person of "mature sexual orientation" would have to be either a zero/heterosexual or a six/homosexual.

36. An important comparison is made in the passage between:

A & E 4

A. homosexuals and lesbians.

WRONG: There is no comparison made between homosexuals and lesbians in the passage. There *is* a late comparison between the "fluidity" of men and women, but this should *not* be confused with this answer.

B. homosexuals and heterosexuals.

WRONG: There is no comparison made between these two. The differences in 'behavior' are understood without explanation in the passage. The two separate terms are used because they are consistently described as *contrasting*, or at the opposite ends of the spectrum.

C. society's labeling and self-labeling.

CORRECT: This is the best answer. Lines 1–6 compare these two concepts, for one, and then they are referred to again at lines 53–59. The entire passage concerns "defining sexual orientation" in the most accurate way possible. It appears from the passage, following the first paragraph and explanation of the ill-defined "trichotomous labeling" of society, that researchers settled upon self-labeling as the most accurate method.

D. gender identity and gender.

WRONG: This would presumably be where, for instance, a male believes or fantasizes that he is actually a female. There is no strong comparison between these two other than a brief mention in paragraph three.

37. Implicit in the author's conclusion that "Thus, for one to label oneself "gay"/"lesbian," it seems crucial that they have both homosexual behavior and desire" (lines 51–53), is the assumption that:

This author's conclusion is a peculiar statement based upon information available in the passage. It is almost as if something was left out, since Laumann only cites one group who "labeled themselves homosexual," yet the author failed to provide *any* other information about them!

A. both homosexual behavior and desire were expressed by the "1.4% of women and 2.8% of men" in Laumann's survey.

CORRECT: The author's conclusion in the question actually *requires* this answer! The "Thus …" refers back in the same paragraph to the survey conducted by Laumann. The *only* group to label themselves homosexual were the "1.4% of women and 2.8% of men" in Laumann's survey, yet the author failed to provide *any* other information about them! It is as if the author forgot to put in the information which would lead us to the same conclusion (see question explanation).

B. both homosexual behavior and desire were expressed by the "59% of women and 44% of men" in Laumann's survey.

WRONG: This answer is *not* implied by the author's conclusion and *contradicts* passage information. This group did *not* identify themselves as "gay/lesbian and [did *not* engage] in homosexual behavior" (lines 47–48) (see question explanation).

C. both homosexual behavior and desire were expressed by the "[t]hirteen percent of men and 22% of women "" in Laumann's survey.

WRONG: This answer is *not* implied by the author's conclusion and *contradicts* passage information. Though this group did participate in homosexual behavior, they did *not* report same-sex desire (lines 48–51) (see question explanation).

D. both homosexual behavior and desire were expressed by the "development models" in Cass's survey.

WRONG: This answer is *not* implied by the author's conclusion. The "development models" (line 64) were from Cass's study. However, the author's conclusion and the question are in regard to the Laumann survey (lines 51–53), not Cass's study (see question explanation).

38. According to passage information, whose method of assessment would best describe a physical male who is attracted to other males but does not self-label as homosexual because he desires to physically become a female?

This question and the correct answer *require* a system that recognizes "'gender identity,' the psychological self-identification of the individual as being male or female" (lines 29–30), as well as gender. Since we do not know if the 'self-label' depends upon behavior, fantasy, or desire, this is not a requirement for the correct answer.

A. Laumann

WRONG: This method would *not* offer the best description (see question explanation). Laumann's survey provides *no* method for describing "'gender identity,' the psychological self-identification of the individual as being male or female" (lines 29–30).

B. Kinsey

WRONG: This method would *not* offer the best description (see question explanation). Kinsey's continuum provides *no* method for describing "'gender identity,' the psychological self-identification of the individual as being male or female" (lines 29–30).

C. Cass

WRONG: This method would *not* offer the best description (see question explanation). Cass's "development models" provide *no* method for describing "'gender identity,' the psychological self-identification of the individual as being male or female" (lines 29–30).

D. Doctors Shively and DeCecco

CORRECT: This method would offer the best description (see question explanation). Only Doctors Shively and DeCecco provide a method for describing "'gender identity,' the psychological self-identification of the individual as being male or female" (lines 29–30).

39. Which of the following would Cass regard as in an "interim 'phase,' rather than a mature sexual orientation" (lines 69–70)?

    I.   Heterosexuals

        WRONG: Cass and others "assume that, eventually, the individual arrives at a relatively fixed outcome [openly acknowledging his sexuality]" (lines 70–71). One *can* infer from this that it would include heterosexuals who, being the majority in society, are rather universally accepted by one another and have reached a 'relatively fixed outcome' from a sexual perspective. If this explanation seems unsatisfying based upon passage information, *reconsider* what the question is asking. Can we consider 'heterosexuals' to be an "interim phase" (even if they are not clearly acknowledged as fitting a "fixed outcome")? The answer is clearly 'No,' and, therefore, 'heterosexuals' is *still* a wrong answer.

    II. Homosexuals who had not revealed their sexuality publicly

        CORRECT: Unlike bisexuality, the 'openness' is significant to this answer. Cass and others "typically describe the movement of the individual from initial blocking of homosexual desires to a sense of ease regarding homosexual feelings and practices. Thus, even these models view homosexual desire as a progression in which open homosexuality is the final destination" (lines 64–68).

    III. Bisexuals who were 'open' about their sexuality

        CORRECT: Cass views "bisexuality as an interim phase, rather than a mature sexual orientation" (lines 69–70). The 'openness' would make no difference in this case.

A. I only

B. III only

C. II and III only

    CORRECT: See above answer explanation.

D. I, II, and III

40. If the passage information is correct, what inference is justified by the fact that studies conducted after Kinsey's have consistently failed to support his finding that 37% of men have participated in same-sex encounters "at least once," more than fifty years after the period described?

A. Kinsey's study was not based solely on behavior.

    WRONG: This inference is certainly *not* justified. Kinsey's "continuum was based solely on sexual behavior" (lines 21–22).

B. Kinsey's continuum offered more limited choices.

    WRONG: This is *not* true. For instance, none of the other research is described as offering questions regarding same-sex encounters "at least once" (line 20).

C. Kinsey admitted that trichotomous labeling produced inaccurate descriptions.

    WRONG: This inference is certainly *not* justified. Kinsey had nothing to do with society's trichotomous labeling (lines 1–6).

D. The subsequent studies do not seem to concern themselves with single same-sex encounters.

    CORRECT: Remember that you are not required to assume or know anything beyond the passage information. Based upon passage information, none of the subsequent research described in the passage addresses 'single same-sex encounters.' We have no way of knowing if any other research studied the same thing or if any other research even took place. Notice the "softener" in this answer; the studies do not *seem* to concern themselves. Finally, the other answers are clearly *wrong*; this answer is the only answer left after the process of elimination. This is the best answer.

A & E 4

Verbal Reasoning Test 5
Answers & Explanations

TEST 5 ANSWER KEY

1.	B	11.	C	21.	C	31.	B
2.	D	12.	D	22.	B	32.	D
3.	C	13.	C	23.	C	33.	D
4.	A	14.	A	24.	C	34.	B
5.	B	15.	C	25.	C	35.	C
6.	C	16.	B	26.	B	36.	D
7.	C	17.	B	27.	D	37.	C
8.	A	18.	C	28.	B	38.	B
9.	A	19.	A	29.	C	39.	C
10.	D	20.	D	30.	A	40.	D

Passage I (Questions 1–6)

1. The *author* of the passage characterizes the "new music" as:

   A. exemplified by rap music and international music.

   WRONG: "One way to *expand* understanding of 'new' music would be to *include* into the curriculum rap music and international music ..." (lines 53–55). The author suggests *including* these types of music into the genre of new music, therefore indicating that they are *not now* a part of it.

   B. arousing increasing interest by the public.

   CORRECT: "This seemed clearly at odds with everything I [the author, writing in the first-person] saw, which pointed to *expanding interest by the public in modern music*" (lines 3–5).

   C. exemplified by that of the twelve-tone composers.

   WRONG: This is *not* the author's opinion but Mr. Rothstein's, with whom the author *disagrees.*

   D. engendering a lack of interest in the public.

   WRONG: This is *not* the author's opinion but Mr. Rothstein's, with whom the author *disagrees*

2. If the public reception of Einstein's theory of relativity repeated the reception that the author claims was given to Schoenberg and Babbitt's compositions, most people would:

   A. view Schoenberg and Babbitt's compositions as too radical.

   WRONG: This answer is wrong because it responds with "Schoenberg's and Babbitt's." The question *requires* a comparative response regarding Einstein and his theory.

   B. only have heard of Einstein's theory in an appreciation class.

   WRONG: This comparison is false. Schoenberg's and Babbitt's compositions would *never* be presented in an appreciation class. The author believes it is because they are too radical, while Mr. Rothstein believes it is because they were not made popular by being included in the curriculum in the first place.

   C. only have heard of Schoenberg's and Babbitt's compositions in an appreciation class.

   WRONG: This answer is wrong because it responds with "Schoenberg's and Babbitt's". The question *requires* a comparative response regarding Einstein and his theory.

   D. view Einstein's theory as too radical.

   CORRECT: "Those who [like Schoenberg and Babbitt] choose to pursue radically different approaches to composition may achieve personal artistic satisfaction, but they must also be prepared never to gain popular acceptance for their work"

(lines 21–24). A repeated reception would view Einstein's theories as too radical.

3. The claim that "[o]nly recently did I realize we were both right" (lines 5–6) is most in accord with the view that:

   The author is clearly taking Mr. Rothstein's arguments and statements out of context and using them to his own advantage.

   A. the author and Mr. Rothstein are in agreement.

   WRONG: Clearly not.

   B. Mr. Rothstein and Babbitt are in agreement.

   WRONG: The question is in the first person, as is the passage, and so the question is referring to Mr. Rothstein and the author. Babbitt is not relevant to this question.

   C. Mr. Rothstein's statements can be reinterpreted by the author.

   CORRECT: The author is clearly taking Mr. Rothstein's arguments and statements out of context and using them to his own advantage. For instance, "If this is the case, he is *partially* correct, in that there is no public interest in them, and *partially* wrong, by attributing this to music appreciation courses" (lines 10–12). The author condescendingly twists Mr. Rothstein's arguments as an adult can do to a child's.

   D. Mr. Rothstein presents primarily valid points.

   WRONG: This is not the case. Line 46, along with lines 9–12, concedes only a partial and limited validity to Mr. Rothstein's statements for the purpose of further supporting the author.

4. The author probably mentions that "some of them do feel contempt for their audience, honestly considering the masses to be asses for not accepting their own extreme theories" (lines 18–20) in order:

   A. to show intellectual elitism.

   CORRECT: One can only have "contempt" for one who is beneath him; an 'ass.' The author clearly feels that *professor* Rothstein and the composers he promotes are outside "mainstream America"— "masses" and "asses." Rothstein is alleged to only appreciate composers with "radically different approaches" that are "so self-consciously opposed to the current understanding of music that it alienates the majority of the public, and appears to do so *deliberately*" (lines 15–17). According to the passage, one would be led to believe that Rothstein fancies himself an intellectual who knows better than the "asses."

   B. to prove the composers' lack of popularity.

   WRONG: The quote in the question provides no additional evidence for the composers' popularity or lack thereof.

C. to identify the cause of the problem.

WRONG: What problem? 'Specificity' is a problem with this answer. Further, if the "problem" is considered to be the lack of popularity for Rothstein's chosen music, then this answer is no better than Answer B.

D. to use alliteration in argumentation.

WRONG: "Masses to be asses" is a fine case of alliteration, as is this answer, but this is not the best answer.

5. According to the passage, which of the following is most likely to be true about the relationship between music appreciation courses and the music or musicians featured in these courses?

"According to the passage," in this case, indicates that it is the *author's* opinion that we are looking for.

I. These courses have created a "lack of interest in the new music" (line 2).

WRONG: According to the passage, this "lack of interest" is a result of the music and musicians themselves who are *not* featured in the courses! They are those promoted by Rothstein.

II. The courses present musical works "that have somehow influenced or represented the mainstream of their time" (lines 34–36).

CORRECT: "The academically 'Certified Masterpieces,' … [used in the music appreciation courses, are] those that have somehow influenced or represented the mainstream of their time" (lines 32–36).

III. "[S]elected musicians only achieved their fame after and because of their inclusion into the curriculum" (lines 42–44).

WRONG: According to the author, "It would *not*, therefore, be logical to conclude that the selected musicians only achieved their fame after and because of their inclusion into the curriculum" (lines 41–44).

A. I only
B. II only

CORRECT: See above explanations.

C. I and III only
D. I, II, and III

6. An appropriate theory of the relationship between artists and their work derived from the information contained in the passage would state that popular acceptance involves:

The key to this question is *"popular acceptance."*

I. achieving personal artistic satisfaction.

WRONG: "Those who choose to pursue radically different approaches to composition *may achieve personal artistic satisfaction,* but they must also be prepared *never to gain popular acceptance* for their work" (lines 21–24).

II. influencing or representing the mainstream.

CORRECT: "The study of popular music … [includes] those that have somehow influenced or represented the mainstream of their time" (lines 32–36).

III. creating within the current understanding of the genre.

CORRECT: The *antithesis* of the idea that *unpopular* music has been produced—described as "pieces so self-consciously *opposed* to the current understanding of music that it *alienates* the majority of the public" (lines 15–17)—is this answer. The implication is that popularly accepted music would fall within the current understanding of music.

A. I
B. I and II
C. II and III

CORRECT: See above explanations.

D. I, II, and III

Passage II (Questions 7–11)

7. Evidence shows that in Leonardo da Vinci's drawing of an old man, probably a self-portrait, the artist has overlaid the picture with a square subdivided into rectangles, some of which approximate Golden Rectangles. This fact tends to support the hypothesis concerning the "repetitiveness and prevalence of these proportions" (line 17) because:

Notice how much extraneous information is provided in this question. This is purposeful.

A. this was "probably a self-portrait."

WRONG: This is not why the "fact tends to support the hypothesis." This answer makes little sense in the context of the question.

B. it is likely that da Vinci knew Fibonacci.

WRONG: This is not why the "fact tends to support the hypothesis." This is not responsive to the question, and there is *no* evidence from the passage that da Vinci knew Fibonacci.

C. it is unlikely that this is mere coincidence.

CORRECT: This answers "why" the "fact tends to support the hypothesis." This is the best answer. The other possible answers are not responsive to the question regarding the "repetitiveness and prevalence of these proportions" (line 17).

D. it is unlikely that da Vinci knew Fibonacci.

WRONG: This is not why the "fact tends to support the hypothesis." This is not responsive to the question, and there is *no* evidence that da Vinci knew, or did not know, Fibonacci.

8. Assume that a scroll was unearthed during an archeological dig in Cyprus, and it appeared to instruct architects of the Parthenon to design using Golden Proportions. This information would increase the likelihood of which of the following answers to the author's question, "[w]as this simply an inherent characteristic of 'beauty' that artists unknowingly produced again and again?" (lines 20–21).

We do know from the passage that the Parthenon is given by the author as an example of the use of the Golden Rectangles. However, what ever else the author may or may not believe is of little help on these types of questions. You must first quickly understand and accept the premise of the first sentence. **Warning:** Make sure that you understand that the premise, or assumption, is new information and *distinct* from the passage and not necessarily the author's viewpoint when you answer the remainder of the questions for that passage!

A. No, the artists had been specifically instructed to use Golden Proportions.

CORRECT: This answer is the best answer. Based upon the assumption we are asked to make in the question, the artists did NOT "unknowingly" produce these proportions again and again.

B. No, the artists were not aware of this characteristic but used it repeatedly.

WRONG: The assumption in the question *tells us* that they *were* instructed in, and thus "aware of," the Golden Proportion.

C. Yes, the artists simply strove for "beauty," and the better ones again and again produced the Golden Rectangles.

WRONG: The first part of the answer, "Yes," is not correct. If the artists were "instructed" to use *traditional* proportions (i.e., proportions that had been used repeatedly in the past), and these proportions are those of the Parthenon, which used Golden Proportions, then the artists did *not* do this "unknowingly."

D. Yes, the scroll indicates that traditions were important to the Greeks.

WRONG: The first part of the answer, "Yes," is not correct. If the artists were "instructed" to use *traditional* proportions (i.e., proportions that had been used repeatedly in the past), and these proportions are those of the Parthenon, which used Golden Proportions, then the artists did *not* do this "unknowingly."

9. The author claims that Leonardo of Pisa's "great book on arithmetic *The Liber Abaci* (1202), was a standard work for 200 years and is still considered the best book ever written on arithmetic" (lines 40–43). The support offered for this conclusion is:

A. weak; the author provides only the discovery and prevalence of the Fibonacci series in furtherance of this claim.

CORRECT: There is no support or further mention of the book beyond the information provided in the quote; the claim is "weak." The second part of the answer is also accurate.

B. weak; the passage suggests that Fibonacci stole the concept of the series from the Greeks.

WRONG: There is no support or further mention of the book beyond the information provided in the quote; the claim is "weak." The second part of the sentence is inaccurate. There is no suggestion that Fibonacci "stole" anything.

C. strong; the passage repeatedly refers to *The Liber Abaci* in furtherance of this claim.

WRONG: There is *no* reference or further mention of the book beyond the information provided in the quote; the claim is "weak." The author also provided that Fibonacci "discovered the [Fibonacci] series of numbers …" (line 43).

D. strong; Fibonacci's discovery of leaves, flowerheads, and seeds is provided as support.

WRONG: There is no evidence that Fibonacci discovered anything having to do with plants.

10. The passage indicates that the author would NOT agree with which of the following statements?

Questions asked in this *negative* sense are inherently more difficult than others.

A. The Golden Proportion is an inherent characteristic of beauty.

WRONG: The author would agree. The author offers this question (lines 19–21) and then its answer (lines 54–57) when referring to plastic surgeons.

B. The discoveries of the occurrences of the Golden Proportion continue today.

WRONG: The author would agree. "The discoveries of the occurrences of this Proportion and this series continue today" (lines 78–79).

C. It is fascinating that the Golden Proportion seems to occur repeatedly throughout nature.

WRONG: The author would agree. The author offers proof that the Proportion does occur repeatedly throughout nature (phyllotaxis, teeth, flowers, etc.), and then defines it as "fascinating" while discounting the "happenstance" aspect (line 68).

A & E 5

The image "sticks" in the author's mind because it is "amazing."

D. It is purely coincidental that the Proportion seems to appear in plants.

CORRECT: The author would *not* agree. He does *not* believe that the occurrences are "happenstance" [i.e., coincidence] (line 69).

11. Suppose the author had inserted the following sentence at line 60: "The Fibonacci series has been used to accurately predict the number of male drones that a given hive will produce." This example would best illuminate the author's discussion of:

These types of questions on the MCAT do *not* require you to refer back to the passage and a specific line number to see the context of the proffered sentence. This takes too much time! You could probably answer this question without even having read the passage.

A. the relationship between the series and the Proportion.

WRONG: The proffered sentence does *not* "illuminate" this answer. The supposition in the question makes no reference to the Proportion.

B. how each succeeding number in the series is derived.

WRONG: The proffered sentence does *not* "illuminate" this answer. The supposition in the question makes no reference to derivation of the series.

C. the Fibonacci numbers are replete throughout nature.

CORRECT: The proffered sentence *does* illuminate and further support our understanding of this answer.

D. discoveries of the occurrences of this series are continuing, even to this day.

WRONG: The proffered sentence does *not* "illuminate" this answer. Though the sentence *is* a discovery of the occurrence of the series, there is no indication from the sentence that would give us an idea *when* it was discovered that the series could be used in this manner: The ancient Greeks might have been the ones who first began predicting hive outputs.

Passage III (Questions 12–17)

12. Which of the following research findings would most seriously *challenge* the hypothesis that "spanking may enhance the internalization of appropriate behavior, which has been explained through reasoning" (lines 65–67)?

"Internalization" seems to mean that the child has wholeheartedly adopted the behavior and made it a part of

who he is. The behavior should therefore manifest itself whether the parent is present or not. The answer must *challenge* this.

A. Evidence that the children were behaving appropriately

WRONG: This does *not challenge* the hypothesis.

B. Proof of enhanced and appropriate spanking

WRONG: This does *not challenge* the hypothesis. Further, this answer is meaningless.

C. Further correlation of appropriate behavior by children, in the absence of their parents

WRONG: This answer *supports*, rather than *challenges*, the hypothesis. If the children are behaving when the parents are away, then they have truly internalized the behavior.

D. Confirmation of inappropriate behavior by the children in the absence of their parents

CORRECT: This answer challenges the hypothesis. Remember, that "internalization" seems to mean that the child has wholeheartedly adopted the behavior and made it a part of who he is. The behavior should therefore manifest itself whether the parent is present or not. "Whenever their parents were absent" implies that the child behaved when the parent was present, and explicitly states that the child misbehaved when the parents were gone. This is the antithesis of "internalized" appropriate behavior.

13. Which of the following suppositions is most clearly believed by the author?

It is apparent from the quote offered at the beginning of the passage—"Spanking is love and scolding is affection" (line 1)—and the context of the passage that the author "believes" in spanking.

A. Spanking may not promote discipline, but it is harmful.

WRONG: As evidenced by the quote, the author believes in "tough love." He does not believe that spanking "may not promote discipline," and he does not believe that it is harmful. The entire final paragraph is provided in support of spanking.

B. The trend towards spanking is increasing and should not be studied further.

WRONG: Neither reference is clearly believed by the author. The "trend" is the government's banning of physical punishment in schools. There is no evidence that the author believes that "spanking is increasing," nor that this nonexisting trend "should not be studied further."

C. Many parents are spanking their children, and there is nothing wrong with that.

CORRECT: The author clearly believes that many, if not most parents, spank as a "prevailing parental practice" (line 18). He cites statistics that "nearly half of U.S. parents now use physical punishment for disciplining their children" (lines 15–16). Further, the author goes to great lengths, first to prove that there is no harm in spanking, and then to try to prove that spanking may be beneficial. This is the best answer.

D. It is undisputed that spanking has proven to be an effective means of discipline.

WRONG: "Undisputed" should have alerted you. This *seems* like a possible answer since the author is in favor of spanking. Yet he fails to provide irrefutable proof, nor does he state that spanking has been proven. He actually admits, "Recent research has *failed to determine* whether spanking is an effective form of behavior modification or whether it has long-term negative consequences" (lines 25–28). The author realizes that he is fighting an uphill battle in his arguments, which is why he first goes to great lengths, first to prove that there is *no harm* in spanking, and then to try to prove that spanking may be beneficial. Yet, the evidence provided in the last paragraph in support of spanking is specious reasoning at best and not proof.

14. In Canada, there are laws against any kind of corporal punishment of children. According to the passage, this trend could lead to:

Of course, the passage does not mention Canada or its laws. The question is, A trend which precluded spanking might lead to *what*? Extrapolate.

A. less internalizing of appropriate behavior in children.

CORRECT: In the last paragraph, the author offers the U.C. Berkeley article. The second proposition is that "spanking may enhance the internalization of appropriate behavior that has already been explained through reasoning" (lines 65–67). Therefore, if a trend that precluded spanking were to continue it might lead to "less internalizing of appropriate behavior in children": the answer.

B. more aggressive behavior in children.

WRONG: The author offers research in the passage that states that, "there is no empirical evidence to support the theory that spanking is related to ... aggressive behavior in children" (lines 73–75). Therefore, a trend that precluded spanking, would *not* lead to "more aggressive behavior in children."

C. a lower level of nurturing in children.

WRONG: This does not really make sense. "Nurturing" is referred to as an "interaction" whereby parents were evaluated in three groups of above-average, average, and below-average levels of spanking. There is no mention of "nurturing in children" or of "children nurturing."

D. less child abuse.

WRONG: The author offers research in the passage that states that "there is no empirical evidence to support the theory that spanking is *related* to child abuse ..." (lines 73–75). Therefore, a trend that precluded spanking would *not* lead to "less child abuse"; the two phenomena are not proven to be related.

15. What is the intended relevance of the quote "Spanking is love and scolding is affection"?

The quote does not exist by itself, but must be interpreted in the *context* of the author's passage.

A. To explain the relative futility of nonphysical forms of punishment

WRONG: This is not the best answer. If this were the intent, then something like, "Spare the rod; spoil the child" might be more apropos. The author at least allows that scolding is "affection."

B. To express that the more you spank your children, the more you love them

WRONG: This is not a belief of the author's. As a matter of fact, "Two groups with above-average use of spanking shared a high prevalence of parent depressive symptoms and a *low level of nurturing* [love?] ..." (lines 46–48).

C. To indicate that those who use physical punishment may care for their children more than those who don't

CORRECT: The quote is relevant for this reason. Notice the use of "may" as a *softener* to make the answer more appropriate. Remember, too, that "parents who reported below-average spanking had relatively low levels of ... *nurturing interactions*" (lines 50–52).

D. To provide a moral justification for requiring obedience in children

WRONG: This answer is not relevant and is wide of the mark. If it had read, "To provide a moral justification for *spanking*" it would be *more* relevant, but still in correct.

16. On the basis of the passage quote, "Despite the fact that over the course of 20 years, 27 states have banned school corporal punishment, nearly half of U.S. parents now use physical punishment for disciplining their children" (lines 13–16), it is reasonable to conclude that the author believes that:

A. spanking is neither good nor bad.

WRONG: This is not a reasonable conclusion. The author clearly thinks that spanking *is* a "good" strategy for discipline.

A & E 5

B. teachers should be able to spank students.

CORRECT: This is the only reasonable conclusion *"on the basis of the passage quote."* This is a difficult question, but it can be answered by eliminating the other choices. The government is banning spanking in the *schools*. By *whom*? Presumably, spanking by teachers. From the disparaging tone, one can assume that the author disagrees with this "trend" and would like to see it reversed. Ergo, this answer choice, "teachers should be able to spank students."

C. parental spanking of children will soon be outlawed.

WRONG: This is not *as* reasonable a conclusion as Answer B. See the explanation to Answer B. The government is banning spanking in the *schools*, presumably by teachers. There is no actual evidence provided in the passage that would allow you to conclude that this "will soon" extend to parents spanking their own children. Thus, this answer requires extrapolation *beyond the quote*, while Answer B is a more direct conclusion.

D. pediatricians strongly endorse spanking.

WRONG: This is not a reasonable conclusion. Pediatricians are *equivocal* regarding whether spanking is harmful, and even more so regarding whether it is helpful.

17. The claim that "[p]arents who used average levels of spanking ... had high levels of nurturing interactions" (lines 52–54), *and* that nurturing interactions are the equivalent of love, is most in accord with the view that:

Lines 39–54 provide information regarding "nurturing" and "nurturing interactions" in a study of people with above-average, average, and below-average levels of spanking. The hypothesis suggests that high levels of "nurturing interactions" are equivalent to high levels of love, and vice versa.

A. parents who use above-average levels of spanking love their children the most.

WRONG: Parents "with above-average use of spanking shared a ... low level of nurturing ..." (lines 46–48). The assumption suggests that "a low level of nurturing" corresponds to a *low* level of love for their children.

B. parents who use average levels of spanking love their children the most.

CORRECT: "Parents who used average levels of spanking ... had high levels of nurturing interactions" (lines 52–54). These parents had higher levels of "nurturing interactions" than the 'above-averagers' or 'below-averagers,' and thus, according to the hypothesis, had higher levels of love.

C. parents who use below-average levels of spanking love their children the most.

WRONG: "[P]arents who reported below-average spanking had relatively low levels of ... nurturing interactions" (lines 50–52). The assumption suggests that "a love level of nurturing" corresponds to a *low* level of love for their children.

D. parents who use below-average levels of spanking love their children the least.

WRONG: "[P]arents who reported below-average spanking had relatively low levels of ... nurturing interactions" (lines 50–52). The assumption suggests that "a love level of nurturing" corresponds to a *low* level of love for their children. However, their level of nurturing (and hence, love) is *no lower than* that of the "above-average" spankers.

Passage IV (Questions 18–24)

18. One of the references used in the passage is to "Historian [Ms.] West" (line 56). What is the most likely reason for the choice of these words?

A. Ms. West probably has a first name that would not clearly indicate her gender.

WRONG: This is *not* the most likely reason. Remember, the author *could* have chosen "Mrs." or "Miss" to indicate her gender. Answer C incorporates this answer (if necessary) and is *more responsive* to the true reasoning. In other words, yes, "Ms." was necessary to "indicate her gender," but *"why?"* Answer C tells us why? in a much more specific fashion.

B. The author felt it important to indicate that she is a historian.

WRONG: This is *not* the most likely reason. The 'historian' component seems secondary to the bracketed 'Ms.' Further, historian [Ms.] West is presented as a supporter of *feminist* legal theory.

C. It was deemed important to indicate that historian West is a woman.

CORRECT: This is the most likely reason. Historian [Ms.] West is presented as a supporter of *feminist* legal theory. This answer is not the same as Answer A. However, as indicated in Answer A, "Ms. West probably has a first name that would not clearly indicate her gender." But there is more to it than that. This answer tells us that *and* also tells us much more specifically why? the author did it.

D. It is surprising that a female historian would disagree with feminist legal theory.

WRONG: This is *not* the most likely reason. This answer is inaccurate, for one thing. historian [Ms.] West is presented as a *supporter* of feminist legal theory.

19. The statue of Justice is a blindfolded woman holding scales, indicating that Justice is eminently fair and unrelated to anything other than reason. The author of the passage would be most likely to respond to this information by:

This is a classic MCAT question. Consider your best answer choices those that would allow the author to either *support* or, in the worst case, *resurrect* or *rehabilitate* his main arguments and thesis. No author is likely to admit he was completely wrong or to abandon his thesis.

A. suggesting this entire concept of justice has been largely undermined and superseded.

CORRECT: This is how the author would most likely respond since he already offers this statement almost verbatim. After explaining the older concepts behind the 'scales' and ideas of neutrality, the author ends the first paragraph unequivocally: "Recent academic discussions have largely undermined the image of an impartial legal process based on logic" (lines 27–28).

B. proposing that the statue of the woman not be blindfolded but gagged.

WRONG: This is *not* a likely response of the author. Though the passage has quite a bit of information on how judges 'hide' behind the verbiage that is used, and further, that these words are more favorable towards the male gender, this answer *fails* to note the presence of the misleading 'scales' that are mentioned explicitly several times in the passage. This is not the best answer.

C. asserting that justice is not fair to women and that only the scales are representative.

WRONG: This is *not* a likely response of the author. The scales represent objectivity, which neither the passage nor the author supports.

D. explaining that the idea of the scales has been refuted.

WRONG: This is *not* a likely response of the author. This answer ignores the presence of the blindfold, which also symbolizes objectivity. Answer A is a much more complete and responsive answer, and one that we know the author would likely provide since it is almost verbatim from the passage.

20. Which of the following conclusions about the author's beliefs can be inferred from the passage?

A. The more radical option of feminist legal theory is the more appropriate.

WRONG: This is *not* clearly one of the author's beliefs. Though the author is a supporter and admirer of feminist legal theory, it is not at all clear that he favors one "option" over the other. This "more radical option" is simply one of two options. Though the author clearly favors feminist legal theory over

the ideas of the legal realists, who "dropped the ball," the author favors critical legal studies more than feminist legal theory (lines 72–85).

B. critical legal studies offers the best ideas for changing the methodology of legal reasoning.

WRONG: This is *not* clearly one of the author's beliefs. "... critical legal studies offers the most *revolutionary* prospect for changing the inadequacies of the current methodology of legal reasoning" (lines 72–74). Does "revolutionary" mean "best?" Although, it is clear that the author favors critical legal studies, it is *not* completely clear that he thinks it is the best option for changing the methodology of legal reasoning. It is certainly not as clear as Answer D, which is almost verbatim from the text. Thus, this is not the best answer.

C. Traditional legal reasoning was the most satisfactory.

WRONG: This is *not* clearly one of the author's beliefs. We can only surmise that "traditional" legal reasoning refers to the entire first paragraph and Judge Hodgekin. However, the author does *not* think that this type of reasoning was at all satisfactory.

D. The current methodology of legal reasoning is inadequate.

CORRECT: This is clearly one of the author's beliefs. From the quote, "... critical legal studies offers the most revolutionary prospect for changing *the inadequacies of the current methodology of legal reasoning*" (lines 72–74), we can easily surmise that this answer is one of the author's beliefs.

21. What is the relation of other passage information to the assertion that "an objective standard, independent of the whim of any ruler (as well as of the judge), governs the outcome" (lines 11–13)?

A. The implication that Judge Hodgekin disagreed undermines it.

WRONG: This answer does *not* show the proper relation of passage information to the assertion. This assertion is a quote from historians Curtis and Resnick who are presented in the *same* line of reasoning as Judge Hodgekin. Judge Hodgekin neither disagreed with the assertion, nor did his *agreement* (not *disagreement*) undermine it.

B. The difference between judges Holmes and Posner weakens it.

WRONG: This answer does *not* show the proper relation of passage information to the assertion. There were really no differences between the two judges that were brought out/emphasized in the passage. Instead their similarity was emphasized (lines 29–46). Both judges actually supported the assertion.

A & E 5

C. The information concerning Oliver Wendell Holmes weakens it.

CORRECT: This answer shows the proper relation of passage information to the assertion. Holmes's idea that "the true basis for judicial decisions was usually the underlying (and sometimes subconscious) *social* policy judges wished to promote" (lines 34–36) *does weaken* the assertion.

D. The contrast between judges Holmes and Posner clarifies it.

WRONG: This answer does *not* show the proper relation of passage information to the assertion. Though the two judges did actually support and "clarify" the assertion, it was not through their "contrasts." There were really *no contrasts* between the two judges that were brought out in the passage.

22. What assumption is implicit in the phrase "hermetically self-justifying" (line 5)?

A. A judge's legal decisions are not subject to the ravages of time in the way that 'oxidation' or rust can affect metals.

WRONG: This assumption is *not* implicit in the phrase. The Verbal Reasoning section is not a science test. If it is implied at all, it is almost indiscernible. This is not the best answer.

B. A judge's legal decision stands alone and is unrelated to peripheral influences.

CORRECT: This assumption is implicit in the phrase. "[B]y virtue of their superior 'artificial reason,' modern judicial reasoning continued to evolve to a point where it could become hermetically self-justifying, without needing reference to external authority or divine right" (lines 3–7).

C. If there are no external authorities to challenge a decision, it is self-justifying.

WRONG: This assumption is *not* implicit in the phrase.

D. When the legal language is genderless, there will be less conflict.

WRONG: This assumption is *not* implicit in the phrase.

23. The passage argument suggests that judicial methodology might benefit from:

I. clearer explanations of the true reasons for a decision.

CORRECT: The author seems to adopt Holmes's ideas that "the true basis for judicial decisions was usually the underlying (and sometimes subconscious) *social* policy judges wished to promote [and] … he suggested only

that judges explain their reasoning and policy choices more honestly" (lines 34–39).

II. less bias in a judge's decision making.

CORRECT: "The legal realists had noted that the neutral, mechanical language of judicial reasoning often obscured the vast discretion judges possessed in deciding outcomes" (lines 49–52). Historian [Ms.] West explains how this 'disadvantaged' women and other minorities.

III. more women in judicial positions.

WRONG: This is not suggested or implied in the passage. It is a change in the "methodology of legal reasoning" and not in the personnel that is suggested.

A. I only

B. II only

C. I and II only

CORRECT: See above answer explanations.

D. I, II, and III

24. Elsewhere, the author of the passage states that people are the sum of their experiences, and thus, true objectivity is not possible. This statement most directly supports the passage assertion that:

Note that in order for the answer to be correct it must satisfy two criteria. It must not only be supported by the statement, but it must also actually be a passage assertion.

A. those in positions of authority try to hide the fact that they have tremendous discretion in the decisions that they make.

WRONG: Most importantly, this answer is *not clearly a passage assertion*. Though Holmes apparently suggested that "judges explain their reasoning and policy choices more *honestly*" (lines 38–39), perhaps implying an effort to hide, he also admitted that a judge's promotion of an agenda might be *subconscious* (lines 34–36). Further, the "vast discretion" (line 51) has more to do with the 'language' of judicial reasoning than any implied attempts to "hide."

B. the male interest is typically privileged over the female.

WRONG: This answer is vague. However, if one assumes that it has to do with "legal" interests then it is implied throughout the third paragraph that males who devised the language of legal reasoning are at an advantage. However, this answer is *not* clearly supported by the statement of the author in the question. Are males *never* able to subordinate their interests to females? This is not the best answer.

C. Holmes suggested only that judges explain their reasoning and policy choices more honestly.

CORRECT: This answer is a passage assertion (lines 38–39) and is almost verbatim. Further, it is supported by the author's assertion in the question, particularly when taken in the context of what else Holmes was saying: "the true basis for judicial decisions was usually the underlying (and sometimes subconscious) *social* policy judges wished to promote" (lines 34–36). If the judges were subconsciously promoting an agenda, then it was ingrained in them, and they were unable to do otherwise.

D. logic was presented as the intellectual equivalent of mechanical scales.

WRONG: This answer is a passage assertion. However, it flies in the face of the statement in the question and is not supported by it.

Passage V (Questions 25–29)

25. In the context of the passage, the term *sanctity* refers primarily to:

Some of the answers are more right than others. Which one is the most responsive to the question?

A. the fundamental rights on which America was established.

WRONG: This is not the *best* answer available. It is a *possible* answer if your thinking was that "fundamental rights" refers to "human life." See lines 18–22.

B. certain truths and values.

WRONG: Taken out of context and standing alone, this answer is very vague. It is not the best answer available. It is a *possible* answer if your thinking was that the "certain truths and values" refers to "human life." See lines 18–22.

C. the human life.

CORRECT: From the passage; "until all citizens recognize the dignity of *human life* and strive to support and defend *its sanctity*" (lines 20–22).

D. the Catholic Church.

WRONG: By virtue of the fact that the author uses the Catholic Church as a point of authority, he obviously is a proponent and supporter of the Church. However, he does not mention the Church in relation to sanctity.

26. The author's argument is based upon the idea that:

What is the *basis* of the author's argument? This passage argues for the sanctity of life; it argues against abortion. However, notice that this sort of question does not provide you with "the author's argument." Nevertheless, if one of

the answers refutes anything that the author is arguing, it should not be considered as a possible correct choice.

A. everyone is called to recognize the Catholic Church.

WRONG: This is not the basis for the author's argument. The author might think that this is a grand idea, but it is not an idea that is suggested in the passage.

B. freedom can be lost.

CORRECT: This is the basis for the author's argument. Evidence for this answer as the best answer is replete throughout the passage. "This [referencing abortion in the previous sentence] poses a serious threat to our nation, for "the future of democracy …'" (lines 11–12). Moreover, 'further rights will be forfeited [i.e., freedoms lost], until all citizens recognize the dignity of human life" (lines 20–21). Catholic politicians should defend right to life because this "represent[s] the fundamental rights [i.e., freedoms] of humanity" (lines 55–56). Failure to protect the unborn "could be devastating for this country [freedom could be lost]" (lines 59–60). The last paragraph warns how freedom can be lost if the wrong choice (abortion) is made.

C. politicians have undergone a radical moral decline.

WRONG: This is not the basis for the author's argument. It is actually the country that has undergone a radical moral decline.

D. our country has flourished because of a good political system.

WRONG: This is not the basis for the author's argument. "Our country has flourished because *it has embodied a commitment to human freedom, human rights, and human dignity*" (lines 3–5). This does not equate to a "good political system."

27. Which of the following assertions in the passage is NOT supported by an example, argument, or reference to an authority?

Remember that an assertion *might* be supported within the same sentence. For instance, "The issue of abortion is not religious, but scientific *when you consider that researchers have proven again and again that life begins at the moment of conception*" (Note: the italicized part of the sentence is fabricated and not from the passage). Additionally, the support that is provided for the assertion does not have to be satisfying or necessarily sway your opinion.

A. A political community is supposed to exist for the common good.

WRONG: This assertion is offered at lines 33–34. Support is provided in the next sentence

B. Catholic politicians should defend the principle of sanctity.

WRONG: This assertion is offered at lines 25–32. Extensive support is provided at lines 39–46.

C. Freedom implies the ability to choose.

WRONG: Do not be confused and equate this answer with the commonly heard pro-choice slogans. The author would obviously *not* support such an idea. You might therefore believe that the answer/assertion is NOT supported and choose this answer! This assertion itself is offered at lines 64–65. Support for it can be found *by example* within the same sentence: "to choose between two roads: one which leads to life: the other, death."

D. The issue of abortion is not religious but scientific.

CORRECT: There is no support for this assertion prior to or beyond its first mention. The author asserts this opinion (lines 49–50) as *fact* and proceeds on with "Furthermore …"

28. Which of the following would the author probably consider the best evidence of the moral regeneration of the country?

The article is about the sanctity of life. The author's idea of evidence of moral regeneration would have to be linked somehow with a reduction in abortions or the abolition.

A. Catholic churches have been reporting that ever-increasing numbers of parishioners are donating money to the Church.

WRONG: There is no mention or implication that tithing, or donating money, has anything to do with the sanctity of human life. The author's concepts of moral regeneration have nothing to do with money.

B. Findings that young people are more supportive than ever of an unborn child's right to life.

CORRECT: The article is about the sanctity of life. The author's idea of evidence of moral regeneration, as mentioned previously, would be linked to efforts to reduce abortions or perceptions of this kind.

C. Catholic politicians, when asked, admitted that they always tended to vote in a manner that was very representative of their constituency.

WRONG: This would obviously mean that *at least sometimes* Catholic politicians voted for abortion rights—not something the author would believe signified moral regeneration. The passage specifically argues against this response to the "perceived demands of democratic pluralism" (line 49), arguing that "Catholic politicians should defend these principles [regarding the sanctity of human life]" (lines 53–56).

D. Voters are voting increasingly for Catholic politicians.

WRONG: The author might approve of this, but by way of omission he admits that Catholic politicians

at least sometimes vote for abortion. Therefore, even if everyone voted for Catholic politicians, these would still be politicians who sometimes voted for abortion. This is not the best answer.

29. The author's reasoning that "the common good cannot be obtained without recognizing and standing up for the right to life because all other inalienable rights of humanity are founded upon and derived from it" (lines 36–39) could most reasonably be extended to questions about:

The question necessarily refers to the right to human life, and by its omission, the cessation of that life: human death. The best answer must embody at least one of these concepts.

A. communism.

WRONG: References to the "common good" notwithstanding, the passage addresses democracy and America rather specifically. It is difficult to imagine how the author's reasoning might be extended to communism.

B. animal rights.

WRONG: Though this answer is vague, "animal rights" as an issue/question is well known enough that one can clearly understand there *are* issues of life and death involved. However, the passage clearly refers to "*human* life." Only the "rights of *humanity*" are expressed as "inalienable."

C. capital punishment.

CORRECT: There are no arguments within the passage that the unborn deserve any special recognition because of their unborn 'innocence.' The question of capital punishment, the execution of convicted criminals, is a logical extension of the author's reasoning.

D. the elderly.

WRONG: This is too vague. With more specificity and information (for instance, references to mercy killing, or euthanasia) this could have been a good answer, but not the best.

Passage VI (Questions 30–34)

30. According to the passage, which of the following is most likely true about the JV policy?

A. The policy was also fashioned by managers of the SOEs.

CORRECT: This is the most likely to be true. "This JV policy, [was] … shaped … even by the managers of the SOEs themselves" (lines 5–10).

B. The policy heavily favored foreign investors.

WRONG: This is not necessarily true. There is no evidence or implication that this is true from the passage. The passage fails to mention *any* motivation that foreign investors might have for these joint ventures.

C. The policy heavily favored the SOEs.

WRONG: This is not true. There is no evidence or implication that this is true from the passage. The SOEs were being transformed *into* JVs. Because of this, SOE managers, and presumably their SOEs, "stood to gain little from the success of the JVs" (lines 43–44).

D. The sole architect of the policy was the Communist Party.

WRONG: This is not true. "This JV policy, [was] … shaped *not only by the national Communist Party* itself, but also by regional officials and even by the managers of the SOEs themselves" (lines 5–10).

31. Which of the following assertions most clearly exemplifies the motivations of the central government?

A. The central government delayed JV implementation in order to assess the foreigners' motivations.

WRONG: This does not exemplify the motivations of the central government. It was *not* the "central government," but the "enterprise-level SOE managers" who delayed the implementation. "Thus, Argentinean managers acted rationally in delaying JV implementation to gain a fuller knowledge of the partner's motives and capabilities" (lines 53–55).

B. The central government hoped that transition to joint ventures would render the SOEs more efficient.

CORRECT: This most clearly exemplifies the motivations of the central government. One can infer this answer from the passage information: "The national government had strong interests in encouraging cooperation between domestic firms and foreign investors; in the short run, it was hoped the union would *remove the drain of unprofitable SOEs* on the national budget" (lines 18–22). The SOEs were to be turned into the presumably more efficient JVs.

C. The central government presumed that the profitable SOEs could be maintained.

WRONG: This does not clearly exemplify the motivations of the central government. There is no support for this assertion. Further, it presumes *incorrectly* that there is passage information that *any* of the SOEs were *ever* profitable.

D. The central government intended to convert all of the manufacturing into SOEs.

WRONG: This does not clearly exemplify the motivations of the central government. This is the opposite of the intent of the policy. The plan was to have "SOEs converted to JVs" (line 38).

32. On the basis of the passage, it is reasonable to conclude that:

A. The SOE managers did their utmost to comply with the reforms, though the reforms were not a good idea.

WRONG: This is not a reasonable conclusion. *Both* of the assertions in this answer are inaccurate. First, "As a group, [the SOE managers] *hindered* the implementation of the JV policies favored by the central and local authorities" (lines 41–42). Secondly, "The central government's decision to move away from a planned economy was *pragmatic*, considering the unsuccessful record of economic planning in Argentina" (lines 11–13).

B. The JV managers attempted to hinder the transition to becoming SOEs.

WRONG: This is not a reasonable conclusion. The passage provides no information specifically on JV managers. It is *possible* that one could assume that the transitioning SOE managers would become the JV managers, but this is speculative. This is *not* the best answer.

C. Foreign investors were not highly motivated to help with the reforms.

WRONG: This is not a reasonable conclusion. What little we do know of the foreign investors indicates that they were at *least* "anxious to return home with a signed contract" (line 67).

D. Though the reforms were a good idea, giving the SOE managers so much responsibility for the reforms was not.

CORRECT: This is the most reasonable conclusion. It is clear that the SOE managers had nothing to gain, and everything to lose. There was no incentive for them in the policies. "While managers gained relatively little, in either money or prestige, from organizing a profitable JV, they stood to damage their political careers in the Party hierarchy if their hastily contracted JV encountered visible problems" (lines 49–53).

33. On the basis of the passage, one may assume that central and local authorities might benefit by:

A. advancing heavy industry over consumer manufacturing.

WRONG: This is not a valid assumption. There is no evidence for this answer. Further, we know that heavy industry was a part of the "unsuccessful record of economic planning in Argentina" (lines 13–17).

B. indefinitely delaying the signing of a contract.

WRONG: This is not a valid assumption. It is only clear that the SOE managers felt that they "could hold out indefinitely in the hope of receiving a bargain from the foreign delegation, which *was*

A & E 5

anxious to return home with a signed contract" (lines 65–67). On the other hand, the central authorities would clearly benefit by *not* delaying the signing of a contract for reason outlined in lines 18–36.

C. hindering the joint venture policies.
WRONG: This is not a valid assumption.

D. promoting the joint venture policies.
CORRECT: This is a valid assumption. The passage provides that "the JV policies [were] favored by the central and local authorities" (line 43). The central authorities would clearly benefit for reasons outlined in lines 18–36. There is no direct evidence that local authorities might benefit from the JVs. However, since they were in favor of the policy, one can presume, in the absence of conflicting information, that the local authorities knew something that we don't. This is the best answer.

34. Which of the following conclusions about the pre-1978 Argentinean economy can be inferred from the passage?

A. Its emphasis on heavy industry was closed to the world market, relying primarily on JVs.
WRONG: This is not a valid inference. The reference to "heavy industry" and "closed to the world market" is accurate. However, the JVs were part of the *post*-1978 economic reform plan, *not* the pre-1978 economy.

B. It was a planned economy that focused on heavy industry and state-owned enterprises.
CORRECT: This is a valid inference. "The central government's decision *to move away from* a *planned economy* was pragmatic, considering … Prior planning had favored heavy industry" (lines 11–14). We can infer that since the plan was to reform SOEs into JVs, the focus in the pre-1978 economy had been on SOEs.

C. It was a planned economy that had a fairly successful record.
WRONG: This is not a valid inference, particularly "considering the unsuccessful record of economic planning in Argentina" (lines 12–13).

D. It was closed to the world market, but open to some foreign investors.
WRONG: This is not a valid inference. There is no evidence for the latter aspect of this answer. The pre-1978 economy *was* closed to the world market, but there is no information that it was open to "some foreign investors."

Passage VII (Questions 35–40)

35. Which of the following statements is an example of what the author probably means in implying that it may be more difficult to undress your child depending on the day or time of year (lines 34–36)?

"Next, you must undress your child; depending on the day or time of the year, this may be relatively easy or a chore" (lines 34–36).

A. In the summer, the child would not want to be undressed.
WRONG: This statement is *not* an example of the author's intended implication. The implication is that at certain "*times*" of the day or year undressing the child is more difficult. If in the summer, the child actually did not want to be undressed, then undressing would be more difficult. However, this is not "what the author probably means." Not wanting to be undressed "in the summer" is a peculiarity and singularity that would not be common knowledge. This is not the best answer.

B. People usually wear more clothes while they sleep.
WRONG: This statement is *not* an example of the author's intended implication. The implication is that at certain "*times*" of the day or year undressing the child is more difficult. This answer addresses "*a*" time, but not the question of "time" and its relation to "difficulty." Additionally, this answer flies in the face of common knowledge.

C. Undressing the child in the dead of winter would take more time.
CORRECT: This statement is an example of the author's intended implication. The implication is that at certain "*times*" of the day or year undressing the child is more difficult. It is common knowledge that in the winter one wears more clothing in order to keep warm. This is emphasized by "in the dead of winter." Removing this additional clothing for the purpose of letting the child use the toilet would be more difficult at this "time of year."

D. For instance, Christmas day would be easier than Easter.
WRONG: This statement is *not* an example of the author's intended implication. The implication is that at certain "*times*" of the day or year undressing the child is more difficult. However, there is no obvious reason why it would be easier on Christmas day than Easter.

36. Which of the following assertions is most clearly a thesis presented by the author?

A. Toilet training a child early will only save you time.
WRONG: This is an antithesis. The author admits that "the expense of either disposable diapers or

cleaning cloth ones is forgotten, but you *pay for it with your time*" (lines 16–18).

B. Most parents assume that life gets easier after their children are toilet trained.

WRONG: This is a thesis but is only one small aspect. This answer may be *included* in Answer D, though Answer D is *not* a subset of this answer. This is not the best answer.

C. You don't save any money through early toilet training.

WRONG: This is not accurate. The author admits that "the expense of either disposable diapers or cleaning cloth ones is forgotten, but you pay for it with your time" (lines 16–18).

D. There are many false assumptions regarding toilet training.

CORRECT: This is a clear thesis. Beginning with the false assumption that a 'regular bowel movement' indicates that the child has 'control' or 'awareness,' to the false assumption that 'a toilet trained child saves time,' to 'it's easier,' to 'she will help you,' etc. Examples are replete throughout the passage.

37. According to the passage, what is the period of time between when a child may first become "regular" and the age at which the "average" child becomes reliably trained?

A. "forever"

WRONG: This answer is not mentioned in the passage. Further, the author reminds us that, regarding this period of time before the child is toilet trained, "It doesn't last long" (line 67).

B. 1 year

WRONG: This is the *age* when the child may first become regular.

C. Two years

CORRECT: There are two years between the end of the first year to three years of age. "Towards the *end of their first year of life*, … babies have … become regular in their … bowel movements" (lines 1–4). Your child "will, on average, be able to keep herself reliably clean and dry by her *third year*" (lines 65–66).

D. Three years

WRONG: This is the *age* when your child "will, on average, be able to keep herself reliably clean and dry by her *third year*" (lines 48–50).

38. Which of the following suppositions is most clearly believed by the author?

A. The psychological implications of early toilet training are exaggerated.

WRONG: This is *not* most clearly believed by the author. The only reference that this answer can be based upon is, "Remember that we haven't even approached, nor will we, any of those sacred-cow psychological implications of toilet training 'too early'" (lines 48–50). However, this does not provide any evidence for this answer. The "sacred cow" remark is not derogatory without additional information.

B. A child with a soiled diaper does not have to be changed immediately.

CORRECT: This is most clearly believed by the author. If need be, "more pressing needs can bet met, and *the soiled diaper can wait*" (lines 23–24).

C. You can't really toilet train a child until three years of age.

WRONG: This is *not* most clearly believed by the author. "Research has shown that no matter when you begin toilet training your child, she will, on average, be able to keep herself reliably clean and dry by her third year" (lines 63–66). The law of averages tells us (and the author) that a large number of children must be toilet trained prior to reaching the age of three. There is no evidence to support this answer.

D. It seems as if you'll be changing diapers 'a long time.'

WRONG: This is *not* most clearly believed by the author. There is no evidence for this answer. Further, the author reminds us that, regarding this period of time before the child is toilet trained, "It doesn't last long" (line 67).

39. What is the author's response to the standard story about the one- or two-year old child who is already toilet trained?

A. The parents are wasting their money.

WRONG: This is *not* a likely response, because the author does not believe this. The author admits that "once a child is potty trained, … the *expense* of either disposable diapers or cleaning cloth ones *is forgotten*" (lines 15–17).

B. This is actually not that hard to teach a child.

WRONG: This is *not* a likely response because the author does not believe this. The passage cautions the parent that, though the child may be defecating regularly, this "child is not truly in control of his bowels, nor is she necessarily aware of the fact that she is eliminating at all" (lines 12–14). The "time-out" scenario also provides a reason why it would not be easy to toilet train a young child.

C. The parents are probably just leaving the child on the toilet until she poops.

CORRECT: This is a likely response, based on an example in the passage. From the first paragraph, the author tells us that "if the child is left in this position long enough a bowel movement in the toilet will result. However, this should not be construed as toilet training" (lines 8–11). *However*, the "child is *not* truly in control of his bowels, *nor* is she necessarily aware of the fact that she is eliminating at all" (lines 12–14).

D. At any rate, the parents now have more time on their hands.

WRONG: This is *not* a likely response because the author does not believe this. "Sure, the expense of either disposable diapers or cleaning cloth ones is forgotten, but you pay for it with your time" (lines 16–18).

40. The statement that towards the end of their first year of life, many babies may have "regular bowel movements" (lines 3-4) probably means that:

A. these babies have movements in their bowels.

WRONG: Yes, the statement does mean this, but this is not an explanation. This is not the best answer. The question pertains to "when." A common mistake is to "begin placing the child on the toilet or a child's toilet seat *around the time of the child's regular bowel movements*" (line 8).

B. the baby's defecations are of a regular size.

WRONG: This is not a likely meaning. There is no mention of size in the passage, and size would not pertain to the *when* of placing the child on the toilet. A common mistake is to "begin placing the child on the toilet or a child's toilet seat *around the time of the child's regular bowel movements*" (lines 6–8).

C. these babies defecate at least once a day.

WRONG: This is not a likely meaning. We have no idea if the regularity refers to "at least once a day" or "six time a day." This is speculative.

D. these babies defecate at regular times each day.

CORRECT: This is the most likely meaning. A common mistake is to "begin placing the child on the toilet or a child's toilet seat *around the time of the child's regular bowel movements*" (lines 6–8).

ANSWERS &
EXPLANATIONS

Verbal Reasoning Test 6
Answers & Explanations

TEST 6 ANSWER KEY

1.	D	11.	C	21.	D	31.	B
2.	C	12.	D	22.	B	32.	D
3.	B	13.	C	23.	C	33.	C
4.	D	14.	A	24.	A	34.	C
5.	A	15.	A	25.	D	35.	A
6.	D	16.	C	26.	C	36.	D
7.	C	17.	B	27.	C	37.	B
8.	C	18.	C	28.	D	38.	C
9.	D	19.	A	29.	C	39.	A
10.	B	20.	B	30.	A	40.	D

Passage I (Questions 1–7)

1. The passage implies that video games may help children with difficulties in:

    I. visual skills.

    CORRECT: "[V]ideo games, as opposed to other forms of media, *encourage* the active development of visual skills … " (lines 13–15).

    II. spatial ability.

    CORRECT: "[V]ideo games, as opposed to other forms of media, encourage the active development of … spatial ability … " (lines 13–15).

    III. abstract thinking.

    CORRECT: "[T]he dynamic imagery in the medium [of video games] and its ability to help children with difficulties in abstract thinking was often noted" (lines 29–31).

    A. I only
    B. I and II only
    C. II and III only
    D. I, II, and III
       CORRECT: See above answer explanations.

2. According to the passage, a child who played more video games will also be likely to:

    A. have better spatial ability and watch less television.
       WRONG: The second aspect of this answer is not accurate "children who played *more* video games tended to watch *more* television" (lines 44–45).

    B. display more creativity and watch less television.
       WRONG: The second aspect of this answer is not accurate "children who played *more* video games tended to watch *more* television" (lines 44–45).

    C. watch more television and display more creativity.
       CORRECT: This is the most "likely" answer: "children who played *more* video games tended to watch *more* television" (lines 44–45), and "video games … encourage the active development of … creativity" (lines 13–15).

    D. watch more television and display diminished hand-eye coordination.
       WRONG: The second aspect of this answer is not accurate: "video games … *encourage the active development* of … hand-eye coordination …" (lines 13–15).

3. Dr. Greenfield writes, "The interactive quality of both video games and computers forces children actively to create stimuli and information, not merely consume them" (lines 16–18). What question might this information reasonably suggest about the author's comment that "video game violence has evolved with violence in other media" (lines 38–39)?

The best answer to this type of question is going to *accurately* encompass components of *both* statements to the greatest extent possible.

A. Aren't video games and television equally responsible for violence in children?
   WRONG: This question is not reasonable based upon the information. This first presupposes that children are violent, which the passage does not assert. Moreover, neither of these statements has anything to do with the 'responsibility for violence in children.'

B. Won't children learn violence from video games rather than just consume it on television?
   CORRECT: This question is reasonable. The parallelism of 'video game violence evolving with television' begs more comparisons. Dr. Greenfield's statement tells us that children are more likely to *learn* from video games than they are from inactively consuming television.

C. Is television as stimulating as video games?
   WRONG: This question is not reasonable based upon the information. Based *solely* on Dr. Greenfield's statement, this is a reasonable question. However, this question pertains to neither violence nor the parallel aspects of the author's comment.

D. Didn't video game violence evolve after the violence we see on television?
   WRONG: This question is not reasonable based upon the information. It presupposes a 'time' or 'before-and-after' aspect that is completely absent from Greenfield's statement and the author's note.

4. The author of the passage would be most likely to agree with which of the following ideas expressed by other researchers?

A. Since it is still a new topic, very little research has been done into how violent video games influence children's behavior.
   WRONG: The author would not agree. "The medium was receiving considerable attention in the world of research even when the home video game market took a turn for the worse" (lines 22–24). Further, lines 32–41, though admitting that no conclusions can be drawn, offer that at least several studies have been done.

B. Children's behavior is tremendously influenced by the increasing violence of video games.
   WRONG: The author would not agree. "Conflicting evidence has been found regarding how violent video games influence children's behavior" (lines 33–35).

C. Violence in video games has little, if any, influence on children's behavior.

WRONG: The author would not agree. "Conflicting evidence has been found regarding how violent video games influence children's behavior" (lines 33–35).

D. No real inferences can be drawn from research into how violent video games influence children's behavior.

CORRECT: The author would be most likely to agree. "Conflicting evidence has been found regarding how violent video games influence children's behavior" (lines 33–35).

5. The passage argument suggests that children might benefit from:

    I. certain types of video games.

    CORRECT: This is suggested based upon Greenfield and other references in the passage. "Dr. Greenfield writes that video games, as opposed to other forms of media, encourage the active development of visual skills, spatial ability, hand-eye coordination, and creativity" (lines 12–15).

    II. certain types of television programming.

    WRONG: This is not suggested in the passage. Lines 12–18 contrast the benefits of video games with television which is merely "consumed." Though "[T]he link [between television and video games]… is strong in part because they are both primarily visual media that involve many of the same cognitive and spatial skills" (lines 45–47), this refers to "*watching*," *not* learning or benefiting from television.

    III. violent video games.

    WRONG: This is not suggested in the passage. Though the author does not say that violence influences children's behavior, and, in fact, offers that "[c]onflicting evidence has been found regarding how violent video games influence children's behavior" (lines 33–35), there is no indication that suggests this answer.

A. I only

CORRECT: See above answer explanations.

B. II only
C. III only
D. I and II only

6. One can infer from the passage that the underlying goal of creating "an all-encompassing popular culture for children" (line 49) was:

"In recent years, video games, television, and film have been used together to create an all-encompassing popular culture for children" (lines 48–50).

A. to aid the active development of visual skills, among others.

WRONG: This is not a valid inference since there are *no* benefits of this type, or any other, linked to *television*, for one.

B. to sell more video games.

WRONG: This is not a valid inference. The only reference to sales is 'popularity,' which is unrelated to the "culture" reference in the quote, or "market." However, the video games, television, and film are apparently "used to market a *specific set of characters*" (line 51), not more video games.

C. to offer an alternative to violent programming and games.

WRONG: This is not a valid inference. It is not implied in the passage.

D. to get children to play more video games and watch more television.

CORRECT: This is a valid inference. Given the positioning of the information that Dr. Dominick "found that children who played *more* video games tended to watch *more* television" (lines 44–45), prior to and in the same short paragraph as the quote in the question, this can be inferred. This might lead to Answer B. But that answer is premature and speculative compared with this one.

7. The author's argument that video games are becoming increasingly realistic is most *weakened* by which idea that is implicit in the passage?

Remember that the correct answer must 1) be *implicit* in the passage, and 2) *weaken* the author's argument.

A. Video game violence is still not very realistic because it has evolved with television violence.

WRONG: This idea is *not* implicit in the passage.

B. Video games, television, and film are creating a culture for children.

WRONG: This *does not weaken* the author's argument.

C. The main characters in the games are not very realistic.

CORRECT: This idea *weakens* the author's argument *and* is implicit in the passage: "With some notable exceptions, typically, the image of the aggressive male hero and the submissive, curvaceous female persists" (lines 6–8). These are stereotypical figures and are not realistic.

D. If you are killed in a video game you get another chance.

A & E 6

WRONG: This *does not weaken* the author's argument. It is pretty clear that this level of realism is not expected and not what the author meant by "one has another chance if one gets hurt or dies in video games" (lines 62–63).

Passage II (Questions 8–13)

8. The author would look upon "whistleblowers" with:

From the passage, remember that "whistleblowers are invariably castigated by their employers and then punished" (lines 9–10). Yet they are responsible for "selfless decrying of wrongs" (lines 11–12).

A. suspicion.
WRONG: There is no evidence for this.

B. envy.
WRONG: There is no evidence for this.

C. admiration.
CORRECT: From the passage, remember, "whistleblowers are invariably castigated by their employers and then punished" (lines 9-10). Yet they are responsible for "selfless decrying of wrongs" (lines 11–12). Altruism and selfless acts are universally admired; it is clear from the passage that the author is no exception.

D. altruism.
WRONG: This is an inappropriate use of the word.

9. The author's reasoning about "societal acts" could most reasonably be extended to questions about:

Societal acts are "behaviors that we laud and endorse and vow to cultivate more fully in ourselves" and "could not have evolved without a *corresponding* readiness to catch, and to punish, the Cheat" (lines 29–34). The author's reasoning would not necessarily have to *agree* with that of a correct answer. However, the correct answer should promote questions, issues, or ideas common to both "societal acts" and the answer.

A. "Eat Meat" and vegetarianism.
WRONG: There is no connection here. This is a nonsensical answer.

B. "Give a hoot, don't pollute" and littering.
WRONG: This answer fails to provide any consequences (or rewards) for the do-gooder, other than his having to carry the trash to the nearest receptacle rather than immediately throwing it on the ground.

C. "Don't do the crime if you can't do the time" and prison sentences.
WRONG: There is no connection here. There are no questions that can reasonably be asked of this reasoning and the author's.

D. "Just say 'No'" and drugs.
CORRECT: We could reasonably extend the author's reasoning to questions about this slogan. This answer is challenged by the author's reasoning. The implication of "Just say 'No'" is that this will help protect society. There is no selflessness here or altruism. In fact, the author would say, "Turn in someone trying to sell you drugs" regardless of the consequences. Many questions can be extended to both. For instance, one can ask, "Is it better to simply say 'no' and turn away without exposing and punishing the person selling the drugs, the transgressor?" Is not society harmed "[i]f the selfish cheater can continue to cheat without rebuke or consequence?"

10. Suppose researchers discover that only in nondemocratic forms of government are high-ranking transgressors punished, whereas in the United States those found cheating at the highest levels of government are almost never punished. Which of the following hypotheses is most compatible with passage information?

There are two clues from the passage. "If the selfish cheater can continue to cheat without rebuke or consequence, the functioning of the *group (society) begins to decline*" (lines 39–41). In addition, "researchers propose that the threat of such punishment may have been crucial to the evolution of human civilization and all its parallel achievements" (lines 57–60).

A. Nondemocratic forms of government will decline.
WRONG: This hypothesis is not compatible with passage information.

B. Democratic forms of government will decline.
CORRECT: This hypothesis is most compatible with passage information. "If the selfish cheater can continue to cheat without rebuke or consequence, the functioning of the group (society) begins to decline" (lines 41-43). Though "democratic" forms of government are not specifically mentioned in the question, the U.S. (a democratic form of government) is referred to, and "democratic forms" are clearly implied by contrast with "nondemocratic forms."

C. The United States is exceptionally corrupt.
WRONG: This hypothesis is not compatible with passage information. The nondemocratic forms of government may actually be more corrupt, yet more likely to do something about it.

D. Democratic forms of government prefer rehabilitation not discipline.
WRONG: This hypothesis is not compatible with passage information. Reference to "rehabilitation, not discipline" (line 17) is made about perspectives on prison.

11. The people who cheat are described as "transgressors." What is the most likely reason for the choice of this word?

   A. The word contrasts with the author's use of "moralistic" aggressors.

   WRONG: This is not likely. The author does mention "moralistic aggression" (line 47), but transgressors has nothing to do with this.

   B. This is a commonly known biblical term, that evokes shame in all of us.

   WRONG: This is not likely. The author does not attempt to "evoke shame in all of us."

   C. The word is widely encompassing and applies to breaking civil or moral rules, whether expressed or implied.

   CORRECT: The word is very descriptive of a wide spectrum of acts. This is intentional on the part of the author and the *most likely reason* why he chose such a word. The author does *not* intend to provide more specificity regarding "cheaters" and "transgressors" because the passage is about our feelings and reactions to these acts, not the acts themselves.

   D. It can be used to describe anyone who follows the rules.

   WRONG: This is not accurate.

12. The aphorism "No good deed goes unpunished" (lines 68–69) means that whistleblowers should:

   A. not go unpunished.

   WRONG: This makes no sense.

   B. expect their transgressors to be punished.

   WRONG: The transgressors are not performing the "good deed."

   C. be better protected for whistleblowing.

   WRONG: This is not suggested by the passage.

   D. expect retaliation for whistleblowing.

   CORRECT: The author would not only admire whistleblowers and say that they are doing 'good deeds' but argue that they are necessary to society. However, he offers the aphorism at the end of the passage: "*But always* remember …" expect to be punished for your good deed; expect retaliation.

13. The ideas discussed in this passage would likely be of most use to:

   This is an ethics passage.

   A. a general preparing for battle.

   WRONG

   B. a senator engaged in a serious debate.

   WRONG: Not unless you assume the debate is on ethics or whistleblowers.

   C. a casino manager promoting ethics.

   CORRECT: The casino manager should give you a clue, and the ethics part should have decided this answer for you.

   D. a zookeeper training animal behaviorists.

   WRONG

Passage III (Questions 14–18)

14. The passage states that "school districts across the country report experiencing significant increases in both the number of students expelled and the length of time they are excluded from their schools" (lines 19–22). According to the author, this increase would probably have resulted from:

   This could have been a difficult question. Remember, on questions of this type, if there are *two* good choices, you should choose the answer that includes *both* of them, if it is available. *However*, and most importantly, if there is *no* answer that includes what you consider to be two good choices, then you must pick the *best possible* choice. *Qualify the rightness* of your choices and then look for the answer that includes the best ones.

   I. the passage of the Federal Gun-Free Schools Act of 1994.

   CORRECT: The consequences of the Act of 1994 are that the student will receive "a minimum 1-year expulsion." Immediately following this information is line 18 giving you the result. This is the best answer and a necessary part of any correct answer.

   II. National School Boards Association (NSBA) reporting of the increasing violence within their schools during the past five years.

   WRONG: Read the sentence structure of this choice carefully. The passage provides no information that the *reporting* of the NSBA resulted in anything.

   III. the lack of alternative schools and other support services while students are away from their regular schools.

   WRONG: The author clearly states the *consequences* of choice III, "Without such services, students generally *return to school* no better disciplined and no better able to manage their anger or peacefully resolve disputes. They will also have fallen behind in their education, and any underlying causes of their violent behavior may be unresolved" (lines 26–31). It is a weak extrapolation to think that a cycle is established and that this would be the correct answer. It is clearly not as good an answer as the explicitly mentioned choice I.

A. I only

CORRECT: See above answer explanations.

B. II only

C. III only

D. I, II, and III

15. The contention that "[r]esearch has shown a link between suspension/expulsion and later dropping out of school, with resulting personal and social costs" (lines 31–33) can most justifiably be interpreted as support for the idea that:

Note that the question does not ask which answer supports the quoted idea, but vice versa. You are *not necessarily* looking for answers or familiar phrases that were mentioned or supported in the passage.

A. reduced prison costs may be achieved through providing educational services that will keep students in school.

CORRECT: This idea is supported by the contention. This is an If/Then type of answer. The quoted contention supports this idea, which can be restated as, '[therefore] keeping students in school by providing educational services may achieve reduced prison costs.' "Reduced prison costs" (line 45) are a "social cost."

B. in cases of suspension/expulsion and later dropping out of school, alternative education may cost a great deal of money.

WRONG: This idea is not supported by the quoted contention. It is attractive because the *separate* clauses are each inferred in the passage.

C. students who are expelled and return to school are able to modify their behavior and peacefully resolve disputes.

WRONG: This answer is not supported by the quoted contention. This answer attractively uses phrases and verbiage taken directly from the passage but makes no mention of any "resulting personal and social costs."

D. personal and social costs should prompt us to link suspension/expulsion and later dropping out of school.

WRONG: This answer actually implies that we should look for the information provided in the question. It makes little sense. The idea is not supported by the contention. The quoted contention already establishes the link.

16. Evidence shows that violent youth have a greater tendency to end up in prison as adults. This fact tends to support the hypothesis concerning "the violence of youth in the school setting [may] bear the fruit of criminal adulthood" because:

This question can and should be answered without referring to the passage. Do not go back and look for the reference to "fruit of criminal adulthood." The question *gives* you the hypothesis whether it stems from the passage or not! What is the "fruit of criminal adulthood?" In this instance, the "fruit" refers to prison, which is emphasized by the given 'fact.'

A. most people in prison are violent criminals.

WRONG: This does not tell why the 'fact' tends to support the hypothesis. Neither the given 'fact' nor the hypothesis would suggest this.

B. adult criminals are usually violent.

WRONG: This does not tell why the 'fact' tends to support the hypothesis. Neither the given 'fact' nor the hypothesis would suggest this.

C. criminal adulthood can lead to incarceration.

CORRECT: This *does* tell why the 'fact tends to support the hypothesis.' The "fruit of criminal adulthood" can lead to "prison" = "incarceration."

D. adults in prison who were violent as youths probably were expelled or suspended from school.

WRONG: This concept is attractive because it *might* be extrapolated from the passage. However, this does not tell why the 'fact' tends to support the hypothesis. Further, neither the 'fact' nor the 'hypothesis' states anything about being expelled or suspended.

17. Which of the following conclusions can justifiably be drawn from the required removal of disruptive and dangerous students as mentioned in the passage?

Note that this question could have been asked without the last part, "as mentioned in the passage." This inclusion considerably tightens the parameters for choosing the best answer.

A. Society has tired of "coddling" troublemakers.

WRONG: This is not a justifiable conclusion. The "coddling" in the passage refers to the costs of alternative education and "the problem of limited resources" being used for students who are perceived as "troublemakers." This would be a natural extrapolation based on general knowledge, but *not* one supported in the passage and not the best possible answer.

B. It has been decided that this is one method that can be used to ensure a safe school environment.

CORRECT: This is a justifiable conclusion. Lines 12–14 give the specific reason why the disruptive and dangerous students are required to be removed. This is the best possible answer.

C. Violent students should be placed directly into alternative schools.

WRONG: This is not a justifiable conclusion. The passage explains clearly that the students were removed to ensure a safe school environment. Further, this was enacted *without* specific thought given to where the students who are expelled/suspended should go or what they should do.

D. Youth violence has increased dramatically.

WRONG: This is a true statement according to the passage. However, it is not a conclusion that can be drawn from the limited information given in the question: particularly with this answer's inclusion of "dramatically."

18. The passage suggests that alternative education should be:

A. provided not just to expelled students, but to all other students who might benefit as well.

WRONG: This is not a suggestion promoted by the passage but an admission by the author that there are *impediments* to alternative education's acceptance. This misleading answer refers to lines 68–70.

B. provided primarily to students who were expelled because of violence at school.

WRONG: The passage begins with school violence and mentions violent students frequently, which might lead one to believe that all expelled/suspended students are violent. However, this is not stated in the passage. There is no suggestion that this answer is correct. It is clear that the services are meant to be provided for all students while they are away from school.

C. provided to all expelled students despite the problem of limited resources.

CORRECT: The passage is certainly pro-alternative education for expelled/suspended students. The passage specifically addresses the problem of limited resources in the area of costs (lines 34–46) and argues that it is cheaper to provide alternative education in the long run; i.e., that the "limited" part of the resources may be an invalid perception.

D. carefully managed by the National School Boards Association (NSBA) in order to husband scarce resources.

WRONG: Resources are admittedly a point of contention according to the passage; however, the NSBA is only mentioned as providing statistical information (lines 5–8).

Passage IV (Questions 19–23)

19. Which of the following statements best summarizes the main idea of the passage?

A. When being questioned by police, any information you provide can and will be used against you.

CORRECT: The author is not equivocal about this point. He does not say that it *may* be used against you. "[y]ou should *never* agree to waive any of your rights. … You are simply providing information to people and a system that *will use it against you, regardless* of your guilt or innocence" (lines 40–43). He emphasizes it will be used against you *regardless* of your guilt or innocence!

B. The police, and law enforcement in general, are dishonest and unscrupulous.

WRONG: The author does not imply this. It would be a false conclusion to assume that because questioning sometimes "occurs under circumstances that the police are aware of and you are not" (lines 25–26) that the police are dishonest. Further, "unscrupulous" is a rather extreme term.

C. John Walker is most probably innocent.

WRONG: Walker is used as a prominent example of what can occur when you waive your rights. His guilt or innocence is irrelevant and not implied in the passage.

D. Always have an attorney present when you answer questions from police.

WRONG: Though the author would agree, this is not mentioned in the passage. The references to "attorneys" are used to support the author's ideas. The author simply points out that "[n]o attorney who had been assigned to provide representation to John Walker would ever have allowed him to speak with law enforcement officers or other agents of the United States" (lines 44–47).

20. The "'American Taliban,' John Walker Lindh" (lines 1–18) best illustrates the author's point that:

A. if you are not being detained by police, they do not have to read you your rights.

WRONG: This point is not illustrated by the reference. This answer *is* a true statement. However, it does *not* apply to Walker in any way. Walker was clearly being detained. Thus, this answer does not illustrate the author's point.

B. cooperating with the police when you are under suspicion will not benefit you.

CORRECT: This is one of the author's points, and it is illustrated by the reference. The author is clear that "innocence" does not matter; it is *always* a mistake to cooperate. "If you are ever read your rights, or 'Mirandized,' you should never agree to waive any of your rights. ... You are simply providing information to people and a system that will use it against you, *regardless of your guilt or innocence*" (lines 39–43).

C. cooperating with the police may help to allay their suspicion of you.

    WRONG: This is neither stated nor implied. The author would strongly disagree with this answer. The author is clear that *innocence* does not matter; it is *always* a mistake to cooperate. See the quote from Answer B.

D. you may wish to help the police for the benefit of everyone else.

    WRONG: In an aside, the author ponders whether Walker's cooperation and waiving of rights "may have been for selfless reasons, because Walker realized that what he had gotten himself involved with was wrong and he wished to help right these wrongs" (lines 44–51). However, the author is clearly against any form of cooperation with the police for any reason. See Answer B.

21. Which of the following statements, if true, would most WEAKEN the author's contention that Walker, if found guilty, will have "put himself in this position" (line 13)?

"You are simply providing information to people and a system that will use it against you, *regardless of your guilt or innocence*" (lines 41–43).

A. The incriminating information provided by Walker to law enforcement was, in fact, not true.

    WRONG: This statement does not weaken the author's contention. It does not matter if the statement was true or not. It could still be used against him. Additionally, you are assuming that everyone involved knew it was true. This answer does not say, "The incriminating information provided by Walker to law enforcement was found by law enforcement and the judicial system to be untrue, *and was not used by them*."

B. The information provided by Walker is the sole evidence used to place him in prison for life.

    WRONG: This would clearly *strengthen* the author's statement.

C. The defense counsel files a legal brief outlining its evidence for an insanity plea.

    WRONG: This has no bearing on the question's premise. This statement does not weaken the author's contention.

D. The prosecution announces that it has several witnesses to its allegations and will not be using Walker's statement.

CORRECT: This statement *does* weaken the author's contention. It is the author's contention that *providing information* to police will always harm you, "*regardless of your guilt or innocence*" (lines 44–45). "Significantly, as pointed out by Ashcroft, these charges are based *almost exclusively on information that Walker provided* voluntarily to law enforcement officers ..." (lines 8-10). Thus, Walker's *statement* put him in this predicament. It is ONLY by somehow *completely eliminating* Walker's statement and information that he provided to law enforcement that the author's statement can be weakened.

22. In advising a group of foreign exchange students who are preparing to go out 'partying' in New York, the author would most likely tell them to:

A. ensure that they have an attorney before they get into any trouble.

    WRONG: This is not supported anywhere in the passage.

B. call an attorney and refuse to answer any questions from police if they get in trouble.

    CORRECT: The author clearly advocates never providing law enforcement with information when being questioned by them because "You are simply providing information to people and a system that will use it against you, *regardless of your guilt or innocence*" (lines 43-45). Therefore, the author clearly believes in the second part of the answer. Further, the author does expand on the help an attorney would have provided to Walker if he had not waived his right to one. Though this first aspect of the answer is less explicit, it is not inappropriate, and it enhances the second aspect.

C. not get into any trouble while they are in the city.

    WRONG: Good "safety tip" as the saying goes. He might advise them this way, but this would be drawing an inference for which there is little evidence, and Answer B is correct in a much more *explicit* way.

D. ask the police officer if they are being detained.

    WRONG: *What* police officer? Did you assume that the students had gotten into trouble or were being questioned? This answer is attractive because it is part of a true statement from the passage. However, when viewed in conjunction with the question it makes little sense.

23. The California Highway Patrol has found that when their troopers simply asked for permission to search the vehicles that they had pulled over, drivers invariably consented, even when the drivers knew that the vehicle was filled with illegal drugs. If the author were to include this description in the passage, it would probably be used to:

A & E6

A. illustrate the point that if you are under suspicion, you will probably be arrested.

WRONG: The author *never* says that if you are under suspicion "you will probably be arrested." You probably misinterpreted the following information: "At that point, you may be detained or arrested by them, but not because you refused to answer their questions. *They were going to arrest you anyway* and were attempting to lull you into a false sense of security" (lined 33–37). However, this does *not* refer to being arrested simply because you are under suspicion. It refers to the police attempting to get more information from you *prior* to letting you realize that you were not free to go (i.e. being detained) and going to be arrested anyway.

B. emphasize that you should cooperate if you want leniency.

WRONG: The author *strongly* urges readers *not* to cooperate with police officers when being questioned by them. He never mentions anything about "leniency." Rather emphatically he declares that "… you should *never* agree to waive any of your rights. … You are simply providing information to people and a system that will use it against you, regardless of your guilt or innocence" (lines 40–43).

C. support the point that we all want to cooperate.

CORRECT: The author makes a point regarding *cooperation* in the passage: "They were playing upon the fact that *deep down* we *all want to cooperate* and want others to like and respect us" (lines 37–39).

D. explain the author's own experiences with being pulled over.

WRONG: This is pure conjecture and is unsupported in the passage.

Passage V (Questions 24–29)

24. According to the passage, Gondwana was:

Questions such as this one that ask for specific information that can be found verbatim in the passage are unusual on the MCAT, but they do occur.

A. a collection of present-day southern continents.

CORRECT: "The largest landmass during this time was Gondwana, which was then a collection of today's southern continents" (lines 16–17).

B. concentrated in the southern hemisphere.
WRONG

C. the second largest landmass.
WRONG

D. predominantly an ice age phenomenon.
WRONG

25. According to the passage, the growth in the number of major new animal groups during the Cambrian period is best shown by analysis of the:

A. shifting southern continents.
WRONG

B. mass extinctions during the ice ages.
WRONG

C. metazoan phylum.
WRONG

D. fossil record.

CORRECT: "More startling still, when the *fossil record* is scrutinized closely, it turns out that the fastest growth in the number of major new animal groups took place … " (lines 7–10).

26. According to the passage, the Cambrian Explosion is considered a result of all of the following factors EXCEPT:

A. rising sea levels opening up new habitats.

WRONG: This is not an exception. "These rising sea levels opened up new habitats where marine invertebrates, such as the trilobites, radiated and flourished" (lines 31–33).

B. high levels of dissolved oxygen.

WRONG: This is not an exception. "This made dissolved oxygen available to the emerging diversity of animals and may have helped trigger the 'Cambrian Explosion'" (lines 45–47).

C. high numbers of oxygen-producing bacteria.

CORRECT: This is an exception, because "only during the Cambrian period did the numbers of oxygen-depleting bacteria become sufficiently reduced in numbers to permit the high levels of oxygen we know of today" (lines 42–45).

D. warmer climates.

WRONG: This is not an exception. "In fact, the global climate was probably warmer and more uniform than it is today" (lines 27–28), which resulted in "rising sea levels" (line 32).

27. The author implies that "previous theories of evolution" (lines 5–6) included the idea that:

A. diversification is always a dramatic process.

WRONG: This idea is not implied by the author regarding '*previous* theories of evolution.'

B. diversification can occur within relatively short "explosions" of time.

WRONG: This idea is not implied by the author regarding '*previous* theories of evolution.'

C. diversification usually occurs over many millions of years.

CORRECT: This idea is implied by the author. "According to the fossil record, animals showed dramatic diversification during this episode of Earth's history. With this diversification occurring over a time period that was short enough to call our previous theories of evolution into question, it has rightly been called an explosion—the 'Cambrian Explosion'" (lines 2–7).

D.   the continents did not develop from a single large landmass.

WRONG: This idea is not implied by the author regarding 'previous theories of evolution.'

28. According to the passage, which of the following is most likely to be true about the relationship between the oxygen and the emerging diversity of animals?

A.   Oxygen diffused from the oceans into the atmosphere and may have helped trigger the Cambrian Explosion.

WRONG: This is not accurate: "... during the Cambrian, oxygen first mixed *into* the world's oceans in significant quantity" (lines 39–40).

B.   Bacteria helped to produced the high levels of oxygen necessary to the Cambrian Explosion.

WRONG: This is not accurate: "... only during the Cambrian period did the numbers of oxygen-depleting *bacteria* become sufficiently *reduced* in numbers to permit the high levels of oxygen we know of today" (lines 42–45).

C.   Atmospheric oxygen may have helped trigger the Cambrian Explosion.

WRONG: This is not accurate. "Although there was plentiful atmospheric oxygen by the opening of the Cambrian, *only during* the Cambrian period did the numbers of oxygen-depleting bacteria become sufficiently reduced in numbers to permit the high levels of oxygen we know of today" (lines 40–45).

D.   Oxygen in the oceans may have helped trigger the Cambrian Explosion.

CORRECT: This is most likely to be true. "Also during the Cambrian, *oxygen* first mixed into the world's oceans in significant quantity. ... This made dissolved oxygen available to the emerging diversity of animals and may have helped triggered the 'Cambrian Explosion'" (lines 39–47).

29. According to the passage, if we were to compare the global climate of the Cambrian world with today's climate, we would find that:

Questions such as this one that ask for specific information that can be found verbatim in the passage are unusual on the MCAT, but they do occur.

A.   the climate of today is more uniform than the climate of the Cambrian.

WRONG

B.   the climate of today is warmer than the climate of the Cambrian.

WRONG

C.   the climate of the Cambrian was more uniform than the climate of today.

CORRECT: "In fact, the global climate was probably warmer and more uniform than it is today" (lines 27–28).

D.   the climate of the Cambrian is colder than the climate of today.

WRONG

Passage VI (Questions 30–35)

30. In discussing the theory of property the author argues that there should be a legal market for selling babies "because the social benefits would outweigh the social costs" (lines 11–12). According to the passage, all of the following would fall under the category of "social costs" EXCEPT:

   I.   abortions of babies.

   CORRECT: This is an exception. It is not included as an economic or a moral cost to society.

   II.   establishing ownership claims of babies.

   WRONG: This is not an exception. The author specifically delineates "the [social] costs of establishing and enforcing those ownership claims" (lines 5–6).

   III.   proving identity of babies.

   WRONG: This is not an exception. The author specifically delineates "the costs of proving identity" (lines 33–34).

A.   I only

CORRECT: See above answer explanations.

B.   II only
C.   III only
D.   II and III only

31. According to the passage, "ownership claims should be granted" (lines 2–3) for all of the following EXCEPT:

According to the passage, "ownership claims should be granted to any resource if [this] ... will lead to a *more efficient use of that resource* and thus an increase in *social wealth* ..." (lines 2–5).

A.   a toxic waste site bought in order to be restored and made into a park.

WRONG: Based solely upon the information given in this answer, this is *not* an exception. This is an *efficient* use of this "resource."

B. a precious gold mine purchased for the purpose of shutting it down.

CORRECT: Based solely upon the information given in this answer, this is an *inefficient* use of this resource. Thus, this *is* an exception. Ownership should not be granted based upon this reason.

C. a baby purchased by a family who intends to raise him as their own.

WRONG: Based solely upon the information given in this answer, this is *not* an exception. This is an *efficient* use of this "resource."

D. an airline acquired for expansion.

WRONG: Based solely upon the information given in this answer, this is *not* an exception. This is an *efficient* use of this "resource."

32. In order to evaluate if the author's idea of 'selling babies' is viable under the economic theory of property, one would first have to determine:

A. if the selling of babies is a moral or a theoretical issue.

WRONG: This is not offered as a basis for determining the viability "*under the economic theory of property!*"

B. whether "surrogacy" actually has "positive social benefit."

WRONG: Not according to the passage.

C. whether "surrogacy" is more advantageous.

WRONG: Not according to the passage.

D. if the costs of production are lower than the value placed upon the child by childless parents.

CORRECT: According to the second paragraph, which defines the economic theory of property as it relates to selling babies, "*if* the costs of 'production' to natural parents are lower than the 'value' that many childless people attach to children, *then* there *should* be a legal market for selling babies …" (lines 8–11).

33. The author's discussion of 'selling babies' includes the assumption that:

A. surrogacy allows the transfer of children to parents.

WRONG: This is not an assumption of the passage but a stated fact.

B. legalizing "child-selling" has not been tried yet.

WRONG: The passage does not address, nor does it assume, this idea.

C. parents who are abusive despise their children.

CORRECT: This is an assumption in the author's discussion. "[L]egalizing child-selling should reduce instances of child abuse, as parents who despise their children would probably choose to sell rather than keep them" (lines 20–23).

D. parents usually want the best for their children.

WRONG: Since the passage discusses parents who "despise," "abuse," and "abort" children, and would cease to do so only because of economic incentives, this is certainly not an assumption.

34. According to the passage, a central problem to be solved in an emerging lucrative "free-market" is:

A. the cost of "production."

WRONG: This is not offered as a problem.

B. hoarding of available resources.

WRONG: This is not offered as a problem.

C. a proportional increase in crime.

CORRECT: This is a problem that needs to be solved. The bulk of the fourth paragraph is devoted to the problems of crime arising from the emerging market of babies who are suddenly "worth" money.

D. the success of the program itself.

WRONG: This is not offered as a problem.

35. The author argues that "our society has conditioned us that it is 'wrong' to sell people, regardless of circumstances" (lines 43–45). According to the passage, these beliefs imply that:

A. society is not as moral as it could be.

CORRECT: The author's argument and beliefs imply this. The author finds it ironic that his economic idea would be "reflexively" rejected for moral reasons. "Thus, most people would rather doom unwanted children … rather than consider new approaches … *may be more moral than the status quo*" (lines 45–48).

B. society is more moral than it should be.

WRONG: This is a vague and rather 'tortured' way of answering the question, and it is not the best answer.

C. the status quo is more concerned with theory than morality.

WRONG: This is neither implied nor argued.

D. the legacy of slavery has left its impact on society.

WRONG: This is neither implied nor argued.

A&E6

Passage VII (Questions 36-40)

36. Which of the following statements is the most reasonable conclusion that can be drawn from the author's description of the "countermajoritarian difficulty" (line 38)?

  A. The Court will lose perceived legitimacy if it votes for a particular branch of government.

  WRONG: This is not a reasonable conclusion. The Court does not vote in this manner.

  B. The Court will lose faith in the government if it makes findings based solely on the popular vote.

  WRONG: This is not a reasonable conclusion. It is not the Court that will lose faith in the government, but that faith will be lost *in* the Court.

  C. The government and the voting public will lose faith in the Court if the Court goes completely against the majority vote.

  WRONG: This is contrary to the passage conclusion. The circumstance is if the Court makes "purely-political decisions on behalf of the electorate," *not* if it "goes completely against the majority vote."

  D. The voting public will lose faith in the Court if the Court makes findings based solely on their majority vote.

  CORRECT: This is the most reasonable conclusion. "[T]he 'countermajoritarian difficulty,' which posits that the Supreme Court's perceived legitimacy among the government and *electorate* will *drop* if it arrogates to itself the right to make purely political decisions on behalf of the electorate" (lines 38–42).

37. If the averred "number of problematic assumptions" *are* true, that "the executive is persuadable, and can be punished by some extralegal mechanism such as election, impeachment, or perdition" (lines 25–27), then which of the following must also be true?

  A. The members of the executive are going to hell.

  WRONG: This is not necessarily true. The passage and the quote offer a *choice*. *If* the executive are persuaded by some extralegal mechanism, *then* they will not be subject to "perdition."

  B. The members of the executive care enough about something to modify their behavior.

  CORRECT: This must be true. *If* "the executive are persuadable" *then* they must have "care[d] enough about something to modify their behavior."

  C. The executive does not care about impeachment, among other things.

  WRONG: This is not necessarily true. The passage and the quote offer a *choice*.

  D. The executive is not going to be re-elected because they are persuadable.

WRONG: This is not necessarily true, and it misconstrues the meaning of the quote in question. If the Executive could be punished by some extralegal mechanism, such as not being "re-elected," then they *might* be persuaded.

38. According to the passage, Judge Bracton felt that "it was not his proper role to judge the king's actions" (lines 20–21). Bracton's reasoning behind this idea paralleled his other belief that:

  A. a judge was accountable only to those he represented.

  WRONG: Bracton's *other* belief is as follows: "He popularized the enduring common law image of an all-powerful judge ... held to account ... by God himself" (lines 60–63).

  B. a judge was accountable only to his appointer.

  WRONG: Bracton's *other* belief is as follows: "He popularized the enduring common law image of an all-powerful judge ... held to account ... by God himself" (lines 60–63).

  C. a judge was accountable only to God.

  CORRECT: Regarding the *first* idea, his right to judge the king, Bracton "felt it was not his proper role to judge the king's actions. Bracton left that responsibility to the 'Divine Law' ..." (lines 20–21). Bracton's *other* belief is as follows: "He popularized the enduring common law image of an all-powerful judge ... held to account ... by God himself" (lines 60–63).

  D. a judge was accountable only to the king.

  WRONG: Bracton's *other* belief is as follows: "He popularized the enduring common law image of an all-powerful judge ... held to account ... by God himself" (lines 60–63).

39. According to the passage, a practical problem for the Court is that the executive branch of government provides:

  A. for the actual enforcement of the Court's decisions.

  CORRECT: This is a practical problem for the Court. "This loss of legitimacy would present a very real practical problem for a *Court that relies on the executive branch for its enforcing 'sword'*" (lines 42–44).

  B. the actual monies from which the Court operates.

  WRONG: Not according to the passage.

  C. some of the most difficult issues with which the Court struggles.

  WRONG: Not according to the passage.

  D. little, if any, popular support for the Court.

  WRONG: Not according to the passage.

40. The contention that "it seems that this admiration of the activist judicial figure, as popularized by the 'great judge' view of legal history, is currently strong among the electorate, if not academics" (lines 74–77) can most justifiably be interpreted as support for the idea that:

In order to answer this question, you must have gleaned the meaning of *activist* from the passage. Beyond later attempts in the passage to provide a definition, "activism" is contrasted with "restraint" at some length. Activism has some dangers: "This leads straight into the 'countermajoritarian difficulty,' which posits that the Supreme Court's perceived legitimacy among the government and electorate will drop *if it arrogates to itself the right to make purely political decisions on behalf of the electorate*" (lines 37–42).

A. those who study and teach law for a living do not think so highly of the electorate.

WRONG: The contention does not support this idea. There is no mention made of the "academics" regard, or lack of regard, for the "electorate."

B. the academicians generally admire an activist judge, while the public prefers a more populist one.

WRONG: The contention does not support this idea. The last aspect of the quote, "if not academics," denies this answer.

C. the electorate strongly supports the idea of a "great judge" who can discern the truth, as do academicians.

WRONG: This answer almost does not make sense. However, the quote in the question clearly indicates that the "electorate" and the "academicians" do not find the same type of judge "popular."

D. the public loves the idea of a judge who will "stand up" to Big Government.

CORRECT: The contention does support this idea. The quote provides that an "activist judicial figure" is popular with the "electorate" (i.e. "the public"). What is left, then, is to determine if "a judge who will 'stand up' to Big Government" fits this definition. It does. An "activist" Court, for instance, "*arrogates to itself the right to make purely political decisions on behalf of the electorate*." See question explanation.

A & E 6

Verbal Reasoning Test 7
Answers & Explanations

TEST 7 ANSWER KEY

1.	B	11.	A	21.	B	31.	B
2.	B	12.	B	22.	D	32.	C
3.	D	13.	D	23.	A	33.	C
4.	B	14.	A	24.	C	34.	A
5.	C	15.	B	25.	B	35.	A
6.	A	16.	D	26.	D	36.	C
7.	D	17.	B	27.	C	37.	A
8.	D	18.	B	28.	A	38.	D
9.	C	19.	C	29.	B	39.	C
10.	B	20.	D	30.	D	40.	B

Passage I (Questions 1–6)

1. According to information in the passage, evolution would be most likely to occur when an animal exhibits:

   A. long generation spans.

      WRONG: This is a limiting factor. "Many factors work to *limit* large animals' capacity for natural-process change, or evolution" (lines 25–26)—among them, "*long generation spans* (the time between birth and the ability to give birth)" (lines 31–32).

   B. simple social structures.

      CORRECT: This answer is based upon what the author contends 'limits' evolution. "Many factors work to *limit* large animals' capacity for natural-process change, or evolution" (lines 25–26)—among them is "their relatively *advanced* cultural and social structures" (lines 35–36). Therefore, we can conclude this answer.

   C. high complexity of morphology.

      WRONG: This is a limiting factor. "Many factors work to *limit* large animals' capacity for natural-process change, or evolution" (lines 25–26)—among them, "*high complexity of morphology*" (lines 333–34).

   D. small population levels.

      WRONG: There is no support for this answer. This is a limiting factor: "relatively *small population levels*" (lines 30–31).

2. According to information in the passage, "r-strategists" (line 24) would be characterized by:

The article is primarily about K-strategists. However, there is enough information on r-strategists to determine that they are the antithesis of K-strategists. Thus, their characteristics can be determined through contrast.

   I. low numbers of progeny produced per adult.

      WRONG: This is a K-strategist characteristic (lines 32–33).

   II. generalized food supplies.

      CORRECT: r-strategists are the *antithesis* of K-strategists. "Humans are *large animals* that fall under the categorization of *K-strategists*" (lines 21–22). Further, K-strategists are limited and characterized by "their *specialized* food supplies" (line 35).

   III. advanced cultural and social structures.

      WRONG: This is a K-strategist characteristic (lines 35–36).

   A. I only

   B. II only

      CORRECT: See explanation above.

   C. I and III only

   D. I, II, and III

3. If the public reception of scientific creation repeated the reception that the author claims was given to Darwin's ideas, most people would:

The "science editors" of a "textbook" are characterized as implying that anyone who doesn't believe in Darwin is 'crazy.'

   A. resist the theory initially but gradually modify their view of natural selection.

      WRONG: *If* the public received scientific creation as they had received Darwin, they would *not* resist the theory initially but gradually modify their view of natural selection.

   B. claim to believe the theory but ignore its profound implications.

      WRONG: *If* the public received scientific creation as they had received Darwin, they would *not* claim to believe the theory but ignore its profound implications.

   C. reject its version of reality as contrary to common sense.

      WRONG: *If* the public received scientific creation as they had received Darwin, they would *not* reject its version of reality as contrary to common sense.

   D. accept the theory readily and quickly revise their theories about natural selection.

      CORRECT: The "science editors" of a "textbook" are characterized as saying that anyone who does not believe in Darwin is '*crazy*' (lines 4–7). This means that they believe in complete and ready acceptance. *If* the public received scientific creation in this fashion, they *would* think that anyone who did not believe in this theory, which had "overwhelmed" evolution, had "abandoned reason."

4. Which of the following statements is most clearly NOT supported by the author?

   A. Evolution is possible.

      WRONG: The author supports this. The author never argues that evolution is not possible. He actually implies that it is very possible with r-strategists, which *H. sapiens* are not.

   B. An occurrence of a new species has never been proven.

      CORRECT: This is *not* supported by the author. "New species of *K-strategists* actually arising (evolving) Phoenix-like from these ashes has never been proven to have occurred" (lines 48–50). The author never says that new species of r-strategists have not occurred, and even seems to imply that they might.

C. A K-strategist's capacity for change is limited.

WRONG: This is supported by the author. Though humans are K-strategists, the author is arguing that something besides evolution has helped create and perpetuate the species.

D. *H. sapiens* did not evolve.

WRONG: This *is* supported by the author. However, the author is arguing that something besides evolution has helped create, evolve, and perpetuate the species.

5. The author's characterization of the science editors who reviewed Darwin's works suggests that the retort/comment "in the ensuing half a century, this rather haughty point of view has *evolved*" (lines 7–8) meant that:

The editor's point of view has "evolved." This means *changed* or *grown*.

A. the editors have abandoned Darwin's ideas.

WRONG: "Abandoned" is too strong a term. The editor's point of view has "evolved." This means changed or grown.

B. the editors probably embrace the concept of scientific creation.

WRONG: "Embrace" is too strong a term. There is no evidence for this in the passage. The editor's point of view has "evolved." This means *changed* or *grown*.

C. the editors' arrogant perspective has changed.

CORRECT: The author does think that the editor's are arrogant, as indicated by their rather extreme quotes, and the use of the word "haughty" (i.e. proud, arrogant, conceited). The editor's point of view has "evolved." This means *changed* or *grown*.

D. the editors had been wrong.

WRONG: This is vague and simplistic compared to Answer C. It is not completely clear that the editors had been "wrong." This is not the best answer.

6. The claim that "a species capable of significant evolutionary advance rather than doomed to eventual extinction must have a population of one quadrillion individuals, a generation time of three months, and a body size of one centimeter" (lines 51–55) necessitates which of the following conclusions?

A. *H. Sapiens* will become extinct.

CORRECT: This is a logical conclusion necessitated by the claim. *H. sapiens* does not qualify under any of the criteria and is thus "doomed to eventual extinction."

B. There is no species capable of "significant evolutionary advance."

WRONG: This is not a logical conclusion. r-strategists seem to be eminently capable of "significant evolutionary advance."

C. All species are doomed to eventual extinction.

WRONG: This is not a logical conclusion. r-strategists seem to be eminently capable of "significant evolutionary advance."

D. *H. sapiens* must increase their generation time to three months, or else they will become extinct.

WRONG: This is not a logical conclusion. Even given this increase in "their generation time," *H. sapiens* still does not qualify under the other criteria, and is still "doomed to eventual extinction."

Passage II (Questions 7–11)

7. In the context of the passage, the word *containment* (line 38) means:

Containment is used to describe the Cold War strategy. Thus, any correct answer must refer *back* to this period.

A. poor allocation of resources and competition from the private sector for talented staff.

WRONG: *Containment* is used to describe the Cold War strategy. Thus, any correct answer must refer *back* to this period. This answer is part of the description of the problems *currently* plaguing our overseas presence.

B. an interagency process for each agency to pay their share of the cost of maintaining and renovating facilities.

WRONG: *Containment* is used to describe the Cold War strategy. Thus, any correct answer must refer *back* to this period. This answer refers to current issues.

C. outmoded administrative and human resources practices.

WRONG: *Containment* is used to describe the Cold War strategy. Thus, any correct answer must refer *back* to this period. This answer is part of the description of the problems *currently* plaguing our overseas presence.

D. countering political movements hostile to American interests.

CORRECT: *Containment* is used to describe the Cold War strategy. Thus, any correct answer must refer *back* to this period. "A vital concern of this period was … countering political movements hostile to American interests" (lines 27–30). For this entire paragraph, the author describes the "strategy" of *containment*, and then names it "containment." Though this answer is *not* a *complete* definition of containment, in providing *at least part* of the meaning, it becomes the *best* answer.

A & E 7

8. The author's reference to the relationship of "our nation's message" and "antiquated technologies" (lines 57-59) implies that:

"It is ironic that, at the moment when *our nation's message* resonates through history, its voice has been rendered nearly mute by *antiquated technologies*" (lines 53–55). Do not assume that the technology must be a communication technology.

A. as a result of older technologies, it is more difficult to communicate throughout the world.

    WRONG: This is not the implication. This is vague and not the best answer.

B. the people of the world would have no recourse but to use old radios to get their information.

    WRONG: This is not the implication. Old radios could be construed as antiquated technologies, but the quote does *not* refer to the technologies of the *recipients*.

C. America's values of freedom and the principled pursuit of global commerce are antiquated.

    WRONG: This is not the implication. America's *values* expressed in the answer refer specifically to "our nation's message," while the adjective "antiquated" refers to things/ways-of-doing-things/"technologies," *not* to values.

D. as a result of archaic technology, our nation's message cannot be adequately expressed throughout the world.

    CORRECT: This is implied by the author's reference. The passage places America's motivation and goals on a high moral plain (lines 10–15 for instance). The archaic technology "lack [of] a common Internet/e-mail-based communications network through which to communicate with one another" (lines 47–49), in addition to "[i]nsecure and often decrepit facilities, *obsolete information technology*, outmoded administrative and human resources practices, poor allocation of resources, and competition from the private sector for talented staff" (lines 3–7). The "antiquated technologies" would not have to be communicative technologies in order to affect the ability to broadcast the nation's message.

9. According to the passage, "system failure" of United States overseas presence would result in all the following EXCEPT:

"Our overseas presence is perilously close to the point of system failure. Such failure would have serious consequences" (lines 55–57).

A. U.S. citizens traveling abroad would not get the assistance that they need and deserve.

    WRONG: This is *not* an exception. "Such failure would have serious consequences … U.S. citizens traveling abroad would not get the assistance that they need and deserve" (lines 57–65).

B. Our nation would be less able to solve global environmental problems.

    WRONG: This is *not* an exception. "Such failure would have serious consequences …[o]ur nation would be less able to … solve global environmental … problems" (lines 57–67).

C. a loss of U.S. imports.

    CORRECT: This is an exception. "Our overseas presence is perilously close to the point of system failure. Such failure would have serious consequences" (lines 55–57). Nowhere in the passage are imports mentioned.

D. a loss of U.S. jobs.

    WRONG: This is *not* an exception. "Such failure would have serious consequences: … a loss of U.S. … jobs" (lines 57–59).

10. According to the passage, the Cold War design (line 36) is considered a result of all of the following factors EXCEPT:

A. denying adversaries access to military technology and sensitive information

    WRONG: This is not an *exception*. This answer is described as a "vital concern of this [Cold War] period" (line 27).

B. circumventing international terrorism.

    CORRECT: This is an exception. Terrorism is *not* mentioned until line 63. It is a challenge of the post-Cold War design and strategy. Terrorism is a fairly recent threat and was not of great concern during the Cold War.

C. countering political movements hostile to American interests.

    WRONG: This is not an *exception*. This answer is described as a "vital concern of this [Cold War] period" (lines 27–30).

D. the need for secrecy and tight control.

    WRONG: This is not an *exception*. This "need for secrecy and tight control" is a categorizing of Answers A and C at line 30 and refers directly back to them.

11. According to the passage, why is "[o]ur overseas presence … perilously close to the point of system failure" (lines 55–56)?

The author *may* offer *several* reasons. Not all of them may be offered in any *single* answer choice. Choose the best *possible* answer.

A. Our country's overseas presence has not adequately adjusted to the end of the Cold War.

CORRECT: This is responsive to the question and is part of the reasoning of the author. Yes, "decrepit facilities, obsolete information technology," etc., are also to blame and are *not* included in this answer. However, it is the best *possible* answer.

B. We are no longer maintaining a robust global presence.

WRONG: This lack of maintenance is a *byproduct* of the system failure, not the author's reason for it; it is a symptom, not the cause. "Only by *maintaining a robust global presence* can our government protect U.S. interests and promote its values throughout the world" (lines 67–70).

C. Our Cold War strategy was enormously successful.

WRONG: According to the author, it is *not* the success of the Cold War strategy, but our failure to continue to evolve our strategy after the Cold War was over, that has brought us to this point.

D. We are less effective in promoting democracy and the rule of law.

WRONG: This is actually referred to as something that *may come to pass* if we do not avert failure, not as a *cause* of the failure.

Passage III (Questions 12–17)

12. An important comparison is made in the passage between:

A. weapons and drugs.

WRONG: There is no comparison made between weapons and drugs. When they are mentioned, they are mentioned together, as if they were one entity (lines 1–5).

B. school officials and law enforcement officers.

CORRECT: This is one of the most important comparisons in the passage. "The Court has determined that this interest justifies a more flexible standard of reasonableness for searches of students that are conducted by *school officials* as opposed to *law enforcement officers*. Thus, the Court has held that *school officials*, unlike the *police* ..." (lines 25–30). Whether you are a school official or a law enforcement officer is *the* determining factor regarding who, what, where, and why you can conduct a search.

C. a student's jacket and book bag.

WRONG: There is no comparison between the two articles. "Thus, a search of a student's jacket or book bag requires less suspicion" (lines 65–66). They are mentioned together as if they were the same thing. And, indeed, they can be described as one; they are the "accompanying possessions" (lines 22–235).

D. searches and seizures.

WRONG: There is no comparison between the two concepts. They are mentioned together as if they were the same thing.

13. If a local police officer, assigned to provide security at a public school, heard of an infraction that would require the search of a student, the author's ideas suggest that the police officer should:

"Thus, the Court has held that school officials, *unlike the police*, do not need to obtain a warrant prior to conducting a search" (lines 29–31). The implication of this statement is clear; the police require a search warrant.

A. be careful in how he conducts the search.

WRONG: This is *not* suggested by the passage. There is *no* evidence that a law enforcement officer *can*, or is authorized to, conduct a search based upon an infraction.

B. first place the student under arrest.

WRONG: This is *not* suggested by the passage. There is nothing to indicate this from the information in the passage.

C. handcuff the student for his safety.

WRONG: This is *not* suggested by the passage. There is nothing to indicate this from the information in the passage.

D. obtain a warrant prior to conducting the search.

CORRECT: This is suggested by the passage. "Thus, the Court has held that school officials, *unlike the police*, do not need to obtain a warrant prior to conducting a search" (lines 29–31). The implication of this statement is clear; the police require a search warrant.

14. The phrases "*more stringent legal standard*" and "*school officials*" can be connected, respectively, to:

"A *more stringent legal standard* likely applies to searches conducted in conjunction with or at the behest of *law enforcement officers*" (lines 43–45).

A. "law enforcement officers" and "more flexible standard of reasonableness."

CORRECT: Both relate to the standards of the searches, which they perform respectively. As "law enforcement officers" goes with "more stringent legal standard" (lines 43–45), "more flexible standard of reasonableness" goes with "school officials." "The Court has determined that this interest justifies a *more flexible standard of reasonableness* for searches of students that are conducted by *school officials* as opposed to law enforcement officers" (lines 25–28).

B. "law enforcement officers" and "nature of the infraction."

WRONG: "Nature of the infraction" is not necessarily related to "school officials."

C. "school officials" and "more flexible standard of reasonableness."

WRONG: This makes no sense. "More stringent legal standards" to "school officials"?

D. "school officials" and "premised only on probable cause."

WRONG: "School officials" is not necessarily related to "premised only on probable cause."

15. If the information that "students have a legitimate expectation of privacy for their persons and accompanying possessions" (lines 21–23) is accurate, then:

A. students have an expectation of privacy with respect to their wall lockers.

WRONG: "The Supreme Court has held that students have a legitimate expectation of privacy for their persons and *accompanying possessions*" (lines 21–23). A "wall locker" would not be an accompanying possession, and therefore the student would not have an expectation of privacy there.

B. students have no expectation of privacy with respect to their wall lockers.

CORRECT: "The Supreme Court has held that students have a legitimate expectation of privacy for their persons and *accompanying possessions*" (lines 21–23). A "wall locker" would not be an accompanying possession, and therefore the student would not have an expectation of privacy there.

C. students have no expectation of privacy with respect to their clothing.

WRONG: "The Supreme Court has held that students have a legitimate expectation of privacy for their persons and *accompanying possessions*" (lines 21–23). A jacket is probably an "accompanying possession" if it is with the student at all. While the student is wearing the clothing, to search it would be a pat down search.

D. students should never be strip searched.

WRONG: "Courts consider strip searches highly intrusive of an individual student's privacy; thus, they should be premised only on probable cause" (lines 67–70). However, they *can* be conducted; students can be strip searched.

16. Which of the following more likely *violates* the basic dictates of the Fourth Amendment, as described in the passage?

There is no indication from the question whether or not there is "reasonable suspicion." Unless we are to assume that none of the answers is correct, we must assume that there is. Note that the question asks which "*more likely* violates"? Which has the higher legal standard?

A. A female school official opens and searches the wall locker of a male student.

WRONG: This does not *violate* the basic dictates of the amendment. The gender in this case is irrelevant. "The Supreme Court has held that students have a legitimate expectation of privacy for their persons and *accompanying possessions*" (lines 20–23). A "wall locker" would not be an accompanying possession and therefore the student would not have an expectation of privacy there.

B. A female school official asks for a male student's book bag, which she then searches.

WRONG: This does not *violate* the basic dictates of the amendment. Since the female school official is not searching the person of the male student, the gender is irrelevant. "The Supreme Court has held that students have a legitimate expectation of privacy for their persons and *accompanying possessions*" (lines 20–23). The student has an expectation of privacy regarding the book bag, but there is *no* information that the school official does *not* have reasonable suspicion. This is not the best answer.

C. A male school official physically pats down a male student.

WRONG: This does not *violate* the basic dictates of the amendment. Gender is the same for official and student. If the school official has reasonable suspicion, he can clearly pat down a student of the same gender.

D. A male school official physically pats down a male student at the behest of a male police officer.

CORRECT: This would "most likely violate" the amendment. Gender is the same for the official, the officer, and the student, and so it is rendered moot. However, "A more stringent legal standard likely applies to searches conducted in conjunction with or at the behest of law enforcement officers" (lines 43–45). This search would be held to the highest standard because of the police officer who can be inferred to be *also* patting down the student.

17. According to the passage, "reasonable suspicion" (line 49) would best be described as:

"In interpreting and applying the 'reasonable suspicion' standard set forth by the Supreme Court, lower courts generally have required more than general suspicion, curiosity, rumor, or a hunch to justify searches of students and their possessions" (lines 46–50).

A. balancing school officials' and police interests.

WRONG: If there is a "balance" to be struck, it is between school/police's *and* the students' interests;

the ones *doing* the searching and the ones *being* searched.

B. more than general suspicion or a hunch.

CORRECT: "… the 'reasonable suspicion-standard set forth by the Supreme Court, lower courts generally have required more than *general suspicion, … or a hunch*" (lines 46–49).

C. specific curiosity or rumor

WRONG: "… the 'reasonable suspicion' standard set forth by the Supreme Court, lower courts generally have required more than curiosity [or] rumor" (lines 46–49). "Specific" does not apply or alter the "curiosity or rumor."

D. the Court's reaction to a strip search.

WRONG: This answer does not make sense.

Passage IV (Questions 18–23)

18. According to the author, his perceptions of his shortcomings were in large part the result of his:

A. apathy.

WRONG: This is not the *reason* for the author's *perceptions* of his shortcomings. Apathy was the *result*, not the *cause*. "[I]t does sink me into the abyss and tend to *breed* apathy" (lines 30–21).

B. unrealistic expectations.

CORRECT: The author berates himself for not *marketing* the products that he *actually hadn't even created*. "What I usually have to remind myself of is, in the first place, that *I've never actually* written a novel, bought any stock, or gone out and tried to sell any of my ceramics pieces" (lines 11–14).

C. being too late to do anything about them.

WRONG: This is not the *reason* for the author's *perceptions* of his shortcomings. This doesn't make much sense in light of the question.

D. inability to write, choose stocks, or create ceramic art.

WRONG: This is not the *reason* for the author's *perceptions* of his shortcomings. Further, it is not clear that the author is *unable* to create ceramic art.

19. What is the author's initial response to the standard story about the successes of others?

A. "That guy is such a loser."

WRONG: The author "covets" the successes of others and admires these people.

B. "I could do that."

WRONG: This is not accurate. "How come they can do that and I can't?" (line 4).

C. "They got the last piece of pie."

CORRECT: "*Initially*," the author whines, "The pie is shrinking and I haven't even gotten my piece yet! Well, there's nothing to be done about it now. Too late. Too late" (lines 35–37). It is only later that he opines, "Hey, the pie gets bigger all the time. … Someone else's good fortune actually increases the opportunities for all of us" (lines 50–53).

D. "I've got to sell one of my books."

WRONG: The author apparently hasn't written any books.

20. The assertion that "[p]erhaps though, it is an inability to be satisfied that drives them" (lines 47–48) is NOT clearly consistent with the information about:

A. Theodore Roosevelt.

WRONG: This answer is not responsive to the question and has no clear relationship to the question. It is not clear whether Roosevelt was able to be satisfied or not. Thus, the consistency of this answer cannot be judged.

B. those who are successful.

WRONG: The author gives us no clear idea or evidence regarding why successful people are successful. Thus, the consistency of this answer cannot be judged.

C. the author's background and interests.

WRONG: This answer is not responsive to the question and has no clear relationship to the question. Thus, the consistency of this answer cannot be judged.

D. the author's own situation.

CORRECT: This answer is *not* clearly consistent with the question. The author is clearly *not* driven. He admits that he is apathetic and actually takes no action. Yet, he is clearly *not* satisfied! "I do hope for their sakes that those whose successes I so admire and covet are more satisfied with what they have at the moment than I seem to be" (lines 45–47).

21. Which of the following descriptions most clearly exemplifies the skills of the author?

A. professional artist

WRONG: This does *not* clearly exemplify the skills of the author. "I've never actually … gone out and tried to sell any of my ceramics pieces" (lines 12–14).

B. ceramic hobbyist

CORRECT: This most clearly exemplifies the skills of the author. We know from the following that the author *has created* ceramic pieces, yet has *not sold* any. "I've never actually … gone out and tried to sell any of my ceramics pieces" (lines 12–14). And "people are always telling me that I should sell my pottery and sculptures" (lines 26–27).

C. stock analyst

WRONG: This does *not* clearly exemplify the skills of the author. "I've never actually … bought any stock" (lines 12–13).

D. novelist

WRONG: This does *not* clearly exemplify the skills of the author. "I've never actually written a novel …" (lines 12–13).

22. The author's characterization of himself suggests that the comment "My image of myself as a rich author includes my rather simple and unpretentious (given the large amounts of money that I will be making, and that everybody knows that I make) house in Cornwall" (lines 15–19) meant that:

A. he plans on making large amounts of money.

WRONG: This is the author's "image" of himself. He has described his seeming inability to put forth the effort in the areas required to acquire wealth and other trappings of success. The passage is on the author's "plans" to improve his outlook on life and his own self-esteem.

B. he is very serious.

WRONG: This is not the most likely meaning. The components of the statement are incompatible: "*unpretentious*"?

C. he is a humble person.

WRONG: This is *not* clear. Though the *statement* is self-aggrandizing, there is no information for us to say that the author is a humble person. This is not as good as Answer D.

D. he was being sarcastic.

CORRECT: This answer, unlike Answer C, refers specifically to the author's *comment*, rather than make a sweeping generalizing about the author himself. Comparing a "rather simple and unpretentious" lifestyle with "large amounts of money" "that everybody knows that I make" is startling (the comparison is incompatible) and can only be construed as sarcasm and self-aggrandizing.

23. Which of the following assertions is the most effective argument *against* the author's suggestion that "[s]omeone else's good fortune actually increases the opportunities for all of us" (lines 57–58)?

A. The early bird gets the worm.

CORRECT: This assertion is effective against the author's suggestion. This saying means that the first person to arrive gets what limited resources are available. This is the author's *initial* feeling in the

passage. However, it is his *final* conclusion that the question is asking you to respond to.

B. Slow and steady wins the race.

WRONG: This assertion is *not* effective against the author's suggestion because it is not related to the author's suggestion.

C. A stitch in time saves nine.

WRONG: This assertion is *not* effective against the author's suggestion because it is not related to the author's suggestion.

D. Alls well that ends well.

WRONG: This assertion is *not* effective *against* the author's suggestion. This would somewhat *support* the suggestion.

Passage V (Questions 24–29)

24. It is clear from the passage that the author believes that the state should administer sentences to criminals in order to:

I. abuse the criminal.

WRONG: It is clear that the author supports the reasoning of the Founding Fathers who felt that criminals "should not be abused by the majority" (lines 8–9).

II. protect society.

CORRECT: "The state should be accorded the same leeway, because its intent is not to harm, not to kill for cruelty, revenge, or selfish gain, but to protect us from those who do" (lines 51–54).

III. punish the criminal.

CORRECT: It is clear that the author believes that we (in this first instance, "we" *as* the state) "we seek to punish" (line 43, and he explains why "we" punish (lines 47–48).

A. II only
B. III only
C. II and III only

CORRECT: See above explanations.

D. I, II, and III

25. Which of the following opinions would the author be most likely to endorse?

A. The Founding Fathers were against punishment that might be considered "cruel."

WRONG: The author would not agree or endorse this opinion. "Thus, the Eighth Amendment should not be taken to mean that the Constitution's framers objected to any sort of punishment that might be considered 'cruel'—what punishment, after all, could be considered kind?" (lines 13–16).

A & E 7

Apparently, the author believes that those who had something to do with the Eight Amendment were also the "Constitution's framers" (i.e. the Founding Fathers).

B. Capital punishment is cruel, but not unusually so.

CORRECT: The author would be most likely to endorse this opinion. There is an oblique reference to this at lines 8–13. More specifically, "the Eighth Amendment should not be taken to mean that the Constitution's framers objected to any sort of punishment that might be considered 'cruel'— what punishment, after all, could be considered kind?—but that they forbade penalties that were *unusually* cruel" (line 13). The author believes that any punishment is cruel. But, only arbitrariness is unusually cruel.

C. Capital punishment is cruel.

WRONG: The author *would* agree with this opinion. He believes that any punishment is cruel. However, the author would "be *most* likely to endorse" Answer B, because it is *more* explanative, conditional, and complete. This is *not* the best answer.

D. The Founding Fathers meant to single out only certain people for capital punishment.

WRONG: The author would not agree or endorse this opinion. The "Founding Fathers instituted the rule of law to do away with *arbitrary* justice" (lines 1–2).

26. Assume that recently obtained medical studies of capital executions over the last twenty years show conclusive evidence that lethal injection is by far the most painless method of execution. This finding:

In order to answer this question it is necessary to understand what the author is arguing. See Answer explanation D.

A. increases the probability that the author's argument is valid.

WRONG: Though the new information indicates that the author's reference to the 'gas chamber' is outdated, the revelation that lethal injection is more humane than the gas chamber has little relevance to the author's arguments or ideas. See explanation at Answer D.

B. increases the probability that the use of capital punishment will become greater.

WRONG: Though the new information indicates that the author's reference to the 'gas chamber' is outdated, the revelation that lethal injection is more humane than the gas chamber has little relevance to the author's arguments or ideas. See explanation at Answer D.

C. decreases the probability that the author's argument is valid.

WRONG: Though the new information indicates that the author's reference to the 'gas chamber' is outdated, the revelation that lethal injection is more humane than the gas chamber has little relevance to the author's arguments or ideas. See explanation at Answer D.

D. reveals nothing about the validity of the author's arguments.

CORRECT: The author does offer, by way of example, that "we have striven to develop increasingly painless methods of execution, culminating in the gas chamber" (lines 34–35). It would *seem*, then, that this "decreases the probability that the author's argument is valid," Answer C, because the author seems uninformed and not up to date. However, the author is not arguing relative degrees of pain in execution. The author's main points are: 1) the Founding Fathers were not against capital punishment, but sought to eliminate arbitrary punishment, 2) all punishment is cruel so yes, capital punishment is also cruel, and 3) capital punishment is a necessary cruelty. Therefore, the revelation that lethal injection is more humane than the gas chamber has little relevance to the author's arguments or ideas.

27. If the author were a warden in a prison, he would most probably tend to place the *least* emphasis on:

A. ensuring that the prisoners did not escape.

WRONG: The author would place emphasis on this area since he believes that part of the state's responsibility is to 'protect' society (line 53).

B. ensuring that the prisoners had adequate nutrition.

WRONG: The author would place more emphasis on this area than on Answer C. To diminish nutrition below the level of "adequate" means that there is not enough food or nutrition. This would be considered "cruel and unusual" by the author, and an "abuse by the majority" (line 9).

C. ensuring that adequate rehabilitative programs were available.

CORRECT: The author would place little emphasis on this area. He mentions absolutely nothing about rehabilitation. To the author, the purpose of incarcerating prisoners is apparently to 'protect society' and to 'punish.'

D. ensuring that the prisoners were not beaten.

WRONG: The author would place *more* emphasis on this area than on Answer C. Thus, this is not the best answer.

28. According to the passage, one drawback to eliminating capital punishment is that it can lead to:

A. cruel and unusual punishments.

CORRECT: This would be a drawback. "By limiting the right of the state to punish by obvious and direct channels [capital punishment], we leave the justice system little choice but to invent truly cruel and unusual punishments" (lines 61–63).

B. excessive fines on the citizenry.

WRONG: This is not correct. The author mentions this in comparing state and citizens' rights.

C. an equivalence of state and citizens' rights.

WRONG: There is no information in the passage that would lead to this answer.

D. prison overcrowding.

WRONG: There is no information in the passage that would lead to this answer. You are basing this on outside ideas and information.

29. According to the passage, the Founding Fathers would consider the *amende honorable* (line 23) to be:

A. unusual and unjust.

WRONG: Probably unusual, but it was *not* "unjust." There is no information that the innocent suffered this terrible fate. It was clearly imposed on murderers. This is not the best answer.

B. arbitrary justice.

CORRECT: The Founding Fathers wanted to eliminate "arbitrary justice" (line 2) and "forbade penalties that were *unusually* cruel, meaning those that singled out certain people for 'special' retribution. A study of the practices of that period suggests that, by including this provision, they sought to save the American people from practices like the *amende honorable*" (lines 17–23).

C. appropriate, given the circumstances of the crime.

WRONG: The Founding Fathers thought this penalty 'arbitrary' and "special retribution," and "they sought to save the American people from practices like the *amende honorable*" (lines 20–21).

D. cruel and unjust.

WRONG: They would certainly have considered it cruel. But it was *not* "unjust." There is no information that the innocent suffered this terrible fate. It was clearly imposed on murderers. This is not the best answer.

Passage VI (Questions 30–35)

30. The word *chastity* (line 6) is most likely being used to describe:

The play is "a story about enticing a widow to lose her chastity" (lines 5–6).

A. a woman who is religious.

WRONG: This is not the real meaning of the word and it is not implied in the passage.

B. a woman who is pure.

WRONG: This is vague when compared with Answer D.

C. a woman who has never had sexual intercourse.

WRONG: This is a possible meaning of the word. However, the passage describes the woman as a "widow." Thus, she was at one time married and is probably not a 'virgin.'

D. a woman who is currently celibate.

CORRECT: This is the most likely meaning of the word. As noted in Answer C, the passage describes the woman as a "widow." Thus, she was at one time married and is probably not a 'virgin.' Yet 'chastity' refers to 'not having sex' or, in other words, being "celibate."

31. According the passage description, Sergei Yanin waits outside of the church in order to draw Svetlana "out of safety using the lure of propriety" (lines 58–59). What was this "lure of propriety"?

A. He offered her a position within the top category of women.

WRONG: The passage does not tell us this. In fact, we are told that if Svetlana had openly taken another husband, "then she would *not* have rated in the top category of women" (lines 38–39).

B. The passage does not specify.

CORRECT: We can only guess how Sergei would use the fact that Svetlana prized "propriety" as a "lure." The passage does not provide this information.

C. He was wealthy and, thus, she would have owned property as well.

WRONG: The word in the question is "propriety" (based upon 'proper') *not* "property." Sergei might have been wealthy, but we do not know this from the passage.

D. He offered to have sex with her.

WRONG: Offering to have sex out of wedlock with a 'proper' woman is the antithesis of a "lure of propriety."

32. According to the passage, "Knowing such 'historical' precedents allows readers to make definite inferences about the characters in this tale" (lines 16–18). The author most likely meant that:

A. historical precedents were not often included in plays such as this one.

WRONG: The "early Russian readers' expectations" (line 2) were based upon the fact that "most Russian

A & E 7

short stories of the period" (lines 7–8) contained these precedents. We know that this play was very unique. Therefore, there may not even have been any other "plays such as this one." This is not the best answer.

B. the readers were bound to be surprised at the characters when they read a play.

WRONG: They would have been surprised when they read *this* play, but *not* "a" play that was representative of that era. What allows the author to make sweeping generalizations about Russian plays of that period (lines 1–10) was the fact that they were very formulaic. There was an "established literary precedent" (line 14).

C. the readers were expected to add their own details to the story based upon previous dramas.

CORRECT: The passage expounds on the differences between this play and "readers' expectations" (line 2) based on "most Russian short stories of the period" (lines 7– 8).

D. without such precedents it would not be possible to understand the play.

WRONG: It is *not* implied that the precedents were so critical that they were required to understand the play. This is too extreme.

33. Based upon the numerous quotations in the passage from the play, we can discern that the play was most likely:

A. written from Sergei's perspective.

WRONG: Sergei could not know that Svetlana was in the church lighting candles.

B. written from a second-person perspective.

WRONG: A "second person" is still a person and could not be both inside the church to see Svetlana lighting candles and outside the church to see Sergei waiting for her.

C. written in the third person as a narrative.

CORRECT: Line 33–34 refers to the "narrator … saying …" Further, this "third-person" narrator can apparently be both inside the church to see Svetlana lighting candles and outside the church to see Sergei waiting for her.

D. written without the character of a narrator.

WRONG: Line 33–34 refers to the "narrator … saying …"

34. On the basis of the passage, it is reasonable to conclude that:

A. the author who wrote this play would have been considered somewhat radical by his peers.

CORRECT: The storyteller "is definitely leading readers to question the value of tradition" (lines

46–47). "In White Russian literature, which elevates acts of maniacal loyalty, his compromising moral attitude is puzzling, perhaps even risqué." (lines 47–49). "Yet whereas traditional Russian short stories often pay homage (or at least lip service) to conventional morality … this *storyteller* unexpectedly softens his rebuke of Svetlana to the point of almost a backhanded compliment" (lines 25–29). Additionally, he does not praise Svetlana's morals, but criticizes them (lines 29–41), and (line 49–51).

B. the author who wrote this play would have been widely accepted.

WRONG: This is not likely. Certainly not as likely as Answer A.

C. this play is indicative of White Russian literature.

WRONG: Considering "White Russian literature, which elevates acts of maniacal loyalty, [the author's] compromising moral attitude is puzzling, perhaps even risqué" (lines 47–49).

D. White Russian literature questioned the value of tradition.

WRONG: Considering "White Russian literature, which elevates acts of maniacal loyalty, [the author's] compromising moral attitude is puzzling, perhaps even risqué" (lines 47–49).

35. Assume that the following statements are true. Which one is *consistent* with the assertion that "[t]here is the strong implication that it was not neglect of, but excessive preoccupation with, propriety that led Svetlana to ruin" (lines 49–51)?

Notice that this type of question could be answered *without even having read the passage*. You certainly do not need to refer back to it.

A. Sergei specifically chose to victimize Svetlana because it was well known that she was chaste and had not left her home in over ten years.

CORRECT: This answer is consistent with the assertion. Here Svetlana is victimized *not* because she is not as 'proper' as possible, but *because* she is so proper, as required by the quote in the question.

B. Ten years of almost total isolation had left Svetlana with an unquenchable sexual desire, which Sergei was able to take advantage of.

WRONG: This answer is *not* consistent with the assertion. This answer would indicate that Svetlana *neglected* her propriety.

C. It was well known that Svetlana's chastity was a front, and that her "No," really meant "Yes."

WRONG: This answer is *not* consistent with the assertion. This answer would indicate that Svetlana *neglected* her propriety.

D. Svetlana had led a very poor life and would do almost anything for money and property.

WRONG: This answer is *not* consistent with the assertion. Do not confuse "propriety" with "property." This answer has nothing to do with the question.

Passage VII (Questions 36–40)

36. Which of the following conclusions can justifiably be drawn from the experience of the pair of inquisitive graduate students mentioned in the passage?

A. Don't assume that someone has done something incorrectly.

WRONG: This is *not* a justifiable conclusion. It would be more accurate, yet still not the best answer, to say "Don't assume that someone has done something *correctly*."

B. Don't assume that an experiment has been performed inaccurately.

WRONG: This is *not* a justifiable conclusion. It would be more accurate, yet still not the best answer, to say "Don't assume that an experiment has been performed *accurately*."

C. It is sometimes helpful to question that which has been accepted.

CORRECT: This is a justifiable conclusion. Apparently, after "years," the students figured out that there had been a false assumption or error in the experiment that pointed towards 'immortal' cells. Notice the use of the softener "sometimes," which make the answer even more palatable.

D. Grad students are more careful than professors.

WRONG: This is *not* a justifiable conclusion. We do not even know that 'professors' were the ones who came up with the errant conclusion in the first place.

37. The author asks, "However, would this merely extend our longevity or have a direct bearing on aging?" (lines 62–64). By "longevity" he most probably means:

A. living longer with a decreasing level of functionality.

CORRECT: This answer is what the author most probably means. "Longevity" obviously has to do with "longer," and in this case, living longer. Further, we can identify what "aging" means in the bull semen experiments: "it was noticed that throughout cellular division the cells exhibited an "*aging* effect" similar to the *decreasing level of functionality noticed in elderly adults*" (lines 49–51). Since the question uses "or" to separate 'longevity' and 'aging,' we know that they are not one in the same, and may contrast.

B. maintaining our functionality into old age.

WRONG: This is *not* what the author probably means. This answer mixes the meanings of the two. It is the "aging" that has to do with the maintenance of functionality (lines 49–51). "Longevity" has to do with "old [or long] age."

C. staying young but not living any longer.

WRONG: This is *not* what the author probably means. This answer is almost exactly the same as Answer D. "Staying young" implies 'continued functionality,' which is an aspect of "aging" (lines 49–51), not longevity.

D. living longer without aging.

WRONG: This is *not* what the author probably means. This answer is almost exactly the same as Answer C. "Without aging" implies 'continued functionality,' which is an aspect of "aging" (lines 49–51), not longevity.

38. The author contrasts our inability to understand why we are getting older with:

A. people living longer today than at any other time.

WRONG: This answer is *not* contrasted with "our inability to understand why we are getting older."

B. the field of biogerontology.

WRONG: This answer is *not* contrasted with "our inability to understand why we are getting older."

C. a pun.

WRONG: This answer is *not* contrasted with "our inability to understand why we are getting older."

D. what the impact will be on this country.

CORRECT: This is the contrast. "By means of surveys, statistics, and other data sources, we can measure and attempt to foresee the impact this will have in the future. However, we may feel uncomfortable with our ability to understand *why* America is getting older" (lines 5–9).

39. According to the passage, in the graduate students' experiment, cells that had already divided twenty times prior to freezing, when thawed would:

A. divide a finite number of times while exhibiting almost no aging.

WRONG: It is accurate that they would divide a finite number of times. However, in addition to this not being as specific and responsive to the question as Answer C, the second aspect of the answer is inaccurate. "Also, it was noticed that throughout cellular division the cells exhibited an 'aging effect' similar to the decreasing level of functionality noticed in elderly adults" (lines 49–51).

B. continue to divide endlessly.

WRONG: We know that, but for the three types of exceptions, all other human cells "had a limited number of divisions, *around fifty*" (lines 38–39).

C. divide around thirty more times.

CORRECT: "Every cell that they defrosted completed its fifty divisions from the point of freezing. The cells somehow remembered where they had left off" (lines 46–49). We also know that, but for the three types of exceptions, all other human cells "had a limited number of divisions, *around fifty*" (lines 38–39). Fifty minus twenty equals "around thirty."

D. divide around fifty more times.

WRONG: This would be a total division of seventy times. The cells remembered where they had stopped dividing and finished off dividing for "around fifty" times upon thawing.

40. Based on passage information, if bulls have shorter lifespans than humans, their semen after freezing would probably divide:

You may know from your science that semen will not divide at all, which would still bring you to Answer B, "less than fifty times." Note that "not divide at all" *is* "less than fifty times." This is a prime example of choosing which is the *best* answer offered to you!

A. endlessly.

WRONG: We are provided with the fact that "bulls have shorter lifespans than humans." "A species with a short life span has fewer divisions than a species with a long one" (lines 57–58). Thus, the bull's cells will divide "less than a human's," or "less than fifty times."

B. less than fifty times.

CORRECT: Notice that the freezing has nothing to do with this answer, since we are not given any number of divisions prior to freezing. Additionally, the cell type (semen) is *not* one of the three that divide endlessly; though you don't have to know it to answer this question correctly, *semen actually does not divide at all!* Finally, we are left with the fact that "bulls have shorter lifespans than humans." "A species with a short life span has fewer divisions than a species with a long one" (lines 57–58). Thus, the bull's cells will divide "less than a human's," or "less than fifty times."

C. around fifty times.

WRONG: We are provided with the fact that "bulls have shorter lifespans than humans." "A species with a short life span has fewer divisions than a species with a long one" (lines 57–58). Thus, the bull's cells will divide "less than a human's," or "less than fifty times."

D. more than fifty times.

WRONG: We are provided with the fact that "bulls have shorter lifespans than humans." "A species with a short life span has fewer divisions than a species with a long one" (lines 57–58). Thus, the bull's cells will divide "less than a human's," or "less than fifty times."

A & E 7

A & E 7

Verbal Reasoning Test 8
Answers & Explanations

TEST 8 ANSWER KEY

1.	B	11.	A	21.	A	31.	B
2.	C	12.	A	22.	D	32.	D
3.	C	13.	C	23.	A	33.	D
4.	D	14.	B	24.	C	34.	A
5.	A	15.	B	25.	A	35.	B
6.	D	16.	D	26.	D	36.	D
7.	D	17.	A	27.	B	37.	B
8.	B	18.	B	28.	C	38.	B
9.	C	19.	D	29.	C	39.	C
10.	C	20.	B	30.	D	40.	D

Passage I (Questions 1–6)

1. Suppose an armed bank robber has failed in his robbery attempt and has taken several hostages within a nearby building. The robber knows nothing about Proxemics but that the concept exists and that the negotiator has been trained in its use. Which of the following negotiating scenarios would be most advantageous to the bank robber, based solely upon passage information about Proxemics?

   This will obviously be an adversarial negotiation. Beyond recognizing that you *need to be able to see* whoever it is you are reading in order for Proxemics to work, the only important aspects of this question are: 1) The robber knows that the negotiator holds an advantage in somehow being able to "read" body language, and 2) What would the bank robber wish to do to *negate* this perceived advantage?

   A. The robber would meet the negotiator within a dimly lit room inside of the building.

   WRONG: This is not the best answer. The robber knows that the negotiator would still be able to *see* the robber and use his training to "read" the body language of the robber.

   B. The robber would insist on negotiating over the telephone from the building.

   CORRECT: The negotiator will only be able to *hear* the robber. In this scenario the robber, who knows that the negotiator hold the advantage in somehow being able to "read" his body language, has negated this advantage by not allowing the negotiator to see him.

   C. The robber would wait until after darkness and meet the negotiator from a short distance away.

   WRONG: This is not the best answer. The robber knows that the negotiator might still be able to *see* the robber and use his training to "read" the body language of the robber.

   D. The robber would seek a face-to-face meeting with the negotiator on the roof of the building.

   WRONG: This is the worst answer choice and ignores all of the information in the question and the passage. The robber knows that the negotiator would be able to *see* the robber and use his training to "read" the body language of the robber.

2. Which of the following statements most strongly *challenges* one of the assertions made in the passage?

   A. The biggest obstacle to Proxemics is that it is only as accurate as a polygraph.

   WRONG: This does not challenge a passage assertion. It is *accurate* that those trained in Proxemics are "every bit as accurate as a polygraph." However, this comparison is obviously being used *favorably* by the author.

   B. An understanding of body language can make all of your statements seem more truthful.

   WRONG: This does not challenge a passage assertion. "Thus, learning to use body language can make all your statements—true or not—seem more truthful" (lines 60–61).

   C. The main stumbling block to the passage's "universal language" is the need for everyone to learn it and stay proficient in its use.

   CORRECT: This challenges the author's "universal language" idea and his "Esperanto" analogy, among others. A language is not "universal" if everyone can speak it, but only a few people can actually understand what is being said! The author would like to have it both ways. He describes his analogous "Esperanto" as so "all pervasive that people could not help but communicate in it, even when they refused to say a word" (lines 2–4). Yet he forgets that this is not communication. It is, in fact, "babbling"; everyone is *attempting* to speak and making noise, but no one understands what is being said.

   D. Apparently, everyone speaks this language but few are actually fluent in it.

   WRONG: This is accurate and an inherent weakness in the author's argument. However, it does not *challenge* any passage assertions. Everyone "speaks" or conveys body language, yet "few" besides those who are trained, or perhaps lovers and "poker players," can "accurately" read the language. Thus, "few are actually *fluent* in it."

3. Which of the following suppositions is most clearly believed by the author?

   A. The untrained negotiator must rely more heavily on the polygraph, which is often not convenient.

   WRONG: This is not clearly believed by the author. The polygraph is used in a comparative fashion in order to show that a human can be trained to be "every bit as accurate as a polygraph."

   B. The ability of the negotiator to convey his messages depends very much on the training of the recipient.

   WRONG: This is not "most clearly believed" nor is it set forth by the author. However, it is probably true.

   C. Proper training in nonverbal communication will allow you to read and convey messages more clearly.

   CORRECT: This is a major thrust of the passage and is reiterated several times. The concept of reading is covered in the first part of the passage, and the accurate 'conveyance' of body language is addressed in lines 41–61.

   D. Esperanto will someday be the primary form of nonverbal communication.

WRONG: This is not put forth or implied as a belief by the author. The idea of Esperanto is used for as an analogy.

4. The passage implies that, without formal training in the area, who among the following may already be proficient in 'reading' nonverbal cues?

A. 95% of the world

WRONG: This is not implied. This percentage refers to the imagined number of people in the world who 'speak' the Esperanto language. However, paradoxically, though these "people could not help but communicate in it … *they refused to say a word*" (lines 2–4). They have no actual "proficiency" in Esperanto (or the question-required "nonverbal cues") because they *cannot* "read" or understand it without more formal training.

B. polygraphers

WRONG: This is not implied. The polygraphers are certainly proficient in reading nonverbal cues. However, the polygraphers *have* received "more formal training" in using the machine called a polygraph.

C. professional negotiators

WRONG: This is not implied. It is clear from the passage that professional negotiators are *not* proficient in reading nonverbal cues *if* they have not been formally trained in this area. "Ironically, research studies show that professional negotiators who have not been trained in the vagaries of Proxemics are actually no more accurate at discerning falsehoods [than other untrained people]" (lines 33–36).

D. poker players

CORRECT: This is implied. "However, any poker player will tell you that their veiled negative emotions will still be apparent" (lines 47–48).

5. The ideas discussed in this passage would likely be of most use to:

A. detectives.

CORRECT: Detectives are constantly interviewing and investigating, *talking* to people, albeit *sometimes* on the telephone. It can certainly be assumed that at some point they are speaking to people face to face. At this point nonverbal training would be very useful to them. Additionally, the thrust of the passage is on discerning or reading "lying" more than truth. The ideas would be of more use to a detective than many others.

B. lovers.

WRONG: Lovers (notice that this is plural, meaning that there are at least *two* of them), who are already in a high state of emotion and becoming increasingly proficient in conveying their feelings "physically," could presumably already send and receive nonverbals. "The ability to read body language is also important because it is easier to convey emotion physically than with words. Words are often clumsy tools for describing feelings" (lines 41–44). Additionally, the thrust of the passage is on discerning or reading "lying" more than truth. The ideas would be of more use to a detective than many others.

C. radio disc jockeys.

WRONG: The entire concept of nonverbal communication *assumes sight* or, though not implied in the passage, constant, intimate touching. A radio disc jockey usually can neither see nor be seen by his audience.

D. police dispatchers.

WRONG: The entire concept of nonverbal communication *assumes sight* or, though not implied in the passage, constant, intimate touching. A police dispatcher is, like the disc jockey, *visually isolated from* those he is communicating with.

6. The passage asks that the reader "[i]magine that 95% of the world shared a language, called 'Esperanto'" (lines 1–2), and then uses Esperanto as an analogy for Proxemics. However, the passage *weakens* this analogy through which of the following quotations?

I. "[P]eople could not help but communicate in it."

CORRECT: This weakens the analogy. Communicate *requires* a *transference* of information. Yet, the author stresses that without proper training, the majority of people cannot read or properly interpret nonverbals. Thus, no communication is taking place without the training; nonverbals are only babble, which everyone is putting out but no one can understand. This is a far cry from a "shared language" that "people could not help but communicate in." In the Esperanto-to-Proxemics analogy, the Proxemics aspect is weakened.

II. "Esperanto [is] spoken by even the deaf, … blind, insane …"

CORRECT: This weakens the analogy. If Esperanto is "spoken," then how can the "deaf" hear it? Thus, in the Esperanto-to-Proxemics analogy, the Esperanto aspect is weakened. This is a far cry from a "shared language."

III. "Esperanto [is] spoken by even the … dumb, blind, … and children."

CORRECT: This weakens the analogy. How can Esperanto be "spoken" by the "dumb" (who are unable to speak)? Thus, in the Esperanto-to-Proxemics analogy, the Esperanto aspect is weakened. This is a far cry from a "shared language."

- A. II only
- B. III only
- C. II and III only
- D. I, II, and III

  CORRECT: See above explanations.

Passage II (Questions 7–11)

7. The passage suggests that the self-esteem of individual homosexuals:

   A. is somewhat higher than the self-esteem found in individuals of other populations.
   WRONG: This is not suggested in the passage.

   B. is somewhat lower than the self-esteem found in individuals of other populations.
   WRONG: This is not suggested in the passage.

   C. varies widely depending upon social stigmatization.
   WRONG: This is not suggested in the passage. There is no mention of a dependency on social stigmatization.

   D. is similar to the self-esteem found in the individuals of any other population.
   CORRECT: This is most strongly suggested. "In fact, most research has found that homosexuals are as diverse with regard to their self-esteem as any other population" (lines 42–44).

8. Which of the following best characterizes the study by Crocker and Major (1989)?

   A. They hypothesized that homosexuals were experiencing prejudice.
   WRONG: This is generalized and, thus, vague and not the best answer. Though the passage doesn't say so, this was probably an assumption of Crocker and Major's.

   B. Their hypotheses and assumptions prior to the study were disproved.
   CORRECT: This is the best characterization. *Both* of the hypotheses mentioned, the "reflected appraisals theory" and the "self-fulfilling prophecies" theory, were found to *not* be applicable to minority group members.

   C. Their hypotheses and assumptions prior to the study were proved.
   WRONG: This is not the best characterization. *Both* of the hypotheses mentioned, the "reflected appraisals theory" and the "self-fulfilling prophecies" theory, were found to *not* be applicable to minority group members.

   D. They hypothesized that being part of a group would insulate individuals from diminished self-esteem.
   WRONG: They did not hypothesize this. This answer is counter to what they originally believed.

9. The author of the passage would be most likely to agree with which of the following ideas expressed by other researchers of societal prejudice?

   A. Members of stigmatized groups may develop negative self-concepts because society as a whole devalues their group.
   WRONG: The author would not agree. "Thus, belonging to a hated or socially ostracized group appears to be a buffer against lowering the individual's self-esteem" (lines 52–54).

   B. The individual will often come to accept and believe societal perspectives about his group.
   WRONG: The author would not agree. *Or*, we do *not know* if the author would agree or not because this idea is not really alluded to in the passage therefore, this is not the best answer.

   C. Being part of a group seems to buffer the individual from the prejudice and stigmatization of society.
   CORRECT: The author would agree. Almost the entire passage refers to this idea. Lines 5–7, 19–21, and lines 52–54: "belonging to a hated, or socially ostracized group appears to be a buffer against lowering the individual's self-esteem."

   D. Societal prejudice falls more heavily upon those whose 'unacceptable' proclivities may be hidden.
   WRONG: The author would not agree. If their proclivities are "hidden," then society is unaware of them! Thus, though they may feel ashamed, they will not be suffering directly from societal prejudice.

10. In the context of the passage, the term *global self-esteem* refers primarily to the:

    A. sense of worth that the world provides you.
    WRONG

    B. way in which the individual believes the world values him or her.
    WRONG

    C. sense of worth the individual has about himself.
    CORRECT: "'global' self-esteem—feelings about one's own self-worth—as opposed to feelings about the minority group" (lines 29–31).

    D. feelings about society's perspective.
    WRONG

11. Regarding the ability of homosexuals to forge a group identity, the passage strongly implies that:

A. this was only possible because of diminished societal stigmatization.

CORRECT: This is strongly implied at the beginning of the passage. "Societal stigmatization of homosexuals declined throughout the 1970s to such a degree that homosexual groups *were able* to forge a group identity" (lines 1–3).

B. this was a unique phenomenon in a global sense.

WRONG: This answer makes little sense but merely plays upon the word "global" to lure you in.

C. prior to this, it was rare for a homosexual to "come out".

WRONG: This is mildly implied, but not as strongly as Answer A. One would have to assume that because of social stigmatization, "prior to this" homosexuals "rarely came out." This is not the best answer.

D. the self-esteem of individual homosexuals might have been stronger.

WRONG: This is not implied at all. It is clear from the first paragraph that the "rise of consolidated groups of gays, lesbians, and bisexuals has helped to change the feelings of those who discover themselves as such from shame to pride" (lines 5–7).

Passage III (Questions 12–17)

12. Which of the following statements is the most reasonable conclusion that can be drawn from the author's description of why cults might value celebrity members?

A. Most people have an unrealistic image of themselves.

CORRECT: This is the most reasonable conclusion. "This works especially well if those others are either like them or like *what the target believes himself to be.* For this reason, having a celebrity member is priceless, since *most people have no trouble picturing themselves as rich, famous, attractive, and adulated*" (lines 15–19). It is common knowledge that "most people" are *not* "rich, famous, attractive, and adulated"; at least not all at the same time.

B. Celebrities would be difficult to recruit into a cult.

WRONG: Though a celebrity *might* require a different 'bait' (his/her self-image might be even grander), this answer is *not* as reasonable a conclusion as Answer A. This is not the *best* answer.

C. Celebrities are no more difficult than anyone else to recruit into a cult.

WRONG: Though a celebrity *might* require a different 'bait,' because his/her self-image might be even grander, this answer is *not* as reasonable a conclusion as Answer A. This is not the *best* answer.

D. An ordinary person would be the best 'bait' for a celebrity.

WRONG: This is not a reasonable conclusion. This is most likely simply not the case.

13. Evidence shows that in the heat of battle, a soldier is much less hesitant to kill in order to defend himself than a civilian alone in an urban environment. This fact tends to support the hypothesis concerning "socially unacceptable" behavior (lines 12–26) because:

A. the civilian, in this instance, is not affected by 'reciprocity.'

WRONG: This is *not* why the given "fact" tends to support the hypothesis; "reciprocity" (lines 27–36) has nothing to do with the hypothesis or the fact.

B. the civilian does not have the soldier's background and training.

WRONG: This is *not* why the given "fact" tends to support the hypothesis. This is pure speculation and not based upon passage information. "Background and training" have nothing to do with encouraging someone to do something that is socially unacceptable, according to the passage.

C. the soldier is surrounded by killing and is seeing many others doing the same as he is.

CORRECT: This is the best reason for why the given "fact" tends to support the hypothesis. "Psychological studies show that the best way to encourage a person to do the socially unacceptable (or to conquer an abnormal phobia) is to show *many others doing the same*" (lines 12–15). This answer provides the "socially unacceptable" behavior: killing. And, "many others doing the same": he is surrounded by killing.

D. the soldier has been trained to consider this behavior acceptable.

WRONG: This is *not* why the given "fact" tends to support the hypothesis. This is pure speculation and not based upon passage information. "Background and training" have nothing to do with encouraging someone to do something that is socially unacceptable, according to the passage.

14. According to the author, what motivates a member of a cult to remain loyal even "after their 'doomsday' has come and gone without incident" (lines 69–70)?

A. strong beliefs

WRONG: This is not suggested by the author. The quote in the question suggests that the member's beliefs have been *dashed*. They exist no longer, so what *then* motivates him?

B. shame

CORRECT: This is suggested by the author. Just prior to the quote in the question is the information:

"If the recruit has to suffer, sacrifice all, and burn his bridges to join, *he will be more loyal*. After all, *how could he admit afterwards, to himself or to others, that he did it all for nothing?*" (lines 65–68).

C.   generosity

WRONG: This is not suggested by the author. Additionally, the member has nothing more to give once he has 'burned all his bridges, renounced his job and family, and donated all of his possessions'!

D.   stubbornness

WRONG: This is not clearly suggested by the author. Answer B is the best answer.

15. Implicit in the passage is the assumption that:

A.   the cult cannot survive without the outside world.

WRONG: This is not implied in the passage. The cult tries to distance itself from the outside world. There may be an argument made that the cult is a parasite to society and needs additional recruits all of the time. But this idea is not nearly as clearly implied as Answer C. This is not the best answer.

B.   cults should be made illegal.

WRONG: This is not implied in the passage.

C.   peer groups are tremendously influential.

CORRECT: This idea is implied over and over again in the passage as the cult attempts to isolate the target and ensure that the cult members become his peer group and the "norm." "Thus, inside the headquarters, the cultists become the only role models to follow; within that context, their behavior becomes the 'norm,' lending it an air of legitimacy" (lines 42–45). "This not only removes him from the steadying influence of outsiders, but ensures his commitment" (lines 66–68).

D.   after her first visit to the cult compound, the target is inevitably going to become a member.

WRONG: This is not implied. There is no inevitability promoted in the passage. Further, it is not on the "first visit" but, "Finally, after one or several visits, the target is ready for the 'pitch.' He is asked to join the cult" (lines 62–63).

16. According to information in the passage, the best way to overcome a fear of heights would be to:

A "fear of heights" would fall under the category of "abnormal phobia" (line 14).

A.   take a friend and stand on the edge of a tall cliff.

WRONG: This answer lacks "many others doing the same thing" (see Answer D) and has the person with the phobia standing "on the edge of a tall cliff." However, the passage does not suggest that the person with the phobia engage in the behavior to get over it.

B.   gradually stand on higher and higher platforms or places.

WRONG: The passage does not suggest that the person with the phobia engage in the behavior to get over it. Additionally, this answer lacks "many others doing the same thing" (see Answer D).

C.   parachute out of a plane with a friend.

WRONG: This answer lacks "many others doing the same thing" (see Answer D) and has the person with the phobia parachute out of a plane. However, the passage does not suggest that the person with the phobia engage in the behavior to get over it.

D.   go to a drop zone and watch as many people as possible skydiving.

CORRECT: This answer contains the passage idea of "many others doing the same thing," and has the person with the phobia 'watching,' rather than participating. "Psychological studies show that the best way to encourage a person to do the socially unacceptable (or to conquer an abnormal phobia) is to show many others doing the same" (lines 12–15).

17. In describing the first meeting with the cult leader, the author writes, "Great effort will be made to display how the cultists obey the leader absolutely, in the same manner that televangelists 'salt' their audience with paid applauders, vocal supporters, faked testimonials, and actors casting off their crutches" (lines 54–58). In the context of the passage, this most reasonably implies that:

A.   some of the cultists are not genuine in their support for their leader.

CORRECT: This is the most reasonable implication offered. Clearly, the televangelists "paid applauders, vocal supporters," etc. are not genuine in their support for their leader. Likewise, as this answer suggests …

B.   televangelists are just like cult leaders.

WRONG: This is not a reasonable implication. The comparison is in the "effort [that] will be made to display how the cultists obey the leader absolutely." Nothing else is implied. If A then B does *not* mean if B then A!

C.   belief is critical to the success of the cult.

WRONG: This is a reasonable implication; however, it is *not* the *most* reasonable implication, given the quote in the question. There is much less use of the information provided in the quote in this answer than in Answer A. This is not the *best* answer.

D.   the "pepper" is composed of all new recruits.

WRONG: This is not a reasonable implication and is very vague. Remember not to choose an answer if you don't know what it means. These are usually not the best answers. *If* the "pepper" is everyone else (and this is not at all clear), surely there are *some older* recruits among them.

Passage IV (Questions 18–23)

18. Which of the following opinions would the author be most likely to endorse?

    A. A person without hair could never achieve the facial beauty of one with hair.

    WRONG: The author would *not* likely endorse this opinion. "Never" is an absolute term and, without some *specific* references in the passage, should immediately identify this answer as unlikely. The hairstyle can merely create an "optical illusion" that enhances good features and distracts attention from the bad. "While the issue of what constitutes facial beauty is much debated and still unresolved, most psychometric research suggests it depends largely on the *proportions of the facial features in relation to each other*, rather than the exceptional beauty of each individual feature" (lines 14-19). Given the answer, it is conceivable that the "person with hair" could have perfect features in perfect proportion, while the "one with hair" would have hideous features. If the answer allows for extreme examples such as the aforementioned, consider if the choice would still be correct and appropriate.

    B. A person without hair might be more facially beautiful than a person with hair who had a 'perfect' haircut.

    CORRECT: The author *would* likely endorse this opinion. Compare the softer "*might*" in this answer choice with the "*never*" in Answer A. The hairstyle can merely create an "optical illusion" that enhances good features and distracts attention from the bad. "While the issue of what constitutes facial beauty is much debated and still unresolved, most psychometric research suggests it depends largely on the *proportions of the facial features in relation to each other*, rather than the exceptional beauty of each individual feature" (lines 14–18). Given the answer, it is conceivable that the "person with hair" could have perfect features in perfect proportion, while the "one with hair" would have hideous features.

    C. A 'perfect' haircut can render anyone facially 'beautiful.'

    WRONG: The author would *not* likely endorse this opinion. The hairstyle can merely create an "optical illusion" that enhances good features and distracts attention from the bad. "While the issue of what constitutes facial beauty is much debated and still unresolved, most psychometric research suggests it depends largely on the *proportions of the facial features in relation to each other*, rather than the

exceptional beauty of each individual feature" (lines 14–18). If a person were physically hideous in the face, the haircut could only distract the viewer from these characteristics or completely cover the face and hide the features.

    D. All hairstylists use scientific principles, whether they realize it or not.

    WRONG: The author would *not* likely endorse this opinion. Based upon the significance the author gives to the scientific principles, this would be tantamount to saying that "all hairstylists are very good at what they do." This is not averred. Notice that "all" is a very extreme term, that should immediately make you suspect of this answer, unless the author himself *specifically* endorsed this statement in the passage.

19. With which of the following opinions would the author be most likely to *disagree*?

    A. A hairstyle rendered without regard for the scientific principles can never improve the client's appearance.

    WRONG: The author would, and *does*, agree with this opinion. "Hairstyles that follow these scientific principles will be successful; that is, they will improve the client's appearance. Those that go against these principles, or are executed without regard for them, can *never* do so" (lines 7–11).

    B. Without applying certain fixed principles, consistent results in hairstyling cannot be achieved.

    WRONG: The author would, and *does*, agree with this opinion. "Styling is in fact a science, which can achieve its consistent results *only* by applying certain fixed principles" (lines 2–4).

    C. Scientific styling principles are more important than execution by the stylist.

    WRONG: The author would agree with this opinion. Consider the very strong statement that hairstylists that "go against these principles, or … [execute a haircut] without regard for them, can *never* [improve the client's appearance]" (lines 9–11). "But knowing such principles gives every stylist the potential to recognize the best possible haircut, and produce a finished product equal to that of overpriced 'top' designers" (lines 65–68). The nod to the importance of "execution" (lines 65–68), on the other hand, is an *afterthought*. Nowhere does the author give "execution" the significance of the "principles."

    D. Classical standards of beauty vary over time and from place to place.

    CORRECT: The author would disagree with this opinion. The author never considers this. "The most important function of hairstyling is to make the facial proportions appear to conform to classical standards of beauty" (lines 12–14). Black, white, oriental,

354 • Examkrackers 101 Passages in MCAT Verbal Reasoning

ancient, modern, it seems to make no difference.

20. Assume that recently obtained lesson plans from an ancient art school in Venice indicate that students were taught classical facial proportions in order to more beautifully recreate the subjects of their portraiture. This finding:

A. increases the probability that artists do not require scientific principles.

WRONG: This is not likely. The passage already equates "facial proportions" with "scientific principles." "While the issue of what constitutes facial beauty is much debated and still unresolved, most psychometric research suggests it depends largely on the proportions of the facial features" (lines 14–17).

B. increases the probability that beauty depends on the proportionality of the features.

CORRECT: This is the most likely answer. "While the issue of what constitutes facial beauty is much debated and still unresolved, most psychometric research suggests it depends largely on the proportions of the facial features" (lines 14–17). The assumption tells us that in "ancient" times, students getting ready to paint portraits studied facial proportions. Portraits are paintings or pictures of "real people." Why study facial proportions unless you were going to render your subjects more beautiful? Why not simply concentrate on painting them with all of their warts, blemishes, big noses, etc., in a gritty realism? Because the students are expected to "more beautifully recreate the subjects of their portraiture."

C. decreases the probability that hairstyles can alter our perceptions of beauty.

WRONG: This is not likely. For one thing, the assumption offers no additional information on hairstyles. If anything, the assumption "*increases*" the probability of this answer, not "decreases" it. The students are being taught that "facial proportions" can enhance beauty. The author has provided ample evidence and argument that hairstyles can do the same, which is not refuted by the assumption.

D. reveals nothing about beauty and proportionality.

WRONG: This is clearly not likely. Based upon the assumption *alone*, without having read the passage, you should be able to discern that this is not the correct answer. The assumption provides a clear link between beauty and facial proportions.

21. An unstated assumption in the author's discussion of hairstyling is that:

Note: On these types of questions, do not discount an answer merely because it is a "stated" or explicit assumption, rather than an "unstated" assumption. That is

just window dressing for the question and broadens the list of possible answers so that the test makers can paraphrase instead of quoting verbatim from the text. The most important aspect is that it is an *accurate* assumption.

A. people generally get their hair styled in order to become more attractive.

CORRECT: This is a correct assumption. "The most important function of hair styling is to make the facial proportions appear to conform to classical standards of beauty" (lines 12–14).

B. a person without hair could enhance his appearance with this information also.

WRONG: This is not an accurate assumption. Based upon passage information, there is no advice for a person without hair. You could *perhaps* extrapolate that this "person without hair" could get a toupee or get some plastic surgery, but that is about it.

C. overpriced designers need to learn scientific principles.

WRONG: This is not a clear assumption. It is implied that these "top" designers either know the principles and are not telling or are using them unconsciously (lines 68–70).

D. anyone who learns hairstyling's scientific principles can give a good haircut.

WRONG: This is not a valid assumption. Though the importance of principles predominates, execution is still important. "The fact that hair styling is governed by such scientific principles does not detract from the importance of stylists' skill at haircutting; a well-conceived style can still be ruined by clumsy execution" (lines 62–65).

22. In the passage, when the hairstyle assumes a "certain shape," it is described as creating an "optical illusion" (lines 26–27). What is the most likely reason for the choice of this phrase?

A. A false impression can be created that the actual hairstyle has changed.

WRONG: This is *not* the most likely reason. If the hairstyle assumes a 'certain shape,' it has definitely changed! More importantly, the "optical illusion" clearly has to do with a perception that facial features, or the shape of the face, has changed.

B. The face can be changed to a shape more nearly similar to the hairstyle's.

WRONG: This is *not* the most likely reason. How? Through plastic surgery? Think about this answer and how you would *actually* change the shape of the face.

C. The eye cannot quickly grasp the true nature of the changes.

WRONG: This is *not* the most likely reason. This *may* be true, but there is no evidence or implication that this is so in the passage. This is not the best answer when Answer D is so clearly supported by the passage.

D. The hairstyle can create the impression that the actual shape of the face has changed.

CORRECT: This *is* the most likely reason. "Hair, by virtue of 'framing' the face, has the ability to create an optical illusion; when the hairstyle assumes a certain shape, the face itself is seen as having a shape more nearly similar to the hairstyle's" (lines 25–28).

23. According to the passage, if a client has a roughly ovoid face with generally unattractive facial features, the hair stylist should:

Notice that the "roughly ovoid face" can be ignored. This is the 'perfect' shape and you wouldn't want to do anything to change it. "Ideally, the 'perfect' face should be roughly oval shaped" (lines 18–19). Thus, we are looking for an answer to what the hairstylist should do about "generally unattractive facial features."

A. leave the client's hair longer.

CORRECT: This is something that the hairstylist should definitely do. "Longer hair, measuring four inches or longer, deemphasizes the face. While it is often the better choice for those with unattractive facial features ..." (lines 48–50). Since there is no information in the question regarding whether the client is a man or has an "acceptable occupation," we can *ignore* the additional caveat regarding long hair. This is the best answer.

B. provide a flat-top style.

WRONG: This is *not* something that the hairstylist should do: "round faces are enhanced by the flat top style" (lines 32–33).

C. advise the client to let the hair hang down over the face.

WRONG: This is *not* something that the hairstylist should do. "As for the vertical proportion, the most easily altered proportion is the top third of the face. It may be reduced by wearing the hair hanging down over the face" (lines 37–39). However, 'our' client has a problem with *all* of his features. This answer only responds to the top third of the face. What about the *other* two thirds of the face? This is not the best answer.

D. frame the face by leaving the hair longer on the sides.

WRONG: This is *not* something that the hairstylist should do. "Framing" the face will alter the appearance of the shape of the face, not the individual features. 'Our' client has a perfectly shaped ovoid face and

doesn't require this framing. "Hair, by virtue of 'framing' the face, has the ability to create an optical illusion; when the hairstyle assumes a certain shape, the face itself is seen as having a shape more nearly similar to the hairstyle's" (lines 25–28).

Passage V (Questions 24–28)

24. Which of the following assertions is the most effective argument *against* the author's supposition that "[i]n combat, there is no equal opportunity" (line 70):

Lines 4–8 clearly specify combat in the passage as "being exposed to hostile fire and to a high probability of direct physical contact." Further, "equal opportunity" (lines 70–73) seems to refer to *surviving* and *helping others to survive*, not necessarily fighting *effectiveness*.

A. Men who were less physically fit were more likely to be killed during sustained ground combat.

WRONG: This is not an effective argument *against* the author's supposition. It actually supports his premises.

B. Female soldiers are not as strong as male soldiers are.

WRONG: This is not an effective argument *against* the author's supposition. It actually supports his premises.

C. Women fighting in the Battle of Stalingrad were frequently better able to survive and help their comrades survive than their male counterparts.

CORRECT: This answer precisely responds to the author's references to "equal opportunity."

D. Men are smarter than women are.

WRONG: This is not an effective argument *against* the author's supposition. If it were true, it would actually support his premises.

25. Suppose it could be established that Civil War diaries and memoirs indicated that women disguised as men and fighting alongside them were rarely discovered to be females. Which of the following hypotheses is most compatible with passage information?

Remember that the answer has to be "*compatible* with passage information."

A. In combat, strong men tend to help their weaker comrades without question.

CORRECT: This is most compatible with passage information. The passage stresses with argument and study that women are physically "unable to stand shoulder to shoulder with men" (lines 23–24). Thus, we are faced with explaining how these *weaker* women soldiers could have avoided the questioning of their performance, which would have lead to their discovery as females.

B. The Civil War offered more "equal opportunity."

WRONG: This is not the most compatible with passage information. This answer is appealing but is not one the author would agree with. The passage provides that the problems are primarily physical and offers no indication that the situation has ever been different than it is now.

C. Women in the Civil War were weaker than women today.

WRONG: There is no basis for this in the passage. Further, this answer actually contradicts a possible hypothesis regarding why women were able to fight undetected during the Civil War.

D. It is the women's perceptions of men in combat that leads to problems.

WRONG: This answer makes no sense in the context of the passage.

26. If the author of the passage admired the exploits and life-saving actions of the Revolutionary War battlefield nurse Betsy Ross, this admiration would be most *discrepant* with the passage assertion that:

The question specifies "lifesaving actions" and reminds us that Betsy Ross was a "nurse."

A. while under fire, women were unable to "dig in" to hard ground.

WRONG: This is a passage assertion. However, the hypothesized admiration would *not* be most discrepant with this assertion. What relevance this assertion could have with Betsy Ross is not apparent.

B. these types of stories are not politically correct.

WRONG: This is not responsive to the question.

C. physical differences can be ignored.

WRONG: This is *not* a passage assertion. It is taken out of context.

D. in combat, there is no equal opportunity.

CORRECT: The hypothesized admiration would be most discrepant with this assertion. Equal opportunity refers to "equal opportunity to survive and to *help their fellow soldiers to survive*" (lines 71–72). Admiration and recognition of Betsy Ross's ability to save lives (i.e., help fellow soldiers to survive) is clearly *discrepant* with the author's assertions.

27. What is the intended relevance of the comment, "These types of stories and reports are not 'politically correct'" (lines 51–52), to the rest of the passage?

A. To explain that the stories and reports are not accurate

WRONG: This is *not* the intent. The author clearly

believes their accuracy as he offers them for the proof of his thesis.

B. To indicate that the occurrences are more prevalent than they appear

CORRECT: This is the intended relevance of the comment. With reference to 'politically correct', "[t]his means that the seriousness and frequency of these problems are being underreported not the opposite" (lines 52–54).

C. To show that women are as strong as men

WRONG: This is *not* the intent. There is no evidence for this.

D. To provide a feminist viewpoint

WRONG: This is *not* the intent. The author would not seem to be interested in a feminist viewpoint. His reference to 'politically correct' can be construed as disparaging.

28. Because of a shortage of people, the Israeli Defense Force (IDF) has traditionally relied upon women to fill the ranks of its armed forces. The argument presented on the cost of placing women with previously all-male units suggests that this policy most probably:

A. increased physical standards.

WRONG: This answer is not suggested. The author implies that physical standards were *lowered* as a result of gender mixing.

B. decreased morale throughout the IDF.

WRONG: This answer is not suggested. Though decreased morale in mixed-gender units is suggested, it is *not* suggested "throughout."

C. decreased morale in IDF mixed-gender units.

CORRECT: This is explicitly suggested in the passage. "[T]here are the additional negative repercussions of decreased ... morale within these mixed-gender units" (lines 60–62). The passage information would "suggest" that this answer would be a logical "cost" of the IDF's placing women in previously all-male units.

D. increased combat effectiveness.

WRONG: This answer is not suggested. Almost the entire passage argues against this answer.

Passage VI (Questions 29–33)

29. According to the passage, which of the following is most likely to be true about the relationship between the person providing the hospitality and the person enjoying the hospitality?

A. Though uninvited, the child of a famous person would be generously welcomed by a good host.

WRONG: This is not necessarily true and not as "likely to be true" as Answer C. There is no real way of knowing, because "the Greeks had no requirement that hosts entertain an uninvited guest" (lines 49–50).

B. If respectful, a host of good character could count on many visits by people of fame.

WRONG: This is not necessarily true and not as "likely to be true" as Answer C. This is pure speculation, and has no support in the passage.

C. A host of good character would generously welcome the child of a famous person.

CORRECT: This is most likely to be true. First, "the Greeks of Homer's time considered the treatment a host accorded his visitors to be a crucial indication of his character" (lines 23–25). Second, "If he himself is an unknown, then his welcome depends on his father's renown. Thus, the renowned Odysseus's young son, Telemachus, finds his first visit to the courts of foreign kings very warm, owing to his father's fame" (lines 37–40).

D. Less respect would be accorded a famous person who was invited by a host.

WRONG: This is not true. This person would likely get the most respect and the greatest welcome. "As a rule, the respect accorded to a stranger is based on his fame" (lines 35–36).

30. Some of the first outsiders to make contact with scattered tribes of Arctic Eskimos brought home stories of frequent instances in which they were encouraged to have sexual intercourse with the women in the tribe. Given the information in the passage, this 'hospitality' was probably due to:

A. a strong sense of welcome and nothing more.

WRONG: This is pure conjecture. It is not based upon any passage information.

B. the Eskimos requiring compensation for the services of their women.

WRONG: This is also pure conjecture. It is not based upon any passage information.

C. Eskimo religious customs, which prohibited being inhospitable.

WRONG: This is not a probable reason. "Social and religious customs often have their basis in worldly necessity" (lines 11–12). This is the *second* best answer. It provides one facet of passage information, but makes no mention of the "basis" of the custom coming from some sort of "worldly necessity."

D. a perceived necessity by the Eskimos, perhaps to enlarge their genetic pool, that had become a social custom.

CORRECT: This is the most probable reason. "Social and religious *customs* often have their basis in worldly *necessity*" (lines 11–12). This answer

responds to the question based upon passage information, and provides the components of a worldly "perceived necessity" as an explanation of what the question calls 'hospitality.' This answer uses passage information the *most fully* to attempt to answer the question.

31. The contention that "[s]ocial and religious customs often have their basis in worldly necessity" (lines 11–12) can most justifiably be interpreted as support for which of the following ideas?

A. Certain religious customs and restrictions, such as not eating meat on Fridays, were handed down through apostolic tradition.

WRONG: This idea is *not* supported by the quote in the question. "Apostolic tradition" does not equate to "worldly necessity."

B. Out of the need to determine that another person was not armed arose the custom of shaking hands upon first meeting.

CORRECT: This idea is supported by the quote in the question. The "need to determine that another person was not armed" can definitely be interpreted as a "worldly necessity." Therefore, the social custom of shaking hands had a basis in the worldly necessity of determining that another person was not armed.

C. Customary observances, such as stores being closed on Sundays, can be traced back to historical religious requirements.

WRONG: This idea is *not* supported by the quote in the question. The quote does *not* say that "social and religious customs often have their basis in" *religious requirements*. A "religious requirement" does not equate to a "worldly necessity."

D. Carrying a young bride 'over the threshold' had its basis in the belief that this would ensure a long and happy marriage.

WRONG: This idea is *not* supported by the quote in the question. A "long and happy marriage" was not necessarily a "worldly necessity"; it is described as an ideal, something to aspire to.

32. Evidence shows that during the early days of expansion westward from the Mississippi River, the small isolated groups of settlers tended to be initially cautious of strangers but were extremely welcoming and generous to the travelers arriving by stagecoach. This fact tends to support the hypothesis concerning the wide range of Greek 'hospitality' because:

"In the Hellenic legendary world, a sea-roving traveler could expect to encounter a wide range of 'hospitality,' ranging from the embarrassingly generous to the horrific" (lines 33–35). This depended to a large degree on whether he was famous or not. However, we also know that it depended upon whether he was "uninvited," too. Most importantly, the question provides a metaphor for the following: The Greeks, "with their small-capacity longships and primitive food-preservation techniques … were dependent on frequent stops in various city-states to rest and replenish supplies" (lines 20–22).

A. the settlers had often learned that uninvited strangers meant trouble, and this attitude carried over to the stage travelers who were actually like the Greek's 'uninvited' guests.

WRONG: The attitude obviously did *not* carry over to the stage travelers if the settlers "were extremely welcoming and generous" to them. This is *not* why the "fact" in the question supports the passage hypothesis.

B. the stage travelers had learned that, though uninvited, they could rest and replenish their supplies since they and the settlers needed one another.

WRONG: This does *not* explain why the settlers "were extremely welcoming and generous to the [uninvited stage] travelers." This is *not* why the "fact" in the question supports the passage hypothesis.

C. the settlers were not obligated to trust and welcome the stage travelers since they were uninvited guests.

WRONG: This is true, if we compare the settlers with the Greeks. However, this is *not* why the "fact" in the question supports the passage hypothesis.

D. though the stage travelers were not invited guests, they, like the Hellenic travelers, were frequent and regular visitors upon whom the settlers were dependent for news, if nothing else.

CORRECT: This is why the "fact" in the question supports the passage hypothesis. This answer provides an analogy to the Greeks, who "with their small capacity longships and primitive food-preservation techniques … were dependent on frequent stops in various city-states to rest and replenish supplies" (lines 20–22).

33. On the basis of the passage, it is reasonable to conclude that:

A. Zeus was the patron of supplicants, and his patron god was Poseidon.

WRONG: This is not accurate. Poseidon was not the patron god of Zeus.

B. Poseidon was the patron god of supplicants and the ruler of the gods.

WRONG: This is not accurate. Poseidon was not the patron god of supplicants.

C. Poseidon was the ruler of the gods, and Zeus was the patron of supplicants.

WRONG: This is not accurate. Poseidon was not the ruler of the gods.

D. Zeus was the patron of supplicants and the ruler of the gods.

CORRECT: This is the only reasonable conclusion. "Zeus (patron of supplicants)" (line 47), and "Zeus, the ruler of the gods" (line 10).

Passage VII (Questions 34–40)

34. Evidence shows that juries tend to assume that a clergyman who is giving testimony in a court of law is telling the truth, unless proven otherwise. This fact tends to support the hypothesis concerning authority because:

A. the clergy are perceived as having connections with a higher authority.

CORRECT: The higher authority being the Deity. Yet, at the end of the day, a clergy person is still just a person.

B. the clergy can generally authorize people to do certain things.

WRONG: The "clergy" is a generalized term for religious persons. There is no 'generalized' authority by which they can authorize people to do anything.

C. a clergyman would not have sanctioned Milgram's experiments.

WRONG: This is purely conjectural.

D. a clergyman would not make specific threats but only say, "You have no choice. You must continue."

WRONG: This is purely conjectural.

35. It is currently possible to more accurately evaluate a person's perceptions of who is in authority by standardized psychological testing. Such information would be relevant to Milgram's theory presented in the passage because it would:

A. show that the results of Milgram's experiment were accurate.

WRONG: It *might* have shown this, or it *might* have shown that they were inaccurate. Yet this answer does not provide that the testing might also show the opposite.

B. indicate whether the participants might have merely enjoyed inflicting pain.

CORRECT: The other answer choices are too specific in that they reach a conclusion. This answer offers that the testing *might* indicate "whether," *and* though not specified, that it might indicate "not."

C. prove that the participants truly believed that Milgram was in charge.

WRONG: It *might* have proven this, or it *might* have proven the opposite. Yet this answer does not provide that the testing might also show the opposite.

D. prove that Milgram's experiment was flawed.

WRONG: It *might* have proven this, or it *might* have proven the opposite. Yet this answer does not provide that the testing might also show the opposite.

36. According to the passage information, what would have happened if the participant administering the shocks had refused to continue the experiment?

A. Nothing. However, he or she would have been denied the travel stipend.

WRONG: "The *most* he could have done was to deny the subjects their small, promised travel stipend, though he had assured them that they would receive it whether or not they completed the experiment" (lines 56–59).

B. He would have been unstrapped from the apparatus.

WRONG: We cannot know this for certain, except that *eventually* they would have been unstrapped from the apparatus. This is not the best answer.

C. They would certainly have lost his Yale affiliation.

WRONG: There is no evidence that all or any of the participants had any Yale affiliation. It merely says that the *professor* "may have had some authority by virtue of his position, but it did not extend over people unaffiliated with Yale" (lines 54–56).

D. There were no specific threats made.

CORRECT: "At no time did the experimenter make specific threats; he only said, 'You have no choice. You must continue'" (lines 59–61).

37. Which of the following scientific advances would most seriously *challenge* the hypothesis involving Milgram's experiments and authority?

A. Association of obedience with perceived authority

WRONG: This would have ratified the hypothesis, not challenged it.

B. Proof of the predictions made prior to the experiment taking place

CORRECT: This would have challenged the hypothesis. "*Contrary to all predictions*, an amazing 63% of volunteers were willing to administer a shock … " (lines 38–39).

C. Further correlation of the necessity of obedience for human survival

WRONG: This does not clearly have anything to do with the hypothesis. Thus, evaluating whether it challenges the hypothesis or not is fruitless.

D. Confirmation of the extreme tension shown by the participants

WRONG: This would not have challenged the hypothesis.

38. If the hypothesis of the passage is correct, one should find that if a policeman ordered several bystanders to restrain someone while the policeman "beat information out of him" that:

A. it is unlikely that the bystanders could be enlisted to help the policeman.

WRONG: According to the passage, this is *not* unlikely.

B. it is likely that the bystanders might cooperate by doing so.

CORRECT: This answer uses a 'softener': "might." The passage provides that "we tend to generalize the obedience we must give to the powers that be … by allowing someone in a position of authority to exceed his jurisdiction" (lines 68–72).

C. a small majority of the bystanders might come to the aid of the person being restrained.

WRONG: If *any* bystanders came to the aid of the person it would *not* be a "*small majority*." The author states that "an *amazing 63%* of volunteers were willing to administer a shock of 450 volts to a person who had stopped responding to questions and was likely unconscious" (lines 38–41).

D. a majority of the bystanders might not stand by and do nothing.

WRONG: This is a double negative. Therefore, "they might not stand by and do *something*." At *best*, "they might do *something*," which is vague. Are they going to help the policeman or the person being beaten? It makes little sense. Don't choose answers that don't make sense.

39. Which of the following suppositions is most clearly believed by the author?

A. The experiment was meant to measure people's tolerance for electric shock.

WRONG: This is clearly not believed by the author.

B. Identifiable criminal tendencies are not an indication of future problems.

WRONG: This is poor logic. The quote refers to "a man *without* identifiable criminal tendencies." It is incorrect to make assumptions regarding what the author believes about those who *have* identifiable criminal tendencies.

C. To follow instructions that will result in hurting another is immoral.

CORRECT: "If asked beforehand, those 26 would doubtless have asserted that neither they nor most anyone else would submit to an *immoral authority*, yet the *fact* remains that they did." (lines 46–49).

D. Most people will obediently submit to rightful authority.

WRONG: The passage does *not* provide information regarding a "rightful authority." It is about perceptions of authority.

40. The quotation by Von Lang & Sibyll refers to the notorious Nazi Adolf Eichmann, who was responsible for ordering the deaths of millions of Jews. According to the passage, the behavior of the soldiers who followed Eichmann's orders could be described as:

A. quite normal.

WRONG: Killing millions of people is rather extreme behavior to be characterized as "normal." This answer is not as appropriate as Answer D.

B. criminal.

WRONG: Certainly the behavior was "criminal." However, the passage provides more specific characterizations.

C. aberrant.

WRONG: As much as the described behavior is too extreme to be characterized as "normal," the experiments indicate that many people will respond to authority in this fashion. It is not, then, "aberrant." This answer is not as appropriate as Answer D

D. socially conditioned.

CORRECT: This is the best description of the soldiers' behavior. "Milgram theorizes that a hierarchy of obedience became necessary for human survival, so it became *socially conditioned*" (lines 62–64). This is the best answer. None of the other answers are specifically addressed within the body of the passage.

Verbal Reasoning Test 9
Answers & Explanations

TEST 9 ANSWER KEY

1.	A	11.	B	21.	A	31.	B
2.	C	12.	D	22.	A	32.	C
3.	C	13.	C	23.	D	33.	A
4.	B	14.	D	24.	B	34.	C
5.	A	15.	C	25.	D	35.	C
6.	D	16.	A	26.	A	36.	B
7.	B	17.	B	27.	B	37.	D
8.	A	18.	C	28.	C	38.	C
9.	C	19.	C	29.	D	39.	D
10.	C	20.	D	30.	B	40.	C

Passage I (Questions 1–6)

1. Which of the following sections of a text would be the most effective areas upon which to focus in order to glean the most useful details, according to passage indications?

    A. conclusory paragraphs or summaries within the text
    CORRECT: "Sometimes, it may require picking out a certain *useful detail* and ignoring the others. To that end, readers should focus on any *summaries within the text* or *conclusory paragraphs*" (lines 28–31).

    B. a chapter's introductory or conclusory paragraphs
    WRONG: This is an area to focus upon if Answer A does not work. "*Failing*" (lines 32) to find the details in the "*summaries within the text* or *conclusory paragraphs*", the reader should look to the chapter's introduction.

    C. a paragraph's opening or concluding sentences
    WRONG: This is an area to focus upon if Answer A does not work. "*Failing*" (lines 32) finding the details in the "*summaries within the text* or *conclusory paragraphs*," the reader should look to the paragraph's opening.

    D. summaries within the text or a paragraph's opening
    WRONG: This is an area to focus upon if Answer A does not work. "*Failing*" (lines 32) finding the details in the "*summaries within the text* or *conclusory paragraphs*," the reader should look to the paragraph's opening.

2. Some timed verbal reasoning tests, such as the MCAT, require the test-taker to be prepared to answer questions that may be drawn from any area of the text or passage. An appropriate clarification of the passage would be the stipulation that the author's argument applies only to:

    A. tests other than the verbal section of the MCAT.
    WRONG: This is not an appropriate stipulation. Granted, given the supposition, some of the speed-reading strategies are not good for tests such as the MCAT. However, "*Some* timed verbal reasoning tests," means *that there are other* "timed verbal reasoning tests" besides the MCAT. This answer is not inclusive enough.

    B. back-skipping when not taking a timed verbal test.
    WRONG: This is not an appropriate stipulation: "back-skipping" is a "waste of time" (lines 52–54) and should always be avoided if possible.

    C. skimming when the reader already knows what information he requires from the text.
    CORRECT: Given the supposition in the question, the author's argument should "*apply only to*" "skimming when …" When you are reading the MCAT passages, you *do not* "already know what

information you require from the text." You do not already know "what information [you] need to extract" (lines 6–7). Therefore, "skimming over details" would *not* be a good idea. "While reading, readers should concentrate the bulk of their time on those sections most likely to contain valuable information. Usually, this means concentrating on understanding the main point/plot while skimming over details" (lines 24–28).

    D. concentrating on those sections most likely to contain valuable information.
    WRONG: This does not help clarify the supposition. When you are reading the MCAT passages you *do not know* which sections are "most likely to contain valuable information."

3. For which of the following conclusions does the passage offer the most support?

    A. Subvocalization is an important skill for reading comprehension.
    WRONG: This conclusion is covered only from lines 56–60.

    B. Readers must skim over details that are not important.
    WRONG: This conclusion is covered only from lines 24–28.

    C. Readers should practice learning efficient eye movements.
    CORRECT: The support for eye movements is in line 4, then in lines 36 through 60. There is vastly more support and discussion of this topic in the passage than there are for any of the other choices.

    D. Readers should test the effectiveness of their efforts.
    WRONG: This conclusion is covered only at the end of the passage, from lines 61–66.

4. According to the passage, the effectiveness of a course in speed reading could be determined by first having the reader speed-read a passage and then measuring:

    A. the reader's attention span.
    WRONG: There is really *only* one section of the passage that refers to testing the effectiveness of the reader's "efforts." This is not it.

    B. the ability to recall the plot.
    CORRECT: There is really *only* one section of the passage that refers to testing the effectiveness of the reader's "efforts." "After reading, readers should test the effectiveness of their efforts by attempting to recall the major points, or plot, of the passage that they have read" (lines 61–63).

    C. the ability to recall each paragraph's opening and concluding sentences.

WRONG: There is really *only* one section of the passage that refers to testing the effectiveness of the reader's "efforts." This is not it.

D. the reader's ability to concentrate.

WRONG: There is really *only* one section of the passage that refers to testing the effectiveness of the reader's "efforts." This is not it.

5. In the context of the passage, the word *primacy* (line 18) means:

A. the first or start.

CORRECT: This is the most similar to "beginnings." From the passage, we know that "primacy" and "recency" effects dictate that students tend to remember the *beginnings* and endings of passages" (lines 18–20).

B. the most important.

WRONG: This is not similar to "beginnings."

C. apelike.

WRONG: Not unless you think that *primacy* is related to *primate*. This is not similar to "beginnings."

D. the main.

WRONG: This is not similar to "beginnings."

6. According to the passage, a very common problem is:

A. eye control.

WRONG: Eye control is not specifically mentioned as a "problem" or a "very common" problem. This answer is too vague and not as responsive to the question as "back-skipping."

B. structuring time poorly.

WRONG: This is not described as a "problem" or a "very common" problem.

C. inability to recall major points.

WRONG: This is not described as a "problem" or a "very common" problem.

D. back-skipping.

CORRECT: "The larger *problem* is back-skipping to already-read sections, which is an obvious distraction and waste of time but is *very common*" (lines 52–54).

Passage II (Questions 7–12)

7. The passage states that the Hippocratic oath "was a direct response to physicians of the day purposely giving mortal doses of medicines for rather minor ailments" (lines 20–22). According to the author, this ancient form of euthanizing would probably have resulted from:

According to the passage, support for euthanizing results from misconceptions and incorrect assumptions about the association between pain and the wish to die.

A. ever increasing health care costs.

WRONG: References to cost are made by the author only in reference to "supportive institutions" (lines 53–55) and in the last paragraph where he is imagining a grim future.

B. empathy for the person suffering

CORRECT: The passage emphasizes repeatedly that the healthy do not understand suffering and pain (lines 4–6, 23–28). Further, it emphasizes that the healthy *inaccurately* perceive an "association between pain and the wish to die" (lines 35–37 and 42–46). It is true that the passage does not say specifically that doctors have suffered from the same misconceptions and associations. However, doctors are people, and like most people, normally healthy. This answer is a reasonable assumption and the best answer.

C. poor understanding of the ailment.

WRONG: "This oath was a direct response to physicians of the day purposely giving mortal doses of medicines *for what they knew to be rather minor ailments*" (lines 19–22). They did NOT have a "poor understanding" of the ailment. Further, this passage is not about actual medical conditions, but about misconceptions of *suffering* and *pain*. We have no information from the article that *misdiagnosis of the actual medical conditions* leads to support for euthanasia. The "poor understanding" is not of the ailment, but of "a perceived association between pain and the wish to die" (lines 36–37). One could argue that a "poor understanding of the ailment" would lead the physician to believe that the patient was experiencing more pain that he actually was, but this is a stretch and besides the point. According to the passage, pain plays little role in motivating a *patient* towards suicide (lines 45–46). This is not the best answer.

D. a desire to rid society of the aged.

WRONG: The sole reference to age, at lines 11–14, is presented as an argument by proponents of assisted suicide. Yet there is no evidence in the passage that assisted suicide is actually carried out as a result of this. Further, the reference still relates to the individual *wanting* to die, not society deciding that he should die as inferred in this answer.

8. Based upon information in the passage, which of the following statements would NOT be an argument given by *proponents* of assisted suicide?

The author is quite clear in pointing out that proponents of assisted suicide are misinformed. The author implies that these proponents "can scarcely relate to or understand" those who are suffering (because the proponents *are not suffering*; they are healthy).

A.   Those fearing a lack of social supports and suffering extreme emotional pain should be allowed to die if they wish.

CORRECT: We find through reading the passage that "[i]t is, in fact, not physical pain, but depression and emotional pain that leads patients to consider suicide" (lines 45–46). At lines 50–52, lack of social supports is mentioned as leading New York HIV patients to consider suicide. However, this information is given by way of revelation with the clear understanding that this is not common knowledge. Nor does the article say or imply that these are arguments that are being currently used to promote assisted suicide.

B.   Medical advances now allow people to live far beyond the point at which they would have naturally passed away.

WRONG: Proponents give this argument at lines 11–14.

C.   Often, people are kept alive artificially against their will.

WRONG: Proponents give this argument at lines 28–32.

D.   Extreme physical pain can commonly lead someone to consider suicide.

WRONG: Lines 23–26 and 35–37 explain that this is a common misconception and, thus, *might be* given by a proponent of assisted suicide. This answer is not as clearly correct as Answer A.

9. According to the author, a healthy person's perceptions regarding what the suffering are feeling are:

A.   based upon a variety of factors.

WRONG: This is a true statement, but one so vague as to be precluded by all but the most incorrect answers.

B.   a valid component of the assisted-suicide debate.

WRONG: It is only a valid component of the debate when you consider that a healthy person's perceptions are inaccurate and misleading (lines 35–37 and 42–46).

C.   what may determine our fate.

CORRECT: The author takes pains to point out that healthy people frame this debate. He does this by specifically designating that the proponents are healthy or identifying them by their misconceptions and their separateness from the suffering who understand because they are there. He also alludes to the fact that the healthy frequently believe the suffering would wish to die when this is far from

the truth (lines 4–6, 23–26, 35–37). In the last paragraph, the author extrapolates into the future, strongly arguing that healthy people [by *implication* the one's doing the deciding] could ultimately determine our fate: "Would you be required to die though you cried out to live?"

D.   how children and the elderly really feel.

WRONG: This is a very vague answer and not the best one.

10. Which of the following is most clearly believed by the author?

A.   A human can never live too long.

WRONG: The statement that "continuing medical advances now allow people to live far beyond the point at which they would have naturally passed away" (lines 12–14) is that of proponents of assisted suicide, which the author is not.

B.   Suicide is wrong.

WRONG: The author is clearly against *assisted* suicide but makes no mention regarding suicide.

C.   Those who wish to die can be helped through means other than assisted suicide.

CORRECT: After pointing out that the wish to die is not based upon pain and suffering (which presumably cannot be helped). The wish to die is based upon "fear of a loss of control or of dignity, of being a burden, and of being dependent" (lines 48–50), and "depression, hopelessness, and having few—and poor-quality—social supports" (lines 51–52). The author provides the means to help those afflicted with these problems, mentioning impediments (labor and money), but not insurmountable ones.

D.   Healthy adults are sound advocates for all of society.

WRONG: Clearly not. Advocacy and representation require understanding. The author takes pain to point out that A) the healthy do not understand the suffering, B) the healthy *already* do a poor job of representing "the unconscious, the demented, [etc.]" (lines 69–73), and C) he points out that ultimately, you might be forced to die (lines 61–62).

11. The passage provides that the wish to die is "a societal problem requiring more supportive institutions and mental health care" (lines 52–54). The reason given is that:

Restated the question reads, "The passages provides that blah-blah *because* …[answer]".

A.   there are poor quality "social supports" for depressed HIV-infected patients in New York.

WRONG: The reference is to lines 50–52. However, this twists the meaning by simply moving the words around. According to the passage, depression (*for an unspecified reason) and* poor quality social supports were some of the leading factors driving patients to request assisted suicide. Nowhere in the passage does it say that AIDs patients in New York were depressed *because of* poor quality social supports.

B. the requests for assisted suicide were driven by a fear of a loss of control or of dignity.
CORRECT: This is responsive to the question because "the leading factors driving requests for assisted suicide were fear of a loss of control or of dignity" (lines 47–49).

C. at some point you would have no choice but to die and have your organs harvested for the good of all.
WRONG: This answer is attractive because it is information provided by the author. However, it is not responsive to the question. The question and "the institution of more supportive institutions and mental health care" would not lead you to this answer. This answer relates to the issue of the institution and legalization of assisted suicide and euthanasia. Whereas the question relates to the issue of why people wish to die and what can be done about it.

D. in the long run, this would cost society less money.
WRONG: There is no explicit or implicit reference to saving money in the long run, or to saving any money at all. The author admits that instituting the aforementioned would be "a labor- and money-intensive proposition" (lines 54–55) without mentioning any monetary returns.

12. The author probably mentions having "your organs harvested for the good of all" (line 63) in order:

A. to illustrate that society could make good use of your body after you have died.
WRONG: There is no mention made of what would happen to the organs after they were harvested. Some mention of this might give you an idea regarding whether the author thought their use would be good or not. Maybe they would be eaten.

B. to support his argument that the debate surrounding assisted suicide is an old one.
WRONG: There is no indication that organ harvesting is an old practice or an old debate.

C. to offer an alternative to an otherwise bleak prediction.
WRONG: On the contrary, the author mentions organ harvesting for emphasis, in order to make a bleak prediction even bleaker.

D. to provide an example of mandatory euthanasia.
CORRECT: This furthers the author's argument that we might be forced to die. "[A]t some point you would have *no choice* but to die and have your organs harvested for the good of all" (lines 62–63).

Passage III (Questions 13–18)

13. The passage provides examples for the assertion that copywriters often use "provocative visuals" (line 15). Which of the following examples would be commonly considered "provocative"?

I. images of puppies and kittens
WRONG: This is an example, but it is not commonly considered to be provocative.

II. pictures of babies' faces
WRONG: This is an example, but it is not commonly considered to be provocative.

III. attractive women used to sell cars or beer
CORRECT: This is an example, and it is provocative, not just because attractive women are in the advertisement, but because the attractive women have *nothing to do with the product*. It is clear that they are included to provide sexual suggestion and innuendo.

A. I only
B. II only
C. III only
CORRECT: See above answer explanations.
D. I and II only

14. Which of the following approaches to selling horses would be most likely to be stressed by an advertiser who had an understanding of how best to translate a product's features?

A. Describe the height of the horse.
WRONG: This would not likely be stressed. "What is consistently compelling to the reader is how the company's product can meet his needs and/or wants" (lines 32–34). Without some additional information, for example, "The rider is short and wants to know the height of the horse," the "height of the horse" is a "technical feature" and not nearly as compelling to a consumer.

B. Explain the different types of horses that are available.
WRONG: This would not likely be stressed. "What is consistently compelling to the reader is how the company's product can meet his needs and/or wants" (lines 34-36). Without some additional information, for example, "This little Arabian mare is the perfect horse for your little boy to ride," "different types of horses" is a "technical feature" and not nearly as compelling to a consumer.

C. Emphasize that the reader shoulder 'buy now' or the horse will be sold.
WRONG: This answer is attractive because it offers accurate and memorable passage information almost

verbatim. However, this answer is *not* responsive to the question and would not likely be stressed by an advertiser trying to "*translate* a product's features." This answer is responsive to a question regarding a "call to action," as described in the last paragraph.

D. Depict how the entire family will enjoy riding the horse.

CORRECT: This would likely be stressed. "What is consistently compelling to the reader is how the company's product can meet his needs and/or wants" (lines 32–34). An advertiser using this approach to sell horses would be helping the consumer to "understand exactly what the product will do for him, and also let him picture himself enjoying the product" (lines 38–40). The advertiser is "*translating*" [per the question] the product's features into "tangible benefits."

15. Which of the following products most clearly exemplifies a "generic commodity" (line 54)?

This question is based upon information in the passage that suggests that "if the product is a *generic commodity*, such that the item itself is fairly similar across all sellers, the copywriter must stress another 'feature,'" (lines 53–56).

A. Dishwashers

WRONG: This is not the clearest example of a "generic commodity." A dishwasher could have more "features" than "contact lenses." A dishwasher could come in a different color, with more or fewer cycles, buttons as opposed to knobs, etc.

B. Computers

WRONG: This is not the clearest example of a "generic commodity." A computer could have more "features" than "contact lenses." A computer could come with more or less RAM, ROM, a CD, CDRW, or a faster or slower processor, etc.

C. Contact lenses

CORRECT: This is by far the clearest example of a "generic commodity" among the four. What are the distinguishing features of contact lenses between manufacturers? There may be some, yet they would not compare in number with, nor be as obvious as, the other three commodities. This is the best answer.

D. Running shoes

WRONG: This is not the clearest example of a "generic commodity." Running shoes could have more "features" than "contact lenses." Running shoes could come in different colors, for men or women, fast runners or slow or long-distance runners, be light or heavier, have different types of bottoms, etc.

16. According to the passage, all of the following may be considered product "features" EXCEPT:

A. free and useful information.

CORRECT: This is an exception and may not be considered a product "feature." This answer is a *technique* that is used to get a consumer to read the entire advertisement. "The more effective approach is to offer the promise of free and useful information if the reader reads the rest of the advertisement" (lines 24–26).

B. service.

WRONG: This is not an exception and may be considered a product feature. In a generic product, advertisers must stress "another 'feature,' such as the manufacturer's *service*, expertise, or warranty" (lines 55–57).

C. manufacturer's expertise.

WRONG: This is not an exception and may be considered a product feature. In a generic product, advertisers must stress "another 'feature,' such as the manufacturer's service, *expertise*, or warranty" (lines 55–57).

D. warranties.

WRONG: This is not an exception and may be considered a product feature. In a generic product, advertisers must stress "another 'feature,' such as the manufacturer's service, expertise, or *warranty*" (lines 55–57).

17. According to the passage, which of the following would be the most effective "call to action" (line 65)?

A. "Let's leave now."

WRONG: This is a "call to action," but this would *not* be the most effective technique. "Psychological research shows the most effective call to action is the *threat of loss*" (lines 70–71). In this instance, there is no "threat of loss."

B. "If we don't leave now, then I'm not going."

CORRECT: This is a "call to action," and this would be the most effective. "Psychological research shows the most effective call to action is the *threat of loss*" (lines 70–71). In this instance, the "call to action" is "Let's leave now," and the directly stated "threat of loss" is the loss of a person going along.

C. "I want you to leave now."

WRONG: This is a "call to action," but this would *not* be the most effective technique. "Psychological research shows the most effective call to action is the *threat of loss*" (lines 70–71). In this instance, there is no "threat of loss".

D. "If you leave now then I'll go with you."

WRONG: This is a "call to action," but this would *not* be the most effective technique. "Psychological research shows the most effective call to action is the *threat of loss*" (lines 70–71). In this instance, there is no *direct* "threat of loss." Though it is *implied* that "if you don't leave now, then I'm not going," this is *very* indirect. The greater emphasis in this answer is on the positive aspect of "*I'll go with you* if you leave now." This is not the best answer.

18. According to the passage, which of the following would be the most effective in credibly promoting a movie?

This question requires that you use information provided in the passage in a new situation. In this case, advertising for a movie.

I. Publicized positive audience responses

CORRECT: This would be effective. An audience would be a "third party." "Much more effective are *testimonials from third parties*, such as customer testimonials, reviews, and industry awards" (lines 61–63).

II. An Academy Award

CORRECT: This would be effective. An Academy Award is an "industry award." "Much more effective are testimonials from third parties, such as customer testimonials, reviews, and *industry awards*" (lines 61–63).

III. Positive interviews with the more famous actors who starred in the movie

WRONG: This would not be very effective, according to the passage. Regardless of whether they were "famous," the "actors who starred in the movie" would be perceived as having ulterior motives for promoting the movie. People would "tend to distrust their claims." "Naturally, neither the manufacturer nor its copywriter is necessarily *objective, so people tend to distrust claims originating from these sources*" (lines 61–63).

A. I only
B. II only
C. I and II only
   CORRECT: See above answer explanations.
D. II and III only

Passage IV (Questions 19–24)

19. Regarding the increasing persecution of homosexuals (lines 1–15), the passage strongly implies that:

A. persecution increased as society felt that this 'disease' could be passed on to others.
   WRONG: This is not implied. It is fairly clear in the passage that the reference to a 'disease' is a psychological, not a physiological, one.

B. homosexuals were increasingly perceived by society as immoral.
   WRONG: This is neither "strongly" nor clearly implied. References to "immoral" relate to homosexual "*activity,*" not necessarily to just *being* a homosexual. Therefore, this answer is highly speculative. This is not the best answer.

C. this might not have occurred without the increasing openness of homosexuals themselves.
   CORRECT: This is strongly and very clearly implied. In one sentence there is a clear causal relationship being put forth by the author. "Historians examining the increasing trend of homosexuals as a persecuted and ostracized American minority cite the 1870's to 1930's as the period in American history when there first emerged an actual 'community' of people who openly recognized erotic interest in members of their own sex" (lines 4–9).

D. the sexuality aspect has always been recognized.
   WRONG: This is not implied, nor is it accurate. Until they emerged openly, "homosexuality was not considered a sexuality but a deviant and disgusting (sinful or immoral) activity" (lines 11–12).

20. According to the passage, Freud's theory of psychosexual development most clearly resulted in:

A. only increased persecution of homosexuals.
   WRONG: This is not a clear result. This is an extreme and very specific answer because of the inclusion of the word "only." Actually, "The 'disease' model removed some prejudices attendant to homosexuality, as those who believed in this model concluded that homosexuals should not be punished for their sexual orientation" (lines 28–31). And, "Freud's famous essays on sexuality, played a large role in influencing the 'disease' model" (lines 35–37).

B. increasing homosexual openness.
   WRONG: This is not a clear result; this is clear *speculation.* You are speculating that because some prejudices may have been removed by Freud's "disease" model, that homosexuals were increasingly open. Freud's theory had mixed results, but there is no reason given for "increasing homosexual openness" mentioned in the first paragraph.

C. impacting only the perception of the medical community.
   WRONG: This is an extreme, very specific, and *wrong* answer because of the inclusion of the word "*only.*" Yes, the medical community was impacted, but the passage is not specific that it was "only" the medical community. "Freud's famous essays on sexuality, played a large role in influencing the 'disease' model" (lines 35–37). And, "The

A & E 9

'disease' model removed some prejudices attendant to homosexuality, as those who believed in this model concluded that homosexuals should not be punished for their sexual orientation" (lines 28–31).

D. diminishing punishment for homosexual behavior.

CORRECT: Do not confuse "prejudice" with "punishment." The only punishment mentioned in the passage is that "imposed by law" (lines 17–18). There is no implication that Freud's theory resulted in any diminishing of punishment.

21. In order to distinguish the nature of who was being persecuted and punished, the author of the passage implies a distinction between:

Be aware that there may be *many* 'distinctions' within any given passage. However, the question calls for the distinction that was implied for the purposes of "distinguishing the nature of *who* was being persecuted and punished." This is a very specific distinction. How do we distinguish the nature of "Who?"!

I. orientation and activity.

CORRECT: This is an implied distinction in the passage. Further, it is offered to "distinguish the nature of *who* was being persecuted and punished." Throughout the passage, we learn that those with homosexual "orientation" were not persecuted and punished to the extent that homosexual "activity" was. For instance, because of the 'disease' model, some people came to believe that "homosexuals should not be punished for their sexual *orientation*. Still, those who engaged in *homosexual practices* were viewed as disordered individuals" (lines 30–32). Additionally, in the first paragraph, it was the openness and "activity" of the homosexual community that apparently aroused the increasing ire of society, not necessarily the orientation ("sexuality"), which had never been considered.

II. homosexuals and bisexuals.

WRONG: There is a distinction. However, it is not offered to show any differences in the nature of *who* was suffering from persecution and punishment. There is no effort in the passage to compare the persecution and punishment of bisexuals with homosexuals.

III. religious institutions and the law.

WRONG: There is a distinction. However, it is not offered to show any differences in the nature of *who* was suffering persecution and punishment. This answer may be attractive because we would naturally equate religious institutions with being the persecutors while the law would punish. The passage mentions

"moral condemnation imposed by religious institutions and punishments imposed by law" (lines 16–18). But this is not the distinction the question is asking for. The distinction must answer "Who?"!

A. I only

CORRECT: See the above answer explanations.

B. II only
C. III only
D. I and III only

22. The contention that "a fair number of psychologists maintain that a theory assuming bisexual tendencies is necessary to explain psychosexual development in 'normal' individuals" (lines 62–64) can most justifiably be interpreted as support for the idea that:

Ask yourself if the author offered the quoted contention in support of his ideas or as a counterpoint to his ideas. This will begin steering you in the right direction in your search for the correct answer.

A. homosexuals are normal individuals.

CORRECT: This answer is similar enough to Answer B that in order to answer it correctly, you must first determine what the meaning of "*normal*" individuals is. Based upon the contention, "normal" individuals are obviously what *society* considers normal (i.e. heterosexuals). The contention *is* suggesting that homosexuals are 'normal,' yet it is *not* suggesting that they are heterosexual!

B. homosexuals are "normal" individuals.

WRONG: This answer is similar enough to Answer A that in order to answer it correctly, you must first determine, what the meaning of "*normal*" individuals is. Based upon the contention, "normal" individuals are obviously what *society* considers normal (i.e. heterosexuals). The contention *is* suggesting that homosexuals are 'normal,' yet it is *not* suggesting that they are heterosexual!

C. homosexuals are abnormal.

WRONG: The contention is not offered in support for this idea. The author clearly favors the view that homosexuality is normal. The author would disagree with this answer's idea. The contention was offered for the purpose of supporting the author, not as a counterargument.

D. homosexuality is a disease.

WRONG: The contention is not offered in support for this idea. The author clearly favors the view that homosexuality is normal. The author would disagree with this answer's idea. The contention was offered for the purpose of supporting the author, not as a counterargument.

A & E 9

23. Which of the following statements, if true, would most directly *challenge* the principles of Freud?

A. A child is not sexually attracted to the same-sex parent.

WRONG: This does *not challenge* the principles of Freud. For one thing, the passage is *not clear* that 'a child is sexually attracted to the same-sex parent' or any parent for that matter. "Over the course of psychosexual development, the child learns to identify with the same-sex parent" (lines 39–41). However, if you choose to equate the word "identify" with "sexual attraction," this answer *still* does *not* challenge Freud; it supports him.

B. Homosexuality is not a disease.

WRONG: This does *not directly challenge* the principles of Freud. Freud's ideas "played a large role in *influencing* the 'disease' model" (lines 36–37). Yet it is not clear that Freud himself ever referred to homosexuality as a "disease." This is not the most "direct" answer, and it is not the best one.

C. Bisexuality is a 'normal' phase in development.

WRONG: This does *not challenge* the principles of Freud. Freud believed that "bisexuality was innate" (line 54).

D. Homosexuality is probably genetic.

CORRECT: This does *directly challenge* the principles of Freud. Freud's theory of psychosexual development left no room for genetic sexual predisposition. Remember that "Freud's famous essays on sexuality, played a large role in influencing [read *promoting*] the 'disease' model" (lines 35–37). It was all nurture and no nature. Reread lines 34–61. Freud believed that we all began the same way sexually when we were born. What happened from there was based upon a number of factors.

24. Which of the following opinions would the author be most likely to endorse?

A. The medical community has finally accepted homosexuality as normal.

WRONG: This is not likely to receive an endorsement from the author. The author offers this very arcane and very tepid endorsement, presumably to indicate support in the *psychological* community. "Today, a *fair number* of psychologists maintain that a theory assuming bisexual tendencies is necessary to explain psychosexual development in 'normal' individuals" (lines 62–64). Psychologists are not MDs. However, even if you did not know that, the quote still does not support this answer. Further, there is no indication that the medical community has "finally accepted homosexuality as normal."

B. The idea that homosexuality is abnormal and can be treated still endures.

CORRECT: The author is most likely to endorse this opinion. "… the search for a biological abnormality as the cause of homosexuality, along with the idea that homosexuality should be 'cured,' *persists*" (lines 65–67).

C. The American Psychological Association still believes that homosexuality is a disorder.

WRONG: This is not likely to receive an endorsement from the author. "In fact, homosexuality was recognized as a disorder by the American Psychological Association as late as 1973" (lines 67–69). That was *thirty* years ago. This is not the best answer.

D. Nowadays, most Americans accept homosexuality.

WRONG: This is not likely to receive an endorsement from the author. There is no support for this opinion in the passage.

Passage V (Questions 25–30)

25. What is the author's response to the passage statement that "approximately half [of the researchers] believe the condition [IBS] is caused primarily by stress or a similar psychosomatic factor" (lines 7–9)?

A. Further research has indicated that this theory is probably correct.

WRONG: This is not accurate. See explanation for Answer D.

B. The likelihood that this is true renders finding a cure more problematic.

WRONG: This is not accurate. See explanation for Answer D.

C. The likelihood that this is true renders finding a cure much easier.

WRONG: This is not accurate. See explanation for Answer D.

D. The likelihood that the condition is inherited shows that this is probably not correct.

CORRECT: "The fact that the condition seems to be, at least to some degree, hereditary vitiates against the theory that it is psychological" (lines 11–13).

26. According to passage information, a person whose large intestine is devoid of cilia would most likely be exhibiting which of the following symptoms?

I. probably not constipation, but constant diarrhea

CORRECT: "[I]f a … patient's large intestine [was] "smooth"—devoid of the cilia … the symptoms would include chronic to constant diarrhea, though likely not frequent constipation" (lines 20–24).

370 • EXAMKRACKERS 101 PASSAGES IN MCAT VERBAL REASONING

II. alternating attacks of diarrhea and constipation

WRONG: This answer is appealing because it is mentioned in the passage. However, this partly describes the symptoms of IBS (lines 3–4), *not* "a person whose large intestine was devoid of cilia."

III. primarily constipation with some diarrhea

WRONG: This is not accurate. See explanation for Answer I.

A. I only

CORRECT: See above explanations.

B. II only

C. III only

D. II and III only

27. If certain patients were to eat large amounts of primarily soluble fiber instead of insoluble varieties of fiber, how would their elimination be affected?

A. This would prevent both diarrhea and constipation.

WRONG: "[F]iber is known to prevent both diarrhea and constipation" (lines 47–48). But this *requires* that the fiber *contain both* soluble and insoluble varieties (lines 50–54).

B. They would tend towards being constipated.

CORRECT: "[S]oluble [fiber] … tends to slow movements" (line 51).

C. They would tend towards having diarrhea.

WRONG: "[I]nsoluble varieties [of fiber tend towards] … making elimination easier" (lines 51–52), which might be diarrhea.

D. They would experience alternating bouts of diarrhea and constipation.

WRONG: This answer is appealing because it is mentioned in the passage. However, this partly describes the symptoms of IBS (lines 3–4).

28. An unstated implication of diarrhea in the author's discussion of treatments is that:

A. laxatives may actually be helpful.

WRONG: This is not implied in the passage. Laxatives cause the bowels to relax. It is clear from the passage that they are used in the treatment of constipation and not diarrhea.

B. it is not easily treated by available medicines.

WRONG: "… simple diarrhea is easily treated" (lines 54–55).

C. those who are afflicted may experience spasms.

CORRECT: This is an unstated implication. Because the passage tells us that "simple diarrhea is easily

treated by commonly available *antispasmodics*" (lines 54–55), it is implied that diarrhea may cause spasms.

D. the medicine is not available over-the-counter.

WRONG: Medicines for both diarrhea and constipation are apparently available "over-the-counter" (line 56).

29. What is the intended relevance of the comment, "In a 'take two aspirin and call me in the morning' approach …" (lines 41–42), to the rest of the passage?

It is not necessary to recognize or completely understand the meaning of this quote. This question can be answered by determining which answer choices are correct extrapolations of passage information and then realizing that the quote involves a doctor's 'treatment.'

A. To explain the prevailing belief that IBS is caused primarily by stress or a similar psychosomatic factor.

WRONG: First, this is not the "prevailing belief"; "approximately *half* believe the condition is caused primarily by stress or a similar psychosomatic factor" (lines 7–9). Second, the quote has to do with 'treatment.'

B. To show that to conveniently label an unknown case as "IBS" often prevents further investigation.

WRONG: The quote has nothing to do with 'labeling' or 'investigation.' It has to do with 'treatment.'

C. To express the general inadequacy of any treatments of IBS.

WRONG: The main symptoms of IBS, "Constipation [and] … Similarly, simple diarrhea [are] easily treated" (lines 52–55).

D. To indicate that physicians do not understand the underlying causes of IBS and treat it like a syndrome.

CORRECT: The passage tells us that physicians consider IBS a 'syndrome' (lines 4–7), and that they do not understand the underlying causes of it (lines 38–39). This answer, like the quote in the question, has to do with 'treatment.'

30. The author suggests that the difficulty of using medicines to treat constipation and diarrhea results from the fact that those afflicted:

A. must get a prescription because the medicines are addictive.

WRONG: The medicines may be "addictive," but there is no information that they are not all available "over-the-counter" (line 56).

B. can become addicted to the medicine, though it can be purchased without a prescription.

Copyright © 2008 Examkrackers, Inc.

CORRECT: "While these over-the-counter laxatives and antispasmodics will effectively cure or prevent the symptoms of IBS temporarily, their addictiveness and increasing side effects do not permit their continuous use" (lines 56–59).

C.   must get a prescription for the medicine, though there is no danger of addiction.

   WRONG: See the quote accompanying Answer B.

D.   must decide if the increasing side effects of the medicine are worth the trouble.

   WRONG: There is no suggestion that a 'decision' must be made by the patient about medicines.

Passage VI (Questions 31–35)

31. According to one authority on illiteracy and public safety, efforts to render all public transportation signs and directions into more easily understood 'symbols,' rather than written directions and words, must continue. This authority would probably:

   The premise of this question closely approximates lines 11–12: "Occasionally, cryptography was even used without any intention of hiding the messages."

A.   agree with the passage suggestion that written communication is sometimes unclear.

   WRONG: This is comparatively vague. It is much less responsive to the question than is Answer B. This is not the *best* answer.

B.   agree with the passage suggestion that what is communication for one group is a code to another.

   CORRECT: The additional information of this question closely approximates lines 11–12: "Occasionally, cryptography was even used without any intention of hiding the messages." However, in this instance, the 'accidental encryption' and/or failure to effectively communicate becomes a safety issue because many foreigners and illiterate persons may not be able to "read" signs.

C.   disagree with the passage suggestion that encryption promotes simpler communication.

   WRONG: There is no such "passage suggestion."

D.   disagree with the passage suggestion that codes are most often used by the military.

   WRONG: This is a passage suggestion. However, the additional information in the question has nothing to do with any military applications or the military.

32. According to the passage, the Spartan's "scytale" (lines 61–66) was characteristic of:

A.   the substitution code.

   WRONG: It was not a "code," and it was not characteristic of the "substitution" system. "An

alternate type of enciphering methodology is the *transposition system* … Ancient Spartans, who invented a primitive enciphering machine [called the "scytale"], used this type" (lines 54–58).

B.   the substitution cipher.

   WRONG: It was not the "substitution" cipher. "An alternate type of enciphering methodology is the *transposition* system … Ancient Spartans, who invented a primitive enciphering machine [called the "scytale"], used this type" (lines 54–58).

C.   the 'alternate' type of cipher.

   CORRECT: "An *alternate type* of enciphering methodology is the transposition system … Ancient Spartans, who invented a primitive enciphering machine [called the "scytale"], used this type" (lines 54–58).

D.   the 'alternate' type of the "code."

   WRONG: It was not a "code." "An alternate type of *enciphering* methodology is the transposition system … Ancient Spartans, who invented a primitive enciphering machine [called the "scytale"], used this type" (lines 54–58).

33. According to the passage, which of the following was a *drawback* to the "code" (line 19)?

A.   Every intended user required a copy of the dictionary.

   CORRECT: This was a big *drawback* to the code. "More importantly, every intended user of the code must be given a copy of the dictionary" (lines 35–36).

B.   Without the dictionary, it was virtually indecipherable.

   WRONG: This is not a *drawback*.

C.   An interceptor who had found the pattern could decipher it.

   WRONG: This is not accurate. The "code" did *not* have any pattern. This was another big advantage.

D.   It was a flexible system.

   WRONG: This is not accurate: "A code is inflexible" (line 32). Moreover, had this been a true statement, this would have been an *advantage* and thus, not one of the possible choices for the correct answer.

34. An important comparison is made in the passage between:

A.   computers and "scytales."

   WRONG: There really is no comparison implied in the passage.

B.   cryptograms and substitution ciphers.

   WRONG: This is a little bit like comparing "fruit" to "navel oranges" or a very specific type of fruit.

Cryptograms encompass the *whole of encoding*, from "codes" to the two types of ciphers: substitution ciphers and transposition ciphers.

C. businesspersons and the military.

CORRECT: Lines 5–16 refer to this comparison. We are told the military primarily used encryption, but so, too, did businesspeople. Then the military *intention* of 'hiding information' was contrasted with the *unintentional* 'hiding of information' by businesspeople.

D. scrambling and encoding.

WRONG: This is, similarly to Answer B, a little bit like comparing "fruit" to "navel oranges" or a very specific type of fruit. Encoding was apparently synonymous with encryption, enciphering, scrambling, substitution, etc.

35. According to the passage, all of the following are true of the cipher EXCEPT:

A. The scrambled message itself is transmitted instead of code words.

WRONG: This is true: "… what is transmitted is the message itself, rather than a series of unrelated code words, that represent the message. But the message is 'scrambled'" (lines 43–45).

B. The cipher must follow some regular predictable pattern.

WRONG: This is true: "But, since enciphering must follow some regular predictable pattern, it can be deciphered by an interceptor who finds the pattern" (lines 68–70).

C. The system was relatively inflexible.

CORRECT: This is an exception and not true. "The cipher offers the advantage of flexibility" (line 66).

D. The "scytale" is an example.

WRONG: This is true: "Ancient Spartans, who invented a primitive *enciphering* machine, used this type [of device called a 'scytale']" (lines 57–58).

Passage VII (Questions 36–40)

36. The author suggests that a school-uniform policy is likely to be much more effective when it:

A. includes an "opt-out" provision.

WRONG: This is not suggested.

B. enlists parental involvement.

CORRECT: Lines 30–41 are replete with evidence for this answer.

C. responds to growing levels of violence.

WRONG: This is one of the *purposes* of the uniform policy. It is a *response* to "growing levels of

violence;" it is *not* more *effective* when it "responds to growing levels of violence."

D. is voluntary.

WRONG: There is no such suggestion.

37. Given the information in the passage, Los Angeles inner-city schools that are experiencing increasingly violent levels of gang activity most likely are undergoing this tribulation because:

A. the school has allowed an "opt-out" provision.

WRONG: The author does not express whether an "opt-out" provision is deleterious to the uniform policy or not.

B. the school is accommodating of the parents' wishes.

WRONG: This is not likely.

C. the school has not enlisted parental involvement.

WRONG: Though the passage provides that parental involvement is critical to the success of a uniform policy, you are assuming that there exists any uniform in Los Angeles. This is not provided in the question.

D. the school is permissive with its dress policy.

CORRECT: *Unlike* Answer C, this answer could be correct even if there was *no existing* dress policy. The permissiveness could be such that the dress policy is nonexistent. References to gangs in the passage refer to gang insignia and clothing. Uniform policies are "helping prevent gang members from wearing gang colors and insignia at school" (lines 10–12), and "schools have implemented dress codes *to encourage a safe environment* by, for example, prohibiting clothes with certain language or gang colors" (lines 25–27).

38. The commonly recognized meaning of the word "uniform" is most DISCREPANT with which of the following ideas from the passage?

"Uniform" commonly means *consistent*, *unvarying*, *standardized*.

A. Many schools that have successfully created a uniform policy first survey parents to gauge support for school uniform requirements and then seek parental input in designing the uniform.

WRONG: This is not discrepant with the word's meaning.

B. Religious messages may not be singled out for suppression, but rather are subject to the same rules as generally applied to comparable messages.

WRONG: This is not discrepant with the word's meaning.

C. Some schools have adopted wholly voluntary school-uniform policies that permit students to freely choose whether and under what circumstances they will wear the school uniform.

CORRECT: This is discrepant with the meaning of the word *uniform*. It just doesn't make much sense. What about *uniformity* of the *uniform*?! *If* students are permitted to wear, or *not* wear, or choose to wear only *parts* of a school "uniform," then it *cannot* truly be called a uniform, because it is *not uniform*. There is no standardization, consistency, or uniformity.

D. Some schools have determined that it is both warranted and more effective to adopt a mandatory uniform policy.

WRONG: This is not discrepant with the word's meaning.

39. The passage indicates that its author would agree with all of the following statements regarding the potential benefits of school uniforms EXCEPT:

A. help school officials to recognize intruders who come to the school

WRONG: This is not an exception. "The potential benefits of school uniforms include … helping school officials recognize intruders who come to the school" (lines 7–15).

B. help parents to resist peer pressure

WRONG: This is not an exception. "The potential benefits of school uniforms include … *helping parents* and students *resist peer pressure* … " (lines 7–15).

C. help students to concentrate on their school work

WRONG: This is not an exception. "The potential benefits of school uniforms include … helping students concentrate on their school work …" (lines 7–15).

D. help to overcome religious persecution

CORRECT: This is an exception. This is not a potential benefit offered in the passage or implied by the author. It is clear that religion is to get no more, or less consideration than other types of beliefs. "Religious messages may not be singled out for suppression, but rather are subject to the same rules as generally applied to comparable messages" (lines 50–52).

40. What distinction is implied in the passage between dress codes and uniform policies, respectively?

A. uniform requirement versus a certain style of dressing

WRONG: A dress code does not stipulate a uniform.

B. mandatory style of dressing versus voluntary policy

WRONG: A dress code does tell you what you *cannot* wear, but not in a "mandatory" fashion , just

as a uniform policy is not usually voluntary, since it is *uniform* or common to all.

C. prohibiting certain clothing versus adopting a type of clothing

CORRECT: A dress code would be *restrictive,* "for example, *prohibiting* clothes with certain language or gang colors" (lines 26–27), whereas a uniform policy would be generally *inclusive* or "*adoptive*," describing the uniform that is common to all.

D. adopting guideline codes versus adopting restrictions

WRONG: This is the opposite. A dress code would be restrictive, whereas a uniform policy would be generally inclusive.

A & E 9

Verbal Reasoning Test 10
Answers & Explanations

TEST 10 ANSWER KEY

1.	B	11.	A	21.	C	31.	D
2.	B	12.	A	22.	C	32.	B
3.	D	13.	D	23.	C	33.	A
4.	D	14.	B	24.	C	34.	D
5.	C	15.	C	25.	B	35.	D
6.	B	16.	A	26.	D	36.	A
7.	B	17.	D	27.	A	37.	C
8.	A	18.	A	28.	B	38.	D
9.	A	19.	B	29.	C	39.	B
10.	C	20.	D	30.	C	40.	C

Passage I (Questions 1–5)

1. According to the passage, an existing solution that closely resembles some aspects of OptiMark is:

    A. the system of "order matching."

    WRONG: This is an "existing solution." "Instead of buying on the open market, the institutional buyer may use the "*order-matching*" system, whereby it advertises its offer price *to large institutional sellers only*. However, this does not resolve the problem entirely, since posting the 'buy' order still tips their hand, albeit to a smaller group of players" (lines 19–23). However, it does *not* resemble an aspect of OptiMark, certainly not to the extent that "crossing sections" does (see Answer B explanation).

    B. the tactic of "crossing sections."

    CORRECT: This is an "existing solution" that closely resembles OptiMark. "Another currently available tactic is 'crossing sessions,' in which a computerized system attempts to *match* a large buy order with an equally large block seller" (lines 23–26).

    C. the NYSE's "rents."

    WRONG: This is *not* an "existing *solution*," but an apparent gripe of the author.

    D. a "contingent" purchase.

    WRONG: This is *not* an "existing solution" since it is a "result" of OptiMark (lines 35–36).

2. On the basis of information in the passage, one would generally expect the required use of OptiMark to be received most favorably by:

    A. institutional investors and NYSE member traders.

    WRONG: NYSE member traders who receive "large fees" and "are the only ones allowed to take orders on the NYSE" would *not* receive the "required use of OptiMark" favorably.

    B. ordinary traders and institutional buyers.

    CORRECT: These two groups would receive this news favorably. There are obvious advantages for the institutional buyers/investors, which are outlined at length in the passage. Additionally, "If ordinary traders could place trades through OptiMark for a smaller commission, they would not need to place them with NYSE brokers" (lines 59–62).

    C. NYSE member brokerages.

    WRONG: NYSE member brokerages who receive "large fees" and "are the only ones allowed to take orders on the NYSE" would *not* receive the "required use of OptiMark" favorably.

    D. broker-dealers and institutional buyers.

    WRONG: Broker-dealers would *not* receive the "required use of OptiMark" favorably. "… if

OptiMark could convince the exchanges to *require* its use (*over broker-dealers' protests*), it could earn commissions from exchange trading" (lines 49–51).

3. Which of the following statements is the most reasonable conclusion that can be drawn from the author's description of OptiMark?

    A. If OptiMark could develop a computerized block-trading service they could become profitable.

    WRONG: This is *not* a reasonable conclusion. OptiMark *already is* a "computerized block-trading service" (line 30).

    B. It is likely that OptiMark would be charging monopolistic "rents" if it became widely accepted.

    WRONG: This is *not* a reasonable conclusion.

    C. The larger the number of shares an institution is willing to buy, the better the price that institution may obtain for those shares.

    WRONG: This is *not* a reasonable conclusion. The only information we have regarding buying large numbers of shares is that it happens infrequently (lines 47–48), institutional investors do it, and if sellers find out about it, they will raise the prices of the shares they hold to take advantage of this.

    D. Institutional investors attempting to acquire voting control of a corporation is an infrequent occurrence.

    CORRECT: This is the most reasonable conclusion among the answer choices. OptiMark "could still earn commissions even if it were used only by institutions trading outside the traditional markets [who are attempting to obtain large numbers of shares], though apparently there is not enough volume in those markets to make OptiMark worthwhile" (lines 45–49).

4. If the description of OptiMark in lines 29–40 is correct, one could most reasonably conclude that:

    A. using OptiMark, a "match" of the seller's offer must be made with the buyer's offer before any intent is revealed.

    WRONG: This is *not* the most reasonable conclusion. It is *not* clear if the seller's intentions are *ever* revealed! Thus, this answer is based on an assumption and lacks the specificity of Answer D. "If supply is insufficient, the trade is automatically reversed, *with no seller learning about the buyer's intentions*" (lines 37–39).

    B. using OptiMark, the buyer would know the seller's intentions, but not vice versa.

    WRONG: This is *not* a reasonable conclusion. It is *not* clear if the seller's intentions are *ever* revealed! Additionally, it is clear that the buyer's intentions may, at some point, be revealed. "If supply is insufficient, the trade is automatically reversed, *with no seller learning about the buyer's intentions*" (lines 37–39).

C.   using OptiMark, the seller would know the buyer's intentions, but not vice versa.

WRONG: This is *not* the most reasonable conclusion. It is clear that the buyer's intentions will, at some point, be revealed. "If supply is insufficient, the trade is automatically reversed, *with no seller learning about the buyer's intentions*" (lines 37–39).

D.   using OptiMark, a seller's offer must match the buyer's offer before the buyer's intent is revealed.

CORRECT: This is the most reasonable conclusion. "If supply is insufficient, the trade is automatically reversed, *with no seller learning about the buyer's intentions*" (lines 37–39).

5. According to the passage, in the existing system, institutional investors looking to buy large numbers of shares cannot avoid:

A.   the price-creeping problem.

WRONG: This *can* be avoided. "If successful, [the currently available tactic of crossing sessions] would of course solve the price-creeping problem" (lines 26–27).

B.   paying large commissions to NYSE brokerages.

WRONG: This *can* be avoided. It is not inevitable. For instance, if the buyers wanted to buy stock shares that were not offered by the NYSE but by the NASDAQ or some other exchange system, they would not have to pay *any* commissions to NYSE brokerages.

C.   revealing their intentions to other sellers.

CORRECT: This *cannot* be avoided in the currently existing system. None of the existing systems "resolve the problem entirely, since posting the 'buy' order still tips their hand, albeit to a smaller group of players" (lines 21–23).

D.   buying their shares in a piecemeal fashion.

WRONG: This *can* be avoided. "Another currently available tactic is 'crossing sessions' in which a computerized system attempts to match a large buy order with an equally large block seller" (lines 23–26). *If* this is successful, then there is no piecemeal buying.

Passage II (Questions 6–11)

6. It can most justifiably be said that the main purpose of the passage is:

A.   to describe the life and difficulties of a prostitute.

WRONG: This is not the main purpose of the

passage. This answer is devoid of any references to the pimp who is described at length in the passage in five of the six paragraphs. According to the passage, the prostitute's life essentially revolves around her pimp. She begins her career with the pimp and hopes to end it and retire with him (lines 56–60). This answer is, therefore, not as responsive to the question as Answer B. This is not the best answer.

B.   to explain the relationship between a prostitute and her pimp.

CORRECT: Of the six paragraphs in the passage, *five* of them are devoted to explaining this relationship. The prostitute begins her career with the pimp and hopes to end it and retire with him (lines 56–60).

C.   to illustrate the reasons why a woman would become a prostitute.

WRONG: This is not the main purpose of the passage. The only real mention of this is at the tail end of the last paragraph (psychologists' views) and early on in the passage where it explains that many prostitutes have illegitimate children before they begin their careers.

D.   to deemphasize the role of prostitutes as bad mothers.

WRONG: This is not the main purpose of the passage. It may not even be a purpose of the passage, though the short mention in paragraph two to attempts at day care point to strong mothering characteristics.

7. What is the most serious apparent *weakness* of the research described?

Upon first reading the passage, the nuances of the weaknesses in the author's argument may be difficult to discern. This would normally, then, make this a difficult question. However, the other wrong choices are fairly obviously not "weaknesses." Thus, by *process of elimination*, Answer B can be chosen without recognizing the nuanced arguments necessary to support it.

A.   The penalties for prostitution are notoriously low.

WRONG: This is not a serious weakness of the passage. The author provides an example. Further, the truth of this statement does not seriously reflect upon other major tenets of the passage.

B.   The mature prostitutes are described as both delusional and realistic.

CORRECT: This is a serious *weakness* in the passage. The author states, "The reasons [women tend to become prostitutes] appear to be *delusional* rather than *rational*" (line 55). *However*, the prostitutes are then described in several places as being completely and realistically aware that their "man doesn't do anything" and that "[the prostitutes] themselves *realize* [the pimp] takes their hard-earned money

A & E 10

in exchange for nothing tangible" (lines 49–51). Yet this idea is countered by the pimp as a day-care provider and banker, if nothing else. Even the author admits that "while a young and *naïve* prostitute may be excused for believing it, more experienced streetwalkers, who have been abandoned by a succession of pimps, *cannot still harbor the hope of it happening*" (lines 61–64). The author cannot seem to decide if the prostitutes are "delusional," rational, or just psychologically traumatized.

C. A long record of arrests makes obtaining credit impossible.

WRONG: This is not a serious weakness in the passage and may not be a weakness at all. There is no indication whether this is true or not true, and outside knowledge regarding the truth of this statement would not be considered common knowledge.

D. A prostitute's wages are tax-free.

WRONG: This is not a serious weakness of the passage. The author provides explanation and evidence that the wages are not reported to the government. They are hidden through the means of the pimp as a banker (lines 25–28).

8. Which of the following opinions would the author be most likely to endorse?

A. In the case of more mature prostitutes, their pimps are often their lovers and boyfriends.

CORRECT: The author would most likely endorse this opinion. "Pimps often promise their women that, at the end of their careers, after they have accumulated enough money for them, *the pimp will marry them*" (lines 56–58). If they believe that the pimp will marry them, it stands to reason that they have some sort of romantic relationship with him to base this on.

B. In the case of more mature prostitutes, they realize the importance of what they pay their pimp.

WRONG: The author would not *clearly* endorse this opinion. This presentation of these concepts is simply not clear. The author contradicts himself in the passage. On the one hand, the prostitutes are described as "delusional." The author states, "The reasons [women tend to become prostitutes] appear to be *delusional* rather than *rational*" (line 55). *However*, the prostitutes are then described in several places as being completely and realistically aware that their "man doesn't do anything" and that "[the prostitutes] themselves *realize* [the pimp] takes their hard-earned money *in exchange for nothing tangible*" (lines 49–51). Even the author admits that "while a young and *naïve* prostitute may be excused for believing it, more experienced streetwalkers, who have been abandoned by a succession of pimps, *cannot still harbor the hope of it happening*"

(lines 61–64). The author cannot seem to decide if the prostitutes are "delusional," rational, or just psychologically traumatized.

C. In the case of a novice prostitute, the pimp provides them valuable information on safety.

WRONG: The author would not *clearly* endorse this opinion. We have no way of knowing if the author would agree or not. There is, surprisingly, no mention of "safety" anywhere in the passage. "And for a novice prostitute, a pimp's advice—on the most profitable and least competitive streets, on avoiding police patrols and arrests, and on ways of extracting the most money from clients—may indeed be valuable" (lines 38–41).

D. In the case of the novice prostitute, they recognize the pimp provides them with little.

WRONG: The author would not endorse this opinion. It is fairly clear that the "novice prostitute" does gain some benefit from the pimp's advice (lines 38–41). Further, he acts as a day-care provider and banker.

9. The author of the passage would be most likely to agree with which of the following ideas expressed by other researchers?

A. Pimps usually remain with the prostitute for her entire working career.

WRONG: The author would not clearly agree and would most probably disagree. Mature prostitutes might find themselves "perhaps replacing their current pimp with another, similar one" (lines 48–49). The "promise" of marriage, a house, investments with the pimp "is rarely fulfilled" (lines 58–60).

B. Prostitutes enjoy their work.

WRONG: The author would not clearly agree. He does not mention or imply this idea in the passage.

C. Prostitutes often drift away from stable upbringings.

WRONG: The author would disagree. "Most of the women who turn to street prostitution share a remarkably similar upbringing: a lack of a strong father figure early in childhood (e.g., raised by a single mother or an abusive father/stepfather), and an early and traumatic experience with sex (e.g., a teen pregnancy, rape, or often incest)" (lines 66–71).

D. The pimp acts as a father figure for the prostitute.

CORRECT: The author would clearly agree with this idea. "Also, it leaves them with the craving for a powerful male figure *to substitute for the absent father/husband figure*. The pimp appears to fill this need, as an exploitative and abusive but powerfully macho and 'male' figure" (lines 74–78).

10. The author claims that "the pimp acts as a banker to his stable" (lines 25–26). The support offered for this conclusion is:

This is a typical MCAT question. Remember to first ascertain if the second clause of the answer is accurate and true, thereby eliminating some choices. Then decide if the accurate second clause strengthens (strong) or weakens (weak) the author's claim.

A. strong; the author argues that, for obvious reasons, a prostitute cannot deposit a thousand dollars a day in a bank without declaring taxable income.

WRONG: The second clause is accurate and true. However, it *weakens* the author's claim. "For obvious reasons, a prostitute cannot deposit a thousand dollars a day in a bank without declaring taxable income" (lines 26–28). "However, the *primary beneficiary* of these earnings is often not the prostitute herself, but her pimp, who, for 'managing' a prostitute, usually keeps for himself an amazing 85% of her earnings." (lines 6–9). Therefore, this second clause offers "weak" support; *a prostitute doesn't actually have a thousand dollars a day to worry about* because her pimp has 85% of the money!

B. strong; the author argues that prostitution penalties are notoriously low.

WRONG: The second clause of this answer is accurate and true. However, it has nothing to do with the author's claim.

C. weak; the author argues that, for obvious reasons, a prostitute cannot deposit a thousand dollars a day in a bank without declaring taxable income.

CORRECT: The second clause is accurate and true. However, it *weakens* the author's claim. "For obvious reasons, a prostitute cannot deposit a thousand dollars a day in a bank without declaring taxable income" (lines 26–28). "However, the *primary beneficiary* of these earnings is often not the prostitute herself, but her pimp, who, for 'managing' a prostitute, usually keeps for himself an amazing 85% of her earnings" (lines 6–9). Therefore, this second clause offers "weak" support; *a prostitute doesn't actually have a thousand dollars a day to worry about* because her pimp has 85% of the money!

D. weak; the author argues that prostitution penalties are notoriously low.

WRONG: The second clause of this answer is accurate and true. However, it has nothing to do with the author's claim.

11. The passage states that prostitutes are:

A. likely to have an illegitimate child before beginning prostitution.

CORRECT: "Many prostitutes *begin* their professional careers *after* having an illegitimate child at an early age" (lines 15–17).

B. not likely to care for their illegitimate children.

WRONG: This is not true. Their "first goal" is to get the children to come and live with them, and then they do what they can to keep them in day care.

C. likely to have an illegitimate child early on in their career.

WRONG: This is not true. "Many prostitutes *begin* their professional careers *after* having an illegitimate child at an early age" (lines 15–17).

D. likely to keep their children with them while they work.

WRONG: This is not true. They keep them in day care of one type or another.

Passage III (Questions 12–17)

12. The central thesis of the passage is that:

   I. a person can learn to 'read' others in order to gain a more accurate impression of them.

   CORRECT: This is the central thesis of the passage, and a pretty easy answer to this question. Look at the first sentence in the form of a classic "topic sentence." This is a passage about "people-reading" and predicting behavior through these readings.

   II. a person can learn to convey the appropriate impression to others.

   WRONG: This is neither the central thesis nor a thesis of this passage. "Conveyance" of an impression is not implied. It is the "reading" of traits and characteristics for the purposes of predicting behaviors that is promoted.

   III. a person can learn to 'read' the impression he is conveying to others.

   WRONG: This is neither the central thesis nor a thesis of this passage. "Conveyance" of an impression is not implied. It is the "reading" of traits and characteristics for the purposes of predicting behaviors that is promoted.

A. I only

CORRECT: See above answer explanations.

B. II only
C. III only
D. I and II only

Copyright © 2008 Examkrackers, Inc.

13. According to the passage, the only real limitations to "people-reading" would be the evaluator's:

    I.   inability to hear.

        WRONG: This would *not* be a limitation to "people-reading" as described in the passage. Though some verbal interaction *might* be *helpful* in confirming some characteristics, it is not required. Even the terminology indicates that hearing is irrelevant: "reading," "visible characteristics and appearance," "observer," "focus."

    II.   lack of background information on the 'target.'

        CORRECT: This would be a very real limitation. The "predictive traits" (lines 34–54) such as "compassion, satisfaction, and socioeconomic fulfillment," which reveal character, would take a long time to observe, if they could be observed at all, and would be better confirmed through some kind of background information.

    III. inability to see.

        CORRECT: This would be a very real limitation, and given only the information in the passage, would render "people-reading" impossible. The art of "people-reading" is primarily a visual one, as indicated by the terminology used: "reading," "visible characteristics and appearance," "observer," "focus," "look for."

A. I only
B. II only
C. III only
D. II and III only

    CORRECT: See above answer explanations.

14. The author's example of the significance of "a man who is usually on his best behavior, but is prone to rare fits of anger or cursing" (lines 64–65) is most *weakened* by which idea that is implicit in the passage?

Notice that the correct answer choice must *first* be an idea that is implicit in the passage. *Then* it must weaken the author's example.

A. Traits that deviate from the norm are also good predictive traits.

    WRONG: This is an idea that is implicit in the passage. "Other predictive traits tend to be those that deviate from the norm" (lines 55–56). However, this idea in no way *weakens* the author's example given in the question. Therefore, it cannot be a correct answer.

B. To determine general behavior over time, patterns should be used.

    CORRECT: This is an idea that is implicit in the passage. "The experienced observer will seek to locate patterns of behavior rather than isolated traits or gestures since patterns are more predictive of general behavior over time" (lines 20–22). Additionally, this idea *weakens* the author's example given in the question. If the "fits of anger or cursing" are "*rare*," it is difficult to see how they can form a pattern. This is the best answer.

C. Almost everyone has gotten very angry at one time or another in their lives.

    WRONG: This is *not* an idea that is implicit in the passage; therefore, though it *weakens* the author's example, it cannot be a correct answer.

D. Anger and cursing is usually caused by situational factors that can be ignored.

    WRONG: This is *not* an idea that is implicit in the passage; therefore, though it *weakens* the author's example, it cannot be a correct answer.

15. According to the ideas presented, people-reading must be done systematically to avoid snap judgments, and "uncaring people tend to be critical, intolerant, harsh and punitive, and prone to impetuous snap judgments" (lines 40–42). If both of these premises are true, what conclusion is most reasonable?

A. A good people-reader should be somewhat critical.

    WRONG: This is *not* a reasonable conclusion. A "good people-reader" should "avoid snap judgments," according to the first idea. Based upon the second idea, it seems at least possible that a "somewhat critical" person would be "prone to impetuous snap judgments." Even if this is not the case, there is reason to conclude that this answer would be correct based upon the ideas in the question.

B. A critical person would make a poor people-reader.

    WRONG: This is *not* a reasonable conclusion. A "good people-reader" should "avoid snap judgments," according to the first idea. Based upon the second idea, it seems at least possible that a "somewhat critical" person would be "prone to impetuous snap judgments." However, take the sentences apart. If you know logic, you will realize that "If A then B" does *not* also mean "If B then A." Simply because "uncaring people" = critical + intolerant + harsh + punitive + prone to impetuous snap judgments, does *not* necessarily mean that "critical"= "prone to impetuous snap judgments" and thus a poor people-reader. Because of the necessity of 'stretching' your reasoning, this is not the best answer.

C. Uncaring people would make poor people-readers.

    CORRECT: This is the most reasonable conclusion. Here we have a very direct relationship. A "good people-reader" should "avoid snap judgments,"

A & E 10

according to the first idea. The second idea tells us that "uncaring" people *are* "prone to impetuous snap judgments." This is the best answer.

D. The best people-readers are usually uncaring people.

WRONG: This is *not* a reasonable conclusion. This is the opposite of the correct answer and not supported in either of the ideas in the question or in the passage. You got mixed up somewhere in your reasoning. See the explanation for Answer C.

16. In the last paragraph, the author writes, "If a seemingly nonconformist trait has its basis in the person's foreign ancestry, it may actually signal a desire for conformity, rather than a rebellion against society" (lines 68–71). By this, the author most likely means that:

A. this person is attempting to conform to his/her own culture.

CORRECT: This is clearly the most likely meaning of the last paragraph. Read the last paragraph carefully. The author suggests that the person *is* signaling "a desire for conformity" to a "culture"/"society"/"ancestry." The *only* real question is conformity to *whose* "culture"/"society"/ "ancestry?" If the person is 'foreign' to us yet is conforming to a culture, it must be *his own* or some culture *other than our own*. This is the best answer.

B. the person is wrongly perceived as rebelling against his/her ancestry.

WRONG: This is clearly *not* the most likely meaning of the last paragraph. The person is "foreign" and is clearly perceived as rebelling against *our* society and culture because he is conforming to his *own* ancestry.

C. the person is attempting to conform to his/her new culture.

WRONG: This is clearly *not* the most likely meaning of the last paragraph. The person is "foreign" and, therefore, his/her "new culture" is *our* culture/ society. We can only assume that the apparent nonconformity in a person who desires to conform and is conforming is due to that person conforming to his/her own culture.

D. the person's ancestry is nonconformist.

WRONG: This is clearly *not* the most likely meaning of the last paragraph. The author suggests that the person *is* signaling "a desire for conformity." Arrival at this answer involves some tortured reasoning and consideration of facts that are not in evidence. Look carefully at the other answer explanations.

17. According to the passage, an inexperienced people-reader might most easily make the mistake of:

A. making a snap judgment about a "rogue" trait.

WRONG: This is not a *mistake*. Remember that just because an "inexperienced" person does something 'unwittingly' does not mean that it is necessarily a "mistake." A mistake is an inaccuracy or an error. The passage provides, "A person's 'rogue' traits are those inconsistent with his other apparent attributes and *are almost always predictive of his true nature*" (lines 61–64). Therefore, in this instance, a "snap judgment" would be very valuable, regardless whether the "inexperienced people-reader" recognized that this was a "rogue trait" or not.

B. trying to observe only traits that he/she felt were relevant to their purposes.

WRONG: This would not be a mistake. Remember that just because an "inexperienced" person does something 'unwittingly' does not mean that it is necessarily a "mistake." A mistake is an inaccuracy or an error. The passage provides that "*expert* people-readers focus on observing only those traits that are relevant to the purposes for which they are evaluating their target" (lines 17–19).

C. making broad generalizations regarding compassion or socioeconomic fulfillment.

WRONG: This would not necessarily be a mistake. Remember that just because an "inexperienced" person does something 'unwittingly' does not mean that it is necessarily a "mistake." A mistake is an inaccuracy or an error. This answer does not tell us that the "broad generalizations regarding …" were inaccurate or in error. Look at the author's stereotypical generalizations of these traits. If these aren't "broad generalizations" nothing is.

D. dismissing a "rogue trait."

CORRECT: This would be a mistake. A mistake is an inaccuracy or an error. "A person's 'rogue' traits are those inconsistent with his other apparent attributes and *are almost always predictive of his true nature*" (lines 61–64). Discovering a "rogue trait" is therefore very important. Dismissing it, or ignoring the finding, would be a big mistake.

Passage IV (Questions 18–22)

18. According to one authority on the Bible, "centuries of faithless secular analysis of the Bible was one of the primary reasons for the Protestant exodus from the Catholic Church." This authority would probably:

"The Muslims have the benefit of hindsight of the European experience, and they know very well that once you start questioning the holy scriptures, you don't know where it will stop" (lines 16–19).

A. consider the fears of extrareligious examination of the Koran by followers of Islam as valid.

CORRECT: This answer exactly parallels the question. The only item missing is a specific description of the Islamic "fears." However, we know from the question that there was an "exodus from the Catholic Church," which any religious faith could validly fear.

B. support further analysis of the Koran within the context of diacritical marks.

WRONG: This answer contains some true information and terminology from the passage. However, this answer is not responsive to the quote in the question.

C. not consider either the Koran or the followers of Islam to have any valid concerns.

WRONG: Answer A exactly parallels the question. This answer exactly opposes Answer A.

D. approve of analysis by Middle Eastern Jews and Christians only.

WRONG: One of the main ideas of the passage is that most followers of Islam *oppose* "extrareligious examination" in any form. Further, the likelihood that they would "approve" of those outside of their faith conducting this analysis is ludicrous in light of the passage.

19. The author suggests that the difficulty of performing a critical analysis of the Koran and then publishing the findings results from:

A. the Judeo-Christian experiences of studying the holy Psalms.

WRONG: You need it to say "Scriptures" or "Holy Scriptures," *not* "Psalms." If you are in a hurry, *and* skipped the last sentence of the passage, this answer looks pretty good. However, it is too *specific*. The "Psalms" are one very small portion of the Bible. They are certainly not indicative of Jewish *and* Christian *Scripture.* "'The Muslims have the benefit of hindsight of the European experience, and they know very well that once you start questioning the *holy scriptures*, you don't know where it will stop,'" (lines 16–19).

B. reluctance to criticize other cultures.

CORRECT: "[I]t's not possible to say anything other than sugary nonsense about Islam," said one scholar … referring to … the widespread reluctance … to criticize other cultures" (lines 64–69).

C. instructions within the Koran "to kill" those who would perform such an act.

WRONG: There is no information from the passage that the Koran has within it instructions "to kill" those would critically analyze it.

D. an inability to understand the ancient Aramaic scripts.

WRONG: This causes problems and variations in interpretation, but it is *not* an obstacle to critical analysis.

20. What is the intended relevance of the comment that "between fear and political correctness, it's not possible to say anything other than sugary nonsense about Islam" (lines 63–65), to the rest of the passage?

A. Islamic people are difficult to understand.

WRONG: This is not responsive to the question. Further, there is no passage information to indicate that Islamic "people" are difficult to understand.

B. Religious books such as the Koran and the Bible cannot be critically analyzed without danger.

WRONG: If not read carefully, this answer would seem to be the correct answer. However, when the words "*and the Bible*" are added, this answer is placed completely outside of any passage information. There is no passage evidence that analyzing "the Bible" is "dangerous." It may be deleterious to the Church, but apparently not dangerous.

C. The Koran is probably not "the very word of God.".

WRONG: This is not responsive to the question.

D. A critical analysis of the Koran has not been accomplished

CORRECT: Based upon the *entire* last paragraph, one may assume that this answer is correct. "*Mr. Berlin would love to see a 'critical edition' of the Koran produced …*" Yet, "between fear and political correctness, it's not possible to say anything other than sugary nonsense about Islam," said one scholar … referring to the threatened violence as well as the widespread reluctance on United States college campuses to criticize other cultures" (lines 59–69).

21. Assume that scientists and physicists studying Genesis, the first book of the Bible, discover that it actually gives an accurate explanation of the beginnings of the universe. Which of the following hypotheses does this assumption suggest?

A. Scientists and physicists have a great deal to learn about the Koran.

WRONG: This is not suggested by the assumption in the question.

B. Extrareligious examination and interpretation of sacred texts continues to undermine their credibility.

WRONG: The assumption provided in the question refutes this answer.

C. Extrareligious examination and interpretation of sacred texts does not necessarily undermine their credibility.

CORRECT: The question gives *specific* information, which is then *generalized* in this answer. "Scientists and physicists," as opposed to theologians, can be assumed to be doing an "extra-religious examination and interpretation." The Bible is considered a "sacred text." Finally, anything that furthers, or supports, the ideas of a sacred text does not undermine its credibility.

D. Extrareligious examination and interpretation of the Koran will help to prove its accuracy.
WRONG: If this answer read "*might* help to prove" instead of "*will* help to prove," it would have been a contender for the correct answer. The assumption of the question certainly does not indicate that what happened with the Bible "will" happen in a completely different instance.

22. According to the passage, which of the following is most likely to be true about the relationship between Muslims and Jews?

It is very important with these types of questions not to draw heavily on outside experiences and sources of information, such as the Israeli-Palestinian conflicts, etc.

A. They are both people of great religious fervor.
WRONG: There is no evidence in the passage to support this. You are drawing upon experience and information from outside the scope of the passage.

B. Centuries of hatred have brought them to the brink of war.
WRONG: There is no evidence in the passage to support this. You are drawing upon experience and information from outside the scope of the passage.

C. The language of the Muslim's Koran is closely related to Jewish Aramaic.
CORRECT: Though the author admits that it is a "*radical* theory," "many of the text's difficulties can be clarified when the text is seen as *closely related to Aramaic, the language of most Middle Eastern Jews* and Christians at the time" (lines 45–48). In the case of this question, none of the other answer choices are acceptable.

D. They have learned not to allow their Koran to be criticized.
WRONG: Read this answer carefully. There is no passage information that "*Jews* learned not to allow *their* Koran to be criticized." "Muslims and *Jews*" have little in common other than Answer C.

Passage V (Questions 23–28)

23. The main argument of the passage is that:

A. Oakland wished to teach Ebonics to African-American children.

WRONG: This is only one aspect of the passage. The passage also points out, "There was an absolute failure of communication between the Oakland School District and the world at large" (lines 39–41).

B. it is incontrovertible that Ebonics is a proven method of teaching Standard English.
WRONG: This extreme statement is not supported by the passage. "There seemed to be good and positive evidence" (lines 8–9) that AAVE helped the children, yet even this statement is equivocal. Ebonics came later, and the author actually provides no information regarding its effectiveness.

C. we cannot learn from one another if we cannot communicate.
CORRECT: "What is ironic is that, in a larger sense, communication relates not only to the issue of Ebonics, but also to the debate *about* Ebonics. There was an absolute failure of communication between the Oakland School District and the world at large" (lines 37–41). The children could not learn from the teachers if they could not communicate, and the world at large could not learn from the Oakland School District what it planned to do with AAVE because they could not communicate.

D. the label Ebonics was being used in a pejorative way.
WRONG: There is no passage information to support this assertion.

24. In the context of the passage, the phrase "rough seas" refers primarily to the:

The ship and its fate are a *metaphor* and thus have at least two meanings: "the AAVE ship '*Titanic*' … was filled with young African-American children this time out as she moved deeper into the waters of the world, and they were unable to communicate with others about the rough seas ahead" (lines 67–71).

A. cultural attacks on the children's primary language.
WRONG: This is not an aspect of the metaphor.

B. opportunity offered to teach AAVE in Oakland.
WRONG: The "opportunity" was going to encounter trouble, but it is not meant to be a part of the metaphor.

C. children's chances for success in the outside world.
CORRECT: The African-American children were in the "AAVE ship '*Titanic*'." AAVE was to "sink" in the "world." The "rough seas" would be their inability to learn to communicate with their teachers. "Unable to communicate, they did poorly in school and thus were failing to learn the skills and *ways of speaking* that were required in order to be successful in the world outside of their local neighborhoods" (lines 19–22).

A & E 10

D. death of the original *Titanic* passengers.

WRONG: The whole *Titanic* scenario is used as an extreme metaphor and certainly does refer to the doom of the original passengers. But *not primarily* so. See Answer C.

25. The passage implies that teaching is less effective when it:

A. is attempted in the native tongue.

WRONG: This is not implied: "the missionaries [who are teaching] … are less effective if they simply ignore the native tongue" (lines 35–36).

B. is performed in a demeaning fashion.

CORRECT: This is implied: "the missionaries [who are teaching]… are less effective if they … *demean* [the native tongue] as inferior to English" (lines 35–37).

C. is scrutinized by the media.

WRONG: This is not implied. Though the media gave Oakland poor press, this was due to poor communication, not mere scrutiny.

D. involves missionaries.

WRONG: This is not implied. Though the passage refers to problems the missionaries may have had, there is no implication that their involvement with teaching rendered the teaching less effective. Moreover, *involvement* assumes other teachers or organizations. In this case, there is no information that would suggest that *any* teaching would have taken place *without* the missionaries.

26. The passage suggests that objection to the phrase "primary language" derives from the fact that:

A. most people did not want their children to be taught to speak AAVE.

WRONG: This is a very poor second choice to the correct answer. This answer uses the word "their" children, indicating that the "people" were the *parents* of the children. There is *no* passage information that refers to *parents* of the children not wanting them to learn to speak a language. The sole passage mention that might lead you to believe that this Answer, or Answer B, is correct, would be, "None of the efforts lasted long, mainly because there was a negative reaction to using the [1969 AAVE] readers" (lines 11–12). However, this is completely nonspecific regarding why there was a negative reaction.

B. most people did not want their children to be taught to speak Ebonics.

WRONG: The reasons for choosing this answer would have been better supported by incorrect Answer A. There is little indication that parents did not want their children to be taught to speak

Ebonics. The sentence, "None of the efforts lasted long, mainly because there was a negative reaction to using the [1969 AAVE] readers" (lines 11–12), as indicated, refers to *AAVE*. It does go on to say, "This issue and the use of this dialect were to resurface, and they were characterized as Ebonics" (lines 13–14), but this is very weak.

C. Standard English is the only acceptable primary language.

WRONG: This is not supported by passage information. It is an inference that can only be drawn if one misses the main passage thrust regarding a failure to communicate. This is the weakest of the answer choices.

D. the true meaning of this phrase was not communicated.

CORRECT: Question 23 resolves that the main theme of the passage was a failure to *communicate*, not just between the children and their teachers, but also between the school district and the world at large. But *what* was it that they failed to communicate? "This phrase '*primary language*,' but not necessarily its meaning, was seized upon by the outside world [and misinterpreted by it]" (lines 51–52). From line 42 to line 71, the entire section is about *primary language*. Finally, "The misunderstandings revolving around this phrase [*primary language*] were only the tip of the iceberg [yet, still the critical example for the arguments offered in this passage] in this ironic debate about communication in which no communication took place" (lines 64–66).

27. According to the passage, why did the school district refer to AAVE as the "primary language"?

A. This was the language spoken at the children's homes with their friends and families.

CORRECT: What [*primary* language] meant was that it was the children's primary *home* language, "the language they spoke with their families and friends" (lines 45–46).

B. This was to be the language that all African-American children learned to speak in school.

WRONG: AAVE and Ebonics were meant only as temporary measures to help facilitate communication; "it was hoped that AAVE would serve as a 'bridge' to help the children learn to speak a more commonly used dialect: Standard English" (lines 25–27). Like the missionaries, it was the teachers who were to learn to communicate in this dialect; the African-American children, for the most part, already knew how.

C. This name was more acceptable than 'Ebonics.'

WRONG: The name AAVE actually came first. Further, there is no information that 'Ebonics' was an 'unacceptable' name.

D. This language was considered the equivalent of Standard English.

WRONG: This answer is not supported by the passage. AAVE and Ebonics were meant only as temporary measures to help facilitate communication; "it was hoped that AAVE would serve as a 'bridge' to help the children learn to speak a more commonly used dialect: Standard English" (lines 25–27).

28. The discussion of missionaries and their efforts to teach English in other countries (lines 32–37) shows primarily that:

A. teachers must speak only English when trying to teach English.

WRONG: This idea is refuted in the passage. "[T]he missionaries are less effective if they simply *ignore* the native tongue" (lines 35–36).

B. teachers can teach more effectively if they learn to speak and understand the native language.

CORRECT: "One of the first jobs of missionaries … is to *learn the local language* and to help the natives to learn to speak English, in order for them to be able to understand one another. Moreover, the missionaries are *less effective if they simply ignore the native tongue*" (lines 32–36).

C. missionaries never demeaned their pupils.

WRONG: This *cannot* be inferred from the passage. However, the *opposite* idea can be inferred from the passage. If we know that "the missionaries are less effective if they … demean [the native tongue] as inferior to English" (lines 35–37), it is reasonable to assume that we know this because it *had* happened.

D. students are more willing to learn if their teacher is a missionary.

WRONG: This is not supported by passage information. There is *no* indication regarding whether the students of the missionaries were willing to learn or not to learn, much less is there a comparison between teachers who were and teachers who were not missionaries.

Passage VI (Questions 29–34)

29. The author's central thesis is that:

A. there should be two sets of standards for judging morality.

WRONG: This is the antithesis of the passage. The author asserts that civil and military atrocities should be viewed the same way by the same standard: control.

B. violence is inevitable.

WRONG: This is not a thesis of the passage. In fact, "inevitability" infers that there is no control.

C. "control" determines culpability.

CORRECT: The author proposes that "our moral judgment [culpability] of a specific action is intrinsic to the control held by an actor over his situation" (lines 11–13).

D. the Germans were amoral.

WRONG: This *might* be inferred by the author's use of the adjective "innocent" to describe the people gassed to death. However, it is not the central thesis and is not as good an answer as Answer C.

30. The passage suggests that if a perfectly functioning precision "smart bomb" hits a hospital, producing many civilian casualties, it may be reasonable to assume that:

"However, if calculated and premeditated *control* is introduced to the bombing … the act is judged immoral and unacceptable" (lines 46–49). Who had *control* of the bomb when it hit the hospital?

A. the pilot who caused the bomb to hit the hospital should not be held responsible.

WRONG: This answer provides that the pilot "*caused*" the bomb to hit the hospital. The pilot had "control" over this "smart bomb." He *is* responsible.

B. 'smart bombs' are not as useful as one might think.

WRONG: The question includes a "perfectly functioning 'smart bomb'" to preclude the consideration of error in the answer. The bomb is not the problem.

C. the pilot who caused the bomb to hit the hospital should be charged with murder.

CORRECT: The question includes a "perfectly functioning 'smart bomb'" to preclude the consideration of error in the answer. This answer provides that the pilot "*caused*" the bomb to hit the hospital. The pilot had "control" over this "smart bomb."

D. the officer back at the base, who initially ordered the bombing of the area but not the hospital, is at fault.

WRONG: This officer ordered the bombing "of the area *but not the hospital*." *Once the plane was away, he no longer had "control." The question includes a "perfectly functioning* 'smart bomb'" to preclude the consideration of error in the answer.

31. Which of the following assertions does the author support with an example?

I. Criminal laws accurately reflect the concept of "control."

CORRECT: Example: "*For instance*, an insane man has no control over his own actions and cannot be held responsible; he can commit no crime" (lines 15–17).

A & E 10

II. Unpredictable circumstances in battle induce our empathy.

CORRECT: Example: "In comparison, other war crimes, *such as* the shooting of momentarily unarmed combatants during a battle, do not conjure up the same intensity of outrage" (lines 34–37).

III. In wartime, where intricate control is possible, we require detailed explanations of any loss of noncombatant life.

CORRECT: Example: "Moreover, in the intricate control of which pinpoint bombing is capable, *as was done in Baghdad*, we require detailed explanations for any loss of noncombatant life" (lines 50–52).

A. I only
B. I and II only
C. I and III only
D. I, II, and III

CORRECT: All three of the assertions are supported with examples (see above).

32. The men, women, and children whom the Germans herded into the gas chambers are described as "innocent." What is the most likely reason for the choice of this word?

A. They all were actually innocent of any crimes.

WRONG: This is not implied and is *very* unlikely given the millions of people who were killed. For this answer to be incorrect, it would only require that *one* of the millions of "men, women, and children" had committed some type of crime in his or her life.

B. To more intensely convey the horror of this fate.

CORRECT: The author is attempting to make a rather extreme analogy between the "innocent" people who were gassed and the "innocent" people who were bombed by the Allies. The number of people killed and the way in which they died are underscored by the use of the word "innocent."

C. They were sentenced to death even though a jury had found them innocent.

WRONG: There is no evidence that they were *actually* sentenced to death, and there is certainly no evidence that they all were found to be innocent. See incorrect Answer A.

D. This is only the author's opinion.

WRONG: It is the author's opinion, since their state of innocence *cannot* be completely true (see Answers A and B). However, there is more to it than this. This is not the best answer.

33. According to the passage, which of the following actions is/are unacceptable?

I. A soldier killing an armed enemy soldier

WRONG: Acceptable: An enemy soldier has the *will* and *orders* to kill. An "armed" enemy soldier has the ability to kill. Given this information, with *no* other information regarding whether the soldier has any ability to *control* the situation, the action is acceptable

II. A soldier killing an armed child who is trying to kill him

WRONG: Acceptable: The child is trying to kill the soldier (i.e. presenting a threat) and is *armed* (i.e. he has the ability to kill the soldier). Given this information, with *no* other information regarding whether the soldier has any ability to *control* the situation, the action is acceptable.

III. A soldier killing a restrained enemy soldier who has surrendered within the last two days

CORRECT: This is unacceptable. The soldier has *control* and can *avoid* the killing. The enemy is "restrained" (i.e. tied up, or handcuffed, or being held), and he had surrendered (i.e. willfully given himself up) as opposed to simply having been captured against his will.

A. II only
B. III only

CORRECT: See above answer explanations.

C. II and III only
D. I, II, and III

34. The author suggests that high-ranking German generals were considered "criminals" because they:

A. had the ability to prevent civilian deaths.

CORRECT: Though they probably did not directly or personally commit the atrocities, these German generals would have had the ability to prevent the civilian deaths, and thereby had *control* of the deaths.

B. were on the losing side of the conflict.

WRONG: There is no suggestion to this effect by the author.

C. did not have precision-bombing capabilities.

WRONG: There is no suggestion to this effect by the author. Further, the "pinpoint bombing" in Baghdad did not, according to the author, preclude civilian casualties.

D. actually put to death innocent men, women, and children.

A & E 10

WRONG: It is very unlikely, and the passage does not say specifically, that the "German generals" *actually* were the ones to put anyone to death. Yet they would have been the ones who ordered the actions and were ultimately responsible.

Passage VII (Questions 35–40)

35. The passage suggests that fluoride provides:

A. an excuse to medicate tap water.

WRONG: The complaint offered in a slogan is "'It is not the business of government to use the water supply to medicate the population without their consent.'" (lines 50–51). However, there is no suggestion that fluoride is being used as an excuse to medicate tap water.

B. an alternative to tap water.

WRONG: This makes no sense. Fluoride is not a fluid but is used as an *additive* to tap water. We *must* drink something.

C. no benefits whatsoever.

WRONG: The author does not believe this. He admits that children who did *not* get fluoride at all "might miss out on a possibly *small* [but *not* non-existent] topical benefit" (lines 55–56).

D. prevention from tooth decay.

CORRECT: The author never refutes the findings of Dr. McKay in Texas, which indicate that fluoride prevents tooth decay, nor does he refute the idea that children who did *not* get fluoride at all "might miss out on a possibly *small* [but *not* nonexistent] topical benefit" (lines 55–56).

36. According to the passage, outside of fluoridated tap water, where might one look to obtain fluoride?

The question does not ask whether the "benefits" of fluoride may be obtained from this alternative source.

A. Foods that have been grown using fluoridated water

CORRECT: "Fluoride may also be found … in fact, in all foods that have been grown … using fluoridated water" (lines 27–30).

B. Nonfluoridated mouthrinses

WRONG: "[N]onfluoridated" products will not contain fluoride.

C. Coffee or tea

WRONG: There is no information "according to the passage …" that coffee or tea contain, or could be used to "obtain," fluoride.

D. Fluoride tablets

WRONG: "Fluoride tablets" are *not* mentioned in the passage. Therefore, this answer is *not* correct because it is not "*according to the passage …*"

37. Suppose that researchers discovered that the human body safely regulated the amount of fluoride that it absorbed even when increasingly large amounts of fluoridated water are drunk. The lesson of this experience for local water districts, in general, would be:

The answer is premised on lines 57–61 of the passage. See Answer C.

A. to attempt to medicate the population more regularly during winter months.

WRONG: Even if we assume that "to medicate" refers to fluoridation, this still makes little sense.

B. to compete more intensely for fluoride contracts during the winter months.

WRONG: This makes little sense unless we extrapolate in an extreme fashion to assume that fluoride would be cheaper in the winter, because we need less, therefore …

C. to focus less attention on monitoring levels of fluoride in relation to the weather.

CORRECT: Given the author's premise at lines 57–61 (above), this is the best answer. "Consider that the amount of fluoride we get depends on how much water we drink, *which is strongly influenced by the climate in which we live*. In warmer climates people usually drink more water, and in cooler climates they drink less."

D. to cooperate more fully with the government on fluoride research.

WRONG: There is no basis for this answer.

38. According to the passage, unlimited intake with respect to fluoride is characteristic of:

I. "Texas teeth."

CORRECT: See below.

II. staining.

CORRECT: See below.

III. decay resistance.

CORRECT: See below.

A. II only
B. III only
C. II and III only
D. I, II, and III

CORRECT: The children from Texas in the first paragraph were drinking unregulated and, therefore, unlimited amounts of fluoride from the ground water. "McKay found a condition … known as '*Texas teeth*.' In 1928, he concluded that such teeth, although *stained*, showed 'a singular absence of decay,' and that both the *staining* and the *decay resistance* were caused by something in the water. In 1931, the 'something' was identified as fluoride" (lines 4–10).

A & E 10

39. Which of the following conclusions can justifiably be drawn from the experience of the authors who wrote the article entitled "Fluoridation: Don't Let the Poisonmongers Scare You!" (lines 40–41) mentioned in the passage?

A. The "Poisonmongers" have some solid scientific bases for their warnings.

WRONG: This is not a justifiable conclusion. "These *dentists and doctors* [as opposed to the Poisonmongers] argue that the scientific community is so solidly in favor of fluoridation that the "Poisonmongers" must resort to conspiracy theories and worse to advance their cause" (lines 45–48).

B. Many communities that may need fluoridated water have been deprived of it.

CORRECT: This is a justifiable conclusion. "The scare tactics of misguided Poisonmongers have deprived many communities of its benefits" (lines 43–45).

C. Many communities are fortunate enough to have been able to choose.

WRONG: This is not a justifiable conclusion.

D. The government may try to medicate the population for its own good.

WRONG: This is not a justifiable conclusion that can be drawn from the *authors of the quoted article*. It is mentioned by the *author of the passage*, but denigrated by him: "And it is easy to find anti-fluoride websites with such slogans as 'It is not the business of government to use the water supply to medicate the population without their consent'" (lines 48–51).

40. Assume that the FDA official who was instrumental in pushing legislation requiring "warning labels" was interviewed. If this official remarked that he had done this only to avoid class-action litigation against the government, this remark would *weaken* the passage assertion that:

A. fluoride can cause "Texas teeth."

WRONG: The "warning labels" have nothing to do with "Texas teeth."

B. fluoride can cause staining.

WRONG: The "warning labels" have nothing to do with "staining."

C. fluoride can be dangerous.

CORRECT: This is a passage assertion that would be weakened by the remark. "Further, fluoride can be dangerous. Since 1997, all toothpaste tubes have carried a warning label that cautions, 'If you swallow more than used for brushing, contact a poison control center immediately'" (lines 37–39).

D. fluoride can prevent tooth decay.

WRONG: The "warning labels" have nothing to do with "tooth decay."

Verbal Reasoning Test 11
Answers & Explanations

TEST 11 ANSWER KEY

1.	B	11.	D	21.	C	31.	D
2.	B	12.	A	22.	C	32.	A
3.	A	13.	B	23.	B	33.	C
4.	D	14.	A	24.	D	34.	D
5.	C	15.	B	25.	C	35.	B
6.	B	16.	D	26.	A	36.	C
7.	C	17.	B	27.	D	37.	C
8.	D	18.	A	28.	B	38.	B
9.	B	19.	B	29.	B	39.	B
10.	B	20.	A	30.	C	40.	C

Passage I (Questions 1–7)

1. The contention that "[b]y 1990, more American homes had a Nintendo than a personal computer" (lines 41–43) can most justifiably be interpreted as support for the idea that:

Essentially, this question asks, "Why did the author even use this contention?" What was the purpose of the contention? This question is based upon *common knowledge*. That common knowledge is that there has been an explosion of personal computers in American homes. It is not necessary, nor assumed, that you know at what date or point this began.

A. there were not many personal computers in American homes by 1990.

WRONG: This idea is *not* most justifiably supported by the contention. In order for the contention to support this idea, you would have to have some idea of how many Nintendos there were in American homes. Unlike the common knowledge that there 'are a lot of personal computers in American homes,' most people would probably *not* know how many Nintendos there were. Most importantly, *what is the author trying to tell us?* Is this a passage on personal computers or on video games? This is a *possible* answer, but certainly *not* the *best* answer.

B. there were many Nintendos in American homes by 1990.

CORRECT: This idea is most justifiably supported by the contention. Most importantly, *what is the author trying to tell us?* Is this a passage on personal computers or on video games? It is obvious that the author has offered this contention attempting to support the idea that Nintendo had "revived the home video game craze in America" (lines 38–39), and that there were a lot of Nintendos. Further, this answer's idea is supported by the contention because it is *common knowledge* that there 'are a lot of personal computers in American homes.'

C. there were not many Nintendos in American homes by 1990.

WRONG: This idea is *not* justifiably supported by the contention. Most importantly, it is obvious that the author has offered this contention attempting to support the idea that Nintendo had "revived the home video game craze in America" (lines 38–39). Common knowledge tells us that there are a lot of personal computers in American homes. Therefore, this answer choice makes no sense.

D. there were many personal computers in American homes by 1990.

WRONG: This idea is *not* justifiably supported by the contention. Though it is common knowledge that this answer's idea is correct, you cannot base the idea on Nintendos because most people would probably *not* know how many Nintendos there were. Most importantly, *what is the author trying to tell us?* Is this a passage on personal computers or on video games? It is obvious that the author has offered this contention attempting to support the idea that Nintendo had "revived the video game craze in America" (lines 38–39), and that there were many Nintendos.

2. According to the passage, which of the following is most likely to be true about the relationship between the video games and the home computer?

A. The advent of the personal computer enabled children to play the video games at home.

WRONG: This is *not* most likely to be true. There is absolutely no passage information in support of this contention. This answer is attractive because of your knowledge of computers and video games, not passage information. Be careful not to base your answer choices on outside information that is not common knowledge. "According to the passage, …"

B. Prior to the advent of video games, children had little contact with computers.

CORRECT: This is most likely to be true. "Video games *introduced* children in the United States to the world of microcomputers …" (lines 1–2). "Introduced" indicates that the children had not "met" the computers or come into contact with them before.

C. Video games became increasingly realistic because of home computers.

WRONG: This is *not* most likely to be true. There is absolutely no passage information in support of this contention. This answer is attractive because of your knowledge of computers and video games, not passage information. Be careful not to base your answer choices on outside information that is not common knowledge. "According to the passage, …"

D. Initially, video games were played in front of the television.

WRONG: This is *not* most likely to be true. There is absolutely no passage information in support of this contention. Even without remembering specific dates, you should have gleaned that the games were not played "*initially*" in front of the television: "Shortly *thereafter*, a variety of other video games could be played in front of the television …" (lines 14–15). In the first paragraph, you can see that the history of video games begins in 1971, and it is not until "shortly thereafter," in 1976 (*at least five years later*) that they could be played in front of the television.

A&E 11

3. According to the passage, which of the following is most likely true about "game arcades" (line 11)?

A. Video games thrived in arcades without decline.
CORRECT: This is most likely true. In "between 1983 and 1985, home video games experienced an immense downward plunge in the market… Meanwhile, video *arcade* games, which had been thriving from the introduction of the first games, *continued* to provide a social gathering place for children" (lines 22–35).

B. Video games experienced an immense downward plunge in arcades between 1983 and 1985.
WRONG: This is *not* true, according to the passage. You may have confused "home video games" with "video arcade games." In "between 1983 and 1985, *home video games* experienced an immense downward plunge in the market… Meanwhile, video *arcade* games, which had been thriving since the introduction of the first games, *continued* to provide a social gathering place for children" (lines 22–35).

C. Pong never gained wide acceptance in the arcades.
WRONG: This is probably *not* true, according to the passage. Pong came out in 1971, fully five years before home video games, so it was an arcade game that had to be played somewhere. "Pong … gained wide acceptance in a relatively short amount of time. It was eased into polite society by appearing in airports, train stations, and other establishments that were not of the typical seedy quality that one associates with game arcades" (lines 6–11). However, this may simply mean that the arcades of the day were different from the "seedy" arcades of nowadays. If that seems like tortured reasoning, consider only that there is *no* support for "*never* gained wide acceptance in the arcades." This is an extreme answer.

D. Early on, children were not allowed in the arcades.
WRONG: This is *not* true, according to the passage. "Meanwhile, video arcade games, which had been thriving since the introduction of the first games, *continued* to provide a social gathering place for children" (lines 33–35).

4. The ideas in the passage seem to derive primarily from:

A. facts observable to the author.
WRONG: This is not likely. There is no information in the passage to support this answer.

B. speculation based upon written accounts.
WRONG: This is not likely. There is no information in the passage to support this answer.

C. evidence from studies and research.
WRONG: This is not likely. There is no information in the passage to support this answer.

D. conversations with others knowledgeable in these areas.
CORRECT: This seems to be where the ideas primarily derived from. There are only two sources of information mentioned in the passage: 1) "Critics are not specific about what was bad about Atari's marketing strategies" (lines 26–27), and 2) "A few *conversations* with experts and enthusiasts revealed that the graphics were much better than those of the Atari video game system" (lines 48–50). The second clearly supports this answer choice.

5. It has been said that in violent video games, children usually identify with the villains because they have superhuman strengths. The author would probably:

A. agree, pointing out how realistic today's games have become.
WRONG: The *first* aspect of this answer is inaccurate. This answer is attractive because the *second* aspect of the answer is fairly accurate. The author would *not* "agree." See the last line of the passage.

B. agree, pointing to the companies as the main culprits.
WRONG: The author would *not* "agree." See the last line of the passage.

C. disagree, arguing that most players identify with the hero.
CORRECT: This is the author's most probable response. "Nintendo's advertising slogan 'Now You're Playing with Power!' gives some insight into the connection that these games have with a feeling of self-efficacy that is partially dependent on a player's *identification with the protagonist*" (lines 66–70). This "protagonist" is the hero.

D. disagree, citing Pong and Donkey Kong as nonviolent examples.
WRONG: It is *true* that the author would disagree with the question's premise. However, there is *no* passage information that supports the *second* aspect of the question. This is pure conjecture. It may be attractive because you have *personal* knowledge that Pong and Donkey Kong *may* be nonviolent by today's standards. However, that is *not* common knowledge. This is not the best answer.

6. Based upon the passage, if the society of the 1970's were a person, this person would most likely be:

A. a well-educated soldier.
WRONG: This is not likely. There is no reason to consider that society was either "well-educated" or "militaristic," unless you take a long, long reach for Vietnam or something of the like.

B. a well-mannered gentleman.

CORRECT: This is the most likely choice. There are strong passage suggestions that the games, the people who played them, and society became more violent over time. Primarily though, this answer can be based upon the author's striking reference to a "polite society" (line 8). This answer supports that idea in an almost *redundant* way: the "well-mannered gentlemen" (who one would probably consider 'well-mannered' or 'polite' anyway).

C. a rude businessman.

WRONG: This is not likely, particularly given the author's striking reference to a "polite society " (line 8).

D. a violent young person.

WRONG: This is not likely, particularly given the author's striking reference to a "polite society " (line 8).

7. According to the passage, which of the following descriptions was/were common to Atari *and* Nintendo?

   I. Japanese company

    WRONG: Though we know from the passage that Nintendo was "a Japanese company" (line 36), there is no information that Atari was a Japanese company also.

   II. Video arcade games

    CORRECT: Both Atari and Nintendo made video arcade games at one time or another.

   III. Home video games

    CORRECT: Both Atari and Nintendo made home video games at one time or another.

A. I only

B. III only

C. II and III only

CORRECT: See above answer explanations.

D. I, II, and III

Passage II (Questions 8–13)

8. If the author of the passage is right about stuttering, then it follows that:

A. stuttering begins with psychological manifestations.

WRONG: If the author is right, this does *not* follow. "It is doubtful that stuttering's *genesis* is of a psychological nature; it is most likely organic" (lines 19–20).

B. the PET scans were wrong or misinterpreted.

WRONG: If the author is right, this does *not* follow. The PET scans serve to buttress Webster's research, which the author uses to support his idea of a physiological basis for stuttering. "Positron

Emission Tomography (PET) scans have further supported these findings" (lines 67–68).

C. stuttering is not a communicative disorder.

WRONG: If the author is right, this does *not* follow. "This classification as a communicative disorder is only *partly correct*" (lines 18–19), but apparently, the author believes that it *is* "partly correct." Even if the difficulty in communicating is only a manifestation of physiological anomalies, it is still probably somewhat a communicative disorder by virtue of the fact that it disrupts the ability to communicate.

D. he holds a rather extreme point of view.

CORRECT: If the author is right, then this idea does follow. "At the other *extreme* is the position that stuttering reflects a physiological or neurological anomaly, and that whatever emotional or psychological concomitants there may be are consequences and not the cause of stuttering" (lines 42–46). The author apparently believes all of lines 47–68, which, though hypotheses, point to a physiological basis for stuttering. Notice the "softener" in the answer: "rather." This makes this answer even more 'flexible' and 'more correct.'

9. Regarding the research of Dr. William Webster (lines 60–68), the passage strongly implies that:

A. finger tapping is the same as stuttering.

WRONG: This is not strongly implied. It is strongly simplistic; stuttering is verbal, and tapping is not. Further, "These [tapping] errors in proper sequencing pointed to an inherent inefficiency in motor coordination, *which is also involved* in the generation of speech" (lines 64–67). If they were the same, the author would not have said "is *also* involved."

B. stutterers had more difficulty with the sequencing of tapping.

CORRECT: This is strongly 'implied.' The author leads us from brain information and what occurs during speech production. "This was confirmed to some degree by Dr. William Webster in 1993 when he undertook to compare repetitive finger tapping [in stutterers and presumably nonstutters]" (lines 59–61). That the phrase "This was confirmed …," immediately follows "during speech production" also indicates that the experiment had to do with stutterers.

C. PET scans were conducted subsequent to the tapping.

WRONG: When one looks closely at this answer, it is clear that this is *not* strongly implied. The term "subsequent" specifies that the PET scans were performed *after* the tapping, not before, or during. There is no way of knowing or inferring this from the passage information.

D. these experiments were conclusive.

WRONG: This is *not* strongly implied. For one thing, the phrase "This was confirmed *to some degree* by Dr. William Webster" (lines 59–60) is rather equivocal. Further, the author admits, "There is no single, accepted, and *provable explanation for stuttering*" (lines 71–72).

10. Suppose it could be established that the majority of those who stutter are, in fact, morbidly fearful in speech situations. The author of the passage would be most likely to respond to this information by:

With these types of questions, one must attempt to use the author's ideas, motivations, and arguments. The author would be more likely to attempt to explain or justify the supposition within the framework of his beliefs than to admit that he was completely wrong about something. Where the supposition seems to refute the author's arguments, look for the answer that would best 'rehabilitate' or 'salvage' the author's line of reasoning.

A. suggesting that this indicates it is even more necessary to find a cure.

WRONG: This is *not* a likely response. The author unequivocally believes that "there is no cure" (line 71).

B. proposing that this still does not prove that stuttering's primary cause is anxiety.

CORRECT: This is the most likely response. You must recognize that the question directly refers to the quote by Dominick Barbara, who describes "a morbidly fearful person in speech situations" (line 37). The author clearly does not agree with Barbara. However, the question tells us that the supposition "*could be established*." Therefore, the author most likely would respond to the rest of Barbara's supposition that stuttering's "cause is primarily due to the anxiety of the stutterer" (lines 32–33), which the author does not believe. *If* this reasoning seems circuitous or tortured, rest easy by recognizing that this answer can most *easily* be chosen by *process of elimination*. The other answer choices are not acceptable, given passage information.

C. asserting that 'left hemisphere explanations' account for this.

WRONG: This is *not* a likely response. "Fear" is an emotion. If a hemisphere of the brain is to account for emotional activity, it would be the right hemisphere, not the left, according to passage information. The "emotional functions [are] purportedly subserved by the right side of the brain" (lines 50–51).

D. explaining the psychological genesis of stuttering.

WRONG: This is *not* a likely response. The author does *not* believe in the "psychological genesis of stuttering"! "It is doubtful that stuttering's genesis is

of a psychological nature; it is most likely organic" (lines 19–20).

11. For which of the following of the author's assertions is NO support provided in the passage?

Remember that the correct answer choice must *first* be an *accurate assertion of the author* before you even begin to consider whether it has no support! Don't be misled into scanning down the answer choices and selecting *any* assertion for which no support is provided. If it is not an assertion of the author, it probably will not have any support, but it also will not be the correct answer.

A. There is no single, accepted, and provable explanation for stuttering.

WRONG: This *is* an assertion of the author; however, there *is* support for this assertion within the passage.

B. Speech is not a communicative disorder.

WRONG: It is true that there is *no* support for this in the passage; however, this is *not* an assertion of the author's! "This classification as a communicative disorder is only partly correct" (lines 18–19), but it *is* "partly correct."

C. Abnormal speech is not dangerous.

WRONG: It is true that there is *no* support for this in the passage; however, this is *not* an assertion of the author's! Though the author does not really think that stuttering should be included in the DSM-IV, the DSM-IV does not assert that speech is dangerous, and neither does the author.

D. Speech is not a behavior.

CORRECT: This *is* an assertion of the author for which *no* support is provided. The author points out that stuttering is listed in the DSM-IV "despite the fact that speech is not a behavior" (lines 15–16). However, he never explains what he means by this assertion, nor does he support it.

12. The author implies that a person who stutters is not:

A. stuttering because of a psychological problem.

CORRECT: This is an implication of the author. "It is doubtful that stuttering's genesis is of a psychological nature; it is most likely organic" (lines 19–20).

B. suffering from any psychological problems.

WRONG: This is *not* implied by the author. This is an extreme statement for one thing. It would be difficult, if not impossible, to argue that *any* group of persons "is not suffering from *any* psychological problems"; no neuroses or anything? Further, the author does not refute (and probably accepts) "the other extreme … that whatever emotional or psychological concomitants there may be are consequences and not the cause of stuttering" (lines 42–46).

C.   suffering from any physiological problems.
   WRONG: This is not implied by the author. Similarly to Answer B, but even more so, this is an *extreme* statement for one thing. It would be difficult, if not impossible, to argue that *any* group of persons "is not suffering from *any* physiological problems"; no stomach aches, hangnails, or pimples?

D.   constipated.
   WRONG: This is not implied by the author and is rather silly. The reference to "constipation" is by the "Freudian" who is using this as a metaphor. The author does not think highly of "spewing" from the "Freudians."

13. Which of the following suppositions is most clearly believed by the author?

A.   There is relatively little information available on stuttering.
   WRONG: This supposition is not believed by the author. The author provides that there is a "*jungle* of information available on stuttering" (line 70).

B.   Stuttering reflects a physiological or neurological anomaly.
   CORRECT: This supposition is most clearly believed by the author. For one thing, "It is doubtful that stuttering's genesis is of a psychological nature; it is most likely organic" (lines 19–20). The author goes on to support this "extreme" position, which he seems to wholeheartedly embrace, from lines 47 to line 68.

C.   The basis for stuttering is the left hemisphere of the brain.
   WRONG: This is not believed by the author. The physiological problems begin in the right side of the brain. Any problems the left hemisphere is experiencing "is further hypothesized to be the *result* of interference effects of the right hemisphere on the left hemisphere's functional executive control of the motor systems, both at cortical and subcortical levels of the brain, during speech production" (lines 55–59).

D.   There are only two irrefutable facts with regard to stuttering.
   WRONG: This is not believed by the author. If you chose this answer, you were focusing too closely on similarities between this answer choice and the last paragraph, which reads in part, "Despite differing opinions, two irrefutable truths emerge from the jungle of information available on stuttering" (lines 69–70). First, it is rather silly to say that "there are only two irrefutable facts with regard to stuttering." This answer is too extreme and rigid. How about

the fact that some people stutter and some people don't, or that stuttering has to do with verbal communication, or that people who are mute do not tend to stutter, etc. Further, the author does *not* say that "*only* two irrefutable facts emerge."

Passage III (Questions 14–19)

14. The author's claim that "in public schools today, there is an emphasis on mediocrity" (lines 1–2) is supported by:

A.   testimony adopted by the author.
   CORRECT: The author respects and believes ["adopts"] Bill Gates's views with regard to Gates's speech ["testimony"] and uses them to support his thesis.

B.   examples of specific public schools.
   WRONG: There are no specific schools mentioned.

C.   comparison with private instruction.
   WRONG: There is no comparison with private instruction.

D.   an analysis of job performance.
   WRONG: There is no real analysis of job performance. Further, this answer choice is not as responsive to the question as Answer A.

15. The author most likely believes that one of the main purposes of pre-college education should be to provide students with:

A.   an awareness of their own importance.
   WRONG: The use of the word "importance" is vague. The author (and Gates) would argue that self-worth should be tied to actual accomplishments and successes in life.

B.   a sense of self-discipline.
   CORRECT: "These rules [which the author adopts from Gates] provide a framework of self-discipline within which to succeed, and a healthy dose of reality" (lines 63–65).

C.   a sense of self-esteem.
   WRONG: "Rule 2: The world won't care about your self-esteem. The world will expect you to accomplish something BEFORE you feel good about yourself" (lines 30–32).

D.   engaging experiences.
   WRONG: See Rules 9 and 10. Though not specifically referred to, this would be viewed as "pandering" by the author.

16. Given the information in the passage, if a "concept of reality" (line 26–27) were taught to students in public schools, which of the following outcomes would most likely occur?

A. There would be fewer students who would have to be "flipping burgers."

WRONG: There would probably be more students doing this because Rule 5 defines this activity as an "opportunity."

B. Politically correct concepts could be utilized more effectively.

WRONG: The author is clearly against "political correctness" (lines 25–28).

C. Teachers would be more accountable for what they are teaching.

WRONG: There is no indication from the passage that this would occur.

D. Students would be much more successful in the real world.

CORRECT: "[Bill Gates] talked about how feel-good politically correct teachings have created a generation of kids who have no concept of reality, ,and how this lack of a concept sets them up for failure in the real world" (lines 25–28).

17. The author suggests that praise and rewards are much less effective when they:

"[T]here is a conscious effort to praise and lift the self-esteem of malingerers. It is politically correct to ensure that everyone feel good about themselves, regardless of what they are not doing or have not accomplished" (lines 7–10). And with extreme sarcasm, "Let's promote the accomplishments of one and all, even if there are actually no accomplishments to speak of" (lines 13–15).

A. are given only to actually promote accomplishments.

WRONG: The opposite is true. The author suggests that praise and rewards are much *more* [not "less"] effective when coupled with this answer.

B. are doled out indiscriminately.

CORRECT: The author offers with extreme sarcasm, "Let's promote ['praise,' from the previous lines] the accomplishments of one and all, even if there are actually no accomplishments to speak of" (lines 14-16).

C. enhance the performance of all the students.

WRONG: The author does *not* think that they enhance the performance of *all* students. However, if praise could accomplish this, the author would probably have to agree that it is more effective.

D. are given only to those who make a lot of money.

WRONG: The author would probably tend to praise those who made a lot of money, though he couches his admiration of Gates in terms of the amount of money that Gates "gives away."

18. Suppose that the majority of high-school students have, at one time or another, held a rather low-paying job, such as working in a MacDonald's restaurant. This new information would most CHALLENGE the claim that:

This question is made easier by the reference to a MacDonald's restaurant, which is related to "flipping burgers." The test might have used another more obscure and more difficult example of a "rather low-paying job."

A. students believe that this type of work is beneath their dignity.

CORRECT: This claim is most challenged by the new information. This "claim" is made indirectly by a reference of Gates in Rule 5: "Flipping burgers is not beneath your dignity. Your grandparents had a different word for burger flipping; they called it opportunity" (lines 38–40).

B. your school may have done away with winners and losers, but life has not.

WRONG: This claim is not challenged by the new information. This answer is not responsive to the question.

C. employers are not interested in helping you find yourself.

WRONG: This claim is not challenged by the new information. Unless you believe (since the passage does not provide) that MacDonald's employers *are* interested in helping you find yourself, this is an incorrect answer.

D. you won't be a vice-president with a car phone, until you earn both.

WRONG: This claim is not challenged by the new information. Unless you believe (since the passage does not provide) that MacDonald's employers *do* provide you with a car phone and make you a vice-president, this is an incorrect answer

19. According to the passage, the author feels that Bill Gates is successful because:

A. he has the most money.

WRONG: "I choose Bill Gates for this, *not* because he has the most money in the world ..." (lines 18–19).

B. he gives away the most money.

CORRECT: "[I]t might do us well to listen to those who ... are actually successful. I choose Bill Gates for this ... because he gives away the most money in the world" (lines 16–20).

C. his money is what made him successful.

WRONG: "His money is a *byproduct* of his success" (lines 20–21).

D. he seems to understand the problems with the school system.

A & E 11

WRONG: The author would agree that Gates seems to understand these problems, but this is not really implied to have anything to do with Gates's success. This is not the best answer.

Passage IV (Questions 20–24)

20. The passage suggests that the author is most likely:

    A. a martial arts instructor.

    CORRECT: This is the most likely suggestion. "My students often ask me what I consider to be the most practical style of martial art for real fighting and self-defense" (lines 1–3). Notice that this answer can assume and probably *include* Answer B, but Answer B alone does *not* necessarily include Answer A. That is the reason that only Answer A is correct.

    B. a martial arts student.

    WRONG: This *is* a likely possibility. So, you ask, what is wrong with this answer? Assuming that the author is now an instructor (Answer A, which is true) then he was probably at one time a student. However, though Answer A (which is definitely suggested) *can* and *probably does* include this answer, this answer *may exclude* Answer A. Thus, this answer might not be correct and is not the *best* answer. It is certainly not as good an answer as Answer A.

    C. the developer of his own martial arts style.

    WRONG: This is not a likely suggestion. There is no passage information that would suggest this.

    D. a historian.

    WRONG: This is not a likely suggestion. There is no passage information that would suggest this.

21. The author of the passage characterizes modern martial arts *dojos* as:

    A. schools of serious self-defense.

    WRONG: This is not an accurate passage characterization. See Answer C for the quote. However, the author certainly does *not* characterize these as schools of serious self-defense.

    B. intentionally deceptive.

    WRONG: This is not an accurate passage characterization. There is no sense that they are intentionally deceptive. Rather, the author *disagrees* with them regarding the effectiveness of their teachings.

    C. schools that should adapt to the times.

    CORRECT: "Most of all, martial arts *dojos* that advertise themselves as schools of serious self-defense, rather than simply schools of Asian history and tradition, *should adapt their martial arts for the demands of modern self-defense*" (lines 48–51).

    D. practitioners of Asian history and tradition.

    WRONG: This is not an accurate passage characterization. *Dojos* are schools, not practitioners.

22. Regarding the concept of modern martial arts instruction, the author asserts that the teaching should concentrate first on:

    A. being safe and effective.

    WRONG: There is no assertion that this should be the *first* area of concentration.

    B. eliminating training in the use of ancient weapons.

    WRONG: There is no assertion that this should be the *first* area of concentration.

    C. making students less of a target for street crimes.

    CORRECT: "They should *begin* by teaching students how to make themselves less of a target for street crimes" (lines 39–40).

    D. hand weapons.

    WRONG: This is not asserted at all, since "hand weapons are no longer carried; if they are, they are guns rather than swords."

23. According to the author, the real effectiveness of a martial artist depends upon:

    I. his athleticism.

    WRONG: There is no information in the passage to support this answer.

    II. how long the artist has trained.

    CORRECT: "In reality, the effectiveness of any fighter depends not on the fighting style he uses, but (of course) on how long he has trained in it" (lines 3–5).

    III. the type of attacks he is more likely to encounter.

    WRONG: There is no assertion in the passage that this has anything to do with a martial artist's "real effectiveness."

    A. I only
    B. II only

    CORRECT: See above answer explanations.

    C. III only
    D. II and III only

24. Assume that many forms of martial arts arose first as spiritual mind-body exercises and only secondarily as forms of self-defense. The author of the passage would be most likely to respond to this information by:

    With these types of questions, one must attempt to use the author's ideas, motivations, and arguments. The author would be more likely to attempt to explain or justify the supposition within the framework of his beliefs than to admit that he was completely wrong about something. Where the supposition seems to refute the author's arguments, look for the answer that would best 'rehabilitate' or 'salvage' the author's line of reasoning.

A. suggesting that this is not contrary to modernizing the combat aspects of the art.

WRONG: This is not a likely response. The author does not mention, nor does he seem at all interested in, any spiritual aspects of martial arts.

B. proposing that the primary emphasis should always have been placed on the martial aspects of the art.

WRONG: This is not a likely response. The futility of this type of change-history argument is not representative of the author's other arguments in the passage. The author is in favor of "calling a spade a spade." See the explanation for Answer D.

C. asserting that the spiritual aspect of martial arts is indeed very important.

WRONG: This is not a likely response. The author does not mention, nor does he seem at all interested in, any spiritual aspects of martial arts.

D. explaining that if spirituality is the primary focus, then the discipline should not be called a 'martial' art.

CORRECT: This answer is based upon and parallels the author's opinion: "Most of all, martial arts *dojos* that advertise themselves as schools of serious self-defense, rather than simply schools of Asian history and tradition, *should adapt their martial arts for the demands of modern self-defense*" (lines 48–51). The author would want to change the name to a spiritual art.

Passage V (Questions 25–29)

25. An unstated assumption in the author's example of "a person who has often been victimized by racism (or who *believes* he has)" (lines 45–46) is that:

A. beliefs are not as important as actual events.

WRONG: This is *not* an "unstated assumption" or an assumption at all. There is no support for this as an implication. The point regarding "who *believes* he has" is that perceptions of an event *are* just as important as the actual event. The idea that beliefs are as important as the actual events is reiterated again and again in the passage with references to "construals" and "misconstruals" of the *same* event.

B. memories can be misleading.

WRONG: Though it is accurate from the passage that events can be "misconstrued," this is *not* as clearly an "unstated assumption" or any kind of assumption as Answer C, *for this specific example.*

In this example, the author meant to convey Answer C. He did not specifically intend to convey this answer. This is not the best answer.

C. repeated injury can increase sensitivity.

CORRECT: This is an unstated assumption. "This will depend largely on the person's own experiences and sensitivities; for example, a person who has *often* been victimized by racism (or who *believes* he has) is *more likely* to assume that injurious acts are motivated by racism" (lines 43–47). "Often" or "repeated," means "more likely to assume" or "increased sensitivity."

D. most people probably weren't actually victims.

WRONG: This is *not* an "unstated assumption" or an assumption at all. This is particularly untrue with this answer's inclusion of the word "most." There is no support for this as an implication. The point regarding "who *believes* he was" is that perceptions of an event *are* just as important as the actual event.

26. In another essay, the author is quoted as saying, "Instead of seeing it as an unqualified disappointment, I prefer to look at a setback as an 'alternative'." This quotation could best be used in the passage to illustrate the concept of:

Notice in the quotation that the author is *not* describing a 'problem,' but a *positive* strategy or outlook that he uses. Thus, any 'negative' or symptomatic answer can be immediately eliminated.

A. categorical thinking.

CORRECT: This answer is illustrated by the quotation. The passage describes "'categorical thinking' (viewing events as total successes or absolute failures, preventing one from recognizing partial successes)" (lines 62–64).

B. catastrophizing.

WRONG: This answer is *not* illustrated by the quotation. 'Catastrophizing' is not a good thing! The author writes that instead of "'catastrophizing,' or overestimating each setback's importance, one should attempt to put it into perspective by considering the setback's *worst possible* consequence, which often reveals it is really quite acceptable" (lines 57–61).

C. misconstrual.

WRONG: This answer is *not* illustrated by the quotation. "Misconstrual" is not a good thing. It is definitely not something that the author would want to attribute to himself unless he was making a revelation of one of his inherent weaknesses.

D. positive thinking.

WRONG: This answer is illustrated by the quotation. However, it does not directly respond to any concept that is specifically outlined in the passage. Of course, 'categorical thinking' (Answer A) could be described

A & E 11

398 • Examkrackers 101 Passages in MCAT Verbal Reasoning

as 'the power of positive thinking.' Nevertheless, 'categorical thinking' is specifically in the passage, while 'positive thinking' is not.

27. The passage discussion most clearly suggests the hypothesis that we must learn:

A. to live with and accept our emotions for what they are.

WRONG: This is *not* suggested and is the antithesis of the passage. The author clearly suggests that we can 'change' the perceptions and the ways in which we 'construe' events in order to avoid 'sudden emotions' and inappropriate responses.

B. to avoid acting on our impulses through re-channeling our emotions during events.

WRONG: This is *not* suggested. The author suggests 'prevention.' It is our perceptions and construals of events that must be dealt with, rather than "re-channeling our emotions *during* events," which we may *not* be able to do anyway. "Unfortunately, prior research has demonstrated conclusively that some sudden emotions, most notably anger, are often accompanied by the release of various hormones and chemicals that contribute to sustaining the emotional reaction [and are not controllable through conscious thought]" (lines 3–7).

C. to control our sudden emotions and sustained emotional reactions.

WRONG: This is *not* suggested. This answer is not even very clear in terms of its meaning. It may be attractive because of the literal terminology contained therein. "Unfortunately, prior research has demonstrated conclusively that some sudden emotions, most notably anger, are often accompanied by the release of various hormones and chemicals that contribute to sustaining the emotional reaction [and are not controllable through conscious thought]" (lines 3–7). However, it is questionable, depending on the "sudden emotions," whether they *can* be controlled consciously. The author would like to see us prevent them in the first place.

D. to understand the ways in which we perceive in order to avoid inappropriate emotions and actions.

CORRECT: This is suggested. This answer restates the following quotation: "One of the best ways to avoid triggering improper impulses is to cultivate an awareness of one's personal 'construals,' or the ways in which one perceives an event" (lines 16–18).

28. The author suggests that the difficulty of controlling some sudden emotional reactions results from:

A. our giving in to them.

WRONG: This is suggested. However, it is not as responsive to the question as Answer B, particularly

when Answer B responds specifically to "*some sudden emotions.*"

B. uncontrollable physiological responses.

CORRECT: This is the most clearly suggested answer. "Unfortunately, prior research has demonstrated conclusively that *some sudden emotions*, most notably anger, are often accompanied by the *release of various hormones and chemicals* that contribute to sustaining the emotional reaction … Thus, emotions, *once triggered*, tend to bypass the conscious mind and are temporarily *beyond its effective control*" (lines 3–13).

C. our not being 'level-headed.'

WRONG: This is suggested, but it is *vague*. It is not as responsive to the question as Answer B, particularly when Answer B responds specifically to "*some sudden emotions.*"

D. recent experiences.

WRONG: This is not suggested, primarily because it is too *specific*. There is no distinction between "recent" experiences and those that may have occurred long ago. "This will depend largely on the person's own experiences and sensitivities" (lines 43–45).

29. According to information in the passage, the best way to avoid 'misconstruals' and develop emotional control would be to:

A. use self-correction.

WRONG: This is not the best way. The author stresses 'prevention' first, in the form of becoming aware of "one's personal 'construals,' or the ways in which one perceives an event" (lines 17–18). Only after this would you attempt to "counter by a corresponding rational pattern."

B. become aware of your irrational thought patterns.

CORRECT: This is the "best way," according to the passage. "One of the *best ways* to avoid triggering improper impulses is to cultivate an awareness of one's personal 'construals,' or the ways in which one perceives an event" (lines 16–18).

C. use 'categorical thinking.'

WRONG: Categorical thinking, "viewing events as total successes or absolute failures, preventing one from recognizing partial successes" (lines 62–64), is a *problem!* It is not a method to help or avoid anything.

D. not overestimate a failure.

WRONG: This is a very small aspect of the author's self-help program and is not the best answer.

Passage VI (Questions 30–35)

30. Based upon its metaphorical usage in the passage, one can make the following extrapolation about the bumblebee:

From lines 36–40, "In hindsight, what Dirac was trying to do was mathematically impossible. But, *like the bumblebee* who doesn't know it can't fly, through a series of inconsistent assumptions, Dirac tapped into a secret of the universe."

A. A bumblebee knows that it cannot fly, but flies nonetheless.
   WRONG: Yes, but this is vague and not as responsive to the question as Answer C.

B. Inconsistent assumptions would add up to show that a bumblebee can fly.
   WRONG: This is not a correct extrapolation.

C. Common assumptions about flight would tend to show that a bumblebee cannot fly.
   CORRECT: Bumblebee flight, like Dirac's mathematics, was theoretically "impossible" given the common assumptions at the time about flight. But, Dirac's "inconsistent *assumptions*" led him to his discovery. In hindsight, the assumptions were only inconsistent based on what was then known about mathematics, like flight and the bumblebee.

D. A bumblebee doesn't know that it can't fly, which allows him to do so.
   WRONG: A *cow* doesn't know that it can't fly either, yet it is *not* able to do so. This is not the best answer.

31. According to the passage, Dirac's "feat is always dragged forth as Exhibit A" (lines 30–31). The defensive context of this statement would lead one to the conclusion that:

The context of this statement is from lines 30–32: "His feat is always dragged forth as Exhibit A in the argument *to show that mathematics really does seem to have something to do with reality.*"

A. mathematics is usually considered to be reality-based.
   WRONG: This is the antithesis of the correct answer.

B. mathematicians require examples of successes to reassure themselves.
   WRONG: This might be the case, but we cannot infer it from the passage. In the context of the statement, Answer D is most correct.

C. Dirac was unwilling to have the 'exhibit' brought forth.
   WRONG: There is no evidence of this. The reference to "dragging" could just as well have something to do with something like the 'weight of importance'

that was associated with this discovery, or dragging something down out of the attic.

D. mathematics often seems to have nothing to do with reality.
   CORRECT: If this "feat" is "always" dragged forth because of an ongoing "argument *to show that mathematics really does seem to have something to do with reality*," then it *must* be in response to Answer D.

32. The statement that "even Einstein was a piker compared with the British theorist Paul Dirac" (lines 1–3) could lead one to the following conclusion:

Lines 1–3: "*When it comes to the quest for beauty in physics*, even Einstein was a piker compared with the British theorist Paul Dirac."

A. Einstein sought beauty in his equations.
   CORRECT: See the quotation on which the question is based, above.

B. Dirac did not care for Einstein.
   WRONG: This is not implied nor alluded to in the passage.

C. Einstein did not care if his equations fit the experiment.
   WRONG: This is a stretch and not as correct as Answer A when the *entire* sentence is examined. See question explanation above.

D. Dirac felt it important to have his equations fit the experiment.
   WRONG: According to the passage, this was obviously *not* important to Dirac! Dirac is quoted as saying that "it is more important to have beauty in one's equations than to have them fit [the] experiment" (lines 3–5).

33. One source provides that, unlike applied mathematicians, pure mathematicians "see their work as an art and judge its value by the brilliance and beauty of its logic. They pay no attention to the practical application of their research." Dr. Steven Weinberg (line 51) is most likely:

A. a pure mathematician.
   WRONG: He is not a mathematician but a physicist (line 52).

B. a physicist who loves applied mathematics.
   WRONG: We know that Weinberg is a physicist, and he says, "It is always *hard to realize* that these numbers and equations we play with at our desks *have something to do with the real world*" (lines 55–57). If it is hard for him to realize this, then he is probably not too interested in applied mathematics.

C. a physicist who enjoys pure mathematics.

CORRECT: We know that Weinberg is a physicist, and he says, "It is always *hard to realize* that these numbers and equations we play with at our desks *have something to do with the real world*" (lines 55–57). If it is hard for him to realize this, then he is probably not too interested in applied mathematics.

D. an applied mathematician.

WRONG: He is not a mathematician but a physicist (line 52).

34. The passage describes Dirac's antiparticles variously as all of the following EXCEPT:

Note that the question is asking for which answer was NOT used as a description.

A. a positron

WRONG: This is not an exception. Lines 23–24: "its antiparticle, the *positron*, was a hole."

B. a hole

WRONG: This is not an exception. Lines 23–24: "its antiparticle, the positron, was a *hole*."

C. evanescent

WRONG: This is not an exception. "Dirac had started out thinking of electrons and their opposites, the 'holes,' as fundamental entities to be explained, but the fact that they could be created and destroyed meant that they were really *evanescent* particles" (lines 41–44).

D. fields

CORRECT: This is an exception. Neither the particles nor the antiparticles are ever described as "fields." Thus, this is the correct answer.

35. The word *cathedral* (line 61) is used in the sense of:

"… and so his equation survives, one of the cathedrals of science" (lines 60–61).

A. a place of worship

WRONG: The metaphor is not appropriate for either a "place" or "worship."

B. an enduring symbol of truth

CORRECT: This answer comes closest to describing the metaphor. It provides "enduring," which goes with "survives," and "truth," which is an aspect of Dirac's equations.

C. a perpetual icon of veneration

WRONG: "Perpetual," though somewhat extreme, does go with "survives." However, the "veneration" aspect is too heavy-handed. This is not as good an answer as B.

D. a vessel of adoration

WRONG: "Vessel" is not really appropriate, and neither is "adoration."

Passage VII (Questions 36–40)

36. In the context of the passage, the word *incentivize* (line 74) means:

A. to induce recipients to distribute their funds in a nonfraudulent manner.

WRONG: Recipients do not "distribute" their funds. They "receive" them from the foundations.

B. to stimulate the foundation to give more to the beneficiaries.

WRONG: The word *incentivize* acts *upon* the beneficiaries, not upon the foundation.

C. to motivate recipients to use funds as the foundation had intended.

CORRECT: This is the primary thrust of the passage. The examples of declining grants and matching grants are methods that will ensure this answer.

D. to encourage beneficiaries not to mislead the foundations.

WRONG: This would be a small *part* of the correct answer but is not the complete meaning of the word. This is not the best answer.

37. The passage suggests that public statements by foundations on what types of programs they will or will not fund are effective because:

A. funds that are misused can be recovered through a lawsuit for breach of contract.

WRONG: This has nothing to do with "public statements." This answer has to do with the "monitoring process". "Presumably, if the beneficiary diverts the money for other purposes, the foundation can recover the money through a lawsuit for breach of contract" (lines 56–58).

B. they will prevent fraudulent abuse by recipients.

WRONG: "First, *foundations can issue public statements* on types of programs they will—or will not—fund. This will prevent mistaken misuse by recipients, *though not fraudulent abuse*" (lines 19–22).

C. they may persuade beneficiaries with less money to apply.

CORRECT: This responds to *why* the public statements are effective. "Conversely, [the foundation] may affirmatively announce types of projects that they *will* fund. This … may also encourage beneficiaries who … lack … funds, to apply" (lines 25–30).

D. a foundation can specify what type of funds it will, or will not, reimburse.

   WRONG: "Reimbursement" of funds is *not* an aspect of the effectiveness of public statements by foundations. The "projects" are "funded"; "expenses" are "reimbursed." Reimbursement is considered during "the *budgeting stage*. Most fundamentally, a foundation can specify what types of *expenses* it will, or will not, reimburse" (lines 36–38).

38. According to passage information, at what point is the foundation's control over a beneficiary's activities the greatest?

A. When the monies can be distributed in partial disbursements

   WRONG: "This is done at the *budgeting stage* ... foundations can grant themselves more discretion, and retain more of their bargaining power with beneficiaries, by disbursing only part of the total projected cost at regular intervals" (lines 36–41).

B. Prior to the foundation committing money to the beneficiary

   CORRECT: "Needless to say, a foundation's power over beneficiaries' activities is greatest *before* it has committed money to them" (lines 14–15).

C. Upon the signing of a conditional grant

   WRONG: The only *conditional* aspect is the "grant" mentioned at line 55.

D. When a foundation can appoint a monitor to work with the beneficiary throughout the project

   WRONG: This is helpful, but it is not when the foundation's control is the greatest.

39. According to the passage, all of the following are *true* regarding the advantages of "partial disbursement" (line 46) of funds by the foundation EXCEPT:

   I. allows the foundation to monitor a project to ensure that it has not strayed from the desired parameters

   WRONG: This *is* an advantage of "partial disbursements." "This allows them to monitor a project to ensure it has not strayed from the desired parameters" (lines 41–43).

   II. encourages recipients to apply for grants from other philanthropic sources as well

   CORRECT: This *is not* an advantage of "partial disbursements." "*Matching grants*—in which the foundation matches contributions made by the beneficiary or third parties—encourage recipients to apply for grants from other philanthropic sources as well" (lines 77–80).

   III. encourages beneficiaries to meet deadlines and disclose results

   WRONG: This *is* an advantage of "partial disbursements." "Also, this partial disbursement encourages beneficiaries to meet deadlines and disclose results" (lines 45–47).

A. I only

B. II only

   CORRECT: See above explanation.

C. III only

D. I and III only

40. According to the passage, informal control mechanisms that are not contractual arise at all of the following periods EXCEPT:

A. during the initial screening of projects.

   WRONG: This is *not an exception.* "[I]nformal non-contractual control mechanisms ... arise at three points: in the initial screening of projects ... " (lines 8–13).

B. when making the decision regarding how much funding to allocate.

   WRONG: This is *not an exception.* "[I]nformal non-contractual control mechanisms ... arise at three points: ... in the decision of how much funding to allocate ... " (lines 8–13).

C. as the foundation decides which projects to support.

   CORRECT: This *is* an exception; it is not mentioned as one of the "three points."

D. upon conferring a conditional grant.

   WRONG: This is *not an exception.* "[I]nformal non-contractual control mechanisms ... arise at three points: ... in the contract between foundation and beneficiary" (lines 8–13). This "conferring" of a conditional grant is tantamount to determining and signing the contract between the foundation and beneficiary.

A&E 11

A & E 11

Verbal Reasoning Test 12
Answers & Explanations

TEST 12 ANSWER KEY

1.	A	11.	A	21.	B	31.	C
2.	B	12.	D	22.	B	32.	C
3.	C	13.	A	23.	B	33.	B
4.	C	14.	D	24.	D	34.	D
5.	A	15.	C	25.	C	35.	A
6.	C	16.	C	26.	D	36.	C
7.	A	17.	B	27.	A	37.	B
8.	B	18.	A	28.	C	38.	C
9.	D	19.	D	29.	C	39.	A
10.	D	20.	D	30.	D	40.	A

Passage I (Questions 1–5)

1. Which of the following suppositions is most clearly believed by the author?

   Notice that the answer must first satisfy the requirement of being a passage supposition.

   A. The recording industry's complaints about CD piracy are legitimate.

   CORRECT: Though some of the other beliefs of the author are equivocal (such as regarding downloading free music), this supposition is most clearly believed by the author. "I cannot condone actual music piracy, which benefits no one but the pirates themselves" (lines 36–38).

   B. Most band members make plenty of money.

   WRONG: This is *not* clearly believed by the author. In the first paragraph, the author gives the example of two band members who are making a lot of money. However, notice that *neither* of them is making any money *because* of being "band members." There is further reason to doubt this supposition. Paragraph four and the discussion of "boot" CDs gives examples of former, disenfranchised, and even wrongly dismissed band members who are *not* making "plenty of money."

   C. The recording industry's complaints about 'boot' CDs are legitimate.

   WRONG: This is *not* clearly believed by the author. First, it is *not* at all clear that there actually *are* "recording industry *complaints*" about "boot" CDs. However, "In the case of boot CDs, it cannot be said that former band members should have *no* right to release and profit from music that they themselves created [even though they signed a contract with the record company]" (lines 56–58).

   D. All reissued CDs are a poor value.

   WRONG: This is *not* clearly believed by the author. Quite the opposite, in fact. "*Typically*, the record label reissues a band's CDs in a multi-CD boxed set, of which three-quarters of the songs are previously unreleased. *This is still good value for the money*" (lines 62–65).

2. According to the passage, the author's primary reason for justifying individuals' copying CDs off of a website seems to be that:

   A. there is no specific law against doing this.

   WRONG: This is not only not a primary reason, but it is also probably not any reason at all, based upon passage information. This is pure conjecture.

   B. record labels and band members make plenty of money.

   CORRECT: This seems to be the author's primary reasoning. Lines 1–14, culminating in "Fans' hearts should not be bleeding," indicate that the author has little sympathy for the record labels and band members. Further, the entire second paragraph indicates that the author feels that they are making plenty of money, with the author asking, "What happens to the money?"

   C. record label rereleases invariably contain mostly reissued music.

   WRONG: This is *not* accurate, for one thing. "Typically, the record label reissues a band's CDs in a multi-CD boxed set, of which *three-quarters* of the songs are previously *unreleased*" (lines 62–64).

   D. everybody else does it.

   WRONG: This is *not* the primary reason. It is questionable whether this could even be inferred from the passage.

3. For which of the following of the author's assertions is NO support provided in the passage?

   A. CD markups are exorbitant.

   WRONG: This is an assertion, and there *is* support for this assertion. An explanation at lines 20–26, ends with the question, "What happens to the money?"

   B. Fans shouldn't feel sorry for record industry executives, because they make plenty of money from the industry.

   WRONG: This is an assertion, and there *is* support for this assertion. "Danny Goldberg, who parlayed a career as a hanger-on to the popular band The Doors into a *record industry executive position*, will not be getting his five-million-dollar bonus this year" (lines 7–10). Lest you point out that it says that he "will *not*" be getting the bonus, consider that, if this amount is his 'bonus,' how much is his salary? Finally, this information comes before, and is referred to directly by, the "Fans' hearts should not be bleeding" comment.

   C. Fans shouldn't feel sorry for band members, because they make plenty of money in the band.

   CORRECT: There is *no* support for this assertion. In paragraph one, The Doors hanger-on Danny Goldberg and Metallica drummer Lars Ulrich are provided as examples for why "Fans' hearts should not be bleeding." The author gives examples of the impressive amounts of money they are making. In Goldberg's case, though he is *not* getting a five-million-dollar bonus, a rather large salary is nevertheless *suggested* based upon the size of the *bonus!* However, notice that Goldberg is making money because he is now a *record industry executive*, and Ulrich is making money from selling some *paintings. Neither* of these two provides an example of making any money "in the band." This is the best answer.

D. 'Boots' usually come from someone connected with the band.

WRONG: This is an assertion, and there *is* support for this assertion. "[A 'boot'] is usually created after material is lifted from the band's recording studio archives by someone connected with the band" (lines 42–44).

4. Which of the following conclusions about the author's beliefs can be inferred from the passage?

A. There is no real value in record company re-releases anymore.

WRONG: This is *not* a valid conclusion. "*Typically*, the record label reissues a band's CDs in a multi-CD boxed set, of which three-quarters of the songs are previously unreleased. *This is still good value for the money*" (lines 62–65).

B. Music piracy and downloading songs for free using Napster are basically the same thing.

WRONG: This is *not* a valid conclusion. For one thing, the author says that he "cannot condone actual music piracy, which benefits no one but the pirates themselves" (lines 36–38). Why, what is the difference? With downloading, like piracy, no one connected with the band or its promoters sees any profit. Lines 32–36 tell us that the difference is because the pirates make a *profit*, plus it is *illegal* and pirates pay *no taxes* on their profits.

C. The only difference between actual music pirates and downloading off Napster is in the selling of the CDs.

CORRECT: This is a valid conclusion about the author's beliefs. The author says that he "cannot condone actual music piracy, *which benefits no one but the pirates themselves*" (lines 36–38), yet he doesn't clearly seem to have a problem with Napster. This is confusing because with Napster it is still the case that "no one connected with the band or its promoters see any profit from sales of pirated CDs" (lines 33–34). What is the difference? It is in the *selling* of the CDs that one becomes a "pirate" (lines 27–36). The pirates are the only ones to profit from the CDs, plus it is *illegal* and pirates pay *no taxes* on their profits.

D. Band members who sign record-company contracts should be bound by them.

WRONG: This is *not* a valid conclusion. The "[U]nder the *record company's standard contract*, dismissed band members *give up their right to most of the band's profits*, even if they were fired without good cause. [However] In the case of boot CDs, it cannot be said that former band members should

have *no* right to release and profit from music that they themselves created" (lines 53–58).

5. What distinction is implied in the passage between a "pirated" CD and "bootleg" CD, respectively?

A. no one connected with the making of the CD makes a profit, and unreleased material

CORRECT: This distinction is implied "Needless to say, *no one* connected with the band or its promoters sees any *profit* from sales of pirated CDs" (lines 32–34), and "A 'boot,' short for 'bootleg,' is a recording of previously *unreleased* material" (lines 39–40).

B. illegal, and illegal.

WRONG: This is *not* a distinction; it would be a *similarity* (if it were true). Further, it is not clear that "bootleg" CDs are "illegal."

C. cannot be condoned, and should not be condoned.

WRONG: This is not implied. The first aspect, "cannot be condoned"= "pirated" CD, is accurate. However, there is *no* implication that the "bootleg" "should not be condoned," and there is implication that perhaps it '*should* be condoned.' Though the band members sign (presumably on their own volition) a standard record contract, "In the case of boot CDs, it cannot be said that former band members should have *no* right to release and profit from music that they themselves created" (lines 56–58). The author seems to believe that some inherent right of theirs to make money supersedes the written contract.

D. someone connected with the band, and an officially released song.

WRONG: This answer is not respective. The aspects are reversed. The "pirated" CDs are of "officially released songs" (line 29), and the "bootleg" is "by someone connected with the band" (lines 43–44).

Passage II (Questions 6–10)

6. According to the passage, when studying the works of Thucydides, one must take into account:

A. the abstract characteristics of Greek political philosophy.

WRONG: This is the antithesis. Thucydides "provides valuable insight … which is *far removed* from the intellectual abstractions characteristic of Greek political philosophy" (lines 1–6).

B. Thucydides's own views.

WRONG: This is not indicated by the passage. However, if Answer C were not here, then this *might* be inferred *because* of the reason given for Answer C.

C. that he fabricated the statements of historical figures.

A&E 12

CORRECT: The author quotes Thucydides as admitting that "my method has been … to make the speakers say what, in my opinion, was called for by each situation" (lines 10–13).

D. the *History of the Peloponnesian War.*
   WRONG: This *is* a work of Thucydides.

7. Regarding the concept of Athenian democracy, Thucydides asserts that:

A. a powerful state will never be esteemed.
   CORRECT: This is an assertion of Thucydides. "Thucydides notes that a powerful state will never be loved, as shown when he says to the Athenians... (lines 65–66).

B. the Athenians were the most powerful of the nation states.
   WRONG: This is not an assertion of Thucydides. The Athenians were "mighty," but there is no indication that they were the *most* powerful.

C. the Athenians were actually living under tyranny.
   WRONG: This is not an assertion of Thucydides. "[W]hat you do not realize is that your empire is a tyranny exercised over subjects who do not like it" (lines 69–70). These "subjects" were *not* Athenians, but were the "subjugated enemies" conquered by the Athenian army. The Athenians lived under a democracy.

D. their existence depended upon the goodwill of their subjects.
   WRONG: This is not an assertion of Thucydides. Their existence depended upon a strong army. This answer cannot be the case since Thucydides asserts that the Athenian "subjects" did not like being subjects and were constantly plotting against them (lines 69–71), yet Athens was expanding and prospering.

8. Passage information indicates that if a strong nation were to begin empire-building, it would probably most benefit from:

The question is asking what can be learned *now* from a nation that no longer exists. In responding to this question, you must remember that though Thucydides may view Athens as the apogee of success, and that for Thucydides an army may be a "yardstick of political power," the passage itself is *not* so compelling. What does the author think?

A. using most of its resources to expand its military.
   WRONG: This may be Thucydides belief, but that is not what the question is asking. According to the passage, this answer is not a strategy for success or longevity. This use of resources begins a cycle that cannot be maintained.

B. offering full citizenship to those it has conquered.
   CORRECT: What were the *mistakes* that Athens made? The passage does *not* attempt to argue that Thucydides's perspective was the best for all-time. The question is asking what can be learned *now* from a nation that no longer exists. "[W]hat you do not realize is that your empire is a tyranny exercised over subjects who do not like it and are always plotting against you ... your leadership depends on superior strength and not on any goodwill of theirs." (lines 69–72). As Athens conquered a "city's population [it] was either destroyed or enslaved by Athens" (lines 59–60).

C. destroying or enslaving those it has conquered.
   WRONG: This may be Thucydides's belief, but that is not what the question is asking. This answer is not a recipe for success or longevity. It begins a cycle that cannot be maintained.

D. requiring only obedience.
   WRONG: This is a reference to a *failing*, not a strategy for success. "It is never mentioned that [the subjects] should be content or prosperous, *only obedient*, nor does it seem especially important whether they are given good laws or secure lasting peace and freedom from fear" (lines 74–77).

9. An important relationship is suggested in the passage between:

A. political philosophy and the Athenians.
   WRONG: "[P]olitical philosophy" is "far removed" from Thucydides, the Athenians, and the thrust of the passage.

B. mercantile trade and power.
   WRONG: "We *might* expect he is referring to mercantile trade" (lines 19–20), but Thucydides is *not*.

C. strong armies and suppressing revolts.
   WRONG: Remember, "Thucydides suggests *wealth is the key to power*" (line 17). This answer is valid, but not as important as Answer D because it does *not* include wealth. This is not the best answer. "In Thucydides's account of 'cyclical' empire-building, a stronger nation conquers a people and exacts tribute, then uses these spoils to expand its military, and finally finds that added soldiers must be stationed in the conquered province to suppress revolts" (lines 24–28). However, strong armies and suppression would *not* be possible without the *wealth* extracted from the subjugated cities.

D. wealth and armies.
   CORRECT: This concept, and the relationship, is key to the passage. "Thucydides suggests *wealth is the key to power*" (line 17). However, "Thucydides does not consider a state's wealth useful other than

to expand its army, which for him is the yardstick of political power" (lines 22–24).

10. The opinion that "[t]he purest instance of political realism in *Peloponnesian War* is the frank discussion between the Melians and invading Athenians" (lines 31–33) is *challenged* in the passage by the argument that:

A. Thucydides did not focus on political thought.

WRONG: If those who are told to focus on Thucydides are any indication, then this answer is not correct. "Modern students of political thought should focus on the speeches and debates recorded by Thucydides" (lines 7–8). If these students are told to focus on Thucydides's works, he must have in part focused on political though.

B. this discussion was not really "frank."

WRONG: There is no information to support this.

C. the Athenians were not invading at that point.

WRONG: This is a poor answer and is not supported by the passage. For instance, the Athenians could have invaded, been repulsed, been engaged in discussions with the Melians, and *still* been correctly referred to as "invading."

D. Thucydides fabricated what people said.

CORRECT: Thucydides *admits* that "my method has been … to make the speakers say what, in my opinion, was called for by each situation" (lines 10–13). Yet the author *still* refers to Thucydides writings as the "*purest* instance of political *realism*."

Passage III (Questions 11–16)

11. The passage indicates that its author would NOT agree with which of the following statements?

A. The West actually had little to do with the Ch'ing dynasty's collapse.

CORRECT: The author would *not* agree with this statement. Though the author stresses that he believes both "Euro centrists" and "Chinese nationalists" place *too much* emphasis on the Western role (for different reasons), and though he does not believe that it was "Western influence alone" (lines 1–15), he is still forced to admit that the West had a good deal to do with the collapse. After taking into account 'social deterioration' and the 'ill-advised' official tax freeze, collapse came about because of "forced dependence on *foreign* capital in order to build the armies necessary to repel *foreign* military influence" (lines 25–26). Further, the British Opium Wars (with Chinese help and collusion), the 'completely reversed trade deficit in Britain's favor,' the British 'draining silver currency' from the Chinese, and other points in the passage indicate that the author would not agree with this statement.

B. The activities of the West were not the sole reason for the Ch'ing dynasty's collapse.

WRONG: The author would agree. The author stresses that he believes both "Euro centrists" and "Chinese nationalists" place *too much* emphasis on the Western role (for different reasons) in the collapse (lines 1–15).

C. Many Western historians place too great an emphasis on European activities.

WRONG: The author would agree. The author stresses that he believes both "Euro centrists" and "Chinese nationalists" place *too much* emphasis on the Western role (for different reasons) in the collapse (lines 1–15).

D. Many Chinese historians place too great an emphasis on European activities.

WRONG: The author would agree. The author stresses that he believes both "Euro centrists" and "Chinese nationalists" place *too much* emphasis on the Western role (for different reasons) in the collapse (lines 1–15).

12. The author is primarily concerned with demonstrating that the causes of the Ch'ing dynasty's collapse:

A. began with the First Opium War (1839–42) and British armed intervention.

WRONG: The author *refutes* this idea. "*Traditional historiography* [which the author does not think much of] makes the First Opium War (1839–42) the *watermark* for imperialist intervention and unequal trade agreements. *But* the war began as an economic reaction by Great Britain against its trade deficit with the Chinese" (lines 35–39).

B. have been accurately described by both Western and Chinese historians.

WRONG: The author stresses that he believes both "Euro centrists" and "Chinese nationalists" place *too much* emphasis on the Western role (for different reasons) in the collapse (lines 1–15).

C. were much more the fault of China than of any Western activities or influences.

WRONG: This is *not* clear. Though the author stresses that he believes both "Euro centrists" and "Chinese nationalists" place *too much* emphasis on the Western role (for different reasons) in the collapse (lines 1–15), he is still forced to admit that the West had a good deal to do with the collapse. After taking into account 'social deterioration' and the 'ill-advised' official tax freeze, collapse came about because of "forced dependence on *foreign* capital in order to build the armies necessary to repel *foreign* military influence" (lines 25–26). Further, the British Opium Wars (with Chinese help and collusion), the 'completely reversed trade deficit in

A & E 12

Britain's favor,' the British 'draining silver currency' from the Chinese, and other points in the passage indicate that the author would not agree with this statement. This is not the best answer.

D. stemmed from longstanding problems within China that were aggravated by Western activities.

CORRECT: This is a more balanced and accurate description of what the author is trying to demonstrate than Answer C. Lines 16–34 argue for 'longstanding problems' within China. Further, the author downplays the traditional "watermark" of the First Opium Wars. He does, however, imply that the collapse would not have occurred without at least some Western activities and intervention.

13. Which of the following discoveries, if genuine, would most *weaken* the author's arguments?

A. The Chinese army at Canton in 1839, for various reasons, had been rendered almost completely ineffective.

CORRECT: This would seriously weaken the author's argument that "[i]t would have been a relatively easy matter for the Ch'ing military, at full strength, to destroy the British expedition [at Canton in 1839]" (lines 63–65). Do not be *misled* by later references to "ineffectiveness." "… in *later* encounters, widespread theft and embezzlement among the Chinese military leaders reduced their impressive army to complete ineffectiveness" (lines 65–67).

B. The British had badly miscalculated the strength of their armed forces necessary for a successful engagement at Canton in 1839.

WRONG: This does not *weaken* the author's arguments. This discovery would actually *support* the author's argument that "[i]t would have been a relatively easy matter for the Ch'ing military, at full strength, to destroy the British expedition [at Canton in 1839]" (lines 63–65).

C. The Chinese naval commanders considered the number of British ships at Canton in 1839 to be inconsequential.

WRONG: This does not *weaken* the author's arguments. This discovery would actually *support* the author's argument that the "British attackers numbered *only* 2,400, in ships *of not much more sophisticated capabilities than those that the Chinese navy had at its disposal*" (lines 59–62).

D. Many modern Chinese historians are at a loss to explain why the British were not simply destroyed at Canton in 1839.

WRONG: This does not *weaken* the author's arguments. This discovery would actually *support* the author's argument that "[e]xactly why the Chinese

defenders were defeated is *unclear*. It would have been *a relatively easy matter* for the Ch'ing military, at full strength, to *destroy* the British expedition" (lines 62–65).

14. Passage information indicates that which of the following statements must be true?

A. In 1839, the Chinese were defeated in Canton because of widespread theft and embezzlement.

WRONG: This is a false conclusion. Even the author admits, "Exactly *why* the Chinese defenders were defeated is unclear" (lines 62–63). References to "theft and embezzlement among Chinese military leaders" occurred "*in later encounters*" (lines 65–66), apparently not in 1839.

B. Opium was legal in China in 1839.

WRONG: This is a false conclusion. Opium was banned as early as 1729 (line 46). The *purpose* of the British sending an "armed force to Canton [was] to *legalize* opium" (line 64).

C. Silver was more popular with the British because it was actually worth more than copper.

WRONG: This is a false conclusion. There is no information or indication in the passage that silver was "worth more" than copper.

D. Those Chinese who were not peasants, or poor urban laborers, dealt predominantly in silver.

CORRECT: Passage information indicates that this must be true. We know from passage information that the two metal currencies were silver and copper. Further, "the copper currency [was] held mostly by peasants and poor urban laborers" (lines 79–80). Therefore, everyone else "dealt predominantly in silver."

15. According to one historical authority on the 1729 ban of opium in China, "because no national [Chinese] consensus existed [on the ban], even a concerted effort by customs inspectors and the government was unable to stem the tide of opium into Canton." This authority would probably:

Remember that this quote is from some "historical authority," *not* from the passage.

A. support the author's assertions fully.

WRONG: No. The quoted authority *completely* disagrees with the author. See Answer C.

B. approve of the author's description of the government's efforts, but disagree with the idea of a 'consensus.'

WRONG: This is incorrect. The author describes the "government officials" as "collaborators." Further, there was "disunity and profiteering … both inside and outside the government" (lines 55–56).

C. not consider the author's portrayal of customs inspectors and government officials to be accurate.

CORRECT: This is the author's probable reaction. Unlike the quoted "historical authority," the author describes the "customs inspectors" and "government officials" as "corrupt" and "collaborators" in the smuggling of opium.

D. consider the author's narrative regarding this ban to be completely incorrect.

WRONG: The author does *not completely* disagree with this "historical authority." The author's narrative asserts that there was *no* consensus, based upon his assertion that "*had* a national consensus existed [on the ban/prohibition]" (lines 53–54), the opium imports could have been stopped. However, unlike the quoted "historical authority," the author describes the "customs inspectors" and "government officials" as "corrupt" and "collaborators" in the smuggling of opium.

16. According to the passage, which of the following is most likely to be true about the relationship between the government and the Chinese people during the period of the First Opium War?

A. After the 1839 initial British invasion at Canton, the government ministers armed the Chinese people to repel the invaders.

WRONG: This is not just unlikely, but is also not true. In later encounters with the British, after 1839, "vital militia units that could have reinforced the Canton defenders were withheld because government ministers were more wary of the threat from arming their own people than the threat from outside attack" (lines 68–71).

B. Both the government ministers and the Chinese people dealt primarily in copper currency.

WRONG: This is not true. Though the British were draining silver, "the copper currency [was] held *mostly* by peasants and poor urban laborers" (lines 79–80). There is no information that "government ministers" dealt primarily in copper.

C. Government ministers were less worried about the British than they were about an internal revolt.

CORRECT: This is most likely true. In later encounters with the British, after 1839, "vital militia units that could have reinforced the Canton defenders were withheld because government ministers were more wary of the threat from arming their own people than the threat from outside attack" (lines 68–71).

D. The Chinese people unsuccessfully revolted against higher government taxes.

WRONG: There is no information or indication in the passage that would lead to this conclusion.

Passage IV (Questions 17–22)

17. According to the passage, "With sunrise, came the daunting realization of the full extent of casualties; as accounts came in, they showed fully 100,000 dead" (lines 25–27). Roughly how many men did Attilla have left in his army?

A. 250,000

WRONG: See explanation to Answer C.

B. 200,000

CORRECT: "On the Catalaunian Plains, Attilla's force of a *quarter million* joined battle with a roughly equal army" (lines 18–20). In the morning, "as accounts came in, they showed fully *100,000 dead*, with roughly equal losses on each side" (lines 26–28). Thus, Attilla's 250,000 minus 50,000 equals 200,000 left alive. The figure 50,000 is half of the 100,00 dead because losses on each side were "roughly equal."

C. 150,000

WRONG: See explanation to Answer B.

D. 50,000

WRONG: See explanation to Answer C.

18. Which of the following statements is the most reasonable conclusion that can be drawn from the author's description of the battle at Catalaunum?

A. The Huns were stalemated.

CORRECT: We know from the body counts alone that both sides started with the same number and ended with the same number of soldiers (see previous Question 17 and explanation). Further, "Fearing desertion by their allies, the Roman armies *retreated*. Attilla, dismayed by his losses, waited long enough to watch the Romans leave, then himself called a *retreat*" (lines 29–32).

B. King Merovich was the victor.

WRONG: *Not* according to the "author's description." King Merovich was only the victor as portrayed on the armoire.

C. Attilla was the victor.

WRONG: *Not* according to the "author's description." See Answer A.

D. The Gauls stalemated the Romans.

WRONG: The Gauls were allied with the Romans! "The Roman army … was forced into an unlikely alliance with its bitter enemies, the Visigoth tribesmen of Gaul, for mutual defense" (lines 14–18).

19. The passage states, "Ostensibly, this artwork commemorates the brilliant victory of King Merovich over Attilla the Hun in 451 A.D. on the plains of Catalaunum" (lines 8–10). According to the author, this rendition of the battle would probably have resulted from:

A. the fact that Merovich was the only surviving Visigoth king.
WRONG: This answer may be attractive because it is regurgitating information from the passage that is technically correct. We know from the author's description of the battle that the artwork is historically innaccurate. Though Merovich was the sole surviving Visigoth king, this is *not* the *reason* for this specific French rendition.

B. a renewed interest in this time period and that battle.
WRONG: This is vague and not as accurate as Answer D. Further, consider that if this answer *were* correct, then it would indicate that the battle was rendered on the armoire 'recently,' not in the 19th century (line 1). This is not the best answer.

C. Roman attempts to rewrite the battle.
WRONG: The artwork is French, and the artist is French.

D. French efforts to rewrite history.
CORRECT: We know from the author's description of the battle that the artwork is historically inaccurate. Lines 49–62, the entire last paragraph, explain how the artwork attempts to evoke the "conception of national identity in a period of renewed French nationalism." This *rendition* of the battle results *specifically* from French efforts to rewrite history.

20. The contention that "[t]he … artwork produced in that period shows how history can be as much a blank canvas for the historian as wood and metal can be for the artist" (lines 60–62) can most justifiably be interpreted as support for the idea that:

A. artists often more accurately illustrate on blank canvas than with wood and metal.
WRONG: This is not an idea put forth by the author.

B. historians should restrict their portrayals to books.
WRONG: This is not an idea put forth by the author.

C. historians must be free to recreate history as they see it.
WRONG: This is not an idea put forth by the author.

D. artists are not restricted to realistic portrayals of their subjects.

CORRECT: We know from the author's description of the battle that the artwork is historically inaccurate. Therefore, artists are not restricted to realistic portrayals *and* neither are historians.

21. On the basis of the passage, one may assume that from the perspective of Attilla, Roman society was characterized by:

We see Roman society through Attilla's eyes, who "while a hostage in Rome, wisely used his time to study the *weaknesses* of the Romans" (lines 40–41).

A. equality between men and women.
WRONG: From Attilla's observations as a hostage in Rome, we know that Roman society was *not* characterized by "gender equality …" (lines 43–45).

B. social stratification.
CORRECT: From Attilla's observations as a hostage in Rome, we know that in Roman society Romans were *not* "free to enjoy greater *social mobility* …" (lines 43–45). Thus, there *was* social stratification.

C. great wealth.
WRONG: There is no information in the passage that this was a characteristic of Roman society.

D. vast empires.
WRONG: There is no information in the passage that this was a characteristic of Roman society.

22. According to the passage, which of the following statements is true about the alliances in 451 A.D. on the plains of Catalaunum:

A. The Spartans and the Romans were led by King Merovich against the Huns.
WRONG: The Spartans were not allied with the Romans.

B. In an unusual arrangement, the Romans had allied themselves with their former enemies, the Gauls.
CORRECT: "The Roman army … was forced into an unlikely alliance with its bitter enemies, the Visigoth tribesmen of Gaul, for mutual defense" (lines 14–18).

C. The Visigoth tribesman had allied themselves with the Romans in order to attack the Huns.
WRONG: "The Roman army … was forced into an unlikely alliance with its bitter enemies, the Visigoth tribesmen of Gaul, *for mutual defense*" (lines 14–18).

D. The Gauls and the Visigoth Tribesman had allied themselves for mutual defense against the Huns.
WRONG: The Visigoth tribesmen *were* Gauls.

Passage V (Questions 23–28)

23. According to the passage, when a person is found "not guilty," one must take into account:

References to "not guilty" come from the author providing counterpoint to his own arguments.

A. that he was accused in the first place.

WRONG: There is no reference to this in the passage.

B. that he has not been "proven innocent."

CORRECT: The author points out that simply because the state cannot prove its case, this does *not* prove someone's innocence. "[A] finding of 'not guilty' or the inability of the state to pursue a prosecution does not mean that the accused has been "proven innocent" (lines 51–53).

C. that he may still have committed the crime.

WRONG: There is no reference to this in the passage. This answer is not the same as, and not as good an answer as, Answer B.

D. that he has been "proven innocent."

WRONG: This answer is the antithesis to the author's point. "[A] finding of 'not guilty' or the inability of the state to pursue a prosecution does not mean that the accused has been "proven innocent" (lines 51–53).

24. The passage implies that "our system of justice" should:

Beyond the subject of the death penalty, the entire passage implicates "our system of justice." This is first specifically mentioned in the statement "Our system of justice was not designed so that we let no guilty man go free" (lines 60–61).

A. ensure that no guilty man go free.

WRONG: This is the antithesis to the passage (lines 60–61).

B. eliminate costly appeals for those facing death.

WRONG: This is not implied in the passage. On the contrary, the author implies that even with costly appeals "human justice remains fallible."

C. ensure that all death sentences are carried out swiftly.

WRONG: This is not implied in the passage. The length and costs of the legal processes are alluded to, yet because "human justice remains fallible" the author would clearly not wish to hasten the processes.

D. ensure that mistakes are not made that cannot be rectified.

CORRECT: The author is clearly not a proponent of the death penalty, which is an "*irrevocable* act from which there is no appeal" (lines 11–12) and "an *irreversible* act of violence by the state, and it will inevitably claim innocent victims" (lines 64–65), to give only a few examples.

25. On the sole basis of the passage, determine which of the following acts the author would most want to see forbidden by international law, regardless of the heinousness of the offense.

The answers to these types of questions can rarely be found verbatim in the passages and *often* deal with completely different, albeit parallel subjects.

A. Using private property for state purposes

WRONG: There are no parallels or relationships that can be drawn between this answer and the passage.

B. Placing certain restrictions on prosecution investigators in death penalty cases

WRONG: The author probably thinks that the prosecution has enough advantages and would *not* want to forbid placing restrictions on investigators. He believes that mistakes are made in the judicial process and that it is *not* an equitable process; "it is irrefutable that for a *disenfranchised* individual who cannot afford his own attorney, the likelihood that he will obtain good representation and counsel at this critical first trial is slim" (lines 27–30).

C. Suspending appeals in death penalty cases

CORRECT: The author *would* most want to see this forbidden. "The death penalty entails the risk of judicial errors, which, unlike imprisonment, can never be corrected" (lines 37–39). The author is *not* a proponent of the death penalty, which is an "*irrevocable* act from which there is no appeal" (lines 11–12) and "an *irreversible* act of violence by the state, and it will inevitably claim innocent victims" (lines 64–65), to give only a few examples. He would therefore, NOT wish to see appeals suspended.

D. Torturing prisoners facing the death penalty

WRONG: This is not as good an answer as Answer C. Being 'tortured' is not as serious as "being put to death." For instance, given the two alternatives, if "torturing prisoners was forbidden," but appeals in death penalty cases were "suspended," what would the probable result be? Most likely this would result in prisoners who were *not* tortured but *were* more routinely put to death.

26. Which of the following statements most strongly *challenges* one of the assertions made in the passage?

A. One only has to watch an execution to see that lethal injection is more humane than Old Sparky.

WRONG: This answer does *not* challenge a passage assertion. "Perhaps this is due to the *seemingly* more

A & E 12

humane method of lethal injection as opposed to Old Sparky" (lines 5–7).

B. Death row is actually very different from the movie, *The Green Mile*.

WRONG: This answer does *not challenge* a passage assertion. Though the movie *The Green Mile* is mentioned, there is *no* assertion that death row is *either* the same or different from the movie.

C. Our system of justice ensures that society is protected from those who commit violent crimes.

WRONG: This answer does *not challenge* a passage assertion. There is no assertion in the passage regarding violent crimes that can be challenged.

D. The death penalty saves money in the long run.

CORRECT: This answer clearly challenges the passage assertion that the death penalty is *more expensive* in the long run. "From a purely economic standpoint, the costs of the death penalty are not intuitive [the remainder of this paragraph goes on to describe the hidden costs of capital punishment]" (lines 13–20).

27. Which of the following conclusions about the death penalty can be inferred from the passage?

A. It is possible that people have been put to death for crimes they did not commit.

CORRECT: This is clearly implied from lines in the passage, and covered at length in the paragraph 40–59. "It is difficult to know if the innocent have been put to death by the state for crimes that they did not commit... Yet this perspective is becoming increasingly naïve in the face of the fact that several individuals who were awaiting executions on death row have been freed recently " (lines 40–46).

B. It is unlikely that people have been put to death for crimes they did not commit.

WRONG: This is exactly opposite the correct answer. See Answer A.

C. Our system of justice ensures that no innocent people are convicted.

WRONG: This is not implied and flies in the face of the author's reasoning. The author believes that mistakes have probably been made. If the innocent have been put to death, then innocent people *are* convicted. See Answer A.

D. Our system of justice ensures that no guilty people go free.

WRONG: "Our system of justice was *not* designed so that we let no guilty man go free" (lines 60–61).

28. With regard to our present system of justice, the author most clearly believes that:

A. justice is blind.

WRONG: There is no mention of this. Further, lines 21–39 argue strongly that the "disenfranchised" receive short thrift at the hands of justice.

B. a minority person is at a disadvantage.

WRONG: This is *not* the best answer. The author admits that it is not clear that minorities are at a disadvantage. "From a purely statistical standpoint, it is difficult to ascertain if these arguments [regarding *minorities*, among others] are relevant" (lines 25–27).

C. a poor person is at a disadvantage.

CORRECT: While admitting that statistical evidence regarding discriminatory practices is not irrefutable, the author argues that being poor means that you begin the judicial process at a disadvantage. "[I]t is irrefutable that for a disenfranchised individual who *cannot afford* [i.e. is "poor"] his own attorney, the likelihood that he will obtain good representation and counsel at this critical first trial is slim" (lines 27–30).

D. DNA testing will always determine innocence.

WRONG: The author does not believe that everyone who is accused, convicted, or put to death is innocent. The point is that *mistakes* are made in the process. The reference to DNA is that it has spotlighted some of these mistakes.

Passage VI (Questions 29–34)

29. In order to distinguish the nature of the Japanese loss at Midway, the author of the passage draws a distinction between:

I. the Aleutian Islands and Pearl Harbor.

WRONG: In order to answer the question correctly, there must *first* be a distinction drawn. There is *no* distinction drawn in the passage between "the Aleutian Islands and Pearl Harbor."

II. planes and aircraft carriers.

WRONG: In order to answer the question correctly, there must *first* be a distinction drawn. There is no explicit distinction drawn in the passage between "planes and aircraft carriers."

III. strategic and tactical objectives.

CORRECT: The author repeatedly draws a distinction between 'strategic' and 'tactical' objectives and plans. The 'strategic' objective/plan/goal was to destroy the rest of the American carriers (lines 13-23). This was the *more* important, *large*-scale, overarching goal of Yamamoto. What occurred was an emphasis on the 'tactical' objective/plan/goal, which was the *less* important, *smaller*-scale attempt to actually take Midway. Midway was "simply a [tactical] ploy" (line 16) to lure the American carriers to battle.

A. I only
B. II only
C. III only
   CORRECT: See above explanations.
D. I, II, and III

30. From the Japanese perspective, an important lesson of war implied in the passage is:

A. never split available forces.
   WRONG: This answer is too extreme. Though the Japanese reserve forces were too far from Midway to be of use, "this reserve force did have tactical value" (lines 29–30). If a reserve force can have tactical value, then it is too extreme to suggest that available forces "never [be] split." This is not the best answer.

B. a reserve force has little tactical value.
   WRONG: Though the Japanese reserve forces were too far from Midway to be of use, "this reserve force *did* have tactical value" (lines 29–30). It is then questionable how much tactical value "a" reserve force has. Notice that the "a" renders this answer a generalization. There is not enough information in the passage for this to be the best answer.

C. position reserve forces to protect against reinforcements.
   WRONG: This is not the best answer. The answer tells us part of what the Japanese were trying to do. "Although this reserve force did have tactical value (it served to protect Japanese invasion forces in the Aleutians from Allied reinforcements), *its remote position eliminated its threat to the American carriers*" (lines 29–32). However, the *end* of the quote points to a more important lesson. The *primary* purpose of the reserve force was to help win the battle of Midway!

D. position reserve forces closer to the battle.
   CORRECT: The passage tells us that the reserve force was ineffective because "its remote position eliminated its threat to the American carriers" (lines 31–32). This "large group in reserve [was] too far from the battle to be of any use" (lines 28–29).

31. What distinction is implied in the passage between tactical and strategic, respectively?

A. long term, short term
   WRONG: This is not "respectively"; it is backwards. If it was "short term [tactical], long term [strategic]," then this would have been correct.

B. more important, less important
   WRONG: This is not "respectively"; it is backwards. If it was "less important [tactical], more important [strategic]," then this would have been correct. "Once again, the strategic objective was sacrificed for the *less important tactical objective*" (lines 55–57).

C. small scale, large scale
   CORRECT: The author, again and again, draws a distinction between 'strategic' and 'tactical' objectives/plans/goals. The 'strategic' objective/plan/goal was to destroy the rest of the American carriers (lines 12–22). This was the *more* important, *large*-scale, overarching goal of Yamamoto. What occurred was an emphasis on the 'tactical' objective/plan/goal, which was the *less* important, *smaller*-scale attempt to actually take Midway. Midway was "simply a [tactical] ploy" (line 16) to lure the American carriers to battle.

D. Pearl Harbor, Midway
   WRONG: There is no relationship between the two battles in the passage regarding a "tactical and strategic" distinction.

32. Suppose it is discovered that Yamamoto wanted the American carrier forces split at Midway in order to ensure that Nagumo's advantage in carrier strength was overwhelming. Does this discovery support the author's argument?

A. Yes. The Aleutian invasion would have accomplished this.
   WRONG: The beginning of the correct answer cannot be "yes." This does not support the author's argument, because the author does not ever suggest "splitting" the carrier forces. There is no indication that the Aleutian invasion "would have accomplished" "splitting" the American carrier forces. All that the passage provides is that it could have drawn the American carrier forces north (lines 40–42).

B. Yes. This would have enhanced chances of Nagumo's victory.
   WRONG: The beginning of the correct answer cannot be "yes." This does not support the author's argument, because the author does not ever suggest "splitting" the carrier forces.

C. No. The author asserts that a feint at the Aleutians was a poor decision.
   CORRECT: First, this does *not* support the author's argument. The author asserts that the Japanese invasion of Midway was a tactical "ploy to bring the remaining enemy carriers to battle at a numerical disadvantage" (lines 16–17), which would have been accomplished by "splitting" them, per the question. The author *admits* that the Aleutians was

a "feint" and admits that the Americans could have been drawn north (lines 40–42), but *never suggests* that the *purpose* was to "split" the American fleet. In fact, the author felt that drawing the carriers 'north' was a *bad* decision.

D. No. Nagumo still should not have been using bombs.

WRONG: The beginning of the correct answer must be "no;" however, using bombs has nothing to do with splitting the American forces. This is the worst choice among the four.

33. Passage information indicates that which of the following statements must be true?

A. Strategic objectives should remain within the confines of the overall tactical plan.

WRONG: This is diametrically opposed to the passage information. We know that a strategic objective is *more* important and wider in scope and should not be "sacrificed for the less important tactical objective" (lines 56–57). Thus, it makes no sense to say, "Strategic objectives should remain within the confines of the overall tactical plan."

B. Tactical objectives must remain subordinate to the strategic plan.

CORRECT: This is strongly reiterated throughout the passage. It can be inferred from references such as the "strategic, and more important, objective" (line 18), and "less important tactical objective" (lines 56–57). And, "In their tactical positioning of the reserves, the Japanese [who lost Midway] overlooked the strategic implications" (lines 32–34).

C. The Japanese strategic plan was flawed.

WRONG: This does not have to be true. We cannot know this based upon the passage, because the strategic concept of concentrating all of the American carriers, then striking them with the full Japanese forces armed with torpedoes, was never carried out.

D. If the Japanese had destroyed the American carriers at Midway, they might well have won the war.

WRONG: This does not have to be true. The final statement, "Clearly, if the Japanese had maintained their focus on the sinking of the carriers, they could not have lost" (lines 63–64), is a reference to the battle of Midway and *not* the *entire* war.

34. According to the passage, all of the following are true about Nagumo's decision to rearm his airplanes with bombs (lines 46–57) EXCEPT:

A. This decision may have saved the American aircraft carriers from destruction.

WRONG: This is true. "This decision alone may have saved the carriers" (lines 54–55).

B. This was an example of a tactical decision taking precedence over the strategic plan.

WRONG: This is true. Nagumo chose to rearm with bombs in order to support the invasion forces at Midway. However, since torpedoes were a better weapon against carriers, this tactical decision made little sense from a strategic standpoint, since the strategic goal of "ploy" invasion was to destroy the carriers.

C. Nagumo seemed to be more concerned about the welfare of his Midway invasion forces.

WRONG: This is true. "Nagumo chose to soften Midway for the invasion force and felt that this called for the rearming of the planes" (lines 52–54).

D. This tactic had been used successfully at Pearl Harbor.

CORRECT: This is *not* true and is thus an EXCEPTION. The planes were "*rearmed*" with bombs. The "planes had been *previously* armed [with torpedoes]" (lines 49–50).

Passage VII (Questions 35–40)

35. The claim that "[w]e must remember that humankind had existed in its primitive, prehistoric state for millions of years before the period of recorded civilization, which has lasted a mere 3,000 years" (lines 3–6) necessitates which of the following conclusions?

Notice that this type of question is prefaced on the "claim" that is a quote from the passage. It does not say *Based on passage information*, the claim that …"

A. Most of humankind's responses evolved during prehistory.

WRONG: This conclusion is *not* necessitated by the claim. This is an inference drawn from the passage as a whole; it is not suggested by the question.

B. Most of humankind's responses evolved during the last 3,000 years.

WRONG: This conclusion is *not* necessitated by the claim; nor is it supported by passage information.

C. Before humans developed the ability to record, there was no civilization.

WRONG: This conclusion is *not* necessitated by the claim. The reference to "recorded civilization" might just as well suggest that there was a period prior to writing when there was an "*un*recorded civilization." Answer D is the best answer.

D. Writing heralded the end of prehistory.

CORRECT: This conclusion is necessitated by the claim. According to the quote, "prehistory" occurred "before the period of recorded [written] civilization." Thus, writing signaled or heralded the end of prehistory.

36. The author claims that in order to maximize the chances that his children would survive and then reproduce themselves, "the main quality sought by men in women was youth, beauty, and easy availability" (lines 47–49). The support offered for this conclusion is:

This is a classic MCAT question. *Before* you decide whether it is "strong" or "weak" go to the *second* clause of the answer and determine if: 1) it is accurate, 2) it is from passage information, and 3) it is supportive or nonsupportive of the question. If the second clause is *in*accurate or *not* from passage information it *cannot* be a correct answer, no matter whether it is "strong" or "weak." However, a *nonsupportive* and *accurate* second clause can be correct *if* it is prefaced by "weak." By the same token a *supportive* and *accurate* second clause must be prefaced by "strong" in order to be a correct answer.

A. strong; the passage indicates that beauty would not help his female children reproduce.

WRONG: The second clause is inaccurate; if one of the main qualities being sought by men is "beauty," then beauty certainly *would* help his female children reproduce. The first part of the answer, "strong," has no bearing on this answer since it is not accurate.

B. strong; the passage indicates that beauty would help his male children reproduce.

WRONG: The second clause is inaccurate; there is no indication that women sought "beauty" in their mates. As a matter of fact, "transient good looks" were far down the list of female values for a man. The first part of this answer, "weak," has no bearing on this answer since it is not accurate.

C. weak; there is no indication that beauty would help his male children reproduce.

CORRECT: The second clause is accurate. There is no indication that women sought "beauty" in their mates. As a matter of fact, "transient good looks" were far down the list of female values for a man. Therefore, the support offered for this conclusion is "weak," and this can be a correct answer.

D. weak; there is no indication that beauty would help his female children reproduce.

WRONG: The second clause is inaccurate; if one of the main qualities being sought by men is "beauty," then beauty certainly would help his female children reproduce. The first part of this answer, "weak," has no bearing on this answer since it is not accurate.

37. The author's argument that men's culture evolved to focus around the hunt is most *weakened* by which idea that is implicit in the passage?

A. This had to have occurred within a relatively short time.

WRONG: This is not suggested by the passage, unless one considers "millions of years" (line 4) to have been a relatively short time. Remember that outside information (and your opinion) on the time required by evolution is not required to answer the question, nor is it helpful.

B. Women's culture also included hunters.

WRONG: This is not implied by the passage.

C. Women were not as physically capable of hunting as men.

WRONG: It is implied in the passage that women were weaker than men; however, if this is assumed to be true, it actually reinforces the author's argument in the question.

D. This had to have occurred prior to agriculture.

CORRECT: This supposition is even provided by the author himself: "For most of (pre-agricultural) prehistory, men assumed the role of 'hunter'" (lines 14–15). And it does weaken the author's argument by limiting the amount of time available for this evolution to have taken place. This answer is not a very satisfying answer, but it can be arrived at by process of elimination. None of the other answers is appropriate. This is a good example of some of the less appealing choices you may find on the actual MCAT. Don't agonize on a question during the test. Make your best choice and move on.

38. Taking into consideration passage information on male desires, the claim that "women desired 'pair bonding' (later institutionalized as marriage), and were conditioned to seek a long-term sexual bond with one male" (lines 60–62) necessitates which of the following conclusions?

A. Men probably ensured that divorce was an option.

WRONG: We know from the passage that men wanted "opportunistic sex with many [preferably young] women," which is diametrically opposed to the idea of 'pair-bonding.' However, divorce is never mentioned or alluded to in the passage. This is quite a stretch.

B. Men would stay married just long enough to inseminate the women.

WRONG: We know from the passage that men wanted "opportunistic sex with many [preferably young] women," which is diametrically opposed to the idea of 'pair-bonding.'

C. Marriage was developed and promoted by women.

CORRECT: This is the only conclusion necessitated by the passage information and the claim. We know from the passage that men wanted "opportunistic sex with many [preferably young] women," which is diametrically opposed to the idea of 'pair-bonding.'

A & E 12

Yet marriage was "institutionalized." By whom? "Taking into consideration passage information on male desires," the answer is, by women.

D. Women and men evolved in their desires for marriage.

WRONG: There is no indication that women evolved in their desires for marriage or that the 'pair-bonding' idea was ever different than presented in the passage.

39. An unstated assumption in the author's discussion of humankind's evolution is that:

A. it was predominantly determined by women.

WRONG: This is not assumed in the author's discussion either explicitly or implicitly.

B. it has been outstripped by civilization.

CORRECT: "Outstripped" merely means "beaten" in the sense of a race. The passage provides that "[evolutionary] responses that evolved during this vast but influential [3,000-year period of recorded civilization] are often startlingly inapplicable to the recently modernized world" (lines 8–10).

C. the majority of this evolution took place over a period of 3,000 years.

WRONG: "Thus, most of human evolution occurred during the prehistoric period" (lines 6–7). This was "before the period of recorded civilization, which has lasted a mere 3,000 years" (lines 5–6).

D. it was predominantly determined by men.

WRONG: This is not assumed in the author's discussion either explicitly or implicitly.

40. Suppose it could be established that many, many women and men do *not* exhibit the tendencies described in the passage. The author of the passage would be most likely to respond to this information by:

This is a classic MCAT question. Consider your best answer choices those that would allow the author to either *support* or, in the worst case, *resurrect* or *rehabilitate* his main arguments and thesis. No author would be likely to admit he was completely wrong or abandon his thesis.

A. claiming that they had "adapted" to their more modern surroundings.

WRONG: This would seriously depart from the author's strong thesis that "[these evolutionary responses] persist, a testament to the durability of evolutionary influences" (lines 12–13).

B. arguing that, most likely, this supposition was flawed.

WRONG: This is a weak and obvious choice. However, we cannot ignore that the supposition in the question tells us that "it could be established" that the supposition is true.

C. explaining that his arguments were obviously generalizations.

CORRECT: With *this* explanation, the author could stand by the premises of his passage *and* yet not be required to argue with "established" information to the contrary. He could "have his cake and eat it, too."

D. describing evidentiary research that backs his claim.

WRONG: This is pure speculation. It presupposes that there is evidentiary research to back his claim. Given that there are no references, studies, or research mentioned, this answer is a stretch of the imagination.

A&E 12

Verbal Reasoning Test 13
Answers & Explanations

TEST 13 ANSWER KEY

1.	D	11.	B	21.	A	31.	C
2.	A	12.	A	22.	B	32.	C
3.	B	13.	C	23.	B	33.	C
4.	C	14.	C	24.	C	34.	B
5.	D	15.	A	25.	B	35.	D
6.	C	16.	D	26.	A	36.	C
7.	A	17.	C	27.	D	37.	A
8.	B	18.	D	28.	B	38.	B
9.	D	19.	A	29.	D	39.	D
10.	C	20.	C	30.	B	40.	B

Passage I (Questions 1–5)

1. According to the passage, Francis Bacon believed in "setting out a more rigid system of gradual degrees of understanding, with sense perception, aided by observational equipment, as the only feasible means of acquiring information" (lines 10–13). This technique could most reasonably be *contrasted* with:

    A. pure discernment.

    WRONG: This does *not contrast* with the quote. One "discerns" with the senses.

    B. practical testing.

    WRONG: This does *not contrast* with the quote. The quote generally describes "practical testing."

    C. experimentation.

    WRONG: This does *not contrast* with the quote. The quote generally describes "experimentation."

    D. subjective reasoning.

    CORRECT: For one thing, Bacon "denies the importance of intellect" (line 15). He would not believe in "subjective reasoning." This answer clearly *contrasts* with the quote in the question.

2. Which one of the following most closely describes the author's characterization of Bacon's and Descartes's attitude toward the Church, respectively?

    In responding to this question, *respectively* means that Bacon's attitude comes *first*, *followed* by Descartes's.

    A. Criticism while avoiding alienation, avoidance of conflict

    CORRECT: In the first part of the answer (as required) Bacon "attacks theologians" (lines 38–39) but also attempts to "avoid alienating influential ... clerics" (line 42). Descartes attempts to avoid conflict and "goes out of his way to appease churchgoers" (line 52).

    B. Criticism, careful criticism while avoiding alienation

    WRONG: The first part of this answer is not as complete a description of Bacon's attitude as Answer A. Further, the passage does not provide that Descartes provided *careful criticism*.

    C. Avoidance of conflict, avoidance of conflict

    WRONG: Bacon did *not avoid conflict* but, after attacking clerics (lines 38–39), attempted to avoid alienating clerics (line 42).

    D. Blunt criticism and rejection, avoidance of conflict

    WRONG: Bacon did not reject the Church. He attempted to avoid alienating clerics (lines 43–44), for example.

3. According to the passage, which of the following could be an example of Bacon disagreeing with Descartes?

    A. The evidence of the senses must be rejected unless aided by observational equipment.

    WRONG: Bacon did *not* believe this statement, but believed in "sense perception, aided by observational equipment, as the only feasible means of acquiring information" (lines 11–13).

    B. Information cannot be generated by reason.

    CORRECT: Descartes believed that "reason ... becomes the *sole tool* for generating information" (lines 31-33). Bacon, on the other hand, wanting "to reduce subjective-reasoning error, he rejects all conclusions based on pure logic. Thus, he denies the importance of intellect" (lines 13–15).

    C. God does not exist.

    WRONG: We have no information from the passage to form a basis on whether Bacon believed, or did not believe, in God.

    D. There is no way of knowing if our physical bodies actually exist.

    WRONG: This is a belief of Descartes. However, Bacon did *not* believe this statement, but believed in "sense perception, aided by observational equipment, as the only feasible means of acquiring information" (lines 11–13).

4. According to the passage, Francis Bacon "rejected pure logic" and believed that it was possible for "anyone with senses to enter the search for truth on a level field" (lines 15–16). This concept is most *discrepant* with Bacon's specific statement regarding which of the following?

    A. the Church

    WRONG: This answer is not related to the question.

    B. God

    WRONG: This answer is not related to the question.

    C. classical philosophers

    CORRECT: Bacon "reluctantly says that classical philosophers were *intelligent* though misguided men" (lines 43–44). This is *discrepant* because, as the quote in the question points out, Bacon "denies the importance of intellect" (line 15).

    D. ancient philosophers

    WRONG: "Bacon blasts ancient philosophers as superstitious 'spiders'" (line 37). However, this is not related to the question.

5. According to the passage, Descartes's "proof" of the existence of God "rests on faith, and should have been rejected on these grounds" (lines 56–57). This conclusion

of the author's can best be supported from the passage information that:

A. Descartes fails to establish God's omnipotence.

WRONG: This answer is a quote from the passage; however, it does *not* answer the question. "The role [Descartes] assigns to God—the giver of knowledge, to the exclusion of all else—fails to establish God's omnipotence (since God has no power over the existence of the thinker)" (lines 58–60).

B. the senses can deceive.

WRONG: This answer is from the passage; however, it does not answer the question. You would have to assume that "faith" evolved or was brought forth from the senses. This information is not provided by the passage.

C. shows that Descartes goes out of his way to appease churchgoers.

WRONG: This answer is not responsive to the question.

D. indicates that Descartes did not believe faith could generate information.

CORRECT: This information is from the passage *and* supports the author's conclusion. "Since the senses can deceive, their evidence is rejected, and *reason ... becomes the sole tool for generating information*" (lines 30–32).

Passage II (Questions 6–11)

6. According to the passage, water-resistance with respect to skins that have been tanned in some fashion is characteristic of:

    I.   chrome tanning.

        WRONG: Chrome tanning "is also used for hides ... *that will not be exposed to water*" (lines 26–28).

    II. vegetable tanning.

        CORRECT: "Vegetable-tanned leather is used ... because of its natural abilities to remain flexible and malleable *after repeated contact with water*" (lines 48–50).

    III. smoking.

        CORRECT: The "qualities of water-resistance ... are added later through slow smoking " (lines 32–33).

A. I only

B. II only

C. II and III only

CORRECT: See above explanations.

D. I, II, and III

7. On the basis of the passage, it is reasonable to conclude that the term *top grain*, when used to describe leather, refers to:

"Top grain" is never explicitly mentioned or described in the passage. It's meaning must be discerned through comparison and contrast with other terminology, such as "bottom grain" (line 64).

A. the outer surface of the animal's skin.

CORRECT: "Care must be taken that only the 'bottom grain' of the leather, and *not the fine outer surface,* is drawn against the edge, or deep scratching may result" (lines 63–66).

B. the finest leather.

WRONG: If you chose this answer you are drawing upon outside knowledge and experience that is not supported within the passage. There is no mention of "top grain" being the finest leather, or of "bottom grain" being the poorest leather.

C. the inner surface of the animal's skin.

WRONG

D. the least desirable leather.

WRONG

8. An important comparison is made in the passage between:

A. tooling and dyeing.

WRONG: These are unrelated. There is no comparison made between them.

B. dyeing and coloration achieved through tanning.

CORRECT: Chrome-tanned skins are described as such: "The resultant hides, furs, and skins are white and must be dyed if another color or a more natural color is desired." (lines 28–30). "Unlike chemically tanned skins, vegetable-tanned skins assume the soft natural color of the plant used for the tanning" (lines 44–46).

C. clothing and tools.

WRONG: These are offered as one in the same, as "necessities, not as comparisons: "*clothing*, housing, *tools*, and other necessities for the survival of hunter-gatherer societies" (lines 5–6).

D. lye and wood ashes.

WRONG: These are offered as one in the same, not as comparisons: "A strong base, such as *lye, wood ashes*, or lime is applied to the skin until the hair comes away easily" (lines 37–39).

9. The author suggests that the difficulty of tanning leather at home results from:

A. the necessity of reducing the leather's thickness.

WRONG: This is not suggested.

B. the tendency of the hair to "slip."
WRONG: This is not suggested.

C. obtaining the necessary materials.
WRONG: This is not suggested.

D. softening the leather.
CORRECT: Breaking or softening (one in the same, see line 16) the leather "is similar to [the action] of buffing a shoe and is physically quite rigorous and taxing. It is at this point that the home tanner begins to appreciate the price that he pays for fine leather" (lines 60–63).

10. According to information in the passage, the fastest way to "remove the proteins from the hide" (line 12) would be to:

To "remove the proteins from the hide" is to tan the hide or turn it into leather.

A. apply a very strong base.
WRONG: The base is used to remove the hair, not tan the hide.

B. first remove the hair.
WRONG: This is not suggested.

C. chrome tan the skin.
CORRECT: "'[C]hrome tanning' ... is very quick and ... this method is *relatively swift*" (lines 22–24).

D. apply very concentrated legumes.
WRONG: Applying legumes is vegetable tanning. "Vegetable tanning is a much *slower* process" (line 34). There is no indication that applying "very concentrated legumes" would make the process faster.

11. Suppose that "prior to the advent of weaving and creating cloth," the hunter-gatherers were to find themselves in a lush prairie environment, but one that was devoid of trees. In order to make leather, the author's ideas suggest that they should:

A. tan using oak, walnut, or sumac leaves.
WRONG: The supposition of the question *precludes* access to trees (oak, walnut, or sumac) or leaves.

B. gather alfalfa or other legumes.
CORRECT: This is the only possible answer choice that will *allow* tanning with materials that might be *available according to the supposition in the question*.

C. use wood ashes or lime.
WRONG: These bases are used to de-hair the skins, not tan them.

D. first de-hair the skins with the animal's brains.
WRONG: The brains are used to "tan" the hide. This answer implies that the brains will "first de-hair the skins."

Passage III (Questions 12–16)

12. The passage implies that wood finishes are MORE effective when they:

A. protect from moisture and beautify that which is covered.
CORRECT: This answer can be chosen by process of elimination in that each of the other answer choices offers an aspect of wood finishes that is *not* considered to be "more effective" according to the passage. Wood "finishes have been used for *preserving and protecting* wood furniture while *maintaining or enhancing the beauty* of the wood itself" (lines 1–4).

B. inhibit moisture, protect that which is covered, and remain impervious to solvents.
WRONG: Remaining "impervious to solvents" is not necessarily more effective or desirable since it inhibits one's ability to repair the surface. See the comparison/contrast between polyurethane and shellac.

C. beautify the underlying wood, protect from moisture, and penetrate to some degree.
WRONG: It is not implied that to "penetrate to some degree" is more effective. Penetration to some degree is not only unlikely, but may cause "predictable darkening."

D. inhibit moisture, allow for easy repairs to that which is covered, and remain transparent.
WRONG: To "remain transparent" is *not* promoted as being more effective. Paint is not transparent, yet it is not only more suitable in some environments, but it is also highly desirable in covering blemished wood, for instance.

13. The passage suggests that people generally believe that a wood finish will actually penetrate the wood, and that this belief derives from the fact that:

A. the finish appears to penetrate.
WRONG: It does not actually penetrate, nor does it *appear* to penetrate, according to the passage.

B. consumers promote this idea.
WRONG: Manufacturers, not consumers, promote the idea.

C. this idea is actually advertised.
CORRECT: This is why people believe that finishes penetrate the wood. "What [wood finishes] do not do, despite the *promotions of manufacturers* and the

yearnings of consumers, is 'penetrate' the wood" (lines 14–16).

D. there exists a "myth that the older furniture makers knew best."

WRONG: The passage does *not* suggest that this "myth" is related to the 'belief' in the question.

14. According to the passage, any actual penetration that is going to occur is predominantly:

A. going to be only one molecule thick.

WRONG: "[M]olecules" is plural, implying *more* than one. "Cross-sectional analysis of any commonly used finish such as a 'penetrating' Danish oil will reveal the finish to be *only molecules thick*" (lines 23–25).

B. from an oily nondrying finish left to soak too long on oak or cherry.

WRONG: "Only in the *softest of woods such as pine* and the oiliest nondrying finishes is there any discernible penetration of the wood itself" (lines 16–18). Pine is contrasted with "hardwoods, such as black cherry, mahogany, and oak" (lines 22–23).

C. at the 'end-grain' of the piece.

CORRECT: "Moreover, unless this 'oil' is allowed to generously soak into the 'end-grain' of the board … there is no discernible penetration of the wood itself" (lines 25–28).

D. the promotions of the manufacturer.

WRONG: This answer does not make grammatical sense when joined to the question. Further, according to the passage, the manufacturer's promotions are wrong and have nothing to do with whether or not the finish will "*actually*" occur.

15. The central thesis of the passage is that:

A. wood finishes actually coat and protect the wood.

CORRECT: This answer is the central thesis and can be determined as such, or found through process of elimination.

B. it is a myth that the older furniture makers knew best.

WRONG: This idea is mentioned but once in the passage. It is not the "central thesis."

C. wood finishes penetrate very little.

WRONG: This is inaccurate. According to the passage, "Wood finishes are in fact wood 'coverings.' What they do not do … is 'penetrate' the wood" (lines 14–16). This is not equivocal.

D. paint is still the best.

WRONG: This is inaccurate. Paint *may* be the best in *certain* situations.

16. According to the passage, which of the following wood finishes is/are a good choice for a wood surface that will be exposed to an outdoor environment?

An outdoor environment will mean exposure to moisture, temperature variations, and sunlight.

    I. shellac

WRONG: Shellac is not acceptable when it means exposure to moisture. Because it is effected by moisture, for one, "shellac has received a reputation for fragility. Though it is true that … water left on its surface may form white rings" (lines 53–56).

    II. polyurethane

CORRECT: We can discern that polyurethane is impervious to water and other solvents because the author contrasts and compares these characteristics in the final paragraph.

    III. paint

CORRECT: Paint "inhibits moisture, and protects the underlying wood from heat and sunlight" (lines 35–36).

A. II only

B. III only

C. I and III only

D. II and III only

CORRECT: See above explanations.

Passage IV (Questions 17–21)

17. According to the passage, which of the following is most likely to be true about the relationship between Wei Yuan and the followers of Hung Hsiu-ch'uan?

Wei Yuan is the first of two intellectuals quoted by the author. The followers of Hung Hsiu-ch'uan were the rebels.

A. They would have agreed with him.

WRONG: This is not likely since Wei Yuan was outspokenly critical of the rebels.

B. He felt that public interest was sacrificed for technological advancement.

WRONG: *Not* Wei Yuan, but the second intellectual "Ch'u Ch'eng-po wrote of the uselessness of technological advancement without an effort to eliminate the corruption" (lines 61–63).

C. He felt that they were being selfish.

CORRECT: In response to the social disunity, which the rebels were a significant part of, "Wei Yuan angrily proclaimed, 'Away with the nurturing of *private* evils and the tolerating of *private* gain at the expense of the *public* interest!'" (lines 58–59).

D. They believed he was a god.

WRONG: The "god" was not Wei Yuan. Though it is not completely clear, "The form of the revolt … headed by a leader who ruled as an incarnation of a god" (lines 14–17) seems to refer to the "messiah" Hung Hsiu-ch'uan.

18. According to the passage, the question of whether or not the rebellion was purposefully aided by the West is best shown by analysis of the:

A. nationalist Kuomintang regime.

WRONG: The passage offers no causality between the much *later* struggles of the Kuomintang regime and the question of Western involvement with the uprising.

B. West's trade concessions.

WRONG: The passage offers no causality between these trade concessions and the question of Western involvement with the uprising. Further, this answer makes it appear that the *West* made trade concessions, when, in fact, the West *forced* trade concessions from the Chinese.

C. Western nations' seizures in the 1860's.

WRONG: The passage offers no causality between these *later* seizures and the question of Western involvement with the uprising.

D. subsequent Western military actions.

CORRECT: "… there are few indications to suggest that the uprising was in any way planned or even desired by foreign powers. … especially since these same powers rejected the T'ai-P'ing regime's diplomatic overtures and even sent a token military force to aid China's Ch'ing government in putting down the revolt" (lines 20–27).

19. The author is primarily concerned with demonstrating that:

A. the internal dissent in China is deep and longstanding.

CORRECT: The author offers that "this type of revolt has clearly happened *before* in China," covers the revolt, then goes on to outline *continuing* strife in the early 1900's. He also refers to the cyclic nature of history.

B. the Ch'ing dynasty was the root of the strife.

WRONG: "The deep-rooted nature of that dissent was visible later, when *neither the fall of the Ch'ing nor the cutbacks of Western encroachment did anything to stop civil strife in China*" (lines 44–47).

C. Western encroachment was the root cause of the strife.

WRONG: "The deep-rooted nature of that dissent was visible later, when *neither the fall of the Ch'ing*

nor the cutbacks of Western encroachment did anything to stop civil strife in China" (lines 44–47).

D. the rebellion was supported by the intellectuals.

WRONG: This is clearly not the case. While not completely supporting the dynasty by any means, neither of the two quoted intellectuals who had been "traditionally aloof" were supportive of the rebellion. They were more concerned with the "opportunistic costs" of China's social disunity (lines 53–55).

20. The author argues that the uprising was more internal than it was influenced from outside the country. Which of the following claims, if true, would most WEAKEN the argument?

A. Hung Hsiu-ch'uan was not really considered a "messiah."

WRONG: This is not related to the question at hand.

B. The author was wrong about the economic imperialism of the West.

WRONG: The economic imperialism is unrelated in the passage to the question at hand.

C. The author was wrong about Roberts.

CORRECT: This would most weaken the argument. If the author had been wrong that "Hung Hsiu-ch'uan's religious advisor, the American priest Roberts, does not seem to have been anything of a provocateur for foreign nations" (lines 21–24), this would have meant that he *was* a provocateur.

D. The intellectuals were correct.

WRONG: First, the author makes no implication regarding whether the intellectuals were correct or not. Moreover, the intellectuals in the passage seem unrelated to the question at hand.

21. According to the passage, prior to the rebellion, which of the following is most likely to be true about the relationship between the intellectuals and the people?

A. The intellectuals had not been involved with the people.

CORRECT: "Unfortunately for China, the *traditionally aloof intellectuals'* calls for unity and morality went unheard among the people" (lines 69–71).

B. The intellectuals had a strong base within the communities.

WRONG: This is not implied by the passage. The intellectuals had been "traditionally aloof" from the people.

C. The intellectuals had urged the people to try to act in the public interest.

WRONG: This is not implied by the passage. The intellectuals had been "traditionally aloof" from the people.

D. The people had looked to the intellectuals for guidance.

WRONG: This is not implied by the passage. The intellectuals had been "traditionally aloof" from the people.

Passage V (Questions 22–28)

22. Suppose you are in the process of finishing a fine wooden rocking chair and given the availability of 200, 400, 80, and 120 sandpaper, but no scrapers. From the grit used first to the grit used last, which of the following choices of sandpaper "grits" (line 13) would be best when finishing this rocker?

A. 120, 200, then 400

WRONG: This sequence "skips" a grit. "This is one reason why it is important *not to skip* grits of sandpaper when attempting to achieve a highly reflective surface" (lines 20–22).

B. 80, 120, 200, then 400

CORRECT: "One uses successively finer and finer grits of sandpaper. Each *higher* number is a *finer* grit and scratches out the scratches made by the previously used grit" (lines 18–20).

C. 400, 200, 120, then 80

WRONG: This sequence is backwards, from lower to higher, from finer to rougher grits.

D. 80, 200, 120, then 400

WRONG: This sequence goes from lower/rougher to higher/finer, to lower/rougher again, to highest/finest. This is not as it should be according to the passage.

23. According to the passage, the biggest drawback to sandpaper is that:

A. it will never allow one to achieve a 'reflective surface.'

WRONG: This is not indicated by the passage. "This is one reason why it is important not to skip grits of sandpaper when attempting to achieve a highly reflective surface" (lines 20–22). One can assume, then, that a "highly reflective surface" might be achieved with sandpaper.

B. it always leave scratches.

CORRECT: This is the biggest drawback. "Sandpaper, by its nature, will always leave scratches in the wood surface, no matter how minute" (lines 27–28).

C. it is rather labor intensive.

WRONG: It is the preparation of the *scrapers* that is "laborious." There is no information that sanding is "rather labor intensive."

D. almost no one hand-sands.

WRONG: This is not offered in the passage as a drawback of sandpaper. This is a *very* nonspecific choice if you felt that it alluded to the problems of "noise." This is not the best answer.

24. The passage suggests that determining the very finest finish may be best accomplished by:

A. looking closely at the surface to determine that no scratches are visible.

WRONG: "At some point, [*but prior to the point where the scratches may still be felt (next line)*] the scratches may no longer be visible to the naked eye" (lines 22–24). In other words, you would *see* a reflective surface with no visible scratches, yet you would still be able to *feel* the scratches. See the explanation for Answer C.

B. looking for a highly reflective surface.

WRONG: "At some point, [*but prior to the point where the scratches may still be felt (next line)*] the scratches may no longer be visible to the naked eye" (lines 22–24). In other words, you would *see* a reflective surface with no visible scratches, yet you would still be able to *feel* the scratches. See the explanation for Answer C.

C. the sense of touch.

CORRECT: "At some further point [and the *final* point mentioned in this section wherein one is discerning surface quality], the scratches *may no longer be felt by a light caress* of the wood surface" (lines 24–25). And, "Closing one's eyes and lightly caressing the piece will reveal much with regard to the care taken in the production and crafting of the piece" (lines 6–8).

D. ensuring that the maker used the correct sandpaper grits in the right order.

WRONG: This is not the best answer. The passage primarily speaks of finishing the wood surface and sandpapers vs. scrapers, not evaluating the one who is finishing the wood.

25. Which of the following quotations of passage information provides the LEAST support for the author's thesis?

Notice that these are all actual and accurate quotes from the passage.

A. "There are no dust particles to be inhaled or cleaned up when using a scraper."

WRONG: The author's thesis is that a scraper is probably a better tool to use for achieving a fine finish than sandpaper. This answer offers another *supportive* reason for using a scraper instead of sandpaper to achieve the required finish.

B. "Sandpaper, by its nature, will always leave scratches in the wood surface, no matter how minute."

CORRECT: This provides the least support for the author's thesis. The author's thesis is that a scraper is probably a better tool to use for achieving a fine finish than sandpaper. However, if there are scratches in the wood, but *the scratches cannot be seen or felt and the wood is highly reflective, why would you care if you had used a scraper to achieve this or not?!* If you did a good job, you would apparently require some artificial means (a magnifying glass, or possibly even an electron microscope) to discern that the sandpapered surface was *not* perfectly smooth. "At some point, the scratches *may no longer be visible to the naked eye.* At some further point, the scratches *may no longer be felt by a light caress of the wood surface.*" (lines 22–25).

C. "The cost of a set of scrapers is less than a sleeve of sandpaper, which must be constantly replenished."

WRONG: The author's thesis is that a scraper is probably a better tool to use for achieving a fine finish than sandpaper. This answer offers another *supportive* reason for using a scraper instead of sandpaper to achieve the required finish.

D. "[C]onsidering that almost no one hand-sands, the noise of the electric sander, and the lack thereof when using scrapers, should be considered."

WRONG: The author's thesis is that a scraper is probably a better tool to use for achieving a fine finish than sandpaper. This answer offers another *supportive* reason for using a scraper instead of sandpaper to achieve the required finish.

26. What does the author's concept of "an age when tools and materials are 'disposable'" (lines 57–58) imply about the author's values?

A. The author would tend to value more traditional tools and materials that could be reused, even if they were not quite as efficient.

CORRECT: The remark is disparaging, indicating that the author does not think much of disposable materials. Further, he is a proponent of the scraper, though he admits that sandpaper may provide a reflective surface in which scratches are not discernible (lines 22–25), and that the scraper requires "rather laborious preparation." This would tend to show that the author was more concerned with traditional hand tools, regardless of the fact that more modern techniques, tools, and materials might be more efficient.

B. The author would value efficiency and the ability to reuse a material or tool above all else.

WRONG: Certainly not above all else. This is an extreme position ("above all else") that is not indicated by the passage. Ensure that when an extreme answer is provided it is justified by passage information.

C. The author is a proponent of this age and its advances.

WRONG: The author is not a proponent of the age referred to in the quote.

D. The author would probably be considered lazy by today's standards.

WRONG: This answer is not even implied by passage information.

27. The author mentions the use of "sharkskin" (line 32) to indicate a general time period to the reader. According to the passage, the aforementioned period was characterized by all of the following EXCEPT:

A. sharkskin being used as sandpaper.

WRONG: This choice is *not an exception* to the time period. Though this is a convoluted sentence, it still provides, "Harkening back first to its lack of availability, when *sharkskin was actually used as one of the first sandpapers*, other methods were used quite successfully" (lines 31–33).

B. the use of scrapers.

WRONG: This choice is *not an exception* to the time period. "[During this time period] *other* methods were used quite successfully. ... One of the lesser known tools most frequently used in the past was the scraper" (lines 33–38).

C. the use of sharp cutting tools.

WRONG: This choice is *not an exception* to the time period. "[During this time period] other methods were used quite successfully. Most of these methods involved a very *sharp cutting tool* ..." (lines 33–34).

D. the availability of sandpaper.

CORRECT: This choice *is an exception* to the time period. "Harkening back first to [*sandpaper's*] lack of availability, when sharkskin was actually used [*instead*] as one of the first sandpapers" (lines 31–33).

28. According to the passage, "One of the lesser known tools most frequently used in the past was the scraper" (lines 37–38), and "Harkening back first to its lack of availability, when sharkskin was actually used as one of the first sandpapers, other methods were used quite successfully" (lines 31–33). If both of these premises are true, what conclusion is most reasonable?

We know from passage information that the "other methods [that] were used quite successfully" involved "sharp cutting tools."

A. Sharkskin was known as a tool to a greater extent than the scraper.

WRONG: This is not necessarily a valid conclusion. We have no information that would tell us for certain that this is true.

B. Though the scraper was successfully used in the past, it is less well known today.

CORRECT: This can be discerned based upon the premises and passage information.

C. The scraper was used quite successfully, if infrequently, in the past.

WRONG: We know that the scraper was a "lesser-known tool," but that is less well known by more modern craftsmen. The author indicates that the scraper might have been a fairly popular choice among traditional craftsmen. "One of the lesser-known tools most frequently used in the past was the scraper" (lines 37–38).

D. Sharkskin was used quite successfully, although less frequently than the scraper.

WRONG: There is no way to compare the frequency of scraper use with sharkskin.

Passage VI (Questions 29–34)

29. Some scientists believe that the author's "weapons of extinction," such as modern thermonuclear devices, actually do have the capability of exterminating the human race. The author would argue that:

A. these weapons exist only to scare nations and would be used only as a last resort.

WRONG: The author would not argue this. If 1) the weapons could exterminate us, and 2) the "parasite" must keep us alive, then the weapons *cannot ever actually be used*. See the quote at Answer D.

B. the "rules of war" dictate that these types of weapons would actually cause the extinction of the human race.

WRONG: The author would not argue this. According to the passage, the parasite *will not let us die*. See the quote at Answer D.

C. these weapons will, in fact, one day lead to the extinction of the human race.

WRONG: The author would not argue this. According to the passage, the parasite *will not let us die*. See the quote at Answer D.

D. though these weapons exist, the "rules of war" would preclude their ever actually being used.

CORRECT: The author would most likely argue this. If 1) the weapons could exterminate us, and 2) the "parasite" must keep us alive, then the weapons *cannot ever actually be used*. "Through rules, war works on mankind like a parasite, taking as much

as possible from the host *without killing him*. If it killed the host, the parasite would die as well, so it insidiously sucks the life from its host, *taking care to hold him above the threshold of death*" (lines 65–69).

30. Implicit in the passage is the assumption that:

A. weapons will one day cause our extinction.

WRONG: This is not implied. According to the passage, the parasite *will not let us die*. "Through rules, war works on mankind like a parasite, taking as much as possible from the host *without killing him*. If it killed the host, the parasite would die as well, so it insidiously sucks the life from its host, *taking care to hold him above the threshold of death*" (lines 65–69).

B. economics is also a critical factor in determining the "rules of war."

CORRECT: This is implied. Economics and money are mentioned again and again as a factor *throughout* the passage: "Chivalry adjusted" (line 22) by requiring ransom; "[o]nly a minority [of bowmen] could afford armor" (line 30); "[d]ue to more affordable weapons" (lines 42–43). In contrast with "the luxury enjoyed by the captured knight" (lines 47–48).

C. war is an inanimate entity.

WRONG: This is not implied. It is not "inanimate" if it is a parasite. Look at all of the 'action' verbs used to describe war: "works," "taking," "without killing," would "die" as well, "acquires," etc.

D. a limited war will never be fought again.

WRONG: This is not implied. There is no mention of a "limited war." "Unlimited war" is mentioned at line 21.

31. The author provides that the "parasite" (line 65) takes care to hold man "above the threshold of death" (line 69). An appropriate clarification of the passage would be the stipulation that the author's argument applies only to:

A. certain kinds of parasites.

WRONG: This is not an appropriate clarification. Remember that you can answer questions in the Verbal section without knowledge from outside sources. At the least, this answer would suppose that you knew something of "other kinds" of parasites.

B. the period of time preceding the invention of "weapons of extinction."

WRONG: This is not an appropriate clarification. It could be argued that the weapons will never be used. According to the passage, man will not be allowed to die if the parasite has anything to do with it. *If* 1) the weapons *could* exterminate us, *and* 2) the "parasite" must keep us alive, then the weapons *cannot ever actually be used.*

C. extermination of the enemy forces.

CORRECT: This is an appropriate clarification. The "weapons of extinction" (line 58) and "mass annihilation" (line 57), *if used,* must be annihilating and exterminating *someone.* If they exterminate *everyone,* then the passage is *wrong.* The question does *not* ask us to *challenge* the author or *disprove* his theories. This question asks us to help the author out by expanding upon his ideas.

D. the most lethal technology.

WRONG: This is not an appropriate clarification. It is apparent that the author's theory may work with less than the "most lethal technology," for instance, knights and bowmen.

32. The author's major thesis is that:

Don't fret that "your choice" for major thesis is not one of the possible answer choices. This is not an essay question. Pick the best answer available.

A. if we do not change course, our extermination is inevitable.

WRONG: According to the passage, the parasite *will not let us die.*

B. missile warfare has had a dramatic impact.

WRONG: This is not his major thesis. It is not even mentioned in the rather traditional 'opening' or 'closing' paragraphs.

C. the "rules of war" change with increasingly deadly technology to avert our extinction.

CORRECT: The entire passage is about the rules of war changing as technology advances. Further, the last paragraph assures us that the parasite *will not let us die.*

D. the "rules of war" will not prevent our extinction.

WRONG: Yes, they will, according to the passage, as the parasite *will not let us die.*

33. What is the most serious apparent *weakness* of the theory described?

A. Why couldn't the knights in heavy armor tolerate high casualties?

WRONG: This is explained and is therefore not a weakness. "Since only a minority could afford armor, the class of knights could not tolerate high casualties in their warfare" (lines 30–32).

B. How does warfare become less civilized?

WRONG: This is explained and is therefore not a weakness (lines 1–15).

C. Why would the parasite want lethal technology?

CORRECT: This is a serious weakness with the whole parasite simile. "[W]ar works on mankind like a parasite, taking as much as possible from the host without killing him. ... [and] acquires the most lethal technology but in such a fashion as to prevent our extinction" (lines 65–71). What does the parasite get from the lethal technology? More bodies or deaths? The passage does not explain what the advantage would be.

D. What is the difference between mass annihilation and extinction?

WRONG: Since the parasite will not let us die, this doesn't really matter. It is like asking if there is a difference between the "machinegun" and the "airplane."

34. According to the passage, "Chivalry adjusted for [the problems of fighting in heavy armor] by requiring capture for ransom whenever possible rather than killing" (lines 22–23). This 'requirement' is later explained to have meant that:

A. otherwise, huge casualties would have been incurred.

WRONG: This explains "why," but does not explain the "requirement" specifically. Further, this comes "before" and not "*later,*" as the question describes.

B. killing a captured prisoner was actually illegal.

CORRECT: This answer specifically "explains" the "requirement." In the third paragraph, while discussing the bowmen, the passage provides, "Killing a captured prisoner was *still* illegal" (lines 46–47).

C. it was more lucrative to capture than to kill.

WRONG: The passage does *not* "*explain*" this. This is an implication.

D. the new captive was provided with only meager subsistence.

WRONG: This has nothing to do with explaining the question's "requirement."

Passage VII (Questions 35–40)

35. The passage implies that laws in the "Western sense" (line 27) are:

"It is difficult to call [Chinese internal laws] 'laws' in the Western sense, since they are often unpublished, obscure, and very vague even when known" (lines 27–29). These characteristics are the opposite of laws in the "Western sense."

A. ambiguous, though clearly written and published.

WRONG: This is not implied. "Ambiguous" is essentially the same as "obscure" or "vague" and is not the opposite of Chinese internal law. Therefore, they do *not* describe laws in the "Western sense." See the explanation for Answer D.

B. often unpublished, obscure, and very vague.

WRONG: This is not implied. "Often unpublished" is a verbatim description of, and not the opposite of, Chinese internal law. Therefore, they do *not* describe laws in the "Western sense." See the explanation for Answer D.

C. clear, though often unpublished and vague.

WRONG: This is not implied. "Often unpublished" and "vague" are verbatim descriptions of, and not the opposite of, Chinese internal law. Therefore, they do *not* describe laws in the "Western sense." See the explanation for Answer D.

D. unambiguous and published.

CORRECT: This is implied. This description is the *opposite* of the Chinese internal laws, as it should be. Lines 27–29 (quoted in full under the question) describe Chinese internal laws. From this, we can discern that laws in the "Western sense" are the *opposite* of Chinese internal laws.

36. In another publication, the author claims that the Chinese government's "delegation by consensus" is very efficient. The support offered for this conclusion in *this* passage is:

Notice that the question *seems* to be asking you for an *opinion*; did you *think* the "support offered was *weak?*" Like all of the other questions in this book, this is an actual style of MCAT test question. It may be answered by *initially* ignoring the references to "weak" and "strong." These are value judgments. Ask instead, "What support was offered by the author?" You will find that the aspect of the answer following the "weak" or "strong" is either accurate or inaccurate; it *is* either the support offered or it is not. However, if the answer is premised with "weak," it may accurately repeat passage assertions, but *negate* them, if it is the correct answer.

A. weak; those making the final decisions are invariably the State Council members.

WRONG: The statement following "weak" is not accurate. The final decisions are *not* "invariably" made by the State Council members. See the explanation for Answer C.

B. weak; those who are involved often use strong-arm tactics.

WRONG: The statement following "weak" is not accurate. The "strong-arming" refers to the "embarrassing [and unpopular] option" of higher-level authorities approving less-than-unanimous decisions over the objections of subordinates (lines 79–84).

C. strong; those most affected by, and with the most knowledge of, the issue are involved in the decisions.

CORRECT: The second aspect of this answer is accurate passage information, *and* the information strongly supports the author's claim. "Decisions are given for ratification to the subordinate bodies most affected by them" (lines 69–70). "This enables subordinates with greater proximity to, and knowledge of, the issue to be involved in the chain of decision" (lines 74–76).

D. strong; the decisions are only made after it has been determined that raw materials and recruits are available.

WRONG: The statement following "strong" is not accurate. There is no information that decisions are made either "before" or "*after*" the above.

37. According to the passage, after the late 1980's, the regional authorities were able to exert an influence on the national policies by:

Notice that the "after the late 1980's" caveat has nothing to do with the answers. It is not the *key* to answering this question. Three of the answers are inaccurate and one is accurate.

A. electing the members of the Central Committee, who in turn elect the Party leadership.

CORRECT: Lines 56–66 provide information on "reciprocal accountability" and the way in which regional authorities influence the national government. Specifically, "The entire Party jointly elects the Central Committee, a group of 200, from the national and local governments. This Central Committee then elects the top Party leadership. " (lines 57–60).

B. electing their local Party representatives who in turn elect the Central Committee.

WRONG: This is not information that comes from the passage. There is no mention of "electing Party representatives."

C. failing to follow the policies of their elected leaders.

WRONG: This is not an option provided by passage information. In fact, "The regional government/Party members are *compelled* to follow the policies of their elected leaders" (lines 61–62).

D. electing a group of 200 who then elect the Central Committee.

WRONG: The Central Committee *is* the "group of 200." "The entire Party jointly elects the Central Committee, a group of 200 …" (lines 57–59).

38. The claim that the "Chinese Communist Party governs China through parallel rule, which closely resembles the Soviet system" (lines 1–2) necessitates which of the following conclusions?

A & E 13

Since there is no further information provided regarding the Soviets, one can safely assume almost anything about the Soviet system that is based upon information provided about the Chinese system.

A. The Soviet legal system grants little legal discretion to regional governments.

WRONG: This is *not* true of the Chinese system and will not be true of a Soviet system that closely resembles it. "China's legal system grants regional governments broad legal discretion" (lines 12–13).

B. The Soviet Central Committee elects the top Party leadership.

CORRECT: This *is* true of the Chinese system and can be assumed to be true of the Soviet system. "This [Chinese] Central Committee then elects the top Party leadership" (lines 59–60).

C. It is likely that openly radical officials will be promoted within the Soviet Communist Party.

WRONG: This is *not* true of the Chinese system and will not be true of a Soviet system, which closely resembles it. In the Chinese system, it is "*unlikely* that openly radical officials will be promoted within the Party" (lines 10–11).

D. The Chinese system is based upon the Soviet system.

WRONG: This is not a valid conclusion. Maybe this is true. *Or* maybe the Soviet system "is based upon" the Chinese system. There is no information in the passage from which you could draw this conclusion.

39. The term *radical* (line 10) refers implicitly to Chinese officials who:

All four answer choices offer only "opinions that differ" as choices for identifying an "openly radical official." This is a good example of an MCAT question that is *arguable*. In other words, why aren't radicals those whose "actions differ"?! Good point, but it is not an answer choice. Choose the best answer. Whoever wrote the question has decided that "opinions that differ," whether literally supported, implied, or otherwise, by the passage, is the litmus.

A. hold Party positions, but have opinions that differ from the Party.

WRONG: It is clear that the person must hold *both* a government position and a Party position. See explanation for Answer D.

B. hold Party positions, but have opinions that differ from the official government.

WRONG: It is clear that the person must hold *both* a government position and a Party position. They are "simultaneously enrolled." Further, the basis for the "loyalty" is to the party, not to the government. See explanation for Answer D.

C. hold government positions, but have opinions that differ from the Party.

WRONG: It is clear that the person must hold *both* a government position and a Party position. See explanation for Answer D.

D. hold government positions and Party positions, but have opinions that differ from the Party.

CORRECT: This is the implicit reference. "[V]irtually all government officials [are] simultaneously enrolled in the Party. Thus, whatever their official capacity, all government officials are ultimately responsible to their Party superiors, who can promote, demote, or purge them based on 'loyalty.' This makes it unlikely that openly radical officials will be promoted within the Party" (lines 5–11).

40. What assumption is implicit in the sentence, "Both are embarrassing options; the former is an obvious method of strong-arming opposition, while the second is an admission of an unpopular decision" (lines 81–84)?

A. The Party does not like to be embarrassed.

WRONG: This assumption is not implicit in the sentence. *No one* likes to be embarrassed, and, yes, the "higher-level authority" are most likely Party members. However, this is not as responsive to the question as Answer B. This is not the best answer.

B. The higher-level governing bodies prefer unanimous decisions by their subordinates.

CORRECT: We can safely assume that "higher-level governing bodies" do *not* "prefer" embarrassment, which *is* the result of a less-than-unanimous decision by subordinates. "If, however, subordinates cannot agree unanimously, then the higher-level authority may either approve the decision over the objection of the subordinates, or reject it. (Both are embarrassing options …)" (lines 79–82).

C. The provincial authorities will usually make unanimous decisions.

WRONG: This assumption is not implicit in the sentence. This may be true, but it may not be. There is no passage information that would lead you to this conclusion. This is not the best answer.

D. The higher-level governing bodies prefer making the decisions themselves.

WRONG: This assumption is not implicit in the sentence. Not unless they "prefer" embarrassment.

14

ANSWERS &
EXPLANATIONS

Verbal Reasoning Test 14
Answers & Explanations

Passage I (Questions 1–5)

1. Which of the following statements is the most reasonable conclusion that can be drawn from the author's description of "the minor imperfections and dissatisfactions incident to most business contracts" (lines 14–15)?

    A. If the literal terms of the contract were followed as precisely as possible, then both parties to the contract would be always be satisfied.

        WRONG: This is *not* a reasonable conclusion, given the information that "minor imperfections and dissatisfactions [are] incident to most business contracts" (line 15-16).

    B. If the parties to a contract were required to abide precisely by the exact terms of the contract, someone could always be declared in breach of contract.

        CORRECT: This is the most reasonable conclusion. Courts have "learned that defining successful 'performance' (completion) of the contract *too strictly* can give opportunistic parties *ample* occasion to declare their counterparts in breach of the literal terms" (lines 2–6). And courts have learned that they must "accommodate the minor imperfections and dissatisfactions *incident to most business contracts*, thus avoiding complete 'forfeiture' of the entire contract, and the need for extensive reparations" (lines 14–17).

    C. In general, parties should be more careful than they are now when they are writing their contracts.

        WRONG: This is *not* a reasonable conclusion, given that the passage does not mention this anywhere.

    D. Usually, both parties to a contract are satisfied with the work that has been accomplished.

        WRONG: This is *not* a reasonable conclusion, given the information regarding "*dissatisfactions* incident to *most* business contracts" (line 14–15).

2. The word *opportunistic* (line 4) is used in the sense of:

    A. a party that is ruthless in its business dealings.

        WRONG: This is too strong. The parties in the passage are only taking advantage of one another when given an "opportunity."

    B. a party that would attempt to fairly make the most of a business relationship.

        WRONG: Given a common understanding of the word "fairly," this is not accurate. "Often, in these situations, the plaintiff does not actually want the 'error' [or 'minor detail'] corrected, but simply wants money" (lines 35–37). We are also told that in the *Jacob & Youngs* case the owner, who was "opportunistic," was "hoping to extort [a] ... discount".

    C. a party that would take advantage of another, given the chance.

        CORRECT: We are also told that in the Jacob & Youngs case the owner, who was "opportunistic," was "hoping to extort [a] ... discount." And, "Often, in these situations, the plaintiff does not actually want the 'error' [or 'minor detail'] corrected, but simply wants money" (lines 35–37).

    D. a party that will use illegal means to achieve its goals.

        WRONG: This is too strong. There is no information that an illegal act has occurred in any of the given instances, beyond the rather liberal use of the word "extort." However, the plaintiffs are generally simply attempting to use the courts to obtain 'money' or a 'discount.'

3. According to the passage, which of the following is true regarding the "owner" in the "the famous case of *Jacob & Youngs*" (lines 6–11) and (30–31)?

    I.   The owner had used a different brand of sewer pipes than the one specified in the blueprints.

         WRONG: This is not accurate. The *owner found* that the *builder* had used a different brand of sewer pipes.

    II. The owner might have been hoping to extort a discount from the builders.

         CORRECT: "... the owner ... hoping to extort an *ex post* discount" (lines 7–9).

    III. The owner might have been dissatisfied with his newly built mansion.

         CORRECT: "... the owner of a newly built mansion, dissatisfied with the results ..." (lines 7–9).

    A. I only
    B. II only
    C. II and III only

        CORRECT: See above explanations.

    D. I, II, and III

4. Suppose that the court finds that the contractor hired to build a barn had placed the wall studs on 24" centers rather than the specified 18" centers, but that this error was *not* substantial and does not deprive the work of its utility. According to the passage, the court would most likely:

    Notice that most of the details in the given supposition are extraneous. You do not need to know what "wall studs" are or the significance of 24" as opposed to 18" "centers" in order to answer the question. The important phrases are "*not* substantial" or "insubstantial" and "does not deprive the work of its utility."

A. declare the contractor in forfeiture of the contract.

WRONG: "An error, that is found to be 'insubstantial,' may oblige the responsible party to reduce its price or correct the problem, but it *will not void the entire contract*" (lines 20–22).

B. direct the contractor to tear down the barn and rebuild it according to contract.

WRONG: This is too extreme. The court would more likely use its "judicial interpretation" (lines 24–25) and instruct the contractor to 'cure' the problem, or reduce the price.

C. oblige the contractor to reduce his price.

CORRECT: Given the information that the error is 'insubstantial' and "does not deprive the work of its utility," the "courts have the option of awarding merely the resulting reduction in market price" (lines 37–38).

D. decide it was not possible nor necessary to 'cure' this defect.

WRONG: This is *possible*, but only remotely. There is no information from the passage, or from the supposition in the question, that would lead us to believe that this is the direction that the court would take. This is *not* the best answer.

5. An important comparison is made in the passage between:

A. opportunistic parties and the leeway of the court.

WRONG: There is no comparison between the two. There *may* be a link or a *relationship* between the two concepts, but there is no *comparison*.

B. substantial performance and correcting the problem.

WRONG: There is no comparison between the two. There *may* be a link or a *relationship* between the two concepts, but there is no *comparison*.

C. a substantial forfeiture and an entire contract.

WRONG: There is no comparison between the two. There *may* be a link or a *relationship* between the two concepts, but there is no *comparison*.

D. a substantial error and a material breach.

CORRECT: The author transitions without pause from "an error must be 'substantial'" to whether a "breach is material." "The first is 'substantial performance,' the doctrine that an *error must be 'substantial'* to require forfeiture of the entire contract. An error that is found to be 'insubstantial' may oblige the responsible party to reduce its price or correct the problem, but it will not void the entire contract. A number of factors go into deciding whether or not a *breach is material*" (lines 20–24).

Passage II (Questions 6–10)

6. Evidence shows that, under a variety of situations, when left to tie their own knots, knots people tie that are inappropriate for that situation. This fact tends to support the hypothesis concerning Granny knots because:

A. Granny knots should never be used in any situation.

WRONG: This answer *implicitly* assumes that all the people are tying Granny knots. Based upon passage information, "The ubiquitous Granny is the knot most commonly used by the unschooled when he or she is asked to join two pieces of string or rope" (lines 16–18). This assumption is not without merit. However, since *each* knot has its appropriate and inappropriate use, this answer is too specific. Answer C can be correct *without* having to make this *unspoken* assumption.

B. a Granny knot is easy to recognize.

WRONG: This is *not* why the fact tends to support the hypothesis concerning Granny knots.

C. these people are probably tying Granny knots.

CORRECT: This answers 'why' the "fact tends to support the hypothesis." Based upon passage information, "The ubiquitous Granny is the knot most commonly used by the unschooled when he or she is asked to join two pieces of string or rope" (lines 16–18). This is the correct answer. This answer is more correct than Answer A because it does not require a leap of reasoning. It fills in the *implicit* reasoning required for Answer A with an *explicit* assumption.

D. people usually don't know which knot is appropriate in a given situation.

WRONG: This may be true, but not based upon any passage information. The passage does *not* say that most people are "unschooled" in tying knots. Only that the "unschooled" will usually tie Granny knots. That is a big difference.

7. If the hypothesis of the passage is correct, one should find that manufacturers of water-skiing ropes:

A. use ropes made of natural materials as much as possible.

WRONG: This is not accurate. The ski ropes are clearly made from polyurethane and/or nylon ropes that are 'self-lubricating.'

B. use special knots on their ropes to keep them from pulling through under pressure.

WRONG: There is no passage information that a ski rope manufacturer would use or know anything about knots! They *would* apparently know how to *splice*. "The manufacturer usually *splices* these ropes, obviating the need for the end-user to knot them in any way" (lines 58–59).

A&E 14

C.   probably don't recommend that the consumer repair a broken tow rope themselves.

CORRECT: The passage provides a vivid example: "When a knot is improperly tied in a broken ski rope and it pulls through under pressure, the resulting reaction of the rope whipping back into the boat is a scary event to behold" (lines 60–62). Additionally, "The manufacturer usually splices these ropes, obviating the need for the end-user to knot them in any way" (lines 58–59). Given the manufacturers care and the dangerous results of an improper repair, this is the best answer.

D.   know a lot about knots.

WRONG: There is no passage information that a ski rope manufacturer would use or know anything about knots! They *would* apparently know how to *splice*. "The manufacturer usually *splices* these ropes, obviating the need for the end-user to knot them in any way" (lines 58–59).

8. Assume that most children's tree swing ropes are made from thick natural materials. The passage information presented on ropes and knots makes which of the following suggestions the most plausible?

A.   The swing should be checked frequently to make sure the knot hasn't pulled through itself.

WRONG: It is the *synthetic* ropes that are 'self-lubricating' and have a tendency to "pull through." "Ropes made of natural materials are not only less elastic, but they also have the tendency to grip themselves, *which lends to knotting*" (lines 63–65).

B.   When the family decides to relocate and take the swing, the knot will be difficult to untie.

CORRECT: "Ropes made of natural materials are not only less elastic, but they also have the tendency to grip themselves, which lends to knotting. Here the knot selected must usually have the additional quality of being easy to remove" (lines 63–66).

C.   Whoever put up the swing probably didn't use a Granny knot to attach it to the tree.

WRONG: We don't know what was used. However, based upon passage information, it is *more* likely that a Granny knot *was* tied than that a Granny knot *was not* tied.

D.   The swing would have to be retied frequently because of the elasticity of the rope.

WRONG: Elasticity is a characteristic of synthetic rope. "Ropes made of natural materials are not only less elastic …" (lines 63–65).

9. The author claims that the Granny knot is an "often dangerous knot" (line 23). The support offered for this conclusion is:

This is a classic MCAT question. *Before* you decide whether it is "strong" or "weak," go to the *second* clause of the answer and determine if: 1) it is accurate, 2) it is from passage information, and 3) is supportive or nonsupportive of the question. If the second clause is inaccurate or *not* from passage information, it *cannot* be a correct answer, no matter whether it is "strong" or "weak." However, a *nonsupportive* and *accurate* second clause can be correct *if* it is prefaced by "weak." Similarly, a *supportive* and *accurate* second clause must be prefaced by "strong" in order to be a correct answer.

A.   weak; there are no examples or evidence of this.

CORRECT: The second clause is accurate. "There are no examples or evidence of this" and "weak" fits.

B.   weak; the author provides only one example in which this is the case.

WRONG: The second clause is inaccurate; there are *no* examples of this. This answer cannot be correct.

C.   strong; there are no examples or evidence of this.

WRONG: The second clause is accurate. "There are no examples or evidence of this." However, this means there is no support; therefore, "strong" is incorrect.

D.   strong; the author provides an example in which this is the case.

WRONG: The second clause is inaccurate; there are *no* examples of this. This answer cannot be correct.

10. Which of the following *violates* the guidelines and suggestions for wire rope or cable (lines 39–50) described in the passage?

I.   Splicing rarely weakens a cable.

WRONG: This does *not violate* the guidelines and suggestions of the passage. "Splicing, unlike knotting, *rarely* weakens that section of any type of joined rope" (lines 43–45).

II.   Cable should be knotted if possible.

CORRECT: This *does violate* the guidelines and suggestions for wire rope or cable. "It is *never* appropriate to knot wire rope" (lines 42–43).

III.   Crimping of cables should be avoided.

CORRECT: This *does violate* the guidelines and suggestions for wire rope or cable. "It is *never* appropriate to knot wire rope; splicing, or *crimping*, is the method of joining" (lines 42–43).

A.   I only
B.   II only
C.   I and II only
D.   II and III only

CORRECT: See above answer explanations.

Passage III (Questions 11–17)

11. Which of the following statements most clearly exemplifies Mishima's concept of a modern samurai's primary obligation?

   A. The samurai's foremost duty is to himself.

   CORRECT: This answer most clearly exemplifies the concept. "In scanning [Mishima's] *Way of the Samurai*, we see an amazing lack of purpose to the samurai's life outside of his duty to himself" (lines 29–31).

   B. The samurai's main duty is to his lord.

   WRONG: This is not Mishima's concept. There are no lords in post–World War II Japanese society.

   C. The primary obligation of the samurai is to society.

   WRONG: Mishima's samurai has absolutely no "obligation" to society. His philosophy is that society is only necessary to "to observe the demeanor of the samurai" (lines 41–42).

   D. The most important obligation of the samurai is to commit suicide.

   WRONG: It would be *inaccurate* to describe suicide as an "important obligation." It is the culmination of the Mishima-samurai's life.

12. In the passage, the author contrasts *Hagakure* with *Way of the Samurai* by pointing out that:

   A. the modern samurai does not need society.

   WRONG: Though Mishima is "asocial," the passage is clear in explaining that he recognizes a need for society, both to "observe the demeanor of the samurai," and because "the samurai needs a social context [in order] to be meaningful" (lines 22–23).

   B. for the ancient samurai, self-inflicted death brought honor.

   WRONG: There is no mention of this in the passage. In *Hagakure*, death is an "occupational hazard."

   C. for Mishima's samurai, death always comes by suicide.

   CORRECT: This answer provides the contrast. "Here is the major departure from the original *Hagakure*, which recognized death as an occupational hazard … In Mishima's era, when there are neither lords nor battles, where can that death come from, unless it is *self-inflicted*?" (lines 48–53).

   D. for the ancient samurai, death should come immediately after a notable success.

   WRONG: Lines 57–58 describe this as Mishima's idea for the post–World War II samurai, *not* the ancient samurai.

13. Which of the following statements is the most reasonable conclusion regarding Mishima that can be drawn from the passage?

   A. His philosophy required selflessness and strength.

   WRONG: This is not a reasonable conclusion. "Selflessness" implies efforts toward or for something greater than oneself. Mishima's emphasis was on the individual whose primary duty is to himself (lines 29–31).

   B. His goal was to promote the construction of a new society of samurai warriors.

   WRONG: This is not a reasonable conclusion. Mishima castigates postwar society. It is never implied that he seeks a "society" of anything. His emphasis seems to be on the *individual*.

   C. He was a man whose philosophy required the society he reviled.

   CORRECT: This is a reasonable conclusion. Mishima castigates postwar society. "Despite critiques that label Mishima basically *asocial*, he is aware that the samurai needs a social context to be meaningful" (lines 21–23). Further, society was required in order to "observe the demeanor of the samurai."

   D. He hated society, but felt that it could be redeemed.

   WRONG: This is not a reasonable conclusion. Mishima castigates postwar society and does appear to loathe it. However, any redemption that he offers is for the *individual* samurai who commits suicide. There is no implication that society can be redeemed.

14. Given an understanding of *Way of the Samurai*, which of the following would be most *discrepant* with this philosophy?

   A. To be strong and heroic and to look the part

   WRONG: This is not *discrepant*. Mishima urges his samurai to be "always projecting a strong and active image. In order to be thought strong and heroic, it is necessary to look the part" (lines 35–37).

   B. To become primarily devoted to oneself

   WRONG: This is not *discrepant*. "In scanning *Way of the Samurai*, we see an amazing lack of purpose to the samurai's life outside of his duty to himself" (lines 29–31).

   C. To dedicate oneself to being feared by all

   WRONG: This is not *discrepant*. "This must be an audience … of weak and effeminate men, to whom a samurai will be seen as rash and *ferocious*. The beauty that Mishima sees in the samurai is for the sake of being *feared*" (lines 42–45).

   D. To seclude oneself in total devotion to the pursuit of strength and heroism

CORRECT: This is *discrepant* with Mishima's philosophy. To "seclude" oneself means to separate oneself from others, from society. Mishima is clear that the postwar samurai *requires* society and others in order to "to be meaningful" (lines 22–23), and to "observe the demeanor of the samurai." Mishima cannot be a "samurai" in 'seclusion.'

15. During the feudal samurai-era of ancient Japan, committing suicide was considered a final honorable act, which was required as a result of dishonor. This information would be most *discrepant* with which of Mishima's views?

A. The ideal death should come immediately after a notable success.

CORRECT: The information is discrepant with this view of Mishima's. Unlike the feudal samurai-era, for Mishima, suicide is an 'exclamation point' to "either a crisis or a notable success." The connotations of this "notable moment" (lines 57–61) do *not* allude to any previous "dishonor" that must be expunged.

B. The most honorable death is one in the service of a lord.

WRONG: This is *not* one of Mishima's views, which is one of the requirements for a correct answer.

C. Mishima describes death in such a way that it has the power to redeem almost anyone.

WRONG: This answer is *not discrepant* with the "information" in the question.

D. As an act, suicide is above the morality and judgment of others.

WRONG: This *is* one of Mishima's views, yet it is *not discrepant* with the "information" in the question.

16. According to the author, Mishima's sole teaching for living was:

A. to imagine oneself as strong and heroic.

WRONG: This is not a "sole teaching for living." The inclusion of "imagine" renders this answer completely unsuitable. To Mishima, everything was how *others* viewed or imagined one to be.

B. to serve your lord.

WRONG: There was no lord to serve in Mishima's time. "In Mishima's era, when there are neither lords nor battles …" (lines 51–53).

C. to look the part of a samurai.

CORRECT: This answer is almost verbatim from the passage. "… it is *necessary to look the part*. Thus, Mishima transfers his obsession with personal beauty into the *only instruction for living*" (lines 36–39).

D. to serve society.

WRONG: Mishima hated society. He apparently did not even consider attempting to change it.

17. What assumption is implicit in the phrase "conscious anachronism" (line 18)?

A. Mishima is aware that his ideas belong to another time.

CORRECT: This assumption is implicit in the phrase. "He *recognizes* that the samurai is *a relic of the feudal past*, with no place in the postwar world. Yet Mishima sees in this 'conscious anachronism' …" (lines 16–18).

B. The behavior is no longer relevant and Mishima knows it.

WRONG: This answer is vague. However, if we assume that the "behavior" refers to being a samurai, Mishima would certainly not agree that the "[samurai] behavior is irrelevant."

C. Mishima believes that society is out of date.

WRONG: This answer may be accurate in that Mishima yearned for a time long gone because he felt that postwar society was decadent. However, it is not responsive to this question. "[Mishima] *recognizes* that the *samurai* is *a relic of the feudal past*, with no place in the postwar world. Yet Mishima sees in this 'conscious anachronism'" (lines 16–18).

D. Everyone knows that Mishima's ideas are relics, except him.

WRONG: There is *no* implication that "everyone" knows and every implication that Mishima does. "He *recognizes* that the samurai is *a relic of the feudal past*, with no place in the postwar world. Yet Mishima sees in this 'conscious anachronism' …" (lines 16–18).

Passage IV (Questions 18–22)

18. An important comparison is made in the passage between:

A. the boxer mentality and the martial artist's abilities, or lack thereof.

WRONG: There is *no* comparison between the "boxer *mentality*" and the martial artist's abilities. There is a comparison between the abilities and training of the boxer and the martial artist. However, even *if* the latter were offered as an answer choice, it would still not be the best answer. The passage is primarily about women's self-defense courses.

B. the expectations in women's self-defense courses and the martial artist's mentality.

CORRECT: This is an important comparison. "It is the average martial artist's mentality toward his craft that promotes the unrealistic expectations being perpetuated in women's self-defense courses" (lines 29–32).

C. women's self-defense courses and the way in which boxers train.

WRONG: This is not the best answer. There *might* be an implied comparison. However, there is a very *specific* and *explicit* comparison made in the case of Answer B.

D. the women taking the self-defense courses and their assailants.

WRONG: There is no comparison made between the two.

19. The word *tearful* (line 13) is used in the sense of:

"The graduation consists of a pretend 'attacker,' heavily padded, screaming obscenities, but whom the graduate inevitably drives off, to the *tearful* cheers of her classmates" (lines 11–14). The author is obviously ridiculing this entire scenario.

A. outraged.

WRONG: If the tears occurred as the beginning of a real attack in which the woman was powerless to do anything, then this might be appropriate. However, the women feel victorious and able to defend themselves at the time of their graduation. Thus, Answer B is more appropriate.

B. exultant.

CORRECT: This comes closest to describing how the "classmates" are obviously feeling.

C. tragic.

WRONG: The women would not view a victory as tragic.

D. happy.

WRONG: This is too simplistic. The author does not deny that there is a very serious side to this training and the entire discussion. Happiness is not a good description.

20. What would be the author's response to the standard story about the smaller, mild-mannered child who finally turns on and defeats the schoolyard bully?

A. The author would first ask about the gender of the child and the bully.

WRONG: In this instance, the gender aspect is subordinated to the given fact that the child is "smaller" than the bully. The entire third paragraph is devoted to explaining the critical aspect of size differences in fighting. This is not the best answer.

B. The author would respond that this is wishful thinking and unlikely to happen.

CORRECT: The key to this question is "*smaller.*" The entire third paragraph is devoted to explaining

the critical aspect of size differences in fighting. The "mild-mannered" adjective would also be somewhat important, thought to a much lesser degree. However, both would serve to help one predict, based upon passage information, that the "smaller" child is very unlikely to defeat the bully.

C. The author would want to know if the child had any martial arts training.

WRONG: The author does not think much of martial arts training. Thus, he would not care whether the child had received any.

D. The author would think that this was very possible if both the child and the bully were the same gender.

WRONG: In this instance, the gender aspect is subordinated to the given fact that the child is "smaller" than the bully. The entire third paragraph is devoted to explaining the critical aspect of size differences in fighting.

21. A women's self-defense course that would best represent the author's concept of *realistic* as opposed to "unrealistic expectations" (line 31) would probably have:

A. a female assailant attacking females, and vice versa.

WRONG: The author would not think it realistic to have females attacking females.

B. a two-hour block of boxing training.

WRONG: Though the author seems to be a proponent of boxing, he points out that "those who box train for *years* in their craft" (lines 18–19). A "two-hour" block of training would seem to the author to be as token as a "foolproof" technique taught in a two-day seminar.

C. more martial art's–type sparring.

WRONG: The author is clear regarding his dim view of unrealistic martial art's sparring.

D. an assailant attacking to the utmost of his abilities.

CORRECT: The author is a proponent of realistic training. This is the best answer. None of the other answers makes sense in the context of the passage.

22. Which of the following assertions is the most effective argument *against* the author's conclusion that "[i]n the end, he should realize that there are other, easier targets of opportunity out there and hopefully he will move on." (lines 65–67)?

A. If a 'stalker' realizes that his victim is wary, he will be dissuaded from further activities.

WRONG: This supports the passage's assertions.

B. Victims are frequently chosen at random based upon their perceived vulnerability at that moment.

WRONG: This supports the passage's assertions.

C. Feelings of vulnerability, denial, and loss of love infrequently motivate the assailant who is looking for targets of opportunity.

WRONG: The first part of this answer makes little sense in the context of the passage. The second part of this answer regarding "targets of opportunity" is *not against* the passage, but supports passage assertions.

D. A stalker's choice of victim is predicated primarily upon his perceptions of such factors as celebrity status and/or affection.

CORRECT: This would be an effective argument "against" the author's conclusions. If this answer were true, it would tend to show that factors beyond making yourself a "hard" target were more important.

Passage V (Questions 23–28)

23. According to the author, which of the following best describes an aspect of Freud's theories?

A. In society, without hedonism man can only realize momentary pleasure.

WRONG: This is not accurate. It assumes that man could realize more than momentary pleasure without society. "Yet to enjoy more than momentary pleasure, he needs the security and leisure provided by society" (lines 17–18).

B. Hedonism is provided by society.

WRONG: This is an incorrect usage of the term. Additionally, hedonism involves the individual. There is no passage information supporting this answer.

C. The nobles' natural aggressive instincts are repressed by society.

WRONG: This is not a theory of Freud's, but of Nietzsche's.

D. Man's aggressive instinct is natural and pleasurable to him.

CORRECT: "Additionally, to keep a society together, man's natural aggressive instinct must be repressed … these repressions reduce man's enjoyment of life" (lines 21–245).

24. Which of the following statements is the most reasonable conclusion that can be drawn from the author's description of Friedrich Nietzsche?

A. Nietzsche felt that the individual needs the security and leisure provided by society.

WRONG: This is not a reasonable conclusion. This was a theory of Freud's, not Nietzsche's.

B. Nietzsche was more interested in civilization as it reflected dominance.

CORRECT: This is the most reasonable conclusion. "Nietzsche … is more interested in [society] … as a reflection of the dominance of certain groups …" (lines 28–31).

C. Nietzsche felt that societal conflict produced progress, but not necessarily universal repression.

WRONG: This is not a reasonable conclusion. "For Nietzsche, the conflict that has historically accompanied civilization produced neither universal repression nor progress" (lines 32–34).

D. Nietzsche felt that societal conflict produced universal repression, but not necessarily progress.

WRONG: This is not a reasonable conclusion. "For Nietzsche, the conflict that has historically accompanied civilization produced neither universal repression nor progress" (lines 32–34).

25. Which of the following approaches to relieving a patient's neurosis would be most likely to be stressed by a clinician who had an understanding of and belief in the work and theories of Sigmund Freud?

A. The clinician would carefully prescribe the appropriate drug that would alleviate all of the symptoms of his patient.

WRONG: On the contrary, Freud felt that "the cure was not achieved by relieving the outward symptoms" (lines 7–8).

B. The clinician would compare his patient's neurosis with the societal problems during that time.

WRONG: This is not accurate. There is no information from the passage that Freud used societal analysis to psychoanalyze the individual. The opposite is true.

C. The clinician would spend however long was required attempting to determine the origin of the neurosis.

CORRECT: "Freud's clinical work taught him that, when people developed neuroses, the cure was not achieved by relieving the outward symptoms, but by finding the origin of the problem, usually in the patient's early childhood" (lines 6–9).

D. After extensive psychoanalysis, the clinician would be able to trace the neurotic manifestations back to their sexual roots.

WRONG: There is no mention in the passage of Freud's perhaps well-known tendencies to draw psychosexual conclusions.

26. The assertion that civilization is "a reflection of the dominance of certain groups who were able to produce 'knowledge' (i.e., make their texts the socially accepted ones)" (lines 31-33) is NOT clearly consistent with the information about:

A. lower classes countering with a passive Judeo-Christianity.

CORRECT: The assertion is not clearly consistent with this information. Nietzsche's characterization, as presented in the passage, of Judeo-Christianity as "passive" is not at all consistent with his idea of groups who "produce 'knowledge,'" or "a power struggle."

B. society providing security and leisure.

WRONG: This answer is a concept of Freud's, while the question concerns Nietzsche. Thus, this answer has nothing to do with the question. Sorry for the double negative, but it is not "NOT clearly consistent with" the question. This is not the best answer.

C. repression being used by one faction to stifle another.

WRONG: This answer is consistent with the question.

D. man needing to repress his natural aggressive instinct.

WRONG: It is not that this answer is "NOT clearly consistent" with the question, as it is true that this answer is not related to the question. The question has to do with a theory of Nietzsche's, while this answer has to do with Freud. According to the passage, Nietzsche gloried in the "nobles' natural aggressive instincts" (lines 47).

27. Which of the following statements is the most reasonable conclusion that can be drawn from the author's description of Sigmund Freud's theories?

A. Society can be 'cured' if one can only determine the origin of its problems.

WRONG: There is nothing in the passage that would indicate that Freud felt society could be cured.

B. The individual would be happiest if allowed to do exactly as he pleased.

WRONG: This is not accurate. Freud felt that "to enjoy more than momentary pleasure, [the individual] *needs* the security and leisure provided by society" (lines 17–18). Yet the perpetuation of society required voluntary repressions that reduced man's enjoyment of life (lines 19–27).

C. Until society is fully developed, the individual will not be able to fully enjoy life.

WRONG: This is not accurate. There is no indication that society will ever be fully developed. Further, "Freud [was] … aware of society's seeming inability to provide lasting happiness for its people" (lines 1–3).

D. The individual will never be able to fully enjoy life without periodic repressions of this enjoyment.

CORRECT: This is the most reasonable conclusion. Freud felt that "to enjoy more than momentary pleasure, [the individual] *needs* the security and leisure provided by society" (lines 17–18). Yet the perpetuation of society required voluntary repressions that reduced man's enjoyment of life (lines 19–27).

28. On the basis of the passage, it is reasonable to conclude all of the following EXCEPT that:

A. Nietzsche felt that he had natural aggressive instincts.

WRONG: This is a reasonable conclusion and not an exception. "Nietzsche … clearly identifies himself with the repressed nobility" (lines 48-49). The nobles are characterized as having "natural aggressive instincts."

B. Freud felt that he had natural aggressive instincts.

WRONG: This is a reasonable conclusion and not an exception. Freud was a man, and would have agreed that he shared "man's natural aggressive instinct" (line 22).

C. Nietzsche fancied himself a hedonist.

WRONG: This is a reasonable conclusion and not an exception. "Nietzsche … clearly identifies himself with the repressed nobility" (lines 48-49). And "the nobles adopted a hedonistic … morality" (lines 37-38).

D. Nietzsche was religious.

CORRECT: This is an exception. Or, not a reasonable conclusion. For Nietzsche there were only the "nobles" and the "passive" religious. "Nietzsche … clearly identifies himself with the repressed nobility" (lines 46–47). According to the article, he denigrates the "lower classes [religious]" as "useless."

Passage VI (Questions 29–35)

29. The author of the passage states that, "though of course it would have been perfectly legal to simply go in alone and set up a branch office in China" (lines 34–36), Morgan Stanley expects to enjoy which of the following advantages through cooperating with and helping the existing state-owned companies?

A. Morgan Stanley expects challenges in the staffing of its Chinese offices.

WRONG: This is not an "advantage."

B. Morgan Stanley foresees great autonomy in the terms it will dictate, based primarily upon its close relationship with these companies.

WRONG: This is not true according to the passage. It will actually "have to govern through compromise and negotiation, which is not a role it is accustomed to assuming in its American operations" (lines 42–44).

C. Morgan Stanley anticipates creating contacts within the Chinese government, which may give them some influence in certain areas.

CORRECT: This is an expected advantage. "Morgan Stanley expects that helping Asian companies … would also create contacts in government, which might perhaps give it influence over legislation on privatization, securities markets, and foreign investment" (lines 24–31).

D. Morgan Stanley looks forward to raising funds from these state-owned companies.

WRONG: This is not accurate. "Morgan Stanley expects that *helping* Asian companies to raise funds …" (lines 24–25).

30. Based upon passage information, one can assume the following regarding the operations of Morgan Stanley in America:

A. Morgan Stanley governs through compromise and negotiation.

WRONG: "[Morgan Stanley] will have to govern through compromise and negotiation, which is not a role it is accustomed to assuming in its American operations" (lines 42–44).

B. Staffing of its offices is not a challenge for Morgan Stanley in America.

WRONG: One cannot make this assumption based upon passage information. Though this is a challenge that the company will face in China, this is not contrasted in the passage with America.

C. From 1992 to 1997, Morgan Stanley enjoyed unusually high growth rates.

WRONG: This is not accurate. "Chinese companies [enjoyed] … high growth rates and return on investment from 1992 to 1997" (lines 13–15).

D. Morgan Stanley does not usually govern through compromise and negotiation.

CORRECT: "[Morgan Stanley] will have to govern through compromise and negotiation, which is not a role it is accustomed to assuming in its American operations" (lines 42–44).

31. Based upon passage information, one can assume the following regarding the Chinese business culture EXCEPT:

A. It is characterized by centralized planning.

WRONG: This is not an exception.

B. It is characterized by rapid decision-making and centralization.

CORRECT: This is the exception. "Also important is bringing quick decision-making to a culture used to consensus management and centralized planning" (lines 67–69).

C. The culture is accustomed to consensus management.

WRONG: This is not an exception.

D. Business is conducted in a different fashion than it is in America.

WRONG: This is not an exception.

32. Based upon passage information, why does Morgan Stanley predict that there may be increased international investment in Chinese companies?

A. These companies are embracing the prospect of capitalism.

WRONG: This is not offered as a reason for the Morgan Stanley prediction.

B. These companies have been dramatically overhauled in the last several years by the state.

WRONG: This is not information that is provided by the passage.

C. These companies are expected to experience tremendous growth once investment barriers are lowered.

WRONG: This is not information that is provided by the passage.

D. These companies have experienced high growth rates.

CORRECT: "Morgan Stanley's managers' analysts have predicted increased international investment in Chinese companies once investment barriers are lowered, two draws being their high growth rates …" (lines 11–14).

33. Which of the following has been ignored under the Chinese government?

A. A strong sales-distribution network

CORRECT: "Morgan Stanley will need to develop a strong sales-distribution network, a factor sorely neglected under the centrally planned Chinese regime" (lines 54–56).

B. Brand recognition

WRONG: There is no information that this has been "ignored." "necessary ingredients include brand recognition. The Chinese central government … may refuse to deal with unknowns" (lines 49–52).

C. Privatization and restructuring

WRONG: There is no information that this has been "ignored."

D. Raising funds

WRONG: There is no information that this has been "ignored." This would be an assumption by the reader based upon the information the Morgan Stanley may help Asian companies in raising funds.

34. According to the passage, which of the following is INACCURATE regarding China?

A. The Chinese market is not limited to the upper ranks.

WRONG: This is accurate. "However, analysts should note that the Chinese market is not necessarily limited to the upper echelon" (lines 18–20).

B. Chinese banks hold high cash reserves.

WRONG: This is accurate. "… high cash reserves held by Chinese banks" (lines 22–23).

C. Chinese consumers choose to save a large portion of their money.

CORRECT: This is not accurate. The passage notes the "high (*forced*) savings rate among Chinese consumers" (lines 20–21).

D. The Chinese government may refuse to deal with unknown brands.

WRONG: This is accurate. "The Chinese central government, anxious to make its first attempts at capitalism a public success, may refuse to deal with unknowns" (lines 50–52).

35. The passage indicates that its author would NOT agree with which of the following statements?

A. Helping Asian companies to raise funds is one of the necessary inconveniences of the Morgan Stanley expansion.

CORRECT: The author would disagree and point out that it is not an "inconvenience," but an *advantage*. "Morgan Stanley expects that helping Asian companies to raise funds would simultaneously allow it to perform due diligence on these companies, allowing Morgan Stanley to recommend increased investment in the more promising companies to their existing clients" (lines 24–28).

B. Western financing is more sophisticated than Chinese financing.

WRONG: The author would agree. "foreigners (who are experienced in the more sophisticated techniques of Western financing)" (lines 63–64).

C. The communications system of the Chinese is often underdeveloped.

WRONG: The author would agree. "… the often underdeveloped foreign communications systems" (lines 58–59).

D. Determining compensation rates for workers will be one of Morgan Stanley's challenges.

WRONG: The author would agree. "Morgan Stanley's challenges will include … setting compensation rates" (lines 60–65).

Passage VII (Questions 36–40)

36. In the context of the passage, the term *utopia* refers primarily to:

"'If you want to know what Utopia is like, just look around—*this is it*,' said Professor Steve Jones of University College London. 'Things have simply stopped getting better, or worse, for our species'" (lines 4–7).

A. the apogee of *Homo sapiens'* evolution.

CORRECT: This answer includes a response to change, "apogee," and refers to our species. "'Things have simply *stopped* getting better, or worse, for our species'" (lines 6–7).

B. Afghani lifestyle and society.

WRONG: Afghani and Indian lifestyles are offered as foils for the abundance in Western lifestyles. The author would certainly not consider them utopias.

C. a perfect futuristic society.

WRONG: This may be a dictionary definition, but it is not the best definition within the "context of the passage."

D. the ability to have more children.

WRONG: There is no natural correlation between utopia and the ability to have more children. Utopia, in the passage, is a reference to *now*, while the answer is a reference to *what may be*. The ability to have more children is postulated to increase as, in the future, we begin to live longer.

37. According to two of the positions presented, evolution as it is occurring nowadays places a premium on sharpness of mind and the ability to accumulate money, *and* Western lifestyle has been postulated to have halted or impeded natural selection. If both of these premises are true, what conclusion is most reasonable?

No natural selection equals no evolution. Thus, "sharpness of mind" and the "ability to accumulate money" are not likely for Westerners who are not evolving.

A. Increasingly, Western societies will be more intelligent and more able to accumulate money.

WRONG: This is not a reasonable conclusion based upon the premises. Western societies are not evolving.

B. Increasingly, Western societies will be less intelligent and less able to accumulate money.

CORRECT: "Western lifestyle has been postulated to have halted or impeded natural selection" (which is necessary for evolution). Further, if evolution results in "sharpness of mind and the ability to accumulate money," then this answer is a reasonable conclusion.

C. Members of Western society will become increasingly able to accumulate money.

WRONG: This is not a reasonable conclusion based upon the premises. Western societies are not evolving.

D. No reasonable conclusion can be drawn.

WRONG: This is not a reasonable conclusion based upon the premises. Western societies are not evolving.

38. According to the passage, "Until recently there were massive differences between individuals' life spans and fecundity" (lines 24–26). This meant that:

From the passage, this meant that "the death rate outstripped the birth rate" (lines 26–27). "Until recently," according to the passage, refers to a *time* when people were living relatively *short* lives.

A. people would live long lives and have few children.

WRONG: This answer provides the "massive differences" requirement of the answer, but is outside of the time context of the question because it refers to "long lives."

B. people would live long lives and have many children.

WRONG: This answer does not provide the "massive differences" requirement of the answer and is outside of the time context of the question because it refers to "long lives."

C. people would live short lives and have few children.

WRONG: This answer does not provide the "massive differences" requirement of the answer, but falls within the correct time context of the question because it refers to "long lives."

D. people would live short lives and have many children.

CORRECT: This answer provides the "massive differences" requirement of the answer *and* falls within the correct time context of the question because it refers to "long lives."

39. Assume that in the West, less-educated, poverty-stricken women have three times as many children as their better-educated, wealthier, counterparts. If, in the West, "virtually every member of society" is being kept alive and able to pass on his or her genes, this evidence would *weaken* the passage assertion that:

A. we will have created a new race of fecund individuals.

WRONG: This assertion is not weakened. Those having the babies are *already* fecund and, if this were a genetic tendency, would pass along this characteristic to their children. Additionally, this passage assertion, by one biologist, has to do with *genetic engineering* (lines 54–66). You did not have to remember that it had to do with genetic engineering because the answer itself reminds you of this; "we will have *created*."

B. evolution is certainly based upon the ability of humans to pass on their genetic code.

WRONG: This answer refers to lines 42–43 and is *unaffected* (i.e., not weakened) by the assumptions in the question.

C. our physiques are actually becoming less robust.

WRONG: This answer refers to lines 13–16 and is also *unaffected* (i.e., not weakened) by the assumptions in the question.

D. there is a premium on sharpness of mind and the ability to accumulate money.

CORRECT: This assertion is weakened. "[B]iologist Christopher Wills … argues that *ideas are now driving our evolution,* [and] says, 'There is a premium on sharpness of mind and the ability to accumulate money …'" (lines 48–51). Without disparaging those whose lives *may be* based on circumstance, if there are considerably more genes entering the pool from those *without* the "ability to accumulate money" (let's assume they don't want to be poverty stricken), and who are less "sharp" (it is not a stretch to equate this with education), then this answer/passage assertion is *weakened*.

40. The opinion that "[p]eople will start to produce dozens of children in their lifetimes, and that will certainly start to skew our evolution" (lines 56–58), is challenged in the passage by the argument that:

The answer is required to *challenge* the given *opinion* and be *in the passage*. This question can be easily answered without referring back to the passage for context.

A. wealthy people generally have many children.

WRONG: This is not responsive to the given opinion. This is neither stated nor implied in the passage.

B. populations and birth rates are declining.

CORRECT: This answer, even when not offered in its entirety, as in lines 63–64, is directly responsive to the given opinion and *challenges* it.

C. studies indicate that wealthy people generally do not have many children.

WRONG: This is not responsive to the given opinion. In addition, this assertion is not stated in the passage. It may be *implied* in the question: "Why would these people … who … had more money suddenly decide to start having all of these children?" (lines 64–66). Finally, this answer does not really *challenge* the opinion. This is not the *best* answer.

D. most of these new members of society will be able to pass on their genes.

WRONG: This is not responsive to the given opinion. It is questionable whether this answer is implied within the passage or not.

_____

Raw Score Conversion Chart
& Answer Sheets

RAW SCORE CONVERSION

40	15
39	14
37–38	13
35–36	12
33–34	11
30–32	10
28–29	9
26–27	8
23–25	7
20–22	6
18–19	5
15–17	4
13–14	3
9–12	2
< 9	1

NOTE: Every MCAT has a slightly different scoring scale. This table shows typical score conversions and should be used for general guidance only.

USE ONLY A NO. 2 PENCIL TO COMPLETE THIS ANSWER SHEET. DO NOT USE INK.

NO 2 PENCIL ONLY

● Right Mark   ✓ ✗ ◉ Wrong Marks

MCAT VERBAL REASONING TEST

Mark one and only one answer to each question. Be sure to fill in completely the space for your intended answer choice. If you erase, do so completely. Make no stray marks.

1 TEST NUMBER

1 DATE

MONTH   DAY   YEAR

1.	Ⓐ Ⓑ Ⓒ Ⓓ	21.	Ⓐ Ⓑ Ⓒ Ⓓ
2.	Ⓐ Ⓑ Ⓒ Ⓓ	22.	Ⓐ Ⓑ Ⓒ Ⓓ
3.	Ⓐ Ⓑ Ⓒ Ⓓ	23.	Ⓐ Ⓑ Ⓒ Ⓓ
4.	Ⓐ Ⓑ Ⓒ Ⓓ	24.	Ⓐ Ⓑ Ⓒ Ⓓ
5.	Ⓐ Ⓑ Ⓒ Ⓓ	25.	Ⓐ Ⓑ Ⓒ Ⓓ
6.	Ⓐ Ⓑ Ⓒ Ⓓ	26.	Ⓐ Ⓑ Ⓒ Ⓓ
7.	Ⓐ Ⓑ Ⓒ Ⓓ	27.	Ⓐ Ⓑ Ⓒ Ⓓ
8.	Ⓐ Ⓑ Ⓒ Ⓓ	28.	Ⓐ Ⓑ Ⓒ Ⓓ
9.	Ⓐ Ⓑ Ⓒ Ⓓ	29.	Ⓐ Ⓑ Ⓒ Ⓓ
10.	Ⓐ Ⓑ Ⓒ Ⓓ	30.	Ⓐ Ⓑ Ⓒ Ⓓ
11.	Ⓐ Ⓑ Ⓒ Ⓓ	31.	Ⓐ Ⓑ Ⓒ Ⓓ
12.	Ⓐ Ⓑ Ⓒ Ⓓ	32.	Ⓐ Ⓑ Ⓒ Ⓓ
13.	Ⓐ Ⓑ Ⓒ Ⓓ	33.	Ⓐ Ⓑ Ⓒ Ⓓ
14.	Ⓐ Ⓑ Ⓒ Ⓓ	34.	Ⓐ Ⓑ Ⓒ Ⓓ
15.	Ⓐ Ⓑ Ⓒ Ⓓ	35.	Ⓐ Ⓑ Ⓒ Ⓓ
16.	Ⓐ Ⓑ Ⓒ Ⓓ	36.	Ⓐ Ⓑ Ⓒ Ⓓ
17.	Ⓐ Ⓑ Ⓒ Ⓓ	37.	Ⓐ Ⓑ Ⓒ Ⓓ
18.	Ⓐ Ⓑ Ⓒ Ⓓ	38.	Ⓐ Ⓑ Ⓒ Ⓓ
19.	Ⓐ Ⓑ Ⓒ Ⓓ	39.	Ⓐ Ⓑ Ⓒ Ⓓ
20.	Ⓐ Ⓑ Ⓒ Ⓓ	40.	Ⓐ Ⓑ Ⓒ Ⓓ

1 RAW SCORE

1 SCALED SCORE

EXAM KRACKERS

USE ONLY A NO. 2 PENCIL TO COMPLETE THIS ANSWER SHEET. DO NOT USE INK.

NO 2 PENCIL ONLY ● **Right Mark** ✓ ✗ ◉ **Wrong Marks**

══════════════ MCAT VERBAL REASONING TEST ══════════════

Mark one and only one answer to each question. Be sure to fill in completely the space for your intended answer choice. If you erase, do so completely. Make no stray marks.

1 TEST NUMBER

1 DATE

/ /

MONTH   DAY   YEAR

1.	Ⓐ Ⓑ Ⓒ Ⓓ	21.	Ⓐ Ⓑ Ⓒ Ⓓ
2.	Ⓐ Ⓑ Ⓒ Ⓓ	22.	Ⓐ Ⓑ Ⓒ Ⓓ
3.	Ⓐ Ⓑ Ⓒ Ⓓ	23.	Ⓐ Ⓑ Ⓒ Ⓓ
4.	Ⓐ Ⓑ Ⓒ Ⓓ	24.	Ⓐ Ⓑ Ⓒ Ⓓ
5.	Ⓐ Ⓑ Ⓒ Ⓓ	25.	Ⓐ Ⓑ Ⓒ Ⓓ
6.	Ⓐ Ⓑ Ⓒ Ⓓ	26.	Ⓐ Ⓑ Ⓒ Ⓓ
7.	Ⓐ Ⓑ Ⓒ Ⓓ	27.	Ⓐ Ⓑ Ⓒ Ⓓ
8.	Ⓐ Ⓑ Ⓒ Ⓓ	28.	Ⓐ Ⓑ Ⓒ Ⓓ
9.	Ⓐ Ⓑ Ⓒ Ⓓ	29.	Ⓐ Ⓑ Ⓒ Ⓓ
10.	Ⓐ Ⓑ Ⓒ Ⓓ	30.	Ⓐ Ⓑ Ⓒ Ⓓ
11.	Ⓐ Ⓑ Ⓒ Ⓓ	31.	Ⓐ Ⓑ Ⓒ Ⓓ
12.	Ⓐ Ⓑ Ⓒ Ⓓ	32.	Ⓐ Ⓑ Ⓒ Ⓓ
13.	Ⓐ Ⓑ Ⓒ Ⓓ	33.	Ⓐ Ⓑ Ⓒ Ⓓ
14.	Ⓐ Ⓑ Ⓒ Ⓓ	34.	Ⓐ Ⓑ Ⓒ Ⓓ
15.	Ⓐ Ⓑ Ⓒ Ⓓ	35.	Ⓐ Ⓑ Ⓒ Ⓓ
16.	Ⓐ Ⓑ Ⓒ Ⓓ	36.	Ⓐ Ⓑ Ⓒ Ⓓ
17.	Ⓐ Ⓑ Ⓒ Ⓓ	37.	Ⓐ Ⓑ Ⓒ Ⓓ
18.	Ⓐ Ⓑ Ⓒ Ⓓ	38.	Ⓐ Ⓑ Ⓒ Ⓓ
19.	Ⓐ Ⓑ Ⓒ Ⓓ	39.	Ⓐ Ⓑ Ⓒ Ⓓ
20.	Ⓐ Ⓑ Ⓒ Ⓓ	40.	Ⓐ Ⓑ Ⓒ Ⓓ

1 RAW SCORE

1 SCALED SCORE

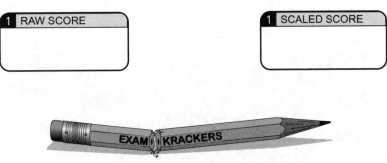

NO 2 PENCIL ONLY ● **Right Mark** ✓ ✗ ◉ **Wrong Marks**

MCAT VERBAL REASONING TEST

1 TEST NUMBER

1 DATE

MONTH / DAY / YEAR

1. Ⓐ Ⓑ Ⓒ Ⓓ	21. Ⓐ Ⓑ Ⓒ Ⓓ
2. Ⓐ Ⓑ Ⓒ Ⓓ	22. Ⓐ Ⓑ Ⓒ Ⓓ
3. Ⓐ Ⓑ Ⓒ Ⓓ	23. Ⓐ Ⓑ Ⓒ Ⓓ
4. Ⓐ Ⓑ Ⓒ Ⓓ	24. Ⓐ Ⓑ Ⓒ Ⓓ
5. Ⓐ Ⓑ Ⓒ Ⓓ	25. Ⓐ Ⓑ Ⓒ Ⓓ
6. Ⓐ Ⓑ Ⓒ Ⓓ	26. Ⓐ Ⓑ Ⓒ Ⓓ
7. Ⓐ Ⓑ Ⓒ Ⓓ	27. Ⓐ Ⓑ Ⓒ Ⓓ
8. Ⓐ Ⓑ Ⓒ Ⓓ	28. Ⓐ Ⓑ Ⓒ Ⓓ
9. Ⓐ Ⓑ Ⓒ Ⓓ	29. Ⓐ Ⓑ Ⓒ Ⓓ
10. Ⓐ Ⓑ Ⓒ Ⓓ	30. Ⓐ Ⓑ Ⓒ Ⓓ
11. Ⓐ Ⓑ Ⓒ Ⓓ	31. Ⓐ Ⓑ Ⓒ Ⓓ
12. Ⓐ Ⓑ Ⓒ Ⓓ	32. Ⓐ Ⓑ Ⓒ Ⓓ
13. Ⓐ Ⓑ Ⓒ Ⓓ	33. Ⓐ Ⓑ Ⓒ Ⓓ
14. Ⓐ Ⓑ Ⓒ Ⓓ	34. Ⓐ Ⓑ Ⓒ Ⓓ
15. Ⓐ Ⓑ Ⓒ Ⓓ	35. Ⓐ Ⓑ Ⓒ Ⓓ
16. Ⓐ Ⓑ Ⓒ Ⓓ	36. Ⓐ Ⓑ Ⓒ Ⓓ
17. Ⓐ Ⓑ Ⓒ Ⓓ	37. Ⓐ Ⓑ Ⓒ Ⓓ
18. Ⓐ Ⓑ Ⓒ Ⓓ	38. Ⓐ Ⓑ Ⓒ Ⓓ
19. Ⓐ Ⓑ Ⓒ Ⓓ	39. Ⓐ Ⓑ Ⓒ Ⓓ
20. Ⓐ Ⓑ Ⓒ Ⓓ	40. Ⓐ Ⓑ Ⓒ Ⓓ

1 RAW SCORE

1 SCALED SCORE

EXAM KRACKERS

MCAT VERBAL REASONING TEST

Mark one and only one answer to each question. Be sure to fill in completely the space for your intended answer choice. If you erase, do so completely. Make no stray marks.

1 TEST NUMBER

1 DATE

MONTH   DAY   YEAR

1.	Ⓐ Ⓑ Ⓒ Ⓓ	21. Ⓐ Ⓑ Ⓒ Ⓓ
2.	Ⓐ Ⓑ Ⓒ Ⓓ	22. Ⓐ Ⓑ Ⓒ Ⓓ
3.	Ⓐ Ⓑ Ⓒ Ⓓ	23. Ⓐ Ⓑ Ⓒ Ⓓ
4.	Ⓐ Ⓑ Ⓒ Ⓓ	24. Ⓐ Ⓑ Ⓒ Ⓓ
5.	Ⓐ Ⓑ Ⓒ Ⓓ	25. Ⓐ Ⓑ Ⓒ Ⓓ
6.	Ⓐ Ⓑ Ⓒ Ⓓ	26. Ⓐ Ⓑ Ⓒ Ⓓ
7.	Ⓐ Ⓑ Ⓒ Ⓓ	27. Ⓐ Ⓑ Ⓒ Ⓓ
8.	Ⓐ Ⓑ Ⓒ Ⓓ	28. Ⓐ Ⓑ Ⓒ Ⓓ
9.	Ⓐ Ⓑ Ⓒ Ⓓ	29. Ⓐ Ⓑ Ⓒ Ⓓ
10.	Ⓐ Ⓑ Ⓒ Ⓓ	30. Ⓐ Ⓑ Ⓒ Ⓓ
11.	Ⓐ Ⓑ Ⓒ Ⓓ	31. Ⓐ Ⓑ Ⓒ Ⓓ
12.	Ⓐ Ⓑ Ⓒ Ⓓ	32. Ⓐ Ⓑ Ⓒ Ⓓ
13.	Ⓐ Ⓑ Ⓒ Ⓓ	33. Ⓐ Ⓑ Ⓒ Ⓓ
14.	Ⓐ Ⓑ Ⓒ Ⓓ	34. Ⓐ Ⓑ Ⓒ Ⓓ
15.	Ⓐ Ⓑ Ⓒ Ⓓ	35. Ⓐ Ⓑ Ⓒ Ⓓ
16.	Ⓐ Ⓑ Ⓒ Ⓓ	36. Ⓐ Ⓑ Ⓒ Ⓓ
17.	Ⓐ Ⓑ Ⓒ Ⓓ	37. Ⓐ Ⓑ Ⓒ Ⓓ
18.	Ⓐ Ⓑ Ⓒ Ⓓ	38. Ⓐ Ⓑ Ⓒ Ⓓ
19.	Ⓐ Ⓑ Ⓒ Ⓓ	39. Ⓐ Ⓑ Ⓒ Ⓓ
20.	Ⓐ Ⓑ Ⓒ Ⓓ	40. Ⓐ Ⓑ Ⓒ Ⓓ

1 RAW SCORE

1 SCALED SCORE

MCAT VERBAL REASONING TEST

Mark one and only one answer to each question. Be sure to fill in completely the space for your intended answer choice. If you erase, do so completely. Make no stray marks.

1 TEST NUMBER

1 DATE

MONTH / DAY / YEAR

1.	Ⓐ Ⓑ Ⓒ Ⓓ			21.	Ⓐ Ⓑ Ⓒ Ⓓ
2.	Ⓐ Ⓑ Ⓒ Ⓓ			22.	Ⓐ Ⓑ Ⓒ Ⓓ
3.	Ⓐ Ⓑ Ⓒ Ⓓ			23.	Ⓐ Ⓑ Ⓒ Ⓓ
4.	Ⓐ Ⓑ Ⓒ Ⓓ			24.	Ⓐ Ⓑ Ⓒ Ⓓ
5.	Ⓐ Ⓑ Ⓒ Ⓓ			25.	Ⓐ Ⓑ Ⓒ Ⓓ
6.	Ⓐ Ⓑ Ⓒ Ⓓ			26.	Ⓐ Ⓑ Ⓒ Ⓓ
7.	Ⓐ Ⓑ Ⓒ Ⓓ			27.	Ⓐ Ⓑ Ⓒ Ⓓ
8.	Ⓐ Ⓑ Ⓒ Ⓓ			28.	Ⓐ Ⓑ Ⓒ Ⓓ
9.	Ⓐ Ⓑ Ⓒ Ⓓ			29.	Ⓐ Ⓑ Ⓒ Ⓓ
10.	Ⓐ Ⓑ Ⓒ Ⓓ			30.	Ⓐ Ⓑ Ⓒ Ⓓ
11.	Ⓐ Ⓑ Ⓒ Ⓓ			31.	Ⓐ Ⓑ Ⓒ Ⓓ
12.	Ⓐ Ⓑ Ⓒ Ⓓ			32.	Ⓐ Ⓑ Ⓒ Ⓓ
13.	Ⓐ Ⓑ Ⓒ Ⓓ			33.	Ⓐ Ⓑ Ⓒ Ⓓ
14.	Ⓐ Ⓑ Ⓒ Ⓓ			34.	Ⓐ Ⓑ Ⓒ Ⓓ
15.	Ⓐ Ⓑ Ⓒ Ⓓ			35.	Ⓐ Ⓑ Ⓒ Ⓓ
16.	Ⓐ Ⓑ Ⓒ Ⓓ			36.	Ⓐ Ⓑ Ⓒ Ⓓ
17.	Ⓐ Ⓑ Ⓒ Ⓓ			37.	Ⓐ Ⓑ Ⓒ Ⓓ
18.	Ⓐ Ⓑ Ⓒ Ⓓ			38.	Ⓐ Ⓑ Ⓒ Ⓓ
19.	Ⓐ Ⓑ Ⓒ Ⓓ			39.	Ⓐ Ⓑ Ⓒ Ⓓ
20.	Ⓐ Ⓑ Ⓒ Ⓓ			40.	Ⓐ Ⓑ Ⓒ Ⓓ

1 RAW SCORE

1 SCALED SCORE

EXAM KRACKERS

USE ONLY A NO. 2 PENCIL TO COMPLETE THIS ANSWER SHEET. DO NOT USE INK.

NO 2 PENCIL ONLY ● **Right Mark** ☑ ☒ ◉ **Wrong Marks**

═══ MCAT VERBAL REASONING TEST ═══

Mark one and only one answer to each question. Be sure to fill in completely the space for your intended answer choice. If you erase, do so completely. Make no stray marks.

1 TEST NUMBER

1 DATE

MONTH / DAY / YEAR

1.	Ⓐ	Ⓑ	Ⓒ	Ⓓ		21.	Ⓐ	Ⓑ	Ⓒ	Ⓓ
2.	Ⓐ	Ⓑ	Ⓒ	Ⓓ		22.	Ⓐ	Ⓑ	Ⓒ	Ⓓ
3.	Ⓐ	Ⓑ	Ⓒ	Ⓓ		23.	Ⓐ	Ⓑ	Ⓒ	Ⓓ
4.	Ⓐ	Ⓑ	Ⓒ	Ⓓ		24.	Ⓐ	Ⓑ	Ⓒ	Ⓓ
5.	Ⓐ	Ⓑ	Ⓒ	Ⓓ		25.	Ⓐ	Ⓑ	Ⓒ	Ⓓ
6.	Ⓐ	Ⓑ	Ⓒ	Ⓓ		26.	Ⓐ	Ⓑ	Ⓒ	Ⓓ
7.	Ⓐ	Ⓑ	Ⓒ	Ⓓ		27.	Ⓐ	Ⓑ	Ⓒ	Ⓓ
8.	Ⓐ	Ⓑ	Ⓒ	Ⓓ		28.	Ⓐ	Ⓑ	Ⓒ	Ⓓ
9.	Ⓐ	Ⓑ	Ⓒ	Ⓓ		29.	Ⓐ	Ⓑ	Ⓒ	Ⓓ
10.	Ⓐ	Ⓑ	Ⓒ	Ⓓ		30.	Ⓐ	Ⓑ	Ⓒ	Ⓓ
11.	Ⓐ	Ⓑ	Ⓒ	Ⓓ		31.	Ⓐ	Ⓑ	Ⓒ	Ⓓ
12.	Ⓐ	Ⓑ	Ⓒ	Ⓓ		32.	Ⓐ	Ⓑ	Ⓒ	Ⓓ
13.	Ⓐ	Ⓑ	Ⓒ	Ⓓ		33.	Ⓐ	Ⓑ	Ⓒ	Ⓓ
14.	Ⓐ	Ⓑ	Ⓒ	Ⓓ		34.	Ⓐ	Ⓑ	Ⓒ	Ⓓ
15.	Ⓐ	Ⓑ	Ⓒ	Ⓓ		35.	Ⓐ	Ⓑ	Ⓒ	Ⓓ
16.	Ⓐ	Ⓑ	Ⓒ	Ⓓ		36.	Ⓐ	Ⓑ	Ⓒ	Ⓓ
17.	Ⓐ	Ⓑ	Ⓒ	Ⓓ		37.	Ⓐ	Ⓑ	Ⓒ	Ⓓ
18.	Ⓐ	Ⓑ	Ⓒ	Ⓓ		38.	Ⓐ	Ⓑ	Ⓒ	Ⓓ
19.	Ⓐ	Ⓑ	Ⓒ	Ⓓ		39.	Ⓐ	Ⓑ	Ⓒ	Ⓓ
20.	Ⓐ	Ⓑ	Ⓒ	Ⓓ		40.	Ⓐ	Ⓑ	Ⓒ	Ⓓ

1 RAW SCORE

1 SCALED SCORE

EXAM KRACKERS

═══ MCAT VERBAL REASONING TEST ═══

Mark one and only one answer to each question. Be sure to fill in completely the space for your intended answer choice. If you erase, do so completely. Make no stray marks.

1 TEST NUMBER

1 DATE

MONTH   DAY   YEAR

1. Ⓐ Ⓑ Ⓒ Ⓓ	21. Ⓐ Ⓑ Ⓒ Ⓓ
2. Ⓐ Ⓑ Ⓒ Ⓓ	22. Ⓐ Ⓑ Ⓒ Ⓓ
3. Ⓐ Ⓑ Ⓒ Ⓓ	23. Ⓐ Ⓑ Ⓒ Ⓓ
4. Ⓐ Ⓑ Ⓒ Ⓓ	24. Ⓐ Ⓑ Ⓒ Ⓓ
5. Ⓐ Ⓑ Ⓒ Ⓓ	25. Ⓐ Ⓑ Ⓒ Ⓓ
6. Ⓐ Ⓑ Ⓒ Ⓓ	26. Ⓐ Ⓑ Ⓒ Ⓓ
7. Ⓐ Ⓑ Ⓒ Ⓓ	27. Ⓐ Ⓑ Ⓒ Ⓓ
8. Ⓐ Ⓑ Ⓒ Ⓓ	28. Ⓐ Ⓑ Ⓒ Ⓓ
9. Ⓐ Ⓑ Ⓒ Ⓓ	29. Ⓐ Ⓑ Ⓒ Ⓓ
10. Ⓐ Ⓑ Ⓒ Ⓓ	30. Ⓐ Ⓑ Ⓒ Ⓓ
11. Ⓐ Ⓑ Ⓒ Ⓓ	31. Ⓐ Ⓑ Ⓒ Ⓓ
12. Ⓐ Ⓑ Ⓒ Ⓓ	32. Ⓐ Ⓑ Ⓒ Ⓓ
13. Ⓐ Ⓑ Ⓒ Ⓓ	33. Ⓐ Ⓑ Ⓒ Ⓓ
14. Ⓐ Ⓑ Ⓒ Ⓓ	34. Ⓐ Ⓑ Ⓒ Ⓓ
15. Ⓐ Ⓑ Ⓒ Ⓓ	35. Ⓐ Ⓑ Ⓒ Ⓓ
16. Ⓐ Ⓑ Ⓒ Ⓓ	36. Ⓐ Ⓑ Ⓒ Ⓓ
17. Ⓐ Ⓑ Ⓒ Ⓓ	37. Ⓐ Ⓑ Ⓒ Ⓓ
18. Ⓐ Ⓑ Ⓒ Ⓓ	38. Ⓐ Ⓑ Ⓒ Ⓓ
19. Ⓐ Ⓑ Ⓒ Ⓓ	39. Ⓐ Ⓑ Ⓒ Ⓓ
20. Ⓐ Ⓑ Ⓒ Ⓓ	40. Ⓐ Ⓑ Ⓒ Ⓓ

1 RAW SCORE

1 SCALED SCORE

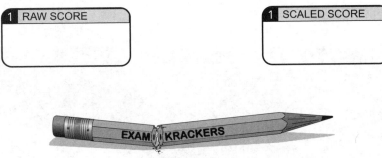

USE ONLY A NO. 2 PENCIL TO COMPLETE THIS ANSWER SHEET. DO NOT USE INK.

NO 2 PENCIL ONLY ● **Right Mark** ✓ ✗ ◉ **Wrong Marks**

═══ MCAT VERBAL REASONING TEST ═══

Mark one and only one answer to each question. Be sure to fill in completely the space for your intended answer choice. If you erase, do so completely. Make no stray marks.

1 TEST NUMBER

1 DATE
___ / ___ / ___
MONTH   DAY   YEAR

1.	Ⓐ Ⓑ Ⓒ Ⓓ				21.	Ⓐ Ⓑ Ⓒ Ⓓ			
2.	Ⓐ Ⓑ Ⓒ Ⓓ				22.	Ⓐ Ⓑ Ⓒ Ⓓ			
3.	Ⓐ Ⓑ Ⓒ Ⓓ				23.	Ⓐ Ⓑ Ⓒ Ⓓ			
4.	Ⓐ Ⓑ Ⓒ Ⓓ				24.	Ⓐ Ⓑ Ⓒ Ⓓ			
5.	Ⓐ Ⓑ Ⓒ Ⓓ				25.	Ⓐ Ⓑ Ⓒ Ⓓ			
6.	Ⓐ Ⓑ Ⓒ Ⓓ				26.	Ⓐ Ⓑ Ⓒ Ⓓ			
7.	Ⓐ Ⓑ Ⓒ Ⓓ				27.	Ⓐ Ⓑ Ⓒ Ⓓ			
8.	Ⓐ Ⓑ Ⓒ Ⓓ				28.	Ⓐ Ⓑ Ⓒ Ⓓ			
9.	Ⓐ Ⓑ Ⓒ Ⓓ				29.	Ⓐ Ⓑ Ⓒ Ⓓ			
10.	Ⓐ Ⓑ Ⓒ Ⓓ				30.	Ⓐ Ⓑ Ⓒ Ⓓ			
11.	Ⓐ Ⓑ Ⓒ Ⓓ				31.	Ⓐ Ⓑ Ⓒ Ⓓ			
12.	Ⓐ Ⓑ Ⓒ Ⓓ				32.	Ⓐ Ⓑ Ⓒ Ⓓ			
13.	Ⓐ Ⓑ Ⓒ Ⓓ				33.	Ⓐ Ⓑ Ⓒ Ⓓ			
14.	Ⓐ Ⓑ Ⓒ Ⓓ				34.	Ⓐ Ⓑ Ⓒ Ⓓ			
15.	Ⓐ Ⓑ Ⓒ Ⓓ				35.	Ⓐ Ⓑ Ⓒ Ⓓ			
16.	Ⓐ Ⓑ Ⓒ Ⓓ				36.	Ⓐ Ⓑ Ⓒ Ⓓ			
17.	Ⓐ Ⓑ Ⓒ Ⓓ				37.	Ⓐ Ⓑ Ⓒ Ⓓ			
18.	Ⓐ Ⓑ Ⓒ Ⓓ				38.	Ⓐ Ⓑ Ⓒ Ⓓ			
19.	Ⓐ Ⓑ Ⓒ Ⓓ				39.	Ⓐ Ⓑ Ⓒ Ⓓ			
20.	Ⓐ Ⓑ Ⓒ Ⓓ				40.	Ⓐ Ⓑ Ⓒ Ⓓ			

1 RAW SCORE

1 SCALED SCORE

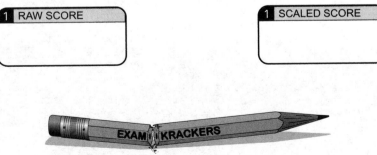

MCAT VERBAL REASONING TEST

Mark one and only one answer to each question. Be sure to fill in completely the space for your intended answer choice. If you erase, do so completely. Make no stray marks.

1 TEST NUMBER

1 DATE

MONTH   DAY   YEAR

1.	Ⓐ Ⓑ Ⓒ Ⓓ	21.	Ⓐ Ⓑ Ⓒ Ⓓ
2.	Ⓐ Ⓑ Ⓒ Ⓓ	22.	Ⓐ Ⓑ Ⓒ Ⓓ
3.	Ⓐ Ⓑ Ⓒ Ⓓ	23.	Ⓐ Ⓑ Ⓒ Ⓓ
4.	Ⓐ Ⓑ Ⓒ Ⓓ	24.	Ⓐ Ⓑ Ⓒ Ⓓ
5.	Ⓐ Ⓑ Ⓒ Ⓓ	25.	Ⓐ Ⓑ Ⓒ Ⓓ
6.	Ⓐ Ⓑ Ⓒ Ⓓ	26.	Ⓐ Ⓑ Ⓒ Ⓓ
7.	Ⓐ Ⓑ Ⓒ Ⓓ	27.	Ⓐ Ⓑ Ⓒ Ⓓ
8.	Ⓐ Ⓑ Ⓒ Ⓓ	28.	Ⓐ Ⓑ Ⓒ Ⓓ
9.	Ⓐ Ⓑ Ⓒ Ⓓ	29.	Ⓐ Ⓑ Ⓒ Ⓓ
10.	Ⓐ Ⓑ Ⓒ Ⓓ	30.	Ⓐ Ⓑ Ⓒ Ⓓ
11.	Ⓐ Ⓑ Ⓒ Ⓓ	31.	Ⓐ Ⓑ Ⓒ Ⓓ
12.	Ⓐ Ⓑ Ⓒ Ⓓ	32.	Ⓐ Ⓑ Ⓒ Ⓓ
13.	Ⓐ Ⓑ Ⓒ Ⓓ	33.	Ⓐ Ⓑ Ⓒ Ⓓ
14.	Ⓐ Ⓑ Ⓒ Ⓓ	34.	Ⓐ Ⓑ Ⓒ Ⓓ
15.	Ⓐ Ⓑ Ⓒ Ⓓ	35.	Ⓐ Ⓑ Ⓒ Ⓓ
16.	Ⓐ Ⓑ Ⓒ Ⓓ	36.	Ⓐ Ⓑ Ⓒ Ⓓ
17.	Ⓐ Ⓑ Ⓒ Ⓓ	37.	Ⓐ Ⓑ Ⓒ Ⓓ
18.	Ⓐ Ⓑ Ⓒ Ⓓ	38.	Ⓐ Ⓑ Ⓒ Ⓓ
19.	Ⓐ Ⓑ Ⓒ Ⓓ	39.	Ⓐ Ⓑ Ⓒ Ⓓ
20.	Ⓐ Ⓑ Ⓒ Ⓓ	40.	Ⓐ Ⓑ Ⓒ Ⓓ

1 RAW SCORE

1 SCALED SCORE

EXAM KRACKERS

MCAT VERBAL REASONING TEST

Mark one and only one answer to each question. Be sure to fill in completely the space for your intended answer choice. If you erase, do so completely. Make no stray marks.

1 TEST NUMBER

1 DATE

MONTH   DAY   YEAR

1.	Ⓐ Ⓑ Ⓒ Ⓓ		21.	Ⓐ Ⓑ Ⓒ Ⓓ
2.	Ⓐ Ⓑ Ⓒ Ⓓ		22.	Ⓐ Ⓑ Ⓒ Ⓓ
3.	Ⓐ Ⓑ Ⓒ Ⓓ		23.	Ⓐ Ⓑ Ⓒ Ⓓ
4.	Ⓐ Ⓑ Ⓒ Ⓓ		24.	Ⓐ Ⓑ Ⓒ Ⓓ
5.	Ⓐ Ⓑ Ⓒ Ⓓ		25.	Ⓐ Ⓑ Ⓒ Ⓓ
6.	Ⓐ Ⓑ Ⓒ Ⓓ		26.	Ⓐ Ⓑ Ⓒ Ⓓ
7.	Ⓐ Ⓑ Ⓒ Ⓓ		27.	Ⓐ Ⓑ Ⓒ Ⓓ
8.	Ⓐ Ⓑ Ⓒ Ⓓ		28.	Ⓐ Ⓑ Ⓒ Ⓓ
9.	Ⓐ Ⓑ Ⓒ Ⓓ		29.	Ⓐ Ⓑ Ⓒ Ⓓ
10.	Ⓐ Ⓑ Ⓒ Ⓓ		30.	Ⓐ Ⓑ Ⓒ Ⓓ
11.	Ⓐ Ⓑ Ⓒ Ⓓ		31.	Ⓐ Ⓑ Ⓒ Ⓓ
12.	Ⓐ Ⓑ Ⓒ Ⓓ		32.	Ⓐ Ⓑ Ⓒ Ⓓ
13.	Ⓐ Ⓑ Ⓒ Ⓓ		33.	Ⓐ Ⓑ Ⓒ Ⓓ
14.	Ⓐ Ⓑ Ⓒ Ⓓ		34.	Ⓐ Ⓑ Ⓒ Ⓓ
15.	Ⓐ Ⓑ Ⓒ Ⓓ		35.	Ⓐ Ⓑ Ⓒ Ⓓ
16.	Ⓐ Ⓑ Ⓒ Ⓓ		36.	Ⓐ Ⓑ Ⓒ Ⓓ
17.	Ⓐ Ⓑ Ⓒ Ⓓ		37.	Ⓐ Ⓑ Ⓒ Ⓓ
18.	Ⓐ Ⓑ Ⓒ Ⓓ		38.	Ⓐ Ⓑ Ⓒ Ⓓ
19.	Ⓐ Ⓑ Ⓒ Ⓓ		39.	Ⓐ Ⓑ Ⓒ Ⓓ
20.	Ⓐ Ⓑ Ⓒ Ⓓ		40.	Ⓐ Ⓑ Ⓒ Ⓓ

1 RAW SCORE

1 SCALED SCORE

EXAM KRACKERS

USE ONLY A NO. 2 PENCIL TO COMPLETE THIS ANSWER SHEET. DO NOT USE INK.

№ 2 PENCIL ONLY ● **Right Mark** ☑ ✗ ◉ **Wrong Marks**

═══════ MCAT VERBAL REASONING TEST ═══════

Mark one and only one answer to each question. Be sure to fill in completely the space for your intended answer choice. If you erase, do so completely. Make no stray marks.

1 TEST NUMBER

1 DATE

/ /

MONTH   DAY   YEAR

1.	Ⓐ Ⓑ Ⓒ Ⓓ	21.	Ⓐ Ⓑ Ⓒ Ⓓ
2.	Ⓐ Ⓑ Ⓒ Ⓓ	22.	Ⓐ Ⓑ Ⓒ Ⓓ
3.	Ⓐ Ⓑ Ⓒ Ⓓ	23.	Ⓐ Ⓑ Ⓒ Ⓓ
4.	Ⓐ Ⓑ Ⓒ Ⓓ	24.	Ⓐ Ⓑ Ⓒ Ⓓ
5.	Ⓐ Ⓑ Ⓒ Ⓓ	25.	Ⓐ Ⓑ Ⓒ Ⓓ
6.	Ⓐ Ⓑ Ⓒ Ⓓ	26.	Ⓐ Ⓑ Ⓒ Ⓓ
7.	Ⓐ Ⓑ Ⓒ Ⓓ	27.	Ⓐ Ⓑ Ⓒ Ⓓ
8.	Ⓐ Ⓑ Ⓒ Ⓓ	28.	Ⓐ Ⓑ Ⓒ Ⓓ
9.	Ⓐ Ⓑ Ⓒ Ⓓ	29.	Ⓐ Ⓑ Ⓒ Ⓓ
10.	Ⓐ Ⓑ Ⓒ Ⓓ	30.	Ⓐ Ⓑ Ⓒ Ⓓ
11.	Ⓐ Ⓑ Ⓒ Ⓓ	31.	Ⓐ Ⓑ Ⓒ Ⓓ
12.	Ⓐ Ⓑ Ⓒ Ⓓ	32.	Ⓐ Ⓑ Ⓒ Ⓓ
13.	Ⓐ Ⓑ Ⓒ Ⓓ	33.	Ⓐ Ⓑ Ⓒ Ⓓ
14.	Ⓐ Ⓑ Ⓒ Ⓓ	34.	Ⓐ Ⓑ Ⓒ Ⓓ
15.	Ⓐ Ⓑ Ⓒ Ⓓ	35.	Ⓐ Ⓑ Ⓒ Ⓓ
16.	Ⓐ Ⓑ Ⓒ Ⓓ	36.	Ⓐ Ⓑ Ⓒ Ⓓ
17.	Ⓐ Ⓑ Ⓒ Ⓓ	37.	Ⓐ Ⓑ Ⓒ Ⓓ
18.	Ⓐ Ⓑ Ⓒ Ⓓ	38.	Ⓐ Ⓑ Ⓒ Ⓓ
19.	Ⓐ Ⓑ Ⓒ Ⓓ	39.	Ⓐ Ⓑ Ⓒ Ⓓ
20.	Ⓐ Ⓑ Ⓒ Ⓓ	40.	Ⓐ Ⓑ Ⓒ Ⓓ

1 RAW SCORE

1 SCALED SCORE

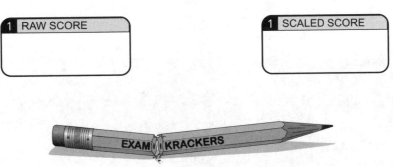

USE ONLY A NO. 2 PENCIL TO COMPLETE THIS ANSWER SHEET. DO NOT USE INK.

NO 2 PENCIL ONLY ➤ ● **Right Mark**   ✓ ✗ ◉ **Wrong Marks**

═══ MCAT VERBAL REASONING TEST ═══

Mark one and only one answer to each question. Be sure to fill in completely the space for your intended answer choice. If you erase, do so completely. Make no stray marks.

1 TEST NUMBER

1 DATE

_____ / _____ / _____
MONTH   DAY   YEAR

1.	Ⓐ Ⓑ Ⓒ Ⓓ	21.	Ⓐ Ⓑ Ⓒ Ⓓ
2.	Ⓐ Ⓑ Ⓒ Ⓓ	22.	Ⓐ Ⓑ Ⓒ Ⓓ
3.	Ⓐ Ⓑ Ⓒ Ⓓ	23.	Ⓐ Ⓑ Ⓒ Ⓓ
4.	Ⓐ Ⓑ Ⓒ Ⓓ	24.	Ⓐ Ⓑ Ⓒ Ⓓ
5.	Ⓐ Ⓑ Ⓒ Ⓓ	25.	Ⓐ Ⓑ Ⓒ Ⓓ
6.	Ⓐ Ⓑ Ⓒ Ⓓ	26.	Ⓐ Ⓑ Ⓒ Ⓓ
7.	Ⓐ Ⓑ Ⓒ Ⓓ	27.	Ⓐ Ⓑ Ⓒ Ⓓ
8.	Ⓐ Ⓑ Ⓒ Ⓓ	28.	Ⓐ Ⓑ Ⓒ Ⓓ
9.	Ⓐ Ⓑ Ⓒ Ⓓ	29.	Ⓐ Ⓑ Ⓒ Ⓓ
10.	Ⓐ Ⓑ Ⓒ Ⓓ	30.	Ⓐ Ⓑ Ⓒ Ⓓ
11.	Ⓐ Ⓑ Ⓒ Ⓓ	31.	Ⓐ Ⓑ Ⓒ Ⓓ
12.	Ⓐ Ⓑ Ⓒ Ⓓ	32.	Ⓐ Ⓑ Ⓒ Ⓓ
13.	Ⓐ Ⓑ Ⓒ Ⓓ	33.	Ⓐ Ⓑ Ⓒ Ⓓ
14.	Ⓐ Ⓑ Ⓒ Ⓓ	34.	Ⓐ Ⓑ Ⓒ Ⓓ
15.	Ⓐ Ⓑ Ⓒ Ⓓ	35.	Ⓐ Ⓑ Ⓒ Ⓓ
16.	Ⓐ Ⓑ Ⓒ Ⓓ	36.	Ⓐ Ⓑ Ⓒ Ⓓ
17.	Ⓐ Ⓑ Ⓒ Ⓓ	37.	Ⓐ Ⓑ Ⓒ Ⓓ
18.	Ⓐ Ⓑ Ⓒ Ⓓ	38.	Ⓐ Ⓑ Ⓒ Ⓓ
19.	Ⓐ Ⓑ Ⓒ Ⓓ	39.	Ⓐ Ⓑ Ⓒ Ⓓ
20.	Ⓐ Ⓑ Ⓒ Ⓓ	40.	Ⓐ Ⓑ Ⓒ Ⓓ

1 RAW SCORE

1 SCALED SCORE

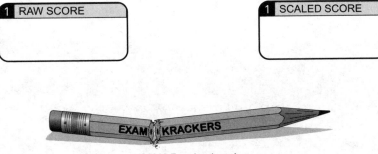

USE ONLY A NO. 2 PENCIL TO COMPLETE THIS ANSWER SHEET. DO NOT USE INK.

NO 2 PENCIL ONLY ● **Right Mark** ✓ ✗ ◉ **Wrong Marks**

MCAT VERBAL REASONING TEST

Mark one and only one answer to each question. Be sure to fill in completely the space for your intended answer choice. If you erase, do so completely. Make no stray marks.

1 TEST NUMBER

1 DATE

MONTH / DAY / YEAR

1. Ⓐ Ⓑ Ⓒ Ⓓ	21. Ⓐ Ⓑ Ⓒ Ⓓ
2. Ⓐ Ⓑ Ⓒ Ⓓ	22. Ⓐ Ⓑ Ⓒ Ⓓ
3. Ⓐ Ⓑ Ⓒ Ⓓ	23. Ⓐ Ⓑ Ⓒ Ⓓ
4. Ⓐ Ⓑ Ⓒ Ⓓ	24. Ⓐ Ⓑ Ⓒ Ⓓ
5. Ⓐ Ⓑ Ⓒ Ⓓ	25. Ⓐ Ⓑ Ⓒ Ⓓ
6. Ⓐ Ⓑ Ⓒ Ⓓ	26. Ⓐ Ⓑ Ⓒ Ⓓ
7. Ⓐ Ⓑ Ⓒ Ⓓ	27. Ⓐ Ⓑ Ⓒ Ⓓ
8. Ⓐ Ⓑ Ⓒ Ⓓ	28. Ⓐ Ⓑ Ⓒ Ⓓ
9. Ⓐ Ⓑ Ⓒ Ⓓ	29. Ⓐ Ⓑ Ⓒ Ⓓ
10. Ⓐ Ⓑ Ⓒ Ⓓ	30. Ⓐ Ⓑ Ⓒ Ⓓ
11. Ⓐ Ⓑ Ⓒ Ⓓ	31. Ⓐ Ⓑ Ⓒ Ⓓ
12. Ⓐ Ⓑ Ⓒ Ⓓ	32. Ⓐ Ⓑ Ⓒ Ⓓ
13. Ⓐ Ⓑ Ⓒ Ⓓ	33. Ⓐ Ⓑ Ⓒ Ⓓ
14. Ⓐ Ⓑ Ⓒ Ⓓ	34. Ⓐ Ⓑ Ⓒ Ⓓ
15. Ⓐ Ⓑ Ⓒ Ⓓ	35. Ⓐ Ⓑ Ⓒ Ⓓ
16. Ⓐ Ⓑ Ⓒ Ⓓ	36. Ⓐ Ⓑ Ⓒ Ⓓ
17. Ⓐ Ⓑ Ⓒ Ⓓ	37. Ⓐ Ⓑ Ⓒ Ⓓ
18. Ⓐ Ⓑ Ⓒ Ⓓ	38. Ⓐ Ⓑ Ⓒ Ⓓ
19. Ⓐ Ⓑ Ⓒ Ⓓ	39. Ⓐ Ⓑ Ⓒ Ⓓ
20. Ⓐ Ⓑ Ⓒ Ⓓ	40. Ⓐ Ⓑ Ⓒ Ⓓ

1 RAW SCORE

1 SCALED SCORE

EXAM KRACKERS

===== MCAT VERBAL REASONING TEST =====

Mark one and only one answer to each question. Be sure to fill in completely the space for your intended answer choice. If you erase, do so completely. Make no stray marks.

1. Ⓐ Ⓑ Ⓒ Ⓓ		21. Ⓐ Ⓑ Ⓒ Ⓓ	
2. Ⓐ Ⓑ Ⓒ Ⓓ		22. Ⓐ Ⓑ Ⓒ Ⓓ	
3. Ⓐ Ⓑ Ⓒ Ⓓ		23. Ⓐ Ⓑ Ⓒ Ⓓ	
4. Ⓐ Ⓑ Ⓒ Ⓓ		24. Ⓐ Ⓑ Ⓒ Ⓓ	
5. Ⓐ Ⓑ Ⓒ Ⓓ		25. Ⓐ Ⓑ Ⓒ Ⓓ	
6. Ⓐ Ⓑ Ⓒ Ⓓ		26. Ⓐ Ⓑ Ⓒ Ⓓ	
7. Ⓐ Ⓑ Ⓒ Ⓓ		27. Ⓐ Ⓑ Ⓒ Ⓓ	
8. Ⓐ Ⓑ Ⓒ Ⓓ		28. Ⓐ Ⓑ Ⓒ Ⓓ	
9. Ⓐ Ⓑ Ⓒ Ⓓ		29. Ⓐ Ⓑ Ⓒ Ⓓ	
10. Ⓐ Ⓑ Ⓒ Ⓓ		30. Ⓐ Ⓑ Ⓒ Ⓓ	
11. Ⓐ Ⓑ Ⓒ Ⓓ		31. Ⓐ Ⓑ Ⓒ Ⓓ	
12. Ⓐ Ⓑ Ⓒ Ⓓ		32. Ⓐ Ⓑ Ⓒ Ⓓ	
13. Ⓐ Ⓑ Ⓒ Ⓓ		33. Ⓐ Ⓑ Ⓒ Ⓓ	
14. Ⓐ Ⓑ Ⓒ Ⓓ		34. Ⓐ Ⓑ Ⓒ Ⓓ	
15. Ⓐ Ⓑ Ⓒ Ⓓ		35. Ⓐ Ⓑ Ⓒ Ⓓ	
16. Ⓐ Ⓑ Ⓒ Ⓓ		36. Ⓐ Ⓑ Ⓒ Ⓓ	
17. Ⓐ Ⓑ Ⓒ Ⓓ		37. Ⓐ Ⓑ Ⓒ Ⓓ	
18. Ⓐ Ⓑ Ⓒ Ⓓ		38. Ⓐ Ⓑ Ⓒ Ⓓ	
19. Ⓐ Ⓑ Ⓒ Ⓓ		39. Ⓐ Ⓑ Ⓒ Ⓓ	
20. Ⓐ Ⓑ Ⓒ Ⓓ		40. Ⓐ Ⓑ Ⓒ Ⓓ	

1 RAW SCORE	1 SCALED SCORE

EXAM KRACKERS

NO 2 PENCIL ONLY

● **Right Mark**   ✓ ✗ ◉ **Wrong Marks**

MCAT VERBAL REASONING TEST

Mark one and only one answer to each question. Be sure to fill in completely the space for your intended answer choice. If you erase, do so completely. Make no stray marks.

1 TEST NUMBER

1 DATE

MONTH   DAY   YEAR

1.	Ⓐ Ⓑ Ⓒ Ⓓ	21.	Ⓐ Ⓑ Ⓒ Ⓓ
2.	Ⓐ Ⓑ Ⓒ Ⓓ	22.	Ⓐ Ⓑ Ⓒ Ⓓ
3.	Ⓐ Ⓑ Ⓒ Ⓓ	23.	Ⓐ Ⓑ Ⓒ Ⓓ
4.	Ⓐ Ⓑ Ⓒ Ⓓ	24.	Ⓐ Ⓑ Ⓒ Ⓓ
5.	Ⓐ Ⓑ Ⓒ Ⓓ	25.	Ⓐ Ⓑ Ⓒ Ⓓ
6.	Ⓐ Ⓑ Ⓒ Ⓓ	26.	Ⓐ Ⓑ Ⓒ Ⓓ
7.	Ⓐ Ⓑ Ⓒ Ⓓ	27.	Ⓐ Ⓑ Ⓒ Ⓓ
8.	Ⓐ Ⓑ Ⓒ Ⓓ	28.	Ⓐ Ⓑ Ⓒ Ⓓ
9.	Ⓐ Ⓑ Ⓒ Ⓓ	29.	Ⓐ Ⓑ Ⓒ Ⓓ
10.	Ⓐ Ⓑ Ⓒ Ⓓ	30.	Ⓐ Ⓑ Ⓒ Ⓓ
11.	Ⓐ Ⓑ Ⓒ Ⓓ	31.	Ⓐ Ⓑ Ⓒ Ⓓ
12.	Ⓐ Ⓑ Ⓒ Ⓓ	32.	Ⓐ Ⓑ Ⓒ Ⓓ
13.	Ⓐ Ⓑ Ⓒ Ⓓ	33.	Ⓐ Ⓑ Ⓒ Ⓓ
14.	Ⓐ Ⓑ Ⓒ Ⓓ	34.	Ⓐ Ⓑ Ⓒ Ⓓ
15.	Ⓐ Ⓑ Ⓒ Ⓓ	35.	Ⓐ Ⓑ Ⓒ Ⓓ
16.	Ⓐ Ⓑ Ⓒ Ⓓ	36.	Ⓐ Ⓑ Ⓒ Ⓓ
17.	Ⓐ Ⓑ Ⓒ Ⓓ	37.	Ⓐ Ⓑ Ⓒ Ⓓ
18.	Ⓐ Ⓑ Ⓒ Ⓓ	38.	Ⓐ Ⓑ Ⓒ Ⓓ
19.	Ⓐ Ⓑ Ⓒ Ⓓ	39.	Ⓐ Ⓑ Ⓒ Ⓓ
20.	Ⓐ Ⓑ Ⓒ Ⓓ	40.	Ⓐ Ⓑ Ⓒ Ⓓ

1 RAW SCORE

1 SCALED SCORE

EXAM KRACKERS